A Culture of Growth

A Culture of Growth

The Origins of the Modern Economy

The Graz Schumpeter Lectures

Joel Mokyr

Princeton University Press

Princeton and Oxford

Published by Princeton University Press, 41 William Street, Princeton, New Jersey 08540

In the United Kingdom: Princeton University Press, 6 Oxford Street, Woodstock, Oxfordshire

OX20 1TW

press.princeton.edu

Jacket art: Change Alley, London, 1853. Street scene depicting events surrounding the South Sea

Bubble (1711-1720). The scene is taking place in front of Garraway's Coffee House, with a pawn

shop at left. Photo credit: HIP / Art Resource, NY

Library of Congress Cataloging-in-Publication Data
Names: Mokyr, Joel, author.
Title: A culture of growth : the origins of the modern economy / Joel Mokyr.
Description: Princeton, NJ : Princeton University Press, 2016. | Includes bibliographical
references and index.
Identifiers: LCCN 2015045838 | ISBN 9780691168883 (hardback)
Subjects: LCSH: Economic development. | Economic history. | BISAC: BUSINESS &
ECONOMICS / Economic History. | BUSINESS & ECONOMICS / Development /
Economic Development. | BUSINESS & ECONOMICS / Economic Conditions. | BUSINESS
& ECONOMICS / Economics / General. | HISTORY / Europe / General.
Classification: LCC HD75 .M65 2016 | DDC 330-dc23 LC record available at
http://lccn.loc.gov/2015045838

British Library Cataloging-in-Publication Data is available

The publisher would like to acknowledge the author of this volume for providing the

camera-ready copy from which this book was printed

This book has been composed in Callisto MT by the author

Printed on acid-free paper.

Printed in the United States of America

10 9 8 7 6 5 4 3 2

Dedicated to

my three siblings

Rob, Miriam, and Ada

who have stood by me

for all those years

It is more easy to account for the rise and progress of commerce in any kingdom, than for that of learning. ... Avarice, or the desire of gain, is an universal passion, which operates at all times, in all places, and upon all persons: But curiosity, or the love of knowledge, has a very limited influence, and requires youth, leisure, education, genius, and example, to make it govern any person ... there is no subject, in which we must proceed with more caution, than in tracing the history of the arts and sciences; lest we assign causes which never existed, and reduce what is merely contingent to stable and universal principles. Those who cultivate the sciences in any state, are always few in number: The passion, which governs them, limited: Their taste and judgment delicate and easily perverted: And their application disturbed with the smallest accident. Chance, therefore, or secret and unknown causes, must have a great influence on the rise and progress of all the refined arts.

—David Hume, 1742

Contents

Acknowledgments

This book had its origins in the Joseph Schumpeter lectures I delivered in Graz in November 2010 and I am deeply grateful to my hosts at the Schumpeter Society for their hospitality and penetrating comments at an early stage. Books based on endowed lectures tend to be relatively short. This book, however, took on a life of its own, and chapters kept being added. Having argued in previous works that the emergence of a cultural phenomenon we think of as the Enlightenment was central to the economic and technological miracles that mark European history since the Industrial Revolution, it became clear that we should ask hard questions about the origins of the emergence of intellectual innovation and a creative elite of scholars and engineers who pushed the envelope. Modern economics has accepted the challenge to understand matters that half a century lay firmly outside its realm: culture and institutions. In this book, I take a closer look at the culture and institutions of Europe between Columbus and the publication of *Principia* and ask how and why it created the conditions for modern economic growth.

Books such as this are never written alone. Many colleagues and friends patiently listened to my often incoherent ravings about various issues in intellectual and cultural history that were remote from their own research. Their questions and doubts made my determination to delve deeper stronger, but I surely did not answer all of them. Among my fellow travelers, who have been thinking along similar lines, I should mention three scholars whose work and friendship have been a source of inspiration even if they have different backgrounds: the sociologist Jack Goldstone, the historian Margaret Jacob, and that incomparable economist, historian, and general-purpose intellectual Deirdre McCloskey.

At Northwestern University, I have had for many years the benefit of two groups of colleagues in two large, vibrant, and utterly different departments, Economics and History. Economists, notwithstanding the stereotype, are often extraordinarily insightful and wide-ranging intellectuals. Many of them are also loyal lifelong friends. Among them, of course, the economic historians are foremost: my friends and fellow economic historians Louis Cain, Joseph Ferrie, Mara Squicciarini, and Regina Grafe (now at the European University). Among the other economists, I should mention especially Larry Christiano, Eddie Dekel, Matthias Doepke, Martin Eichenbaum, Robert J. Gordon, Joel Horowitz, Lynne Kiesling, and Charles Manski. In History, the list of colleagues who have enriched and stimulated this book include Kenneth Alder, Lydia Barnett, Peter Carroll, Sarah Maza, Melissa McCauley, Edward Muir, and Yohanan Petrovsky-Shtern. Much like Rabbi Akiva, however, through my entire career I learned the most from my current and former students: Ran Abramitzky, Gergo Baics, Maristella Botticini, José Espin, Avner Greif,

Ralf Meisenzahl, John Nye, Tuan-Hwee Sng, Yannay Spitzer, Rick Szostak, Chris Vickers, Marlous van Waijenburg, Marianne Hinds Wanamaker, Anthony Wray, Ludovico Zaraga, Nicolas Ziebarth, and Ariell Zimran.

Outside Northwestern, perhaps the best scholarly environment any scholar can imagine is the fabulous Institutions, Organizations, and Growth group run by the Canadian Institute for Advanced Research (CIFAR). This group contains the best minds that social science has to offer in this world, and its interest in economic history is unrivaled. The group has allowed me to interact with and learn from scholars of the calibre of Daron Acemoglu, Roland Benabou, Tim Besley, Rob Boyd, Mauricio Drelichman, Avner Greif, Elhanan Helpman, Joseph Henrich, Roger Myerson, Torsten Persson, James Robinson, Ken Shepsle, and Guido Tabellini, and there exists no research project in social science that will not benefit vastly from the comments and suggestions of this remarkable group of intellects. For four decades now, I have benefited from the inexhaustible wisdom, the learning, and the kindness of my Irish friend and coauthor Cormac Ó Gráda. He and our erudite collaborator Morgan Kelly, also at University College Dublin, have many valuable contributions and suggestions to this manuscript. I am also grateful for the encouragement and sage counsel of Professor Alberto Quadrio Curzio, president of the Accademia dei Lincei. In Israel, I have benefited from being a guest in two departments, the Berglas School of Economics at Tel Aviv University and more recently the Interdisciplinary Center in Herzliya under the inspired leadership of Zvi Eckstein. Other Israelis to whom I owe special thanks are my co-authors and dear friends Amira Ofer and Karine van der Beek, my life-long fellow-traveler, president Jacob Metzer of the Open University, and the ever-thoughtful and wise Manuel Trajtenberg, formerly of Tel Aviv University. Outside those institutions, I owe an enormous intellectual debt to four giants of economic history: Eric L. Jones, the late David S. Landes, the late Douglass C. North, and the late Nathan Rosenberg. More distant in time, but never forgotten, are the memories I have of my late Northwestern colleague Jonathan R. T. Hughes and his wife, Mary Gray.

Beyond those individuals, there are a large number of scholars who have attended seminars and lectures in which I tried out various ideas that eventually became this book. Among those many were seminars in economic history and economics at the following institutions: Bar Ilan University, University of California Berkeley, Ben Gurion University, Cambridge University, Carleton College, Harvard University, the Hebrew University, Interdisciplinary Center Herzliya, MIT Sloan School, the Princeton Center for Advanced Studies, UCLA, University of Peking, the University of Tel Aviv, and Yale University.

My long-standing relationship with Princeton University Press has made the production of this book a special pleasure. Working with Peter

Dougherty and Seth Ditchik on this project, as well as many other projects, has been a joy. The manuscript was edited meticulously and patiently by Cyd Westmoreland and Mary Bearden, and produced with supreme competence by Mark Bellis. I am very grateful to all. Financial support from Northwestern University's Weinberg College of Arts and Sciences, the Center for Economic History at Northwestern University, Valor Equity and especially Antonio Gracias and Chris Murphy, Anthony Melchiorre of Chatham Asset Management, and the International Balzan Foundation is gratefully acknowledged.

Finally, as always, I owe more than I could possibly express to my wife, Margalit Mokyr, whose patience and loyalty are only matched by her smarts, her competence, and her common sense. As is written:

אשת חיל מי ימצא ורחק מפנינים מכרה: בטח בה לב בעלה ושלל
לא יחסר (משלי ל"א יא–יב)

Skokie, IL, March 2016

Preface

Economic history and intellectual history are two dynamic and active disciplines that barely intersect, which is a shame. Except for the crude materialist hypothesis which explains changes in what people believed and knew by arguing for the supremacy of economic structures, not much has been done to show that much of what happened in the economies of the world in the past three centuries was a function of what people believed. Above all, modern economic growth or "the Great Enrichment" depended on a set of radical changes in beliefs, values, and preferences—a set I will refer to as "culture" despite the many justified concerns about the over-usage and ambiguity of that term.

But which beliefs, and whose? In earlier work, I have argued that the European Enlightenment (or at least a substantial segment of it) was pivotal in the propulsion of economic growth in the nineteenth century. This seems an innocuously enough proposition, except perhaps for a fringe who wish to denigrate the Enlightenment as something profoundly retrograde and culpable of the disasters of the twentieth century. But the Enlightenment was not a mass-movement. It was an elite phenomenon, largely confined to intellectuals, scholars, a literate and educated minority that included not just physicians and philosophers but also practical people such as engineers, industrialists, and instrument makers, yet still a small sliver of the population. New scientific insights, the invention of new techniques, their successful application to production—all were the result of the actions of a fairly small proportion of the population. I also have maintained that what mattered was not only what people believed about social contracts, political pluralism, religious tolerance, human rights and so on, but also what they believed about the relationship between humans and their physical environment and role of what they called "useful knowledge" to improve material well-being. The fundamental belief that the human lot can be continuously improved by bettering our understanding of natural phenomena and regularities and the application of this understanding to production has been the cultural breakthrough that made what came after possible.

But how and why did these beliefs emerge? In the two centuries between Columbus and Newton, European elite culture underwent radical intellectual change. In what follows, I analyze this change, using material from intellectual history and the history of science and technology to achieve an explanation of a question posed primarily by economists: how do we explain the "modern economy?" The methodology used to answer the question comes from the social sciences —primarily economics but also from cultural evolution theory. It is meant to attack the deepest questions regarding intellectual innovation. Why do people come up with new ideas? How do new ideas succeed in supplanting old ones? Why one kind of idea and not another one? By asking these questions, I will show how "early modern" Europe prepared the ground for the vast changes in the eighteenth century: the Enlightenment, the Industrial Revolution, and the rise of useful knowledge as the main engine of economic history.

Part I

Evolution, Culture, and Economic History

Chapter 1

Culture and Economics

The world today is richer than it has ever been. We know a great deal about the economic transformations that made it this way thanks to a vast literature examining every possible aspect of modern economic growth taking place since ca. 1800. We know *what* happened, and we know more or less *how* and *where* it happened. What remains very much a mystery is *why*. This book tries to provide an answer.

The basic facts are not in dispute. The British Industrial Revolution of the late eighteenth century unleashed a phenomenon never before even remotely experienced by any society. Of course, innovation has taken place throughout history. Milestone breakthroughs in earlier times—such as water mills, the horse collar, and the printing press—can all be traced more or less, and their economic effects can be assessed. They appeared, often transformed an industry affected, but once incorporated, further progress slowed and sometimes stopped altogether. They did not trigger anything resembling sustained technological progress, and their effects on income were small and in many cases barely enough to offset population increase. As late at 1754 David Hume summarized the economic history of the world until that time by noting that "if the general system of things, and human society of course, have any ... gradual revolution, they are too slow to be discerned in that short period. ... Stature and force of body, length of life, even courage and genius, seem hitherto to have been in all ages pretty much the same" (Hume [1754] 1985, p. 378). As a description of the past, Hume's summary is consistent with much of the consensus in economic history today (leaving aside, perhaps, courage, on which little has been said).

But as a prognostication of what was to come, this turned out to be spectacularly incorrect, and Hume was wise to add the qualification "hitherto." The early advances in the cotton industry, iron manufacturing, and steam power of the years after 1760 became in the nineteenth century a self-reinforcing cascade of innovation, one that is still very much with us today and seems to grow ever more pervasive and powerful. If economic growth before the Industrial Revolution, such as it was, was largely driven by trade, more effective markets and improved allocations of resources, growth in the modern era has been increasingly driven by the expansion of what was known in the age of Enlightenment as "useful knowledge."

What had started in a few counties in the English midlands and the Scottish lowlands soon spread to the European continent and to America. By the end of the nineteenth century, the Industrial Revolution had transformed the economies of much of Europe and the European off-shoots, and it began to spread to Japan and other non-Western economies. Transformative technological change turned from an unusual and remark-able phenomenon to something routine, expected. By 1890, one might not know what kind of and where a wave of technological progress would erupt, but one got accustomed to *something* happening. The results were inescapable: nearly everywhere on the planet men and women lived longer, ate better, enjoyed more leisure, and had access to resources and delights that previously had been reserved for the very rich and powerful, or more commonly, had been utterly unknown. With these blessings came dis-ruptions, environmental disasters, and at times utter destruction. Tech-nology and economic might provide the human race with more powerful tools, nothing more. Today, although the rate of measured economic growth in the industrialized world has slowed down, such blessings and curses are still piling up. Measured economic growth in the industrializing economies in the nineteenth and twentieth centuries approached a rate of 1.5–2.0 percent a year, perhaps ten times faster than before. Moreover, the resulting prosperity turned out to be persistent. Despite a series of self-in-flicted political and economic disasters in the twentieth century, the indus-trialized West recovered miraculously after 1950 and was able to reach living standards that would have been unthinkable in 1914, let alone in 1800.

There can be no doubt that growth of this kind, while of global consequences, started in the West. What used to be known as the literature on "the rise of the west" or "the European Miracle" (following E. L. Jones's seminal 1981 book)—now more commonly referred to as "the Great Divergence" or "the Great Enrichment"—documents and describes the West's leadership in the emergence of Modern Growth. But a consensus on why this happened seems remote.[1] Some scholars have branded the writings of those who point to the Western origins of modern

---

[1] In a recent tour d'horizon, Peer Vries (2013) has surveyed many explanations offered over the years for the origins of the Great Divergence and the escape from poverty. In the end, however, he finds the bulk of them unpersuasive, and even the ones he favors seem to lack precision and are hard to test.

economic growth as "Eurocentric," implying that such explanations suggest some kind of inherent superiority of European culture or institutions. While it is undeniable that some accounts have tried to credit some aspect or other of Western civilization, most scholars have eschewed such simple arguments and tried either to avoid cultural explanations altogether or to come to grips with the question of why certain values and beliefs differed systematically. One can write such histories without sounding "triumphalist" (Goldstone, 2012). The account below should be seen as part of this tradition.

In this book, I propose a new explanation, largely based on events in Europe. It is one that relies on something I call "culture," but unlike most accounts that rely on this vague concept, the notion of culture I deploy will be circumscribed and defined with precision. The great economist Robert Solow once remarked that all attempts to explain differences in economic performance and growth using culture "end up in a blaze of amateur sociology" (quoted in Krugman, 1991, p. 93, n. 3). Perhaps. But if we are to look for institutions to explain historical development, can culture be far behind?

My approach simultaneously resolves two difficulties in the "Great Divergence" literature, one historical and one economic. The *historical* riddle is what might be called the great dilemma of the new institutional economic history: much of the literature in economic history that is trying to explain differences in economic performance and living standards, both by economists and historians, has accepted in one way or another Douglass North's call for the integration of institutions into our narrative of economic growth (Acemoglu and Robinson, 2012; Sened and Galiani, 2014). An economy that grows as a result of favorable institutions requires a world of well-delineated and respected property rights, enforceable contracts, law and order, a low level of opportunism and rent-seeking, a high degree of inclusion in political decision making and the benefits of growth, and a political organization in which power and wealth are as separate as is humanly possible. Such institutions—whether part of the formal political structure (as embodied for example in a constitution) or based on private-order institutions—are credited with many positive economic developments in the past: the rise of more effective product and factor markets (and thus more efficient allocations), the growth of international and interregional trade, and the accumulation of capital, to name a few. But, as other scholars (Vries, 2013, p. 433; McCloskey, 2016b) have argued, the puzzle is that better markets, more cooperative behavior, and more efficient allocations simply do not in themselves account for modern economic growth. What is far harder to explain is the growth of technological creativity and innovation in Europe and especially the surge following the middle of the eighteenth century. The Industrial Revolution, in the sense of an acceleration of technological progress, at first blush does not seem to have been a response to any obvious institutional stimulus. We actually know remarkably little about the kind of institutions that foster and stimulate technological progress and more widely, intellectual innovation.

The second riddle is closely related but looks at the problem from a different, more economic, point of view. If the generation and continuous improvement of new "useful knowledge"—both scientific and techno-logical—is at the core of modern economic growth, the riddle is one of motivation or incentives. Knowledge, as has long been understood, is an unusual commodity, subject to rather serious public good properties: it is very hard to exclude others from using it, and the cost to the owner from sharing it is negligible or zero. As a result, economists suspect that knowl-edge tends to be chronically underproduced, because those who spend resources, time, and effort generating it have difficulty appropriating any returns. As far as technology or prescriptive knowledge is concerned, the existence of a patent system or other ways to reward inventors has provided a (very) partial solution.[2] But advances in natural philosophy and pro-positional knowledge could not be patented. This is especially problematic because the growth of technological knowledge by itself, without the con-stant interaction with some form of formal or informal science, would not have been able to generate growth and development at the rates observed. The issue of the exact role of science in the Industrial Revolution is still debated, but there can be no doubt that as growth accelerated, the input from science increased and became the dominant motive power at some point after 1830.

As this book makes clear, the solutions to the historical and the economic riddles coincide. My focus is on the period from 1500 to 1700, during which the cultural foundations of modern growth were laid. These foundations grew out of a set of political and institutional developments and cultural changes that were not intended to produce these results, and their deeply contingent nature is a recurrent theme in these pages.

A famous distinction made in Jewish law illustrates the difference between the type of phenomena we associate with institutions, on the one hand, and the importance of process and product innovation fed by growing human knowledge of natural forces on the other. The Talmudic tradition distinguishes between affairs that concern relations between the individual and others, and the relations between the individual and *makom*—a somewhat unusual name for the deity, meaning literally "place"

---

[2] For an assessment of the patent system in the early stages of economic growth in Europe, see Mokyr (2009b).

and practically interpreted as one's physical environment.[3] Commerce, the division of labor, effective markets in labor, credit and land, and similar institutions associated with Smithian growth were all outcomes of games between people. They depended on what values people adhered to and what they believed about others' values and behavior. What is less discussed is a set of cultural beliefs that pertain to games against *nature*, in which individuals try to understand natural regularities and exploit them to their advantage. Religious beliefs and metaphysical attitudes condition a society's willingness to investigate the secrets of nature, alter its physical environment irreversibly, and "play God." Technology is at its very core a relation of people with the physical environment and not with other people. For such practical matters as the diffusion and implementation of new techniques, of course, social relations are central to technological progress. But in the end the willingness to challenge nature in some way to reveal one of her secrets is based on metaphysical beliefs held at the individual level.

The drivers of technological progress and eventually economic performance were attitude and aptitude. The former set the willingness and energy with which people try to understand the natural world around them; the latter determines their success in turning such knowledge into higher productivity and living standards.[4] In this book I will be concerned with attitudes. The proposition I put forward here is that the explosion of technological progress in the West was made possible by cultural changes. "Culture" affected technology both directly, by changing attitudes toward the natural world, and indirectly, by creating and nurturing institutions that stimulated and supported the accumulation and diffusion of "useful knowledge." For quite a few years now, economists have become increasingly open to the idea that long-term economic change cannot be seriously analyzed without some concept of "culture" and some idea of how it changes and why these changes matter. McCloskey's massive trilogy (2006, 2010, 2016a) is by far the most significant of these analyses, but many mainstream economists are now committed to the significance of culture in the evolution of modern economies.[5] The reason this is so has been ob-

---

[3] This distinction has also found its way into the writings of Freud, who notes that "civilization" describes the sum of achievements that serve two types of purposes: "to protect men against nature, and to adjust their mutual relations" (Freud, [1930] 1961, p. 36).

[4] Differences in aptitude explain, for instance, why the Industrial Revolution started in Britain and not elsewhere in Europe (Mokyr, 2009a; Kelly, Mokyr, and Ó Gráda, 2014).

[5] Two particularly interesting examples are Doepke and Zilibotti (2008) and Clark (2007). Both stress the growth of certain cultural features associated with entrepreneurial behavior such as hard work and willingness to postpone gratification, and explicitly stress how these features are passed on from generation to generation. For a recent survey, see Alesina and Giuliano (2016).

vious for a long time. Individuals are assumed to have preferences and
beliefs that determine how they are likely to act both toward others and
toward their natural environment. However, these cultural elements can
change, and we want to know why they change, and why at times culture
changes at a tectonic pace, and at others with startling rapidity (Jones,
2006). But "culture" is a vague and mushy word, and as such is not a satisfactory term: here we need to be much more specific about whose culture
and what specific elements of it mattered. Moreover, we must understand
how culture changes and why societies have different cultures. If economists cannot contribute to this literature, they should leave it to other social
scientists, but in that case they must concede much of the explanation of
modern economic growth to others. An alternative is to see what historians
and students of "culture" (in a certain sense) have had to say and incorporate their insights into the economic narrative (Vries, 2001).

To start with: Culture means various things to different people,
and to begin, we need to clarify the concept and our use of it. Given the
rather astonishing popularity of the concept of culture in the social sciences
and the humanities and the mind-boggling number of definitions employed,
it is useful for an economist to start off by defining precisely what is included in and excluded from "culture" and how it differs from "institutions,"
before we examine its role in the origins of modern economic growth.[6] The
definition I use here (and one very similar to the definition proposed by
Boyd and Richerson, 1985, p. 2) is: *Culture is a set of beliefs, values, and prefer-*
ences, capable of affecting behavior, that are socially (not genetically) transmitted and
that are shared by some subset of society. In what follows, my approach is
similar to and inspired by the literature on cultural evolution proposed by
some anthropologists. It will have little in common with "cultural studies"
and the cultural analysis implied by social constructivism.

What does this definition buy us? First, **beliefs** contain statements
of a positive (factual) nature that pertain to the state of the world, including
the physical and metaphysical environments and social relations.[7] Second,
values pertain to normative statements about society and social relations
(often thought of as ethics and ideology), whereas **preferences** are normative statements about individual matters such as consumption and
personal affairs. Third, culture is decomposable, that is, it consists of
separate cultural elements or features. Much like genes, these traits are

---

[6] In a famous essay, Kroeber and Kluckhohn (1952) assembled no fewer than 156
different definitions of the term culture. It goes without saying that since then the term has been
used and abused in different contexts by social scientists and historians, so that the number of
different definitions would be larger today.

[7] As such, "beliefs" should be interpreted as containing knowledge, both codifiable
and tacit, as well as human skills and capabilities. The most important component of these beliefs
for my purpose is useful knowledge.

largely shared by people of the same culture; a single individual cannot have a cultural trait that is not shared by others, but each individual is unique in that it is highly unlikely that two people share precisely the same combination of cultural elements. There is no puzzle here: by analogy, all individuals have somewhat different genotypes (identical twins excluded) yet they share the vast bulk of their genes with other people and even with other mammals that have quite different phenotypes. Furthermore, this definition stresses that culture involves social learning, so that one's beliefs, values, and knowledge are not built-up from scratch for each individual but are acquired from others. The key concepts of attitude and aptitude are contained in the larger category of culture, and they will remain at the center of the discussion.

One could argue whether *behavior* itself (that is, actions) should be included in the concept of culture, but it seems useful to separate actions (which may be driven by a combination of cultural and other causes) from culture that guides and constrains it, although a great deal of culture, much like junk DNA that does not code for any known proteins, just "is" there in our minds and conditions no actions. The use of these evolutionary terms suggests an analogy that treats culture as genotypical and actions as phenotypical. Although tempting (and the subject of a large literature), such analogies should be carried out cautiously, as facile projections from one subject area to another are fraught with pitfalls. The argument that social phenomena or historical developments can be analyzed as analogous *to* biological processes is more misleading than helpful. Rather, my approach here is derived directly from the approach outlined in Aldrich et al. (2008), in which we argued that Darwinism in a historical framework is more of a general tool of analysis. The basic argument is not a facile shoehorning of complex social phenomena into a framework derived from biology but rather a *generalized Darwinism* that "relies on the claim of common abstract features in both the social and the biological world; it is essentially a contention of a degree of ontological communality, at a high level of abstraction and not at the level of detail" (Aldrich et al., p. 579).[8]

Before proceeding, it is important to distinguish between such terms as "culture" and "institutions." For my purposes it seems best to regard culture as something *entirely of the mind,* which can differ from individual to individual and is, to an extent, a matter of individual *choice.* Institutions are socially determined conditional incentives and consequences to actions. These incentives are parametrically given to every individual and are beyond their control. In that way institutions produce the incentive structure in a society. Institutions as "rules" can be seen as a special case:

---

[8] Many scholars have argued for more precise isomorphisms between natural and economic history. For instance, Vermeij (2004, p. 247) has argued that "human history recapitulates the much more protracted history of life as a whole."

the rules specify certain behaviors to be proper and legal, but they also specify the penalties for breaking them and the rewards for meeting them.[9] Beliefs and preferences are the "scaffolds," to use Douglass North's (2005) term, of institutions. In a sense culture forms the foundation of institutions, in that it provides them with legitimacy.[10] In a different context, Leighton and López (2013, pp. 11, 112–22) create a similar framework, in which incentives determine behavior, institutions "frame" incentives, ideas influence institutions (provided circumstances are favorable), and entrepreneurs make change happen. That is not to say, of course, that every institution is necessarily supported by a majority of the population; many institutions serve a small minority that uses its power to extract resources from others (Acemoglu and Robinson, 2012). Regarding beliefs as the foundation of institutions is oversimplified. Greif, in his attempt to define institutions with care, points out a problem with the "institutions-as-rules" idea, namely that without a meta-rule (or ethic) that rules should be respected and followed, rules and laws may well be empty and unenforced suggestions.[11] For him, institutions should be seen as a set of factors that generate regularities in behavior. By this definition, institutions however, inevitably contain in some measure beliefs as well, and thus would violate my attempt to keep them apart. To be sure, institutions in turn affect cultural beliefs in many ways and through many mechanisms (Alesina and Giuliano, 2016, pp. 6–7). Perhaps the best way of thinking of the relationship between the two concepts is to realize that they coevolve, much like a species and its environment. Recent research by economists and other social scientists has examined the details of this coevolution process in detail and concluded that it can easily lead to multiple equilibria outcomes, in which "good institutions" (defined as those that lead to better economic

---

[9] This is a variation on Bowles (2004, pp. 47–48) who defines institutions as "laws, informal rules, and conventions that give a durable structure to social interactions ... and make conformity a best response to virtually all members of the relevant groups."

[10] The mapping from one to the other is far from monotonic, however. The political process that converts beliefs into institutions is noisy and depends not only on beliefs but also on the ability of those who hold the beliefs to persuade or coerce others to accede to the institutions. As Szostak (2009, p. 234) notes, many institutions are little more than the "codification" of beliefs. Thus, an aversion of violence in a society may lead to formal legislation against it, and the conviction that wearing seatbelts in cars (a cultural belief) reduces accident fatalities leads to legislation making them mandatory (an institution). A cultural belief that the use of narcotics is bad may lead to an institution that mandates prison terms for drug use.

[11] As Greif (2006, p. 7) put it, rules "are nothing more than instructions that can be ignored. If prescriptive rules of behavior are to have an impact, individuals must be motivated to follow them. ... By 'motivation' I mean here incentives broadly defined to include expectations, beliefs, and internalized norms."

performance and growth) interact with a culture that enforces them, where-as bad institutions may reinforce a culture that perpetuates them.

Other scholars have used related if somewhat different definitions. Thus Roland (2004) suggests that culture as defined be included as a "slow-moving institution" that affects political and legal arrangements that can be changed faster; he prefers to limit the word "culture" to beliefs about the interaction of individuals, driven by social norms. Either way, however, there is a consensus that the incentive structure of society rests on a found-ation of ideas, some of them about nature, some about human interactions, and still others of a moral nature. In other words, institutions rest on a bed-rock of what people believe and know (or, to be more precise, *think* they know). If the culture and the institutions are misaligned, the foundations become unstable. If there is a clash between culture and institutions, in the sense that the underlying belief or legitimacy for certain institutions has eroded, a political disequilibrium has emerged. Unfortunately, there is no good theory to predict what happens then; in some cases the institutions are overthrown, but in others through political and military means, those who benefit from the institutional status quo can hold on to power and the resources that come with it for a long time.

If institutions have indeed become one of the main explanations of why some nations are economically successful—as the modern consen-sus increasingly seems to suggest—how do institutions relate to cultural beliefs?[12] At first glance the connection between culture and institutions seems tenuous. The institutional variation on our planet suggests that societies with similar cultural and environmental characteristics can have quite different institutional set-ups. The almost hackneyed example is of course Korea, where an arbitrary line dividing a single nation in two created two dramatically different societies. The different development in the past decade between Venezuela and Colombia could be cited as another example. Through sheer bad luck some countries ended up with predatory rulers or aggressive neighbors who created bad institutions that thwarted economic growth and caused a great deal of human misery. While such institutions have low legitimacy, they can survive by using a high level of coercion—which itself is a costly and inefficient way of maintaining bad institutions, thus compounding poverty and backwardness.

Culture, then, helps determine what kind of institutions emerge, but it does not guarantee outcomes. Indeed, one of the first and most in-fluential papers in the analysis of the role of institutions in economic history (Greif, 1994) used the term "cultural beliefs" to identify the forces that underpin changes in institutions and thus to understand how they

---

[12] Acemoglu and Robinson (2012, pp. 56–63) dismiss the role of culture as an independent factor, and stress the importance of institutions without fully recognizing the possible effect of the dominant beliefs and values on the kind of institutions that emerge.

supported markets and exchange. Greif's point was that if the economic game is to have a cooperative equilibrium, what people actually believe about how others behave helps determine how they themselves will act in a variety of situations of interest to the economic historian. In short, if economists admit that economic history cannot do without institutions, it cannot do without a better understanding of culture. They like things, however, clear-cut, precise, and if possible formally modeled and testable. This is a daunting task.

Moreover, as already noted, causality does not run purely from culture to institutions. Institutions create the environment in which cultural evolution occurs. Much of what is to follow describes cultural changes as a result of the incentives and stimuli provided by an institutional environment. Institutional outcomes, moreover, have a large aleatory component. They are the result of battles, dynastic arrangements, power struggles, the arbitrary preferences of unusually influential or powerful individuals, political compromises, and maps drawn by generals or politicians. There was nothing inevitable in the survival of relatively tolerant institutions in the Low Countries and Britain in the seventeenth century, any more than in the emergence of very different institutional outcomes in Korea or Germany after World War II. Such differences often seem to be the outcome of historical flukes rather than of deep cultural processes. Furthermore, institutions, once in place, can display considerable durability and persistence even if they do not conform with the cultural beliefs of most people. As long as the interests of a few powerful groups are served, they can maintain a set of institutions for a very long time (Acemoglu and Robinson, 2006). It is hard to deny that importing such institutions as free-entry markets, fair and general-franchise elections, and freedom of speech and association into a society in which the Enlightenment culture that underpins them is not widely shared is at best an uphill struggle. Yet, perplexingly, it is not impossible.

As already noted, culture is shared, yet individuals will normally differ in some ways from one another in what they precisely believe, just as they differ in genotype. This analogy should also not be pushed too far; above all, cultural beliefs are not like genes in that the latter are "immutable for life." Above all, they are a matter of choice.[13] Individuals can make explicit choices to either accept the default cultural characteristics they were born with or to reject them and replace them with something else that they select from their cultural menu. Of course, we do not always know how

---

[13] To be sure, even in biology, modern research has blurred some of these sharp distinctions. While the inherited DNA sequence is immutable over a lifetime, cells can acquire and pass on to their progeny information acquired over their lives through epigenetic inheritance using methylated bases in the DNA. These do not alter the proteins but affect the chances of their being transcribed. See Jablonka and Lamb (2005, pp. 113–46).

and even when some preferences and beliefs are acquired, and shedding them may be difficult. However, it is not quite correct to compare preferences to accents (Bowles, 2004, p. 372), because accents for most people become fixed as teenagers, whereas a taste for certain forms of art or food can continue to evolve over a lifetime, even if the likelihood of change declines with age.

Some pathbreaking research on the economics of culture and how beliefs can affect economic performance has recently been carried out by theorists and empirical economists alike.[14] One mechanism through which culture is believed to have affected economic performance is through the idea that higher trust and cooperation reduce transaction costs and thus facilitate exchange and emergence of well-functioning markets. Another is civic-mindedness. A spirit of public consciousness and willingness to abstain from free-riding behavior in collective actions supports a higher supply of public goods and investment in infrastructure than is otherwise possible. The beliefs that makes such behavior possible depend crucially on the beliefs regarding the behavior of others; this is a classic example of frequency-dependence in the choice of beliefs, a topic I return to below in chapter 5.[15] The importance of these elements was already pointed out by John Stuart Mill ([1848], 1929, pp. 111–12) and different levels of trust have been shown to explain income differences between nations (Zak and Knack, 2001).

As noted, both theorists and applied economists have shown a growing interest in the economics of culture. Among the theoretical works by economists on the origins of culture are the pathbreaking papers by Bisin and Verdier (1998, 2011), which for the first time brought to economics the important work on cultural evolution done by scholars of cultural anthropology and population dynamics. The empirical work on the economics of culture depends heavily on data from the World Values Survey, Gallup World Poll, and similar data (Guiso, Sapienza, and Zingales, 2006; Tabellini, 2008, 2010; Deaton, 2011). This work has successfully addressed a whole set of issues of supreme importance to economists such as household behavior and female labor force participation, corruption, and migration (Fernández, 2011). It also draws heavily on experimental data, which suggest that culture modifies behavior in many ways that qualify and nuance the standard economic assumptions of individual utility maximization in such obvious set-ups as simple ulti-

---

[14] Much of this work is surveyed in Bisin and Verdier (2011) and Alesina and Giuliano (2016). It is striking that there seems to be very little work so far done on the cultural factors behind scientific and technological progress.

[15] In Greif's (1994, p. 915) terms, cultural beliefs are the expectations that individuals have about the actions that others will take. To that we should add the further belief that individuals hold regarding the morality of a particular action.

matum games (Bowles, 2004, pp. 110–19). A recent essay by Rodrik (2014, p. 189) complains that ideas are "strangely absent" from modern models of political econom—but the same might be said about models of economic growth and innovation, though recent work has made a beginning at coming to grips with the cultural roots of these phenomena (Spolaore and Wacziarg, 2013).

Most research by economists on culture as they see it focuses primarily on social attitudes, beliefs, and preferences supporting informal and formal institutions that increase cooperation, reciprocity, trust, and the efficient operation of the economy (Guiso, Sapienza, and Zingales, 2008; Bowles and Gintis, 2011). More recently, economists have become interested in attitudes toward discipline, education, work, time, self-control, and similar areas. Cultural beliefs also help determine, for instance, whether preferences might be "other-regarding" (that is, whether the consumption of others affects one's well-being) and whether they might be "process-regarding" (that is, whether the utility one derives from being in a particular state of the world depends on the way that state was reached rather than on the intrinsic quality of the state itself). Both of those types of preferences are not normally part of the analysis of economic preferences, but there is no inherent reason they should not be.[16] A good example of process-regarding preferences is when an individual cares whether he or she earns income by creating wealth through entrepreneurial activity or by redistributing it from others through rent-seeking or corruption. Does one regard a dollar in the same way no matter how it was earned, or does one care whether it was made while providing a socially useful activity? Is a dollar earned the same as a dollar stolen? Such preferences could make a difference in the institutions that are critical to the emergence of a civil economy and economic growth (Bowles, 2004, pp. 109–11; Bowles and Gintis, 2011, pp. 10–11, 32–35).

In what follows, I concentrate primarily on the one element in cultural beliefs that economists have so far neglected almost entirely, namely the attitude toward Nature and the willingness and ability to harness it to human material needs. Ultimately the relations with *makom*, or the physical world around us in the end determine the growth of useful knowledge and eventually that of technology-driven growth.[17] Technology is above all a consequence of human willingness to investigate, manipulate,

---

[16] Many modern economists have, of course, seen the obvious connections here. Thus one has summarized that "what people believe what it takes to become prosperous has much to do with how they behave" (M. Porter, 2000).

[17] In her excellent and exhaustive surveys of the literature on culture and economics, Raquel Fernández (2008, 2011) does not deal much science or technology or indeed the accumulation of knowledge in any form, although she stresses that "The relationship between technology and culture also needs to be investigated" (2008, p. 10).

and exploit natural phenomena and regularities, and given such willingness, the growth of the stock of knowledge that underpins and conditions the exploitation of knowledge. The willingness and ability to acquire, disseminate, and harness such knowledge are themselves part of culture and thus determine the intensity of the search for knowledge of nature, the agenda of the research, the institutions that govern the community doing the research, the methods of acquiring and vetting it, the conventions by which such knowledge is accepted as valid, and its dissemination to others who might make use of it. It is in this general area that the roots of modern economic growth should be sought—specifically in events and phenomena that precede the eighteenth-century Enlightenment and Industrial Revolution in the centuries that are known, for better or for worse, as "early modern Europe," roughly speaking between the first voyage to America by Columbus and the publication of the *Principia Mathematica* by Newton. It is the basic argument of this book that European culture and institutions were shaped in those centuries to become more conducive to the kind of activities that eventually led to the economic sea changes that created the modern economies.

Chapter 2

Nature and Technology

I have already noted that there is an obvious limitation to the approach focusing on institutions to explain long-term economic growth. Such phenomena as trust, honesty, cooperativeness, thriftiness, public-spiritedness, and law-and-order can explain a great deal of economic performance: the emergence and growth of trade at arm's length, the evolution of nonpersonal credit networks, better land and labor markets, and thus more efficient resource allocations. But in the end, they cannot explain the miraculous explosion of science and technology in the past two and a half centuries that engendered modern economic growth.

At a high level of abstraction, the difference between "Smithian" and "Schumpeterian" growth is that for the former, exchange and cooperation based on trust or respect for the law are treated as a game between individuals whereas the essence of Schumpeterian growth is based on the manipulation of natural regularities and phenomena and thus au fond should be seen as a game against nature. However, only in the extreme limit is innovation a game against nature *alone*. There can be technological change in a Robinson Crusoe economy, but in any society, coming up with a technical solution to a problem is only the beginning of success. In practice, innovation requires a great deal of social interaction with creditors, workers, suppliers, customers, and the authorities, and all these relations involve elements that are part of a "civil economy." Society can set up institutions that reward innovators in a variety of ways—through patents, prizes, or patronage—or it can try to discourage them by, for instance, accusing them of "black magic." One particular aspect of culture that has been much discussed in recent years as a key to economic development is public sector corruption and the institutional environment in which innovation must operate. Vested interests of incumbents protecting the rents generated by status quo techniques and fear of the unknown and novel create strong incentives to resist innovation. If groups committed to these beliefs control the formal apparatus of the state, they can thwart innovative efforts. Moreover, certain culturally determined preferences will have a positive spillover effect on technology, even if that was not their intention: investment in the human capital of children and a low rate of time preference and risk aversion come to mind.

Culture can thus affect technological creativity through institutions. But growth through innovation is in large part dependent on a direct link between culture and technology, through attitudes toward nature and the beliefs regarding relations between humans and their physical environment. The most direct link from culture and beliefs to technology runs through religion. If metaphysical beliefs are such that manipulating and controlling nature invoke a sense of fear or guilt, technological creativity will inevitably be limited in scope and extent. The legends of the ill-fated innovators Prometheus and Daedalus illustrate the deeply ambiguous relationship between the ancient Greeks' religious beliefs and their attitudes toward technology. If the culture is heavily infused with respect and worship of ancient wisdom so that any intellectual innovation is considered deviant and blasphemous, technological creativity will be similarly constrained. Irreverence is a key to progress. But so, as Lynn White (1978) has pointed out, is anthropocentrism. In his classic work, White stressed the importance of a belief in a creator who has designed a universe for the use of humans, who in exploiting nature would illustrate His wisdom and power.

As White and many authors have stressed, social attitudes toward production and work (and leisure) are another major factor in determining the likelihood of innovation. Technologically progressive societies were often relatively egalitarian ones. In societies dominated by a small, wealthy, but unproductive and exploitative elite, the low social prestige of productive activity meant that creativity and innovation would be directed toward an agenda of interest to the elite. The educated and sophisticated elite focused on efforts supporting its power such as military prowess and administration, or on such topics of leisure as literature, games, the arts, and philosophy, and not so much on the mundane problems of the farmer in his field, the sailor on his ship, or the artisan in his workshop. The agenda of the leisurely elite was of great importance to the lovers of music in the eighteenth-century Habsburg lands, but was not of much interest to their farmers and manufacturers. The Austrian Empire created Haydn and Mozart, but no Industrial Revolution. As McCloskey (2006) has stressed, the bourgeois societies of the Netherlands and Britain of the seventeenth century, in contrast, were prime candidates for technological advances. Technological progress might take place in areas that interfaced with the military or with civil administration, such as the advances that the Romans scored in hydraulic and construction engineering, but agriculture and manufacturing made little progress during the heyday of the Roman Empire.

A somewhat different link between potential technological creativity and underlying cultural values has to do with individualist vs. collectivist cultural norm (Gorodnichenko and Roland, 2011; see also Triandis, 1995). Gorodnichenko and Roland define a variable they dub "individualism" which measures the degree that societies reward such personal accomplishments as innovations. Placing low values on individualism means that collective actions are easier to achieve, but it flattens the reward structures and thus discourages individuals from standing out. Hence individualism stimulates innovation by not penalizing heterodox intellectuals who come up with unconventional and possibly heretical ideas and think outside the box (Triandis, 1995). The cultural beliefs underpinning the institutions that set these incentives are a good example of how such cultural beliefs can influence innovation, but they concern how society should operate, not the relation between individuals and their environment. Societies and nations differ in their valuations of such cultural norms, and it seems plausible that more individualist cultural norms will be more consistent with technological progress—if indeed the institutions they undergird encourage technological creativity and not more destructive forms of individualism such as military prowess. Gorodnichenko and Roland argue plausibly that in fairly poor societies collectivist values may lead to more productivity growth but that for truly original innovations, individualist values are more important. While their data are for a cross-section of modern countries and show an unambiguous relation between their measure of individualism and economic outcomes, there is not much evidence to indicate that historically individualism played a similar role.[1]

A related and important literature focuses on the distinction between *general* and *specialized* (or limited) morality (Tabellini, 2008, 2010). In a specialized morality society, individuals care primarily about themselves and members of their immediate environment (say, close relatives and friends) and much less about the larger society in which they live, so that they tend to be more opportunistic when they deal with unknown persons. A general morality means one also cares about people one does not know. Innovation, because its benefits affect a larger community (and possibly humanity at large), is at least in part more likely to occur in a society that has opted for a more general morality, in which innovators are motivated by a desire to do something for a large number of people, or at least acquire the respect of others who care about such things. Especially because in the production of useful knowledge nearly all the economic surplus thus created accrues to consumers (that is, anonymous people),

---

[1] MacFarlane (1978) has argued explicitly that late Medieval England was very much an individualist society and drawn a link between that individualism and eighteenth-century industrialization.

general morality encourages more research that has no direct and immediate payoffs to the creator than specialized or "local" morality.

That said, culture can affect technological progress in many ways
other than metaphysical beliefs and individualism, and they will be at the
center of this book. Cultures can be backward- or forward-looking in the
sense that some may hold the knowledge and learning of previous generations in such high esteem that novel ideas run a serious risk of being
viewed as apostasy. At the other extreme, cultures can regard everything
new as an improvement, so that only the newest beliefs and gadgets are
held in high regard. Religions, with some notable exceptions, have tended
toward conservatism in this regard. For most of its post-temple history,
Judaism was, on the whole, committed to the unchallenged authority of the
writings of previous generations, and new ideas had to be camouflaged as
commentary and exegesis of ancient texts. In Christianity, physics and
metaphysics often collided, and as a result the revolutionary theories of
Copernicus and Darwin, in very different eras, ran into serious resistance
from people with strong religious beliefs. Scientific and technological
innovation, of most interest to economic historians, often ran and still runs
into resistance in backward-looking cultures, in large part because every invention is an act of rebellion against time-honored beliefs and deeply entrenched customs.

A critical cultural belief that drives economic growth and comple-
ments the belief in the "virtuousness of technology" is a belief in progress,
and specifically in economic progress. Such a belief has positive, normative, and prescriptive components. First the positive component means the
acceptance of the belief that material progress is *possible*, that is, history
shows an upward trend and not just stationary cyclical movements and this
trend can be continued. It opposes the "Ecclesiastes view of history," which
stipulates that long-term change is impossible, because "there is nothing
new under the sun." A belief in future progress, of course, requires an
implicit model of what could have brought about such progress as well as
evidence that such progress had happened in the past. As I argue in detail
in chapter 14, such a model and the evidence supporting it emerged in
seventeenth-century Europe and became a major force in the age of Enlightenment. The model postulates that what contemporaries called "useful
knowledge" (roughly speaking, science and technology) could become an
engine of economic progress through improving production techniques.

Second, the normative component postulates that economic progress is *desirable*, eschewing any notions that the accumulation of wealth and
material goods is somehow sinful or vain. Such beliefs are a good illustration of the kind of dilemma faced by economists trying to think about
culture. Were the beliefs that wealth accumulation was sinful— embodied
in the famous New Testament statement that it was unlikely for a rich man
to enter heaven and Plato's belief that the more riches and rich men are
honored in the state, the more virtue and the virtuous are dishonored—

simply a rationalization of the inevitable poverty that a static technology and extractive institutions imposed on economies incapable of growth? Or were they in part an autonomous cultural force that was itself a cause of poverty by guiding the motives and incentives of the best and brightest members of society toward activities that were not conducive to economic growth? A similarly Weberian distinction can be made about whether intellectual activities were mystical and other worldly, with an attitude of resignation toward the environment, or directed toward the world, practical and materialist, believing that virtue and salvation were to be attained by confronting and achieving control over natural forces and using those resources for the good? Whatever the case, what is crucial is to see how that circle was broken in Europe and eventually led to the Industrial Revolution and the beginnings of modern growth (McCloskey, 2006, 2016a).

Third, once the possibility and desirability of economic progress had been accepted, a concrete *agenda* of policy measures and institutional change had to be formulated, elaborated, proposed, and implemented for long-term progress to take place. This agenda became increasingly concrete and detailed in the eighteenth century and was implemented, in different ways, in some European nations the late eighteenth century and then more widely in the nineteenth century. There was, of course, no unique way of carrying out this agenda. In some countries the "policies" were largely based on private initiative and spontaneous organization. In others the state needed to play a proactive role. Whatever the exact agenda, the policies had unintended consequences. At least in that regard they were like all evolutionary processes: messy and imprecise, full of false starts and dead ends.

These three cultural elements have roots that go far back into early European history, certainly to the late Middle Ages and possibly before. But before 1750 they did not produce anything like an Industrial Revolution or sustainable economic growth propelled by technological progress. Although held by a few individuals in earlier times, such attitudes were not sufficiently widespread to make a difference. The emergence of such beliefs among some individuals is never sufficient to generate economic growth; they must emerge in the right environment—one that is somehow conducive to rapid changes in attitudes and beliefs, which ultimately affect every aspect of society. The key element here is that those who propose the new ideas must have the opportunity to persuade others. Cultural change is to a large extent about *persuasion*. What makes persuasion possible— though not inevitable— is a technology for discourse and communication that is sufficient to reach the audience that matters, and the establishment of rhetorical rules sufficient to convince them (McCloskey, 1985, pp. 27–28). Another critical element is that entrenched conservative elements trying to resist intellectual innovation for some reason are weakened. Finally, we would expect to observe the proliferation of new ideas in societies where there is some compelling reason to doubt the traditional wisdom as inconsistent with indisputable new facts that have come to light in recent years. Such an anomaly between beliefs and facts could occur, for instance, when two societies that were hitherto unconnected establish contact, so that they learn about each other. The environment described is a fair (if schematic and oversimplified) description of Europe in the two centuries after 1500.

Chapter 3

Cultural Evolution and Economics

In this chapter I use an evolutionary approach to culture.[1] As already noted, it can be extremely misleading to "shoehorn" the methodology of one field into another. Economics in particular and the social sciences in general are decidedly not like biology. Looking for forced parallels and analogies is not a useful strategy. But using the parallels that do exist and pointing out the differences can be illuminating.

Evolutionary models have had a mixed record in economics; despite the influence of Nelson and Winter's (1982) seminal book, mainstream economics has typically relegated evolutionary models to niches, such as evolutionary game theory. An attempt to use gene-culture coevolution to explain the emergence of successful cooperation in human societies can be found in Bowles and Gintis (2011). In economic history, except for a few attempts to use evolutionary models of technology, these ideas have had little impact.[2] Their introduction into economic history, at first blush the research area most amenable to evolutionary models, has been slow. Recently, Darwinian models of selection have been proposed to explain the economic transformation of Western Europe and the emergence of modern growth (Galor and Moav, 2002; Clark, 2007). Such models mark a considerable advance in applying Darwinian models to economic growth. The idea in this literature is that the agents who are most likely to perform well in the economy and thus to be agents of economic growth also tend to have differential reproduction rates, so their share in the population keeps rising. The cultural traits these agents embody might be called "middle class values." They emphasize investment in human

---

[1] For a recent summary of this literature, see Mesoudi (2011) and Richerson and Christiansen (2013).

[2] See for instance Constant, 1980; Vincenti, 1990; Ziman, 2000.

capital, industriousness, thrift, and other elements of what is sometimes misleadingly thought of as "the Protestant ethic." As Deirdre McCloskey (2006) has stressed the bourgeois ethic involves an implicit recognition of the value of progress: hard work and education can make one better off, and thus collectively and cumulatively generate a trend of progress. A rise in the prevalence and social prestige of such "bourgeois values" would be a powerful factor in explaining economic performance. But can such a rise be better understood with Darwinian models? The rigid evolutionary approach, while different from the one used here, employs the important assumption that culture is essentially hereditary and thus passed on from parent to child. This somewhat restrictive assumption permits the possibility of using models of Darwinian selection. The basic idea is that differential reproduction, working mostly through the larger number of surviving "high-quality" children, leads to an expansion of middle class culture and thus eventually to successful economic growth.

There is a great deal of validity in these arguments, even though it would take many centuries for a relatively small group even with significantly higher reproduction rates to become a majority in the population.[3] The agents who constitute the engine of technological progress are usually a fairly small proportion of the population, the right tail of the human capital distribution. Beyond the great inventors, the Industrial Revolution required a larger cadre of mechanics, highly skilled artisans, entrepreneurs, financiers, merchants, and organizers of different kinds. But the world of useful inventions remained to be conquered what Robert Hooke called "a Cortesian army, well-Disciplined and regulated, though their numbers be but small" (cited in Hunter, 1989, p. 233). The Industrial Revolution did not require, or cause, the transformation of an entire economy or labor force, and evolutionary models that depend on the numerical growth of this key group through differential reproduction are missing the boat. In mechanical Darwinian models, culture is assumed to be set for life at conception; there is little room in these models for learning, persuasion, or imitation.

The more plausible way to use evolutionary models in economic growth is to take the "cultural element" to be the unit of selection rather than its carrier. That gets rid of the knotty problem of selection on humans, which generates slow cultural change because of the long length of a

---

[3] One constraint on the success of Darwinian models in the preindustrial West is the institutional constraint of monogamy, which placed limits on the most successful males to propagate their genes (unlike, say, the Yanomanö Indians documented by Napoleon Chagnon, where the most aggressive males were allowed to have more wives). Leaving out their undeniable potential to have illegitimate offspring (who were, however, severely handicapped in most Western societies), the only way in which more successful individuals could have a reproductive advantage in these societies is through lower infant mortality, which has been documented for small samples in seventeenth-century Britain but seems a relatively weak quantitative reed to lean on.

human generation. The cultural elements themselves, and not their carriers, are subject to evolutionary forces. It is important not to push the analogy too far, looking for particulate and discrete units such as "memes" that would be isomorphic to genes and even might be "selfish" like them. Evolutionary models are larger than Richard Dawkins, even larger than Charles Darwin (Hodgson and Knudsen, 2010). Above all, they involve selection, but the selection here is not the natural selection that occurs through population dynamics but the conscious choices made by individuals.

Every person forms a unique cultural phenotype much like every person forms a unique biological genotype, but how is this phenotype formed? Cultural evolution sees this as essentially a quasi-Lamarckian process, in which individuals acquire cultural characteristics through learning and imitation during their lifetimes and pass these on to others. They choose their cultural elements (or stick to the default, which are the beliefs and preferences they acquire from their parents during socialization). It does not rule out a genetic component in the choices made.[4]

Darwin was the first to point out in his *Descent of Man* that culture exhibited certain evolutionary characteristics.[5] Three elements make these frameworks Darwinian, as much of this extensive literature has noted (Aldrich et al., 2008, p. 583). One is that cultures, much like species, contain a great variation of traits, the results of past innovation. Many of these traits are shared among certain groups of individuals and distinguish them from those belonging to other groups. Yet the lines are often blurry, as they are between species, and cultural overlaps are common. Jews and Muslims share a belief in a single God and a taboo on the eating of pork, yet they are distinct groups in a way not dissimilar from two species that share the vast bulk of their genes and yet are phenotypically quite distinct.

The second is that culture, much like genes, is passed on among individuals, either vertically from generation to generation or horizontally among separate units. Genetic transmission occurs through mitosis in eukaryotic cells, cultural transmission through socialization and learning in

---

[4] Recent work by James Fowler and others indicates that ideology and other cultural variants may have a genetic component, working through dopamine receptor genes that are inherited (Fowler and Schreiber, 2008).

[5] Darwin made this point especially poignantly with respect to language, one of the main components of any culture. See Darwin (1859/1871, p. 466). The classic works in the mid-1980s by Cavalli-Sforza and Feldman (1981) and Boyd and Richerson (1985) both stress the evolutionary features of culture. Recent research in anthropology and social sciences has shown that evolutionary approaches can indeed be quite fruitful if still controversy-ridden (Henrich, Boyd and Richerson, 2008; Hodgson and Knudsen, 2010; Mesoudi, 2011). These approaches have also become a cornerstone of a certain line of cultural argument associated with Richard Dawkins and his followers, who have tried to identify units of cultural analysis equivalent to genes.

cultural processes. Children are being socialized by parents, but socialization (that is, the vertical transmissions of information from parents to
children) is not all there is to choice-based cultural evolution; children are
socialized by other children and non-parents, and as adults they can still be
subject to persuasion and other forms of cultural ontogeny and engage in
choice-based learning albeit at a declining rate with age.[6]

The third is that there are "too many" cultural features so that
individuals have to choose among menus. In biology, what drives evolution is superfecundity: species have the capability to reproduce at a rate
much faster than is needed for replacement, which means that not all those
who can be born will be, or that those born will actually survive. This is the
Darwinian "struggle for existence." Natural selection is driven by a process
in which those with the most fit features have a better chance to survive
and reproduce. Cultural features are "superfecund" in that there are far too
many of them produced for an individual to absorb, so that selection must
take place among sometimes enormous menus. There are 10,000 distinct
religions in the world, and 6,800 different languages. No individual can
believe in all religions and speak all languages. One has to choose. The
same is true, say, for a belief about the causes of business cycles: does one
believe they are primarily generated by real productivity shocks or by finan-
cial-sector shocks? In many other cases, however, new information is piled
on top of old, and by accepting the new as valid, one does not necessarily
have to make a choice. In this regard the superfecundity feature of the evolutionary model is a constraint that is not invariably binding.

These three characteristics—variation, inheritability, and superfecundity—as Darwin showed, are sufficient to ensure that selection is
adaptive: when there is a change in the environment, cultural traits trend
to change through the retention of some and the elimination of other elements. The exact unit of this selection is the "cultural element" that
remains at the center of the debate (Mesoudi, 2011). The cultural evolution
literature has argued that cultural evolution does not require the much
stricter conditions imposed on evolution after Darwin by the neo-Darwinian synthesis. These additional conditions postulated further constraints on
evolution: the so-called Weismann barrier (acquired phenotypical characteristics are not passed on to following generations); the random ("blind")
occurrence of mutations (so that *all* direction in evolution is imparted by
selection); and the particulate nature of transmission by discrete units

---

[6] Social values may be part of the changing life cycle, as illustrated by the famous
quote attributed to Winston Churchill but actually first stated by the French historian François
Guizot that if you are not a left-leaning liberal when you are 20 you have no heart but if you're
not a conservative at age 40, you have no brain, implying that people become more conservative
with age. As argued by Tuschman (2014), personalities may be hard wired for shifts over the life
cycle and changes in gene expression may alter openness to new ideas, conscientiousness, and
other traits.

(genes) (Mesoudi, 2011, pp. 40–47). Darwin had a theory of evolution without knowing about the neo-Darwinian synthesis, and while the latter has worked miracles in making the theory of evolution a coherent biological doctrine, Mesoudi makes a persuasive case that these principles are not needed for an evolutionary theory of culture. Where the use of biology is unnecessarily confining, it should simply be abandoned. Evolution occurs on cultural variants, which are neither random mutations on existing variants nor necessarily slow cumulative variations that are retained selectively. The discrete units (memes) are purely imaginary and not all that useful. Above all, learned characteristics can be passed on—indeed, this is the very engine of cultural change. Of the various aspects of cultural change, what is of central interest here is changes in useful knowledge, leading ultimately to changes in technology and economic welfare.

The odd thing is that when otherwise insightful cultural evolutionists come to the history of technology, they seem to fall into the same errors they warn against in almost the same sentence. Thus, after they dismiss the idea of sudden and discrete leaps in genotypes leading to major differences in phenotypes, they mechanically extend the notion of gradualism to the history of invention. The history of technology, Richerson and Boyd (2005, p. 51) assert, depended on "complex artifacts ... built up piecemeal by the cumulative improvements of technologies at the hands of many innovators ... each contributing a small improvement to the ultimately amazing instrument" (see also Mesoudi, 2011, p. 33 for a similar view). It is far from obvious on what evidence this extension of evolutionary gradualism to the history of technology is based. To say that *every* technique embodies some previous technological component (as does Basalla, 1988) is no more a refutation of saltationism than to point out that even Goldsmith's hopeful (and possibly fanciful) monsters and the rapidly changing species in Gould's and Eldredge's punctuated equilibria involved pre-existing DNA. In fact, few examples are more striking than the one ironically deployed by Richerson and Boyd (Harrison's H-4 marine chronometer) and Mesoudi (Newcomen's steam engine) to show that discrete leaps in technology did in fact take place. The history of technology is, in fact, full of major discontinuities in which novel designs created totally new options. From time to time, one can observe a "hopeful monstrosity—indeed no better one than Thomas Newcomen's Dudley Castle engine, installed in 1712.[7] More broadly, it is easy to spot discontinuous leaps in culture. Each of them inevitably contains elements of earlier features, but they are phenotypically and functionally sufficiently different from what came before to qualify as hopeful monsters. None of this refutes the point

---

[7] The term "hopeful monstrosity" was coined by the evolutionary biologist Richard Goldsmith (1940) in his now largely discredited view that evolution could at times advance by discrete quantum leaps in which altogether new species emerged quite suddenly.

that for every successful radically new design, there are far more that languished largely forgotten on inventors' workbenches. Consider the Stirling engine, invented in 1816, or funicular railroads.

To be sure, most technological progress and productivity growth are very much the result of the slow and gradual accumulation of small changes. Saltationism does not deny that. However, such small changes—or microinventions as I have elsewhere called them (Mokyr, 1990)—tend to run into diminishing returns after a while. What is needed for sustained innovation is the injection of a new idea, or at least an idea from a very different area, what Matt Ridley (2014) has called in a memorable phrase "ideas having sex." Improve a horse and buggy all you will, it will never become a bicycle; improve a bicycle all you will, it will never become a Segway. The statement that even such novel designs contained some existing components detracts nothing from the revolutionary nature of the new design.[8] More to the point, perhaps, is that fundamentalist incrementalism as proposed by George Basalla and others overlooks the complex interplay between prescriptive knowledge (technology) and the propositional knowledge that underpins it (its epistemic base). The positive feedback between those two can create rapid, even explosive, advances that clearly refute any loose analogies to evolutionary gradualism (Mokyr, 2002). Hopeful monsters who catch on for one reason or another are not only to be found in technology. The history of culture is full of rather sudden discontinuities that may appear inevitable and obvious ex post but were hard to predict ex ante, from Newton's *Principia* to Beethoven's *Eroica* to Darwin's *Origins*. Whatever the origins of these successful "monsters," they led to discontinuous changes.

There are many caveats to borrowing concepts from evolutionary biology for understanding of cultural change. It is far from obvious, for instance, what exactly is meant by the biological concepts of species and speciation in cultural models, since if species are defined by reproductive isolation, they have no meaning in a cultural context. The same is true for the concept of a "generation" in cultural evolution. Intergenerational information in neo-Darwinian models is transmitted only during mitosis, although by now it is quite clear that certain bacteria can actually acquire genetic information from other entities through such mechanisms as transduction. Cultural evolution places no upper bound on the number of sources of culture. Furthermore, there is no reason to believe that innovations occur wholly at random, much like mutations. In biology we do not get more mutations of a particular kind just because we need them. In culture the relation between innovations and perceived needs may be noisy,

---

[8] In Mokyr (1991), I provide five examples of such macroinventions during the Industrial Revolution: gaslighting, the breast wheel, the Jacquard loom, chlorine bleaching, and hot-air ballooning.

but a correlation seems plausible. Those who create the innovations do not exert their efforts at random, and while often they discover unexpected novelties, and innovations have many unintended and accidental consequences, these point to a noisy but not a wholly random process. For instance, a large literature in the economics of technological progress points to a search for labor-saving innovations in economies that have expensive workers, and while this literature has been heavily criticized, it is still true that one would expect inventors to work on issues that they deem for one reason or another to be a socially high priority, whether finding a smallpox vaccine or developing a nuclear bomb.

What, then, is actually gained from an evolutionary approach to culture? As explained in Aldrich et al. (2008, p. 589), such an approach supplies a framework for explaining the evolution of complex, undesigned outcomes over time, and it involves both the adaptation of cultural beliefs to changing circumstances and the elimination of others through selection. Economists still committed to the Popperian notion that science has to make some kind of falsifiable predictions will find little of use here. For the economic historian, the great advantage of evolutionary thinking is that it tries to explain why the present is the way it is and not some other way by using history. It encourages us to look at how the past shaped the present using Darwinian concepts, above all the concepts of choice and selection, and how such choices are made from past choices and innovations. Evolutionary thinking does not provide a clean and ready-made methodology like standard economics, but for a historical analysis of intellectual innovation, it has certain merits. Below I list some of the main advantages of an evolutionary approach to the history of culture.[9]

First, evolutionary systems are characterized by a fundamental duality of information and action, of genotype and phenotype. Distinctions between genotype and phenotype are hazardous to extend to cultural history, but all the same something can be learned from them. Culture is about matters of the mind; behavior and actions are the observable outcomes of preferences and knowledge (Mesoudi et al., 2013). But, as already noted, the mapping from beliefs to behavior is no simpler than that from genes to phenotypes; at best there are loose statistical associations masking the interactions of many variables.[10] One reason is that beliefs, much like other genotypical processes, affect "adjacent" beliefs. We can indeed speak of cultural *pleiotropy*, much like in evolutionary processes. Pleiotropy means

---

[9] For a similar argument, with a slightly different emphasis, see Mesoudi et al (2013).

[10] A good example can once again be found in the history of technology. In Mokyr (2002), I distinguish between propositional and prescriptive knowledge, the former roughly corresponding to a genotype, the latter to an observable technique. There is no easy mapping between the two. Sometimes techniques are used with virtually no understanding of why and how they work. At other times, the necessary underlying knowledge may well be there, but the techniques fail to emerge. Moreover, there is no clear-cut causal arrow between them; the best we can say is that they coevolve.

that a certain genotypic change leads to more than one phenotypical effect, because of the spillover effects on genes in the proximity of the mutation, in a sort of genetic packaging. A parallel phenomenon is *epistasis,* in which more than one piece of information is required to jointly bring about a certain trait or behavior. Such bundling often occurs in cultural evolution: a growth in the belief in the virtue of commercial activity may be associated with a growth in the belief in the value of useful knowledge although there is no necessary association.

Second, evolution is about the interaction between a pre-existing environment (in which an innovation is introduced) and the innovation itself. Innovation, as noted, remains a stochastic variable, even if it is in some sense directed and not purely random (as mutations are supposed to be in a pure Weismannian world). We do not know precisely why a certain idea occurs to an individual at a particular time, and why in some societies certain ideas simply never occur at all. The likelihood of an idea occurring to anyone is affected by the environment and perceived needs. But even if the flow of innovations were wholly predictable, we would not be able to predict with any certainty their success unless we could measure their "fitness" relative to the environment in which they take place, which determines whether they will catch on. What makes matters even more complicated is that even if it were possible somehow to predict the likelihood of an innovation succeeding in a given environment, that success is likely to produce complicated feedback effects because it is likely to change the environment itself.

Third, evolutionary systems are based on the dynamics produced by superfecundity and selection. The system throws up more variants than it can possibly accommodate, and so some form of winnowing must take place. The notion of natural selection in biology is purely metaphorical. Nobody actually makes choices, and the selection mechanism is wholly driven by differential reproduction and survival. In contrast, people actually make conscious choices choosing one cultural element over another from a menu of options, and then display the behavior implied by this choice. Like species, some ideas may go "extinct" in the face of a powerful new competitor (for example, geocentric astronomy or miasma theories of disease) but in other cases new ideas may coexist with the old ones in some kind of mixed equilibrium in which the competitive environment is insufficiently stringent to bring about a complete domination of the innovation. As I shall argue below in chapter 5, this can happen when knowledge is *untight,* that is, not very certain and not easily verifiable by the rhetorical criteria of the time. The idea of a niche is appropriate here: some environments provide an opportunity for minority cultural beliefs to survive and sustain themselves—one thinks of the Amish, flat-earthers, or Trotskyites.

Fourth, evolutionary models are rich: they allow change to occur on different levels. There is a long debate whether this occurs in biological systems and what the appropriate unit of selection is. Some biologists, led by George Williams and Richard Dawkins, feel that all selection happens at the level of the gene and nowhere else, but others strongly argue for selection at the level of the cell, the organism, the species, or even populations. Whatever the outcome of this literature, it seems beyond question that in cultural evolution selection can happen at many levels. To see this, consider a novel cultural trait offered to an individual in a particular society. If the individual chooses the variant and not another, this is one level of selection at which choice-based cultural evolution occurs. Now assume, however, that this variant increases the fitness of the individual and thus extends his life expectancy and/or the number of surviving children who resemble him. This increases the chances that the trait will be passed on, either vertically through the socialization of offspring or horizontally through "infecting" his immediate neighbors. Furthermore, suppose that society as a whole has now adopted the trait, and that it increases the fitness of the group (for example, through more cooperation or adopting a superior technique); this may mean a higher population growth rate in a society that has adopted the trait, and thus it is likely to increase its relative frequency in the global population. Evolution is not a single process, but a complex and intertwined system of conscious choices and "natural selection" at different levels.

Fifth, like all evolutionary systems, culture is resistant to change. In the technical language of evolutionary dynamics, prevalent cultural variants are evolutionarily stable strategies with respect to most conceivable innovations ("mutants"). There are built-in mechanisms that maintain a certain stability and provide an advantage to incumbent cultural variants against innovations, but the effectiveness of these mechanisms is itself a function of the content of the system. Ernst Mayr (1989, p. 35) has suggested that genes "perform as teams" and that "epistatic interactions form a powerful constraint on the response of the genotype to selection." Cultural elements, too, form a coherent system, which may resist change because of the interdependence of its components (Bateson, 1979, pp. 176–80).[11] For instance, a complex religious culture in which some elements are out of tune with perceived reality may either adapt to reflect new beliefs or cling to increasingly antiquated beliefs. The power structure within the organizations that depend on these beliefs (as is the case with the Catholic church today) may either dig in and fiercely resist change or adapt. In cultural systems (with no obvious parallel in biology), culture is tied up with what we could call cultural capital, investments that people have made in the current beliefs that would decline in value if the current beliefs

---

[11] The idea of inertia and resistance to radical change is common to all evolutionary systems (see Cohen and Stewart, 1994, pp. 92ff, 332), who define a concept of "canalization." See also for example Mayr (1991, pp. 160–61) who uses the term "cohesion."

were to be modified or overthrown. Physicists resisted quantum mechanics, physicians the germ theory, and chemists the atomic theory for precisely such reasons. No matter what kind of cultural system we are looking at, there will be some resistance to change, and many seemingly "fit" innovations will fail in a hostile environment biased toward conservatism.[12] In other cases "cultural species" can coexist for long periods indeed. The "new science" that emerged in the sixteenth and seventeenth centuries did not replace the Aristotelian orthodoxy in a few years or decades, but shared the same environment, at times as substitutes but often in some kind of harmony or compromise that may seem implausible to us now.

Sixth, an evolutionary framework implies that any easy generalizations or predictions about the speed and direction of cultural change are doomed. Most of the time culture changes at a tectonic pace, surviving dramatic institutional and political shocks. But at times culture changes quickly as a result of weakened resistance, perhaps, or some powerful exogenous shock that challenges existing cultural beliefs deeply (Jones, 2006). Much like evolutionary science, the strength of the methodology is that it helps us make sense of the past rather than predict the future. Precisely because the unit of analysis continuously interacts strongly with its environment and because there are few time-invariant relations, it becomes unpredictable (Saviotti, 1996, p. 31). Moreover, as John Ziman (2000, p. 50) has pointed out, selectionist models stress that often what matters is not statistical averages over large numbers of similar states or agents, but rare events that are amplified and ultimately determine outcomes.[13] The challenge to historians then becomes to try to understand which rare events take on that function, and under what circumstances they are "selected." In principle, of course, there is no reason to presume that evolutionary models should be confined to finitely lived beings endowed with a genotype derived from one or two parents, subject to differential reproduction. In other words, thinking in evolutionary terms boils down to what Mayr (1982, pp. 46–47) sees as the main power of evolutionary models: what he called "population thinking." This idea stresses the importance of individual variation within populations and its ability to bring about changes in the many starting from the few. If we are interested in

[12] Recently, economists (Benabou, Ticchi, and Vindigni, 2014) have developed models to formalize the problem, pointing out that certain kinds of innovations reduce the value of existing ideas by being "belief-eroding," even if that was not their original intent. This creates an obvious conflict between those whose beliefs are being threatened and society at large, which stands to benefit from such ideas because they increase economic performance.

[13] This has long been realized by evolutionary biologists, who have postulated that major evolutionary advances come from unusual and exceptional genotypes with opportunities to dominate their own small populations and radiate into marginal habitats. See Stebbins (1969, p. 142).

economic change at the macro level, such population thinking is critical. Much economic change is brought about by the few affecting the many.

Finally, an evolutionary approach gives us a more reasonable way of thinking about how and why historical trajectories were followed. It places the analysis between the extremes of a materialist analysis that regards historical outcomes as inexorable and foreordained and a nihilist approach that sees nothing but randomness everywhere. The Great Divergence and the Industrial Revolution that caused it were neither fluke nor necessity, to paraphrase Jacques Monod's (1971) famous title. Nor were the Scientific Revolution or the Enlightenment.[14] They arose because historical circumstances were conducive to the sprouting of seeds that were already present in the soil. Evolutionary innovation occurs because a mutation takes place that happens in an environment favorable to it. But such a mutation is a minute subset of all favorable mutations that might have happened, as well as the smaller set of all mutations that actually did happen but turned out to be unviable. Evolutionary theory reminds the historian that contingency is everywhere: not everything that happened had to happen, and that many things that could have happened did not. It also reminds us that similar circumstances do not always lead to the same outcomes and that similar outcomes do not always have identical causes. The language of evolution suggests the distinction between homologies (similar outcomes resulting from similar origins) as opposed to analogies or homoplasies (similar outcomes with different origins). The work by economists on the interaction between culture and institutions reinforces this interpretation by recognizing that these models have multiple equilibria and that societies may start from similar circumstances and yet end up in very different situations "depending on historical idiosyncrasies" (Alesina and Giuliano, 2016, p. 44). In both approaches, a guiding principle is that nothing was inevitable about the actual historical outcomes we observe. And yet, it seems plausible to argue that even if developments on different parts of the globe were never quite independent, they still can yield insights about some role for historical regularities and causation; not everything is accidental in history. As Vermeij (2004, p. 250) remarks, comparative history helps us separate chance and necessity. Hence it is important to compare the experience of Europe with that of another culture, for example China (see chapters 16 and 17).

---

[14] For a powerful statement in the same vein about the Scientific Revolution, see Cohen (2012, p. 204). He argues that the emergence of a "realist-mathematical" (that is, modern) science was always a possibility, but its realization was not foreordained—we might still be living in a world in which Archimedes and Ptolemy represented the summit of scientific achievement and the astrolabe and mechanical clock the supreme examples of toolmaking, with "death within a year of birth as the likeliest human fate by far."

Furthermore, evolutionary systems have been argued to generate a general trend toward progress, at least in the sense of growing complexity and diversity. While the matter is still quite controversial, one eminent biologist has pleaded with his colleagues to adopt a view in which this trend in history is a central organizing principle. "History, then, is not random change. Among competitive dominants, there is a trend toward increased power through time ... a trend toward increased diversity of membership and increased productivity" (Vermeij, 2004, p. 252). Others are much more skeptical (for example, Futuyma, 1986, p. 366). As we shall see in chapter 14, concepts of a discernable trend in history became part of the culture of the period between 1500 and 1700. If we see the history of culture and that of living species as instances of a generalized Darwinian system, a discourse on the plausibility of some kind of trend that can be viewed as progress is apposite.

Episodes of scientific and technological flourishing have occurred throughout history, but the one that occurred in Europe after 1700 was in many ways unique. It was not the ineluctable culmination of Western history, nor a sign of the greater dynamism of Western culture, but the unintended and unanticipated result of a set of circumstances that affected the culture of some parts of Europe and through them the institutions that set the parameters of intellectual development. Neither the classical world, nor the medieval church, nor the Renaissance made the material successes of the West inevitable (Goldstone, 2012). Indeed we can view the economic developments of the past two centuries much as we view the emergence of *Homo sapiens* in the past half million years, after sixty-five million years of mammal evolution in which species came and went, but none had the fortune of developing the central nervous system that changed the world (Vermeij, 2004). It could have happened at another point in time, and it could easily not have happened at all or been nipped in the bud at an early stage. The story of evolution is, by and large, the story of species that survived—at least for a while.

The literature of cultural evolution is largely concerned with the emergence of tools in ancient societies. Imitation and learning-by-doing are the mechanisms of change. In such a world technological progress will be slow because "it is typically more difficult to make large improvements by trial and error than small ones" (Boyd, Richerson and Henrich, 2013, p. 135). But when cultural evolution began to involve *persuasion* regarding the natural principles that make techniques work, the game of innovation was changed forever, and increasingly discrete leaps in technology became increasingly frequent. That, in the end, is the tale underlying the Great Enrichment.

Chapter 4

Choice-based Cultural Evolution

Any evolutionary approach to culture needs to be explicit about how culture is passed from one generation to the next, a process often referred to as "socialization." Socialization occurs through direct imitation, often unconsciously so, or through symbolic means—spoken and written language, images, and examples. Economists have recently come to recognize the importance of intergenerational cultural transmission as a fundamental determinant of economic performance (Spolaore and Wacziarg, 2013; Giuliano, 2016). Of course, childhood socialization is not all there is to social learning. Individuals can change their values and beliefs throughout their lives, but much like languages or the ability to play a musical instrument, new capabilities and beliefs become increasingly difficult to acquire as an individual ages. All the same, adults make cultural choices about religion, social relations, political beliefs, the value of time, material consumption, and anything else. In the intellectual community such lifetime learning is itself a skill that is required from successful members.

Choice-based cultural evolution has been an important stream of research in the social sciences since the appearance of the seminal works in that area in the mid-1980s, and it has been adapted by some scholars to economics with considerable success as embodied in the important papers of Bisin and Verdier (1998, 2001). Their model allows parents to choose whether to socialize their child themselves (that is, imbue him or her with their cultural traits) or to relegate this duty to a random individual in society, whose cultural traits may or may not resemble the parents'. Bisin and Verdier's work has been quite influential and has inspired other work using this framework to explain important phenomena such as corruption (Hauk and Saez-Marti, 2002), morality (Greif and Tadelis, 2010), and situations in which the parents, in contrast with Bisin and Verdier, want their children to differ from themselves or in which socialization can be influenced by media and other outside sources (Christopoulou, Jaber, and Lillard, 2013).

Cultural evolution of any kind, then, consists of social learning and persuasion. Much social learning occurs *vertically*: most people are socialized first and foremost by their parents. In past societies this was the source of the bulk of socialization, but rarely was it the only one. Parents could farm out the socialization process to individuals they selected (but did not fully control) such as schoolteachers and masters. Or they could leave the socialization to an individual or organization of their choosing. In some settings, such as a Kibbutz or an extended family living together, parents were supplemented by others (for example, grandparents) who possessed similar cultural features. But as they age, individuals themselves can also choose among cultural traits and among individuals whose traits they want to emulate or adopt. The proportion of learning from these horizontal and oblique channels relative to vertical learning depends on how much contact an individual has with sources of information outside his or her family environment. Institutional factors play a role here as well. Ultra-orthodox Jewish boys in fundamentalist sects are rarely exposed to much secular cultural information, but this is not because of technology. Rather, it is because of a set of institutions that limit their access to such sources.

The socialization approach to cultural choices abstracts from the more general scenario, in which parental decisions are only one of many factors that determine socialization, that is, the culture of the next generation. In a more general set-up, an individual has the option to stick with the default, that is, the cultural features that she receives from her parents, or can select cultural features that deviate from her parents'. The problem for all social scientists is that it is far from clear how individuals make such choices. There is no obvious maximization process that leads people to believe in the immorality of a high income inequality, the evils of narcotics use, or the theory of evolution.

Choice-based cultural evolution is not an unconstrained choice. Clearly every individual is constrained by his or her environment, which determines the set of possible choices. One can choose, but normally only from a pre-existing menu. The menu of choices is parametrically given to most individuals. One is exposed to certain information and influences, and these produce options; someone who has never listened to the music of Schubert cannot possibly develop a preference for it, nor was it likely for a person born and raised in medieval Mongolia to adopt, say, the metaphysical beliefs of Maimonides. It is thus likely that individuals will culturally resemble their parents, but the exact extent of resemblance is endogenous to the culture itself and the institutional and technological environments. In a way, this explains the dilemma implicit in Eric Jones's (2006) book on culture and economics: Jones points out that neither the view of culture as a fixed exogenous environment constraining economic behavior nor the opposing view of culture as fully adaptable and malleable to economic needs is very persuasive. He views culture as somewhere in between, at times flexible and adaptive, at times displaying astonishing stickiness. But we need to know more regarding the conditions under which cultural change will be fast or slow, and if we can, in which direction it may move.

Technology clearly mattered. The printing press, rising literacy and mobility, improved postal networks, and interaction with others in city squares or near water coolers provide sources of information that illiterate peasants never had. Television, the Internet, and social media have augmented the array of sources of information in ways that were unimaginable as late as 1914. Choice-based social learning has increased exponentially in importance over the past two or three centuries with rising access to information and literacy. The historical implications of that phenomenon are profound.

Choice-based social learning is at the heart of cultural evolution, as many scholars, above all Boyd and Richerson (1985, 2005), have noted. An adaptation of Boyd and Richerson's work is useful for this purpose. Consider Figure 1. An individual's total set of preferences, attitudes, and beliefs come from two sources: his or her parents (whether through genes or through vertical socialization), and "all others" which are either oblique (diagonal) sources such as schools and role models, or horizontal transmission from peers or the media. If vertical socialization is dominant, society can only change through differential rates of reproduction and errors in the transmission process creating genetic drift.[1] In the limiting case, in which all cultural elements are passed on error-free from parent to child, we are back in a Clark (2007) and Galor (2011) world in which children are cultural carbon copies of their parents, and in which the main driver of change is the Darwinian selection of individuals exhibiting certain features that in some way make them fitter.

As noted, the degree to which people deviate from their default and adopt new cultural features is the critical variable that allows for dramatic cultural change. Useful knowledge, including science and technology, are very much part of culture and hence a good example of a sudden acceleration of cultural change with profound economic implications is the Industrial Revolution. How much horizontal and oblique information appeared on the menu? This depends, as Bisin and Verdier point out, to

---

[1] This is strictly speaking only true if vertical cultural transmission occurs through one parent only; in the case of two parents, recombinations of cultural traits taken from both parents could produce cultural features that make an individual different from his or her parents.

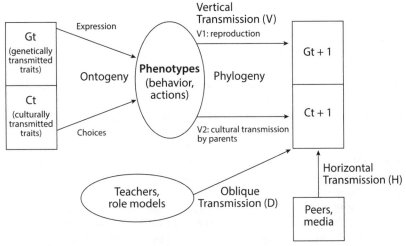

Figure 1: Intergenerational transmission of cultural traits

some extent on the parents themselves. On the whole, parents prefer their children to reflect their own culture, a feature that they refer to as "imperfect empathy." Given that home-schooling was costly and not very efficient, parents preferred to appoint an outsider to socialize their children. Schoolteachers reflected to a large extent the cultural beliefs of the parents, but given that schoolchildren came from families with heterogeneous cultural beliefs, a perfect reproduction of the parents' cultural traits was not fully possible. Children who went to school were inevitably exposed to a larger cultural menu than if they were entirely socialized by their parents. But other elements of society in the past always played a role in this, especially organized religion of any kind, which was designed to impose a set of cultural beliefs (and the behavior they implied) on youngsters. Hence the large role of religious education through most of the European past. Other ideologies and sets of cultural beliefs were transmitted by similar mechanisms, such as Confucian schools in China.

A modern economy is characterized by a rapid growth in nonparental transmission, and in fact such mechanisms of intergenerational transmission are one of the hallmarks of modernity. In a Bisin and Verdier (1998) framework, the change is explained by a rise in the opportunity costs of parents socializing their children. Once those costs rise, it makes sense for parents to sacrifice some similarity to their own cultural beliefs and outsource socialization to others. More was at play, however. Schoolteachers replaced home-schooling in part because of the advantages of specialization, but also because there were other economies of scale in education, and the public sector decided to subsidize schooling. In a modern age, single-channel vertical transmission paths are unrealistic. The division of knowledge has made it impossible for most parents to master all the knowledge and culture that becomes part of required socialization for their children. Moreover, culture and knowledge are changing at a rate that is rapid relative to the length of a single generation, meaning that by the time parents have to socialize their children, their skills and knowledge may already be outdated. Learning about new cultural variants, be they religious, scientific, or technical, was facilitated by the radical revolution in access to information, which has made the transmission of cultural components easier and faster than ever before. Beyond skills and knowledge, the other cultural menus that individuals can choose from in the twenty-first century have expanded enormously: the range of religions, ideologies, philosophies, literature, art, music, and much else has expanded beyond anyone's wildest dreams. Parents increasingly struggle to maintain any kind of "imperfect empathy" in view of the torrent of cultural variants to which young people and adults are exposed and from which they are free to choose. Parents, of course may have had little choice as far as schooling is concerned, but the popularity of after-school programs and summer camps for working parents indicates that this model indeed has some bite. Home-schooling has survived in modern America, but its niche is not large and is mostly confined to non-mainstream religious groups.[2]

Children as well as adults make cultural choices themselves. Biographies are full of rebellious sons and (less frequently) daughters who rebelled against dominant parents or established religion and chose a different culture in some form; scions of wealthy bourgeois families who became Marxist, sons of Orthodox rabbis who became Catholic bishops or secular-minded physicists, and so on. Often this is not only *because* their socialization by parents and parent-substitutes was incomplete but also as a reaction to it.

Why do children differ culturally from their parents? One reason is that the "imperfect empathy" postulated by Bisin and Verdier may not be a full characterization of the behavior of the parents; it is more persuasive to write an altruistic utility function in which the parents cared exclusively about the happiness of their children as they saw it, which may mean that the culture they acquire for their children diverges significantly from their own culture if they regret their own past cultural choices (Christopoulou, Jaber, and Lillard, 2013). Alternatively, even if the parents choose an outsider to socialize their offspring in their own image, there

---

[2] In 2007, the National Household Education Surveys Program of the US Department of Education estimated that about 1.5 million children or 2.9 percent of all school-aged children were home-schooled. Of those, 36 percent reported that the main reason for them doing so was "to provide religious or moral instruction," another 21 percent a concern with the "school environment," and 17 percent a more general dissatisfaction with the academic instruction at schools (US Department of Education, 2008).

may be a serious principal-agent problem, because the parents can only monitor their children's socialization process imperfectly.

It might be thought that in the modern age vertical transmission has become relatively unimportant. In her popular *The Nurture Assumption*, Harris (2009) amasses a great deal of evidence to show that the cultural impact of parents on their children in today's society is limited. In her view, the evidence suggests that social behavior is largely the result of the interactions of children with their peers (that is, other children) and that parents have only limited effect on their children past the toddler years. But while there is no question that peer socialization of children is important, Harris's views are only part of the story.[3] For one, while children may be socialized more by peers that we often realize, peers are often chosen by parents, often indirectly (through a choice of residential location and school). Moreover, peers less frequently set moral and religious values and political ideology, and they do not systematically convey skills and technical knowledge. Nor, it would seem, do children learn from peers the willingness to accept discipline, observe punctuality, self-control, and respect for superiors that are required for capitalist production. Moreover, technological change depends on nonconformism, someone willing to suggest something that is novel and perhaps unusual. But, as Harris herself stresses, child culture is highly conformist; loners and rebels are "nails that stick up and are hammered down" (Harris, 2009, p. 158). In other words, culture is an enormous and heterogeneous mass of information, but most of what matters to economic development may still come vertically from parents and teachers, and quite a lot of this may still be malleable at adulthood and subject to persuasion through spoken and written media.

In any event, in modern times the state has entered in a big way into the socialization scene, partly in competition with the parents. Socialization of children is seen to have major externalities, and hence compulsory education and military service have been introduced at least in part to imbue children with cultural elements that people in power feel they ought to have. This process of socialization extends to all subsets of culture: beliefs and knowledge (in that science education transmits a set of propositions about how the world operates); certain skills such as the three R's viewed as indispensable; values (such as religious or ideological beliefs, nationalism, and a loyalty to the dominant political discourse in the nation); and preferences (for example, music, art-appreciation, drug-

---

[3] In a famous paper, Cavalli-Sforza et al. (1982) examined which cultural traits among Stanford students were strongly correlated with their parents. The central finding was one of fairly high correlation on some matters such as religion where the correlation was .57 but a much lower correlation for belief on "contentious issues" such as horoscopes and UFOs. The conclusion is that individuals clearly *choose* whether they want to adopt the default option or adopt a different belief, acquired horizontally or obliquely.

education). Political socialization is often far from waterproof: communist education did not succeed in fostering loyalty to totalitarian socialism, and Catholic schools in the United States produce a remarkable number of agnostics. To some extent, of course, the state replaced the church in this regard, but it is more powerful and leaves people fewer alternatives.

Here is one example: a particular cultural feature of interest taught to children by industrial society are those that concern the attitudes toward time and punctuality (Levine, 1998). None of these preferences seem to be hard-wired; they are taught and passed on through cultural diffusion and thus can differ significantly among societies. Punctuality is a good example of how technological and cultural factors interact to produce enormous differences. On the supply side, accurate, inexpensive, and omnipresent devices that show time in an accurate and reliable fashion were required for punctuality; on the demand side, there must be sufficient need for a high degree of coordination and monitoring. Both of those were present by the mid-nineteenth century in the industrialized market economies of the West, and the result is a governance (some would say a tyranny) of time that has affected daily life to a degree barely recognized by those who do not realize how different things used to be (Landes, 1983). How the socialization process was used to imbue children with the need to be punctual is illustrated by an 1881 American fifth-grade school textbook, illustrating the disasters that could happen because of a variety of failures stemming from a lack of punctuality, including a somewhat ahistorical account of Napoleon's defeat at Waterloo because one of his marshals was behind schedule (O'Malley, 1990, p. 148).

As noted, becoming an adult does not mean that the absorption of new cultural information is complete. Adults who interact with others are amenable to learning and persuasion (including simple imitation). The rate of cultural change thus depends on the degree of cultural interconnectedness, that is, how many interactions adults have with one another and with how many others (Henrich, 2009). For a given population size, individuals influence one another in direct proportionality to the number of social interactions between them, as well as whether those ties are "strong," typically meaning intra-household, or weak, that is, with outsiders (Granovetter, 1973, 1983).

To see this, all we need to do is assume that innovations occur as a by-product of some other activity and are thus generated randomly. Once such an innovation is made, the speed of its diffusion in a simple model of imitation depends on the number of other members of society who can observe or find out in some other way about an improved technique. In this model, the rate of technological progress depends on two parameters: the (given) probability that an individual will stumble on an invention, and the number of people she is connected to. In a simple functional form, Henrich demonstrates that the outcome of interest (how many individuals end up using the new technique) is far more sensitive to the number of connections between individuals than to the probability of making an invention.

In fact, the importance of the degree of interconnectedness to technological change is still understated by Henrich's model. The main reason interconnectedness is important to technology is that inventions are mostly not accidental events. The probability of an invention occurring is related to an epistemic base underpinning it, that is to say, to an understanding of the natural regularities and phenomena that make the technique work. Some inventions required a rather extensive understanding of the underlying science—nuclear reactors are not built by accident. Many others do not, yet even in those cases *some* knowledge is usually required.[4] Even if many inventions were not wholly based on prior scientific insights, Fortune favored "prepared minds." Sustained progress demanded a widening epistemic base of technology so as to make the process faster, more efficient, and better able to avoid blind alleys and reinvented wheels.[5] Inventors can acquire this knowledge by accessing it through a variety of social connections, such as consulting or hiring individuals who possess it (as Edison famously did by hiring formally trained experts at his Menlo Park facility). Hence the degree of interconnectedness described by Henrich in modern society includes many factors that determine access costs to useful knowledge; hence it affects not only the rate of diffusion but also the rate at which innovations themselves occur.

Moreover, the interconnectedness described by Henrich implicitly assumes that the transmission of cultural features occurs typically on a one-to-one basis. But it is easy to see that information can take the form of one-to-many, in which a single source transmits information to many recipients, and a many-to-one form in which individuals can absorb information from a very large number of sources (Cavalli-Sforza and Feldman, 1981). The rising power of technology to support the one-to-many transmission mechanism should be obvious, and electronic communications (of which Twitter and blogs are just relatively recent examples) have vastly amplified what the printing press and radio did in earlier times.

---

[4] The classic example is the development of the steam engine in the eighteenth century; the exact understanding of how and why a steam engine worked and what determined its efficiency were not really mastered until the second quarter of the nineteenth century, but some knowledge of atmospheric pressure and the behavior of steam under pressure was essential for the machine to be built at all. Much of the improved understanding was the result of practical experimentation with the engine.

[5] Moreover, more widely diffused and more accessible knowledge of other techniques facilitated the rate of technological progress because many inventions involved the recombination of other technological components and analogies from different techniques. Thus knowledge of the existence of other techniques, learned presumably from others, would have accelerated and lubricated the emergence of innovations.

The parameters underlying the communication technology needed for choice-based social learning were critical to the development of modern technology. Hence, the techniques of transportation and communication were of historic importance, since they helped determine the access costs to knowledge. Cultural innovation post-1500, from the Reformation to Copernican astronomy to calculus depended on the printing press, better postal services, and the improved capability of ships and land-based modes of transport to spread information around the world. But institutions mattered as well. An important development is the rise of scientific and intellectual societies and academies in which useful knowledge was exchanged. While a few of those academies preceded the Enlightenment, they came to their full blossoming as formal and organized institutions in the second half of the eighteenth century and became part of what has become known in England as the "associational society" (Clark, 2000). In it, the business and technical elite met to exchange useful knowledge; the rise of the number of people who were part of this associational society is a striking example of Henrich's idea of "interconnectivity."[6]

The degree of interconnectivity itself was in part determined by culture, that is, the preference that people had for interacting with others and their growing belief that useful knowledge should be shared and distributed. Enlightenment society realized instinctively that such knowledge was non-rivalrous and hence distributing it was a means of improving society. Interaction, however, was similarly a function of technology, and advances from better postal service to streetlights to the telegraph and telephone implied improved access and more rapid innovation and diffusion. The prediction of this model is that the veritable explosion of communication technology in the late twentieth century will lead to an acceleration of technological progress as social interactions and information exchanges have become essentially costless regardless of distance.

---

[6] Most of the associations were quite different from the scientific and learned societies so beloved by economic historians: political clubs, musical groups, eating and drinking clubs, regular attendants of coffeehouses, and so on.

Chapter 5

Biases in Cultural Evolution

The richness of cultural evolution as a tool for understanding historical development is illustrated by the work of two biologists, Eva Jablonka and Marion Lamb (2005). They discern four dimensions of evolution. In their view, there are biological and nonbiological ways in which cultural traits are passed from generation to generation. The four dimensions really boil down to two: biological transmission (either through genes or through epigenetic transmission) and cultural, through learned cultural elements (either through imitation or through symbolic transmission). The kind of cultural evolution models that affected the early modern intelligentsia I have in mind here are mostly part of Jablonka and Lamb's "fourth leg," coded information was exchanged by intellectuals through letters, publications, and meetings that affected the beliefs and information of participants.

The power of the multiple mechanisms of evolution described by Jablonka and Lamb is that they allow biological and cultural evolution to take place cheek-by-jowl in the coevolution of genes and culture. Human history in the long run was obviously affected by both, but the more we focus on recent history that unfolds in centuries rather than millennia, the more important the cultural element looms, whereas the biological selection mechanism sinks into comparative insignificance. Change has simply occurred too fast to be accounted for purely in genetic terms. All the same, there is some reason to believe that genetic change may be faster than the slow drift that pure differential reproduction implies.[1]

---

[1] Epigenetic mechanisms, shown recently to have been more important in human populations than was hitherto thought, could provide an additional explanation for rapid changes in populations that could not be brought about by classic genetic selection (Spolaore and Wacziarg, 2013, p. 25). Recent studies have found that pure Darwinian selection can work faster

Recent work on evolution and human culture has not necessarily drawn an extremely detailed and testable picture of how cultural change occurs, but it has been made obvious that simple Darwinian models relying purely on differential reproduction cannot by themselves explain the cultural and economic changes in the West. It is sometimes argued that the term "Lamarckian" really applies here, because in cultural evolution characteristics acquired from others can be retained and passed on. Yet as Hodgson and Knudsen (2010, pp. 64–65) point out, this is a misunderstanding, since Darwin himself never denied that acquired phenotypic characteristics could be passed on—that insight is associated with August Weismann, a generation later. In some ways, therefore, the dynamics of culture resemble an epidemic more than they do differential survival and fecundity. Unlike what happens in biological evolution, cultural selection is not natural but is mostly conscious. The questions are what happens during the acquisition process and how are such choices made.

The rational or even boundedly rational optimization process often assumed by economists does not seem terribly helpful when people make once-in-a-lifetime or very rare choices (or do not choose at all and instead simply stick with the default cultural characteristics they were socialized to adopt). But neither are they the mindless replicators of evolutionary biology. Instead we are looking at a rather subtle and complex process that lies somewhere between those two mechanisms. In Bowles's words, they are "adaptive agents," who learn when exposed to new cultural variants and choose whether or not to adopt them (Bowles, 2004, p. 60), using a variety of criteria. Analyzing history through this perspective is more suitable to the issues at hand.

Intellectual innovations are new items placed on the choice menu of the educated elite. But why and how were these people persuaded by new information, ideas, beliefs, and values? During 1500–1700 innovations of many kinds were made. Some of them concerned new information about the physical environment or new mathematical concepts and techniques, some contained new religious or philosophical ideas, still others considered what a "good society" should be like. If they were deemed sufficiently attractive (meaning that they represented an improvement in some environments), they were "fit" in an evolutionary sense and spread through persuasion in a choice-based cultural evolution among individuals.

The choices apply to all three main classes of what I have defined as "cultural elements." Preferences changed, for instance, through fashion

---

than was hitherto supposed. A gene named *HIF* was shown to have become fixed in a Tibetan high-altitude population that gave it a higher fitness through avoiding the blood thickening that lowlanders typically experience when they move to high-altitude areas. See Simonson et al. (2010) and Nielsen et al. (2010).

changes which applied to art, music, clothes, and even the human body. Values, too, were subject to such processes. At times they change imperceptibly slowly, at others more rapidly, bordering on revolution, such as the rapid rise of Calvinism in the sixteenth century or the acceptance of religious tolerance in the second half of the seventeenth century. Beliefs about how the physical and visible world worked could sometimes change dramatically and abruptly because of rhetorical standards that "test" them. Aristotle's notion that a vacuum was impossible was shown to be wrong by a series of experiments and observations that were irrefutable, as was the existence of Jupiter's moons.

Such tests did not always work well in filtering out beliefs that most would regard as erroneous or superstitious. Knowledge and beliefs can be "tight" or not. By "tight" beliefs I mean that they are held by a large majority and with a high degree of certainty, that the belief is trusted by most people relying on it and thus does not require verification. Few people hold on today to the Ptolemaic geocentric universe, or believe that smoking tobacco is safe, or that collectivist regimes can bring about economic prosperity. But many other beliefs are *untight*, simply because our ability to come up with evidence that would be persuasive (that is, satisfy the rhetorical standards of our age) is limited. This was true a fortiori for an earlier age: did the world consist of small corpuscular bodies that were the building material of all matter? What was heat and how was it related to combustion? What caused fever? Could one substance be transformed into another? Did God have consciousness? As a result, cultural evolution often throws up a great diversity of ideas that are incompatible with one another but that cannot be resolved, and it leaves matters unsettled until a better way of testing the competing views is found.

Persuasion and the diffusion of new ideas depend on many factors. One seemingly unassailable factor is that when knowledge is *effective* (that is, when techniques or predictions based on this knowledge work well), beliefs can change quickly. Once people see an airplane fly, they will accept the propositional belief that objects heavier than air can actually defeat gravity and the underlying aeronautic physics. A classic example is the set of beliefs around the causes and modes of diffusion of infectious disease in the last third of the nineteenth century. Once it was shown that certain actions that killed bacteria could reduce the rate of infection, few doubted the proposition that infectious diseases are caused by microbes. From a purely logical point of view this can lead to false inferences, as it is quite possible that a technique works on the basis of false premises. If one believes that bad air, caused by swamps, causes malaria, draining the swamps and the consequent disappearance of the disease might seem to corroborate the hypothesis that miasmas are behind infection. But it would be wrong.

The rhetorical criteria by which knowledge is tested and accepted and is thus transmitted successfully are themselves social conventions that are subject to cultural evolution (see McCloskey, 1985). To say that propositions are accepted when they are supported by evidence is not much help, since it has to be specified what "supported" really means and which kinds of evidence are admissible. A society in which "evidence" is defined as support in the writing of earlier sages would be very different from one that relied on experiments, but even the latter has to determine what experimental design is regarded as permissible and what outcome is accepted as decisive. When is a statistical test that says that a hypothesis cannot be rejected at some level of certainty because a regression coefficient is much larger than its estimated standard error seen as persuasive, and does the fact that it cannot be rejected make it true or at least believable? Perhaps the best we can do is simply assign subjective probabilities that a statement is true, though some of these probabilities are clearly equal to one.

There are different approaches to cultural evolution. The most extreme and popular approach is one that was proposed originally by Richard Dawkins and is an analogy to genetics, in which the gene, the classic replicator, is replaced by a "meme." Susan Blackmore (1999) has pushed this idea further and argued that memes are "selfish" evolutionary replicators. In her view, cultural evolution must be understood as the result of the interactions of two kinds of selfish replicators, genes and memes. Much like the gene-culture coevolution discussed by Bowles and Gintis (2011), she sees the world as the result of meme-gene coevolution with people being nothing but the temporary depositories and unwitting vehicles of these two kinds of replicators (Blackmore, 1999, pp. 235–36). Whether this kind of reductionist approach is helpful in a historical narrative remains to be seen. The problem with memes, as has been pointed out many times, is that knowledge is not just "copied" the way genes make copies of themselves when they multiply. Instead, they are sent, received, and then interpreted (Sperber, 1996, pp. 101–6). What matters is persuasion, the decision by the receiver to choose to accept the cultural message and add it to his or her set of beliefs or preferences. This could be because the new knowledge is believed to be correct, because it is consistent with one's prior propensities, or a variety of other criteria. The receiver of a gene has no such choice.

Historically, then, people made selections from cultural menus, but how and why they chose one item is often hard to establish. What we can trace, however, is who wrote the menus, why some things appeared on it and others did not, and how attractive items were made to look. When economists write about people making choices, they tend to formulate it in some kind of optimizing framework. Choices subject to constraints, in either static or dynamic contexts, constitute the bread and butter of economic models. Cultural choices, arguably, are difficult to fit into this framework. Are they made rationally? How does one decide to become a Marxist, or to believe in evolution, or that one likes Thai food?

The diversity of the literature on the economic significance of culture was well described by Jones (2006, pp. 31–51) as "fluid and sticky." One approach is pure materialist considerations: culture adapts to the economic environment. Do people really choose their beliefs because these cultural elements are consistent with and enhance their economic interests? Historical materialism asserts that when the economic conditions are ripe, the appropriate culture will somehow emerge as a consequence of hard and concrete conditions on the ground and people will buy into a culture that is congenial to their material interests. Powerful impersonal forces determine outcomes, and there is little room for human agency. In a recent wide-ranging and erudite book, Ian Morris (2010, pp. 476, 568, 621) repeatedly states that each society "gets the ideas it needs" and subscribes to the "maps, not chaps" view of history (p. 427). But this is not altogether satisfactory. What determines those needs? What guarantees that they actually emerge? And what if different segments or classes in a society have different needs or disagree about what the needs are? In contrast, cultural determinists believe that culture is "almost everything" and determines a society's economic fate (Landes, 2000). This view raises even harder questions of why some societies end up with different cultural beliefs than others and why some cultural traits are more persistent than others. It also ignores the possibility that ideas and circumstances might be complementary and synergistic. The "right circumstances" may become a missed opportunity without the necessary ideas popping up, whereas good ideas may fall on barren ground unless other conditions are satisfied.[2] It seems an ahistorical and overly simplistic way to characterize cultural choices. But if not a maximizing framework, how should we think of these choices? Sociobiologists and evolutionary psychologists have proposed a functionalist approach. Many cultural features were selected for in the countless generations that humankind spent in hunter-gatherer tribes, and these features need to be adapted to or clash with the needs of modern society. The human brain evolved in an environment that made split-second decisions often crucial for survival (Cosmides and Tooby, 1994). Cultural choices, however, are not usually made in split seconds and rarely matter for immediate survival.

A key to the understanding of the emergence of modern economic growth can be gained by recognizing that both the technology of the Industrial Revolution and its subsequent development and the propositional knowledge underpinning it were cultural phenomena subject to evolutionary forces. Technological or prescriptive knowledge, which is partially tacit knowledge, is passed among individuals who teach one another how

---

[2]   John Stuart Mill expressed this well, albeit in a different context: "Ideas, unless outward circumstances conspire with them, have in general no very rapid or immediate efficacy in human affairs; and the most favourable outward circumstances may pass by, or remain inoperative, for want of ideas suitable to the conjuncture. But when the right circumstances and the right ideas meet, the effect is seldom slow in manifesting itself" (Mill, [1845] 1967, vol. IV, p. 370).

to make things or produce a service, from music lessons to apprenticeships. The propositional knowledge (science) on which techniques are based is taught as well, although typically in a somewhat different settings and not always to the same people (although all engineers and technicians need to be trained in mathematics and physics). Propositional knowledge is almost always codified in some way. Both types of knowledge allow vertical, horizontal, and oblique transmission between generations, and thus can be fast- or slow-changing or even stagnant subject only to evolutionary drift. But much as in the Jablonka-Lamb world of multiple evolutionary processes superimposed on one another, the evolution of the two kinds of knowledge, prescriptive and propositional, can affect and complement each other in multiple ways to produce what became an explosive, self-reenforcing positive feedback dynamic (Mokyr, 2002).

How, then, did the intellectuals of early modern Europe make decisions to select from the menu of cultural choices an item that is different from the default? Choice-based social learning or cultural evolution is subject to what Richerson and Boyd call "bias." What they mean by bias here is that cultural choices follow certain identifiable patterns that make people choose one cultural element over another (Richerson and Boyd, 2005). The more credible options a child or adult can choose from when exposed to menus of cultural variants different from the ones offered by her or his parents, the more important such biases will be.

The type and rate of bias depend on the technological parameters of cultural transmission and on its cultural and institutional structure. The printing press, mandatory schooling, and mass communications through the Internet and social media are examples of technological developments that clearly affected the significance and power of such biases. At times, of course, even with oblique or horizontal transmission, parental culture was reproduced. If parents choose teachers much like themselves, or if there is little cultural variance in the community, the biases may be quite small. Examples are the Israeli kibbutz before 1970 or ultra-Orthodox communities, in which children were not socialized by their parents as much as by the representatives of a culturally homogeneous community.

A variety of biases can be distinguished. These can be conveniently classified into the following categories (mostly based on Richerson and Boyd, 2005).

Content-based bias: People pick cultural variants different from the ones they were taught by their parents because of the inherent qualities and content of these variants. But how do people exactly assess content? By what means is knowledge validated, legitimized, and ultimately accepted? If the subject is a statement of a fact, it seems reasonable that they consider the evidence, but as noted, how they interpret the evidence and when they consider it sufficient are functions of the rhetorical conventions of the society. They are convinced by seemingly irrefutable new facts (or at times try to ignore them, as in Benabou, 2008), or by new and persuasive theories. In addition, if cultural beliefs yield palpable results (e.g., successful techniques), this could produce "results bias" (Shennan, 2013). Marxism and the theory of evolution were novel cultural variants in the second half of the nineteenth century that persuaded many—but by no means all—people to change their beliefs on the basis of the inherent logic of the new set of beliefs and its power to fit the facts, and allowed people to re-interpret their environment and life in the light of the new theories. For these people, Marxism or Darwinism simply seemed true.

In many cases, however, when knowledge is untight or more complex to evaluate, beliefs may not become fixed in the population—indeed, ironically, that was the fate of both Marxism and the theory of evolution (Darwin's theories remained highly controversial and disputed for many decades after the publication of his *Origin of Species* in 1859). The lack of tightness often leads to unpredictable distributions: nearly all Americans do not believe that the earth is flat or that infectious diseases are caused by miasmas, but the number who do not believe in the theory of evolution is another matter.[3] Theistic religion, an inherently untight belief, is subject to a very diverse set of distributions, with far fewer atheists in the United States than in Europe. What it is precisely that convinces people that a belief is correct depends in part on the kind of information supporting it. If it is readily testable through procedures that are deemed admissible (for example, double-blind experiments carried out on large samples) and rather simple to comprehend, or (as argued above) if it supports techniques that demonstrably work, content bias can be expected to guide cultural selection.

Direct bias: A central feature of all social learning is that society appoints cultural authorities as an information-cost-saving device who have great influence on others' cultural beliefs. Such authorities are especially important in religious contexts (such as priests), but they are just as central in modern society, in which experts such as scientists and physicians become central in helping others decide what is true and moral. The obvious reason is that social knowledge depends on specialization, simply because the set of total knowledge is far too large for a single mind to comprehend. Complex social and physical processes are often impossible for laypersons to comprehend, yet the information may be essential to guide certain important behaviors. Subtle statistical models and sophisticated experimentation may be needed to discriminate between important hypotheses about, say, the effects of certain foods on human health or the causes of crime. Especially for propositional knowledge (the knowledge underpinning

---

[3] A 2009 Gallup Poll reported that 39 percent of Americans believed in the theory of evolution whereas 25 percent did not and 36 percent had no opinion. The proportion of believers in evolution rose, as would be expected, with education and declined with the frequency of church attendance. See http://www.gallup.com/poll/114544/darwin-birthday-believe-evolution.aspx (accessed July 5, 2010).

techniques in use), authorities and the division of knowledge are indispensable because such knowledge can operate effectively only if a fine subdivision of knowledge through specialization is practiced. Some cultural authorities illustrate the one-to-many form of cultural transmission identified by Cavalli-Sforza and Feldman (1981, p. 62). It can be shown that under reasonable assumptions, such forms of transmission are associated with more rapid cultural change (Seki and Ihara, 2012). Cultural "authorities" often have no special expertise and yet somehow become the source of authority or focal points in cultural choices. Some of these, such as Oprah Winfrey or Dr. Ruth, can have a large impact on their societies, despite the absence of obvious qualifications.

The authority-based social learning process at work in direct bias requires society to solve three major problems. The first is who appoints such authorities, who monitors their reliability, and who appoints the appointers and the monitors and so on.[4] The second is what to do when experts disagree and how to choose among conflicting propositions. One simple rule is simply to go with the majority (as in the "the preponderance of experts today believe that ...") although the pitfalls here are obvious. The third and most pernicious problem with direct bias is that if the authorities become too powerful and entrenched, they may act to crystallize their beliefs and possibly reduce contestability. Such actions make further progress increasingly hard. It is a hallmark of open and culturally dynamic societies that all authorities are contestable and are subject to continuous critique and scrutiny. When for some reason their pronouncements become incompatible with reality or some other source of doubt arises, they can be readily dethroned. The eighteenth-century chemists who adhered to the ruling phlogiston theory of chemical reactions were unceremoniously forced to accept the powerful evidence of the new chemistry put forward by Lavoisier and Dalton. Some chemists resisted, but within one generation this battle was over. The same happened a century later with medical authorities and the miasma theory of disease, doomed by the germ theory. **Consistency and confirmation bias:** Unless there is a relatively straightforward and unequivocal way of evaluating a cultural belief, people may prefer to choose cultural variants that are somehow compatible with their other beliefs and form a coherent whole. Individuals tend to filter out information and ideas that contradict their held beliefs and stereotypes.[5] If

---

[4] Normally, authorities are appointed by their peers (that is, practitioners themselves). One is reminded of Einstein's famous remark that to punish him for his contempt for authority, fate made him an authority himself—though this was of course a perfectly normal development.

[5] Cognitive scientists have shown that there is a general preference for ideas that confirm existing beliefs. An example is the statement that "People tend to seek information that they consider supportive of favored hypotheses or existing beliefs and to interpret information in ways that are partial to those hypotheses or beliefs. Conversely, they tend not to seek and perhaps even

people think they know how the world works, they often will discount or somehow find fault with evidence inconsistent with their views. As Rodrik (2014, p. 194) and others have pointed out in a different context, limitations on cognitive capability mean that agents often will twist and distort new information and logic to confirm existing cultural variants. Thus cultural innovation will always and everywhere run into resistance, not just from entrenched economic interests but also from those who have committed to an existing cluster of beliefs that they are protecting from disruption.

To put it in evolutionary terms, cultural variants are subject to pleiotropic effects, that is, adjacent beliefs tend to occur together. Cultural beliefs mostly occur in clusters. For instance, those Americans who adhere to evangelical religion commonly also think that widespread gun ownership is desirable, that marriage should be confined to heterosexual couples, that climate change is not a reality, and object to large scale federal redistribution policies, although logically these beliefs are not all obviously connected. Even when faced with powerful evidence that contradicts their beliefs, people may try to discredit the evidence, blithely ignore it, or cling to a supposed authority. Thus, for example, Darwinism, which cast a new light on the evolution of species, had deep (and unintended) consequences for the cultural beliefs of certain groups. It was judged by many on the basis of its merit, but for some it clashes with other beliefs and is thus rejected. This consistency bias is what makes knowledge systems stable and conservative.

All the same, throughout history, and more pronouncedly in the West after 1500, this effect has not been powerful enough to condemn the cultures to complete stasis. When an educated elite is willing to consider new information on its own merits (which may or may not be content bias alone), it may overcome confirmation bias and accept radically new views of the universe, life or other central issues.

Model-based bias: Cultural evolution scholars have long recognized that a great deal of cultural learning of traits occurs through imitation. The beliefs of people who are role models and thus appear worth imitating create an example that others follow, because these traits are correlated with others that are deemed desirable. Here the issue becomes not so much what cultural traits to choose from, but which individuals are worth imitating. Obviously, part of socialization is imitation of the immediate family in which children grow up. Beyond that, individuals (or groups) observe cultural elements of the most successful and prestigious members of society and might adopt their preferences and beliefs. Other factors in the

---

to avoid information that would be considered counterindicative with respect to those hypotheses or beliefs and supportive of alternative possibilities" (Nickerson, 1998, p. 177). See also, for instance, Wason (1960), Henrich (2001), or Lyons and Kashima (2001). The psychological intuition is that stereotype-consistent information is easier for individuals to accept than stereotype-inconsistent information because it is more readily understood and more likely to be perceived as true.

choice of models worth imitating may have been age and self-similarity, for instance, older siblings. In the past, such direct bias was often associated with individuals with political power and noble birth whom others wanted to emulate. The importance of upper class individuals in sponsoring and at times participating in intellectual innovations of certain kinds in the early modern period raised the social prestige of these activities and the credibility of their findings. In our time, successful movie or sports stars are used to sponsor products or behaviors in the hope that the endorser's irrelevant but desirable qualities will induce others to adopt their apparent preferences or cultural beliefs.

Rhetorical bias: A bias can be imparted through persuasion, in which some charismatic and persuasive individual is simply good at convincing others of the correctness of his or her views. Commercials and propaganda campaigns are rhetorically sophisticated attempts to persuade people of certain cultural variants (they can be beliefs, values, or preferences) on the basis of form as much as or more than of content. In many cases, new ideas are successful not just thanks to the contents of the message itself but also because of the *framing* of it.[6] Theories and propositions are often described as "elegant" referring to their aesthetic qualities. Rhetorical bias can be created by the originator or by the acolytes or epigones. Thus, for instance, Calvinism was spread not just through the persuasive talents of Jean Calvin but also by those of his followers John Knox and Guido de Bres. The doctrines of Adam Smith were taught with great effect by his follower in Edinburgh, Dugald Stewart, a highly effective teacher. Those of Marx spread by such influential followers as Lenin, Gramsci, or Mao Zedong, whose own cultural innovations were comparatively marginal. The cultural variants that emerged as the result of this dissemination process were often modified by apostles and interpreters: Marxism did not always follow what Marx wrote, any more than Calvinism was wholly described by Calvin.[7]

Frequency dependence bias: Individuals tend to choose some cultural beliefs by simply determining what the majority of people around them believe. The economic logic of this bias is similar to direct bias: to save on information costs by assuming that others have already tested the new cultural variant and found it acceptable. In part, frequency bias occurs to

---

[6] A case in point is the famous "Rose Diagram" (or "coxcomb") produced by Florence Nightingale in 1858 to illustrate the effectiveness of sanitary measures in the Scutari hospital during the Crimean War. As a contemporary commentator puts it, "she realized that the truth about public health was so vital that it could not be recited in a monotone [of dry statistics]. It needed to sing." (Harford, 2016, p. 17).

[7] As Landes (2000, p. 11) remarks in his discussion of Calvinism, its original "hard belief in predestination did not last more than a generation or two (it is not the kind of dogma that has lasting appeal)." One might even be tempted to surmise that the belief in predestination was doomed from the start.

avoid possible social sanctions against nonconformists, though of course individuals who disbelieve the conventional wisdom held by the majority can falsify their preferences (Kuran, 1997). But institutions differ in the way they treat cultural deviants, from persecuting heretics and banishing innovators, to pursuing a liberal let-a-hundred-flowers-bloom policy. In that sense, cultural choices are reflexive. One important cultural value is pluralism: whether to tolerate incompatible values and beliefs, and whether to give new cultural elements—no matter how outrageous they sound—a fair chance to compete in the market place for ideas and values is itself a value that needs to be accepted. A belief in cultural (including religious) tolerance and free speech and thought, and the institutions it implies (such as the first amendment to the US Constitution) can be of great economic value when it is relatively rare; it allows an economy to attract and absorb religious and political refugees, who tend to be creative and well-networked.[8] The willingness of the Netherlands and later Britain and the United States to tolerate Jews and dissenting Christians contributed a great deal to their economies, especially in high-skilled manufacturing and financial services.

Conformism bias would tend to create homogenization, if it worked only in one direction. But a perverse frequency dependence can arise through "rebellious" or deliberate nonconformist behavior in a "deviant" group, if such contrarian behavior is not penalized too severely. In the Bisin-Verdier framework, frequency dependence bias is built in, because parents can only choose between socializing their children themselves or having them socialized by a randomly chosen other individual in society. The randomness here seems implausible: as already noted, parents are likely to choose another individual who holds their values, but because of agency problems, a larger chance of transmission errors is introduced. Moreover, children are subject to conformist biases when in contact with peers. But there, too, it is likely that contrarian biases will emerge among a small minority, and of course it is likely that precisely that a member of such a rebellious and minority group will create the innovations that eventually will add significantly to or overthrow the conventional wisdom. One thinks of Alan Turing.

Rationalization bias: Cultural change can take place or be resisted through the rationalization of an existing set of institutions, thus creating feedback from institutions to culture. There is an inherent tendency to internalize existing social customs, norms, and socially mandated rules and associate them with desirable values. Suppose a law or social norm penalizes a

---

[8] As Cipolla, (1972, p. 52) has remarked, "Throughout the centuries the countries in which intolerance and fanaticism prevailed lost to more tolerant countries the most precious of all possible forms of wealth: good human brains. ... Inflow of good brains and receptiveness to new ideas were among the main sources of the success stories of England, Holland, and Sweden in the sixteenth and seventeenth century. It is gratifying to be able to say that tolerance pays off."

certain action. Such penalties eventually may make the action seem undesir-
able merely because a penalty is associated with it. While "crime" is a viola-
tion of institutional rules, "sin" is a transgression against morals, that is,
against cultural beliefs. Projecting rules onto morality might occur when
attempting to rationalize an institution (if an action is punished, there must
be a reason for it), or it may happen during the process of socialization by
parents imbuing their children with a sense of sin for some action punish-
able by law. It is rational for parents to indoctrinate their children in the sin-
fulness of crime, to minimize the probability of them violating the rule and
being punished. Many rules, such as "do not kill," reflect both law and
morality, but the dietary laws of Jews and Muslims or the marijuana laws
in the United States are examples of morality grafted onto rules. What was
once forbidden now becomes taboo. Some people tend to eat according to
strict table manners even when they eat alone, simply because they have
internalized the rule of holding the knife with the right hand and a fork with
the left. The internalization of institutions and norms into preferences is
probably fairly unstable, unless it is supported by some deeper ethical or
other knowledge. Thus people eating by themselves may eventually drop
their formal table manners but still wash their hands before eating for
hygienic reasons, and parents may be less emphatic in warning their
children against marijuana than against the use of substances such as PCP
or methamphetamines.

Coercion bias: In a highly authoritarian or coercive society, cultural beliefs
can be affected by force. As noted, no government or religious authority can
ever force people to actually believe certain propositions, only make them
pretend as if they do, which can create preference falsification and what
Greif and Tadelis have called crypto-morality (Kuran, 1987, 1997; Greif and
Tadelis, 2010). On the whole, such schemes are unstable and can lead to
sudden collapses, such as the fall of totalitarian states and the sharp decline
of the ideologies that supported them. But while coercive regimes cannot
control what goes on in people's minds, they can control and manipulate
oblique and horizontal transmission mechanisms (schools, churches, media)
and thus try to influence beliefs and enforce what could be called political
and ideological socialization. Repressive regimes can also arrest people
known to have deviant or inconvenient beliefs or force them to leave the
country, and thus to try to homogenize the distribution of beliefs in the
country. Before the completion of the Berlin Wall, East Germany experimented with such policies, but in the long term these turned out to be
ineffective. The historical evidence that coercion actually works at the level
of values, based on the experience of political revolutions from the French
to the Russian to the Iranian, is rather mixed. But clearly government-
controlled entities, such as schools and the military, can reproduce certain

elements of socialization including a belief in punctuality, discipline, temperance, and the virtuousness of obedience, hard work, and technology.[9] **Salient events bias**: Highly dramatic and traumatic events can have a discontinuous effect on culture through powerful framing effects. Such catastrophes as the Black Death, the Holocaust, or 9/11 changed ideology and beliefs through their powerful challenge to existing beliefs. Such salient events are especially important for political ideology and the area of social "values" that pertain to the role of the state. Major and dramatic failures of the free market create more support for a regulated and managed economy (as happened in the industrialized West during the Great Depression of the 1930s), whereas major failures of a managed economy such as the former Soviet bloc increased ideological support for a free market economy both in the affected areas and in those competing with them.[10]

Biases should not be regarded as parametrically given; they are time-variant and historically contingent. Content bias, for instance, depends crucially on what the rhetorical criteria are: what counts as proof or at least what is felt to be convincing. In mathematics, astronomy, medicine, and botany, what was admissible as evidence changed dramatically in the early modern period: experimental evidence became increasingly central to the intellectual discourse, as was mathematization, and the inductive method of looking for empirical regularities in the data. As Shapiro (2000, p. 106) and Wootton (2015, pp. 251–309) have emphasized, what was regarded as a "fact" changed dramatically in the seventeenth century and the distinction between *verum* and *factum* was eroded. Ideas in science were increasingly viewed in an almost legalistic fashion, to be decided by evidence that was regarded as sufficient as opposed to the *obiter dicta* of ancient writings. The laws of nature were the laws of God, the trick was to discover them.

How did these biases change in early modern Europe? All beliefs about the physical world had to be confronted by the best tests that could be designed. Technology accelerated these developments: the appearance of

---

[9] Recent work on the impact of the Nazi regime on cultural beliefs shows that the cohorts most exposed to Nazi indoctrination held significantly stronger anti-Semitic views than cohorts born before and after (Voigtländer and Voth, 2015). The success of the Nazis in installing these beliefs was, of course, a combination of coercion and rhetorical bias, and possibly confirmation bias as well. Voigtländer and Voth (2015, p. 7935) cite Joseph Goebbels's famous statement that "propaganda can only be effective if it is broadly in line with pre-existing notions and beliefs."

[10] For an interesting analysis of the effect of such traumatic events in nations with a relatively uneventful history, see Broomé et al. (2011). For a Swedish sample (on the basis of somewhat mixed evidence) these authors claim that "defining moments engrave themselves on the minds most particularly of those coming of age at the time they occur." Events that sweep away "isms" and forms of government and also damage families can reorient "one's life and values" (Broomé et al., 2011, p. 31). The authors are non-committal about predicting the exact direction of such changes.

the microscope, the telescope, the barometer, and other new instruments, opened new worlds of observation to curious and skeptical natural philosophers. New tools helped change the minds of the intellectuals under their influence. The emergence of the tools of science and their dissemination depended on technological developments in glass, in papermaking, in shipbuilding, navigation, and watchmaking.

Equally dramatic was the change in direct bias: as stressed throughout this book, the authority of the ancient canon of classical civilization lost out in this age, replaced by new experts who had to earn their place at the top of the knowledge pyramid by gaining a reputation among their peers. To become an authority, with all the privileges thereof, it was not enough to be learned; one was expected to have contributed to the body of knowledge. Rhetorical bias and framing changed, too, thanks to new techniques: the effect of the printing press was comparable to that of radio and television in the twentieth century. Publishing in the vernacular languages instead of in Latin, too, was a powerful rhetorical device, allowing intellectual innovations to reach people who had not been trained in Latin. In France, by the time of Louis XIV, works written in Latin would be either translated into French or ignored (Fumaroli, 2015, pp. 63–64).

Part II

Cultural Entrepreneurs and Economic Change, 1500–1700

Chapter 6

Cultural Entrepreneurs and Choice-based Cultural Evolution

How does cultural change occur? Why do cultural choices and their consequences differ among different societies? Is there room for human agency, and if so, what is it? As Greif (1994; 2005, pp. 269–71) has noted, normally each individual makes cultural choices, taking as given what he or she thinks others believe. There are, however, exceptions, and they matter. A small number of individuals, Hooke's "Cortesian army" if you wish, not only choose a set of cultural traits for themselves from a given menu but also add to the menus available to others. Such individuals might be called "cultural entrepreneurs" and they are the ultimate form of the one-to-many transmission mechanism. This term is akin to Greif's (2009) "moral entrepreneur."[1] Perhaps the closest concept is that proposed by Douglass North (1981, p. 65) of the "ideological entrepreneur," who perceives anomalies between people's beliefs about the world and their actual experiences, and takes advantage of the disparity to promulgate a novel ideology or interpretation.[2] Richard Swedberg (2006) has argued that a concept of "social entrepreneur" can be extracted from the early writings of Schumpeter, a "man of action" who carries out ideas whose time has come.

The essence of the argument made here is contained in George Bernard Shaw's Maxim # 124 in his *Maxims for Revolutionists* (1903), where he noted that "The reasonable man adapts himself to the world: the unreasonable one persists in trying to adapt the world to himself. Therefore

---

[1] Greif notes that "moral entrepreneurs are individuals with new moral visions who seek to gain followers. When they fail, they enter the history books, if at all, as anarchists, rebels, false prophets, cult leaders, and heretics. When they win, they write the history book" (Greif, 2012, p. 31). The analogy of influential figures with entrepreneurs is also used by Ringmar (2007, p. 96) but in a somewhat different sense. The same idea, applied to politics, can be found in Leighton and López (2013, pp. 179–82).

[2] As Virgil Storr (2011) has noted, North's concept has remained underdeveloped and needs to be enriched by supplementary theories of entrepreneurship.

all progress depends on the unreasonable man." Cultural entrepreneurs can thus be regarded as the exceptional and unusual specimens who are the sources of evolutionary change: they are the ones who do not take the cultural choices of others as given, but try consciously to change them. But they also have a straightforward interpretation in economics. Their function resembles that of entrepreneurs in the realm of production: people who think "outside the box," refuse to take the existing technology or market structure as given and try to change it—and benefit personally in the process. Most of them were willing to take large risks; were obsessive and hard-working individuals; often charismatic; and of course also lucky. Much like economic entrepreneurs, nearly all cultural entrepreneurs made fairly marginal changes in the cultural menus. However, a few stand out as having affected the menus in a substantial and palpable way; they changed beliefs, values, and preferences of significant subsets of society.

We can thus think of successful cultural entrepreneurs as the individuals who successfully contested and overthrew existing authorities in a specific area of culture and created a competing variant: this is one way of thinking about Mohammed, Martin Luther, Adam Smith, Karl Marx, and Charles Darwin. In terms of the cultural evolution models, cultural entrepreneurs can be seen as the arch-example of the one-to-many transmission we saw before in chapter 5. Cavalli-Sforza and Feldman (1981) point out that such transmissions occur quite rapidly and have the effect of reducing within-population variation. Cultural entrepreneurs function at least as much as coordinators as they do as innovators. They coordinate disparate beliefs, creating a more coherent set of cultural traits that form a focal point in the tradition of Thomas Schelling. Thus there were many forms of socialist thought before Marx, and his great achievement was to unify and coordinate these belief into a cohesive doctrine. Psychiatry was a messy body of knowledge until Freud came along. Scholarship on the great cultural entrepreneurs in history is vast. Multitudinous bookshelves are devoted to the works of Adam Smith and Sigmund Freud, and even more minor cultural entrepreneurs such as Ayn Rand, Joseph Schumpeter, Michel Foucault, and Herbert Marcuse. Some may find a great deal of interest in parsing and exegesizing the exact words of cultural entrepreneurs to find out what the Master "really meant." However, because my purpose is to uncover how cultural change affected actual events and outcomes, what is of concern to us is what people actually extracted and learned from the cultural entrepreneurs and how they changed their economic behavior as a result.

In recent years economists have become increasingly interested in the way in which some influential individuals affect the beliefs and preferences of others. Thus Glaeser (2005) has shown how certain political entrepreneurs, or "entrepreneurs of hate," convince others to dislike some group in a way that may benefit them. In a very different context, Acemoglu and Jackson (2015) show that the leadership of prominent agents can affect future social norms whether to be more or less cooperative (in the sense of generalized trust). This work focuses on the relationships between agents and others, and the economic consequences of trust and cooperation. My interest here is in the attitudes of people to their natural environment and their willingness to comprehend and manipulate it for their needs. But before, it is worth discussing the concept of a cultural entrepreneur a bit in detail.

The degree to which history is driven by a "vital few" and their indispensability has been controversial. Most modern historians have tended to dismiss the impact of individuals on history by mocking the "intellectual prowess and persuasive capabilities of a few men" and stressing cultural change as "a confluence of available ideas," although one is left wondering where such influential ideas might have come from in the first place.[3] In contrast, Jonathan Hughes (1986, p. 2) wrote that "to ignore the impact of individuals on our historical development would be like studying physiology without considering the actions of the organs and cells on the body and each other." Most economic historians today would still agree with David Hume that "what depends upon a few persons is, in great measure, to be ascribed to chance, or secret and unknown causes; what arises from a great number may often be accounted for by determinate and known causes" (Hume [1742], 1985, p. 112). In other words, Marxist and similar interpretations that minimize the role of individuals can write down aggregative dynamic models that they believe drive the behavior of masses, but making any predictions about the rise of a person like Mohammed or Hitler seems futile. Did successful entrepreneurs really matter? Perhaps the safest thing to say is that even if no single individual was truly indispensable, some persons made a clear difference in that historical developments would have been noticeably different without them, although the degree of difference remains a matter of debate.

What seems beyond dispute is that the "great number" of people that Hume wrote of needed to be coordinated to converge on a more or less coherent set of beliefs and this coordinating role is crucial. At times, most of the coordinating is left to apostles and acolytes who build on the entrepreneur's prestige and name recognition (as was the case with the emergence of Christianity). Such coordinators were not just pawns of deeper historical forces, but also had considerable agency themselves. When that agency becomes important to the outcome, we may say that history is at a bifurcation point or a "critical juncture" (Acemoglu and Robinson, 2012) and that fairly small events and decisions made by a single individual or a

---

[3] The quote is from Lowengard (2006, p. 6). Tolstoy famously wrote in *War and Peace* that "to study the laws of history we must completely change the subject of our observation, must leave aside kings, ministers, and generals, and the common, infinitesimally small elements by which the masses are moved."

few of them may set the process on a different trajectory. It is this kind of evolutionary mechanism that such evolutionary theorists as John Ziman had in mind when they pointed to the rare and unusual events that may have cascading effects in evolutionary systems. Such individuals are responsible for the "chance" part in Monod's (1971) dyad. But not all is chance: there are rules, regularities, and constraints that constitute the "necessity."

What is it precisely that cultural entrepreneurs do? They are persons who become sufficiently influential to change the cultural menus of enough people and who persuade many of them to adopt the cultural variants they are proposing. The number of converts has to be large enough to affect institutions and behavior in significant ways. How many that is, of course, depends on the context. A cultural entrepreneur like John Maynard Keynes needed only to persuade a relatively small number of economists and policy makers to make a significant impact on the institutions of his age. Hitler, however, needed to persuade a large number of German voters and citizens. How, exactly, these individuals themselves arrive at their novel ideas is, as Hume suggested, in the final analysis unknowable, but usually they build on existing but diffuse notions, and formulate them in a sharper and coherent body of propositions or beliefs, which serve as a focal point for their contemporaries. In that sense they create something new.

The term "entrepreneur" calls up the notion of a market. Choice-based cultural evolution can be regarded as taking place in a market setting. The idea of a "market for ideas" is not new (Polanyi, 1962; Stigler, 1965; Coase, 1974; Gans and Stern, 2003; Mokyr, 2007).[4] In this market, people try to persuade an audience of the correctness of their beliefs and the merit of their values and to provide information to others who do not have it.[5] Cultural choices are not quite like other choices in economics, and hence the concept of a "market for ideas" does not correspond neatly to other markets. We use the idea of a market for other areas in which goods are not bought and sold for a price, such as the "marriage market" and the "political market." But at least in the marriage market, the opportunity cost of picking a partner is well defined in monogamous societies. In the market for ideas, the opportunity costs of adopting a new idea are less clear-cut. In

---

[4]   The term "marketplace for ideas" is quite common in discussions of higher education in the United States (e.g., Menand, 2010) and has been used in connection with free speech and first amendment law by the American Supreme Court.

[5]   The concept is more natural to economists, perhaps, but Cook (2007, p. 411) describes a world in which knowledge was wholly commodified. It was, in his words, produced, accumulated, and exchanged. Habermas (1989, pp. 36–37), in his discussion of the rise of informal public groups where much of the discourse of the Enlightenment took place, also speaks of a "market" that made cultural products and information accessible, which only makes sense if he means by that a metaphorical market for ideas.

some cases, much like the marriage market, the choice is clear: one cannot be a Catholic and a Jew or believe in a Ptolemaic and Copernican universe at the same time. But in many other cases a new notion may not crowd out existing beliefs but simply be added to them.[6] There is no obvious cultural equivalent to the budget constraint, which is central to the operation of markets in which goods and services are sold at well-defined prices. That said, the idea of a market in which sellers and buyers meet and transact is still a valid and useful metaphor.

Cultural entrepreneurs were very successful sellers in this market. Like all successful innovating entrepreneurs, cultural entrepreneurs combined an ability to "read" their market with their original insights, altering the culture by adding items to the menu of cultural choices but not being so outrageously different as to become ineffectual. Some of them did so by sensing a latent demand: a dissatisfaction with some cultural beliefs or knowledge, or diffuse and incoherent earlier attempts to cope with a new reality. For cultural entrepreneurs to be successful, some disconnect must exist between the prevalent cultural elements and some new information that does not quite square with it. This is much like Thomas Kuhn's cognitive dissonance or what he called "awareness of anomaly," caused by the accumulation of evidence inconsistent with the current paradigm and thus leading to scientific revolutions. What was true for astronomy in the sixteenth century was equally true for anatomy and theology. Because such dissonances evolved independently, they elicited responses that tended at first to be diffuse and required coordination and standardization. Thus, for instance, we can easily document the growing disenchantment of Europeans with the established church in the fifteenth century, but it required a Luther and a Calvin, armed with the printing press, to create a coherent new alternative.

Most successful cultural entrepreneurs stand on the shoulders of those who came before them. Marx lived at a time when the prevailing interpretations of society were no longer consonant with a new industrial and urban reality, and his work appeared in the wake of myriad disparate socialist ideas. He created historical materialism as a hybrid of classical political economy, utopian socialism, Hegelian historicism, and other elements. Combining these elements and adding new ones, he was able to create a new standardized synthesis which became Marxist orthodoxy. Adam Smith, perhaps the most successful cultural entrepreneur in eco-

---

[6] In evolutionary terms, this would be equivalent to saying that the selection environment is not very stringent. A different way of seeing this is to allow for the possibility that even if A and B are mutually exclusive, one might take the position that *both* are possible at nonzero probabilities. The selection criteria for any kind of cultural belief are contingent, and it is easy to envisage a cultural environment in which the question "but is it true?" can be routinely answered satisfactorily by "sometimes," or "maybe," or "if God wills it."

nomics, was successful by synthesizing and reformulating the economic doctrines he gathered from others.[7] Keynes explicitly acknowledged his precursors in his "notes on Mercantilism" in the *General Theory*.

To function as a focal point, the beliefs and ideas of a cultural entrepreneur have to be widely disseminated and believed by most people to be believable to others and thus to reduce dispersion. Such dispersion is never quite eliminated altogether, and different interpretations, say, of the Koran and *Das Kapital* co-exist. But part of the success of cultural entrepreneurs is in steering people toward cultural convergence. They thus set out to alter the beliefs or preferences of others by proposing a more comprehensible and compact set of cultural elements, but one that can be related to by people "shopping" in the market for ideas.

Cultural entrepreneurship operates through many of the transmission biases that cultural evolution has proposed, as described above. At first glance, Mohammed and Adam Smith had little in common. All the same, we can see certain similarities. What determined their success was not only content but also rhetoric: the effective cultural entrepreneur needs to find a formulation and a language that resonates with his intended audience. Moreover, most cultural entrepreneurs operate in concentric "layers," that is, they reach their audience through disciples, apostles, acolytes, and epigones who transform and in some cases translate their messages. In some case in the past, these transmissions altered and distorted the teachings of the master. Few will quibble with the statement that twentieth-century Marxism-Leninism as interpreted by Stalinists bears only a superficial resemblance to the writings of *The Communist Manifesto* and *Capital*. Adam Smith was not a prophet of unbridled laissez-faire, but that seems to matter little to many of his modern-day acolytes. The exact content of the writings of cultural entrepreneurs sometimes mattered less than the message that future generations chose to distill from it. Moreover. the stature of some cultural entrepreneurs was puffed up by followers whose careers may have been affected by the way the Master was viewed.

The success of cultural entrepreneurs depends on an environment that is conducive to intellectual innovation. Like all evolutionary systems, cultural systems resist change. If institutions are extremely conservative and conformist, and have the power to repress innovators by branding them as blasphemers and apostates, the risk to which cultural entrepreneurs and their followers are exposed is higher and the likelihood of their success is reduced. Such institutions therefore discourage cultural entrepreneurship. The main reason for the resistance is quite clear. The new ideas proposed by a cultural entrepreneur replace incumbent ideas, and the social and

---

[7] Schumpeter maintained, somewhat unfairly, that "the *Wealth of Nations* contained no really novel ideas and ... cannot rank with Newton's *Principia* and Darwin's *Origin* as an intellectual achievement." See Schumpeter, 1954 p. 185.

economic rents accruing to those invested in a dominant set of ideas imply that there will be strong incentives for entrenched interests to discredit them or even using force to suppress them (Benabou, Ticchi, and Vindigni, 2014). Such resistance can be built into the institutions: religions maintained orthodoxy by persecuting heretics. For potential intellectual innovators the resistance to innovation and the fear of persecution or other forms of sanctions create a negative incentive. Scientists, too have designed many ways in which incumbents try to protect themselves from what they feel to be excessive innovation. Max Planck famously noted (with some exaggeration) that a new scientific insight never triumphs by convincing its opponents, but only because these opponents eventually die off. Within technology there was and still is considerable resistance to inventors coming from vested interests, known (somewhat unfairly), as Luddism. Deirdre McCloskey (2016a, p. 94) points out that such words as "innovation" and "novelty" in the past often had negative connotations. An emotional attachment to traditional ways of doing things made novelty look suspect.[8]

If the environment, however, is sufficiently open to new ideas, entrepreneurs and their personal qualities will in turn help change the environmental parameters, creating a feedback effect that makes future entrepreneurs more likely to succeed. The same is true, mutatis mutandis, for cultural entrepreneurs. To say, therefore, that Martin Luther, Adam Smith, and Karl Marx were merely the product of their respective environments is to impoverish the historical narrative and marginalize all elements of discretion and agency. Similarly, the influential intellectuals whose work jointly produced the eighteenth-century Enlightenment and the economic miracles it produced were products of their time, but in turn shaped their environment through the political and intellectual changes they brought about.

The cultural biases identified by Richerson and Boyd (2005) and discussed in chapter 5 can help identify the roots of success of some cultural entrepreneurs. Some new ideas just resonated with known facts and conditions on the ground and the entrepreneurs persuaded their audience simply because the message sounded right at the time. Some succeeded because they and their followers were rhetorically gifted. Almost all of them relied on direct bias through influential and authoritative followers and disciples.

The interaction of a gifted and lucky cultural entrepreneur with a suitable environment is what created dramatic and at times revolutionary cultural changes. In that sense, again, cultural entrepreneurs are no different from the standard innovator-businessperson model of entrepreneurship envisaged by economists. The idealized perfectly competitive baseline model of economics has no room for entrepreneurs because nobody can

---

[8] In 1492 the Abbott of Sponheim, Johannes Trithemius, wrote *In Praise of Scribes* in which he made a series of powerful arguments against the use of the printing press and favoring hand-copying. He then promptly proceeded to have the book printed.

affect market outcomes on their own. But in economic history individual entrepreneurs do matter to outcomes, from Josiah Wedgwood and Matthew Boulton to the great entrepreneurs of late nineteenth-century America. They changed what was produced and how production took place. Cultural entrepreneurs change what people believe, and if enough important people are converted, they will change institutions to conform with the new beliefs and thus the environment in which the next generation of cultural entrepreneurs find themselves. Such feedback effects can lead to unpredictable dynamics. Arguably, entrepreneurs drive history mostly in the limited sense that they take advantage of opportunities created by an environment larger and stronger than themselves. But in their absence, these opportunities may well have been missed, or at least exploited in different ways, leading to different outcomes.

The question is not only why some environments spawned such entrepreneurs and others did not, but rather why some cultural entrepreneurs are successful. What determines their success? Success was a function of personal characteristics, the capability to inspire a devoted set of followers who would spread the new message, the content of the message, and the lucky coincidence of having the right message at the right time. One can think of Jesus and Charles Darwin, for instance, as unusually successful cultural entrepreneurs. There are many others in almost every realm of culture who changed the beliefs and preferences of their contemporaries and subsequent generations, from Caravaggio to Beethoven to Shakespeare to Joyce. Being the right person at the right time in the right place sounds like the confluence of many contingencies, and of course it is.

Spectacularly successful cultural entrepreneurs have been few and far between. But precisely because of that, it is hard to accept the fundamentalist gradualist agenda at face value; cultural evolution includes definable events and individuals who abruptly changed the cultural menus for many individuals. The publication of *The Origin of Species* in 1859 is a good example of a "hopeful monstrosity" in the cultural realm; so was the discovery of the structure of DNA in 1953. Such innovations never appear entirely ab nihilo but if they are significantly different from incumbent knowledge and if they start appearing on the cultural menu, they make a difference. Not all cultural entrepreneurship was favorable to an advance in useful knowledge. One could cite the case of the Islamic philosopher Al Ghazali (1058–1111), a Persian whose influence on thought in the Muslim world led to a rising mysticism and occasionalist thinking. He was a key figure in the decline in Islamic science, which had flourished in the first centuries of Islam. In the views of some historians of science it was due to his influence and that of his followers that the "Arabs" never became "a nation of Galileos, Keplers, and Newtons" (quoted in Cohen, 1994, p.

395).[9] Cohen (2012, p. 66) argues that this outcome was far from the author's original intentions, but the very nature of cultural entrepreneurship means that the forces set in motion often exceed what was originally intended.

As in all discussions of entrepreneurship, the counterfactual of what course history would have taken in the absence of some pivotal individual agent remains a matter of speculation. Is it likely to have been radically different? That, of course, depends on what "radically different" means. History is neither fluke nor necessity, but somewhere in between. Individuals mattered, even if they were not all that mattered, and even if their impact was ultimately constrained by the environment. It is useful to study the impact of highly influential persons in relation to their environments, and to examine how and why they changed the beliefs and thus the behavior of others.

In summary, much like in any story of innovation, it is convenient and only a little misleading to organize the tale around a few key entrepreneurial figures who helped organize and standardize the work of many, whose insights (and success) inspired and motivated others. To repeat: this approach does not imply that they were, in some sense, indispensable, nor that they and their work were inevitable products of their times. But within those limits, there remained many degrees of freedom, and much like other great entrepreneurs in history, the details, if not the main tale, would have read differently in their absence. Equally important, like any well-functioning market, the success of able and lucky entrepreneurs is like the proverbial canary in a coal mine. The proliferation of successful entrepreneurs is a telltale sign of well-functioning markets. The success that cultural entrepreneurs in early modern Europe had in persuading others to change from the "default option" of their cultural beliefs to new and sometimes radical ideas indicates that such persuasion was indeed effective: others were willing to listen to and evaluate intellectual innovations. The deep significance of the institutions that governed the market for ideas resides here.

In chapters 7 and 8, I will take a closer look at two of the cultural entrepreneurs whose influence I consider as supremely important for the rise of the Industrial Enlightenment and eventually the emergence of useful knowledge as the main engine of modern economic growth—Francis Bacon and Isaac Newton. It should be made clear, however, that between 1500 and 1700, the European intellectual scene included other remarkable

---

[9] Al Ghazali's famous treatise *The Incoherence of the Philosophers* was increasingly interpreted to imply that foreign learning was incompatible with Muslim religion and that the concept of a natural "law" contradicted the omnipotence of the creator. Chaney (2015) casts an interesting light on Al Ghazali as a cultural entrepreneur. He was influential in part because of a changing environment: the Sunni Revival in the eleventh and twelfth centuries consolidated the political power of religious leaders who believed that the study of scientific subjects using rational methods would undermine their power.

individuals, who dramatically changed the cultural menu of European society. Besides the obvious religious entrepreneurs such as Luther and Calvin, I could have easily picked Descartes or Spinoza as intellectuals whose work left an indelible print on the evolution of culture in Europe both on their contemporaries and future intellectuals. Historians of science and intellectual historians could make the case for Kepler, Galileo, or even Leibniz.[10] Perhaps the most important cultural entrepreneur in terms of his impact on eighteenth-century political thought (and eventually institutional changes in the century after his death in 1707) was John Locke.[11] For the change in the cultural menu of choices regarding useful knowledge, however, we must look elsewhere.

It is not of great importance what our own age thinks of the contributions of these cultural entrepreneurs, because our age did not create the Industrial Revolution or modern economic growth. It is of central importance, however, that Enlightenment thinkers clearly looked up to Bacon and Newton as the most influential thinkers who formed their age, and when they wanted to hand out supreme compliments to other intellectual innovators, these two were the standards. Voltaire, in his discussion of "great men" (which he first dismissed as a "frivolous" question but then engaged in it anyway) began with the three greatest—all of them English: Bacon, Locke, and Newton ("the generals and ministers will have to wait," he added for good measure) (Voltaire [1733–34], 2007, p. 37). The Scottish Enlightenment philosopher and historian John Millar (1735–1801) in a footnote acknowledging his masters in political economy, wrote that "the great Montesquieu ... was the Lord Bacon of this branch of philosophy. Dr [Adam] Smith is the Newton" (Millar, 1790, p. 473). In a similar vein, when the young Jeremy Bentham wanted to praise the French Enlightenment writer Claude-Adrien Helvétius, he wrote that "what Bacon was to the physical world, Helvétius was to the moral. The moral world has therefore had its Bacon, but its Newton is still to come" (quoted in Mitchell, 1974, p. 170). Similarly Condorcet fully realized that the progress made in the hard sciences was the result of "Baconian science" and its "Newtonian legacy" (Williams, 2004, p. 95). Thomas Jefferson, by anyone's definition an emblematic man of the Enlightenment, wrote in 1789 that three

---

[10] Cohen (2012, pp. 179, 362) writes that "Galileo is the first thinker about natural phenomena that a modern scientist can identify with ... the predominant figure of how modern science came into this world" and gives him credit for pioneering "realist mathematical science." He adds, very much in the spirit of model-based cultural bias, "how could [Galileo's work] fail to serve as a source of inspiration ... for younger men sensitive to the attractions of mathematics?"

[11] Peter Gay (1966, p. 321) wrote of Locke that he was "to the Enlightenment what [the poet Abraham] Cowley had said Bacon was to the Royal Society: a Moses, writing the Law, showing the way, dominating the scene, exacting gratitude, but stopping short of the promised land."

Englishmen—Bacon, Locke, and Newton—were "the three greatest men that have ever lived, without any exception, and as having laid the foundations of those superstructures which have been raised in the Physical & Moral sciences" (Jefferson, 1789). As late as 1851, a review of the "Official Catalogue" of the Crystal Palace exhibition, after a rather congratulatory account of industrial progress, noted that "as a nation, we [Britain] cannot claim the distinction of having originated this great lever of industrial progress, but we have at least given to the world the two philosophers, Bacon and Newton, who first lent direction and force to the stream of industrial science" (*Edinburgh Review*, 1851, p. 288).

Chapter 7

Francis Bacon, Cultural Entrepreneur

As a cultural entrepreneur, Francis Bacon was of unique importance to the development of the West. "Baconianism" has meant different things to different people over time, as a philosophical system, an inductive scientific methodology, and a set of policy suggestions, among other things (Pérez-Ramos, 1988, pp. 7–31).[1] Of interest here is his impact on subsequent cultural beliefs that eventually affected economic development. A dated but still useful biography of Bacon (Farrington, [1951] 1979) refers to him in its subtitle as a "Philosopher of Industrial Science." It seems an anachronistic and odd term; "industrial science" even today sounds almost oxymoronic and in any event has little to do with philosophy. For Farrington, a classicist, Bacon was not so much the great advocate of an inductive methodology in science but rather someone who had one great idea: knowledge ought to bear fruit in production, science ought to be applicable to industry, and it was people's sacred duty to improve and transform the material conditions of life. A somewhat different approach is taken by Rossi (1970) who emphasizes a critical innovation in Bacon's philosophy, namely the fundamental complementarity between "truth" and "utility," that is, the "mechanical" and "liberal" arts (or science and technology). For Bacon, scientific and economic progress depended on the integration of the knowledge of technicians into science and natural history (Rossi, 1970, pp. 120,

---

[1] Graham Rees (2000, p. 69) amusingly starts his essay on "Baconianism" announcing that "there is no such thing" and the terms is a reification denoting the alleged influence of Bacon on the "turbulent intellectual cultures of seventeenth century Europe." He then proceeds to describe in detail those influences and dismisses (tongue in cheek) the Royal Society's *History of Trades,* because it "turned out to be very difficult to accumulate technological data [and] derive genuine improvements from the energy invested" and that this aspect of Bacon's program had to wait until the eighteenth century.

146–73). The upshot of the rather voluminous literature on Bacon is that his vision prepared the Western world for what was to become in the eighteenth century the "Baconian program"—the attainment of material progress through propositional and prescriptive knowledge feeding off one another and creating a self-reinforcing (auto-catalytic) feedback loop that changed the economic history of the world.

Bacon's image of how this was to take place sounds uncannily prescient: "The true and legitimate goal of the sciences is to endow human life with new discoveries and resources." He fully recognized that progress of this kind was to be attained by the work of a small elite: "The over-whelming majority of ordinary people have no notion of this ... perhaps occasionally, some unusually intelligent craftsman ... devotes himself to making some new invention, usually at his own expense." He complained that most research and development followed an unfocused agenda and thus led nowhere, and that progress has been hindered by an excessive "reverence for antiquity and by the authority of men who have a great repu-tation in philosophy and the consensus that derives from them" (Bacon, [1620] 1999, pp. 66, 68, aphorisms 81, 84). In a widely cited short essay, written in 1592, Bacon laid out his view of what knowledge was and what it ought to be. Up to his day, he sighs, technological progress had been the result of small and accidental inventions made by craftsmen. Formal knowl-edge (what we would refer to as science or propositional knowledge) had to date done very little to discover the underlying natural regularities that governed technology (Bacon, [1592], 1838, vol. 1, pp. 216–17):

> Is there any such happiness as for a man's mind to be raised above the confusion of things, where he may have the prospect of the order of nature and error of man? But is this a view of delight only and not of discovery? of contentment and not of benefit? Shall he not as well discern the riches of nature's warehouse as the beauty of her shop? Is truth ever barren? Shall he not be able thereby to produce worthy effects, and to endow the life of man with infinite commodities?

It was a theme he repeated over and over again in his later writing and one that the Royal Society subscribed to. In the introduction to *The Great Instau-ration*, Bacon stated that he hoped to establish "a true and lawful marriage between the empirical and the rational faculty... out of which marriage let us hope there may spring helps to man, and a line and race of inventions that may in some degree subdue and overcome the necessities and miseries of humanity" (Bacon [1620], 1999, preface). The closing words of his *In Praise of Knowledge* are particularly prescient: "The sovereignty of man lieth hid in knowledge, wherein many things are reserved which Kings and their treasures cannot buy ... now we govern nature in opinions but we are thrall unto her [enslaved to her] in necessity, but if we would be led by her in invention, we should command her in action" (Bacon, [1592], 1838, vol. 1, p. 217).

The odd thing about Bacon is that he created no science, and was himself a poor scientist: he knew no mathematics and failed to appreciate its importance in the agenda he advocated. He managed to be ignorant of or reject some of the most significant scientific advances of his age: Harvey on the circulation of blood, Gilbert on magnets, Copernicus on the solar system, and Galileo on physics. One expert has concluded that his post-humous encyclopedic work *Sylva Sylvarum* shows the essentially unwork-able nature of Bacon's method (Debus, 1978, p. 105). There are clear signs in Bacon, as there are in so many other writers of the age, of a belief in "Adamite wisdom"—the notion that research consisted not of uncovering new facts and regularities as much as rediscovering a pristine wisdom that had already been revealed in an earlier age and had been lost or distorted by later scholars. It is also the case, as Harkness has argued, that much of what he was pleading for was already taking place in Elizabethan London, namely the growth of a practical natural knowledge with an attention to utility (Harkness, 2007, p. 246). In many areas, especially in his emphasis on the methods and practical relevance of science, he had numerous precursors.[2]

And yet, his influence on European science in the century and a half following his death in 1626 was immeasurable. The intellectual leaders of the Republic of Letters all acknowledged their debt to him. John Locke, for instance, was deeply indebted to Bacon and clearly read his work carefully and Boyle's research was heavily indebted to the agenda of Natur-al History delineated by Bacon in his *Parasceve* or "Preparative" toward a Natural History (Bacon [1620b] 1861–79; Anstey, 2002). Experimental science was not born with Bacon, but it was transformed beyond recog-nition. The concept of an experiment was an ancient one, and examples can be found in earlier times, most brilliantly in the work of the great Muslim optician and astronomer Ibn al-Khaytam or Alhazen (965–1040). But as Long (2011 p. 35) and Dear (1995, p. 30) note, the concept of hands-on research by experimental philosophy was remote from the scholastic tra-ditions of medieval universities, because the notion of an experimental de-sign to solve a specific question was basically alien to Aristotelian method-ology. Deductive knowledge derived by syllogisms was regarded the noblest and most prestigious form of knowledge. But more important, until it was overthrown in early modern Europe, Aristotelian doctrine sharply distin-guished between natural objects and artificial objects, and the rules of one

---

[2] See Stearns (1943). Paolo Rossi (1978, p. 9) explicitly claims that "Bacon was voicing the general opinion of his age ... when he strove to rehabilitate the mechanical arts ... and planned a history of arts and sciences to serve as a foundation for the reform of knowledge and of the very existence of mankind."

did not apply to the other. Taken to its extreme, this would mean that no experiment could shed much light on the natural world and that human-made devices might overcome the constraints that nature imposed on objects. These beliefs were already doubted long before, but the philosophy of science of Bacon together with the work of Galileo showed them to be false.

While the slow transformation toward the acceptance of experiments as a valid means of increasing useful knowledge had begun earlier, its prominence came with Bacon's work. Kuhn (1976, pp. 12–13) has stated flatly that after Bacon experimental science no longer was geared to confirm what was already known, but sought to know how nature would behave under previously unobserved or artificial circumstances, such as a mouse in a total vacuum. Moreover, it became reliant on new instruments and laboratory techniques that themselves were innovations and turned sharply against "thought experiments"—those that were imagined and recognized to make sense but in fact never actually performed. In aphorism II in his *Great Instauration,* Bacon states the point: "Neither the naked hand nor the understanding left to itself can effect much. It is by instruments and helps that the work is done ... as much for the understanding as for the hand (Bacon, [1620], 1999, p. 89). Despite these revolutionary innovations, Kuhn submits that the experimental method did not revolutionize "classical sciences" so much as complemented it. The interaction between the two was partial and slow (though he concedes that Newton and Huygens as well as the French mathematical physicist Edme Mariotte (1620–1684) were exceptions).[3]

Needless to say, Bacon did not start ab nihilo. Intellectually, his most prominent precursor was Paracelsus, who produced a great deal of work on medicine and "matter theory" which was "resolutely practical" (Gaukroger, 2001, p. 176). Paracelsus, an early citizen of the Republic of Letters, was highly influential on the Continent although Bacon usually cited him unfavorably. The French writer and historian Louis (Loys) Le Roy was designated by Frances Yates as "almost a precursor of Bacon," but more of a realist (Yates, 1967). Another forerunner of Bacon's was the Calabrian philosopher and scientist Bernardino Telesio (1509–1588), who pleaded for a purely empirical approach to science and for taking the study of nature beyond the constraints of the Aristotelian-Scholastic straitjacket.[4]

---

[3] Eamon (1994, p. 298) feels that Kuhn's argument diminishes the revolutionary significance of Baconian sciences in that Baconianism completely overthrew the boundaries of research of Aristotelian science and that knowledge of natural causes could be established by careful experiment and disciplined observation. "The inner 'secrets of nature' and not its outer appearances became the object of the new science."

[4] Bacon, indeed, famously referred to him as "the first of the moderns" and saw him as an ally in his rebellion against the authorities (especially Aristotle), even if he did not much care for Telesio's specific theories of nature, which were somewhat eccentric (Giglioni, 2010).

In France, the protestant philosopher Petrus Ramus expressed many of the same ideas, and his influence extended into England where the pugnacious intellectual and poet Gabriel Harvey (1552–1631) was one of his leading followers and Aristotle critics. The Dutch inventor and engineer Cornelis Drebbel was in some ways the incarnation of Bacon's hopes, and many of Drebbel's inventions found their way into Bacon's *New Atlantis* (Colie, 1955). In England itself, there was John Dee (1527–1608), a mathematician and religious mystic (as well as counselor to Queen Elizabeth), who wrote a famous and widely read "Mathematical Preface" to Henry Billingsly's translation of Euclid's *Elements* (1570) that was full of practical applications such as surveying, navigation and hydrography. Dee pleaded for the practical application of mathematics to skilled arts and commerce, geared toward an audience of non-specialists, and was read widely among the growing class of merchants, craftsmen, and skilled artisans (Trattner, 1964, p. 24; Harkness, 2007, pp. 100–7). Another English pre-Baconian author was Sir Hugh Plat (1552–1608), the author of many practical books full of recipes and prescriptions on a range of topics, from meat preservation and pest control to gardening.[5] One could mention many other people, mostly in London, who before Bacon combined mathematics and propositional knowledge with practical innovations and activities: Robert Recorde (1512–1558) a practical mathematician whose activities ranged from running the Bristol mint and developing silver mines in county Wexford in Ireland to a textbook on diagnosis from urine samples; Leonard Digges (1515–1559), another mathematician who authored a successful volume titled *Tectonicon* (1556), a mathematical handbooks for land surveyors and artisans that was reprinted twenty times in the ensuing century and a half; his son Thomas Digges (1546–1595) who wrote books on ballistics, designed a new harbor for Dover, and spread Copernican astronomy in England; Thomas Hood (1556–1620), a physician and lecturer in mathematics who made early versions of the slide rule and a calculating machine as well as books on navigation at sea using cross staffs and Jacob's staffs (early instruments to determine latitude at sea). Yet Hill's (1965, p. 292) suggestion that behind Bacon's writings stood London's craftsmen and practical mathematicians is one-sided: Bacon was also deeply influenced by an odd mixture of sixteenth-century Continental thought and Elizabethan proto-étatism.

By providing a coherent intellectual framework to these activities and bringing together many loose intellectual ends, Bacon's role can be seen as a synthetic thinker. He rephrased and re-organized many ideas in a

---

[5] One of the more skeptical scholars regarding Bacon's legacy remarks that many Londoners who had read Plat's work "must have wondered whether Bacon had done his homework," as Plat had written as early as 1594 that "the end of all our private labors and studies ought to be the beginning of the public and common good of our country"; "in 1605 Bacon could not invent, but merely repeat, this message" (Harkness, 2007, p. 246).

clearer formulation that recognized a comprehensive program for progress through experimental philosophy (Slack, 2015, p. 74). The bewildering plethora of religious and metaphysical notions that were bandied about in England in the seventeenth century, "came to be projected upon a mode of nature-knowledge associated with ... Bacon's name and writings" (Cohen, 2012, p. 585). Bacon's writings were the coordination device that served as the focal point of departure for thinkers and experimentalists for two centuries to come.[6] In this sense he fits the model of a cultural entrepreneur. Within fifty years of Bacon's death, much of Europe's scholarly and professional elite had adopted some version of his notions regarding the role of useful knowledge in society. Hiram Caton (1988, p. 39) summarized Bacon's influence by arguing that "for the first time, natural philosophy became a progressive, expansionist social institution." The full economic effects of these developments remained latent for many decades, but eventually they erupted in the Industrial Revolution and the subsequent processes of technological change.

Any attempt to portray Bacon anachronistically as a prescient and "modern" advocate of the direct application of science to industry seems misplaced, and much of Bacon's thinking is still an odd blend of alchemical and vitalist natural philosophy with more novel approaches (Rossi, 1978, pp. 11–20). One modern author states baldly that Bacon was more interested in magic than in technology and wrote more like a magician than an engineer (Henry, 2002, p. 50).[7] His bottom up inductive methodology, while a refreshing antidote to the barren deductivist approaches of the top-down Aristotelians and Cartesians, was never taken seriously in its pure and literal form. Yet despite doubts voiced by some historians and philosophers of science influenced by Karl Popper's dismissive attitude towards Bacon, his reputation as a prophet of economic progress, as modern economic

---

[6] Hill (1965, pp. 95–96) points to two separate scientific traditions that had developed in sixteenth-century England (mathematical and alchemical) plus an antitraditional heterodox Puritan intellectual tradition. Bacon, he argues, joined the three traditions and turned them into a coherent philosophical entity, thus strengthening a body of ideas that was bubbling up from below.

[7] In fairness to Bacon, note that "magic" at the time may have meant any natural force that was not properly understood and that any claims about what knowledge might be able to do for humankind would seem like magic. Bacon's own definition of magic is clearly different from our use of the term: "natural magic pretendeth [proposes] to call and reduce natural philosophy from a variety of speculations to the magnitude of works [experiments]" Bacon([1623], 1996, p. 143). Brian Vickers, in his notes to this passage, adds that "natural magic" was an eclectic mixture of physics and occult phenomena that had unobservable causes such as magnetism. One of the most accomplished and influential writers on "magic" was the German humanist Cornelius Agrippa (1486–1535), who wrote almost a century before Bacon that the effects produced by magicians are often taken by "the Vulgar" to be miracles "when they are notwithstanding only natural operation" (Agrippa,[1527] 1676, p. 111).

historians should recognize but rarely have, has survived intact.[8] William
Eamon (1991, p. 27) sees Bacon as part of a "complete redefinition of what
constitutes scientific research," in which the logical structures of scholasticism were replaced by "the hunt" for new facts. Yet Bacon never advocated the mindless piling up of empirical facts—his famous entomological
metaphor in *New Organon* clearly points to his clear notion of how good
science was supposed to be carried out. Ants, he explained, merely collect
things and use them. Spiders spin webs entirely out of materials they generate themselves. Bees have the right way: they gather nectar from flowers,
but then are able to transform it into something much better (Bacon [1620]
2000, aphorism 95, p. 79). What he is clearly advocating is a search for
empirical regularities and patterns that can be discerned from the data,
through analogy and conjecture, with creative imagination helping the in-
vestigator fill in gaps in natural history and experimental findings (Eamon,
1994, p. 288). His insight was that science was a product of the interaction
between people and nature producing facts and data, on explanatory
theories can then be built. Rescher, who points this out, remarks that it is
"to the immortal credit of Bacon that he was the first to see this point with
total clarity" (Rescher, 1978, p. 165).

    To be sure, Bacon greatly overrated the potential of purely empi-
rical research in his age. But as a successful cultural entrepreneur, he did not
have to be correct on all issues. He only had to be influential. What mattered in the case of Bacon is not what we think of him today, but the impact
he had in the decades that followed his life, in which intellectual processes
influenced by him changed the metaphysical outlook of European
intellectuals and its scientific and technological elite.[9] His influence was
narrow but deep. Bacon was keenly interested in the concept of knowledge
and suggested radical revisions on how we think about natural phenomena

---

[8] One influential historian of science who explained and supported Bacon's role in
the rise of economic modernity is Charles C. Gillispie. Gillispie noted that the program that Bacon
suggested to attain material progress through technological progress consisted of the application
of inductive and experimental methods to investigate nature, the creation of a universal natural
history, and the reorganization of science as a human activity. He summarized Bacon's vision
memorably as a "program for building an infinity of better mousetraps into a better world"
(Gillispie, 1960, p. 78). For a more recent statement in that spirit, see Zagorin (1998, pp. 97, 121).

[9] One interesting view has been put forward by Barbara J. Shapiro (2000, p. 107),
who has credited Bacon with nothing less than being the "central agent" of applying the notion
of a "fact" from the realm of law to that of science and technology, placing British natural
philosophy on an empirical basis. Other experts have pointed out that a whole series of applied
fields, such as heat, electricity, magnetism, and biology were created and "sanctioned by the
Baconian tradition as properly belonging to the cognitive scope of natural philosophy"(Pérez-
Ramos, 1988, p. 35). As Brian Vickers (1992, pp. 516–17) notes, this constituted an enormous
expansion and legitimization of the study of nature. Vickers adds that "Bacon's influence can be
traced to a great range of scientific pursuits, including geology, topography, statistics, medicine
and much else."

and its "operative" nature, that is the basis for human action and especially practical "works" or *opus* (Pérez-Ramos, 1988, chs. 12–13). His lasting insight was that knowledge was a collective activity, a social phenomenon, to be organized and distributed, and that its purpose was to be applied and used by society for material purposes (Farrington, [1951] 1979). Ferrone (2015, p. 98) adds that Bacon's work highlights the discontinuity between the "ineffable mystical wisdom of the Renaissance magi" and the modern and public methods in research, which was comprehensible to all because it was communicated widely and could be verified.[10]

Bacon himself, as noted, was not a distinguished scientist, but he had excellent instincts concerning the problems with natural philosophy as practiced in his time. He launched a devastating critique of what he called in the *New Organon* the "idols of the theater," which impede the progress of knowledge through bad methodology that was either too deductive (as in Aristotle), or, at the other extreme, too specialized and inductive, teasing excessively general conclusions from a few narrow experiments. Instead, in aphorism 61 in his *New Organon* he insisted on rigor and precision, fully specified by rules and instruments, much as the drawing of a perfect circle or straight line required compass and ruler (Bacon [1620] 1999, p. 103). Bacon and the Baconians stressed that nature was intelligible if the proper method of investigation was used, and the investigating mind was to be guided in the correct way (Shapin, 1996, p. 90). He never advocated the mindless collection of piles of facts; what his method meant was that theory had to be grounded in fact and tested at every step. Researchers should manipulate nature to extract its secrets. The widely cited statement attributed to Bacon that experimenters should "twist the Lion's tail and wait for the results" is apparently apocryphal, and its popularity is a sign of the identification of Bacon with a purely inductive method.[11] His insight that the artificial does not differ from the natural except in its effectiveness in revealing the secrets of nature was a critical deviation from Aristotelian dogma and the key to his copious descriptions of an experimental culture in Salomon's House (Eamon, 1994, pp. 310–11). The basic concepts of experimental philosophy owe much of their focus and formulation to Bacon's writings. This is not to say that had he not existed, modern science would

---

[10] As always, there were earlier expressions of his ideas, not always wholly acknowledged by Bacon. One example is the sixteenth-century French theologian Pierre de la Ramée (Petrus Ramus), with whom Bacon would have agreed that "the union of mathematics and the practice of scholarly arts by artisans would bring about great civic prosperity" (Smith, 1994, p. 36). Hill (1965, p. 292) insists on Ramus's enormous influence on Bacon, on "most of the Great English Puritans" and on such thinkers as Comenius.

[11] For a repetition of this statement, see for instance Heilbron (2003b, p. 287). But the original metaphor cannot be traced to any of Bacon's writing and is apparently due to Ian Hacking. See https://groups.google.com/forum/ #!topic/fa.philos-l/nvF7MYjedKQ, accessed November 24, 2013.

not have emerged. But the influence that Bacon's writings had in the century and a half after his death are a telltale sign of the kind of cultural changes Europe experienced that paved the way for future economic transformations.

Interestingly enough, Bacon has been heavily criticized by some early and modern critics of industrial society (for example, Merchant, 1980).[12] It is ironic, one scholar remarks wryly, that those who were born late enough to have benefited the most from advances inspired by Bacon's insights have heaped the most scorn on his "disastrously mistaken belief that nature and the creation are ordained for man's benefit and rule" (Zagorin, 1998, p. 121). It is even more striking that economic historians who regard the Industrial Revolution and the subsequent process of economic growth as a watershed in economic history have never given the Baconian program much credit for this development. Bacon and his followers planted the seeds of what is now known as the Industrial Enlightenment, and it is hard to think about the Industrial Revolution without considering the preceding cultural developments that made it possible. Recent writings on Bacon seem to have accepted this connection, but without explicitly tying it to later economic growth.[13]

Bacon's views on the method and purpose of useful knowledge influenced intellectuals decades after his death and grew steadily throughout the age of Enlightenment.[14] To be sure, Bacon was a transitional figure in many ways, and he was a product of the end of the sixteenth century, not an enlightened *philosophe*. The adoption of his ideas by the eighteenth century Enlightenment intellectuals was highly selective and was made to suit their agenda.[15] Even writers who disapproved of him gave him credit as

---

[12]   William Blake went so far as to claim that it was Bacon who had ruined England, and he blamed the unholy trinity of Bacon, Locke, and Newton for the "materialism of modern times" (Damon, 1988, p. 35).

[13]   Thus for example Claus Zittel writes, "[Bacon's] philosophy gave birth to the scientific dream of modernity that the advancement of society goes hand-in-hand with the unimpeded development of all technologies" (Zittel et al., 2008, p. xx).

[14]   The Scottish mathematician Colin MacLaurin wrote in the middle of the eighteenth century that "[Bacon] saw that there was a necessity for a thorough reformation in the way of treating natural knowledge. ... He proposed his plan in his *instauratio magna* with so much strength of argument and so just a zeal as renders that admirable work the delight of all those who have a taste for solid learning ... his exhortations had good effects and experimental philosophy has been much more cultivated since his time than in any preceding period" (MacLaurin, 1750, p. 59). Hume, ever the skeptic, disagreed and rated Bacon below Galileo and Kepler—a somewhat misleading comparison.

[15]   As Henry (2002, pp. 138, 163) points out, Enlightenment thinkers regarded Bacon as a hero, but they were making Bacon "in their own image," a "selective and truncated form of what Bacon had in mind," and yet Baconianism was still the foundation of their "concern with practical progress for the amelioration of the human condition."

one of the most influential thinkers ever.[16] Modern scholars from many disciplines seem to agree in general. In the words of one scholar, "The major purpose of Baconian natural philosophy is to produce innovations of which nature unaided is not capable" (Zagorin, 1998, p. 97). Throughout the Industrial Revolution, the set of values implied in Bacon's ideology affected scientists and engineers, whether or not they acknowledged it. Bacon's influence on the Industrial Enlightenment can be readily ascertained by the deep admiration the encyclopédistes felt toward him, exemplified by a long article on *Baconisme* written by the Abbé Pestré and the credit given him by Diderot himself in his entries on *"Art"* and *"Encyclopédie"* in his great Encyclopedia (Diderot, [1751] 2003).[17] The Scottish Enlightenment philosophers Dugald Stewart and Francis Jeffrey agreed on Baconian method and goals, even if they differed on some of the interpretation (Chitnis, 1976, pp. 214–15).[18]

The authoritative text on science and technology in the age of the Industrial Revolution states categorically that "Bacon's influence can be perceived everywhere among men of science in the seventeenth and eighteenth centuries, constantly encouraging them to comprehend workshop practices" (Musson and Robinson, 1969, p. 16). Other typical judgments from different generations of historians are easy to find. "Sir Francis Bacon bears the same relationship to the movement under discussion [the rise of modern science in Britain] as Karl Marx to the rise of communism— but to much better purpose" (R.F. Jones, [1936]1961, p. vii). "In an age dominated by sectarian strife ... the Baconian vision ... urged Westerners to turn to science and its application. At every turn the Baconian legacy inspired visionaries as well as industrialists" (Jacob, 1997, p. 33). Most recently, one authority has defined the "Baconian Ideology" as a double leap of faith in the power of science—a confidence in what natural philosophers could do to improve human destiny and a belief that in doing so they were fulfilling a divine calling (Cohen, 2012, p. 584).

---

[16] The French reactionary writer Joseph LeMaistre blamed Bacon for having initiated a chain of enemies of the human race that led eventually to the French Revolution (Pérez-Ramos, 1988, p. 20).

[17] In his essay on "Arts," Diderot [1751], 2003 wrote that "we are all too inclined to believe that it is beneath the dignity of the human spirit to ... descend to the study, let alone the practice, of the mechanical arts. ... This prejudice has tended to fill cities with useless spectators ... and the countryside with petty tyrants who are ignorant, lazy and disdainful. Such was not the thinking of Bacon, one of the foremost geniuses of England."

[18] A practical later Enlightenment scientist, Humphry Davy, had no doubt that Bacon "was the first philosopher who laid down plans for extending knowledge of universal application; who ventured to assert, that all the science could be nothing more than expressions or arrangements of facts ... The pursuit of the new method of investigation, in a very short time, wholly altered the face of every department of natural knowledge" (Davy,1840, pp. 121–122).

The influence of Francis Bacon on the evolution of what was known at the time as "experimental philosophy" was profound. Even intellectuals not directly involved in experimental work such as Samuel Parker, the bishop of Oxford (1640–1688), felt that "the only way to be fully satisfied of their [apparent certainties] Truth and Sincerity, is to examine them by a wary and discreet Experience, the Test whereof will remove all ground to doubt ... Experimental knowledge is of all others the safest and most unquestionable." And he immediately acknowledges his debt to the Master: "and therefore my Lord Bacon has well noted it as none of the least obstructions to the advancement of knowledge that Men have sought for Truth in their own little worlds ... withdrawing themselves from the Contemplation of Nature and the Observations of Experience" (Parker, 1666, pp. 56–58). The great diarist and intellectual John Evelyn (1620–1706) may have summarized the sentiment of the generation after Bacon's death when he wrote that "the noble Verulam (Bacon) ... outstripp'd all who went before him; so is he celebrated as far as knowledge has any Empire ... the learned rise up at the sound of his very name" (Evelyn 1661, p. A5).[19] It is somewhat ironic, perhaps, to realize that intellectuals who had labored to dethrone Aristotle as the great authority on all learning were transferring some of the personality cult to Bacon. Yet Baconianism never became a rigid dogma—on the contrary, as Hunter (1981, p. 18) has pointed out, Baconianism encouraged pluralism and diversity of beliefs, with the coexistence of different and often contradictory hypotheses, that had to compete with one another for acceptance by testing and logic. Baconianism also led to what Hunter (1985, p. 65) has called a "leveling" effect on natural philosophy: it made the practice of science and the participation in scientific activity possible for people of lesser training and ability who could serve as "minor observers" and collect data and information on anything from seashells to the movement of the tides. This is not to suggest that natural philosophy became a mass-participation activity, only that its medieval exclusivity was a tad mitigated by the rise of literacy and the growing sense of a need for evidence and data.

As Gaukroger (2006, pp. 354–55) notes, the distinction between Baconian experimental philosophy and logical-deductive systems of natural philosophy in the Descartes-Hobbes mode can become blurred, but it is in the end real enough. Bacon's legacy was a concrete and materialistic science based on data and experiments, sharply rejecting what the age called "hypotheses" but which in our lingo would be thought of as speculation. The great experimentalists of the late seventeenth century, Robert Boyle and

---

[19] Lesser intellects similarly acknowledged Bacon, none more so that the astrologer Joshua Childrey (1623-1670), who in his appropriately titled *Britannia Baconica* acknowledges that he tried as much as he could follow his "Master, Lord Bacon" from whom he received "his first light on his way" (Childrey, 1660, p. B-4).

Robert Hooke had no doubts whatsoever on the matter. In his appropriately titled book *The Usefulness of Experimental Philosophy,* Boyle shows his full commitment to the Baconian idea: "I shall not dare to think myself a true Naturalist till my skill can make my garden yield better herbs and flowers, or my orchard better fruit or my field better corn or my dairy better cheese than theirs that are strangers to physiology [natural philosophy]." When an experimental philosopher descends to consider husbandry, he muses, he should be able to improve the precepts of an art that was the result of the "unlearned Observations and Practice of such illiterate Persons as Gardeners and Milk-maids ... if the true principles of that fertill Science [Physiology] were thoroughly known, considered and applied, tis scarce imaginable, how universal and advantageous a change they would make in the World" (Boyle, 1664, part II, pp. 3–4).[20] In his essay on the methodology of science, Hooke went even further: "the intellect ... is continually to be assisted by some method or engine ...of this engine no man except the incomparable *Verulam* [Bacon] has had thoughts ... [he] was able to overcome all the difficulties of prejudice with which Men's minds are usually beset not only to discover the impediments to learning but to free the mind from them" (1705a, pp. 6–7).

Bacon's work reinforced the trend in the West to build bridges between the realm of natural philosophy and that of the artisan and farmer. These bridges are critical to technological progress, because they allow people who generate propositional knowledge to communicate with those who generate and apply prescriptive knowledge (Mokyr, 2002). For Bacon, craftsmen were not only the beneficiaries of propositional knowledge, but also its inspiration. Bacon stressed that technological progress would be successful only if useful knowledge was organized, coordinated, distributed, and made accessible. He felt that for that reason the state needed to "save inventions from the inventors" and knowledge had to be moved from the inventors to the collective, that is to say, the state. In that way, he felt, useful knowledge would be both cumulative and accessible (Keller, 2012, p. 242). Their manipulation of materials and energy showed experimental philosophers how an artificial environment could be created to examine natural phenomena (Cohen, 2012, p. 247). Many of the great scientists of the age were also able instrument makers, as the examples of Galileo, Hooke, and Huygens amply attest. These men, however, were anything but run-of-the-mill craftsmen.

What about the larger population of artisans? As I have emphasized elsewhere (Mokyr, 2002, pp. 63–64), building bridges over the social chasm between scientists and manufacturers was a critical feature of

---

[20] In his *Certain Physiological Essays,* Boyle notes explicitly that his work in natural history was nothing but the continuation of "the Lord Verulam (Bacon)'s *Sylva Sylvarum or Natural History*" (Boyle, 1669, p. 14).

European culture; it entailed a struggle that was won only slowly and haltingly.[21] One of the most remarkable trends in the cultural development of European intellectuals after 1500 was the slowly ripening notion that "intellectuals should involve themselves in practical matters traditionally considered beneath them" and that their priorities "should take artisans newly seriously" (Hunter, 1981, pp. 99, 88).

If technology was to advance in a serious and sustainable way, the two groups had to respect one another and feel that their communication and cooperation could be mutually beneficial and for society at large. One would expect cultural evolution of this kind to take a long time. Any application of formal science such as mathematization and experimental research to engineering, artisanal production, or medicine would take many decades, if not centuries. By 1700 the gap between formal science and artisanal practice "yawned almost as widely" as it had in 1500, largely because those who had put their hopes in the mathematization of nature and the ability of experimental work to make nature reveal its secrets had seriously underestimated the world's messiness (Cohen, 2012, pp. 323, 325). Even in the eighteenth century, clear-cut examples in which scientific insight led to economically significant technological advances are few and far between. In many instances the relationship between science and industry was hazy and fuzzy. Yet it was undeniably there, and blanket dismissals of the Industrial Enlightenment (as in Epstein, 2013) are unwarranted. Many of the important advances of the Industrial Revolution were made by inventors who were either scientifically schooled or had contacts with those who were. Other inventions were actually made by trained scientists venturing into technology, from Joseph Priestley to Claude Berthollet to Humphry Davy.

More than anything else, however, the disappointments over the failure of experimental science to keep its promise and bring about the hoped-for major technological breakthroughs resulting from new discoveries, point to the rhetorical power of Bacon's message. In many way it was a promissory note, and if it was not yet realized by 1680 or 1720, it surely would be so in the future. Clearly science was advancing, but the mountain turned out to be higher than could be seen when starting off from the valley. Yet even if the glass were still largely empty as late as 1750, careful examination revealed that it was filling, albeit at a slower rate than Bacon's enthusiastic disciples had promised. The hope was kept alive by the

---

[21] When Constantijn Huygens, the aristocratic and learned father of the famous scientist, received a letter addressed to "Mr. Huygens, mathematician," he remarked acidly that he was "not aware of having any craftsmen among his children" (quoted in Cohen, 2012, p. 335). Yet as Dijksterhuis (2007) points out, the writer of the letter was none other than the great Marquis de Louvois, Louis XIV's minister of war. He could make this mistake because in practice "pure mathematicians" (*géometres*) and "applied mathematicians" (*mathématiciens*) might be socially distinct, but in practice the two categories overlapped a great deal.

visible successes that scientists accumulated, above all the Newtonian triumph. In addition, clever artisans were able to build many instruments that Bacon dreamed about: pendulum clocks, thermometers, microscopes, and marine chronometers. Observant physicians could inoculate people against smallpox. Science of some kind often played a role in this story, but we should not commit the error of looking for a rapid and direct application of some newly discovered scientific insight to artisanal techniques. Instead, the interplay of what we call science and technology was subtle and complex. It can better be seen through the lens of what I have called the *epistemic base* of a given technique: how much was really understood about why a particular contraption or medication worked? In the case of cinchona bark (used to alleviate the symptoms of malaria) or smallpox inoculation, nothing. In the case of Newcomen engines, some. In the case of the breast-wheel and water turbines: quite a lot.[22]

It is important not to overstate the case for cultural entrepreneurs. It will be objected, with some justification, that Bacon was so admired in Enlightenment Europe because he explained to his eighteenth-century followers why it was correct and virtuous what they wanted to do anyway. But that is, to some extent, what the function of a cultural entrepreneur is: it is not to pull reluctant people into an altogether new direction they would not have gone otherwise, as much as formulating a coherent doctrine that the followers can all accept as the consensus central message. Moreover, in the market for ideas, the acolytes of the Master need to persuade others, since there will always be resistance to the new message. The action is not in persuading fierce opponents, which is not a likely option; the message of the cultural entrepreneur is directed at persuading the fence-sitters in the middle or individuals who can be made to change their minds.

Between Bacon and the Industrial Revolution stood many decades of transitional figures.[23] His call for widespread and productive cooperation between people who knew things (*savants*) and people who made things (*fabricants*) resonated with Industrial Enlightenment. Thomas Sprat, in his *History of the Royal Society,* prophetically noted that "Philosophy will attain perfection when either Mechanic Labourers shall have philosophical heads,

---

[22] Cohen (2012, pp. 606–8) lists the reasons he believes the high expectations of the Scientific Revolution were not fulfilled. One of the factors not mentioned by him is that almost all the great scientists of the age, from Galileo to Newton, were concerned with *motion*, whether of atoms or heavenly bodies or objects in between, and with light. Yet technology had just as much a need for an understanding of *heat* in the processing of materials and the construction of engines. The understanding of heat eluded seventeenth-century natural philosophers, and the best they could come up with, Johann Joachim Becher's and Georg Ernst Stahl's phlogiston theory, does not even get a mention in Cohen's encyclopedic work.

[23] Many of those are documented in Mokyr (2009a), and include men like John Theophile Desaguliers, Henry Beighton, William Cullen, Joseph Black, and Colin MacLaurin, among many others.

or the Philosophers shall have Mechanical Hands" (Sprat, 1667, p. 397).[24]
The long and winding road, in the end, led to such key figures in the
Industrial Revolution as John Smeaton, Josiah Wedgwood, and Isambard
Brunel. The fact that the transition took many decades does not disprove the
continuity. The deep roots of economic development were in cultural
changes that had occurred much earlier.[25] During the transition, the change
in values that began by legitimizing natural philosophy transformed into an
ideology that did much more: it demanded that science be made available
to those who could use it best and built the organizations and means that
could carry out this program.

Bacon was, as noted, far from being a liberal and enlightened
thinker; he was no precursor of Benthamite utilitarianism. For him useful
knowledge was first and foremost an instrument of state power, not human
well-being (Poovey, 1998, pp. 98, 102). While William Harvey's alleged
sneer that Bacon wrote philosophy like a Lord Chancellor is a tad unfair,
there is no question that Bacon's approach to the institutions of useful
knowledge was decidedly étatist. Bacon was worried that unguided knowledge would end up being chaotic and thus his program for intellectual
reform "amounted to an attempt to secure order through ... the state"
(Shapin, 1996, p. 130). Much of his writing, moreover, still bears the marks
of an earlier age. Thus, his suggestion in *New Atlantis* that some big advances in science should be kept secret (at the discretion of the lead scientists
who would decide which of their inventions made there could be published
and which could not) was in direct contradiction to the idea of the open
science that became the hallmark of the Republic of Letters (and that Bacon
himself advocated).[26] As Grafton (2009b) has noted, much of his utopian
book *New Atlantis,* which in some ways foreshadowed modern research
institutes, was informed and inspired by church history rather than by a
forward-looking organized study of useful natural phenomena. Moreover,
it is also true that in some places Bacon legitimized curiosity and scientific
research by a millenarian justification: in places, the *Great Instauration* seems
to indicate that it was no more than regaining knowledge that Man had

----

[24] It was widely observed that this was far from a reality in this era; half a century
after Sprat, Mandeville ([1724] 1755, p. 121) still noted that "they are very seldom the same sort
of people, those that invent Arts and Improvements in them, and those that enquire into the
Reason of Things."

[25] It is interesting to note that in making this point, Cohen (1990, p. 66) cites Rupert
Hall's famous study on ballistics which showed that despite considerable advances in the science,
seventeenth-century gunners on a day-to-day basis took no notice or were unaware of the work
done by scientists.

[26] The *New Atlantis* fellows had to decide which inventions would be published and
which not, and then took an oath of secrecy to conceal those that were better kept secret "though
some of those we do reveal sometimes to the state and some not" (Bacon, [1627], 1996, p. 487).

possessed before the Fall. The "true ends of knowledge," Bacon writes in his *Valerius Terminus*, was not satisfying curiosity or material wealth but a "restitution and reinvesting ... of man to the sovereignty and power ... which he had in his first state of creation" (Bacon [1603], 1838, p. 220). It is hard to know whether such pious proclamations were sincere or whether Bacon believed that what really counted was not the retrieval of some mystical past but the growth of state power and human control of the environment—arguably in his mind the two were not separable.[27] The millenarian aspects of Bacon were in part what made his work so attractive to Puritans. In the end, however, little of that aspect of his work was retained by his eighteenth-century followers. What did matter to them was his view of the role of knowledge: as one of the most insightful students of Bacon in the twentieth century has argued, Bacon saw the interaction of humans with their physical environment as what an economist would call "a constrained maximization problem." There were no limits to the possibilities that people could achieve as long as they observed and respected the laws of nature (Rossi, 1978, p. 18). Yet Bacon's writing helped create a way in which scientific research and religious beliefs could coexist by recognizing that by the study of nature, humans could acquire true and certain knowledge that would then allow them to come up with the correct interpretation of the scriptures. James Moore refers to what he calls a "Baconian compromise," an implicit and informal modus vivendi between religion and natural philosophy in which scientists would offer illustrations of divine omnipotence in exchange for freedom of researchers from religious harassment (Moore, 1986, p. 323). This truce was not specific to the English-speaking world; it is assumed in the writings of many of the prominent members of the Republic of Letters.

After his death in 1626, Bacon's influence expanded through his disciples. The most effective person to take up Bacon's ideas soon after his death was Samuel Hartlib (1600–1662) who was instrumental in spreading the ideas of Francis Bacon to an ever-widening circle of intellectuals committed to the creation, organization, standardization, and dissemination of useful knowledge.[28] Hartlib was a prototypical follower and distributor of information, a highly effective "intelligencer," in the terminology of the

---

[27] Bacon adds immediately (Bacon [1603], 1838, p. 220) that "Better again and more worthy must that aspiring be which seeks the amplification of power and kingdom of man over the world ... this is a world truly divine."

[28] Hartlib and his close friend John Dury (1596–1680), a Calvinist minister, were deeply religious Protestants who strongly felt that the spreading of knowledge in the Baconian fashion would lead to a unification of the deeply Protestant churches of his time. But he was also keenly interested in agriculture, Helmontian chemistry, medicine, and was issued a large number of patents. He and his followers shared a deep belief in the potential of technical progress based on increased knowledge free of the obfuscations and confusions of the past.

time[29] and was appointed in 1649 by the Rump Parliament as the "Agent for the Advancement of Universal Learning," an honorary position that had little direct content but clearly reflected the respect he enjoyed. He was not an original thinker but a central node in a network of information dissemination; he was effective at organizing an intellectual elite to follow a coherent program. He was an inveterate correspondent and was instrumental in disseminating scientific writing in a wide array of applied fields, ranging from medicine to horticulture. He and his collaborator John Dury followed Bacon in the judging of the value of knowledge by its degree of "usefulness" and were firm supporters of the concept of "improvement." As Slack (2015, p. 108) put it, Hartlib "accelerated a process of cultural change which ensured that 'what is wanting in our current age' would be forthcoming in the future." Hartlib was instrumental in disseminating scientific writing in a wide array of applied fields, ranging from medicine to horticulture.[30]

Through a wide network of correspondents and personal acquaintances, Hartlib laid the foundation of the Royal Society, which was established by the end of his life. Hartlib drew his inspiration from other sources as well, such as German Calvinism, and also helped introduce the new chemistry of van Helmont and the metaphysics of Descartes into the Cambridge of the young Isaac Newton (Greengrass, Leslie, and Raylor, 1994, p. 18).

Hartlib and Dury were far from alone. Theodore Haak (1605–1690), another German immigrant, was one of the founders of the Royal Society; spoke many languages; traveled extensively; and had a very wide network of intellectual friends and correspondents including Marin Mersenne. William Petty, well known to economic historians, proposed a *gymnasium mechanicum*, a college for craftsmen and engineers (Petty, 1647). In this academy young men would study the history of crafts; instead of wasting their time "reading hard Hebrew words in the Bible or parratlike repeating heteroclitous nounes and verbs," they would spend ten or twelve years in the "study of Things," "the Theory of their Trades before they are bound to a master" (Petty, 1647, pp. 23–24). Petty added, somewhat naively, that he hoped that "a vast increase of honourable, profitable and

---

[29] The term was apparently first applied to him by John Winthrop, governor of Massachusetts. Webster (1970, p. 3) sees him as the one who undertook the Baconian ideal of organizing Europe's intellectuals in a "noble and generous fraternity"—obviously an early version of the eighteenth-century Republic of Letters. One of his main projects was his "Office of Address and Correspondency," a kind of virtual Salomon's House in which useful knowledge would be circulated and distributed by means of epistolary networks, and a precursor of the basic Enlightenment project to reduce access costs and enhance the dissemination of scientific and technological knowledge.

[30] Hartlib was particularly interested in bee keeping, both as an interesting agricultural pursuit and because he saw the symbolism of bees pollinating flowers in analogy to men of learning spreading information to increase the productivity of the economy.

pleasant inventions must needs spring from the work, when one man ... may see and comprehend all the labour and wit of our ancestors, and thereby [be] able to supply the defects of one trade with the perfections of another" (Petty, p. 22).

After Hartlib's death, the secretary of the Royal Society, Henry Oldenburg (1619–1677), played a similar role (Hunter, 1989, p. 250). Oldenburg, like Hartlib, was a foreigner (born in Bremen), who arrived in England on a diplomatic mission in 1653 and eventually settled there. He became a member of the circle around John Wilkins, and enjoyed the patronage of Robert Boyle. In 1662 he was formally appointed the first secretary of the Royal Society, and he brought the concept of "intelligencer" to new heights not only by corresponding with many of the leading scientists of his time, but also by actively encouraging and supporting promising young scholars, including the astronomer John Flamsteed and the physician Martin Lister. In 1665 he founded the *Philosophical Trans-actions*, the official journal of the Royal Society and the oldest continuous scientific journal in the world. Oldenburg is famous for persuading scholars to publish their findings in it, and thus streamlining his function as a nodal point in ever more efficient networks of useful knowledge diffusion.[31] Another group of Baconians congealed at Oxford's Wadham College around its warden Wilkins, including such notable intellectuals as John Wallis, Christopher Wren, and William Petty. There was also the "Rota Club," a debating club founded by the radical political theorist James Harrington, which met in a coffeehouse for a brief period in 1659, and resembled the Royal Society in some ways (Hunter, 1989, p. 8). Even outside the circles of learned acolytes, there were admirers of Bacon who felt inspired by his writings. An example was his pupil Thomas Bushell (ca. 1600–1674), a mining engineer who helped introduce adits (a drainage device based on horizontal tunnels) into British mines.

The "invisible colleges" that formed in England before 1660 were inspired by if not dedicated to the ideas of Francis Bacon. These informal organizations transformed into the Royal Society in 1660, whose declared purpose it was to increase useful knowledge, and to build bridges between formal science and the actual practical applications of the "useful arts."

---

[31] The influence of Bacon on Oldenburg is easy to detect. In a letter to a new member of his wide correspondence network, he wrote that he wished "to investigate the secrets of nature for the glory of the creator and the benefit of mankind" (quoted in Webster [1975], 2002, p. 502). In the first issue of the Royal Society's *Transactions*, he wrote in the best Baconian tradition that "there is nothing more necessary for promoting the improvement of Philosophical Matters, than the communicating to such, as apply their Studies and Endeavours that way, such things as are discovered or put in practise by others. ... To the end, that such Productions being clearly and truly communicated, desires after solid and usefull knowledge may be further entertained, ingenious Endeavours and Undertakings cherished. ... All for the Glory of God, the Honour and Advantage of these Kingdoms, and the Universal Good of Mankind" (Oldenburg, 1665, pp. 1–2).

Michael Hunter has summarized the purpose of the Royal Society as en-hancing the standing of science in the eyes of the public, as well as providing a forum for carrying out the actual research that would augment useful knowledge (Hunter, 1989, p. 15). The admiration that these people felt for Bacon and their indebtedness to him are noticeable everywhere. William Petty (1647) started his letter to Hartlib by stating that it was un-necessary for him to provide an exact definition of learning or the advance-ment thereof, "it being already so accurately done by the Great Lord Verulam" (1647, p. 1).

The Royal Society clearly was in many ways the embodiment of Bacon's dreams as expressed in *New Atlantis* and *The Great Instauration*, but as Hunter (1989) points out, the timing and precise form of its establishment were contingent on historical circumstances in 1660. Hill (1965, p. 129) has felt that in many ways the Society fell short of the Baconian ideals, by its pandering to the aristocracy, its dilettantism and its failure to establish the utopia of which Bacon and Comenius had dreamed. Even so, most scholars would agree with Lynch that "the Royal Society was a Baconian institution" and that it had " a significant impact on future developments in science and a wider social impact as well ... [that] can be felt during the remainder of the century, throughout the eighteenth century, and beyond" (Lynch, 2001, pp. 233–34). At first, the Royal Society made valiant efforts to concentrate its efforts on technological matters, including sponsoring a special committee looking into the feasibility of planting potatoes as a means of averting famine. Its famous *History of Trades* project was meant to describe and catalog the entire set of artisanal practices in the kingdom, and it collected endless information on such subjects as dyeing, candlemaking, tanning, and the brewing of cider (Ochs, 1985). The declared purpose of the Society was well described in Sprat's *History* in terms that will be sur-prisingly familiar to the modern economist, namely, to reduce the gap between best-practice and average-practice techniques and to allow inven-tors to recombine and hybridize existing production methods and tools.[32] Yet in the end, the *History of Trades* project was short-lived and the Royal Society's early emphasis on technology was toned down, largely because the gap between ambition and achievements was far larger than the Baconians imagined (Hunter, 1981, p. 102; Lynch, 2001, pp. 77–78, 31). Within the Royal Society there was a shift away from the stress on utilitarianism and toward a more elevated notion of the scientist as having a monopoly on the interpretation of nature, assigned to advance the under-

---

[32] In Sprat's (1967, pp. 310–11) own words, "the worst Artificers will be well instruc-ted, by considering the Methods, and Tool of the best; And the greatest Inventors will be ex-ceedingly inlighten'd; because they will have in their view the labours of many men, many places, and many times, wherewith to compare their own. This is the surest and most effectual means, to inlarge the Invention."

standing of the natural world (Hunter, 1995c, p. 178). Yet to ridicule the program just because it was premature seems unwarranted. As Kathleen Ochs observed (1985, p. 130), in the end science did benefit the economy as Bacon had prophesied. It just needed to get better at doing so. The trades historians helped develop further new attitudes toward industry that eventually revolutionized it. Most importantly, the gentlemen scholars of the Royal Society strengthened the fruitful bridges between science and industry that Bacon had envisioned, which became one of the pillars of the Industrial Enlightenment.

Although restoration science was thus self-consciously Baconian, Bacon's intellectual influence on the Royal Society should not be exaggerated. In the end, it was an organization in which very heterogeneous scientists, who worked on their own, met, communicated, and interacted but then went their separate ways just as they had before (Hunter, 1995a, p. 102). Any simplistic causal line that connects the Royal Society with the Industrial Revolution would be misleading, or else the Industrial Revolution would have occurred a century earlier. The Royal Society was one more reflection of a profound cultural change among England's intellectual and technological elite that gathered power and momentum in the later seventeenth century and the first half of the eighteenth. Its debt to Bacon is undeniable.

The Royal Society was explicitly patterned after Bacon's Salomon's House, the fictional academy described in is *New Atlantis*.[33] It started off with boundless enthusiasm for practical technical matters. "The business and design of the Royal Society is to improve the knowledge of naturall things, and all useful Arts, Manufactures, Mechanick practises, Engines, and Inventions by Experiments" (Lyons, 1944, p. 41).[34] Robert Hooke added in his preface to the second edition of his *Micrographia* that the Fellows of the Royal Society "have one advantage peculiar to themselves, that very many of their number are men of converse and traffick, which is a good omen that their attempts will bring philosophy from words to action, seeing men of business have had so great a share in their first foundation" (Hooke, 1667, unpaginated preface). In 1666, the French Académie des

---

[33] In a wonderful piece of doggerel titled "Ode to the Royal Society," written by the now (deservedly) neglected poet Abraham Cowley (one of the Society's co-founders) and reprinted as a preface to Thomas Sprat's (1667) celebrated *History of the Royal Society of London*, the gratefulness of the scholars of the time to Bacon was well expressed: "From these and all long Errors of the Way; In which our wandring Predecessors went; And like th' old Hebrews many Years did stray; in Desarts but of small Extent; Bacon, like Moses, led us forth at last; The barren Wilderness he past; Did on the very Border stand; of the blest promis'd Land; And from the Mountain's Top of his exalted Wit; Saw it himself and shew'd us it."

[34] Hunter (1995c, p. 173) attributes this famous passage to Sir Robert Moray (1608–1673) a Scottish polymath, politician, general, and leading Freemason, and one of the most influential leaders of the Royal Society in its early years.

Inscriptions et Belles-Lettres had a medal made in honor of the slightly younger Académie des Sciences with the slogan *Naturae investigandae et perficiendis artibus* (for the investigation of nature and technological competence).

The Royal Society, as noted, eventually lost interest in practical knowledge, but the spirit of Bacon lived on in many other organizations that came to the fore in eighteenth-century Britain. Thus the Society of Arts, founded by William Shipley in 1754, viewed its purpose as follows "Whereas the Riches, Honour, Strength and Prosperity of a Nation depend in a great Measure on Knowledge and Improvement of useful Arts, Manufactures, Etc ... several [persons], being fully sensible that due Encouragements and Rewards are greatly conducive to excite a Spirit of Emulation and Industry." The second half of the eighteenth century witnessed a veritable explosion of formal and informal societies and academies dedicated to combine natural philosophy (science) with the "useful arts" (technology) by bringing together entrepreneurs and indus- trialists with scientists and philosophers. In 1799, two paradigmatic figures of the Industrial Enlightenment, Sir Joseph Banks and Benjamin Thompson (Count Rumford), founded the Royal Institution, devoted to research and charged with providing public lectures on scientific and technological issues. In the first decade of the nineteenth century, these lectures were dominated by the towering figure of the scientist Humphry Davy, another classic figure of the Industrial Enlightenment.

In addition to organizations, the ideas Bacon supported were expanded and developed by many members of the intellectual elite of the seventeenth century. The great experimentalist Robert Boyle expanded the ideas of the Master, pointing out that Lord Verulam (Bacon) had made a distinction between "luciferous" (enlightening) and "fructiferous" (useful) experiments, but that in fact the one led to the other. He then added a line that summarizes the Baconian influence on the Industrial Enlightenment: "There is scarce any considerable physical truth which is not, as it were, teeming with profitable inventions and may not by human skill and industry, be made the fruitful mother of divers things useful, either to Mankind in general, our at least to the particular Discoverer and dexterous Applyer of that Truth" (Boyle, 1671, p. 45). Elsewhere Boyle added that men study natural philosophy for two distinct ends: "Some men only care to know nature, others desire to command her...some desire but to please themselves ... others would be able to bring nature to be serviceable to their particular ends whether of health, riches, or sensual delight" (Boyle, 1744, vol. 1, p. 199).

Nowhere was there so much promise in carrying out the Baconian program as in medicine, where Thomas Sydenham (1624–1689), a keen follower of Bacon, pioneered applying his empirical method to medical research and was the founder of what today we would call nosology (Trail,

1965; Anstey, 2002, pp. 87–88).[35] The physician and polemicist Marchamont Nedham (1620–1678) wrote a controversial pamphlet titled *Medela Medicinae,* in which he strongly argued for the promise that experimental philosophy held for the future of medicine and sang the praises of Bacon and his followers (Nedham, 1665, p. 6). Nedham argued that Bacon had shown how medicine should be reconstructed from its very foundations and that it had to abandon "that superstitious reverence which has been so long paid to the antiquated Masters of the Profession" (Nedham, 1665, pp. 361–62). The development of nosology was recognized for carrying out Bacon's call for physicians to collect disease histories, an appeal that was part of Bacon's "Great Instauration" (Bynum ,1993, p. 343).[36] Or consider the work of Richard Lower (1631–1691), a remarkably talented English physician and experimentalist, who carried out pathbreaking work on both the blood circulation system and the heart, as well as on the nervous system, and is credited with the first blood transfusion in history. Lower and his coauthor Thomas Willis (1621–1675) were part of the remarkable scientific circle of Baconians at Oxford's Wadham College.

But in other areas, too, data collection and experimentation were intensified: botany, zoology, metallurgy, agriculture, mining—all became legitimate areas of study. A fine example of Baconian philosophy in action was presented by John Ray (1627–1705), one of the founders of modern zoology, for whom natural history and religion coincided. His highly popular 1691 three-volume work, significantly titled *The Wisdom of God Manifested in the Works of the Creation,* went through eleven editions and was still being

---

[35] Merton ([1938] 2001, p. 24) notes that the growth of interest in medical science in the seventeenth century was an aspect of the growth of interest in science. For the vast majority of medical practitioners, this was probably at best only marginally the case. The strong connection between biology and medicine was a product of the nineteenth century. But for the very top medical practitioners such as Sydenham, and his followers such as Richard Blackmore (1654–1729; famous for being a writer of dull poetry), and Thomas Dover (1660–1742; a physician who turned privateer), the impact of Baconian ideology is quite marked. Sydenham's impact on Continental medicine (such as on the great Dutch physician Herman Boerhaave) was also quite large (Poynter, 1973).

[36] The systematic collection of information was extended in this age to surgery, up to then a little-respected craft. Richard Wiseman, the Royalist surgeon who served in the English Civil War, published his *Chirurgicall Treatises* in 1676, in which he listed a catalog of 660 individual cases. While there is no explicit mention of Bacon in Wiseman's book, he sighs in his introduction that "when the young chirurgeon shall find the cure easie in the Theory and appear so at first in the practice too, yet suddenly [the condition] deceive him with a Relapse ... he will then wish that all other practitioners had done what I have done in this *Treatise* viz. recommend their observations both successful and unsuccessful, thereby encreasing Knowledge in our Profession, and leaving Sea-marks for the discovery of such Rocks as they themselves have split upon before" (Wiseman, [1676] 1719, vol. 1, pp. v–vi).

reprinted in 1798.[37] Ray was also a pivotal figure in the rapidly expanding field of botanical taxonomy, which was in part fueled by the burgeoning trade in rare and exotic plants, the collection of which became a widespread hobby of well-to-do Europeans.[38] The scientific networks claiming to be inspired by Bacon's vision were at the core of the flourishing of British experimental philosophy and medicine in the second half of the seventeenth century.

It is true, as Hunter and other have emphasized, that the claims made for Bacon's influence have been at times exaggerated and could be misleading (Hunter, 1995a, pp. 102–04). Yet Baconianism provided an umbrella ideology for people to collect data, believing perhaps a bit prematurely that doing so was helping the advancement of learning and social progress in general. The belief that collecting data and facts about the physical world would lead to social progress was born in the seventeenth century and refused to die, even if its tangible results were slow in coming. A notable Baconian was the Norwich physician and polymath Thomas Browne (1605–1682), the author of a popular encyclopedic book titled *Pseudodoxia Epidemica* (Browne, [1646] 1964), which claimed to expose a multitude of vulgar errors and superstitions on a stunning range of topics including zoology, mineralogy, astronomy, history, and geography. It serves as a perfect illustration of the idea of contestability, which was a hallmark of European intellectual life in this age. Among others, he debunked ideas as far apart as the beliefs that chameleons live only on air, that Jews naturally stink, and that carbuncles give light in the dark.[39] Browne's work, brilliantly written mostly in English, can be seen as an early example of scientific journalism, and clearly it helped disseminate the ideas and beliefs of the "new science" advocated by the Baconians to a larger circle.[40] But he was also an

---

[37] Seventeenth-century writers on farming and natural history explicitly acknowledged their debt to Francis Bacon and especially his *Sylva Sylvarum*, a somewhat indiscriminate collection of real and putative facts, which included the *New Atlantis* as an appendix. Between 1626 and 1685 this work became something of a bestseller, with sixteen English and three Latin editions. See Gaukroger (2001, p. 33).

[38] Ray's *Historia plantarum*, appeared between 1686 and 1704. The first two volumes described 6,100 species, many of which Ray had seen or had had described for him by his botanical correspondents in his network. A third volume detailed a further 10,000 species, largely on the evidence of printed sources. Ray had an enormous influence on eighteenth-century botanists, including Carl Linnaeus (Mandelbrote, 2004).

[39] The popularity of the book is attested to by the fact that it went through six editions between 1646 and 1672 and was translated into at least four other languages. Before we label Browne a "modern thinker," however, it may be worth recalling that he attributed many of these errors to "the advocacy of Satan" ([1646] 1964, p. 75).

[40] Denonain (1982, p. 371) sees Browne's best-selling and highly influential *Religio Medici* ("The Religion of a Physician") published in 1643 to have been structured "in accordance with Bacon's requirement."

experimentalist himself and has been credited as the first to use the word "electricity" in the English language. His work reports on at least a hundred experiments that he carried out himself, but also surveys a very wide literature on almost every field of inquiry practiced by the middle of the seventeenth century. Browne was hugely respected at his time (King Charles II paid him a call during a visit to Norwich and knighted him) and was one of Bacon's most celebrated followers. His thinking is most notable for a deep sense of skepticism and uncertainty and the abjuration of blind faith in venerable ancient authority: the opening page of his book states that "to purchase a clear and warrantable body of Truth, we must forget and part with much wee know" (1646, Preface). He did not become a member of the Royal Society, but corresponded with many of its members and clearly was very much part of the intellectual network of his time.

Of special interest is the remarkable figure of John Wilkins (1614–1672), one of the founders of the Royal Society and its first secretary. Wilkins is a good example of the kind of talented disciples needed by cultural entrepreneurs to disseminate their message. Married to Cromwell's sister, appointed warden of Wadham College in 1648 and later Master of Trinity College and Bishop of Chester, he was a politically savvy intellectual as well as a pivotal figure in the post-Baconian movement in England.[41] Wilkins's career showed how religion and scientific endeavor complemented each other at this time: a practicing Puritan clergyman and widely renowned theologian, he foretold, in Charles Gillispie's words (1960, p. 113), with surprising insight "the accommodation to be reached between Galileo's mathematization and Bacon's socialization of science." This was embodied in his 1648 book, *Mathematicall Magick* which explicitly claimed that there was "much real benefit to be learned; particularly for such Gentlemen as employ their estates in those chargeable adventures of Drayning, Mines, Cole-pits, &c. who may from hence learn the chief grounds & nature of Engines ... and also for such common artificers, as are well skilled in the practise of these arts, who may be much advantaged by the right understanding of their grounds and Theory" (Wilkins, 1648, p. 4). The work stressed practical mechanical devices and labor-saving inventions "whereby nature is in any way quickened or advanced in her defects" (Aarsleff, 1992, pp. 6–7). Wilkins stressed that spreading useful knowledge meant that more people could develop and adopt best-practice concepts and techniques. The distribution of existing knowledge required better language and communi-

---

[41] John Aubrey, the author of brief sketches of the lives of many of his contemporaries, noted that Wilkins was "the principall reviver of experimentall philosophy (*secundum mentem Domini Baconi*) at Oxford, where he had weekly an experimentall philosophicall clubbe, which began in 1649 and was the incunabula of the Royall Society" (Aubrey, 1898, p. 301). His master's lodging at Wadham College in Oxford was quite consciously inspired by Bacon's Salomon's House (Houghton, 1942, p. 201).

cations technology. In his *Essay towards a Real Character and a Philosophical Language*, he became one of the first of many writers who called for the establishment of a common scientific language that would provide a more efficient medium for scientists to interact and, as he pointed out, "repair the ruins of Babel" (Strasser, 1994). In it he proposed the development of an artificial language based on a classification of knowledge. In this work he foreshadowed the heroic attempts to reduce access costs, that formed one of the core projects of the eighteenth-century Enlightenment (Mokyr, 2005).[42] The notion that the interconnectivity of people concerned with innovation depended not only on the technology and culture of language and communication but also on the organization of knowledge was common among the Baconians of the second half of the seventeenth century.[43] Wilkins (1648, pp. 2–3) believed in the unlimited capability of technology to remove the "curse of labor" and restore the dominion of humans over nature. As he saw it, technology ("the arts") could either assist nature or overcome and advance it. Practical knowledge or knowledge "intended for action" was our "best and most divine knowledge" (Wilkins, 1648, p. 3). Wilkins, then, was more than just a link between Bacon and eighteenth-century natural philosophy; he was one of the main figures that formed the transition from the Renaissance to the Enlightenment and a perfect illustration of the role of Puritanism in this historical evolution.

It is interesting to note that Francis Bacon's influence on seventeenth-century British intellectuals extended equally to Puritans and non-Puritans and, as Charles Webster has noted, his system of natural philosophy was framed in the context of a millennial expectation of human's dominion over nature. His writings attained almost scriptural authority among Puritans, and "no figure was more influential in stimulating his countrymen's active participation in experimental science and drawing the natural philosopher and the craftsman in the centre of social scene"

---

[42] Wilkins (1668, dedicatory) wrote, with an innocence not unusual among early Bacon disciples, that "most obvious advantage which would ensue, of facilitating mutual Commerce, amongst the several Nations of the World, and the improving of all Natural knowledge; It would likewise very much conduce to the spreading of the knowledge of Religion. ... This design will likewise contribute much to the clearing of some of our Modern differences in Religion, by unmasking many wild errors, that shelter themselves under the disguise of affected phrases."

[43] In her introduction to Wilkins's *Mercury, or, The Secret and Swift Messenger*, Asbach-Schnitker points out that "When Wilkins's Essay ["Towards a Real Character"] appeared in 1668, published under the auspices of the Royal Society, the impressive volume was in fact to a certain extent the result of the common efforts of a number of scholars, especially Francis Willughby, John Ray, who devised the tables of plants and animals, William Lloyd, the contributor of the Alphabetical Dictionary, Robert Hooke and Francis Lodwick" (one of the pioneers of universal alphabets). See Wilkins ([1641], 1984, p. xxvi).

(Webster [1975] 2002, p. 335).[44] And not just his countrymen either. Samuel Hartlib was Prussian (even if he lived most of his life in England) and Jan Amos Comenius was Czech.[45] The naturalist Jan Jonston or Johnstone (1603–1675), born in Poland from Scottish parents and for most of his career a practicing physician in Leyden and later in Poland, was an ardent disciple as well.[46] In the Netherlands, there were no fewer than forty-five printings of Bacon's work before 1700, and in Italy both the Accademia del Cimento and the Accademia della Traccia were clearly founded along Baconian lines (Gaukroger, 2001, pp. 2–3).[47] Almost a century after the deaths of Hartlib and Comenius (in 1662 and 1670 respectively), Denis Diderot's life work was still explicitly inspired by Bacon's work, and his

---

[44] To pick another example, William Wotton (1666–1727), one of the most wide-ranging and best-read English intellectuals of the later seventeenth century, and who wrote what may be seen as the first deep and clear-eyed analysis on the growth of science in the early modern period, had little doubt how the remarkable progress in knowledge he observed in his own age had started. "My Lord Bacon was the first great Man who took much pains to convince the World that they had hitherto been in a wrong Path, and that Nature itself, rather than her Secretaries, was to be addressed by those who were desirous to know much of her Mind" (Wotton, 1694, p. 306).

[45] Many of the earliest admirers of Bacon were indeed on the European Continent, among them René Descartes who in one letter expressed the view that he and Lord Verulam (Bacon) complemented each other. Two other leading French intellectuals of the era, Pierre Gassendi and Marin Mersenne, were clearly influenced by his work. The French intellectual Nicolas Claude Fabri de Peiresc, one of the pivotal and most influential intellectuals in France in the early decades of the seventeenth century, admired Bacon and expressed regrets that he never met him (Caton, 1988, p. 80). He owned many works by Bacon and his English translator repeatedly referred to *The Advancement of Learning* to describe Peiresc's motivation (Miller, 2000, p. 23). So did the Dutch philosopher and physicist Isaac Beeckman who provided copious commentaries on Bacon's work. Constantijn Huygens, the Dutch man of letters, diplomat, and father of the famous scientist, actually met Bacon and admired his work. His son Christiaan was a convinced Baconian, who even in Paris stressed the importance of Bacon's teaching. "Experiment and observation" he wrote, "provide the only way of arriving at the knowledge of the causes of all that one sees in Nature" (quoted in Bell, 1947, p. 61). While many of these writers agreed with some of the central tenets of Bacon's method, they often misconstrued his work and did not share the aggressive approach toward the exploitation of nature and drive toward technological progress, much less the inductive methodology. See Pérez-Ramos (1996, p. 312).

[46] Jonston wrote glowingly of "practical philosophy" (by which he meant useful knowledge) as capable of producing new metals; making artificial baths of vitriol, brimstone and alum; and producing new plants and animals. Then he added that "the practick part of Philosophy was until now in the greatest darkness. At last in our age the way to it was opened by famous Verulam. ... And those that have afforded anything notable therein were either of the age newly past or of our own times" (1657, pp. 83–84).

[47] The otherwise rather cantankerous French physician and intellectual, Samuel Sorbière (1615–1670), who visited England in the 1660s, wrote that "the Lord Chancellor Bacon has surpassed all the rest in the vastness of his designs [and his work has taught us] to reduce the Knowledge we have of natural things into practice. ...This is no doubt the greatest man for the interest of Natural Philosophy that ever was" (Sorbière [1664] 1709, p. 32).

Encyclopédie was permeated with Baconianism.[48] Progress was to be secured, he felt, if and when artisans understood the principles underlying their techniques and knew why they worked. In his essay on "Art" in the *Encyclopédie*, Diderot noted that Bacon considered the history of the mechanical arts to be the most important branch of true philosophy, and therefore he did not scorn its practice. Elsewhere, he highlights what he sees as critical in Bacon by comparing him favorably to Michel Montaigne, who had doubted the efficacy of the firearms in his time. "Imagine," Diderot writes, "Bacon in the place of Montaigne: you would see him study the nature of the agent and prophesy, if I may say so—grenades, mines, cannons, bombs, and the entire apparatus of military pyrotechnics." Bacon's influence on the intellectuals of the French Enlightenment was pervasive even if their knowledge of the contents of his work was at best superficial.[49] What the French *philosophes* saw in Bacon was a view that stressed science as holding the key to a progressive and optimistic view of history, which questioned the fatalist belief in the inherent and inevitable miseries of humanity (Dieckmann, 1943, p. 328). Moreover, the key to progress for Enlightenment thinkers was the communication and exchange of ideas and useful knowledge, and in Bacon they saw the prophet who first perceived this light (Goodman, 1994, pp. 23–26).

It was not only the liberalism and political critique that accounted for the popularity of Diderot's *Encyclopédie.* As Gillispie (1960, p. 174) noted, "it was the technology, taking seriously the way people made things and got their livings, dignifying common pursuits by the attention of

---

[48] d'Alembert ([1751] 1995, pp. 74–75) referred to Bacon as "the immortal Chancellor ... the greatest, the most universal, and the most eloquent of the philosophers ... [who] conceives of philosophy as being only that part of our knowledge which should contribute to making us better or happier ... confining it ... to the science of useful things." Voltaire, in his *Philosophical Letters* (letter XII) called him "the father of experimental philosophy" and added that the *Novum Organum* "was the scaffold by means of which the edifice of the new philosophy has been reared; so that when the building was completed, the scaffold was no longer of any use. Chancellor Bacon was still unacquainted with nature, but he perfectly knew, and pointed out extraordinarily well, all the paths which lead to it" (Voltaire, [1733–1734] 2007, p. 38). Even the curmudgeonly Rousseau, who had little sympathy for philosophies of technological progress, admitted that "Verulam was perhaps the greatest of philosophers." See Gauss (1920, pp. 58–59).

[49] Michel Malherbe (1985) points out that despite their admiration for him, most of the French *philosophes* had actually read little of his work, and that even the author of the article on *Baconisme* in the *Encyclopédie* (the Abbé Pestré), shows little evidence of having read much of Bacon's work. Even Diderot, Bacon's most enthusiastic disciple, who wrote that Bacon was a philosopher "I never got tired of praising, because I never got tired of reading him," in the judgment of one scholar contented himself with a rather cursory reading of Bacon and never fully came to grips with Bacon's thought as a "complete system of ideas" (Dieckmann, 1943, pp. 326–27).

science."[50] It is exactly on that topic that Bacon's role as a cultural entrepreneur can be discerned. His most powerful impact was indeed on the intellectuals and *philosophes* of the Enlightenment, who admired him as a propagandist of natural inquiry that held the key to social progress. Bacon's basic philosophy could be regarded as what later came to be seen as "Whiggish," and it is not surprising that the arch Whig historian Lord Macaulay, in his long essay on Bacon (Macaulay [1837] 1983), hailed his work as prophetic.[51] On the other hand, idealist German philosophers were less impressed.[52]

How do we explain Bacon's impact on elite culture in the decades after his death? Deborah Harkness, who regards this phenomenon with some regret, attributes Bacon's impact (compared to that of more practical writers, such as Hugh Plat) to our focus on singular men rather than collaborative communities and our preference for a neat scientific story over the messy tale of "humble practitioners on the streets of a busy city" [London]. But above all, she thinks, that "Bacon himself wanted it that way" (Harkness, 2007, p. 252). That interpretation seems wrong: it was not only Bacon, but also his followers who wanted it that way. In the market for ideas, he may have been a more successful salesman than Hugh Plat, but it was the "buyers" who determined which of the two would become a successful cultural entrepreneur and who would be relegated to oblivion. Hill (1965, p. 87) refers to Harvey's sneer mentioned above and notes that

---

[50] Bacon's influence on Robert Hooke, after Newton the most ingenious and talented English scientist of his age, can be seen from Hooke's somewhat exaggerated plan to write the history of every artisanal occupation, including the makers of counterfeit pearls and precious stones, bugle-makers, book-binders, dancing masters, varnishers and so on. See Farrington ([1951] 1979, p. 137).

[51] In his essay, Macaulay noted that "some people may think the object of Baconian philosophy [to provide a man with what he requires to continue to be a man—that is technology] a low object, but they cannot deny that, high or low, it has been attained ... they cannot deny that mankind have made and are making great and constant progress in the road which he pointed out to them" (Macaulay, [1837], 1983, pp. 129–32). These lines are without a doubt triumphalist, but by the time they were published, on the eve of the Victorian era, they were based on real and palpable technological achievements in the British Industrial Revolution. As McCloskey (2010, p. 91) has noted, Bacon and Macaulay were "the foolish optimists of the Enlightenment," yet it was they who were correct about the magnitude of future growth and their pessimist opponents were quite wrong.

[52] Thus Hegel writes somewhat acerbically that "Since Bacon has ever been esteemed as the man who directed knowledge to its true source, to experience, he is, in fact, the special leader and representative of what is in England called Philosophy, and beyond which the English have not yet advanced. For they appear to constitute that people in Europe which, limited to the understanding of actuality, is destined, like the class of shopkeepers and workmen in the State, to live always immersed in matter, and to have actuality but not reason as object ... His practical writings are specially interesting; but we do not find the bright flashes of genius that we expected." See Hegel ([1805-1806] 1892-1896, p. 172-74).

it was important to write philosophy like a lord chancellor so as to elevate to a coherent philosophical system what hitherto had been only partially articulated assumptions of practical men.

Today, to be sure, the significance of Bacon's legacy for the history of science can be disputed, but his impact on the prestige and agenda of scientific endeavors and indeed on all studies of useful knowledge, including technology, is undiminished. The consensus view is still that "the ethos he infused into modern science as something inherently related to social development remains ... part of our categorical framework" (Pérez-Ramos, 1996, p. 311). Baconianism meant that his followers accepted, among other things, a belief in the institutionalization of science and the means of gathering, collating, and disseminating knowledge through planned and cooperative research; they also believed in technological solutions to social problems, not least if money could be made (Rees, 2000, p. 71). In other words, Bacon's heritage was nothing less than the cultural acceptance of the growth of useful knowledge as a critical ingredient of economic growth.

Chapter 8

Isaac Newton, Cultural Entrepreneur

Newton's role as a cultural entrepreneur was quite different from Bacon's. If Bacon's messages about knowledge-based progress were in the end little more than hopeful, Newton's were affirmative. If technological progress consisted of commanding nature by obeying her, someone had to find out the rules. More than anyone else, Newton showed that those rules were within reach.

The connection between the work of Newton and the subsequent rise of Newtonian science and economic development in the eighteenth century is a matter of some dispute. Margaret Jacob has argued strongly that the Newtonians had a powerful impact on what actually was taking place on the shopfloor of British manufacturers (Jacob, 1997, 2000a, 2007; Jacob and Stewart, 2004). Against this, Fara (2002, p. 21) has argued that the eighteenth-century growth in Newton's reputation was a *consequence* of England's growing commercialization in this period. While there is some truth to both views, we should keep in mind that direct applications of Newtonian science to actual inventions before 1800 were quite rare and that Britain was already a highly commercialized and monetized economy by 1687, the year in which *Principia* was published. The main causal model did not lead from Newtonianism to economic development or vice versa, but from a third set of variables that was driving both. Those factors included the growth of an elite culture that increasingly subscribed to the view that the growth and dissemination of useful knowledge was key to material progress, and they were a direct product of two centuries of debate within the institutional context of a competitive market for ideas.

Newton's career and influence on later generations, unlike that of many important cultural entrepreneurs, is an illustration of unintended consequences and willy-nilly effects. Indeed, he may well have become a cultural entrepreneur in spite of himself: his aim in writing, Iliffe (1995, p. 175) has noted, was only to interact with a select band of the mathematically sophisticated. By his own admission, he made his *Principia* abstruse, so as to be understood only by "able mathematicians" who would "concurr with him in his Theory." His personality, moreover, made him an unlikely candidate for a position of great influence on his contemporaries, as Keynes pointed out in his posthumous lecture on "Newton, the Man."[1] If Newton as a cultural entrepreneur had an effect on the Industrial Revolution, it was through his impact in changing the fundamental values and beliefs of a select group of elite agents in Enlightenment society. His impact in the end had little to do with his personality and everything to do with the message. Content bias rather than rhetorical bias was his hallmark.[2]

From a methodological point of view, Newton represents a confluence of the Baconian empirical approach that dealt with observations, data, and experiments, and the mathematical approach to physics that came from Galileo. He eschewed suppositions and conjectures, and confined himself to theories that could be inferred from observation. Indeed, as Barbara Shapiro (2000, p. 156) has noted, Newton might be taken to insist that natural philosophy should be confined "to those realms of fact in which quantification or measurement was possible." Yet it is important to stress that the impact of Newton's work on his contemporaries and future generations referred to a very small part of his intellectual output. In many ways Newton was still an old-fashioned intellectual who wrote a great deal about the scriptures and engaged in numerology, trying to put predictive values on the numerical equivalent of certain passages in the scriptures to decipher the presumably coded dating of the apocalypse. He spent much time and energy scouring the book of Ezekiel to work out the exact dimensions of the first temple (Manuel, 1963, pp. 162–63), and to confirm the future coming of the second kingdom (Fara, 2002, p. 78). He wrote a great deal about history, including Egyptian hieroglyphs, ancient chronology revised on the basis of astronomical data, and the origins of Greek astronomy (Manuel, 1963). Many of his most creative years were devoted to alchemical experimentation, and modern scholars have realized that this research was not the pardonable eccentricities of a hyperactive genius, but part and parcel of a

---

[1] Keynes wrote that "For in vulgar modern terms Newton was profoundly neurotic of a not unfamiliar type, but—I should say from the records—a most extreme example. His deepest instincts were occult, esoteric, semantic-with profound shrinking from the world, a paralyzing fear of exposing his thoughts, his beliefs, his discoveries in all nakedness to the inspection and criticism of the world. 'Of the most fearful, cautious and suspicious temper that I ever knew', said Whiston, his successor in the Lucasian Chair. The too well-known conflicts and ignoble quarrels with Hooke, Flamsteed, and Leibniz are only too clear an evidence of this. ... He parted with and published nothing except under the extreme pressure of friends. Until the second phase of his life, he was a wrapt, consecrated solitary, pursuing his studies by intense introspection with a mental endurance perhaps never equalled" (Keynes, 1946).

[2] Michael White (1997, p. 99) points out that despite his "natural misanthropy," Newton networked well, not with any natural charm, but "solely through the impressive powers of his intellect."

complex intellectual persona that blended seminal intellectual innovation with a strong commitment to ancient writings. But Fara's (2002, p. 27) view that the modern view of Newton as a "scientific hero" was the result of "300 years of media manipulation" is untenable—there is overwhelming evidence that in the highly competitive market for ideas in the late seventeenth century, Newton's mathematical physics was recognized almost right away to be both innovative and correct. First through content bias (the best minds saw the logic of his work) and then through direct bias (his followers were themselves intellectuals of the highest standing), his work got the recognition it deserved in the market for ideas.

To be sure, Newton's influence was on a small elite. The vast bulk of the population even in eighteenth-century Western Europe had never heard of him—Newton, much like Bacon and Galileo within the narrow borders of the Republic of Letters. But it is among that elite where the action was in the market for useful knowledge. It is also true that the selection process operating in the market for ideas sanctified Newton's work on mathematical physics and had little interest in his alchemical work or his biblical studies. This side of him was probably suppressed—in part by himself and in part by his hagiographers in the age of Enlightenment. While this side of his research, as well as his relationship with Fatio de Duillier (a young Swiss mathematician and protégé) may be of interest to some, here the emphasis must be on his impact as the premier natural philosopher of his age and the crowning achievement of the Republic of Letters on the thought and culture of the Enlightenment.

To start with, Newton's work was the last nail in the coffin of the "ancients" in their struggle with the "moderns" on the question whether modern culture could measure up to the achievements of classical civilization.[3] His new physics was almost at once recognized to have overthrown what little there was left of ancient cosmology and physics, and it vindicated the many authors who had been pleading against a sense of inferiority of their own age. Furthermore, his work became a role model for other sciences. Many other branches of knowledge tried to develop elegant models much like Newton's theory of celestial mechanics and followed the lead of his work. His work filled other scholars with hope that such areas as farming, medicine, chemistry, electricity, materials, and even the "science of man" would soon be similarly reduced to well-understood, elegant laws. At first, the tangible results of that program were mixed at best. Newton's excursions in chemistry in the famous "query 31" at the very end of the third edition of his *Optics*, for instance, included a discursion about chemical affinity that later inspired other chemists, such as Etienne François Geoffroy

---

[3] Oddly enough, Newton himself seems to have believed that much of what he had discovered was already known by the ancient Greeks but had been lost subsequently. See Iliffe (1995, pp. 165–68).

(1672–1731), to compile the first tables of chemical affinities (Brock, 1992, p. 76). In the same "query," Newton conjectured that if his scientific method "shall at length be perfected, the Bounds of Moral Philosophy will be also enlarged" (Newton, 1721, p. 381). A group of doctors—of whom the best-known were the renowned Scottish physician Archibald Pitcairne (1652–1713) and his student, the fashionable English physician George Cheyne (1671–1743)—tried to apply Newtonian ideas to physiology in a field known as iatro-mathematics.[4] The movement to "Newtonize" other areas culminated in the work of another Scotsman, James Keill (1673–1719), who published in 1708 a volume on animal secretions in which a theory based on attractive forces operating on particles in animal blood was put forward (Roe, 2003, pp. 400–1).[5] Similarly, the Dutch physician Herman Boerhaave (1668–1738), who taught medicine, chemistry, and botany at Leiden between 1709 and 1738, subscribed to Newtonian principles to explain the human body in terms of gravitation and attraction (Dobbs and Jacob, 1995, p. 85), but it is unlikely that this insight led to any tangible improvements in clinical practice.[6] Even some of the work of the ever-skeptical David Hume, especially his "science of man," has been argued to be modeled in part on Newton's successes in natural philosophy. Hume certainly appears to want, in places, his readers to feel that he is modeling his project on the successes of natural philosophy exemplified by Newton, suggesting that his "science of man" could parallel recent achievements in natural philosophy (Schliesser, 2007). Newton's impact on economics, especially Adam Smith, has also recently been emphasized. Smith (who had a strong interest in natural philosophy) admired Newton's work

---

[4] Iatro-mathematicians imagined the body to be a hydraulic machine filled with fluids that could be explained by Newtonian laws of motion, an original blend of humoral medicine and Newtonian laws of motion. See also Fara (2002, p. 85). Cheyne went so far so to apply Newtonian principles to clinical depression (from which he suffered), concluding somehow that Newtonian science suggested that "melancholy" was centered in body fluids, which could be repaired with a proper diet and moderate exercise (Guerrini, 2004b).

[5] In this work, Keill attempted to apply Newton's model of a chemical attraction somehow similar to gravity to explain the cohesion of the particles of blood, and he developed a mathematical model of the circulatory system (Guerrini, 2004a). The logic here was typical of the optimism of the post-Newton age: "If some things which to former ages have appeared unaccountable are now as clear and demonstrable as the pressure of air, why should we not hope for a discovery of the things that are still hidden from us?... the Animal Body is a pure machine and all its actions from which Life and Health do flow are the necessary consequences of its Oeconomy. ... This Oeconomy depends on attractive power first discovered by the incomparable Sir Isaac Newton" (Keill, 1708, pp. v–vi, 8).

[6] Boerhaave serves as another classic example of the kind of epigone that is instrumental in disseminating the ideas of the true cultural entrepreneurs, in his case Descartes and Newton. Famous and celebrated in his own days, his original contributions were few and middling, yet he helped spread the main cultural beliefs of the Enlightenment, not only in his own country but throughout Europe.

as much as anyone in his generation.[7] Newton's influence on Smith is palpable in the method of moving "bottom-up" by induction from phenomena to principles, and in the willingness to concede that the deep causes of the phenomena he has described may be beyond him (Hetherington, 1983, pp. 503–5).

Newton's impact on the physical sciences was, a fortiori, enormous. His insights more than ever confirmed the belief in a mechanistic, understandable universe that could and should be manipulated for the material benefit of humankind. In some form, the anthropocentric idea of nature in the service of humans had been around since the Middle Ages, but what counted was its triumph over what their proponents regarded as obscurantism and superstition. Seventeenth-century science prepared the ground for the Industrial Enlightenment by stressing mankind's relationship with the environment as based on intelligibility and instrumentality. In Newton's work the emphasis is on mathematics and instrumentality, not on explaining the "deep" causes of things (Dear, 2006, pp. 37–38). The exact cause of gravity, in his view, would be a "hypothesis" (meaning speculation), for which he had nothing but contempt. It was enough for him, he noted in the famous *General Scholium* appended to a new edition of *Principia* in 1713, that gravity exists and that the rules he had uncovered explained the motion of heavenly bodies.

This is precisely what Newton did. He did not claim to understand *why* the principles he discovered existed and described physical reality and *how* two bodies separated at a distance from one another could affect each other, only that these principles were universal and could be understood by generally applicable principles. In that sense his outlook seems similar to Descartes's mechanistic universe. However, his view of the role of science was to establish regularities and show how they could be exploited, but not to provide any top-down "micro-foundations" the way Descartes and Leibniz had tried.[8] Hence he had no need to find the elementary particles of matter that French scientists such as Pierre Gassendi were concerned

---

[7] In his *History of Astronomy,* Smith wrote that "Such is the system of Sir Isaac Newton, a system whose parts are all more strictly connected together, than those of any other philosophical hypothesis ...His principles, it must be acknowledged, have a degree of firmness and solidity that we should in vain look for in any other system. The most sceptical cannot avoid feeling this. ... Can we wonder then, that it should have gained the general and complete approbation of mankind, and that it should now be considered, not as an attempt to connect in the imagination the phaenomena of the Heavens, but as the greatest discovery that ever was made by man, the discovery of an immense chain of the most important and sublime truths, all closely connected together, by one capital fact, of the reality of which we have daily experience" (Smith, 1799, p. 121). For a recent analysis see Montes (2008).

[8] Bernard LeBovier Fontenelle (1657–1757), a French contemporary of Newton and a highly influential intellectual, summed up the difference by noting that Descartes started from what he clearly understood to find the causes of what he saw, whereas Newton started from what he saw to find its causes whether clear or obscure (Fontenelle, [1727] 1728, pp. 11–12).

with. Rather than produce a philosophically consistent system that describes everything, Newton aimed for a more modest goal, namely, to provide a mathematical description of observed phenomena. The implication was that once nature was intelligible, it could be manipulated, controlled, and app-lied to human needs as Bacon had advocated.

Intelligibility, above all, depended on a mechanistic view of the world. The concept of a mechanical clockwork-like universe in which the regularities were predictable and deterministic, although in the air for a long time, was given an enormous boost by Newton's work. Newton himself never committed to a mechanistic view of the world, and firmly believed that the system he had discovered could only "proceed from the counsel and dominion of an intelligent and powerful being" (Newton, 1729, p. 344; Mayr, 1986, pp. 97–98; Snobelen, 2012). The trend toward mechanistic thinking was the product of the thought and labors of many people, some famous such as Descartes, many obscure, who used Newton's findings in ways that he himself would not have approved of.

It stands to reason that Newton's work persuaded a large number of educated and informed people that a project of material improvement, in the Baconian tradition, based on an understanding of the laws of a mech-anistic view of the universe, was feasible—despite the lack of many tangible concrete achievements by the time Newton died (1727). What drove scient-ific and eventually technological progress was the conviction that all natural phenomena and regularities could be explained by a coherent and compre-hensible set of natural laws. Carrying out a project that would uncover them turned out to be a huge undertaking, especially because so many relevant areas (such as medicine, chemistry, and agriculture) turned out to be much more complex and messy than anyone had imagined. To manage and direct the accumulation of comprehensible knowledge, experimental science became increasingly the vehicle of natural philosophy. The Newtonians did not invent the experimental method, but their work helped make it a dominant methodology (Gascoigne, 2003, pp. 289, 302).

Newton's other contribution was the sanctification of the use of mathematics in the generation and processing of useful knowledge. Conti-nental Europe had long accepted this: Galileo, Descartes, Mersenne, Torricelli, Huygens, and Leibniz all used mathematics in their natural philo-sophy. In England, this insight arrived relatively late. Francis Bacon, as already noted, had no interest in mathematics as a tool of research.[9] Nor, it seems, did many of the British scientists between Bacon and Newton.

---

[9] Bacon claimed in the (rarely reprinted) third book of *The Advancement of Learning* that to science's detriment "it is natural for men's minds to delight more in the open fields of generals, than in the inclosures of particulars, nothing is found more agreeable than mathematics, which fully gratifies this appetite of expatiating and ranging at large. ... It is a strange fatality, that mathematics and logic, which ought to be but handmaids to physics, should boast their certainty before it, and even exercise dominion against it" (Bacon [1605] 1875, vol. IV, p. 370).

Robert Boyle, for instance, argued against the use of mathematics in experimental science and his own mathematical aptitude is in dispute (Shapin, 1988b).[10] Some of the leading minds of the Puritan era were of course mathematicians, especially Hobbes and Wallis, but most English scientists and mathematicians of the early days of the Royal Society stayed away from the formal deductive rigorous logic of the Cartesians (a methodology to which Hobbes also subscribed), preferring a more prudent, pragmatic, and experimentalist approach, in which knowledge accumulated bit by bit and was rarely irrefutably true.

Newton singlehandedly combined the deductive powers of mathematical modeling with Baconian stress on experimental data and observations, showing that the two were not only capable of coexisting in the same mind but could actually be complementary. The combination of his formidable mathematical and analytical skills with his continuous reliance on empirical and experimental data was regarded in his own day as a shining example that lesser scientists could only hope to mimic. John Arbuthnot, a Scottish physician and polymath, wrote in 1701 that mathematical learning had unlocked "the grand secret of the whole machine [that is, the universe] which depended on the most known and most common property of matter, viz. gravity ... from this the incomparable Mr. Newton has demonstrated the theories of all the bodies of the solar system" (Arbuthnot, 1701, p. 13).

The classical canon had been largely based on logic and authority; Bacon had wanted to replace it altogether with facts and data that, somehow, would then fall into place. In the end, Newton taught, one should always prefer principles gained by induction from observation (Iliffe, 2003, p. 272). Methodologically, Newton arguably followed the Galilean method, which combined the kind of induction that was proposed by the followers of Paracelsus and the Baconians, rather than the formal-deductive method that was at the base of Descartes's thinking. Moreover, Newton's writing had a provisional tone, one that strongly suggested science was an ongoing, never-ending project. He wrote famously that "to explain all nature is too difficult a task for any one man or any one age. 'Tis much better to do a little with certainty & leave the rest for others that come after you" (quoted by Iliffe, 2003, p. 273). He thus helped establish an important principle, namely that scientific knowledge is defeasible, subject to revision and challenge when new and better evidence becomes available. Anyone who believed in the feasibility and desirability of continuous progress must have found this message congenial.

---

[10] There were exceptions, of course, such as the mathematician John Dee (see chapter 7) who is believed by some to have been more advanced in his thinking than Bacon. In any event, while Dee's widely read introduction to Euclid's works remained quite influential, it is quite clear that his subsequent influence on the practices of natural philosophy was far more limited than that of Bacon.

Moreover, even though he never left England, Newton was deeply integrated in a *European* as opposed to an English academic environment. Self-taught in mathematics, he relied on books written by Frenchmen (René Descartes and François Viète) and a Dutchman (Frans van Schooten). He corresponded (briefly) with Huygens, Leibniz, and Johann Bernoulli, and was universally regarded quite early on as an international scientific superstar, the most successful citizen of the Republic of Letters. As Westfall (1980, pp. 472–73) notes, the two most prominent intellectuals on the Continent, Christiaan Huygens and Gottfried Wilhelm Leibniz, had initial doubts about some aspects of the *Principia*, but Huygens eventually came around to see his genius and went out of his way to meet Newton during his 1689 visit to England. Upon being asked what he thought of Newton, Leibniz once told the Queen of Prussia that mathematics could be divided into two halves, before and after Newton, and that "what [Newton] had done was much the better half" (Westfall, 1980, p. 721). More ebullient was the French mathematician the Marquis de l'Hôpital (1661–1704) who famously asked of Newton "is he like other men?" (Westfall, 1980, p. 473). Despite the innovativeness of his theories, his main scientific fights were not with those who disagreed with him on essential matters, but were instead about priority disputes (Hooke) or access to data (Flamsteed). While his religious views were heterodox, there is no evidence that they stood in the way of his celebrity and the powerful patronage positions he occupied after 1687.

As noted, Newtonianism engaged in a drawn-out battle with its main competitors in the marketplace for ideas in the first half of the eighteenth century. What is interesting is that the battle was fought on the Continent, not in Britain, and that the shock troops of Newtonianism were Dutch: the Leyden University natural philosopher and experimentalist Burchard de Volder (1643–1709), who taught Cartesian principles for decades but late in life defected to Newtonianism (Feingold, 2004, pp. 69–70), his student Hermann Boerhaave, the central figure at Leyden for the first decades of the eighteenth century, and Boerhaave's colleagues Willem 's Gravesande (1688–1742) and Petrus Musschenbroek (1692–1761), both of them leading researchers and prolific authors of textbooks that disseminated the gospel of Newtonianism.

In France, there is some dispute on when the impact of Newton's work was fully felt (Shank, 2008). Some mathematicians clearly were indebted to his work, above all Pierre de Varignon (1654–1722), a leading French mathematician who wrote that reading *Principia* in 1688 "provoked many new ideas in his mind," and who remained immersed in the book for the rest of his life. Varignon's work was as important to the development of analytical mechanics as to the growing reputation of Newton in France (Feingold, 2004, pp. 57–58). There was fierce resistance by the Cartesians, especially by the influential philosopher Nicolas de Malebranche (1638–1715), who respected Newton's work but formulated a neo-Cartesian philosophy that favored his own camp. As time went on, however, the Cartesians saw their domination slip away. The Newtonian camp could count such converts as Pierre-Louis de Maupertuis and Alexis-Claude Clairaut (Glass, 2008; Itard, 2008) and the coup de grâce may have been Voltaire's influential *Élements de la Philosophie de Newton,* published in 1738.[11]

While many French natural philosophers did not choose to fully commit to Newtonianism and maintained a foot in both camps, the triumph of Newtonianism over Cartesianism was part and parcel of the rebellion against traditional learning (Gascoigne, 2003, pp. 300–02). This was less the case in Italy, especially in the south, where the heavy hand of the Jesuits and the Catholic Church, and the threat of being charged with heresy were still present; yet even there Newtonianism gained ground in a circumspect and cautious manner. The evidence and the logic, for those who had access to it, were powerful. Content bias worked.[12] Some other biases unrelated to the actual content of the competing doctrines were operative as well. Many French natural philosophers remained loyal to Cartesianism because Descartes was one of them and satisfied their national pride. All the same, the wave of *anglomanie* that swept France and much of the rest of the Continent, together with the popularity that French philosophers enjoyed in the courts of Potsdam and St. Petersburg, demonstrates how pan-European the market for ideas had become in the eighteenth century.

What, then, was the significance of Newton for the cultural changes that prepared the ground for the Industrial Enlightenment? As noted, Newton's influence can be attributed in large part to content bias. His work was convincing because it met the rhetorical criteria of those who could understand it, that is, those who could follow the mathematics and could verify the experimental and observational data that confirmed it. There was also direct bias (many of his followers were men of substantial authority and scientific prestige, whom others trusted).[13] Direct bias re

[11] Even reactionary writers who found the implications of Newton's work revolting had to admit his genius. An example is the work of the Abbé Augustin Barruel (1740–1821), a conservative Jesuit priest (later to become famous for his accusations that Freemasons and other secret societies were responsible for the excesses of Jacobinism) who blamed Newton for the appearance of "schools of atheism" but then proceeded to attack the materialist view by asking rhetorically if the mind of a Newton could arise in an insect (Shank, 2008, pp. 5–6).

[12] In addition to the Lapland expedition that showed the flattening of the earth at the poles, another piece of evidence that was incontrovertible proof of Newton's physics was the return of Halley's comet in the spring of 1759 on almost exactly the date predicted by Clairaut and his colleague Joseph-Jérôme Lalande, using new mathematical methods of approximating solutions to the three-body problem. The accuracy of the prediction was regarded widely as another vindication of Newton's laws of gravitation (Hankins, 2008; Itard, 2008).

[13] Newton's system was rapidly embraced by the Scottish mathematician David Gregory (1659–1708), professor of mathematics at Edinburgh and later at Oxford, and who had the mathematical skills to recognize straight away the genius of *Principia*. Gregory introduced his students to Newton's work and was the author of the first textbook that integrated Newton's theory of gravitation with known astronomical facts. He became one Newton's protegés, and in

mained essential in a world in which specialization and a division of knowledge were inevitable especially when the discussions were quite abstruse and technical.

Yet despite Newton's enormous prestige, his work was subject to critique and revision. A case in point was his work in optics, and specifically his argument that an achromatic lens (correcting for chromatic aberration) was impossible, which was challenged by Leonhard Euler. Euler argued, in analogy with the human eye, that two lenses with water between them would correct the problem, despite Newton's categorical denial that this was possible.[14] The Royal Society commissioned a London optician, John Dollond, to investigate the matter. That a self-taught former silk-weaver would be asked to test a pronouncement of the greatest mathematician of the age is itself an illustration of the evolution of the unwavering principle of contestability in the eighteenth-century Republic of Letters. At first, Dollond argued flatly that Euler was wrong and that anything Newton had said must be true, but eventually he was convinced by the Swedish mathematician Samuel Klingenstierna, who had taken an interest in the issue, that Euler may have been right. Experimentation with lenses made from different types of glass subsequently persuaded Dollond that Newton had been wrong, and he made a point of building a telescope embodying Euler's correction (Sorrenson, 2001; Fara, 2002, p. 101; Clifton, 2004) and had a drawing of himself made with a copy of the *Opticks* and a bookmark indicating the erroneous passage in the Great Man's work. Another area in which eighteenth-century scholars tested and refuted Newton's work was in hydrostatics or the science of ships, the subject of a long discussion in *Principia*.[15] The Bernoulli father and son team and then Leonhard Euler replaced the impact theory associated with Newton's work with a new theory that dealt with the physical state variables in the whole domain of the fluid.

Newton's impact on the supply of scientists and research is an example of model-based bias: young scientists and mathematicians all knew

---

many ways satisfies the characteristics of an epigone, as his own original contributions were marginal. His student, John Keill (1671–1721), similarly worked in Newton's shadow and famously unleashed the priority dispute between Leibniz and Newton by suggesting that Leibniz had pirated the ideas of calculus from the master. He and Roger Cotes (1682–1716) labored to make the works of Newton more accessible to students.

[14] Interestingly enough, Euler's analogy was flawed; the eye is a flawed lens that suffers from chromatic aberration, which is subsequently removed by the brain.

[15] Newton himself had been guarded about the validity of his work on hydrostatics and resistance, but unfortunately his disciples and adherents were not so cautious. They quickly and uncritically proceeded to apply Newton's theory, which they called "impact theory," to real fluids and to bodies in water and air. "The results were entirely disappointing, but due to Newton's authority such misleading concepts were widespread for a considerable time" (Nowacki, 2008, p. 280).

of his fame and fortune, and the social prestige of a career in science would never be the same.[16] Newton's patronage job as master of the mint and the many attractive offers he declined amply demonstrate his celebrity and prestige.[17] His career illustrated the social status that a truly successful scientist could attain in a society that began to value useful knowledge. He was knighted, elected to Parliament, and became quite wealthy.[18] In 1727 he was given a splendid funeral and interned in a prominent place in Westminster Abbey. Voltaire remarked that he was buried like a well-loved king. No wonder that his life provided an iconic model that other would-be scientists were hoping to follow, much like James Watt's career did for engineers a century later (MacLeod, 2007). In early eighteenth-century France, the new science was especially valued and became part of high society and a new political culture in which a powerful alliance was created between the *savants* of the Republic of Letters and the royal administration (Shank, 2008, p. 88). The effective allocation of talent and human capital in the very extreme upper tail of the distribution of talent is sensitive to such signals.[19]

As president of the Royal Society, Newton was the uncontested leader of Britain's intellectual community for decades, surrounded by admiring and fawning students (most notably John Keill, Richard Bentley, Samuel Clarke, Henry Pemberton, and William Whiston). He was on close terms with all the leading intellectuals and scientists of his age, unless (as Keynes remarks) he had quarreled with them (which was common). His most effective disciple perhaps was John T. Desaguliers (1683–1744), a brilliant engineer and mathematician who spent much of his life spreading

---

[16] Three of the eighteenth century's most influential intellectuals, Buffon, Diderot, and Rousseau—very different men indeed—all were inspired early in their careers by Newton's example (Feingold, 2004, pp. 154–58).

[17] Among others, the visiting French scholar Jacques Cassini conveyed to him in 1698 an offer of a large pension by Louis XIV that would have involved an appointment at the French Royal Academy of Sciences. He was also offered the mastership of Trinity College (Westfall, 1980, pp. 587–89)

[18] Although apparently little interested in acquiring wealth, he left his nieces and nephews a liquid estate of £ 32,000 in 1727 (Westfall, 1980, p. 870).

[19] Shapin (2003) examines the image of scientists in seventeenth- and eighteenth-century England, and he notes that despite their rise in prestige, they were still some distance from being accepted in "polite" (that is, aristocratic) society. Instead, both the state and industrial and commercial entrepreneurs regarded them as "civil experts" whose knowledge could be tapped. There was nothing radically new in such a demand for expertise except for its degree: the eighteenth century witnessed a vast expansion of experts counseling on commerce, geography, botany, chemistry, farming, ceramics, and medicine (Shapin, 2003, pp. 169, 179). The causes of this expansion were both on the supply side (more people chose careers as natural philosophers and other experts) and on the demand side. The growth in knowledge of nature and the improved tools to attain it may have meant growing usefulness in some cases, but above all the Baconian ideology had become so powerful that many people believed in the potential of science to assist in production long before its effectiveness was evident.

and defending the views of the Master against the Cartesians.[20] In Enlightenment Europe, a whole industry sprang up of books interpreting and explaining Newton, often written in languages other than English and then translated further. Of those, the volume by Voltaire (*Elements de la Philosophie de Newton*), was translated back into English, as was that of the leading Dutch Newtonian, Willem 's Gravesande.[21] In Germany a leading Newtonian was the mathematician Jakob Hermann (1678–1733), a relative of Euler, who taught for years in Padua and St. Petersburg as well as in Frankfurt on the Oder and his native Basel. Germany's intellectual elite became definitively Newtonian when Maupertuis became president of the Berlin Academy of Sciences (1746). To be sure, both he and Leonhard Euler modified Newtonianism to include other elements, such as Leibniz's mathematical notation—but there was no question that Newtonianism emerged triumphant. In Italy, the impact of Newton can be measured by the appearance in 1737 of *Il Newtonianismo per le Dame* (Newtonism for Ladies) by Francesco Algarotti (Mazzotti, 2004).[22] Over time, Newton's standing only rose as the embodiment of the Enlightenment's view of the ideal scientist.[23] The impact of Newton on the thin but strategically placed class of European intellectuals in the eighteenth century was immense and was famously summarized by Alexander Pope's epitaph.[24] Similarly, the astronomer Edmund Halley in his "Ode to Newton" (1687) wrote "Come celebrate with me in song the name of Newton, to the Muses dear; for he

[20]   In the preface to his magnum opus, Desaguliers wrote that "When mons. Des Cartes's philosophical romance, by the elegance of its style and the plausible accounts of natural phaenomena had overthrown the Aristotelian Physicks, the world received but little advantage of the change ... it was thanks to Newton's application of geometry to philosophy that we owe the routing of this army of Goths and Vandals in the philosophical world" (Desaguliers, 1745, pp. v–vi).

[21]   See Voltaire (1738). An interesting case in this regard is the career of Voltaire's companion, Emilie the Marquise du Châtelet (1706–49), one of the most remarkable female Enlightenment figures, who published one of the more user-friendly translations of Newton's work into French. In a touching preface, Voltaire dedicated his work to this "vaste et puisante génie, Minerve de la France, immortelle Emilie, disciple de Neuton & de la Verité."

[22]   Algarotti's book became a big best-seller: it was translated into French in 1738, English in 1739, and into many other European languages, a prime example how rhetorical bias affects cultural dissemination through the work of epigones.

[23]   In a famous anecdote, the French mathematician Jean-Baptiste Delambre's in his eulogy of Lagrange recounts that Lagrange often cited Newton as the greatest genius that ever existed but also the luckiest, because there was only one universe the laws of which he could discover. Delambre ([1816] 1867, p. xx).

[24]   Westminster Abbey did not allow the epitaph to be placed on the grave. The original read, "Nature and Nature's laws lay hid in night: God said, 'Let Newton be!' and all was light." Instead it reads (in Latin) "here lies that which was mortal of Isaac Newton."

Unlocked the hidden treasuries of Truth. ... Nearer the Gods, no mortal may approach" (Halley [1687], 1934]).

The only other intellectual of the age whose impact on his age and stature in modern assessment resembles Newton's (despite differing from him in almost every other dimension), John Locke, recognized Newton's achievement—but only after verifying with Huygens that the mathematics were sound.[25] The respectability of scientific research that augments useful knowledge was embodied in the Royal Society that Newton presided over. The implied message was that the work of natural philosophers was destined to become the primum mobile of social progress by carrying out Bacon's call for intelligibility. Newton had shown once and for all that this was feasible. This message became the core motto of the Industrial Enlightenment.

Thus Newton also contributed enormously to the rise of science (or, better put, natural philosophy) as a valuable human activity contributing to the well-being of mankind, worthy of the patronage and support of wealthy people.[26] The physician and botanist Hans Sloane (1660–1753), Newton's successor as president of the Royal Society, basked in the prestige of his predecessor to elevate the prominence of natural history. In this fashion, Newton completed what Galileo and the Puritans had started: to raise the social standing and prestige of science and natural philosophy, because of the realization that this kind of work was destined to become the primum mobile of social progress. People who engaged in it should be respected and supported. Because of Newton and the Newtonians, in eighteenth-century Britain the prestige of useful knowledge had become such that more and more entrepreneurs and manufacturers came to believe in its ability to help them solve practical problems.[27] Newton provided legitimacy and respectability to those who controlled useful knowledge as an independent locus of power in Western societies, a "fourth estate" of experts who served as authorities on the secrets of nature.

As I noted in chapter 6, the apostles and epigones of every cultural entrepreneur adapt and alter the original message, and Newton was no exception. Dobbs and Jacob (1995, p. 61) stress that Newton was not a

[25] "Yet the incomparable Mr. Newton has shown how far mathematics, applied to some part of nature, may, upon principles that matters of fact justify, carry us in the knowledge of some ... particular provinces of the incomprehensible universe." See Locke ([1693], 1812, vol. 9, p. 186).

[26] As Michael Hunter has pointed out, the prestige of the scientific endeavor and culture was by no means assured in Restoration England. Only after 1700, he notes, "under the presiding genius of Newton, science became increasingly orthodox, systematic, and influential" (Hunter, 1995a, p. 119).

[27] An example of this tendency was the career of William Cullen, a Scottish chemist, physician, and professor at the University of Edinburgh, who was much in demand as a consultant to bleachers, farmers, salt miners, and dye manufacturers.

"Newtonian." He showed little taste in his lifetime for applications, and unlike his nemesis Robert Hooke, invented nothing worth mentioning. Newton was more interested in motion than in heat, and yet it is the latter that turned out to be crucial to eighteenth-century advances in power and materials. Mechanical science, as developed by Galileo and Newton, was initially of little direct help to the mechanical inventions in the textile industry. Differential calculus, arguably Newton's most practical invention, did become more useful to engineers in the second half of the eighteenth century, but it is not easy to assess its exact role in technological progress outside a few areas. Most of his epigones, too, were not famous for significant technological advances.[28]

Any direct effect of Newton and even his closest students on concrete technological advances, then, was slight. As is often pointed out, the Industrial Revolution did not begin properly until seven or eight decades after the publication of *Principia*, though the traditional timing schedule tends to slight a substantial number of important technological breakthroughs that date before 1750, including coke smelting, crucible steelmaking, the early steam engines, and the flying shuttle. It is true that some of Newton's followers were able to demonstrate his principles using mechanical devices. But, as Cardwell (1972) and others have noted, the dispute between the Newton measure of force (momentum, or mass times acceleration) and the Huygens-Leibniz notion of *vis-viva* (kinetic energy, or mass times velocity squared) was not altogether in Newton's favor, as the vis-viva concept was more useful to engineers interested in mechanical work, duty, and efficiency (Henry, 2008, p. 113). The confusing dispute regarding which of the two concepts was to be preferred illustrates the fact that Newton's work left a lot to be done by future research. Concepts critical to machinery, such as momentum, force, work, power, and torque were not fully worked out until late in the eighteenth century (Home, 2002, p. 361). Definitions of such critical variables as impulse, momentum, work, power, and force had not been established before the work of Euler in 1750 and Lagrange in his *Mécanique Analytique* (1788). The same indefiniteness is true for Newton's concept of the universe, and the final structure of the classical theory of the movement of heavenly bodies and their stability (using calculus that Newton himself had invented but had not deployed in his work) was not nailed down until Laplace's *Mécanique Céleste* in the late eighteenth century.

---

[28] It is true that the career and work of Desaguliers exemplifies the positive effect of Newtonianism in Britain, focusing on the practical and useful application of the new mechanical science. He experimented a great deal with electricity and machinery without making any breakthroughs of note. During the careers of Desaguliers and that of other similarly-minded Newtonians such as the influential scientist and physician James Jurin (1684–1750), no Industrial Revolution took place.

The connection between the Scientific Revolution and the Industrial Revolution was deeper, and more subtle and less direct than a linear line from Newton's laws of motion or the work of the Newtonians to create new machines (Jacob and Stewart, 2004, pp. 26–60; see also Jacob 1997). The rise of public science and the growth of the appreciation of the value of scientific knowledge through Newtonian lecturers gave rise to a new "technical literacy," which included the ability to do mathematical calculations and the ability to read and understand technical drawings and explanations (Jacob and Stewart, 2004, p. 131). Sometimes known as latitudinarianism, this set of beliefs viewed scientific knowledge as a unifying force among moderate and tolerant Protestants (Hunter, 1981, pp. 27–28). By making science "a fit subject for pulpit discourse" latitudinarianism made science more relevant to daily experience (Jacob, 1997, p. 61). Through a variety of channels, the kind of liberal Anglicanism that the Newtonians (more than Newton himself) represented filtered down from the Newton acolytes via the Boyle lectures first given in 1692. Some of the more influential among them, such as Richard Bentley, Samuel Clarke, and William Derham described what they felt Newtonianism stood for: the pursuit of sober self-interest, an endorsement of human domination over nature, and a full acceptance of the Baconian program (Jacob, 1986, pp. 243–44). Whether the cosmic order propounded in the *Principia* really was a prescription for a stable and progressive Christian society, a long and winding road led from the *Principia* to a liberal Anglicanism and the kind of ideology that was critical in preparing the ground for the Industrial Revolution. Perhaps even without Newton, Britain would have arrived there. By the middle of the eighteenth century, however, Newton had become the emblem of more than just successful science but of a "transcendent entity" embodying "reason, order and genius"—all concepts that the Enlightenment came to adore (Fara, 2002, pp. 130–31).

Perhaps the most important contribution that Newton's work made to the Industrial Enlightenment was the elegance and completeness with which he explained phenomena and regularities that had puzzled people for centuries, which instilled in others confidence about the ability of humans to understand nature. The point was not just that his equations—which explained celestial motions as well as provided a theoretical basis for much that had been known before on the motions of earthly bodies and the behavior of light—provided a world of order and logic. It was also that the Baconian ideal of understanding nature through observation and experiment and thus asserting control over it seemed so much closer after 1687. As Feingold (2004, p. 148) has phrased it, "by becoming science personified … Newtonian Science also became the model to emulate, the manifestation of 'superior knowledge' that summoned all other learning to reorient itself along similar lines." In sum, the importance of Newtonianism lay not so much in its discoveries as in what it implied for the "most fundamental of human problems—that is to say, the relation of man to nature and of both to God" (Becker, 1932, pp. 61–62). This relation is the cultural change on which much of the exponential growth of useful knowledge relied, and the economic consequences thereof cannot be understood without recognizing it.

Newton's work constitutes a crashing crescendo to a century in which natural philosophers had worked to raise the social prestige of "useful knowledge" as both socially beneficial and personally virtuous. Such an elevation of the status of intellectuals and their work was essential if useful knowledge—physics, botany, mathematics, chemistry, technology, medicine—were to play the transformative roles that they did. But Newton also changed the methodological premises of how useful knowledge was constructed. In the age of Enlightenment, Newton became the epitome of the potential of human rationality, and, as Peter Gay (1969, p. 130) has put it, "in the deification of Newton, the Enlightenment of the philosophes and the age of Enlightenment were at one." Deification, of course, was the fate of many of the truly successful cultural entrepreneurs in history—from Jesus to Marx.[29]

As a result of Newton's influence and the triumph of his work over that of Descartes and Leibniz during the Enlightenment, "natural philosophy" became gradually disconnected from philosophy. The former no longer promised a unified theory of everything, and instead confined itself to the explanation of separate phenomena, relying heavily on observation and experimentation. The importance of Newton and the Newtonians for subsequent developments therefore also lies in the change in the function of religion that his work implied. The danger to traditional beliefs was already realized by Newton's epigones, such as Samuel Clarke, who defended Newtonianism's religious loyalty against more radical thinkers such as the highly heterodox John Toland (1670–1722), who saw the gravitational laws as proof of a pantheistic materialism viewed as heresy by Newton and his followers. All the same, during the Enlightenment, "despite constant efforts to exorcize the demon, the specter of radicalism, irreligion, and Spinozism continually haunted discussions of Newtonian attraction throughout the eighteenth century" (Shank, 2008, p. 129).

The irony is hard to miss. Newton was a deeply religious man, for whom his findings affirmed the ever-presence of a wise deity who had created a world of knowable regularities.[30] But Newtonian mechanical

---

[29] Voltaire regarded Newton practically in religious terms, regarding himself as Newton's apostle and admitted that Newton was the "God to whom I sacrifice" (Feingold, 2004, p. 104).

[30] While it surely is far-fetched to see in his Arianist (and thus *heretical*) convictions a driving force for his science, Newton's Christian faith affirmed and supported his scientific work. He could do this by developing eclectic and idiosyncratic religious beliefs that were designed to be consistent with his scientific insights. He ignored the problems that his mechanical theory posed for cosmogenesis and ostensibly adhering to the literal biblical text (Snobelen,

philosophy did not strictly require a personal and conscious God, and it is telling that many of his Enlightenment followers, above all Voltaire, could decouple his scientific works from his faith and adopt the former without paying much attention to the latter.[31] Laplace—who, in terms of his capabilities and insights was in some ways Newton's successor—supposedly declared to the Emperor Napoleon that he had no need for "the God hypothesis."[32] Enlightenment science—especially in England—often coexisted with religion, but it needed religion less than the Puritan scientists did in the mid-seventeenth century. It replaced religion with other beliefs, some of them Utopian and millenarian in their own right, even though they were secular. Economic progress held the promise of a more prosperous and peaceful world (Becker, 1932). Concepts such as virtue were replaced by secular equivalents such as good citizenship and rational behavior. Salvation had to make room for progress.

More than anything in the terminology of defining what was attractive and valid in new cultural variants—always a central part of rhetorical bias—the sacred was replaced by the "natural," but often with similar meaning. This was, for instance, well-expressed by Adam Smith—another cultural entrepreneur of great importance to economic history—who wrote that "Statesmen ... and Projectors [fraudulent speculators] disturb nature in the course of her operations in human affairs; and it requires no more than to let her alone, and give her a fair play in the pursuit of her ends, that she may establish her own designs."[33] Becker's interpretation squares well with the Baconian image of *New Atlantis*'s scientists, who had many attr ibutes of priests and who could remedy human suffering through useful knowledge. The attitude in *New Atlantis* of the Fathers of has a strong reli-

---

1999). Newton had to struggle with the relation between God and his concepts of time and space and to show how the timelessness of one implied the timelessness of the other (Janiak, 2006).

[31] Newton himself realized the danger that science might push him into a Deist position, and in his private notes worried about the conflict between Christian doctrine and "the touch of cold philosophy" (Westfall, 1986, p. 232). By the eighteenth century, conservative writers such as the Jesuits associated Newtonian physics with various heretical philosophies such as deism, Spinozism, or Epicurean materialism (Shank, 2008, p. 381).

[32] There is no documentary evidence for Laplace ever to have uttered those widely cited words, but Hahn (1986, p. 256) notes that the statement was a faithful reflection of his position.

[33] This line comes right after the famous statement (not reproduced in the *Wealth of Nations*) that "little else is required to carry a nation to the highest state of opulence from the lowest barbarism but peace, easy taxes, and a tolerable administration of justice" (Stewart [1793] 1829, p. 64). Dugald Stewart added that the sentences appear in a small 1755 manuscript by Smith that was in his possession, but not to be published.

gious flavor.[34] The Baconian description of the scientist as a fount of wisdom and social leadership seems to predict Newton's almost priest-like
status before and after his death. Alexandre Koyré (1965, p. 18) noted that
Newtonianism, in a "curious mingling with Locke's philosophy," became
the scientific creed of the eighteenth century and that Newton appeared as
a superhuman being who had once and for all solved the riddle of the universe. But replacing the religious core of natural philosophy with a more secular one was not pure metaphysical juggling. It had profound implications
for the way the members of the intellectual elite saw their role in society.

[34] The description of the one of the "fathers" of Salomon's House, despite the
definition of the end of their foundation as "the knowledge of causes and secret motions of things
and the enlarging of the bounds of Human Empire to the effecting of all things possible" includes
his entry in streets lined with people in which he "held up his bare hand as he went blessing the
people in silence." Bacon ([1627], 1996, pp. 479–80).

Part III

Innovation, Competition, and Pluralism in Europe, 1500–1700

Chapter 9

Cultural Choice in Action: Human Capital and Religion

How, then, did culture affect economic development in the past? Before we turn to that question, one preliminary issue should be addressed. Whose culture are we talking about when discussing the cultural origins of economic growth? It bears reiterating that in general when we examine the roots of technological change, what counts disproportionately is the culture of an educated elite. Advances in useful knowledge are made by a relatively small percentage of the population, the trained and literate, and a few technical geniuses with unusual mechanical intuition. Whether it was a culture that favored labor and technology, as Lynn White (1978) has suggested was the case in medieval Europe, or one of appreciation of "bourgeois virtues," as suggested by McCloskey (2006) for early modern England and the Low Countries, the critical element is typically the beliefs and attitudes of a small but pivotal segment of the entire population: monks in the views of White, or the bourgeois merchants and artisans in the interpretation of McCloskey. In the cultural milieu of Enlightenment Europe it was no different. Voltaire proposed that nineteen out of twenty people work with their hands and "never know there is a Locke in the world or not." Among the small minority who read, "there are twenty who read novels for every one who reads philosophy" (Voltaire [1733–34], 2007, letter XIII, p. 45).

What is crucial above all for modern economic growth is the leadership of entrepreneurs, bankers, inventors, and engineers—the generals in Hooke's Cortesian army. Below them was another, somewhat larger, layer of people who supported the leaders and made their work possible. These were the "tweakers and tinkerers," the highly skilled craftsmen and mechanics who read the blueprints, perfected the gears, got the temperatures just right, and scaled-up the prototypes (Meisenzahl and Mokyr, 2012). Intelligent and creative artisans invented, improved, and tinkered with tools and techniques. Many improvements came about through small, cumulative improvements made by unknown craftsmen and diffused through the networks of technically literate masters and journeymen who became increasingly adept at disseminating tacit knowledge. Yet all told, these groups remained a small minority, and economic development in these areas can be viewed as their actions eventually affecting the economic status of the rest of the population, not so much a trickle-down as a dragging-along. The exact modus operandi of this top-down mechanism could vary from situation to situation, but historical outcomes can be analyzed using the various cultural evolution biases delineated in chapter 5. The elites acquired education, studied science, and read books, and others followed and imitated them. Educated individuals, almost by definition, were exposed to more ideas and were more likely to acquire beliefs and information through horizontal and oblique transmission than were the less-educated masses. It is not surprising that intellectual innovations were first aimed at educated people who could access them using printed sources or letters.[1] They were therefore more likely to be persuaded by new information and less committed to the cultural elements they had acquired from their parents or those teachers reflecting their parents' values. However, greater exposure to cultural variants opened doors; it did not force anyone to walk through them. Educated people might have had a vested interest in adhering to the ideas they learned early in life and resisting change.

The values and motives of the elite that spurred them to engage in science, engineering, improved agriculture, and other production-related agendas provide a clue as to why most slave societies usually showed little technological productivity. It is not so much the often-made argument that labor was cheap in slave societies (it was not) and thus there was little incentive to introduce labor-saving technological progress (there was no less such incentive). Instead, technological creativity was lower because the spheres of production and physical work were associated with low-prestige culture and inferior social standing.[2] In most slave societies, educated elites concerned themselves with philosophy, poetry, history, and such entertaining leisure activities as hunting and music. While they were usually interested in military technology, engineering, architecture, and large-scale hydraulic projects, more mundane subjects such as farming, shipbuilding, iron-working, food processing, and textiles were rarely on their agendas. Early-modern Europe's elites were for the most part not very different from the

---

[1] Whether the work of intellectuals criticizing existing political structures from Rousseau to Marx can actually inspire political revolutions remains controversial. Modern authors have often expressed skepticism as to whether and how books can lead to abrupt political change. But the matter remains controversial, as the writing of Israel (2010, p. 87) attests.

[2] There is, of course, no reason to suspect that a priori slave labor was cheaper to its owner than the wages that capitalists paid their hired workers. Moreover, most technological progress in pre-modern societies cannot readily be classified as labor-saving.

slave societies of the past—except for the small group that was to change the history of the world.

Once acquired, the attitudes and aptitudes of a more practical and materially oriented elite eventually reached larger and larger segments of the population. A plausible scenario is that when a technological elite of scientists, engineers, and skilled mechanics designed a set of novel manufacturing techniques, it became necessary for employers to have more educated workers who could operate and maintain the complex equipment—what is known as skill-technology complementarity. Historically, this led to employers investing in their workers' education (or, more accurately, persuading the political system to use the state's resources to do so) and thus eventually changing the living standards and culture of the population at large and altering the dynamics of class relations in the industrialized West (Galor and Moav, 2006). To make a strong case explaining modern economic growth, then, we need to focus on those groups whose culture mattered, what I have called (Mokyr, 2009a, p. 122) "upper tail human capital."[3] Other interpretations might focus on the culture of a larger group, such as the general population gradually increasing its respect and eventually admiration for the bourgeois merchants and entrepreneurs who set out to enrich themselves and in the process enriched society around them (McCloskey, 2016a). Equally important was the rising social prestige of the learned scientists and mathematicians whose research supported the technological advances.

As we have seen, culture can affect Smithian growth through the creation of an ideological environment (or, as some would prefer to call it, social capital) that is conducive to commerce and better-functioning markets. A Lockean belief in property rights, for example, or a belief that most people are trustworthy leads to the reduction of transactions costs and thus stimulates commerce. Related to trust is loyalty, which mitigates principal-agent problems. A belief in the virtuousness of loyalty to an employer or an organization saves monitoring costs and thus enhances both efficiency and trade. Public-mindedness (or *asabiya* in Ibn Khaldun's famous formulation), is a third cultural element related to cooperation: the willingness to avoid free-riding and contribute to a collective good despite the incentive that each individual has to shirk. Ideology is a mechanism by which society overcomes free-rider problems, as North (1981, p. 31) pointed out. Public-mindedness includes the willingness to help punish defectors, even if that comes at a personal price. Such punishment is much like contributing to a public good, because it permits the functioning of a private-order institution

---

[3] An imaginative attempt to test for the quantitative importance of these elites in eighteenth-century France is by Squicciarini and Voigtländer (2015), who define their cultural elite as the number of people who subscribed to the inexpensive edition of Diderot's and d'Alembert's *Grande Encyclopédie*.

that makes exchange happen by minimizing opportunistic behavior. The seminal work of Greif (2005) on the Maghribi traders is perhaps the best illustration of this kind of historical phenomenon, but other examples abound such as Ostrom's work (1990) on communities that help overcome opportunistic behaviors in the setting of a common-pool resource.[4] Certain kinds of cultural beliefs allow society to overcome voluntarily collective action problems, that might otherwise be achieved only by coercion.

Growth can also be supported through the creation of an entrepreneurial or bourgeois culture, a set of Weberian values in which people are willing to work harder, save more, provide for the poor, and take more risks. It involves enhanced respect for labor, production, and technology. The rise of a bourgeois culture, that enunciated respect for merchants and artisans, forms the core of McCloskey's (2006, 2016a) argument regarding the origins of modern growth. Obviously, if such risk-taking and diligence are channeled into productive directions, they can lead to improvements in economic performance.[5] Yet unless accompanied by innovations and productivity growth, growth exclusively based on a cooperative ethic will eventually peter out. There must be something more than an "ethic" that values hard work, honesty, and the people who make their money through it. There must be new ideas on how to produce.[6]

To be sure, a sharp categorization of cultural factors supporting Smithian vs. Schumpeterian growth is misleading. Many of the cultural beliefs and institutions that support Smithian growth also have an impact on technological progress. Technological progress in practice depends on well-defined property rights, as well as on contract enforcement, since it typically involves investment of some kind, as well as contracts with suppliers, workers, and customers. The existence of intellectual property rights, enforced by complex and often ambiguous institutions such as patents and copyright, has also been credited by many scholars as fostering technological progress. Innovation always and everywhere involves risk,

---

[4] Janet Tai Landa, for instance, has demonstrated such networks could enforce contracts among ethnically homogeneous middleman groups such as Chinese immigrants outside China (Landa, 1981, 1995).

[5] It is perhaps not surprising that the the association of commerce with virtue was most intense in the Netherlands. In 1632 the Dutch author and intellectual Casparus Barlaeus published a pamphlet titled *le Marchand Philosophe*, in which he argued point blank that not only was the accumulation of wealth good, but also that a rich merchant could be good without giving away his wealth to charity: "commerce itself could be among the best pursuits of life" (Cook, 2007, pp. 70–71). More and more contemporaries agreed with him.

[6] Hume (1742, [1985], p. 113) felt that this was the far more important but more difficult question. It is easier to account for the growth of commerce than that of learning, he felt, and that in the Netherlands "necessity and liberty" had produced commerce, but it had hardly produced any eminent writers.

and it is the kind of risk that cannot be insured against, unlike the risk of sending out a ship to trade with remote countries. Every invention is made only once, and hence the experience of past inventions is at best a limited guide to the success of a new idea. A willingness to take risks by experimenting with never-before-tried techniques is essential if innovation is to occur.

Perhaps the most obvious mechanism through which cultural values can affect economic growth is formation. Cultural values determine how much time and money parents decided to spend on the education of their children and what would be in the curriculum. To some extent, this is determined by their own preferences: do they care sufficiently about their children so that they act altruistically to maximize the child's welfare? Or are they acting wholly selfishly, to maximize the revenues and other services they can extract from their children? Or are they simply trying to do their best to make their children believe in their own cultural variants, maximizing some kind of similarity index to themselves? Or was there something more elaborate at work, such as a signaling game the parents played with other adults? How do they trade off the number of children against the resources they spend on the education of each one?

Investment in human capital is still widely regarded to be of central importance to all economic development. Education and economic development are both regarded as desirable phenomena. What could be a more reassuring idea than that they were closely associated? The seminal paper on the matter (Nelson and Phelps, 1966) was published almost a half century ago. It postulated that both technological advance and technological catch-up depend strongly on the level of human capital.[7] In his presidential address, Richard A. Easterlin (1981) posed the basic question: Why isn't the whole world developed? His answer was quite unambiguous: modern economic growth depended on the diffusion and absorption of new techniques. But technology has to be learned, and the diffusion of modern technology thus depends on formal or informal schooling. In a more recent paper, Glaeser et al. (2004), criticizing the view that differences in *institutions* are central to the explanation of differences in economic performance, point to differences in schooling and school attendance as the variable that best explains differences in economic outcomes. A large literature has emerged that views investment in human capital as a central factor in economic growth, although it is remote from reaching a consensus on most details.

But who exactly makes the decision to invest in human capital and why? And what form does the human capital take: general erudition? specific skills, and if the latter, productive ones? Clearly decisions about human

---

[7] For a recent restatement and elaboration, as well as empirical support, on this view, see Benhabib and Spiegel, 2005.

capital cannot be understood without cultural underpinnings. Three general categories of human capital can be distinguished: *training*, in which skills and useful knowledge are transmitted to the child; *education,* in which the ability to consume certain goods and services—we can think of them as hobbies—is taught (for example, music, literature, and sports) and in which certain values (moral codes, loyalty, respect for others, nationalism, and religion) are transmitted; and *drilling,* in which a child is taught such behaviors as politeness, table manners, hygiene, punctuality, and obedience. Decisions are made at two levels: how much to invest in children, and what kind of education to provide. These clearly reflect cultural elements, that is, what society believes to be important, and there was enormous diversity and variability in what was conveyed to youngsters and the extent to which "education" and what we would call today "human capital" diverged in the past, from Jewish lads trained to excel in Talmudic exegesis to clockmaker apprentices in London to Chinese youngsters strenuously preparing for the Civil Service examinations by studying the classics of ancient Chinese philosophy. Because the decision is usually made jointly by the child, the parents, and third parties of some kind such as religious or secular authorities, there is often subtle and complex bargaining that occurs among these players.

Interestingly enough, most scholars have paid comparatively little attention to possible differences in human capital and education between East and West in explaining the Great Divergence, though there have been some important exceptions such as Galor (2011), Davids (2013), and Jan Luiten van Zanden and his collaborators (for instance, Baten and van Zanden, 2008; De Pleijt and van Zanden, 2013), who argue for a rise in human capital in Western Europe that started centuries before the Industrial Revolution and is claimed to have had a causal effect on economic growth. It is difficult to compare levels of human capital across such large geographical and cultural distances, but on the whole there is little evidence indeed that by 1700 or so China was, in some sense, less "educated" and "literate" than Europe. Indeed, as we shall see, there is good reason to believe that by most standard measures, it was more so. Yet modern economic growth did not start in China.

The problem with the theory that regards human capital as a driver of technological progress is double. First, it is not at all clear that the education provided to youngsters in the past had much practical or economic value. Schools for the working masses—with some exceptions —did not teach much beyond basic literacy and a great deal of religion.[8] Education for

---

[8]   An example of such education were the projects of famous English writer and educator Hannah More (1745–1833) who founded twelve charity schools in Somerset county in the 1780s. The highly religious character of the evangelical schools, and More's insistence that children be taught reading but not writing (because of her fear that if children were too educated,

the higher classes was richer and far more diverse, but the evidence that this education by itself made major contributions to technology is at best mixed. To be sure, in the upper tail of the distribution we see a small group of scientists, physicians, engineers, and mathematicians who were pushing the frontier of useful knowledge. Yet the fields that mattered, such as mathematics, physics, and engineering, were not taught much in early modern Europe, and it is perhaps only in medicine that some spillovers from education to technology can be discerned (many physicians were also trained in chemistry). Moreover, investing in education on the extensive margin (that is, spreading it to a large portion of the population) did not have much effect. Indeed, David Mitch, the leading authority on the subject, has argued that Britain may have been over-educated on the eve of the Industrial Revolution (Mitch, 1999). The great engineers and inventors who made the Industrial Revolution were rarely well educated.[9] Few of them went to the universities, and many of them acquired their knowledge on their own or through private networks.[10] James Watt was educated at a good grammar school but never had a formal education beyond that, though he networked with some of the best scientists at Glasgow University and was tutored in reading the textbook of the Dutch Newtonian Willem 's Gravesande (1720). John Smeaton, Watt's rival for the position of the best engineer of the age, was also largely self-taught in the art of what was known at the time as "philosophical instruments," though he, too, cultivated friendships and correspondences with people from whom he felt he could learn (Skempton, 2002, p. 619).

The second doubt that arises concerning the relation between education and economic development is simply that neither by comparing today's economies nor by looking at history does it become obvious that

they might communicate dissatisfaction with their status in society), limited the effectiveness of these schools as a source of human capital. Her explicit purpose was to train the lower classes in the habits of industry and piety—and here "industry" means diligence.

[9] Data show that out of 498 applied scientists and engineers born between 1700 and 1850, 329 had no university education at all. The proportion of notable engineers with no university education in the eighteenth century was 71 percent. Out of a sample of 244 inventors born before 1820, only 68 had enjoyed higher-level training. See Birse (1983) and Khan (2006).

[10] The great engineer George Stephenson, who built the famous "Rocket" locomotive that won the Rainhill Trials marking the beginning of the railway age in Britain, was entirely self-trained in engineering skills and learned to read and write at the age of eighteen; later in life he employed a secretary to conduct his correspondence because of his poor literacy skills. Many others in the industry similarly had at best an informal education: the great mechanical engineer Richard Roberts, the inventor of—among many things—the self-acting mule, "received next to no education, and as soon as he was of fitting age was put to common laboring work. For some time he worked in a quarry near his father's dwelling; but being of an ingenious turn, he occupied his leisure in making various articles of mechanism, partly for amusement and partly for profit" (Smiles, 1876, p. 321). More recent scholarship has modified this account but still concludes that he was more interested in making things than learning about them (Hills, 2002, p. 9).

Easterlin's (1981) hypothesis passes with flying colors. Some contemporary development economists have expressed the almost heretical view that despite huge investments in education, the response of economic growth to the "education explosion" has been little or none (Easterly, 2001, p. 73). There has been little visible return to the large amounts invested in education in developing countries in the 1990s. Econometric work (Pritchett, 2001) has found little support for a major role for education in explaining economic progress.

A closer historical examination of the postulated role of human capital in growth also suggests that, alas, education (or human capital more generally) is not a magic formula for rapid economic development. Historically, Britain, the technological leader of Europe and the first industrial nation, had a mediocre record in terms of schooling, whereas Prussia and Scandinavia with high literacy were, in Lars Sandberg's (1979) memorable phrase "impoverished sophisticates" until late in the nineteenth century. Closer to our own time, even European countries that had achieved high levels of human capital under communism do not seem to have been uniformly able to take advantage of it. Belarus and Moldova, two of the more economically backward nations in Europe with the weakest institutions, still have respectable educational statistics, but in these countries the investment in human capital has been more difficult to translate into economic success after 1989 than it has been in Estonia or Poland.

Besides the attitudes toward education, other cultural values may affect technological progress indirectly. As already mentioned in chapter 2, social psychologists classify some societies as more individualistic than others, and it seems plausible that individualistic societies have more incentives for would-be innovators, because they tend to reward individuals who in some sense stand out. Societies may also be "vertical"— promising upward mobility to individuals who excel in some area (Triandis, 1995, pp. 43–52). None of this is enough to generate sustained technological progress: technologically conservative societies could be individualistic, but it seems reasonable that a high level of creativity and originality is probably more likely in highly individualistic societies. As Triandis notes, "collectivism ... often increases the probability of conformity to group norms and results in the development of strong traditions" (Triandis, 1995, pp. 101–2). There is also a related and interesting distinction between "tight" and "loose" societies (Triandis, 1995, pp. 52–57). A society is *tight* if there is wide agreement on what is true and what constitutes correct action, if most people behave very much according to the norms and rules dictated by this consensus, and if deviations are severely criticized and penalized. Triandis suggests the United States as an example of a loose society and Tokugawa Japan as an extreme example of a tight society. Again, it seems plausible that the kind of thinking outside the box and willingness to rebel against accepted practices and norms that are associated with technological creativity would be more common in loose societies.

What has not received enough attention in the recent literature in which economists have begun to reexamine the effect of culture on economic development is the matter of cultural beliefs regarding the relationship between humans and their physical environment and the virtuousness of technology. If the natural environment is treated with too much respect or fear and if the aversion to playing God or angering a deity was too strong, the willingness of humans to manipulate their physical settings for their material benefit could be impeded. Similarly, if nature is regarded as unfathomable and beyond human comprehension, or as totally arbitrary and capricious, there can be little advantage in controlling it for human purposes. These attitudes bring us back to religion.

Early modern Europe, for the first time in many centuries, offered its people a choice between traditional Catholicism and an array of Protestant religions. Moreover, doubts had crept in about the content of religion in the skeptical minds of radical thinkers such as Cremonini, Spinoza, Sarpi, and Toland. Full-blown atheism was still largely in the future despite accusations and trials, but the doubts gnawing at the very core of the beliefs of Christian culture indicate the profundity of the debate in the Republic of Letters. For many, if not for all, religion became a matter of choice, even when such choices had consequences.

Religion was instrumental in the creation of both Smithian and Schumpeterian growth. Its impact on Smithian growth was complex and multifaceted. First, some religions insisted on investment in human capital, above all literacy, so that young people would be socialized to participate in rituals that required reading. The Jewish religion made it more or less mandatory for all males to be literate, and Lutherans insisted on literacy as well. Although the main purpose of literacy was clearly non-economic, it spilled over into economic activities. Recent research on both Jewish and Protestant communities bear this out (Becker and Woeßmann, 2009; Botticini and Eckstein, 2012). Whether such literacy (and the numeracy that usually accompanied literacy when children were taught the three Rs as a package) actually had much of an impact on technology and innovation is anything but clear. It did, however, allow correspondence, written contracts, computations, and bookkeeping which reduced transactions costs and thus facilitated commerce. At a more advanced level, education could train individuals to enable markets and trade through the work of lawyers, notaries, judges, accountants and the like. Some recent research has argued that the founding of universities in Germany in the late Middle Ages and the training of legal expert stimulated economic development through this kind of mechanism, an example of upper-tail human capital affecting the economy at large (Cantoni and Yuchtman, 2014).

Second, in some religions, religious bodies often assumed judicial functions and took it upon themselves to act as the makers of commercial law and third-party arbiters. The Jewish codes that were created in the first half of the first millennium dealt to a large extent with settling commercial disputes.[11] The *responsa*, a body of answers to questions issued by rabbinical authorities, was for many centuries a means of lubricating commerce between Jews. Interestingly, the function of religion as a means toward dispute-resolution seemed a largely Jewish (and later Muslim) feature; Christianity, it appears, had at first little interest in copying the Jewish civil-society institutions and in early Christianity the church was by and large reluctant to enter into commercial disputes.[12] Third, religious communities, especially among minorities, created a shared social identity and a solidarity among its members that created a level of trust that made exchange between its members more likely. In small and highly networked communities, credible information about defectors could be readily diffused, defectors could be fingered and then penalized largely by collective decisions to remove them from a remunerative position. The knowledge that such penalties were enforceable induced agents, on the whole, to maintain above all a reputation of being honest and trustworthy and thus behave cooperatively. This mechanism allowed Maghribi trade to prosper (Greif, 2005). Yet solidarity among members of a small religious minority in other ways provided them with a level of cooperation that bred success. The remarkable success of Quakers in the British Industrial Revolution is an illustration of such groups (Mokyr, 2009a, p. 362). The flip side of this argument is that religious fragmentation between monotheistic religions led to enhanced distrust of others who did not share the same convictions. It often resulted in violent conflicts that seriously disrupted trade both between Christians and Muslims, and in the sixteenth century among Christians of different persuasions.

Finally, an argument has been made that certain types of religion fostered cooperation and discouraged opportunistic and dishonest behaviors. Many religions postulated an omniscient and moral God who meted out divine justice to those who did not play by the rules and exhibited opportunistic behavior. Shariff, Norenzayan, and Henrich (2009) postulate that cultural evolution favored a belief in a committed omniscient deity who cared about cooperation and would punish opportunistic and overly selfish

---

[11] Of the six orders of the Mishna, the fourth, *Nezikin* (torts or damages) deals largely with commercial and real matters, especially the first three known as "the three babas" or (gates).

[12] As one authority has pointed out, "The task of the [early] Church is not to organize courts to govern real estate transactions and decide commercial disputes. Even though it may not have been deemed seemly to turn pagan courts for the settlement of such disputes among Christians, it is not easy to point to literature of the character of the division of Damages, or, all the more so, for this period, to describe a fully exposed Christian system of civil law and government parallel to that of Mishnah" (Neusner, 1980, p. 430).

individuals who committed "sins." This faith, it is argued, led to a significant growth in cooperative behavior in societies in which monitoring costs tended to be high and punishing defectors was difficult. It suggests altruistic behavior and an adherence to certain fairness norms even toward strangers. If cooperation in the group could be maintained, a higher living standard would mean increased fitness, and the group would grow relative to others. There is some theoretical work and experimental data to back up this theory.[13] Strong religious beliefs also contributed to the resolution of asymmetric information situations, as these were an element in trying to encourage truth-telling by making witnesses swear a holy oath, with a strong implication of severe divine punishment if broken. Again, the flip side is that it is not clear how strong the strength of the commitment between members of different religions was. More damaging to this line of argument, Eastern religions lacking a personal God functioning as a moral policeman were still able to develop a great deal of trust and economic cooperation in the trade networks based on them. As late as the eighteenth century the commercial integration of China was comparable to that of Europe, and little evidence suggests that Chinese merchants had less effective cooperative institutions than did Christians. It seems plausible that an omniscient and just enforcer of honest behavior was one but far from the only means toward establishing an efficient commercial economy.

At times, however, religious differences could lead to positive economic outcomes because pluralism fostered a spirit of what eighteenth-century writers called "emulation," the strong desire to avoid "falling behind the competition." The rivalry among different European religions after the Western Christian Church lost its monopoly in the West in the sixteenth century is particularly relevant here. Following the challenge of the Reformation, this position was contested and the resulting response created a large boost to the formation of human capital. Much scholarly and educational work was undertaken for the purpose of demonstrating the superiority of and attaining a victory for a branch of the now divided Western Christianity (Grafton, 2009a, p. 11). The role of the Jesuits, an order established explicitly to defend Catholicism from competing Christian faiths in the formation of human capital in the West and elsewhere, is too well known to need elaboration here. One of the main instruments they relied on was education. What is striking, however, is that Jesuit schools emphasized

---

[13] The argument is basically that in any non-cooperative setting it is costly to punish free riders, while the benefits are shared with non-punishers and thus create an externality and making cooperative outcomes more difficult to attain. Religious beliefs, by postulating an external punisher with low or zero cost of monitoring and punishing, would help solve this problem. This implies that religious societies, in which such beliefs were prevalent, would have higher inclusive fitness. Moreover, even if people were unsure about the existence of this supernatural punishing agency, it would be rational for them to stick to Pascal's wager and behave as if they believed in it. See for instance Johnson and Krüger (2004) and Johnson (2009).

not just religious and moral teaching but also insisted on the inclusion of useful knowledge such as mathematics and physics in the curricula. Many of the great thinkers of the era, including such seventeenth-century luminaries as Peiresc, Descartes, Torricelli, and Mersenne, and Enlightenment writers such as Condorcet, Helvétius, and Diderot went to their schools. As Feingold (2003) has argued, in this way Jesuits made significant contributions to useful knowledge at the time, even if the innovations their former students produced were not always to their taste. Jesuit institutions introduced an element of competition into the market for education in Europe, and in the late sixteenth century they even competed with the distinguished University of Padua, a competition that led to the banishment of Jesuits from the Venetian Republic (Muir, 2007, pp. 24–27). In Catholic France, too, competition among different religious movements led to competition in the educational sphere, such as the competition between Jesuit and Jansenist schools.[14]

The Jesuit Order itself was more than conservative; it was—to use an anachronistic term—reactionary. A notorious committee of the Jesuit Collegio Romano (established in 1601) known as the "Revisors General" mercilessly weeded out from all Jesuit curricula items that were deemed contrary to accepted doctrine—above all Copernicanism. Even the role of mathematics in its teaching was a matter of fierce debate. In their teaching of mathematics in the seventeenth century and beyond, the Jesuits "never deviated from their commitment to Euclidian geometry" because that was a "deeply held ideological commitment ... to demonstrate how universal truth imposed itself on the world" (Alexander, 2014, p. 74).[15] The General of the Order, Claudio Acquaviva, wrote in 1584 that Jesuits should avoid not only innovation but also make sure that nobody "suspects us of creating anything new or teaching a new doctrine ... no one shall defend any opinion that goes against the axioms received in philosophy or in theology" (quoted in Feingold, 2003, p. 18). What they meant by these axioms is clear: the late medieval Thomist synthesis between orthodox Aristotelian and Catholic doctrine (Ariew, 2003, pp. 162–63). For individual Jesuits, who pursued

[14] The fifteen-year-old Denis Diderot switched halfway through his education from the Jesuit school Louis LeGrand to the Jansenist college d'Harcourt (today the Lycée St. Louis), indicating (perhaps) that his sympathies were already moving away from rigid Jesuit thinking (Blom, 2010, p. 12).

[15] Cohen (2012, pp. 146–47) points out that the education of Europe's elites in order to strengthen the counter-reformation was one of the main objectives of the Jesuits and that the Jesuits made a supreme effort to reconcile the Aristotelian system with what Cohen calls "mixed mathematics" by which he means "applied mathematics," used in astronomy, calendar calculation, the analysis of music, and so on. The aging eminent Jesuit mathematician, Christopher Clavius (1538– 1612), at first welcomed Galileo's telescopic discoveries and only later did the order turn against it. In the end, Cohen concludes, Jesuits were constrained by the preconceived notions imposed on the Jesuit intellectuals (Cohen, 2012, pp. 212, 495).

secular studies and may have been sympathetic toward the New Science, this could have created serious conflict.[16] Many of them disguised and hid their views in textbooks between pious pronunciations on the sanctity of classical writing. Yet even the Jesuits were eventually forced to relent in their resistance to the new astronomy and the new mathematics. Confirmation bias and coercion bias had to make way to content bias.[17]

Religious competition was also an important factor in Britain, where the Church of England had to contend with dissenters, who founded the "dissenting academies" (Stone, 1969). These were progressive schools in England, that taught geography, mathematics, chemistry, languages, and useful skills in addition to heterodox religion. In some cases a symbiotic division of labor emerged between a small religious minority and the great majority of people.[18] During the British Industrial Revolution, the entrepreneurial role of dissenters was unusually large because they were barred from many official occupations and they developed a high-quality educational system. In other societies, too, peaceful competition among religions, much like peaceful competition between states, encouraged intellectual innovation and progress.[19]

[16] The Austrian Jesuit mathematician Christoph Grienberger (1561–1636) confided in 1613 to Galileo that "I don't have the same freedom as you" and his colleague Piero Dini told Galileo two years later that "many Jesuits shared his views but have to keep quiet" (Feingold, 2003, p. 23)

[17] The stark contrast drawn by Alexander (2014, p. 177), who juxtaposes the Jesuits who fostered a "totalitarian dream of seamless unity that left no room for doubt or debate" with the Galileans who believed in a vision that "allowed for room and debate ... that opened the way for scientific progress [and] for political and religious pluralism" is somewhat overdrawn. Jesuit scientists had to compete in the marketplace for ideas with the growing strength of the cumulative insights that evolved in Europe after the Galilean breakthroughs, which they could not afford to ignore. By the middle of the eighteenth century, compromises were reached in the writings of moderate Jesuits, such as Francesco Antonio Zaccaria (Dooley, 2003).

[18] In a classic statement, Yuri Slezkine (2004) describes the division of labor between a domestic resident farming community he called "Appolonians" and a service minority ("Mercurians") that provides the kind of support that the locals cannot provide for themselves

[19] Chaney (2008, 2015) has argued that there was a direct connection between the flourishing of Islamic science in the early stages of Islam and the degree of religious competition, both within Islam and between Islam and other religions. He points to the the desire of Muslims to convert others to their religion by means of rational debate and superior knowledge. Forced conversions were discouraged by Islam, and in any case were impractical given the sheer numbers of non-Muslims in the lands they controlled. Muslim authorities encouraged the study of logic for use in winning converts. Chaney argues that this policy fostered an environment in which science could thrive and also led to an increase in intra-Muslim debates that prevented the rise of a repressive orthodoxy. The growth of Sunni power in the eleventh and twelfth centuries reduced religious diversity and pluralism throughout the Islamic world. As religious competition declined through conversion and the growing political power of Sunni clerics, Islamic original science began to decline some time around the twelfth century (Chaney, 2015, pp. 18–19).

Despite the fierce competition among religions for the souls of believers, it is striking how blithely intellectuals bridged or ignored altogether the chasms between different religions. The Republic of Letters on the whole seems to have paid fairly little heed to the religious beliefs of its citizens. Grafton (2009a, p. 12) explains that it was regarded morally wrong to break off scholarly communication with people of different religious convictions, because such "restrictions could only hamper the flow of information and ideas." Moreover, citizens of the Republic of Letters argued against religious persecution, a voice that became louder as wars of religion increasingly showed themselves to be destructive and pointless after 1562. Prominent citizens of the Republic of Letters, from Sebastian Castellio (1515–1563) to Spinoza to Voltaire, argued for religious tolerance and against the persecution of apostates (Zagorin, 2003).[20] Even scholars of fundamentalist religious beliefs, such as the great Swiss Huguenot polymath Louis Bourguet (1678–1742), were able to develop what Barnett (2015, p. 149) has felicitously called a "strategy of toleration" in which deeply felt religious differences were papered over in scientific exchanges and a scholarly civility was maintained despite private outrage at the heretical opinions of "unbelievers." The Republic of Letters is an illustration of Cipolla's (1972, p. 52) remark that the same qualities that make people tolerant also make them receptive to new ideas.

The historical evidence regarding the net effect of religion on Smithian growth is thus rather ambiguous. In antiquity, pagan Phoenicia, Greece, and Rome were able to generate a great deal of trade criss-crossing the Mediterranean and adjacent waterways, whereas the monotheistic Jews were by and large a farming society. Moreover, for whatever reason, the first centuries of Christianity were accompanied by a rise in barbarism and an institutional and commercial decline in Europe, and any suggestion that Christianity as such created a civil society and enhanced economic performance as such is sheer nonsense.[21] The spread of Christianity in its first half-millennium in Europe did not significantly increase the level of commerce—quite the reverse. It could, of course, be argued that the rise of Christianity was to some extent a result of the economic collapse of classical society and

---

[20] Grafton (2009a) points out that Castellio acted on his indignation about the execution of Miguel Servetus in Geneva in 1553 in a scholarly way appropriate to a citizen of the Republic of Letters: he researched the issue and used documentary evidence to demonstrate that the violent persecution of heterodox thinkers was opposed to Christian doctrine. While at first a distinct minority view, Castellio's work was picked up by later writers and eventually became part of a late seventeenth-century ideology of tolerance. "Such characteristic Enlightenment attitudes grew from the speculations of learned men," notes Grafton (2009a, pp. 12–13).

[21] For an extreme view asserting that the roots of all economic and social progress are in medieval Christianity, see Stark, 2003.

that its growth mitigated the worst effects of the decline. All the same, the association appears weak.

What about the influence of religious beliefs on Schumpeterian growth, the kind of growth that was driven by advances in useful knowledge? Early modern Europe was a deeply religious age. As Hooykaas (1972, p. 101) argued, the pervasiveness of religion meant that for *any* idea to become socially acceptable, it made a huge difference whether it was resisted, tolerated, or sponsored by prevalent religious beliefs. Christopher Hill (1967, p. 112) has pointed out that control of the pulpit had huge cultural and political importance, because it was one of the main ways of influencing people, comparable to modern mass media. Powerful orators could impart a great deal of rhetorical bias on the beliefs of the masses, and hence religious control affected the way people thought about their world, including their relationship with their physical environment. In short, religion needs to be considered as a factor in the historical development of useful knowledge.

An earlier generation of historians saw a fundamental and irrepressible conflict between scientific innovation and religion. The great Thomist synthesis, in which Christianity was merged with Aristotelian physics and metaphysics in the late Middle Ages became a deeply entrenched dogma that resisted any encroachment. More than a century ago this classic liberal view was expressed in Andrew Dickson White's book (1896). A serious conflict could easily erupt between the formal institutions of religion (such as the Church) and natural philosophers simply over the question of who had a monopoly over discovering and revealing the Truth, and who had the right to anoint the experts who decided those cases in which there was doubt. After all, direct bias involves such authorities, and part of the conflict was about whose pronouncements on the structure of the universe were to be believed, those of Galileo or of Pope Paul V.

The relationship between religion and the advance of useful knowledge in this age cannot be summarized simply as either the conflict between progressive scientists and benighted clerics, as White would have it, or as Hooykaas (1972) and others argued, that Christian beliefs were the taproot and inspiration of seventeenth-century science. Religion in this age was a large tent that contained a plethora of attitudes toward science; some aspects of modern science were compatible with some religious beliefs, but on the whole the relation cannot be summarized as either one of conflict or one of harmony. A complex and multivariate interlocking of scientific interests and religious beliefs coexisted within the larger European context, in each community, and often in the same person (Lindberg and Numbers, 1986, p. 10).

As in every other aspect of culture, religious beliefs came under skeptical re-assessment in the sixteenth century, not only through the Reformation but also subsequently in each religious group. It is striking how deeply and abruptly theologians, natural philosophers, medical doctors, and astronomers began deviating from accepted religious and scientific doctrines, while clearly staying safely and indisputably within the Christian faith as they saw it. Science and religion in the sixteenth century were deeply intertwined in complex fashions, far more than was the case, say, in the eighteenth century. An example is the Spanish physician Miguel Servetus, who had decided at an early age that the doctrine of Trinity was false, and after he studied medicine this led him to reject, as a parallel, the triadic structure of body functions (nutrition, muscular activity, and mental activity) that was part of the Galenian medical orthodoxy of his time (Mason, 1992, p. 8). Such astronomers as Johannes Kepler and physicists as William Gilbert, after accepting the heliocentric hypothesis, suggested that God might be living in the sun, the center of the Universe.[22]

All over seventeenth-century Europe, science and religion discovered a range of possible symbiotic relations. In England this was expressed in the deep Anglican beliefs of Robert Boyle and the somewhat eccentric but deeply felt religious sentiments of Newton. But everywhere similar compromises can be discerned: Italian Jesuits, English Puritans, French Catholic friars, pre-adamites, unitarians, and devout Dutch Calvinists—all found a way to reconcile their religious beliefs with their scientific activities. The eighteenth century was not an age of atheism (though some of the leading *philosophes* clearly were) but it is striking that religion's role in sustaining and supporting science declined during the Enlightenment. It is not hard to see why: whether Catholic or Protestant, natural philosophers in the seventeenth century found evidence of God in Nature, and this was an impersonal mechanical God who was revealed in his immutable laws, to which he himself was subject. This was not a judgmental entity concerned with enforcing a morality or granting rewards for good behavior, much less engaged in miracles. But in the sixteenth and seventeenth centuries things were still different. As Westfall (1986, pp. 234–35) has put it, the new natural philosophy put forward by such scientists as Kepler, Descartes, and Newton could not avoid the question whether the aspects of Christianity that distinguished it from a more impersonal theism held up in view of their growing knowledge of nature.

Technology involves in a deep sense "playing God," that is, making deliberate and irreversible changes in the original natural physical environment to solve an economic need and further a material interest. Every human society has altered its natural environment permanently to make a living, often with dramatic ecological effects, such as the extinction

---

[22] In his magnum opus, *De Humani Corporis Fabrica* (1543) the Belgian physician Andreas Vesalius, who single-handedly overturned Galen's work on anatomy, felt it necessary to add that "By not first explaining the bones anatomists ... deter [the student] from a worthy examination of the works of God" (quoted in O'Malley, 2008, p. 8).

of large mammals on the American continent or the great deforestation in China in the eighteenth century. Where to draw the line between permissible and impermissible interventions remains a difficult issue. Why do some areas of technological activity—such as cloning humans or creating new forms of life through genetic engineering—find themselves beyond the pale even today? Which activities involve an inadmissable level of "playing God" is clearly a question of cultural beliefs about religion.

In other words, culture determines not just the parameters of interpersonal games but also those of games against nature. Anthropocentric views of the world, as found in Judeo-Christian (but much less in Eastern) religious beliefs, were one way to overcome the sense of guilt that humankind often displays when manipulating nature and altering the landscape. Such beliefs placed humankind in the center of the universe and viewed the rest of nature as having been placed there by the Creator to serve humans. If humans were created in "God's image," they were different from all other living beings, a view that is increasingly contested in our age but was axiomatic in early modern Europe. By harnessing nature for human purposes, engineers did not sin against the deity, but quite the opposite: they demonstrated his wisdom in designing a rational, mechanical universe (Benz, 1966).

Medieval historians have noted that this culture became increasingly important in the high Middle Ages in Europe. As Lynn White (1978, p. 27) has pointed out, if the world was created merely for the *spiritual* edification of humankind and served no other purpose, the simplicity of Eden and harmony with the rest of creation might have been a sufficient road to bliss. What was needed for a progressive culture was to be concerned with *material* conditions and an aggressive attitude toward the manipulation of natural phenomena and regularities. In White's view this cultural change began in the twelfth century, although it came to its fullest and most explicit expression in the writings of Francis Bacon, more than four centuries later.[23] Such attitudes were never a necessary condition for technological advances to occur: societies without a concept of a personal God, such as Confucian China, proved themselves perfectly capable of generating innovations, many of them sufficiently disruptive and pathbreaking to alter the environment in dramatic ways. Medieval China altered its environment no less than Europe did: if in Europe the environment was transformed by the axe to carry out deforestation and the improved plough to cultivate the new lands, in China a lot depended on water management

---

[23] Elsewhere White noted that "The Christian Creator God, the architect of the cosmos and the potter who shaped man from clay in his own image, commands man to rule the world" and as occidental medieval machines became more intricate, "God the builder developed into God the mechanic" (White, 1978, pp. 236, 239).

and irrigation through sluices and ditches (Elvin, 1973, p. 113).[24] It is now widely agreed that White may have underestimated the technological achievements of classical Rome and thus exaggerated the discontinuity that medieval Europe presented in technological development.[25] But despite numerous qualifications and criticisms, his broad emphasis on the religious elements of medieval technology has endured (Livingstone, 1994). Modern research, too, stresses the significance of religion for certain cultural variants that matter to innovation.[26]

Attitudes toward manual labor were another cultural variable in which religion played an important part. In medieval Europe, the "regular" church (monks) developed a set of cultural beliefs encapsulated by the *laborare est orare* slogan of the Benedictine monks (White, 1978). Production and work became virtues, and thus educated and intelligent individuals became involved in them. In medieval times, that meant to a large extent men of the church. Hooykaas ([1956], 1990, pp. 194–96; 1972, pp. 88–94) and Benz (1966), among others, have emphasized the growing cultural belief that physical labor was respectable and that artisans were to be honored and esteemed. In medieval Europe, some monastic orders served as the bridge between propositional knowledge, such as it was, and its technological applications. For centuries these monks were at the cutting edge of technological change in Western Europe. Regardless of whether or not the Western church in the Middle Ages can really carry the heavy historical weight that Lynn White has placed on it, it is clear that any discussion of the origins of technological creativity in the medieval West must consider its religious origins.

The idea that important knowledge was embodied in the work of artisans can be found in the writings of some early sixteenth-century

---

[24] Some modern scholars have argued that the view that stressed the "harmonious" relation between humans and nature in China (as suggested by Needham and others) is overstated, and that even in early dynasties such as the Zhou (1046–256 BC) there are clearcut signs of a merciless exploitation and plundering of the physical environment. For example, see Roetz (2010, p. 217), who argues that "the school of Confucianism discovered clearly positive sides to the subjugation of nature, seeing in it the presupposition of all culture."

[25] The dismissal of White's view that a cultural transformation in the medieval Occident led to a different attitude toward technology and thus to a different agenda, as in Davids (2013), seems unwarranted. The seeds of the notion that work, production, and commerce were "virtuous" and somehow sacred were clearly medieval in origin and were to have long-term consequences in the changing attitudes toward production in the early modern period documented by Zilsel (1942), McCloskey (2006), and others.

[26] Modern social psychology research has established a negative correlation between a variable named "self direction" (independent thought, creativity, willingness to explore) and a single measure of "religiosity," with a correlation of about –.35. Interestingly enough, the correlation was little different between Israeli Jews, Dutch Protestants, Spanish Catholics and Greek Orthodox in Greece. See Schwartz and Huismans (1995).

intellectuals railing against scholastic philosophy, which they claimed was writing about nature without knowing much about it and working with wholly imaginary constructs. Instead, the peasants, the navigators, the craftsmen, and the surgeons were those who interfaced with natural phenomena on a daily basis, and therefore their experiences were all the more valuable. Such ideas were a new departure. The medieval tradition is illustrated by a statement from the master builder who built the Milan Cathedral, who wrote in 1392 that science had been one thing, the useful arts (that is, technology) quite another (cited by Cipolla, 1980, p. 243). In the early Renaissance this became, if anything, worse, but after 1500 we see the cultural tide slowly turning. One of the first and most articulate and respected of the scholars trying to raise the standing of artisanal skills was the Catalan-born Juan Luis Vives (1493–1540), a leading humanist of his age. He spent most of his life in Flanders—at the time a major industrial center—and made a strong argument in favor of the value of artisanal knowledge.[27] By the early seventeenth century this argument had carried the day among many European intellectuals. Tommaso Campanella's utopian work *City of the Sun* (1602) explicitly expounded the dignity of the mechanical arts and manual labor.[28]

The theme of communication between scientists and producers is not new: Edgar Zilsel (1942) emphasized its importance in European development. Zilsel noted that already in the sixteenth century it started dawning on people that something could be gained from an exchange of information between the learned and the skilled.[29] Zilsel pointed out that

---

[27] Vives wrote in his *De Trandendis Disciplinis* (1531) that "He [the student] should not be ashamed to enter into shops and factories, and to ask questions from craftsmen, and get to know about the details of their work. Formerly, learned men disdained to inquire into those things which it is of such great import to life to know. ... This then is the fruit of all studies; this is the goal. Having acquired our knowledge, we must turn it to usefulness and employ it for the common good. Whence follows immortal reward not in money, not in present favour, or pleasures, which are fleeting and momentary. ... We ought therefore, not always to be studying, but our study must be attuned to practical usefulness in life" (Watson, 1913, pp. 209, 283–84).

[28] In his imaginary state, the citizens "considered the noblest man to be the one that has mastered the most skills ... the more laborious and utilitarian tasks, like those of the blacksmith and mason, are the more praiseworthy and nobody shuns them" (Campanella, [1602] 1981, p. 81). He noted, with some exaggeration, that he learned more from the anatomy of one plant than from all the books in the world, a sentiment that reverberated with many intellectuals of the age, none more so than the influential French polymath Peiresc (Miller, 2000, p. 23).

[29] One example is the fictional *Accademia Segreta* described by Girolamo Ruscelli (1518–1566) in the 1540s, in which academicians mixed with apothecaries, herbalists, gardeners, and other craftsmen to study their recipes and techniques. In it "artisans worked side by side with men of leisure and learning," and it serves as a remarkable and early example of the union of scholars and craftsmen (Eamon, 1985, p. 478). This description may have been more of a utopian vision than a reality, but it is clear that the idea was ripening in Europe even before Bacon (Long, 2011, pp. 94–96).

much of the technological change that occurred before 1600 came from the artisans and craftsmen, who were the "real pioneers of empirical observations, experimentation and causal research" (Zilsel, 1942, p. 551). In the late sixteenth and early seventeenth centuries, learned philosophers became interested in the work of artisans, and slowly but certainly a recognition of the value of exchanges between prescriptive knowledge and propositional knowledge began to coalesce. The bridges between propositional knowledge and prescriptive knowledge allowed a mutual inspiration and enrichment that was one of the cornerstones of the Industrial Enlightenment (Mokyr, 2002). Artisanal skills were necessary and thus appreciated by those who carried out experiments. They needed well-built instruments and laboratory equipment, often constructed by the researchers themselves. But they knew whom to learn these skills from. Bacon was not alone and not the first to realize this. The French philosopher and logician Petrus Ramus (1515–1572) wrote proudly that he had visited every mechanical workshop in Paris more than once and advised other philosophers to do the same (Hooykaas, 1972, pp. 99–100).

A good example of the new thinking, anticipating in many ways the Industrial Enlightenment, was the work of the Dutch physicist Isaac Beeckman (1588–1637), a close friend and collaborator of Descartes. Jacob (1988, p. 52) has called Beeckman the first "mechanical philosopher of the Scientific Revolution." What is particularly striking about his work is his effort to build bridges between artisanal knowledge and natural philosophy. A recent biography notes that "Beeckman in a way is the missing link between artisanal knowledge and mathematical science. He is the perfect example of a 'liminal' figure between the world of scholarship and the crafts, someone who was actually able to incorporate an artisanal way of dealing with nature into a new and academically acceptable discourse on nature. ... His mechanical philosophy of nature was grounded in both the practical knowledge of a craftsman and the theoretical knowledge of a scholar" (Van Berkel, 2013, p. 4). At the same time, however, Beeckman was profoundly Baconian in that he fully realized how much the crafts could gain from a theoretical education (Van Berkel, 2013, pp. 139–40).

Another influential writer, from a different point of departure, was the French potter, hydrologist, and geologist author Bernard Palissy (ca. 1510–1590), who wrote a widely read and influential book titled *Discours Admirables*. As a scholar-craftsman, his approach to knowledge was highly experimental and empirical. He was convinced that practice was superior to theory and promised to prove the veracity of his ideas by convincing the human senses. Indeed his book was structured as a debate between theory and practice, in which practice was always correct (Amico, 1996, p. 43). Palissy proudly conceded that he was a modest potter ignorant of classical languages, but would openly challenge the theories of the ancient and modern physicians, alchemists, and philosophers (Deming, 2005, p. 971).

His writings were particularly critical of those academics contemptuous of the mechanical arts and artisanal knowledge. "I have no other book than the sky and the earth," he announced (Palissy, [1580] 1957, p. 148). Artisanal knowledge gained some respect, something that would come to full bloom in the writings of Francis Bacon, who may have attended one of Palissy's lectures when he visited Paris as a sixteen-year-old lad.

A sharp distinction between propositional and prescriptive knowledge (or science and technology if these terms are preferred), useful as it may be for analytical purposes, does not accurately describe the world of early modern Europe. The notion that all propositional knowledge was "open" is clearly not a good description for most of the period between 1500 and 1700, even if the trend toward growing open-ness is clear. Some scholars have proposed getting rid of such categories as "science" and "technology" altogether and instead proposed something like a "mindful hand" (Roberts and Schaffer 2007), which stresses the difficulty of drawing a line separating skill from knowledge.[30] In the process they wish to liberate us from the notion of the importance of past dramatic revolutions such as the Scientific Revolution and the Industrial Revolution and introduce new terms such as "ingenious aptitude" and "social circulation." More controversially, they eschew "a splendid narrative structure that would carry European cultures from primitive accumulation inevitably to industrial enlightenment." Splendid or not, the emergence of an industrial enlightenment remains at the center of what useful knowledge could do for the economy—much as Bacon had hoped for. Inevitable, of course, it was not, and their objection to deterministic models is apposite.

We should indeed stress that knowledge was produced by a continuous range of people, from mindful hands to handy minds, struggling with a large set of issues, described by some of the scholars working in this "new style" of the history of knowledge. In recent years these scholars have correctly pointed to a great deal of knowledge that was accumulated by what we may call practitioners: painters, architects, clockmakers, botanical collectors, even pyrotechnicians created useful knowledge (Smith and Schmidt, 2007). The term "practitioner" is not all that clear, and could include clever and imaginative artisans as well as well-trained scientists who were not afraid to get some dirt under their fingernails. It is not hard to think of natural philosophers such as Huygens and Hooke as dexterous natural philosophers capable of constructing their own instruments, but

---

[30] Roberts and Schaffer (2007, pp. xv–xvi) wish to abandon formulae that equate science with knowledge and technique with application and replace it with a collaborative effort engaged in inquiry and invention. They maintain that their argument is about more than just claiming that philosophers were "a handy lot" and craftsmen "were capable of thought." They are seeking to understand the "hybrid activities involved in the intimately related processes of material and knowledge production."

among the highly skilled instrument makers, physicians, artisans, alchemists, and engineers of the age struggling with a niggardly and recalcitrant nature (to say nothing of highly imperfect materials and tools), a body of applied knowledge arose that was circulated through the practical provinces of the Republic of Letters.[31] Much of the new and improved useful knowledge was indeed the result of what Roberts and Schaffer (2007, p. xxi) call "local technological projects" carried out by the "tacit genius of on-the-spot practitioners," but what made it significant was that it was carried out in a coherent cultural context in which ideas and techniques competed for acceptance and prestige in a larger European environment. The notion that theory and practice or "pure science" and "application" were somehow separate would have seemed strange indeed to scholars and practitioners of the time alike. Indeed most scholars were in some ways practitioners.[32] For a long time the Baconian dream of a production sphere enlightened by best-practice science was little more than an Enlightenment chimera. With a few notable exceptions, there was not all that much that seventeenth- and eighteenth-century artisans could learn from best-practice science to improve their productivity. At the same time, it has become abundantly clear that scientists learned a great deal from craftsmen and practitioners and clearly realized it, as Hooke's proposed catalog of all artisanal practices illustrates.

In addition to cultural beliefs about cooperation and relations with the physical environment, what matters to economic growth are personal preferences. Individuals are not hard-wired with a particular rate of time preference, that is to say, a degree of patience and willingness-to-delay-gratification, or other attitudes toward time, and it is easy to document that these differ a great deal across societies.[33] Such preferences are important, because they help determine not only the rate of savings and thus physical capital accumulation, but also of investment in human capital and skills. Doepke and Zilibotti (2008) argue that such preferences are learned behavior and term it "patience capital." They argue that it requires investment

[31] Long (2011), who provides a summary of this literature, has dated the beginning of this rapprochement between artisans and philosophers to 1400, but it seems clear that it did not switch into high gear until the sixteenth century with the technological descriptions in the work of such authors as Agricola and Ercker (mining), Taccola and Besson (machinery), Ramelli (pumps), which appeared in the sixteenth century.

[32] Hooke (1667) wrote in the preface to his *Micrographia* that "so many are the links, upon which the true Philosophy depends, of which, if any one be loose, or weak, the whole chain is in danger of being dissolv'd; it is to begin with the Hands and Eyes, and to proceed on through the Memory, to be continued by the Reason; nor is it to stop there, but to come about to the Hands and Eyes again, and so, by a continual passage round from one Faculty to another." Clearly the idea of the "mindful hand" was very much around at the time.

[33] These differences are well documented in Levine (1997).

by parents to instill into their offspring the willingness to invest in order to reap a higher income at a later time. Preferences about time mirror those about risk. Were some societies more prudent or risk averse than others? Almost all forms of economic growth require some risk-taking —what determines individuals' willingness to take such risks? At least one factor that seems plausible is the safety net that society provides in case things go wrong on a risky project. England in the centuries before the Industrial Revolution provided such a safety net in a formal way through the Poor Laws. In other societies safety nets were lessencompassing (religious and charitable organizations and extended families) and hence on the whole were less reliable. In this way it can be seen that institutions feed back into preferences in subtle and complex ways.

To summarize, then, in the past attitudes toward education, religion, and a variety of other beliefs and preferences had a significant impact on economic performance and Smithian growth through many channels, although it would be rash to assess them as unequivocally favorable or unfavorable on balance. A high level of commerce and good institutions were consistent with quite a few different sets of beliefs. On the whole, the environment for more efficient markets was becoming more favorable in medieval and early modern Europe, but this does not help us much in explaining the explosive increase in Schumpeterian growth after 1700.

Chapter 10

Cultural Change and the Growth of Useful Knowledge, 1500–1700

If we are to understand the Industrial Revolution and the launching of the West on a trajectory of sustained economic growth based increasingly on advances in science and technology, we must unearth what happened in the two centuries following Columbus's arrival in the New World. It was an age of considerable scientific advances, sometimes dubbed the Scientific Revolution. It was also an age of considerable technological advances in some areas, although these were less dramatic and pathbreaking than the advances made in the century just before or the ones to follow. What changed in this age was the culture—the beliefs and attitudes of the educated elite toward useful knowledge, how to acquire it, how to distribute it, and what it could do. Such changing beliefs led to new institutions reflecting them, and those institutions fed back into the beliefs. The net result was that by the middle of the eighteenth century the attitudes toward technology-driven material progress had changed dramatically, a phenomenon I have called in earlier work the Industrial Enlightenment and which was a foundation of the Industrial Revolution. But what were its cultural origins?

Had religion in the West been more uniformly hostile to mechanical culture and production technology, the medieval inventions so crucial to subsequent technological progress might never have flourished. But, as already noted, there were important elements in the medieval Christian Church that were deeply interested in technical matters. Indeed, some of the most sophisticated and clever writers on technology were monks, such as Roger Bacon (ca. 1214–1294) and Theophilus, author of *De Diversis Artibus* (ca. 1122). Lynn White's argument that monasteries were the spearhead of technological progress in the medieval occident has stood the test of time even if some of his other arguments and theories have not fared uniformly well. Monks were a large component of the intellectual elite of the Middle Ages, and the culture that determined economic outcomes in the past was the culture of the elites. If they had an interest in technology, there was hope

for technological progress, even if eventually the leadership shifted to secular scientists.

The two hundred years before the Black Death and the subsequent
centuries were a period of substantial technological progress in Europe. To
be sure, the contrast between a progressive Middle Ages and a technologically stagnant antiquity can be exaggerated. Earlier scholars, such as
Lynn White and Moses Findlay, underestimated the technological accomplishments of the Romans. New archaeological finds have demonstrated,
for example, that water power was far more widely used than was hitherto
supposed (Greene, 2000; Wilson, 2002). Yet none of this distracts from the
technological achievements of medieval Europe such as the invention of
heavy ploughs, mechanical clocks, spectacles, wind mills, iron-casting, firearms, and the shipping design and navigational equipment that eventually
allowed European to cross large oceans.

All the same, these advances failed to generate rapid and sustainable economic growth based on technological progress. There was no
medieval Industrial Revolution and for good reasons. One is that these
inventions were not based on a deep understanding of why and how the
techniques worked, and therefore they were likely to dead end in technological stasis early on. As I argued in Mokyr (2002), it is the coevolution
and mutual reinforcement of the technology in use and the knowledge on
which it is based that generates the kind of explosive dynamics we associate
with the modern era. Artisanal technology on its own can change conditions on the ground, the result of learning-by-doing on the part of clever
craftsmen, serendipitous inventions, and dogged trial and error. Advances
generated by such events in the past, however, have tended to fizzle out
unless they were accompanied by a parallel growth of the propositional
knowledge that explained why the inventions worked.

All the same, the pragmatic turn of the Occidental Church in the
high Middle Ages was a key event in modern economic history. In a society
that believed that technological activity was meant "to afford help to many
for the glory of God and for the exaltation of His name" as Theophilus put
it (cited in Klemm, 1964, p. 65) technological progress was possible.
Western medieval Christianity was a complex and heterogeneous entity. It
stressed an increasingly anthropocentric view of the world, in which it was
God's will that humans take advantage of the wisdom of his creation. Moreover, actual religious beliefs are quite a different matter from formal established doctrine, and both of them evolved during the Renaissance. Medieval inventions may not have produced sustainable Schumpeterian growth,
but as always, technological progress had unintended consequences, and
these affected the trajectory that Europe took after 1500. The progressive
attitudes of medieval culture were not guaranteed to last, and they did not;
by the fifteenth century, the Catholic Church had become more inward
looking, conservative, and averse to change. But it let the genie out of the
bottle. Technological creativity blossomed in fifteenth-century Europe,

including the invention of the movable-type printing press, the casting of iron, and major advances in shipbuilding and navigational instruments.

How should we think of the cultural changes relevant to subsequent economic development in the centuries between 1500 and 1700? As we have seen, religious beliefs were profoundly transformed in this age and in some ways made to coexist with and even encourage experimental science. Another important cultural element in the growth of technological creativity in early modern Europe is an openness to and willingness to absorb and exploit foreign ideas. Such openness was already noticeable in medieval Europe, but apart from the crusades, intellectual contacts with Islamic civilization in Spain and the Mediterranean, and the occasional Marco Polo type of traveler, Europe was not as much exposed to foreign ideas as it became after 1500. The cultural trait of openness has an interesting analogy in biology. Genetic transmission was long believed to be entirely limited to the genetic content of the organism's parents (combined in different ways). As already noted in chapter 3, it is now known that certain micro-organisms can actually receive genetic material from non-parent peers.[1] In culture, this kind of horizontal transmission is far more common and widespread, but receptivity to foreign ideas is quite variable among societies. A mechanism that has long been known to scholars working in cultural evolution is known as *transmission isolating mechanisms,* or TRIMs (Durham, 1992, pp. 333–35). TRIMs isolate a society from foreign cultural features, thus in some sense making its cultural macro-evolution more like biological evolution. The stronger these TRIMs, the more information is received from parents (and sources collinear with them) than from foreign sources. Such TRIMs can be detrimental to the development of society, but are perfectly rational from the point of view of a powerful entrenched elite, because they may protect the human capital of those who have interests in the existing knowledge and technology. Throughout history, societies have had some TRIMs, from language differences to outright xenophobia and the belief that foreigners were barbarous primitives from whom nothing could or should be learned. None of those TRIMs ever proved wholly effective, although those in Tokugawa Japan before the Meiji revolution came close, and North Korea in our time is making a serious effort in the same direction. Historically, TRIMs have been asymmetric: the TRIMs set up in most European societies were less powerful and effective that those in other societies. Perhaps this was because the internal variation

---

[1] This mechanism is carried out by so-called plasmids, which are essentially free DNA molecules that can replicate independently from the host, and thus constitute one mechanism for horizontal genetic transmission of genetic information within a population and thus can increase fitness. An example is resistance to antibiotics, which is transferred by this mechanism. As already noted, some horizontally acquired characteristics can be passed onto the next generation through epigenesis.

within Europe was quite high in terms of cultural features and political fragmentation: learning from and imitating others was necessary, lest political competitors acquire an advantage in terms of useful knowledge.

The voyages of discovery in early modern Europe opened the floodgates of information on alien societies: novel products, techniques, flora, and fauna all arrived in Europe and were rarely resisted with much effectiveness.[2] New facts and information were proposed not just by researchers who were peering at the sky or examining ill people but also by travelers, sailors, and the traders who ventured to lands hitherto unknown. They brought with them geographical knowledge, of course, but also new products and techniques. It is striking to what extent European culture was willing to accept foreign ideas and cultural elements and how ineffective TRIMs such as xenophobia and ethnocentrism were in blocking the adoption of useful knowledge developed by other civilizations. Margóczy (2014a) has described in exquisite detail how a lively market developed in curiosities, specimens of alien flora and fauna, unusual rocks, and similar examples of a foreign world. Following the great voyages of the late fifteenth and sixteenth centuries, books that summarized the useful knowledge of hitherto unknown cultures appeared, such as the Portuguese physician Garcia de Orta's 1563 work *Colóquios dos simples e drogas da India* (Colloquies on the Simples and Drugs of India).[3] Europeans increasingly would sip tea from chinaware, grew corn (maize), potatoes, raised turkeys, wore damasks and calicots, and practiced a technique of black laquer known as "Japanning."[4] The appreciation of foreign information by Europeans had already manifested itself in the high Middle Ages. The names of medical authorities such as Al Razi (Rhazes) and Ibn Sina (Avicenna) were latinized, and medieval medicine never hesitated to adopt them as the core of the medical canon for centuries knowing full well that they were Muslims. Even more striking is the willingness of theological writers to study and learn from the philosophical writings of Ibn Rushd (Averroes), whose work influenced Thomas Aquinas. As many scholars have noted, this route was mostly one way. There was little in Western culture that Islam adopted

---

[2] Oliver Cromwell allegedly died because of his refusal to take Cinchona bark, an antimalarial drug, not because it came from South America, but because he regarded it as a Jesuit treatment. The story is widely cited, but seems to be apocryphal (McMains, 2000).

[3] Europeans arriving in India were impressed by the quality of local shipbuilding and adopted many of the features they saw in South Asian ships (Unger, 2013, p. 176). While some reverse copying also took place in India, by 1800 European ships were "definitely superior" to Asians ones (Unger, 2013, p. 202).

[4] Eighteenth-century Britain and France experienced a wave of fashionable "chinoiserie," in which Chinese objects, real or imitation, were in fashion. Many of its artistic manifestations are well known, such as the Pagoda built in Kew Gardens in 1762, the orientalist paintings of François Boucher, and the ceramic products of Meissen.

before the nineteenth century unless it was for a highly specific purpose, and some key inventions were resisted for centuries. Compare that with the total lack of scruples with which Europeans conceded the foreign origins of their use of "Arabic numerals," drank beverages that had alcohol in them (derived from the Arabic *al kohl*), and taught their children algebra (from the Arabic *al jebr*).

The parallels between the voyages of discovery and scientific advances were made quite explicitly. Bacon made the point in his *New Organon*. After pointing out that the greatest obstacle to the progress of science was that men despaired from trying to do things they deemed impossible, he notes that "It is fit that I publish and set forth those conjectures of mine which make hope in this matter reasonable, just as Columbus did before that wonderful voyage of his across the Atlantic" and that these explorations into the unknown were "the causes and beginnings of great events" (Bacon [1620], 2000, aphorism 92, pp. 126–27).[5] That Bacon's account and knowledge of the details of the voyages was highly inaccurate subtracts nothing from the effectiveness of his rhetoric (Alexander, 2002, p. 80). Joseph Glanvill (1661, p. 178) felt that the natural philosophy would be "an America of Secrets and an unknown Peru of Nature." Paolo Rossi (1970, p. 42) describes scientific research in the sixteenth century as an attempt to penetrate territories never before explored. Instead of science logically demonstrating things that were already known, argues William Eamon (1991, p. 27; 1994, pp. 269–300), science went after things hitherto unknown, as if hunting for new prey. The "Science as a *venatio* [hunting]" concept is an analogy that spoke to the age, because hunting was very much an upper-class phenomenon and it thus provided natural philosophy with the respectability that its practitioners eagerly sought. Bacon himself pursued the hunting metaphor tenaciously in his *Advancement of Learning*, recounting the myth of Ceres (the goddess of farming) and Pan, who discovered her after all gods had failed, during a hunt. This tale, Bacon explains, "contains a very true and wise admonition; which is not to look for the invention of things useful for life and civilisation from abstract philosophies ... but only from Pan, that is from sagacious experience ... which oftentimes, by a kind of chance, and while engaged as it were in hunting, stumbles upon such discoveries. For the most useful inventions are due to experience and have come to men like windfalls" (Bacon [1605] 1875, p. 326). Contemporaries full well realized that the incentive structures of geographical discoveries and inventions were similar. Simon Stevin (1548–1620), a Dutch polymath, whose strengths were hydraulic engineering and applied

---

[5] The title page of *Great Instauration* famously depicts an English ship passing beyond the Pillars of Hercules (that is, the straits of Gibraltar), traditionally the limits for sailors before Columbus, the inscription reading "Multi pertransibunt et augebitur scientia" ("Many shall go to and fro and knowledge shall be increased," Daniel 12:4).

mathematics (he invented the decimal point), noted in 1585 that "as the mariner, having by hap found a certain unknown Island, spareth not to declare to his prince the riches and profits thereof ... we speak freely of the great use of this invention" (Stevin [1585], 1608, unpaginated preface).

The causal connection between the great voyages and the growth of science and technology is of course not simple to unravel. From the very beginning, however, the realization that the world was very different from what ancient authorities had described undermined their credibility.[6] Alexander (2002) has argued for a strong causal connection from the voyages of discovery to new research in mathematics.[7] He notes that the language of exploration was adopted by mathematicians and natural philosophers. In response to the shock of new knowledge being unleashed by the voyages, a growing number of mathematicians began to see themselves as experimentalists and explorers rather than as the guardians of a fixed, unchallengeable Euclidian truth. In their hands, the quest for a hidden golden land beyond formidable obstacles became a metaphor for the quest for knowledge in general and mathematics in particular (Alexander, 2002, pp. 72, 200). Yet it is not clear to what extent the voyages were a cause of the scientific advances. The causality in part surely ran the other way, as improved navigational capabilities through better instruments, astronomy, and cartography aided navigators. Both the voyages and advances in natural philosophy are likely to have been two aspects of the same phenomenon: the knowledge of foreign countries and their geography were part of the useful knowledge that Europeans were chasing. How to get from A to B and what one can find in B that might be valuable or interesting were just as much part of useful knowledge as the circulation of blood or how to brew a better beer. All the same, the voyages gave the "moderns" a powerful weapon in their struggle to throw off the fetters of stale classical scholarship and the obscurantist scholars who defended it at all cost. Bacon said as much: "the distant voyages and travels" of his time had "laid open and discovered many new things in nature which may let in new light upon philosophy" (Bacon [1620], 2000, aphorism 84, p. 119).

Moreover, following the growing contact with Asian civilizations after 1500, Europeans soon discovered that India and China in many areas

---

[6] As early as 1514, the Italian physician Giovanni Manardi (1462–1536) wrote that "if anyone prefers the testimony of Aristotle or Averroes to that of men who have been there, there is no way of arguing with them ... other than for one to navigate with astrolabe and abacus to seek out the matter for himself" (quoted in Eamon, 1994, p. 272).

[7] In his words, "whereas Columbus and Magellan had sailed actual oceans and mapped unknown territories, their mathematical successors would uncover the secrets of quantity and magnitude in the uncharted lands of mathematics. ... The imagery of exploration thus proved to be ideally suited for the promotion of the experimental philosophy, which sought to explore the intricate pathways of nature and bring to light secrets and wonders never seen before" (Alexander, 2002, pp. 2, 200).

had accumulated knowledge that was far beyond the classical Hellenic and Hellenistic heritage. Bala (2006) has suggested that many of the most important scientific advances made in Europe were aided and stimulated by knowledge that Europeans brought with them. Thus, he argues that Harvey's discovery of the circulation of blood and Copernicus's heliocentric cosmology depended on advances that were imported from China and India. It is hard to establish the extent to which such claims, often plausible, are valid. It is striking, nonetheless, that some major advances occurred in European science right after it had been exposed to quite similar beliefs in Asia and in some cases, such as the widely disseminated work on optics of the Islamic scientist Alhazen, Europe's debt to non-Western science was obvious and indeed generally acknowledged.[8] The difficult problem remains that Islamic science's subsequent development and practical effects were to be found in the West, not in the "Arabic world" as Bala (2006, p. 92) puts it. The same was true, mutatis mutandis, for Chinese and Indian science. Bala's interesting argument is that Europe's leadership in the Scientific Revolution occurred because Europeans found themselves at the confluence of Islamic, Indian, and Chinese useful knowledge. Europe was thus in a unique position to produce the syncretic creation that, Bala argues, constitutes modern science. Yet that argument, of course, raises the question why such a synthesis did not take place elsewhere.

The same is true for technology. By 1500, Europeans dominated in some techniques, such as machinery and weapons, whereas in others, such as Chinese porcelain and Indian textiles, Asia was still far ahead of them (Prak and Van Zanden, 2013, p. 21). The difference between European and Asian culture was that Europeans on the whole saw opportunities in the new techniques and products they encountered and were willing to abandon traditional and trusted techniques. As a result, their technological backwardness in those industries was gradually erased and eventually they found ways to outproduce their Asian competitors in those very fields in which they had lagged earlier. Although in some areas Asians did try to change their technology under European influence, by 1800 a decisive technological gap had opened up, and the European effort had gathered a momentum that would not find an equivalent in the Asian world until after 1970.

---

[8] In some areas, the flow of knowledge is supportable: Tycho Brahe, the founder of modern observational astronomy, adopted Chinese practices when constructing his armillary spheres, an astronomical instrument. Brahe owned astronomical books in Arabic, and the Arabs knew of the Chinese instruments (Needham, 1969a, pp. 80–81). Here, then, it seems that the flow of knowledge from East to West is plausible. However, Bala's argument (2006, p. 104), that Islamic *kalam* philosophy—basically a conservative and occasionalist approach opposed to the Aristotelian physics of Averroes (Ibn Rushd)—was a harbinger of modern science just because it entertained a vaguely atomistic view of the world and that thus "the Newtonian view is a vindication of *kalam* against Averoism," seems a bit of a stretch.

While adopting new and more effective knowledge from other cultures sounds unexceptional to a modern observer, it is striking how difficult it was for non-Western societies before 1900 to adopt Western (and indeed all foreign) ideas and techniques. None of those societies were closed to *all* foreign ideas, but most were suspicious of Western ideas and selective when imitating Western techniques. Some, like Tokugawa Japan, went to the extreme of shutting Western influences out as much as they could.[9] Ming China, as we shall see, admitted European knowledge through the narrow and tightly controlled channel of a Jesuit mission.[10] Others, like the Ottomans, picked up some items from the West such as more advanced firearms, but declined others until (not unlike Japan) they discovered that shutting out Western useful knowledge altogether meant that they would not be able to compete militarily and politically. Russia's uneasy and vacillating attitude toward Western culture is an intermediate case. While obviously suspicious of Western values and anxious to protect its Slavic culture, there were episodes in its history in which Russia made deliberate efforts to westernize. Much like in other non-Western societies, the transfer was partial and spasmodic.

In the rest of Europe, however, the "not invented here" syndrome was overcome and eventually abandoned. The cotton and chinaware industries, two of the paradigmatic industries of the Industrial Revolution, bear the evidence not only of European willingness to adopt foreign techniques and products but also of their total lack of coyness in doing so by explicitly naming products after their (supposed) origins. Smallpox variolation was brought over from Constantinople by the wife of the British ambassador in full acknowledgment of its source. In those cases, the non-European origins of the technique were clearly acknowledged, but then the Europeans set about to make improvements at a rate that eventually forced the originating societies to re-import the technique in much improved and

---

[9] Even when they had some access to Western science, the willingness of the Japanese to adopt other points of view was limited. The Japanese astronomer and physician Mukai Genshō (1609–1679) felt that Westerners were ingenious only in techniques that deal with appearances and utility, but are ignorant about metaphysical matters and go astray in their theory of heaven and hell. He added that "Portuguese scholars are convinced of the superiority of their own learning and go abroad to preach it, but their study is utterly erroneous and prejudiced" (quoted by Nakayama, 1969, p. 91). A hundred and fifty years later, a Japanese Buddhist monk, Fumon Entsu (1754–1834) could still launch a virulent attack on Western astronomy making a strong case for a "Buddhist astronomy" which was supposed to stand guard against Western scientific ideas ands religion. (Nakayama, 1969, pp. 210–12). Only in the first half of the nineteenth century did Dutch astronomy make inroads in Japanese thinking.

[10] Cohen (2012, p. 46) sees in the absence of what he calls "cultural transplantation" in China a central cause of the absence of novelty and creativity in Chinese science. For him the policies of the emperors were responsible for Chinese science remaining "encapsulated inside itself." Yet such a lack of interest in foreign ideas was not just a policy variable but a deeply held cultural belief that seems to have been immune to change for many centuries.

modified form. A hundred fifty years before the Industrial Revolution, Bacon's imaginary *New Atlantis*'s Salomon's House had twelve fellows known as "merchants of light," whose function it was to sail to foreign countries and bring back books, abstracts, and "patterns of experiments" (Bacon, [1627] 1996, p. 486).

The cultural element here was not an enlightened tolerance for non-Europeans or non-Christians as much as a pragmatic recognition that one can usefully distinguish between the character and religion of foreigners, which may be seen as repugnant, and their techniques and knowledge, which can be usefully adapted. The origins of this cultural trait are not fully understood, but some obvious candidates come to mind. The fact that the highly educated intellectual elite in Europe considered itself part and parcel of a transnational community implied that the national and religious identity of the creators of intellectual innovations could be separated from its content and was to some extent immaterial. But other factors played a role, above all the relentless competition among European polities at every level, which had accustomed them to imitate techniques from others they had no liking for. The twentieth-century move toward globalization has reduced TRIMs worldwide, and horizontal transmission of knowledge and preferences has become vastly faster and more encompassing, from taste in food and music to technology at every level.

The other important cultural element that ultimately mattered to economic outcomes was the attitude toward the wisdom and knowledge of earlier generations. To the extent that ancient learning is regarded as sacrosanct and unassailable, one would expect it to serve as a constraint on the rate of intellectual innovation. The relatively fast rate of cultural change in the West can be seen most prominently in the Reformation, which criticized and revised long-standing Christian dogma and worship rituals, and in the revision of the classical scientific canon, which as late as 1400 still had been by and large unassailable. This was especially true in a world in which science, philosophy, and religion were still intimately connected. By the fifteenth century, the intellectual innovations of the twelfth and thirteenth centuries had rigidified into a Ptolemaic-Aristotelian dogma that became increasingly intolerant of deviants. In the picture of the world that emerged, cosmology and theology were deeply intertwined and provided an intellectual foundation for the religious establishment. In this system metaphysics provided a bridge between natural philosophy and theology (Gaukroger, 2006, p. 130). "The resulting system of the Universe was considered impregnable and final. To attack it was considered blasphemy" (White, 1896, p. 120). As Cohen (2012, p. 81) phrases it, "from Coimbra to Cracow and from Vienna to St. Andrews, Aristotelian doctrine and the *quadrivium* were taught as foundation courses ... this state of intellectual affairs was without precedent."[11] The orthodoxy was nothing if not tenacious. In 1624, the parlement of Paris still prohibited the teaching of material that contradicted "ancient and approved authors." The law was not strictly enforced but could be used to intimidate those who deviated too much.[12]

Yet from 1500 on, this seemingly unshakeable conservative cultural system came under increasing pressure and while the battle veered back and forth, much of the orthodoxy eventually collapsed. Tradition remained supremely important to all European intellectual activity, but while nobody disputed that there was a tradition that should be held in great esteem, the conversation about what tradition exactly was became a main topic of discourse. The net result was that "everywhere there seemed to be a looking at things in new ways" (Schoeck, 1982, pp. 308–9). The importance of the empirical, observation-based study of nature was at first legitimized by the belief that it would reveal God's intentions of creating the universe, and thus natural philosophy was justified in large part on religious grounds. Besides religion itself, this onslaught on received wisdom occurred in all important areas of knowledge, such as mathematics, physics, astronomy, and medicine. Eventually, the religious justification had to make room for a much more practical and material motive: the improvement of material conditions through better agriculture, medicine, and industrial technology.

In the sixteenth century an increasing number of iconoclastic scholars attacked the classical canon outright, a few of them showing outright disdain for the canon and often paying a high price for it.[13] The cosmology

[11] In the fourteenth century, Oxford University had a rule on the book that every master who deviated from Aristotle's *Organon* would be fined 5 shillings for every case of deviation (Devlin, 2000, p. 58). This rule was still on the books when Giordano Bruno visited Oxford in ca. 1583. In 1556 A statute at Oxford stipulated the basic texts for the study of fields: Ptolemy for astronomy, Strabo and Pliny for geography and thirty years later students were urged to follow only Aristotle and those who defended him (Rossi, 1978, p. 40). In 1559 a Dr. John Geynes, who had suggested that Galen may not have been infallible, was forced by his furious colleagues to recant (Debus, 2002, p. 174).

[12] Caton (1988, p. 68) comments acerbically that Aristotle might have been amazed that criticism of his views would be a capital offense in a Christian nation, but then, he had never met a Jesuit.

[13] Petrus Ramus (1515–1572), a French philosopher and logician, made a career out of slaughtering the holiest of holy cows, namely Aristotle's logic. His promotion lecture (1536) was actually titled "Everything that Aristotle ever Taught is Wrong." The great physician and medical troublemaker Theophrastus Bombastus von Hohenheim, better known as Paracelsus (1493–1541), at times referred to as the "medical Luther," was a notoriously quarrelsome and provocative physician and chemist, who relentlessly attacked the accepted and revered medical doctrines of his time as codified by such classical authors as Galen, whose books he burned in public to show his contempt for the wisdom of the "ancients." Known as the "wandering Swiss Doctor" he and his followers were anti-establishment and anti-elitist and got in trouble with the authorities (Breger, 1998, pp. 102–3). In 1527, Paracelsus publicly burned the canonical medical

based on Aristotle's *De Caelo* and Ptolemy's *Almagest* was disintegrating as new observations were made that did not square with it. By the early seventeenth century, European intellectuals were increasingly coming to terms with their break with classical science. The English physician and physicist William Gilbert in his *De Magnete* (1600), a widely admired and pioneering work in its time, announced from the onset that he was not going to waste time on "quoting the ancients and the Greeks as our supporters, for neither can paltry Greek argumentation demonstrate the truth more subtly nor Greek terms more effectively, nor can both elucidate it better. Our doctrine of the loadstone is contradictory of most of the principles and axioms of the Greeks." The multiple errors he found in such classic authors as Pliny and Ptolemy were spread "much as evil and noxious plants ever have the most luxurious growth." Ptolemy's erroneous astronomy was "followed by the rabble of philosophasters and astrologers." His view of the universe consisted of "superstition, a philosophic fable, now believed only by simpletons and the unlearned; it is beneath derision." Furthermore, Ptolemy's theories were "of no account" and anyone who held on to them "would reason as stupidly just as those who cling to an opinion because it was held by the antients" (Gilbert, [1600], 1893, pp. 1–2, 208, 321–22, 339–40).

Francis Bacon launched a full-fledged attack on classical wisdom (especially in his *Advancement of Learning* and *New Organon*) and called for nothing less than to junk classical science and start afresh, using observation and experiment rather than syllogisms and authority. He noted, in a telling remark, that the wisdom of the Greeks was but a wisdom of boys, it can talk but not generate, it was "barren of works"(Bacon, [1620] 2000, aphorism 121, p. 59).[14] In the first decades of the seventeenth century the rebellion against the "ancients" was taken further. Famously, Galileo wrote in his 1615 letter to Duchess Christina of Florence that "in disputes about natural phenomena, one must begin not with the authority of scriptural passages but with sensory experiences and necessary demonstrations" (quoted in Reston,1994, p. 137). Many of the scientists and scholars who rose to prominence in the mid-seventeenth century had accepted this critical

books in Basel and barely escaped arrest. By being constantly on the move and considering himself a subject of no king, he succeeded in repeatedly annoying men seemingly more powerful than himself and yet escaped jail or worse, despite repeatedly being threatened by the authorities (Debus, 2002).

[14] Political expediency may have tempered Bacon's tone, and he was careful not to sound too disrespectful lest he infuriate too many powerful intellectuals. Hence aphorism 32 in his *New Organon* "the honour of the ancient authors stands firm and so does everyone's honour. We are not introducing a comparison of minds or talents, but a comparison of ways" (Bacon [1620], 2000, p. 39). The very fact that he felt it necessary to add that remark, however, suggests that many might indeed have seen his revolt against the ancients for what it was: a call for an entirely new way of doing science.

attitude toward received authority. "Whatever the schoolmen may talk," wrote one of them, "yet Aristotle's Works are not necessarily true and he himself hath by sufficient Arguments proved himself to be liable to errour. ... Learning is Increased by new Experiments and new Discoveries ... we have the advantage of more time than they had and Truth (we say) is the daughter of time" (John Wilkins, [1648] 1684, p. 5).[15] Even earlier, George Hakewill's *Apologie* (1627) argued strenuously against the prevalent view of "decay" that held that human capabilities were declining over time. Hakewill pointed to the three Baconian warhorses of technology (the printing press, gunpowder, and compass), but he also presented additional evidence of modern superiority: anatomical discoveries, chemistry, the Copernican theory, and the telescope. Even more rebellious was Nathanael Carpenter (1589–1628) who, in his *Philosophia Libera* (1621) launched a devastating attack on the "servility to the ancients, mainly Aristotle, and made a strenuous plea for a critical attitude of mind and complete freedom of thought" (Jones, 1961, p. 65).[16] The paralyzing respect for the wisdom of previous generations was slowly melting away.

The fear of the new and the strange dissipated in sixteenth- and seventeenth-century Europe. Curiosity, which had been condemned by scholastic writers as sinful, began to acquire a more positive meaning. The "hunt for knowledge" of the rare and the freakish was displayed in the proto-museums known as *wunderkammern*. Weird and exotic exhibits were displayed in these "cabinets of curiosity" and people were invited to gawk (Eamon, 1991, p. 34). Slowly but certainly the fear of the new as disruptive and disturbing was replaced by a fascination with novelty. As Eamon (1991, p. 49) points out, for a book to sell well, it had to be about scientific novelty: discoveries, inventions, secrets, new scientific insights, and descriptions of new lands where Europeans were setting foot for the first time. Daniel Margóczy has recently shown in great detail how a lively trade emerged in "curiosities" that ranged from ancient coins and pinned butterflies to curative plants and exotic fruits. Collecting such curiosities became the rage in Europe, and while they were of course attractive because they "evoked wonder, charmed the eye, and instantiated God's unbound creativity," they were also attractive because of the chance that they could have some use in farming, medicine, or manufacturing (Margóczy, 2014a, p. 31). The spirit of Francis Bacon reached far and deep.

---

[15] Wilkins borrowed this line from Bacon ([1620] 2000, p. 121 aphorism 84). Bacon appended significantly "not of authority" to his statement.

[16] Of the third-century Christian author Lucius Lactantius (who had denied the possibility of life at the antipodes), Carpenter wrote scathingly that while he may have been a pious and eloquent Father, "the childishnesse of his arguments will to any indifferent reader discover his ignorance in the very first rudiments of Cosmographie" (Carpenter, 1625, p. 231).

The other symptom of a cultural change in Europe was the emergence of a peculiar upper class trend known as "virtuosity"—a word that meant something quite different in early modern Europe than it does today. Originally a product of Italian courts and heavily influenced by Italian norms of behavior, it depicted an upper class fascination with learning and the arts, combining the features of scholar and gentleman into a serious if perhaps somewhat amateurish intellectual. But the *virtuosi* provided much-needed respectability to those who contemplated engaging in intellectual endeavors and they turned curiosity, once regarded as a vice, into a virtue. As Eamon (1994, p. 314) observes, in the seventeenth century "virtuoso" was synonymous with "curioso." They collected rare specimens of plants and animals, seashells, archaeological artefacts, and other exotic objects. Virtuosi constituted much of the readership of the works of the great minds of the Republic of Letters, such as Bacon and Comenius. The courtier had become a scholar, and culture for social ornament passed into learning for fame and admiration (Houghton, 1942, p. 61). Their enthusiasm and sometimes naiveté created a dilettantism that made them the butt of ridicule. Nonetheless, these people clearly helped pave the way for the Enlightenment by stressing the compatibility of intellectual activity and "politeness" and "virtue" and by reinforcing the concept of reputation as an incentive for learned individuals to generate knowledge—after all, Robert Boyle himself must be regarded as a virtuoso.

Situating the virtuosi in the seventeenth-century market for ideas is complex because, as Houghton (1942) points out, they came in many stripes. For the virtuoso, the study of any topic was not just an occasional diversion but a serious matter to which much time was devoted, and one hoped to become an authority on the subject. Yet studies were never meant for commercial gains, but were a gentlemanly occupation, intended for people "for whom learning is the means to dispose of wealth and leisure in the happiest fashion" (Houghton, 1942, p. 57). At first, then, it was purely motivated by epistemic purposes, knowledge for its own sake, but as the Baconian influence became more pervasive after 1650, the virtuosi allowed possible utilitarian motives to affect their agendas. John Evelyn, who is often singled out as a paradigmatic virtuoso (Hunter, 1995d; Chambers, 2004), came from a wealthy family (of gunpowder manufacturers), wrote his best-known book on forestry (Evelyn [1664], 1679), and one on horticulture. Evelyn clearly had utilitarian objectives in mind—though he also wrote a book on numismatics and one on sumptuary laws. The aristocratic mathematician William second Viscount Brouncker (1620–1684), the first president of the Royal Society, and the highly accomplished astronomer and instrument-maker Richard Towneley (1629–1707) are other examples of independently wealthy virtuosi with real contributions to make. Books on "curiosities" and mathematical games appealed to these people, and practical utility was not the driving motive behind their researches. Yet they directed the interest of a broader class of intellectuals toward science, toward instruments, experimentation, and eventually toward potential applications. Eamon (1994, p. 307) recounts that the instrument maker John Bate (no dates known) was so often bothered by virtuosi questioning him about his hydraulic devices such as pumps, siphons, and water clocks that he wrote a book describing them, *The Mysteries of Nature and Art* (1634), a copy of which was owned by Newton. Boyle (1690, pp. 6 ff) pointed to the virtuosi as individuals committed to experimental philosophy and insisted that, combined with adherence to Christianity, such persons should enjoy credibility and be valued as helping to reveal the secrets of nature.

Whether the virtuoso movement as a whole was a success in reforming the views of the British aristocratic elite and turning them into a building block of the Industrial Enlightenment remains an open question. There was a continuous gradation from leisurely and possibly bored gentlemen who played with science (such as Boyle and Evelyn) to the serious (if often impecunious) natural philosophers such as Ray and Hooke. In between we see such figures as John Wilkins (Houghton, 1942, p. 202). By the late seventeenth century the movement went into decline and despite the defense by aristocratic intellectuals such as Shaftesbury, by 1700 "the middle ranks of virtuosi were thinned and their sons, to avoid being pedants, were often content to be ignorant" (Houghton, 1942, pp. 216, 219). The torch of learning was passed from the nobility to *homines novi,* who were more talented, better trained, and above all better motivated. The market for ideas had seen to that.[17] The enormous success of its superstars meant that some young people would still choose a career of learning in natural and experimental philosophy—perhaps the eighteenth-century scholar, as Steven Shapin puts it, was no longer a gentleman, but he not only might be tolerated, but even valued and sustained. Because he was not like other people, he might know something useful others did not (Shapin, 1991, p. 314).[18]

Competition for fame and reputation became a central feature of intellectual life in seventeenth-century Europe. The result was that the

[17] Shapin (1991) states flatly that the attempt to combine learning and politeness was a failure; there was no real new role for the scholar-gentleman, and that "polite society" was never persuaded that systematic natural knowledge was a necessary gentlemanly accomplishment (p. 312) and insists that vehicles for the advance of scientific culture developed outside polite society. Yet this argument sets the standard for the elite too high and confines it apparently to a thin slice of upper society. Whether rich aristocratic natural philosophers of international caliber such as Boyle and Cavendish were the exception or the rule seems less relevant than the fact that virtuoso culture helped pave the way for the legitimacy of new "bourgeois dignity," as McCloskey (2006, 2010) has demonstrated, even if (in some cases) this may have been regarded as a "seriously impolite utilitarian culture" (Shapin, 1991, p. 313).

[18] Shapin's image of the post-virtuoso scientist as a lonely and uncivil Newton-like figure is very far from the typical eighteenth-century member of the Republic of Letters either in Britain or elsewhere in Europe. Indeed, the work of such scholars as Larry Stewart (1992) has shown how science and technology increasingly became part of literate and "polite" society in Europe.

market for ideas in sixteenth- and seventeenth-century Europe became deluged with a plethora of competing methodologies to study the world. Aristotelians battled anti-Aristotelians, Corpuscularianism (or atomism) was revived from its Epicurean origins and led by such scientific stars as the Dutch scientist Isaac Beeckman and his French contemporary Pierre Gassendi. They battled vitalists and both of them battled Aristotelians. In medicine, iatrochemists, inspired by the work of Paracelsus and van Helmont, challenged their Galenist opponents. In mathematics, a variety of battles were enjoined, none fiercer than the one whether infinitesimals were an appropriate concept in mathematics (Alexander, 2014). The hardest-fought battle, of course, was the one over heliocentrism and the structure of the heavens, which may not have been fully over until 1758, when the Catholic Church finally dropped books supporting the Copernican universe from its Index of prohibited books.

But the market for ideas extended to meta-arguments about the nature of knowledge and beliefs themselves. The most significant debate was whether civilization and science in their own time could ever measure up to the great achievements of the classics that everyone still studied (Levine, 1991). The meta-argument over free debate itself was superimposed on these disputes: should tolerance and pluralism be values in and of themselves, or are the authorities justified to use the law (that is, violence) to silence heterodox opinion and nip dissent and subversion in the bud so as to maintain law and order? Books were prohibited both in Catholic and in Protestant areas, but the ubiquity of the printing press made a mockery out of these prohibitions, even if suppression of intellectual innovation may well have affected to some extent the pursuit of truly innovative work in countries "where the Inquisition held sway" (Cohen, 2012, p. 438).[19] It is anything but clear whether the decline in the sciences in Catholic Europe was quite as dramatic as it is depicted by Alexander (2014), and even less how much of that decline was actually because of the fear of the Catholic reaction.[20]

---

[19] Galileo's "banned" books were smuggled out of Italy and published in Protestant cities, such as the *Discorsi* published in Leiden in 1638 and the *Dialogo* re-published in Strasbourg in 1635.

[20] John Milton, visiting Galileo in his villa in Arcetri, thought that the tyranny of the Inquisition had "dampened the glory of Italian wits," but in fact scientific advances by active members of the Republic of Letters continued in Italy after Galileo, especially in fields outside the areas in which the reactionary powers had a stake. Thus the Florentine physician Francesco Redi (1626–1697) showed convincingly that the Aristotelian belief in spontaneous generation of plants and insects was false. Giovanni Alfonso Borelli (1608–1679), a talented polymath, made important contributions to the understanding of volcanos, epidemics, and the structure of the solar system. Both Redi and Borelli lived in worlds in which the Catholic reaction was powerful, but they could do their work. Even more impressive in this regard was the career of Marcello Malpighi (1628–1694), the great microscopist who established for the first time the importance of capillary vessels in the circulation of the blood and thus irrefutably established Harvey's theory

Entry into the market for ideas became easier, and competition fiercer. Radical deviations from the conventional wisdom became common: such intellectuals as Paracelsus and his later follower Jan-Baptist van Helmont, Francis Bacon, William Gilbert, Thomas Hobbes, and Spinoza did not hesitate to express opinions that would have been sacrilegious in an earlier age. In the market for ideas, like any market, (relatively) free entry and contestability became increasingly common, and the outcomes were determined by evidence, logic, and other cultural biases. Contestability and skepticism of received wisdom, the hallmarks of the Republic of Letters, found their way into the writings of intellectuals of many stripes and nationalities, from Michel de Montaigne to Giordano Bruno to Thomas Browne. All of them, in one form or another, admitted their doubts about the classical canon. The authority of the ancients was bursting at the seams in every area. One still had to be prudent and polite; empty lip service to powerful vested interests was still sometimes called for. At times, as both Copernicus and Descartes knew, the publication of materials that would annoy some powerful (usually religious) authority could be dangerous. Recklessness could lead to the sad fate of Giordano Bruno (1548–1600), arrogance to that of Galileo. But overall, the system worked well as a competitive market for ideas. After 1650, the power of conservative forces to hold back new ideas dissolved north of the Alps and the Pyrenees.

That said, unlike highly competitive markets for goods or labor, the market for ideas does not invariably converge to an "equilibrium outcome," comparable to the law of one price in markets for goods. The reason is that even if the market for ideas is highly competitive, it may be difficult for "consumers" to choose on the basis of content alone, because knowledge is insufficiently tight and the evidence or data are inconclusive. In that case the market generates multiple solutions. In some sense multiple equilibria in the market for ideas can be viewed as an inefficiency, since if there are two diametrically inconsistent ideas extant about some natural phenomenon, at least one of them is likely to be in error. In these cases, the market for ideas cannot settle on a unique equilibrium outcome until better tools become available to determine the issue. Such was the case in medicine, where best-practice knowledge before 1870 could not produce a tight explanation of infectious disease. But in a well-functioning market for ideas, content bias—the willingness to be persuaded and accept what seems true—should be decisive in matters that can be verified by the best instruments and satisfy the rhetorical conventions of the time.[21] In that case

---

of the circulation of the blood. Despite these radical findings, Malpighi late in life was appointed the personal physician of Pope Innocent XII.

[21] A typical case was that of pre-Galilean Copernicans, who for many decades lacked demonstrative proof of the logically coherent but empirically untight system proposed in *De Revolutionibus*. The central premise was an assumed, unproven, and to many people heretical

something akin to the law of one price should obtain. Hence, when such cultural entrepreneurs as Lavoisier, Darwin, and Pasteur proposed radically new views of natural phenomena, the evidence and logic were judged to be persuasive by the rhetorical standards of their age. Notwithstanding skepticism and resistance, their ideas became eventually accepted and were considered to be sufficiently tight at least among those who mattered for further progress. The same was true for scientists like Copernicus, Harvey, and Galileo in the early modern market for ideas.[22]

How and why did this momentous cultural sea change happen? Perhaps it was not so much an exogenous increase in the supply of innovators that was behind this development, but rather a change in the institutional parameters under which they operated, that drove (and was in turn driven by) changes in the market for ideas. By this time, European cultural entrepreneurs and intellectual innovators operated in an institutional environment that was increasingly more conducive to their work. Their success and growing prestige enabled them to influence the culture underlying these institutions, which led to further institutional change. Tracing these changes is the task at hand.

It is important to stress that nothing suggests that any inherent qualities of Europeans or Christians were systematically different from other societies in a way that would foster the development of useful knowledge. In other words, it stands to reason that potential cultural entrepreneurs emerged in other societies as well, but for one reason or another did not succeed in bringing about a radical shift in the prevailing culture of the groups that mattered for sustained technological change. In fact, as we shall see in chapters 16 and 17, this was indeed the case in China. To understand why they were more successful in Europe, we need to identify those elements in the Occidental environment that facilitated this success. Cultural entrepreneurs, no less than business entrepreneurs, fail more often than they

---

proposition (Westman, 1986). Between its publication in 1543 and the early seventeenth century, the idea clearly was untight: there was no empirical evidence to discriminate between it and competing hypotheses, and it was based purely on mathematical reasoning. Only as evidence piled up from the work of better-equipped astronomers, such as Kepler and Galileo, did the knowledge become tighter and content bias could fully do its work. It is safe to say that by 1700, the geocentric hypothesis had disappeared from the discourse of serious astronomers in Europe.

[22] Harvey's theory of blood circulation was at first rejected by many physicians, including the eminent Danish scientist Ole Worm (1588–1644); yet within a decade or two Worm and many other skeptics bowed to the evidence and accepted it. As Grell (2007, p. 231) points out, Worm does not reveal what precisely made him change his mind, but many of his students traveled through Europe in the 1630s and no doubt kept him informed of changes in best-practice medical knowledge. Fifty years after the publication of Harvey's *De Motu Cordis*, Thomas Browne ([1680] 1964, p. 198) reflected on Harvey's discovery that "at the first trump of the circulation all the schools of Europe murmured ... and condemned it by a general vote ... but at length [it was] accepted and confirmed by illustrious physicians." Experimental evidence was one of the tools by which the citizens of the Republic of Letters could take advantage of content bias.

succeed, but survival bias tends to focus attention on the successful ones. For every Luther and Calvin there were many failed religious innovators, about whom we rarely know much. The most famous, to be sure, was the Bohemian reformer Jan Hus, who was executed in 1415 and his movement suppressed. Other failed cultural innovators included Miguel Servetus (executed in Geneva in 1553) and Jan of Leyden (executed in Munster in 1536).[23]

To see what set Europe apart, it is useful to ask about the circumstances under which the cultural entrepreneurs of the era operated. As noted above, entrepreneurs, generally speaking, take advantage of circumstances and opportunities, and if the environment is repressive or otherwise resistant to innovation, entrepreneurs will not flourish. From 1500 to 1700, many would-be cultural entrepreneurs struggled to make their mark. Far from the unavoidable products of the rise of commerce and industry and the accompanying urbanization that took place after 1500, cultural entrepreneurs struggled against reactionary interests and competed with one another. Nothing guaranteed success. This period in Europe was one in which political circumstances and contingency determined many outcomes, and the cultural sea change we call the Enlightenment that followed it was anything but preordained and ineluctable.

In literate and educated circles in much of Europe, the sixteenth and seventeenth centuries experienced the development and maturation of a "high level of awareness of, and high expectations of understanding, the mechanisms of nature" (Webster, [1975] 2002 , p. 505). But what in the European environment made the growth of this new awareness possible? Prior technological developments played an important role, and in that regard the evolution has clear-cut medieval roots. The great voyages, made possible by the improvements in shipping and navigation technology in the fifteenth century, affected in many ways the attitudes of Europeans to their environment. It certainly increased their confidence in their ability to control the environment and raised their curiosity as to the world around them. It also could be seen by them as evidence for progress and the superiority of their generation, which finally had discovered something that the ancient Greeks and Romans had surely not known.

Scholars have also stressed the central role of the printing press as a causal agent in the post-1500 changes (Eisenstein, 1979; Perkinson, 1995, pp. 64, 74). Without it, it has been argued, many of the cultural changes and institutions that drove them would not have been possible. Printing offered many advantages to science, not least of which was the elimination of corrupted editions and what Eisenstein (1979, p. 113) calls "typographic

---

[23] Persecution was only a minor contributor to such failures—as with all entrepreneurs, we would expect the majority of them to fail simply because their message did not resonate (or resonated less than similar ones) with their audiences, or simply failed to reach them.

fixity"—knowing with certainty what previous writers had written, which she considers a basic prerequisite for the rapid advancement of learning. Perhaps more important is that printing, precisely because it produced hundreds or thousands of identical documents, made it far less likely that any codified knowledge would ever be lost or go extinct. In that regard, the printing press ensured the cumulativeness of knowledge, which was regarded as the logical support for the idea of progress. Beyond that, printing was an important element in the principle of contestability: it turned "private experience into a public resource" and thus, in Wootton's view, created the freedom to contest authority (Wootton, 2015, p. 302). Such freedom had not been entirely absent before, perhaps, but reaching a large audience became much cheaper. Wootton argues that the printing press, more than anything else, undermined the power of authority and thus "was the perfect tool for the Scientific Revolution" (Wootton, 2015, p. 305).

That the printing press had momentous consequences for the development of culture in those countries that adopted it is commonplace and has recently been shown to be consistent with rigorous quantitative analysis (Dittmar, 2011). But it seems exaggerated to argue that without the printing press, modern science would not have arrived and that "printing created the modern world" (Perkinson, 1995, p. 63). For one thing, printing could disseminate and preserve only codified knowledge, and while that clearly had big consequences, codifiable knowledge was not all there was to know. Artisanal knowledge was still predominantly tacit knowledge, and its transmission required personal contact. Codified technological knowledge, as embodied in the many books about machinery and engineering that were published in this age, did not have much of a direct impact on technological practices (Cipolla, 1972). The same was true for large parts of natural history and experimental philosophy, which needed other means of communication such as personal interaction. Moreover, even codified knowledge did not wholly depend on printing, and much of it was transmitted through handwritten personal correspondence. Some of the most influential scientists of the era did not publish and their reputation was almost exclusively based on correspondence and personal relations, the aforementioned Isaac Beeckman being a classic example.[24] Evangelista Torricelli (1608–1647), the brilliant Italian mathematician and experimentalist and Galileo's most distinguished student, published only one book; his reputation among his fellow scientists with whom he had long correspondences was based on personal communications. Yet there is little doubt that the printing press sharpened the competitive level of the market for ideas. Not only authors, but also printers and booksellers had a stake in making certain

---

[24] Beeckman's considerable fame in his time was largely based on his relationship and correspondence with two of France's most influential intellectuals of his age, Descartes and Mersenne, and his unpublished journals, to which a few had access.

ideas and pieces of knowledge look persuasive and interesting to reach a large audience.[25]

The growth of commerce in the sixteenth century may have affected the advances in useful knowledge in other ways. In a subtle and sophisticated argument, Harold Cook (2007, p. 411) has argued that it was no accident that the so-called Scientific Revolution occurred at the same time as the development of the first global economy. In his interpretation, commerce drove a search for accurate information and knowledge about the nature of goods, their prices, their measurable characteristics, such as quantity and volume, and their geographical origins. Instead of "wisdom," more and more highly educated people were in search of the "material details of the world as perceived by the senses," driven by financial interests and the "warm hope of material progress" (Cook, 2007, p. 41). For the decisions that had to be made by merchants, he argues, factual knowledge was essential. To take advantage of the new economies of exchange one had to value facts: the quality of a wine, the therapeutic power of an exotic herb, the price of sugar (Cook, 2007, p. 17). In a leap of faith, Cook then proceeds to argue that trust and credibility, aimed at discovering and accumulating knowledge of the material world, were the values of both the hard-headed merchant and those of the naturalist and physician. The Scientific Revolution, in his view, resulted from the greater mobility of people in the sixteenth century, "leading to countless efforts to find out matters of fact about natural things." Merchants and natural philosophers shared certain values such as seeing things afresh, long-distance connections, and the "hope of a better material future through worldly activity" (Cook, 2007, pp. 81, 57).[26] By itself, commercial expansion cannot explain the whole story: long distance trade was not confined to Europe, and even before Vasco da Gama a fair amount of trade in oriental goods took place, with Arab, Turkish, and Indian merchants sending and receiving goods from remote countries. But even without committing to a more materialist interpretation, it makes sense that the takeoff of long-distance commerce and the great voyages in Western Europe after 1500 enriched research in natural history and underscored the economic benefits of expanding useful knowledge.

---

[25] It seems questionable to argue, as does Perkinson (1995, p. 65), that printing made it possible for people for the first time to distinguish between the culture of the ancients and their own culture. Yet there is no question that after 1500 the wider dissemination and increased standardization of the classical canon contributed to the growing critique of the knowledge of the "ancients," one of the critical components of the changing culture of intellectuals at the time.

[26] Equally interesting, merchant accounts and letters served as sources of information for many well-connected members of the Republic of Letters interested in geography, history, botany, and many other areas in which knowledge from foreign countries was accumulating. Especially Peiresc, well-connected and enormously erudite polymath that he was, was well informed by many of the merchants with whom he corresponded (Grafton, 2015, p. 64).

Another set of favorable circumstances in early modern Europe that created opportunities for cultural entrepreneurs was the growing gap that emerged after 1500 between accepted doctrine and an avalanche of new facts that educated people were exposed to and that often contradicted conventional wisdom. Part of the reason for the growth in this Kuhnian anomaly was again purely technological. The accumulation of a plethora of systematic astronomical observations by astronomers such as Tycho Brahe, who refuted Aristotle's views of comets and the prevailing notion that celestial bodies except the planets were eternal and unchanging.[27] As new facts and data surfaced, in part through the expansion of geographical horizons and in part through more careful observations and better instruments, Europeans began to see the flaws of the canonical works of antiquity. It may not be an accident that Bacon, Galileo, and Newton were spanning a period that witnessed the emergence of the telescope, microscope, thermometer, barometer, pendulum clock, and air pump. Evangelista Torricelli and Blaise Pascal showed that Aristotle's assertion that a vacuum was impossible was contradicted by the facts, and air pumps used by von Guericke and Robert Boyle removed any residual doubt.[28]

Newly discovered continents weakened the image of the world as pictured by classical geography. After all, Aristotle had suggested that the area around the equator would be too hot for survival, a position obviously recognized as mistaken after 1500 or so.[29] Improved navigation was supplemented by better research tools. Kepler showed that the planetary orbits were ellipses, not the perfect circles that classical astronomy had asserted. The work on human anatomy by Vesalius and on blood by Harvey lent further support to the critique raised against the Galenian medical canon by iconoclastic physicians such as Paracelsus. The new knowledge undermined much of the conventional wisdom and what seemed like common sense observations, and scholars such as Peiresc basically refused to take anything for granted "until experience opens the way for us to pure truth" (Miller,

---

[27] In 1572, the young Tycho Brahe was shocked by a glaring counterexample to the Aristotelian view of the immutability of the heavens, as he observed a nova in the sky. As Cohen (2012, p. 274) notes, Brahe overcame the flip side of what we have called confirmation bias, namely, the "human inclination to pass over the unexpected and ignore things whose possible existence is ruled out ... on theoretical grounds."

[28] In a famous quote, often erroneously attributed to Galileo himself, Kepler wrote in his comments on Galileo's *Sidereus Nuncius* written in 1611, "O Telescope, instrument of much knowledge, more precious than any sceptre, is not he who holds thee in his hand made king and lord of the works of God?" (Carlos, 1880, p. 86).

[29] The French polymath, translator, and cosmographer François de Belleforest (1530–1583), wrote in 1568 that "the voyages of modern times have shown that the ancient astronomers and geographers had scant knowledge and even less experience ... to contend that the world beyond the equator was uninhabited, buttressing their contentions with cold and frivolous reasons. Happy is our century to have men like our voyagers" (quoted in Rossi, 1970, pp. 65–66).

2000, p. 27).[30] In sum, then, new discoveries of all kinds weakened the prestige of classical authorities irreparably. The Thomist synthesis was coming apart at many seams, and the accumulation of new facts through observation and experiment, armed with new instruments and new techniques, created growing skepticism.[31]

*   *   *

The evolutionary perspective proposed in Part I suggests that innovations (or "mutations") are more likely to succeed if they increase fitness of the unit under selection in a particular environment. Around 1500, the environment in Europe was changing for a variety of reasons. The voyages to the New World and to Asia created, rather suddenly, a world that was more mobile, monetized, and market oriented. As Europeans discovered hitherto unknown (to them) lands, with new products and new information, their commitment to the old and their resistance to novelties weakened. Tobacco, potatoes, sugar, maize, tea, chinaware, spices, and many more things that had been either very rare or unknown, became common. New and unimagined lands, fauna, and flora shook the familiar world European had hitherto lived in. As Cook has argued, merchants, sailors, and explorers and the writers who disseminated their new information acquired a more prominent voice in society, and these were the very people who would be more friendly to new ideas and techniques, no matter whether they came from China or from Cambridge. Within Europe itself, urbanization, growing intra-European trade, the commercialization of agriculture, and of course the printing press, all helped to change the European environment to create a process that biologists refer to in their quaint terminology as "adaptive radiation"—accelerated evolutionary change. The changes included both the emergence of new species and the rapid adaptation of existing species resulting from the combination of a changed environment and enhanced mutagens. The classic eras of adaptive radiation in the history of the world were the Cambrian Explosion (in which many multicellular phyla appeared) and the spectacular proliferation of new mammalian forms at the beginning of the Cenozoic after the extinction of the

---

[30] Whether this was actually his practice rather than a statement of intent is another matter, as it did not stop Peiresc from believing in various miracles, though he regarded those as a stimulus to further investigation rather that as truly supernatural.

[31] For a similar argument, see Goldstone (2012). This argument forms the center of the interpretation put forward by Jin (2016). Jin analyzes the rise of Western science in the sixteenth and seventeenth centuries through the perspective of cognitive science. The disruption of existing paradigms through new discoveries and new information created what he calls a "knowledge transcendence," in which a unique situation allowed intellectuals in the West to reconstruct their knowledge of nature de novo through new tools and methods.

dinosaurs (Wesson, 1991, pp. 209–15; Eldredge, 1995, pp. 150–51). Both resulted from exogenous shocks affecting environment-population inter-actions, and they led to rapid (by geological standards) speciation. Adaptive radiation occurs when some exogenous event weakens (or eliminates) an existing state of affairs and disturbs an equilibrium. From 1350 on, a combination of demography, information, technology, and politics weak-ened the cultural status quo in Europe.[32] Yet none of these events made the cultural innovations of early modern Europe inevitable—many shocks create not innovation and dynamic development but retrogression and re-treat. Other societies responded to shocks by taking a conservative turn and digging in—as Qing China and Tokugawa Japan both did. Europe was unique.

All the same, this argument only pushes the question one stage up. After all, why was it that Europeans, after being technologically and scienti-fically backward for many centuries, came up with new instruments, built better ships, and invented calculus? China had both a printing press and movable type centuries before Europe, yet it did not produce a Galileo, a Spinoza, or a Newton. It was building powerful seaworthy ships in the fifteenth century, yet Chinese sailors never showed up one day in Europe or on the Gold Coast. The same argument may be applied to India. Parthasarati (2011) has argued that as late as 1700, there was no discernible difference between the scientific and technological achievement of Britain and India. One might ask, had Britain and India been at the same level of economic and institutional development in 1700, why was there no "West-ern-Europe Company" set up in Delhi that would have exploited the deep political divisions within Europe to establish an Indian Raj in London, ex-tracting high rents from Europeans remitted to nouveaux riche nabobs in India and forced Europe to accept Indian calicoes without tariffs?

---

[32] Christopher Hill, in a memorable passage, summarized the sudden acceleration in the rate of cultural change in the era as follows: "men were still surrounded by blind, un-controllable force, whether of nature or society. But some were becoming conscious of new possi-bilities of controlling these forces. The great geographical discoveries, scientific, technical and medical advances, the liberation of thought after the Reformation and after: all this offered quite new perspectives ... they called for fresh thought about the nature of man" (Hill, 1967, p. 201).

Chapter 11

Fragmentation, Competition, and Cultural Change

As we have seen, one bias in cultural evolution is what I call *coercion bias*, the ability of those in power who have a strong stake in the cultural status quo—be it religious, artistic, or scientific—to suppress innovation and persecute heterodox cultural entrepreneurs who deviate from the received wisdom. Innovations can undermine an existing structure of beliefs and in the process "erode beliefs" that provide certain groups with rents and legitimization (Benabou, Ticchi, and Vindigni, 2014). Another way of looking at this bias is to note that incumbents erect high barriers to entry into the market for ideas to protect their monopoly. These barriers often rely on such terminology as "heresy," "apostasy," and "blasphemy" and depend on raw political power to prevent new ideas from competing. In other cases, the educational system may have built-in protection for the intellectual status quo, such as the Chinese civil-service examination system or Jewish religious education. Unlike highly competitive economic systems—where entry and exit in the limit are effort- and cost-free—at some level *all* evolutionary and cultural systems must have such a system in place, to lend some modicum of stability to existing beliefs and prevent complete chaos. The question is to what extent is such resistance too hermetic? If it is too airtight, it may make innovation of any kind practically impossible and condemn a society to cultural stasis. Degree is everything here. By the early sixteenth century, the forces of repression and resistance were beginning to lose ground in Europe in every cultural domain, making accelerated change possible. But the old culture did not leave without a fight. The forces of reaction regrouped in the Counter-Reformation, and the power of the Jesuit order in southern Europe and Latin America slowed down the diffusion of the *nuova scienzia* innovations and the rise of the Enlightenment in these areas. Influential conservative thinkers, such as Hobbes in England and Bossuet in France, fought intellectual innovation tooth and nail. The

proponents of the new philosophies fought back. One common denominator that most citizens of the Republic of Letters (otherwise a diverse and
fractious lot) shared was that they recognized their enemies, the opponents
of new ideas and pluralism.[1]

What changed history was that in Europe, over the long term, the
innovators defeated conservatism. This did not happen anywhere else.
How do we explain the unique European experience? One serious candidate
for explanation is what E. L. Jones (1981) has dubbed the European "states
system," consisting of highly fragmented units, constantly at loggerheads
with one another. Europe enjoyed significant advantages from political
fragmentation although at considerable cost. The idea that political fragmentation yields benefits because of the salutary effects of competition
among those who seek power dates back to the great thinkers of the
Enlightenment.[2] The most widely cited quote stressing the blessings from
political fragmentation is from David Hume:

> Nothing is more favorable to the rise of politeness and learning
> than a number of neighbouring and independent states, connected
> together by commerce and policy. The emulation, which naturally
> arises among those... is an obvious source of improvement. But
> which I would chiefly insist on is the stop [constraint] which such
> limited territories give both to power and authority ... The divisions
> into small states are favourable to learning, by stopping the
> progress of authority as well as that of power. Reputation is often
> as great a fascination upon men as sovereignty, and is equally
> destructive to the freedom of thought and examination. But where
> a number of neighbouring states have a great intercourse of arts
> and commerce, their mutual jealousy keeps them from receiving
> too lightly the law from each other, in matters of taste and of
> reasoning, and makes them examine every work of art with the
> greatest care and accuracy. The contagion of popular opinion
> spreads not so easily from one place to another. It readily receives
> a check in some state or other, where it concurs not with the
> prevailing prejudices Hume, [1742] 1985, pp. 119–20].

Modern scholars such as North (1981, p. 27), Jones (1981, pp. 109–
10), and more formally Karayalçin (2008) have largely interpreted the

---

[1] In 1640, Descartes wrote to the Dutch author and diplomat Constantijn Huygens (the
father of the better-known mathematician) that "he was going to war with the Jesuits" because of
their aversion to intellectual innovation and his radical novel ideas in philosophy and mathematics
(Ariew, 2003, pp. 157–60).

[2] The canonical statement by modern scholars is clearly Eric L. Jones, 1981. For more
recent restatements, see for example Bernholz, Streit and Vaubel, 1998.

advantages of political fragmentation as fiscal and administrative, in the sense that political competition restrained rulers to some extent from misruling their domains and overtaxing and exploiting their most productive but mobile citizens. Historically, the fiscal argument is rather tricky: it is true, of course, that in many European nations competition imposed constraints on the executive that in one form or another limited their ability to tax their citizens into poverty. To be sure, competition among states is not like that among firms or consumers in that there are no enforceable rules (whether imposed by a third party or by a self-enforcing mechanism) to tame and constrain competition and set the parameters on what forms it can take. State competition can often resort to extreme violence or mindless trade restrictions and tariff wars as well as state-sponsored piracy, weakening all economies. But it can also take highly productive forms. The same political fragmentation that led to frequent and expensive wars among the European powers, which required high taxes (and imposed other serious deadweight costs on the population as well), was associated with economic success. The two most progressive nations in eighteenth-century Europe, the Netherlands and Britain, were the most heavily taxed on average, even if their taxes had been consented to by their representative bodies (which rarely represented more than a small fraction of the taxpayers in any case).

There is validity to the argument that interstate competition in Europe at times did mitigate and soften the worst forms of mis-governance in Europe and led to institutional progress, such as it was.[3] Reforms were often introduced after a major military defeat (such as the Prussian defeat by Napoleon in 1806 or the Russian debacle in the Crimean War), or in an attempt to improve the economy so as to expand the tax base. Eric Jones notes that "the states system was an insurance against economic and

---

[3] This was quite keenly noted by Immanuel Kant. In the eighth proposition of his 1784 essay "Idea of a Universal and Cosmopolitan History," Kant observed that

> Now the States are already involved in the present day in such close relations with each other, that none of them can pause or slacken in its internal civilisation without losing power and influence in relation to the rest; and, hence the maintenance, if not the progress, of this end of Nature is, in a manner, secured even by the ambitious designs of the States themselves. Further, Civil Liberty cannot now be easily assailed without inflicting such damage as will be felt in all trades and industries, and especially in commerce; and this would entail a diminution of the powers of the State in external relations. ... But if the citizen is hindered in seeking his prosperity in any way suitable to himself that is consistent with the liberty of others, the activity of business is checked generally; and thereby the powers of the whole State, again, are weakened. Hence the restrictions on personal liberty of action are always more and more removed, and universal liberty even in Religion comes to be conceded. And thus ... the spirit of Enlightenment gradually arises as a great Good which the human race must derive even from the selfish purposes of aggrandisement on the part of its rulers, if they understand what is for their own advantage. Kant ([1784], 2010, pp. 30–31).

technological stagnation" (1981, p. 119). Yet at all times, the benefits of this competition must be weighed against the tremendous costs of destructive warfare and military spending. Indeed, the cultural changes after 1500 poured oil on the fires of war by adding religion as a casus belli and leading to a host of violent conflicts, made increasingly destructive by ever-more sophisticated weapons and larger armies that could be raised in part thanks to the profits made in the New World and in part through expanding economies.

The passage from Hume shows that he was clearly more concerned with culture than with taxes. Edward Gibbon, undoubtedly influenced by his friend Hume, added a somewhat exaggerated picture of the benefits of the European system of political fragmentation:

> Europe is now divided into twelve powerful, though unequal, kingdoms, three respectable commonwealths, and a variety of smaller, though independent, states: the chances of royal and ministerial talents are multiplied, at least, with the number of its rulers ... The abuses of tyranny are restrained by the mutual influence of fear and shame; republics have acquired order and stability; monarchies have imbibed the principles of freedom, or, at least, of moderation; and some sense of honour and justice is introduced into the most defective constitutions by the general manners of the times. In peace, the progress of knowledge and industry is accelerated by the emulation of so many active rivals; in war, the European forces are exercised by temperate and undecisive contests. (Gibbon, 1789, vol. 3, p. 636)

The Age of Enlightenment coined a new term for the competition among people of different nations, regarded as a salutary force. National *emulation* was regarded as the key to the "competitive pursuit of national economic excellence" and produced in this view "proficiency in the arts and sciences" (Hont, 2005, pp. 115–16). But, as Adam Smith pointed out in a memorable passage, "in such [technological and scientific] improvements each nation ought not only to endeavour itself to excel, but from the love of mankind, to promote instead of obstructing the excellence of its neighbours" (Smith [1759] 1969, p. 229). The boundary between "emulation" and "jealousy" was as vague as the boundary between peaceful competition and a more pernicious nationalism that could end in international violence.[4]

---

[4] Hume ([1742] 1985) used the term "jealous emulation" to describe one of the elements that would lead to economic development. Both Adam Ferguson and Adam Smith fully realized the danger of this double-edged sword even before the "national jealousy" erupted with full violence in 1793 (Hont, 2005, p. 122).

Competition among states, then, implied two things for cultural change. One is that rulers competed with one another for the best citizens, be they astrologers, painters, artisans, sea captains, musicians, or armorers. But more important, they provided a major reason for coordination failure among the powerful forces of conservatism trying to suppress intellectual innovators. Unless suppression was well coordinated among the reactionary powers, ingenious cultural entrepreneurs would play these powers against one another and survive. In 1415, Jan Hus still ended up at the stake in Constance, because the emperor and the pope were able to work together to eliminate this dangerous heretic. A century later this strategy no longer worked, and the Reformation could not be stopped. While most peasants may rarely have ventured outside their villages, and even most traveling journeymen stayed within the neighborhood of their place of birth (although more of them moved about than is commonly thought), members of the "creative classes"—top-rated craftsmen, engineers, physicians, architects, musicians, astrologers—moved all over the Continent.[5] Political fragmentation inevitably weakened the forces of reaction. The Jesuit Order, the most effective and consistent conservative force in Europe, did all it could to suppress new ideas, such as Copernican cosmology and infinitesimal mathematics. Had they gained more control in France, Britain and the Netherlands—say, because of decisive Spanish military victories—the intellectual development of Europe inevitably would have been impeded.

The precise reasons Europe remained fragmented the way it was whereas China and the Middle East were unified into coherent empires have been debated at some length (Hoffman, 2015, pp. 107–34, provides an excellent summary; see also Ko, Koyama, and Sng, 2015). Geography has undoubtedly played some role: the Pyrenees and the Alps may have helped preserve Spain and Switzerland as independent political states, and the Dutch rivers repeatedly kept out larger and more powerful neighboring armies.[6] Another argument is the interrelatedness of European monarchs and rulers, who formed coalitions based on family ties and preserved the status quo. Even when relatives fought one another, as happened repeatedly, they usually refrained from dethroning a brother or a cousin. Instead, Hoffman proposes a model based on ideas derived from cultural evolution. Strong beliefs about the value of courage and heroism in battle plus a cul-

---

[5] No more than 75 percent of all engineers working in sixteenth-century Spain were born there; the others came from Italy, Germany, Flanders, and England (Davids, 2013, p. 182).

[6] Ko et al show that through most of its history China faced a severe, unidirectional threat from the Eurasian steppe, whereas Europe confronted several smaller threats from Scandinavia, Central Asia, the Middle East, and North Africa. They argue that empires were not viable in Europe, and political fragmentation turned out to be the norm. In contrast, empires were more likely to emerge and survive in China, because the nomadic threat endangered the survival of small states more than it did larger ones.

turally-learned dislike of other groups were included in the socialization of youngsters, which made it more difficult to create a common European identity that a unifying warlord might exploit. Beyond that, Hoffman argues that Western Christianity was a factor here, as the popes used their religious influence to prevent any European ruler, and above all the Holy Roman Emperor, from amassing too much power (Hoffman, 2015, pp. 132–34). One might add that contingency may have played a role as well: had the Spanish Armada succeeded or Napoleon won at Waterloo, perhaps the story might have ended differently.

What emerged in medieval Europe, and turned out to be of great importance is that political fragmentation was coupled with an intellectual and cultural unity, an integrated market for ideas, that allowed Europe to benefit from the obvious economies of scale associated with intellectual activity.[7] This unity derived from both Europe's classical heritage and the widespread use of Latin as the lingua franca of intellectuals, and the Christian Church. While for much of the Middle Ages the level of intellectual activity (in terms of both the number of participants and the intensity of the debates) was thin compared to what it was to become after 1500, it was *transnational*. This unique combination of political fragmentation with the pan-European institution of the Republic of Letters holds the key to the dramatic intellectual changes after 1500.

Thus, as Jean Baechler (2004) has stressed, the political fragmentation and the concomitant pluralism of Europe became a key to its intellectual development. The dark forces of reaction in the sixteenth century were no less benighted than those of the fourteenth, but it became increasingly difficult for those forces to work together, in part because some defenders of the conventional wisdom were Protestant and others Catholic.[8] The forces of the Catholic reaction were fragmented among themselves.[9] Authorities could not agree on who were heretics and what to do about them, and the heretics took full advantage of this. The unique situation in

---

[7] Cohen (2012, p. 206) refers to these economies of scale, as he points out that one of the factors that may have given early modern Europe (as opposed to early Islamic civilization) an advantage in making scientific breakthroughs as opposed to early Islamic civilization is sheer numbers, in which Europe had an advantage of 1:4.3 (adjusted for time). That number, one should add, is attained by aggregating *all* European scientists—implicitly assuming that Europe constituted a single intellectual community.

[8] Consider Luther's disciple Philipp Melanchthon's denunciation of Copernicus: "some think it a distinguished achievement to construct such a crazy thing as that Prussian astronomer who moves the earth and fixes the sun. Verily, wise rulers should tame the unrestraint of men's minds" (cited by Kesten, 1945, p. 309). Luther himself said caustically of Copernicus, "the fool wishes to turn the entire art of Astronomy on its head" (cited by Merton, 1973, p. 245).

[9] Thus for instance the reactionary Pope Paul IV in the 1550s alienated the main Catholic power, the Habsburgs, as well as the English Catholic legate, Cardinal Reginald Pole, the leader of the Catholic reaction in England whom he denounced as a heretic.

Europe, then, was that intolerance and the suppression of cultural hetero-doxy, long before they fell out of fashion, could not be properly coordi-nated. Many innovators—not least Martin Luther, who was protected by the powerful prince-elector Frederick III of Saxony and later by the latter's brother and successor John—were able to game the political system to avoid persecution. Hostility among the European powers led each ruler to protect the gadflies that irritated his or her enemies. One noteworthy example is Tommaso Campanella, (1568–1639), an Italian monk who studied astro-nomy, astrology, and occult philosophy, like many others became skeptical of the Aristotelian orthodoxy. He was accused from an early age of heresy by the Inquisition; his ability to play one power against another in fragmented Italy failed him when he was sentenced to life imprisonment in 1599 (for anti-Spanish activity rather than for heresy) and spent twenty-seven years in a Neapolitan jail. However, his conditions there were sufficiently benign that he could write seven books in jail as well as a pam-phlet defending Galileo during his first trial in 1616. In the end, he was released from jail through the intervention of Pope Urban VIII, but got in trouble again. He had succeeded, however, in endearing himself to the French authorities (anxious to embarrass the Spanish). Through the inter-vention of the French ambassador he made it out of Italy to France, where he was honored by the court of Louis XIII and eventually accepted even by the suspicious Cardinal Richelieu and died in Paris (Headley, 1997, pp. 117–27).[10] In other cases, the ability of intellectual innovators to move about the Continent to escape potential persecutors left the incumbents powerless to suppress innovations, though the causality between mobility and intel-lectual innovation is of course rather complex.

By the eighteenth century, the attempts of reactionary forces to suppress innovations had become a bit of a charade, and while the more outrageous *philosophes* such as Helvétius and Lamettrie still had to move about when the local authorities became disenchanted with them, they usually found welcoming hosts abroad. By the closing decades of the eight-eenth century the forces of the Enlightenment had become too powerful to resist, and even in much of Catholic Europe persecution of heretics

---

[10] Another, earlier, case is that of Bernardino Ochino (1487–1564), a highly contro-versial Siennese Franciscan monk and preacher, committed to free inquiry and controversy, and famous for an unusual eloquence. He managed to alienate the Catholic Church, especially attracting the hostility of the reactionary hard line Cardinal Giovanni-Pietro Caraffa (later Pope Paul IV, 1555–1559). An equal-opportunity gadfly, Ochino also alienated most protestants. He was summoned to appear before the Roman Inquisition established in 1542 (one of the first "heretics" to be so persecuted) and fled to Geneva in 1547, eventually ending up in England, whence he was driven by the ascension of the intolerant Mary Tudor. Returning to Zurich, he was again expelled and ended up in Poland (at that time a relatively tolerant nation) but was banished from it in 1564 at the instigation of the papacy and he died in Moravia. Among other things he advocated divorce and was suspected of supporting polygamy (Benrath, 1877).

slackened even if heterodox views had to be cast in prudent terms.[11] The Jesuits were suppressed by the pope in 1773, and intellectual pluralism became increasingly the dominant modus operandi everywhere in Europe west of the Elbe river.

Moreover, the fragmentation of Europe into many independent states and statelets was only part of the underpinning for a competitive market for ideas and seriously understates the degree of political fragment-ation. In ostensibly unified countries, such as the Netherlands and Spain, local and regional authorities had a large degree of independence (Grafe, 2012). Moreover, within each state, there were many more or less autono-mous, mostly self-governing entities or "corporations," in which heterodox opinions could flourish.[12] Among those entities in early medieval Europe, monasteries had been in the vanguard. Gradually they were joined by universities, where the sons of the elite were offered information and beliefs beyond their early socialization and could be exposed to intellectual inno-vations. Much like monasteries, universities were quasi-autonomous self-governing bodies. Despite their independence from the central government, European universities were, however, rarely the taproot of intellectual inno-vation. Indeed, as much as any organization, they helped maintain the *auctoritates* of the canon (mostly religious texts, Aristotle, and some of the classical textbooks of medicine), which were the classical books that any educated person was expected to read and discuss. Universities were usually bodies that guarded tradition and the intellectual status quo. They thrived on exegesis and commentary, and made sure that the knowledge of one generation was passed on whole and unaltered to the next. Even those scientists who started their careers as part of universities escaped them when their fame had risen enough to enable them to find better patronage (Galileo and Newton immediately come to mind). Universities in early modern Europe were, then, mostly highly conservative organizations in which, for the most part, "critical learning" meant purging classical texts of distortions introduced through copying and translation errors in a later time. The goal of the typical university scholar was "textual purity rather than scientific truth" (Debus, 1978, p. 4). This was the kind of scholarship that we find in

---

[11] The Spanish Benedictine monk Benito Jeronimo Feijoo (1676–1764), one of the leaders of the Spanish Enlightenment, published essays in which he considered the arguments for and against the Copernican system. While he was careful to remain formally loyal to the scriptures, he laid out the arguments on both sides. His eight-volume book of essays, *Teatro Critico Universal* (1726–1739) was not only approved by the censors; it was actually praised lavishly by them (Castellano, 2004, p. 34).

[12] As Slack (2015, p. 65) points out in the case of England, "in the seventeenth century every aspect of social welfare was being managed by corporate bodies, by parish vestries, charitable trusts, civic corporations, and companies of merchants, whose collective cultures communicated and sustained shared values."

the kaozheng movement in China at the time, and while it was clearly critical and evidence-based, it was fundamentally backward looking.

All the same, some universities, especially newly founded ones or those that had been rejuvenated by the arrival of a few leading scholars, could generate heterodox cultural elements. The newly founded university at Wittenberg was barely fifteen years old when one of its professors famously nailed his ninety-five propositions to the church door. Galileo did some of his best work at the University of Padua, as did Andreas Vesalius; it counted both William Harvey and Nicolaus Copernicus among its graduates.[13] For much of the period between 1500 and 1700, it was the best university in Europe, and the government of Venice bent over backward to accommodate its distinguished if opinionated faculty and protected them from papal and Jesuit obscurantism. The University of Leyden in its golden age in the first half of the eighteenth century was perhaps the most dynamic and successful institution spreading the new Newtonian physics and cutting-edge medicine. In Britain the eighteenth-century Scottish universities famously became a center of innovation in science, political philosophy, medicine, and many other areas. Some, though not all, German universities reformed during the age of Enlightenment and encouraged new styles of learning oriented toward contemporary issues and practical disciplines (Moran, 1991b, p. 178). Progressive universities rose and fell, and few remained innovative over the very long haul. But because they were numerous, of them, it was rare that there was not some innovative activity taking place at *some* university in Europe. When such intellectual innovation occurred, central authorities had difficulty suppressing it. Furthermore, universities had to compete with other scientific organizations, such as the various academies and learned societies that sprang up all over Europe in the seventeenth century.

Something similar can be said about guilds. They, too, were autonomous organizations that to a large extent were self-regulating and enforced their own institutional elements. A long and acrimonious debate has developed over the question whether craft guilds were technologically progressive or conservative in European economic history (for recent summaries, see Prak and van Zanden, 2013 and Ogilvie, 2014). But guilds lasted at least half a millennium in many regions and regulated many crafts. They often crystallized existent skills and techniques and resisted innovation in an attempt to protect the exclusionary rents of incumbents. In other cases they encouraged innovation, diffused new ideas geographically, and encouraged younger members to think for themselves. Guilds, despite their local autonomy, were often allied with kings; hence they were known as *choses du roi*. Kings were often interested in technological innovation as a

---

[13] Another innovative Padua professor was Girolamo Fracastoro (1478–1553), possibly the first physician to propose that diseases were caused by minute invisible organisms.

way of strengthening their tax base or their military capability, and thus guilds could be seen on both sides of the line.

Another of the independent corporations that Europe—and few other societies—offered was the autonomous, largely self-governing city. The Republic of Letters, much like the Reformation, was largely an urban phenomenon.[14] Not all cities were welcoming to heterodox intellectuals: not the Rome of Pope Clement VIII who was personally involved in the execution of Giordano Bruno; not Calvin's Geneva; and not the Utrecht dominated by reactionary theologians such as the Calvinist theologian Gisbertus Voetius (Gijsbert Voet, 1589–1676).[15] But there were always enough towns where one could go, or at least find an audacious publisher who would print one's works. Venice in the first half of the seventeenth century (which included Padua) was an exceptionally tolerant and open-minded environment in which unconventional and heterodox thinkers such as Galileo, Paolo Sarpi (1552–1623), and Cesare Cremonini (1550–1631) could thrive (Muir, 2007). It banished the Jesuits, who fought for a more conservative and orthodox curriculum between 1606 and 1657.[16] Stras-bourg, a cosmopolitan border town, was famous for its tolerance, as was Basel, "a city ever hospitable to refugees from oppression in their native countries" (Grafton, 2009a, p. 7). Wittenberg, Leyden, Louvain, and Mont-pellier were university towns that at one point or another were home to important intellectual innovators and scholars. The miraculous growth of London after 1570 had an obvious cultural effect (Harkness, 2007, esp. pp. 160–69; Slack, 2015, p. 75). The urbanization of the age of the great voyages and the flourishing of commerce in the Renaissance towns thus provided an unintended underpinning for future development. It is also striking that some of the smaller independent political entities in Europe punched above their weight in the Republic of Letters. The important role of the Nether-lands as a site of tolerant pluralism (at least most of the time) is well known. Barnett (2015) has pointed to the Swiss towns as a pivotal location in con-necting the Italian Republic of Letters with its Northern counterparts, as

---

[14] For an argument about the importance of cities in cultural change in the sixteenth century, see Wuthnow, 1989, pp. 41–45.

[15] Hooykaas (1972, p. 100) writes that especially commercial and industrial cities were intellectually dynamic, far more so than sleepy university towns. These cities also tended to be more tolerant of different religions and multilingual. Modern research has found that especially cities involved in Atlantic trade were institutionally dynamic (Acemoglu, Johnson, and Robinson, 2005).

[16] In his play *Life of Galileo*, Bertold Brecht has the University of Padua curator explain to Galileo that while the university may not pay quite as much as some wealthy patrons, "it guarantees freedom of religion and even admit Protestants to our lectures" (cited by Muir, 2007, p. 16).

well as their polyglot character, which produced a set of translators needed when more and more intellectuals began publishing in their vernacular.

Political fragmentation was thus important for more than restrained taxes and effective governance; it was a major factor in the emergence of cultural pluralism. In the sixteenth century, heterodox cultural variants emerged in many fields, meaning that existing barriers to entry were being compromised and penetrated. New people challenged the conventional wisdom in every area of knowledge and thought. To be sure, a variety of conservative bodies made serious attempts to suppress innovators, and some of the most innovative cultural entrepreneurs paid with their lives.[17] No European country was completely free of suppression. Protestant nations were at times more intolerant than Catholic ones. The leading religious reformers were themselves far from paragons of tolerance, and philosophers of the early Enlightenment did not all believe in a level playing field in the market for ideas.

Notwithstanding the formidable powers of conservative forces, dissent and innovation flourished. Fragmentation, footlooseness, and the proliferation of printing presses meant that it became increasingly difficult for politically powerful incumbents to suppress subversive and heretic new beliefs generated by cultural entrepreneurs. Any such suppression would only mean that the persons targeted would flee elsewhere.[18] Studies of European intellectuals show that they had a high rate of mobility, despite the obviously high costs of traveling (Mokyr, 2006c).[19] The Moravian intellectual Jan Comenius (né Komensky, 1592–1670), is an example, albeit an extreme one. His career spanned at least four major and quite different countries (Bohemia, England, Poland, and Holland), as he repeatedly fled persecution for his views. He declined a fifth when he turned down an offer to serve as the first president of Harvard. Desiderius Erasmus was as peripatetic as one could get in an age of poor transport. Born in Rotterdam, he studied in Paris, holding appointments in Basel, Leuven, and Cambridge. During his stay in Leuven he felt victimized by critics, who opposed his

[17] An example is the execution of Jan of Leiden, an early leader of the Anabaptist reformation in 1536—oddly enough by the deposed bishop of Münster, Franz von Waldeck, who had known Lutheran sympathies. Yet it is telling that the harsh violence used against Anabaptists failed to put an end to the movement.

[18] A striking example is that of Pierre Bayle (1647–1707), a highly critical and skeptical French intellectual, who switched from Catholicism to Calvinism and eventually fled to Rotterdam while his works were burned at the stake in France (which greatly increased their popularity); less innocuously, his brother was arrested *faute de mieux* and died in jail. See Labrousse (1983, p. 28).

[19] It is indeed striking that, despite the obvious improvements in inter-European transportation, the distance between place of birth and place of death among notable Europeans, a rather rough measure of footlooseness, has changed little since the Middle Ages (Schich et al., 2014, p. 560).

devotion to a more progressive text interpretation, and took refuge in Basel. Later in his life, when he was the most eminent and widely respected humanist scholar of his age and one who refused to take strong positions on the most disputed issues of his day, there is no evidence that he was ever seriously threatened by people who disagreed with him. Erasmus's close friend, Juan Luis Vives, the son of persecuted Spanish *conversos,* left Spain at age sixteen never to return and spent much of his life commuting between Bruges and England.

Many other intellectuals moved from country to country in search of learning, patronage, and teaching positions, escaping religious intolerance and at times creditors, jealous husbands, and other sources of distraction, but they also traveled to find the newest and best knowledge and to sell their own ideas in larger markets than their place of birth. Traveling, despite the discomforts and the hazards, to study with the best and most prestigious scholars remained a central mode of learning, and few European intellectuals followed the example of Newton who never left England and never ventured north of the Lincolnshire hamlet of his birth near Grantham. Above all, traveling was a safeguard against oppression and intellectual persecution, and the common knowledge that moving elsewhere was an option for heterodox scholars helped cultivate the rise of tolerance in Europe.

It is telling for the way the Republic of Letters worked that Hobbes wrote *Leviathan* in Paris and Locke his *Letter on Toleration* in Amsterdam. The Dutch jurist Hugo Grotius fled the Netherlands and took refuge in Paris. Descartes, who lived for much of his life in the Netherlands, left the country when Prince Maurice took the side of hard-line Calvinists in 1619. Two centuries after Erasmus's death, European intellectuals still took advantage of its fragmentation. Voltaire famously purchased his property in Ferney in the 1750s close enough to the Swiss border to make an escape if push came to shove, but within France to avoid repressive Geneva regulations on having a private theater on his estate. As Gibbon observed, in Europe "a modern tyrant" would discover that "the object of his displeasure would easily obtain in a happier climate, a secure refuge, a new fortune adequate to his merit [and] ... the freedom of complaint" (1789, vol. I, p. 100). The fragmentation of Germany and Italy, as we have already seen, protected many intellectual innovators from the fury of the reaction.[20] Many intellectual innovators were able to thrive by moving with virtuosity on the

---

[20] Thus, for instance, the heterodox friar Paolo Sarpi was protected by the Venetian Republic, which blithely ignored the papal summons by Paul V to send him to Rome and the ensuing excommunication (1607). The pope tried to get the Spanish king to support him militarily, but the equally Catholic king of France supported Venice, and the pope had to resort to a heavy-handed attempt to assassinate Sarpi (which failed).

seams between competing powers.[21] Moreover, even when intellectuals could not move easily, their books and writings did—in great part thanks to the printing press and the growing ease of shipping books. In this kind of world, suppressing heterodoxy became simply unworkable.

Political fragmentation in the early modern period meant not so much that Europeans were more tolerant than those residing in other parts of the world from the outset (the opposite was the case) than that in Europe intolerance became ineffective in the long run. After 1660 or so, tolerance of heterodox views, not matter how objectionable, was on the rise and effective suppression of disruptive or subversive intellectuals (hoping perhaps to become successful cultural entrepreneurs) was fading. Most regimes still felt the need to pay lip service to the accepted orthodoxies and prohibit certain publications, as when the works of Spinoza banned by the Dutch Estates General in 1678 but then published and disseminated clandestinely. Much the same happened to Voltaire's *Lettres Philosophiques* in 1734 (they were actually burned symbolically by executioners). The last person to be executed for blasphemy in Britain was one Thomas Aikenhead, hanged in pre-Enlightenment Edinburgh in 1697, for explicitly anti-Christian beliefs. Unitarianism, which could be a capital crime in the sixteenth century and still left Newton uncomfortable, was more or less tolerated in his later years.[22] The free-thinking Irish intellectual John Toland (1670–1722), whose writings slaughtered virtually every sacred cow imaginable and "generated great hostility," experienced no worse persecution than being ordered by its vice chancellor to leave conservative Oxford (Daniel, 2004). In France, the best-known Enlightenment writers found themselves "playing a game of harmless charades" with the censors (Gay, 1969, p. 77).[23] Most rulers began

---

[21] Another example is Johann Joachim Becher (1635–1682), a German alchemist, engineer, and entrepreneur, one of the founders of phlogiston theory, who worked alternately for a variety of German rulers, including the elector of Bavaria, the emperor, and smaller German princes as a court scientist and counselor, moving each time that his enemies and rivals got the better of him. Becher's ability to exploit the political fragmentation in Europe bordered on the virtuosic, enabling him to move rapidly between the Imperial court and various German princedoms. In Vienna he was able to play the Habsburg emperor against his own Hofkammer. When his German patronage ran out, he ended up in England in 1680 (Smith, 1994).

[22] Snobelen (1999) has pointed out how toothless the laws against heresy had become in Britain after 1700 through the examples of Newton's students and friends William Whiston and Samuel Clarke in the early 1710s. There was a cost in terms of patronage: Whiston's anti-trinitarianism cost him his professorship and any further hope of public office. Clarke's heterodoxy prevented further ecclesiastical preferment. Still, neither man was jailed or fined —let alone defrocked. Whiston wrote a highly successful book popularizing Newton's work and went on to obtain patronage from the nobility, while Clarke retained his rectorship at St James's in London.

[23] Jean-Jacques Rousseau still found himself persona non grata at Montmorency after the 1762 publication of *Émile*, and ended up traveling throughout Europe, especially in Switzerland and Britain, but soon all was forgiven, and he was able to live out his last decade in France. Claude-Adrien Helvétius's *De l'Esprit*, published in 1758, was condemned by the Sorbonne and

to see the futility of the effort and attempts to persecute people regarded as troublemakers were half-hearted at best. David Hume was denied a tenured professorship at Edinburgh because of his alleged heterodox views, but otherwise he was not much harassed. Kant, too, felt the harshest side of suppression when he was "reprimanded" by the king of Prussia for his heterodox views. There remained some uncertainty for authors, but not nearly enough to put an end to the flow of new radical ideas and the people producing them.

By the middle of the eighteenth century it is fair to say that even in so-called absolutist countries, the suppression of dissenting and even heretical voices had become more of a ritualized formality than a real threat. The more conservative rulers of Europe found themselves pushed toward a policy of "if you cannot beat them, join them" and co-opted many of the ideas of the Enlightenment, creating the somewhat oxymoronic "enlightened despots" (Scott, 1990). The liberal ideas of religious tolerance, free entry into the market for ideas, and belief in the transnational character of the intellectual community were essential to Enlightenment thought. These were the cultural underpinnings of the institutions that not only supported a functioning market for ideas, that is, a market in which innovators had a fair chance to persuade their audiences. They also actively encouraged intellectual innovation and thus laid the foundation for the emergence of the modern economy.

the books burned in public; Helvétius had to formally retract his ideas and found himself in England, later on in Potsdam. Yet the entire reaction did not last, and in 1765 he was allowed to return to France and back in favor again. Even more striking is the history of the radical atheist gadfly Julien La Mettrie (1709–1751), whose heretical works first forced him to take refuge in Leyden, but even there his hedonism so annoyed his hosts that he was forced to leave for Berlin, where Frederick the Great delighted in his often outrageous opinions. After 1750, censorship in France was left to Guillaume-Chrétien de Lamoignon de Malesherbes (1721–1794), a kind and somewhat ineffectual lawyer, who actually maintained tight friendships with opposition intellectuals such as Diderot and Grimm.

Chapter 12

Competition and the Republic of Letters

The institutional background of the intellectual community in early modern Europe consisted of a polycentric political environment coexisting with a transnational Republic of Letters, which included scholars and literati. The importance of that community was huge. For one thing, it overcame the limitations of fragmentation by providing the intellectual innovator with a much larger audience than his or her own countrymen. While the power of the ruler was limited by the borders of the realm, the influence of intellectuals paid no heed to political boundaries. Moreover, precisely because the knowledge was not rooted primarily in local conditions, it could make stronger claims to universality. Above all, it was this community that provided a set of institutional incentives encouraging academic and artistic "superstars."[1] Erasmus himself thought of his scholar friends as "amicarum communia omnia" (Schoeck, 1982, p. 303). A century later, Thomas Browne, while he may not have used the exact term, uses terms such as "Latine Republique" and "common wealth of learning" and stressed the importance of the sharing of knowledge as a duty of all its members or citizens (Denonain, 1982, p. 371). The community provided a competitive marketplace not only for ideas but also for the people who generated them in their struggle to gain recognition, fame, and patronage.[2] It was the ultimate

---

[1] The idea of academic superstars over whom patrons would compete was already present in the late sixteenth century: the eminent French classical scholar Joseph Scaliger (1540–1609) was tempted to join the faculty at Leyden University in 1593 with the promise of a salary higher than that of the law professors and a complete release from teaching duties.

[2] Perkinson (1995, p. 74) stresses the importance of a community of scholars forming "a collection of widely scattered readers ... who kept abreast of the state of knowledge in a given field" and who subjected each new idea to a critique and a set of validity tests, yet he insists on ascribing this community entirely to the printing press.

realization of the Talmudic wisdom that *kin at sofrim tarbeh chochma*—the jealousy of the learned shalt increase wisdom.

We should not overrate the quantitative importance of the Republic of Letters. The vast bulk of the women and men who lived in Europe between 1500 and 1700 would have had no idea of its existence. It was a small, often-endangered species, whose precarious existence depended on the power of the minds of its founding parents and those who followed in their footsteps. It was not an enlightened age, and the ideas of tolerance and universalism were still in embryonic form, if that. Yet, as Anthony Grafton (2009a, p. 5) has put it so well, within an ocean of darkness, small bands of intellectuals navigated in fragile crafts, little communities of scholars with their own values and rules. What should be added, however, is that these small bands were not insulated: their strength came from the close ties they maintained with one another and the astonishingly effective network that emerged as a result—not by design, not by intention, but all the same capable of bringing about a historic sea change. Moreover, the emergence of the "state" in early modern Europe is widely believed to be central to the story. "The holders of authoritative positions made decisions with respect to culture producers that greatly enhanced or impeded the work of these producers," argues Wuthnow (1989, p.17). This loses sight of the transnational nature of the community of "culture producers" and the fierce competition among states and wealthy individuals for having the privilege to host the best and the brightest Europeans, whatever their nationality, as Wuthnow acknowledges elsewhere. Authorities had an influence on the evolution of culture, but it was constrained, and often depended on the political accident that determined the persons and personalities in power and thus lacked consistency (Wuthnow, 1989, pp. 167–68).

The Republic of Letters was decidedly not a construct of modern historians. It was very much an institution of which contemporaries were fully conscious, and they realized its significance.[3] Pierre Bayle began publishing his newsletter *Nouvelles de la République des Lettres* from 1684, printing it in his relatively safe abode in Holland. Bayle said of his "citizens" that "we are all equal, because we are all the children of Apollo" (quoted in Dibon, 1978, p. 45). But "all" pertained to an elite that was estimated in Bayle's age to have 1,200 members, and a century later perhaps 12,000 (Brockliss, 2002, p. 8). While the evidentiary base of these estimates can be questioned, there is no doubt that the number of people involved was tiny relative to the population. As noted, it existed primarily as a virtual

---

[3] Marc Fumaroli (2015, pp. 50, 294–96) assigns special significance to the Venetian satirist Trajano Boccalini (1556–1613) who published in 1612 a best-selling work, *Ragguagli de Parnaso* (*Newsletter from Parnassus*), which was translated into many languages. In Fumaroli's opinion, this work established the idea of an independent intellectual community among a large transnational and transreligious constituency and constituted a precursor of Bayle's later work.

entity, kept alive by letters and publications that were open to all. But some of it was clearly located in formal organizations—the Royal Society, the French Royal Academy, and the many Continental academies founded in the eighteenth century.[4] The Republic of Letters was the institution that resolved the problem of rewarding creative individuals for efforts and talent and above all for originality and creativity.

Competitive patronage was the chief, but not the only incentive mechanism in the Republic of Letters. Prince-savants and other patrons were supposed to be able to recognize and value high ability and cultivate it, a signal of their legitimizing wisdom. This tradition was still respected in the eighteenth century by Frederick the Great, whose patronage of the best of Europe's intellectuals is well known. In practice, however, reputation based on peer evaluation was what counted (David, 2008). While patronizing learning and the arts was clearly a form of conspicuous consumption, there were other pragmatic advantages: some wealthy merchants had a deep interest in natural history and the details of the material world in areas that directly affected their activities such as navigation and accounting, as well as in engineering, medicine, and astrology. To inform them, they needed contact with experts and intellectuals. While the superstars enjoyed the tight competition for their services and could bargain for the best appointments, many lesser lights had to struggle for such patronage. In general, the higher one's scientific reputation, the better the chances (David, 2008). Reputations increasingly were no longer based just on erudition and knowledge of the classics; one had to make *original* contributions to be assessed by one's peers in the scholarly community. In this way the system encouraged and incentivized intellectual innovation.

Continent-wide reputations required good communications. During the Renaissance, Europe witnessed the creation of increasingly dense epistolary networks of scholars and engineers that transcended political and ethnic boundaries (Collins, 1998). These networks grew throughout Europe due to commercialization and the growth of medium- and long-distance trade. The improvements in shipping and other transport technologies were key to the expansion of the Republic of Letters. Reputations and correspondence networks were strongly complementary: intellectuals measured themselves by their ability to communicate with the superstars of the scholarly world. D'Alembert, one of the most prominent citizens of the eighteenth-century Republic of Letters, wrote in his eulogy for Jean Bouhier (1673–1746), another respected member and president of the French Academy in 1746 that "nothing is better for furthering the reputation of a man of letters ... than a large epistolary commerce ... and even the great Leibniz

---

[4] Some scholars, such as Goodman (1991, p. 184), see the Parisian salon as the primary form that gave the Republic of Letters a source of organizational order for its social relations and discourse, a somewhat Francocentric point of view perhaps (Melton, 2001, p. 211).

himself employed it responding even to the most obscure writers "
(D'Alembert, 1821, vol. 3, p. 325).

It was expected that in return for patronage, intellectuals display
loyalty to the monarchs and nobles who sponsored them, but such loyalty
rarely extended to a direct control over the writings of scholars beyond
fawning dedications. Many of the most prominent scholars and patrons,
even in the age of religious fanaticism, could be quite flexible in their
religious loyalties.[5] The international competition among courts, rich private patrons, universities, and later academies for the best and most eminent
scholars meant that in the long run the power of the patron and the local
religious authorities to control or dictate their views to the intellectuals he
or she employed was limited. This competition implied a relatively high
level of freedom for people to propose new ideas in an increasingly open
market for ideas.[6] In the seventeenth and eighteenth centuries, some princes
formalized their patronage and rather than having scientists and intellectual
at their courts, they were appointed to formal academies and universities
under their control. While the patronage enjoyed by intellectual innovators
was often fickle and intrusive, on the demand side there was enough competition among rulers to ensure a reasonable amount of independence from
political and religious institutions for most members of the community.

This relative independence from rulers helped turn the scholarly
community into an institution that incentivized the educated elites in
Europe to produce intellectual innovations that led to an unprecedented
flourishing of new ideas in every area. It also led to the emergence of an
impressive number of heterodox scholars who thought outside the box and
promulgated original hypotheses and notions, in the hope of acquiring the
respect of their colleagues and peers. Court patronage provided some of the
best minds of Europe with the freedom and leisure to pursue their interests.
In a few cases, such patronage liberated scholars from universities, when
these were unfriendly to innovative intellectuals. Moreover, for scientists
and artists to be recognized by figures of high social standing and power
mattered because such recognition conveyed respectability in an age in
which outside the scholarly community "whom you knew" conveyed as
much social prestige as "how much you owned" (Hahn, 1990, p. 7). In early
modern Europe, intellectuals as such (with the exception perhaps of a
handful of superstars) still had fairly low social status. Powerful and high-

---

[5] The renowned Flemish philological and humanist scholar Justus Lipsius (1547–
1606), though a lifelong Catholic, seemed to have little trouble conforming formally to Lutheranism while teaching at Jena between 1570 and 1572 and in Calvinist Leyden between 1579 and
1592. The Habsburg Emperor Rudolf II, nominally a Catholic, was the patron of Protestant
scholars, including Kepler (who had steadfastly refused to convert to Catholicism).

[6] This was equally true at a more local level: Cohen (2012, p. 585) points out that it
was during the "unruly" English interregnum in the mid-seventeenth century when censorship
broke down and hence all kinds of "half-baked ideas and projects had a chance to gain a hearing."

status patrons supplied them with an opportunity for a secure existence as well as elevated social status; thus, patronage provided powerful incentives to creative and learned people to exert themselves. In the eighteenth century, as the economic power of the urban bourgeoisie increased, the population of potential patrons and customers widened.

There was a close connection between the competition of the political entities in the European states system and a new feature of the European intellectual elite that arises in early modern Europe, namely, the rise of "open science" (David, 2008). With remarkably few exceptions, European scholars who made discoveries or generated new insights of any kind placed the information in the public realm through books, pamphlets, personal correspondence, and periodicals. Only in that fashion could others know and recognize their work and their reputation grow. In his magisterial work on the topic, William Eamon (1994) has described how science in early modern Europe became less and less secretive.[7] By reducing the secretiveness of knowledge and turning useful knowledge into what today would be called an open-source system, European intellectuals created an institution that reduced access costs. It is easy to dismiss the importance of codifiable (written) knowledge and the networks that diffused them by arguing that "not a single premodern innovation was transferred by print alone" (Epstein, 2013, p. 53). It is also a bit shortsighted. Formal knowledge, be it mathematical or experimental, was largely disseminated through written or printed communications. Can we really dismiss its importance for the subsequent technological development of the Continent?

The growth of open science as the central institutional principle of the intellectual world of early modern Europe did not occur by any conscious design. It was an emergent property, the unintended consequence of a different phenomenon: scholars trying to build reputations among their peers in order to gain various advantages, including the much-hoped-for financial security, freedom, and time to do undisturbed research through patronage positions. The resulting decline in access costs was central to the way that useful knowledge affected technology and eventually productivity and economic performance (Mokyr, 2005). It also serves as a good example of how institutions were internalized and then "fed back" into cultural beliefs: open science and free access to knowledge as a social method of organizing knowledge became itself a value, something to be savored and protected. The question that it resolved was the classic dilemma of an inappropriable but valuable resource: if knowledge was regarded a public

---

[7] Not all members of the Republic of Letters adhered loyally to its principles of openness and transparency; the great Jesuit polymath Athanasius Kircher (1601–1680), for example, still clung to secrecy and concealed much of his evidence. He was concerned that the ancient wisdoms he thought he had unearthed should not fall into the wrong hands and should be kept from the common people (Malcolm, 2004). Such attitudes, however, increasingly fell into disrepute as the Republic of Letters matured during the seventeenth century.

good and dispensed freely, as open science demanded, how would those who created it be incentivized and rewarded? What kind of property rights could intellectual innovators secure?

What do property rights in new knowledge actually mean? As economists have long realized, the economics of useful knowledge is complex precisely because of the appropriability issues associated with all knowledge creation, which makes it practically impossible to impart it to some and exclude others. An innovator can either keep the new knowledge secret and tell know no one or can reveal it to a few, but then there is obviously the risk of losing control and experience full disclosure. The knowledge is, moreover, non-rivalrous in that by sharing it the innovator has no less of it, though he or she risks having a smaller share of the market if they try to sell a newly invented product. For propositional knowledge, in any event, the likelihood that it can be "sold" in any form is small, and so the incentive system is not well structured. One could speculate that most societies that ever existed produced less useful knowledge than they could have, simply because the rewards were not there and the risks were substantial.

It is remarkable that only Western Europe after ca. 1600 managed to create the conditions for this knowledge to accumulate at an ever more rapid pace, enough eventually to affect every aspect of production. But the solutions found were complex. Roughly speaking, the property rights in useful knowledge trifurcated into three categories. First, propositional knowledge was normally placed in the public realm, with the hope that others would recognize it and attribute it henceforth to the author and thus enhance his or her reputation. Here property rights meant credit but not the exclusion of others—on the contrary. Publication and correspondence were critical to the proper operating of the system, spread over most of the continent. Eisenstein (1979, p. 229) noted that "scribal culture ... worked against the concept of intellectual property rights" but in fact stresses that authors and their publishers did all they could to publicize themselves, to the point of writing blurbs and other forms of "the art of puffery."

Second, in contrast, those who generated new prescriptive knowledge—that is, technology—in many cases tried to earn rents by exclusion. In some areas inventions could be patented. In theory that meant that the inventor released the information in exchange for a temporary monopoly or, in some cases, a payment from some public agency. The alternative was to try to keep the knowledge secret. Secrecy could and was still attempted by Italian craft guilds in the eighteenth century (Belfanti, 2004, pp. 574–75) and by some inventors (most famously the British steelmaker Benjamin Huntsman). Secrecy only made sense when the knowledge could not be readily reverse-engineered. In intermediate cases the open-source ethics of the Republic of Letters, in which the free sharing and open distribution of useful knowledge were moral imperatives, applied to the world of technology as well (Allen, 1983).[8] Third, in other cases, engineers and inventors whose work created novel prescriptive knowledge sought publicity, because reputations could gain them lucrative commissions. Many of the successful inventors of the age were rewarded by public recognition, academic status, patronage, and well-paying assignments and consultancies. In that sense they were entirely part of the cultural sphere of the Republic of Letters.[9] This blurring between the spheres of open science and proprietary technology reduced the monetary rewards of many inventors, but it speeded up the dissemination of new technology by applying the ideology of open science to the realm of technology.[10] Many of the great inventors of the British Industrial Revolution, including Abraham Darby (who invented coke-smelting), the innovative potter Josiah Wedgwood, and John Smeaton (the inventor of the breast wheel), largely stayed away from the patent system.

Of those three categories, the first set of incentives may be the poorest understood and yet in the long run it was decisive. To understand how and why this happened, it helps to rely on Elinor Ostrom's idea of a *community-management* of a commons resource, since knowledge shares many of the characteristics of a commons (Ostrom and Hess, 2007). Such a community was essential in creating the norms and rules that in turn generated the useful knowledge necessary for sustained economic growth, rewarding those who play by the rules and punishing those who break them. At first blush, a community of this kind may appear unlikely: as already noted, Europe was heavily fragmented politically, and managing any

---

[8] The English inventor Hugh Plat was knighted in 1605 in recognition of his many inventions which he placed in the public domain through such books as his *The Jewell House of Arte and Nature, Conteining divers rare and profitable Inventions, Together with Sundry new Experiments in the Art of Husbandry, Distillation, and Moulding,* (1594). The book contains a plethora of practical detailed prescriptions but also illustrates the appropriability issues involved in invention by listing "An offer of certain new inventions which the author proposes to disclose upon reasonable considerations." He also considered opening his own shop to sell the "excellent sweet oils and waters" that he had invented, implicitly recognizing an alternative way in which an inventor could be remunerated: first-movers advantage (Harkness, 2007, p. 232). None of this led to much, and he complained that "happy men are rewarded with good words, but few or none, in these days, with any real recompense" (Harkness, 2007, p. 233).

[9] An example is the Dutch engineer and alchemist Cornelis Drebbel (1572–1633), whose inventions included improved (compound) microscopes, clocks, thermostats, pumps, a tin mordant for dyeing scarlet with cochineal, and, most famously, the first submarine. Yet his career depended entirely on a sequence of royal patrons and official commissions, including the Emperor Rudolf, the English Crown Prince Henry Frederick, and the Duke of Buckingham. His older compatriot, the engineer and inventor Simon Stevin, earned many commissions and served on a variety of boards thanks to his reputation as a mathematician and engineer. Most of the engineers in the British Industrial Revolution operated in a similar way (Mokyr, 2009a, pp. 91, 409).

[10] At times, arguments from this blurry area were used by European rulers to acquire private information that they regarded as valuable to the state (Bertucci, 2013).

common resource by a public institution on more than a local scale seems to be beyond the power of any entity. Yet in the late Renaissance, an institution emerged that was able to create conditions that were conducive for sustained knowledge creation.

The community in question was known in its time as the *Respublica Literaria* or the Republic of Letters, an institution already encountered repeatedly. It has received a great deal of attention from historians (Daston, 1991; Brockliss, 2002; Darnton, 2003; Grafton, 2009a; Fumaroli, 2015), but its significance as an institution that generated and diffused useful knowledge has not been sufficiently appreciated. It was an "invisible college" of internationally connected scholars and intellectuals, based on the implicit understanding that knowledge was a nonrivalrous good to be distributed and shared by the community. The community constituted an elite group of intellectuals and scientists who circulated and checked new knowledge through an epistolary network, the printing press, and local meeting places of scholars. The tightness of the network was a testimony to its success: the citizens of the Republic of Letters were morally obliged to respond to letters. As always, the professional network had a social aspect: members of the virtual community could become true friends as well as mortal enemies. Having a lingua franca in which significant work was published was important in the early stages, but by the late seventeenth century the Republic of Letters was efficient and large enough for its citizens to publish in vernacular languages (though French to some extent replaced Latin as the new lingua franca), counting on translators, often themselves distinguished scholars, to make their work available elsewhere in Europe. Indeed, such translations served both as powerful signals as to who was an intellectual star, and as opportunities for epigones to borrow liberally from others and publish it as original work.

The historical roots of the Republic of Letters in Renaissance Europe were a mixture of admiration for the common classical heritage being rediscovered and being made accessible, and a set of traditions (real or imaginary) of an intellectual unity harking back to the classical world, the medieval church, and the *Respublica Christiana* that harked back to St. Augustine's City of God. The scholastic intellectuals of the late Middle Ages had constituted a loose transnational intellectual community under the aegis of the church. What emerged in the sixteenth and seventeenth centuries was a very different institution: originally dominated by Italians, it moved north of the Alps and was infected by Gallicans and Protestants, increasingly skeptical of many tenets that hitherto had been axiomatic. It became increasingly divorced from the "educated aristocracy of the Roman Church." Yet the idea of a mystical but coherent scholarly community working together for a common good was retained until and beyond the Enlightenment (Fumaroli, 2015, pp. 121–23).

In practical terms the Republic of Letters was both an institution supporting the operation of a marketplace and an identity. The market was one in which persuasion was akin to a successful sale, and the payoff was an enhanced reputation. It provided an unusual institutional framework that eventually proved of crucial importance to the economic development of Europe by setting up norms and incentives that made the market for ideas work. In so doing, it motivated talented and educated men and women to explore new ideas in science, medicine, philosophy, and other fields, and placed their findings in the public domain. A more open-minded constituency helped improve incentives: "good" (by the rhetorical standards of the time) intellectual innovations had a better chance of being selected and thus rewarded.[11] The improved incentives in the market for ideas encouraged new entrants on both the extensive and the intensive margins. On the extensive margin, by creating such rewards, it sent a signal to bright young individuals that careers in natural philosophy and other intellectual pursuits could be rewarding, and thus encouraged them to make the substantial investment in human capital necessary to embark on such careers. On the intensive margin, those who did so may have increased their efforts and ventured into more innovative areas.

While the beginnings of the Republic of Letters as a major intellectual institution can be dated to the earlier days of Erasmus of Rotterdam (MacLean, 2008, p. 18; Fumaroli, 2015, pp. 45–47), it developed and progressed over time and reached full maturity in the early decades of the Enlightenment, 1680–1720 (Ultee, 1987, p. 97).[12] From the very beginning, it fully realized that intellectual property was held in common (Grafton, 2009a, p. 9). The Republic of Letters was above all a *virtual* community: it had at first no formal institutions, no annual congress, it did not publish its own periodical, and yet it managed to create and enforce a substantial number of rules that supported the emergence of open science in Europe. Unlike the other self-governing communities that form the basis of Ostrom's critique of the commons "tragedy," the Republic of Letters, then, was not a local affair and was not bound by space (Eisenstein, 1979, p. 138). Its operation by and large transcended distance by means of travel or the written or printed word. In fact, it was the opposite of local—it was a transnational network of individuals connected by letters, books, and pamphlets, punctuated by relatively rare but intense personal visits and study periods

---

[11] A similar view is expressed in Grafton's (2009a, p. 11) summary of the Republic of Letters: "[it] stood, in the first instance, for a kind of intellectual market—one in which values depended, in theory at least, not on a writer's rank but on the quality of his or her work."

[12] The earliest mention of the term actually goes back to 1417 (Waquet, 1989, p. 475). The same idea was expressed by other writers. In a 1517 letter, Erasmus—who could make a credible claim to be one of the founding fathers of the Republic—wrote that "as if on a given signal, splendid talents are stirring and awakening and conspiring together to revive the best learning. For what else is this but a conspiracy, when all these great scholars from different lands share out the work among themselves and set about this noble task" (quoted in Huizinga, [1924] 1984, p. 219).

at foreign universities. The institution was truly cosmopolitan, in the sense of paying little heed to boundaries or religion and mostly ignoring ascriptive characteristics, such as ethnicity or language. It was spread over much of Europe, including areas far from Paris (which is imagined by some Francophile scholars to have been the core of the Republic of Letters). Thus, for instance, the brilliant Croatian mathematician Marin Getaldić (1568–1626) was widely known throughout Europe but he settled back in his place of birth, Dubrovnik. The Greek Theophilos Corydalleus (1563–1646), like so many ambitious scholars from the European periphery, studied at the University of Padua, taught neo-Aristotelian secular thought in the Greek communities in the Ottoman Empire, and refashioned their educational institutions along lines similar to Padua. Probably the most distinguished Polish citizen of the Republic of Letters was probably the mathematician and physician Jan Brozek (1585–1652), a great admirer of Copernicus, who studied at Padua as well and taught at Krakow University. Scholars like Jonston and Comenius worked in Poland, Hungary, and other parts of Central Europe, depending on the religious atmosphere and the presence of a patron or a commission.[13]

The market for ideas supported by the Republic of Letters was somewhat peculiar by the standards of markets. The payoff for successful efforts was enhanced reputation; the magnitude of the payoff usually had little to do with the actual economic or social value of an intellectual innovation to society except insofar as it was judged meritorious by peers, although at times the state was keen on finding a military application, as was the case with the first telescopes. As every academic knows, to be recognized by one's peers as a master is enormously desirable and this was the driving motive behind most scholarly effort in early modern Europe. While positive incentives thus became stronger, the negative incentives became weaker. Repression of innovation by entrenched interests declined in the late seventeenth and eighteenth centuries, so that the study of nature became distinctly less hazardous, even for radical innovators. Intellectual innovators were still constrained by the moral and religious conventions of the times, but these could be readily circumvented.[14] As the generation of intellectual innovations became more attractive, more people in search of fame and patronage tried their hand at suggesting new ideas. Most new ideas were rejected, and not all ideas that were accepted stood the test of

---

[13] The itinerant Venetian historian Giovanni Michele Bruto (1517–1592) spent years working in Transylvania and Silesia, enjoying the patronage of a number of rulers culminating with that of Rudolf II in Prague.

[14] Thus Antonie van Leeuwenhoek used his microscope to identify spermatozoa in 1677, but prudently remarked that the specimen he chose was the result of the excess bestowed on him by Nature in his conjugal relations with his wife Cornelia and was not obtained by any "sinful contrivance" (quoted in Cobb, 2006, pp. 202–3).

time, but with the selection system firmly in place, its long-term effect on technological development was assured. Other conditions were necessary for such new ideas to lead to sustained, technology-driven economic growth, above all sufficient certainty that those who successfully implemented new ideas into the production sphere would keep their profits and gain the respect of their fellow citizens.

The Republic of Letters was not entirely virtual. Some brick-and-mortar organizations helped make it work. Some of its citizens resided at universities, although the relationships were often uneasy because, as noted, most universities tended to be conservative and protective of entrenched knowledge, which limited their ability to transform elite cultural beliefs. Eisenstein points to the role of European printing houses in providing a material base for the institution. They produced periodicals and books, which provided their authors with both income and prominence. Furthermore, print shops were "international houses" where dissident foreigners could find shelter and a meeting place (Eisenstein, 1979, pp. 139, 449).

But publishers did more: they were spread all over Europe, and they rendered censorship by reactionary governments essentially impotent. In that sense they neatly complemented the mobility of intellectuals. In the Age of Enlightenment, Amsterdam became the location for presses that published books prohibited elsewhere, "the central city of the Republic of Letters" in that limited sense (Eisenstein, 1979, p. 420). The most famous French authors of the age of Enlightenment were published primarily by printers outside France. As discussed below in chapter 15, formal academies and scientific societies represented the institutionalization of the Republic of Letters, but did not play a central role until the closing decades of the seventeenth century.

Virtual or not, the Republic of Letters was the main institution behind the meteoric takeoff of useful knowledge in Europe during the Scientific Revolution and the Enlightenment. In this context institutions should be seen as a set of rules by which the economic game is played. In this case, the rules were of a game where the payoff was academic success, fame, and reputation, correlated with some material payoffs and enhanced social status. The main rules governing the Republic of Letters were freedom of entry, contestability, that is, the right to challenge any form of knowledge, transnationality, and a commitment to placing new knowledge in the public domain. This last rule is the key to what we now call open science was the ethical foundation of the Republic of Letters. Free exchange and open circulation of knowledge were the tacit rules of the self-identified "Republic"—these rules "set them morally apart from the world of trade in which information was bought and sold" (Bertucci, 2013, p. 838). On most issues in theology, philology, astronomy, medicine, and natural philosophy, the members of the Republic could differ a great deal. However, they generally agreed on the rules by which such disputes should be conducted and how they could be resolved (as a few disputes were).

The scholars who considered themselves citizens of the Republic of Letters argued not only about points of substance but also about how inquiries into natural philosophy should be conducted and what should be on the agenda. As discussed in Chapter 7, Francis Bacon's writings on the methods of scientific investigation and experimental philosophy influenced the growth of propositional knowledge in this age. His followers took his approach further and established the principles that should guide research. Robert Hooke's famous posthumous *General Scheme* insisted that the senses and intuition would never be enough to understand "Natural Operations, which are the kinds of secret and subtile Actors" (Hooke, 1705a, p. 6). He proposed a kind of "philosophical algebra" which would direct and discipline the application of reason to natural knowledge (Hooke, 1705a. p. 7). At the end of the seventeenth century it was clear what the tools of such an investigation should be: the experimental method and observation relying on scientific instruments.

Within the Republic of Letters, practitioners developed a scientific language of communication and rhetorical conventions that determined which knowledge was tight, that is, what constituted proof and which argument was persuasive. In much of the discourse, of course, this boiled down to the question of who is credible. Shapin (1994, pp. 212 ff) lists seven criteria or "maxims for the evaluation of testimony" as he calls it in the seventeenth century. Among those were plausibility (consistency with what is already known), the integrity and impartiality of the source, internal consistency, and consistency with multiple other sources reporting on the same matter. Some of Shapin's items parallel the biases in cultural evolution discussed in chapter 5. The market for ideas, to repeat, was about persuasion. Persuasion was in part about *what* new knowledge was validated and verified, but it was also in large part about *who* was trustworthy and reliable. In the market for ideas—as in so many markets—what counted was not only the nature of the commodity transacted but also the character of the seller.

Beyond trust, however, there were new methods and standards for research and new criteria for rigor and reliability. The most important of these were the ever-growing use of mathematics where it was applicable (astronomy and mechanics), the validity of experimental data in those fields where experiments were possible, and the collection and careful taxonomy of empirical observations where neither of these approaches worked (e.g., in botany and entomology). Experimental work was also bound by rules: unbiased inference from data, replicability, accuracy in measurement and purity of materials wherever possible, reliance on credible witnesses observing the procedure; clear and transparent delineation of procedures used, and publication of results. None of those conventions were quite new at this time, but they became more central to the enterprise and increasingly overrode other considerations, such as consistency with ancient authorities, aesthetics, or metaphysical or moral concerns. The concept of an experiment as a means of resolving disputes became particularly popular following its advocacy by Bacon. His influence was especially strong among the early members of the Royal Society, whose views were summarized by Bishop Sprat who wrote at length about the many real and imaginary virtues of experimental research (Sprat, 1667, pp. 403–30).[15] Nonetheless, given the cost and difficulty of replicating experimental work, dispute resolution inevitably retained elements of trust and social status (Shapin and Schaffer, 1985).

The Republic of Letters, and the network it created among natural philosophers, is a good example of the efficacy of networks of weak ties to use Granovetter's (1973, 1983) well-known concept. Unlike strong ties, such as families and small communities, the connections among members of the virtual community were not transitive, and the information that members could exchange did not necessarily overlap much. New information and ideas are more efficiently diffused through weak ties than through strong ones because the latter are more likely to provide redundant information. Individuals who are strongly tied are more likely to share the same sources of information and to otherwise be similar to one another. In contrast, weak ties when they are "bridges" (that is, single connections that have no substitutes), are more likely to be the avenue by which new information is introduced to an individual. Hence, more weak ties imply a more effective network for information dissemination.

Precisely because the members of the Republic of Letters often did not know one another very well, it was a highly effective community in which innovation could occur, circulate, and be evaluated. Weak ties provided bridges *between* local communities within which individuals had stronger ties, like universities and local academies (Granovetter, 1983). The main disadvantage of weak-ties networks is that the levels of trust between members may be lower than those in strong-ties network, in which interactions are much more frequent between two individuals. Even when trust is relatively low, weak ties provide more useful knowledge because of their enhanced ability to provide non-redundant information (Levin and Cross, 2004, p. 1480). The concept of ties here modifies the importance of trust, which is widely regarded as an indispensable part of the division of labor, without which no collective scientific endeavor can exist. Direct bias—accepting a new idea on the basis of authority—requires trust. At the same time, however, the emergence of new useful knowledge in the Republic of Letters depended on skepticism, on the contestability of all authority. The

---

[15]   Galileo placed experimental research as an inevitable middle road between a "basement level" of everyday reality observations that were too messy and an "upper level" of idealized reality that was too abstract (Cohen, 2012, p. 196). Robert Hooke made a different point: human observation was limited by the five senses; experimentation provided a sixth and more powerful sense (Cohen, 2012, p. 558).

dilemma is well formulated by Shapin (1994, p. 17): "the distrust, which social theorists have identified as the most potent way of dissolving social order is said to be the most potent means of constructing our knowledge." The key words that defined much of the new thinking in early modern Europe were *doubt* and *skepticism*—about the classics, about the structure of the universe, about the physical and biological environment, eventually even about the immortality of the soul.

In fact the citizens of the Republic of Letters were quite alert to the issue of trust, and such experimentalists as Robert Boyle made supreme efforts to make sure that his social prestige was behind his experimental work, which in that age would be associated with some level of trust associated with gentlemanly "honor" (Shapin and Schaffer, 1985; Shapin, 1994, pp. 185–92). Those who did not have the elevated social standing of a Boyle sought legitimization through the formal sponsorship of high-status patrons to generate some level of trust (Biagioli, 1990). But to introduce a new idea successfully into the market for ideas at this time, obiter dictum was rarely enough; some level of evidence or logic to back up assertions was expected if a "sale" was to take place, that is, if persuasion was to be successful. It is this kind of network that produces the highest chances of innovation in codifiable knowledge that could be readily vetted and verified. By contrast, strong ties in coherent and localized groups may have been preferable in the dissemination of tacit and practical knowledge, such as artisanal skills that were exchanged through apprenticeships and personal contacts (Epstein, 2013).

In a world of codifiable (and codified) intellectual innovations, communicated by letters or printed in books and pamphlets, it was skepticism and not trust that provided an engine of creativity. Of course, knowledge expansion still required some level of trust, since it would be unthinkable for every researcher to start from scratch and verify personally every component of a new theory. But, as Shapin (1994, pp. 19–21) notes, skepticism takes place on the margins of trusting systems and, odd as it may sound, skepticism and trust were complementary in the generation of new knowledge—a variant of Ronald Reagan's famous use of the Russian proverb "trust but verify." It is on these margins that progress occurs, and these margins were mostly found in the codified knowledge that circulated in the Republic of Letters.

It is too easy to dismiss the importance of formal and codified knowledge in technological progress at this time, as Epstein (2013, p. 67) does. Such dismissals fail to recognize that major conceptual breakthroughs are required if artisanal tinkering and local improvement are not to run into diminishing returns. The argument that formal, codified knowledge depends on skepticism while tacit knowledge depends on trust is too oversimplified and schematic. Experimental knowledge always had a tacit component, and no description of what we would call today "materials and methods" could ever be complete. As Dasgupta and David note (1994, p. 495), the complementarity between tacit and codified knowledge is critical to the way knowledge is created and disseminated.

The networks of people who rarely or never met one another turned out, paradoxically, to create a unity of purpose and method in a community that was overlaid on a highly fragmented world. At least in principle, the nationality, religion, and social origins of a scholar were irrelevant to the assessment of his or her scholarly contribution. In practice, this was an age in which these things mattered a great deal, and they mattered more than most citizens of the Republic of Letters would have liked to admit.[16] The Republic of Letters was a transnational institution, but one that had to exist in a political reality. Many of those defending Newton in his priority dispute with Leibniz did so out of national loyalty, although referring to a kind of "philosophical jingoism" in the early eighteenth century (Shank, 2008, p. 181) seems excessive. Whether the sciences "were never at war" as Edward Jenner famously remarked may still be an open question. The ideals of the Republic Letters, in which Diderot could tell Hume that the latter "belonged to all nations" and would never be asked for his birth certificate (Gay, 1966, p. 13), did not always mesh with the reality on the ground. The eighteenth century after all was not just the age of Enlightenment, it was also an age of mercantilism, and the information made available freely in the Republic of Letters was often gathered to serve the interests of the state—as Bacon had advocated. But if enlightened cosmopolitanism could not altogether suppress nationalism in an age of mercantilist ideals, the members of the Republic of Letters argued that the reputation and glory of a country would be enhanced if foreign scholars celebrated the achievements of its scholars (Daston, 1991, pp. 378–79). Despite the many claims of the citizens of the Republic of Letters about the utility of their learning and intellectual innovations, before 1700 it is quite hard to point to many breakthroughs resulting from the work that natural philosophers did that dramatically changed a technological practice. It is arguable that the very fact that so little of the science had many significant useful applications that really mattered made open science possible; had it had more consequential implications for those techniques that states considered vital, rulers may have tried to limit the free exchange of knowledge across national boundaries and imposed secrecy on some findings— precisely as Bacon had advocated. Whether such secrecy would have been successful in the long run is questionable, but it may have weakened the transnational nature of the Republic of Letters.

---

[16] Many Frenchmen remained loyal to Cartesian physics simply because Descartes was French, and British science at times showed signs of Francophobia. Yet at least in theory a citizen of the Republic of Letters was supposed to be a person without a fatherland, or as a 1779 issue of the *Histoire de la République des Letters et Arts en France* put it, he was "a kind of orphan, to whom fortune denies those distinctions for which nature intends them" (quoted in Daston, 1990, p. 97).

The citizens of the Republic of Letters were almost by definition highly educated, and with few exceptions literate both in Latin and their own languages. A large proportion of the membership consisted of people trained in and practicing medicine and law, though of course many of them had a wide range of knowledge and interests. While most of them were still quite religious (including many eminent Puritans in seventeenth-century England), members were open minded, eschewed rigid dogmatism, and accepted (if sometimes reluctantly) the discipline of evidence and logic. Ancient authorities in physics, astronomy, medicine, and other areas were still read with polite respect and paid lip service to, but clearly the community's fundamental premise was that it was acceptable to question anything said by the ancients and overturn their findings if the evidence called for it. It was acknowledged that ancient authorities were wrong on many matters.[17] For communications, the citizens depended on the publication of books, newsletters, periodicals, and pamphlets, and an ever-increasing set of epistolary and personal networks (Collins, 1998). Indeed, correspondence was at the very heart of the modus operandi of the Republic of Letters (Ultee, 1987). Special nodal figures whose responsibility it was to copy letters and send them on to other members were known as "intelligencers."[18] Correspondence clearinghouses or "offices of addresses" were set up, in which private communications were further disseminated.[19] In the century following, periodicals increasingly supplemented epistolary networks. More than a century later, François Rozier (1734–1793), publisher of the *Observations sur la Physique, sur l Histoire Naturelle, et sur les Arts* (widely

---

[17] A typical way of dealing with the ancients by scholars of this period was to assert that if the ancients only knew what they know now, they would have agreed with them. For instance, William Gilbert in the preface to *De Magnete* states that "To those men of early times, Aristotle, Theophrastus, Ptolemy, Hippocrates, and Galen, be due honour ever rendered : for from them knowledge has descended to those who came after them but our age has discovered and brought to light very many things which they too, were they among the living, would cheerfully adopt" (Gilbert, [1600] 1893, p. li).

[18] Examples of nodal figures in these epistolary networks are Samuel Hartlib (1600–1662) and Marin Mersenne (1588–1648), both of whom maintained extensive correspondences with the major intellectuals of their age (Webster, 1970, p. 8; Webster, [1975], 2002, pp. 67–77 and passim; Collins, 1998, p. 528). One recent author has remarked that "writing a letter to Mersenne was akin to publishing an article in a scientific journal" (Van Berkel, 2013, p. 59). Another compulsive letter-writer was Peiresc, whose fame and reputation were largely based on his correspondence, both local and long-distance, with scholars as well as merchants and travelers (Miller, 2015, pp. 54–59).

[19] These clearinghouses often served as exchanges, where employers could find employees, but in other cases they just traded information. One of the first was associated with the French physician Théophraste Renaudot (1586–1653), which was emulated in England by the irrepressible Hartlib, whose office of addresses purported to act as a "Center and Meeting-place of Advices, of Proposalls, of Treaties and of all Manner of Intellectual Rarities" (Webster, 1970, pp. 44–47; Jacob, 2006, p. 48).

regarded as the first independent periodical to be concerned wholly with advances in cutting-edge science), assured the American Philosophical Society that "all of Europe will be informed in less than three months" if they sent the new information first to him and that such correspondence would be "indispensable for the progress of science" (quoted in McClellan, 1979, p. 444).

Eisenstein and others have stressed the importance of the invention of the printing press to the evolution of the Republic of Letters, although Fumaroli (2015, pp. 24, 37) points out that the first use of the term, by the Venetian politician and humanist intellectual Francesco Barbaro, predates the first press by at least three decades. Much less discussed than printing but of great importance in the operation of the Republic of Letters was the improvement in the continent-wide flow of mail. It is this innovation that maintained communication among the leaders of Europe's science and technology, and allowed them to establish the kind of interconnectivity that was at the heart of the dissemination of knowledge. The improvement of the postal system took place thanks to the organizational abilities of de Tasso family, led by Francisco de Tasso (later known as Franz von Taxis) and his brothers who established regular postal services in Italy, Germany, and the Habsburg lands in the early sixteenth century. Their postal system covered much of the Continent by the middle of the sixteenth century and created one of the most durable business dynasties in history. A French system was established in 1603, when King Henri IV allowed royal couriers to accept and distribute postal material from the general public and a few years later appointed his first postmaster general. The emergence of a European continent-wide postal service was a by-product of the growing need for communications in the multinational Habsburg Empire under Emperor Charles V and other increasingly bureaucratic nation-states, as well as the needs for long-distance communication of international religious organizations, such as the Jesuit order. Above all, however, it was the growing needs of commerce and finance for information and communications as it increasingly dealt with long-distance trade, both inter- and intracontinental.[20] The infrastructure on which the Republic of Letters rested was thus an

---

[20] Postal rates remained quite high, in part because they were a convenient revenue-raising device for the state. As Margóczy (2014a, p. 33) remarks, "the price of mail could break friendships and scholarly networks." All the same, there is no question that by the early eighteenth century the cost was sufficiently low to sustain dense epistolary networks. The establishment of the famous London penny post in 1683 and its gradual extension in the eighteenth century meant that by 1764 most of England and Wales received mail daily (Headrick, 2000, p. 187). Postal rates depended, in part, on the cost of internal transportation, and as roads were improved, canals dug, and carriages made faster and reliable, the effectiveness of internal communications increased greatly in the age of Enlightenment.

unintended by-product of other historical phenomena.[21] In that sense cultural change may be seen as being driven by the material world, but in a far more contingent and roundabout way than historical materialism would have us believe.

Thus, the epistolary network, as it developed after 1500, was an essential part of the Republic of Letters. To be a member of the intellectual community of the Republic of Letters was to be connected with others. As Paul Dibon (1978, p. 46) has noted, "it was the strict duty of each citizen of the *Respublica Literaria* to establish, maintain, and encourage communication, primarily by personal correspondence or contact." In the 1660s, the first formal organizations embodying the ideals of the community were established. The English Royal Society was a bottom-up voluntary organization growing out of the "invisible academy" of Baconians that had formed after the death of Bacon, whereas the French Royal Academy was a top-down government initiative by J-B Colbert.[22] In between formal and officially sponsored organizations and the completely virtual epistolary networks there were the many semiformal manifestations of literary clubs such as the *societé amusante* of Berlin, which met every Wednesday at the home of one of its members "with the goal of instructing and diverting themselves at the same time" (Goldgar, 1995, p. 2). These organizations constituted the formal part of "public science" that could also be found in coffeehouses, taverns, and other informal local venues (Stewart, 1992).[23] These institutions soon started to publish scientific periodicals, such as the *Journal des Scavants* and the *Transactions of the Royal Society*, both of which began appearing in 1665 (though neither was at first wholly dedicated to scientific and technological topics). These periodicals became a substitute for printed books and personal correspondence, and they created what we call today the scientific paper (McClellan, 1979, p. 425).[24]

While there were differences in local institutions and styles, the common denominator of most citizens of the Republic of Letters was their education, their commitment to what they believed was the growth and free

---

[21] The commercial postal network was supplemented by a variety of private networks such as publishers, booksellers, merchants, diplomats, and religious connections.

[22] The famous diarist, horticulturist, and Royal Society charter member John Evelyn's (1620–1706) highest praise for the organization was that "Never had the *Republique of Letters* so learned and universal a correspondence as has been procured by this *Society* alone" (Evelyn [1664], 1679, unpaginated preface).

[23] John Houghton (1645–1705), a pharmacist and early writer in the best of the traditions of the Industrial Enlightenment, wrote in 1699 "coffee-houses improve arts, merchandize, and all other knowledge; for here an inquisitive man, that aims at good learning, may get more in an evening than he shall by books in a month" (cited by Cowan, 2005, p. 99).

[24] For more details on the growth of scientific periodicals in the age of Enlightenment, see Mokyr (2005).

dissemination of knowledge, and their Baconian belief that this knowledge may in the end be of service to humankind as a whole. It should be added that the social status of intellectuals was rising during this period. Men (and a few women) of letters increasingly found themselves rising in the esteem of their society, invited to fine salons, and expected to dress well and behave according to the manners and etiquette prescribed by the culture of the elite.[25] To be sure, there was also an intellectual underworld of Grub Street hacks immortalized by Robert Darnton, but its impact —outside that of spiced-up literature—was probably minor.

Within the community, the ideals of openness, contestability, and competition were increasingly prominent. A central pillar shared by the citizens of the Republic was their antidoctrinaire bent. From the earliest stages of the Republic of Letters, its citizens realized that their community was not at peace, but was "an army fighting against formidable and numerous bitter enemies" who wanted to silence the enlightened armies of the Republic. Erasmus himself spoke of "armed citizens" in a figurative sense (Fumaroli, 2015, p. 47). One central issue was what the age of Galileo called *libertas philosophendi*. The freedom to philosophize was an ancient concept revived in Renaissance Europe by the humanist scholar Marsilio Ficino (1433–1499) (MacLean, 2006, pp. 264–65), but it was accepted as a central tenet of the Republic of Letters by its giants, above all Giordano Bruno, Galileo, Campanella, Descartes, and Spinoza (the latter included the term in the subtitle of his *Tractatus*) (Sutton, 1953). They knew full well that they lived in a dangerous world, in which this freedom was not guaranteed.[26] As Stewart (1994, p. 42) points out, the concept of the freedom to philosophize is not quite the same as the modern concept of academic freedom, because it was part of an attempt to preserve disciplinary boundaries.[27] Instead we should see the concept above all as a statement of freedom from dogmatic

---

[25] In this regard, the Republic of Letters is a good example of what Deirdre McCloskey (2010) has called "Bourgeois Dignity"—the growing value that society placed on features that might be of general utility.

[26] Copernicus's student and the editor of *De Revolutionibus,* Georg Joachim Rheticus (1514–1574), had thought it appropriate to cite as an epigraph the dictum of the ancient Platonist Alcinous: "He that would be a philosopher must be of a free (unenslaved) mind" (Stewart, 1994, pp. 34–35). Rheticus himself prudently never published his exposition of Copernicanism titled *Epistolae de Terrae Motu,* an attempt to reconcile heliocentrism with the scriptures (published posthumously in 1651).

[27] The issue came up explicitly in the nasty dispute between Descartes and the Dutch Calvinist professors of theology. The Synod of South Holland eventually took action, imposing the resolution that "there should be no infringement on the freedom to philosophize, but ... this freedom was not to be abused" (Stewart, 1994, p. 41).

thought within the limits of each discipline; stepping outside these borders, as Descartes was accused of doing, could still imply serious penalties.[28]

The Republic of Letters was based on the shared faith that the freedom to philosophize was a foundation of their calling for expanded knowledge, both useful and metaphysical. Research, it was felt, should proceed wherever natural philosophers wanted it to go, and if the evidence ended up contradicting some venerable authority, the view of that authority should be discarded (for classical sources) or reinterpreted (for scripture). It is sometimes believed that "the rebellion against authority" and the "tradition of criticism" were specific to the Enlightenment (for example, Deutsch, 2011, pp. 12–13). While they were central to Enlightenment philosophy, the foundational beliefs of the Enlightenment themselves were born from rebellion and criticism and established in the two centuries before 1700. Knowledge, it was increasingly believed, was never final and always should be further corrected and extended. The experimental method, wrote Bishop Sprat (1667, p. 429) "teaches men humility and acquaints them with their own errors and so removes all overweening haughtiness of mind." As early as the late sixteenth century, Simon Stevin explained that the main reason he published his *Mémoirs Mathématiques* was so that "his errors [could] be corrected and other inventions added" (quoted in Rossi, 1970, p. 72). Some of its most influential leaders, such as Peiresc, called for respect and temperance in scholarly dispute (Miller, 2000, p. 43), a call that was not always heeded.

By the late seventeenth century, the Republic of Letters had come into its own as the institutional underpinning of a competitive market for ideas, in which different schools competed with one another for the minds of the intellectual elite. Bayle wrote in a famous essay that "this commonwealth is a State extremely Free. The Empire of Truth is only acknowledged in it; and under their protection an innocent war is waged against anyone whatever. Friends ought to be on their Guard against friends, Fathers against their children" (Bayle, [1696–1697] 1734, vol. II, p. 389, essay on *Catius*).[29] The Dutch mathematician and physicist Nicolaas Hartsoeker (1656–1725), a rather typical if pugnacious citizen of the Republic of

---

[28] The freedom to express ideas without any constraints was a guiding principle of the French intellectuals who organized in the early seventeenth century in the so-called Cabinet of the Dupuy brothers, an informal French academy established in Paris following the will of Jacques August de Thou (1553–1617), a noted historian and great patron of French learning, and himself one of the most respected citizens of the Republic of Letters of his age. It seems that the idea of this freedom ripened during the bloody French religious wars, which senselessly set the French against one another (Delatour, 2005a, p. 289).

[29] William Wotton, a late seventeenth-century intellectual and a great admirer of the new science as practiced in the Republic of Letters, noted pointedly that in the "Modern Methods of philosophizing as compared with the Ancient ... Des Cartes is not more believed upon his own word than is Aristotle; Matter of Fact is the only thing appealed to" (Wotton, 1694, p. 300).

Letters, wrote many essays attacking sacred cows in his life (among them Newton, Leibniz, and Jacob Bernoulli) and was unrepentant: "I very humbly beg of all whose opinions I have attacked, perhaps with too much liberty, not to take it in a bad way, since I have most often done this only to invite them to do the same to mine ... this philosophical war will likely cost a bit of ink but there will be no spilling of blood" (quoted in Feingold, 2010, p. 183). As a sixteen-year-old he had been taught by no less a figure than Leeuwenhoek himself about microscopes, but in his later work he did not hesitate to criticize and even ridicule the old man. Notwithstanding (and perhaps because of) his disputatious reputation, he was offered a number of patronage positions, including one by Czar Peter the Great (which he declined).

Voltaire, looking back at the history of the Republic of Letters in 1753 reflected that "During the Age of Louis XIV, a Republic of Letters was established, almost unnoticed, despite the wars and despite the difference in religions ... all the sciences and arts received mutual assistance this way. ... True scholars in each field drew closer the bonds of this great society of minds, spread everywhere and everywhere independent ... this institution is still with us, and is one of the great consolations for the evils that ambition and politics have spread through the earth" (Voltaire, [1751] 1785, vol. 21, p. 287).

The Republic of Letters was predominantly male, although at times women did play important roles.[30] The invisible college that emerged in the late seventeenth century in full bloom was successful precisely because it was relatively small. Cooperative behavior was encouraged, and defectors could be recognized and punished. This kind of equilibrium was more likely to emerge if the "game" is played over and over again, if the participants shared an "ethos" of cooperation and knew that others do, and if the numbers remained small enough so that opportunistic behavior could and would be detected and punished. These conditions obtained in the Republic of Letters far more than anywhere else. As David (2008, p. 77) notes, "the norm of cooperative disclosure provided the basis for repeated, reciprocal information transactions that on balance would be conducive to further enhancing the members' reputation." For those reasons, membership in the Republic of Letters was limited and not costless. The norms it set implied that one was expected to reply to letters, to disclose findings and data truthfully, and to acknowledge intellectual debts. The markets for ideas was an arena of both competition and cooperation: the suppliers and the buyers both competed with one another and competition often led to conflict.

---

[30] This matter is still in some dispute. For a useful summary, see Melton (2001, pp. 209–11). In some of the locations were the Republic of Letters was actually organized in concrete locations, such as the French *salons*, women played a pivotal role; elsewhere, such as in English coffeehouses, they were excluded.

Indeed, the marketplace for ideas at the time was often riven by bitter disputes, rivalries, and jealousies, a cutthroat nasty world of selfish individuals, jockeying for positions, patronage, and reputations—something that a modern academic might not regard as very alien. At the same time, its participants shared a set of underlying assumptions and had to cooperate and trust one another. There is no contradiction between the coexistence of such harmonious and competitive forces, as an analysis of any market demonstrates. Economists have understood since Adam Smith that the glory of the market system is this unique combination.

In principle, the Republic of Letters fancied itself to be egalitarian, although this was of course not always the case in practice. Yet its hierarchy was ordered quite differently from that of the rest of society: neither ancestry nor wealth were supposed to count for much. Merit, originality, achievement, and erudition determined one's place in the hierarchy and were always formally contestable. The community dealt on more or less equal footing with the very rich and aristocratic Robert Boyle and his assistant, the impecunious parvenu Robert Hooke, as well as members of the *haute bourgeois* intelligentsia such as Christiaan Huygens and René Descartes.[31] To be sure, the wealthy and socially prominent French intellectual, astronomer, and classical scholar Nicolas Claude Fabri de Peiresc (1580–1637) has been called "the prince of the Republic of Letters," but clearly this distinction was related to his intellectual power and widespread personal and correspondence networks. Of his correspondence, about 10,000 letters survive.[32] It has been argued that the lack of hierarchical organization was effective, because in scientific and technological endeavors the tasks normally delegated in a hierarchical structure "are better left undelegated" (Rosenberg and Birdzell, 1986, p. 255). The more important elements, however, were that the lack of hierarchy guaranteed contestability and that the internal pecking order of science, which was the closest that the institutional setup in Europe came

---

[31] Habermas (1989, p. 33) notes that in the Paris salons the nobility and the grande bourgeoisie met with intellectuals on "an equal footing" and that the sons of watchmakers and shopkeepers associated with princes and counts.

[32] Pierre Bayle, another pivot of the international intellectual community half a century after Peiresc summarized the latter's contribution as "no man ever rendered more services to the Republic of Letters than him" (Bayle, [1696–1697] 1740, pp. 638–39). Fumaroli (2015, pp. 60–61) sees in him a "figurehead" of the Republic of Letters, someone who facilitated and encouraged the work of others but produced little of lasting value himself. Miller (2000, p. 4) sees in Peiresc's celebrity status in his own lifetime the kind of activity and skills that other members of the Republic of Letters found worth celebrating. Many European intellectuals, many of them now obscure, were similar. Truly original minds were complemented and supported by other network members, who shared and distributed their knowledge and helped making access to it easier and faster. Peiresc shared and distributed knowledge and interests with his contemporaries, but he was far from unique. As Grafton notes, Europe's Republic of Letters was teeming with such intellectuals and it was their work that constituted the fabric of the Republic of Letters (Grafton, 2015, p. 65).

to a hierarchy, provided incentives for ambitious practitioners to do their best. Being a scientific superstar, then as now, was enormously desirable.

The ethos of the Republic of Letters conformed in many ways to Robert K. Merton's famous characterization of the ethos of science.[33] The most important operational rule of the community was that new knowledge should be placed in the public realm when it was generated. If one of the important characteristics of good institutions is that they define and enforce property rights, priority rights were the equivalent of ownership for intellectual innovations. The creator would earn a property right as the rightful discoverer of some natural regularity or phenomenon, or the originator of a new idea, but such priority rights did not include the right to exclude others from using it. Instead, the originator was credited by other members of the community as the original innovator. A successful intellectual innovator would have her or his name associated with the new idea so that the idea and its progenitor become a dyad as "Boyle's Law" or a "Poisson process," and thus while the progenitor does not own the new idea (in the sense of excluding others), he or she is credited with it and may therefore gain in terms of reputation. At some stage, the process became more sophisticated. In the second half of the seventeenth century procedures emerged that allowed a scientist to establish priority even before publication by depositing a paper in a sealed envelope or a device with the secretary of a learned society (Pancaldi, 2003). Credit without direct profit became the rule for intellectual property rights in the Republic of Letters—the profit had to come indirectly, from the reputation effect. Pascal was quite explicit in establishing clear and well-defined property rights in new ideas. In his *Expériences Nouvelles*, published in 1647, he noted that he owned experiences "that were proper to me" (quoted in Dear, 1995, p. 186) yet responded with horror when someone suggested that he passed on Torricelli's finding as his own (Wootton, 2015, p. 101).

For intellectual innovation to be an effective force for cultural change among the literate elite, diffusion mechanisms were crucial. It is indeed worth keeping in mind that right below the intellectual superstars such as Bacon, Spinoza, and Newton, the market for ideas depended on learned polymaths such as Browne, Campanella, Hartlib, and Peiresc, who transmitted and tweaked the products of the great minds. Less prominent intellectuals, many of them now obscure, supported this endeavor. Truly original minds were complemented and supported by other network members, who shared and distributed their knowledge, making access to it easier and faster. As Grafton notes, Europe's Republic of Letters was teeming with

---

[33] Merton (1973) notes four basic characteristics: universalism (knowledge is not specific to a single group); communism (the knowledge is shared by placing it in the public domain and it thus becomes a "commons problem"); disinterestedness (researchers and philosophers search for a truth, to be policed and verified by their peers); and organized skepticism (the unwillingness of those in search of knowledge to be constrained by preconceptions).

such intellectuals and it was their work that constituted the fabric of the Republic of Letters (Grafton, 2015, p. 65).

Although the idea of open science explicitly eschewed the notion of excludability and secrecy in the intellectual marketplace, the implicit notion of "credit without profit" did not exclude notions of intellectual property rights. There was growing recognition that new ideas and the reputation that came with them were assets and that the sanctity of property rights applied to them. Queen Anne's Law (1710) established a rather rudimentary form of copyright in Britain, and similar arrangements emerged elsewhere in the eighteenth century. The patent system was a very different idea, since it explicitly excluded others from using the new knowledge without permission, though the knowledge itself was placed in the public domain. In the realm of propositional knowledge, however, in principle priority established some kind of one-to-one relationship between the idea and its originator.

This system did not work perfectly, as the many priority disputes between scientists attest.[34] It is significant that the person who received credit for an idea was not always the person who was historically the first to discover or enunciate it, but was often the one who managed to sell it most effectively in the market for ideas.[35] But as a means of simultaneously ensuring the openness of science and intellectual discourse, and as a means of ensuring adequate incentives to creative and original minds to generate intellectual innovations, it was a resounding success (Dasgupta and David, 1994, pp. 499–500). If the Republic of Letters was the institution that made the market for ideas work, it is important to realize how it enforced these rules, as it had little coercive power and no formal structure. One answer in institutional analysis is that legitimacy—a shared set of beliefs—reduces enforcement costs for any institution. It is this growing legitimacy of the Republic of Letters that made it successful in imposing its rules. These rules, as noted, included contestability, transnationality, independence from authority, and openness.

The incentive structure that drove the market for ideas depended on reputations and the Republic of Letters set the criteria by which repu-

---

[34] The earliest priority fights are found in the sixteenth century, such as that between the astronomers Tycho Brahe and Nicolaus Reimers ("Ursus") Baer. Of the many others, the dispute between Leibniz and Newton over the invention of differential calculus is the most famous, but that between Newton and Hooke over optics and between Hooke and Huygens over the invention of the spiral-spring balance in watches are well documented. Equally nasty, if more obscure, is the fight between two Dutch scientists, Jan Swammerdam and Reinier de Graaf, over the discovery of a technique to study female reproductive organs ca.1665. According to an unsubstantiated account, De Graaf died as a result of the exhaustion caused by the priority dispute.

[35] This was pointed out by Stephen Stigler, and is known as "Stigler's Law." Appropriately enough, Stigler has attributed its original discovery to Robert K. Merton. See Stigler (1999, pp. 277–90).

tations were established. Reputations required openness. Besides the obvious importance of establishing a reputation, openness was in part driven by an ideology regarding the moral duties of scientists in their societies. As Descartes noted, "I believed that I could not keep them [my notions concerning physics] concealed without greatly sinning against the law which obliges us to procure... the general good of mankind. For they caused me to see that it is possible to attain knowledge which is very useful in life... and thus render ourselves the master and possessor of nature" (Descartes, [1641] 2005, p. 50). But an economist tends to suspect that besides morality and ideology, there may also have been material or other selfish motives.[36]

As Richard Westfall (1985), Roger Hahn (1990), and Paul David (2004, 2008) have pointed out, the incentives that drove this system were part of a reputation game that had patronage jobs as its payoffs (although in some cases publishing a successful book could be remunerative). Peer assessment was especially important because unlike artistic and literary genius, the real quality of scholarship and original ideas was hard to establish for outsiders with fat purses.[37] The members of the Republic of Letters thus set up mechanisms that sent out signals about the quality of their peers (David, 2008). Reputations were based on achievement and merit, measured by the quality and originality of the scholarship. With some exaggeration, Hahn (1990, p. 11) states that the "invention of the merit yardstick" as a measure of intellectual worth was a radical innovation. Moreover, merit was global, not local, and was judged by a transnational community in which social connections counted for relatively little.[38] As such it amplified the incentives: a global reputation clearly provided advantages

---

[36] It is telling that even such a wealthy scientist as Robert Boyle eventually became annoyed by people using his work without attribution and instructed Henry Oldenburg to produce a catalog of his writings to secure his intellectual property rights in this research (Shapin, 1994, p. 183; Hunter, 2009, p. 190). At the same time, however, he remained very generous with awarding credit where it was due—as befitted a gentleman. In Boyle (1682, preface) he gives ample credit to his assistant, the French Huguenot refugee and itinerant experimental philosopher Denis Papin, the first to construct a workable model of an atmospheric engine.

[37] Dasgupta and David (1994) and David (2008) make the important point that in many areas of natural philosophy and mathematics, it was impossible for the outsiders who mattered—potential patrons—to evaluate the work themselves, and so reputation *within* the community of scholars determined the reputation one enjoyed vis-à-vis the outside world. In that regard, the Republic of Letters differed from, say, the kind of patronage awarded to painters and musicians, whose work the patrons mostly judged themselves.

[38] Daston puts it well: "the avowed foundation of the ... diffuse and often quarrelsome Republic of Letters ... was *merit* ... and many Enlightenment intellectuals came to believe that foreigners were more trustworthy judges of merit than compatriots" (Daston, 1991, p. 379, emphasis added and slightly rearranged).

in bargaining power for anyone who acquired one.[39] It bears repeating that such reputations required the creation of original knowledge, not just erudition and the interpretation of existing texts.

Princes and kings competed to provide patronage and protection to the most successful and best-known artists and scientists. They bid high for the services of such superstars as the painter Anthonie van Dyck, the composer Jean-Baptiste Lully, and the astronomer Tycho Brahe in a competition for being able to attract the most glorious and talented of Europe's citizens. Prestige, vanity, and a need to demonstrate the ruler's wealth and power in a highly competitive world were motives that drove dukes and kings to try to attract the best and the brightest. It was common for rulers to employ gifted and mathematically trained people in a variety of technical advisory positions. Princes needed mathematicians, architects, map-makers, engineers, and experts in ballistics, fortifications, and metallurgy.[40] The age of mercantilism expected trained mathematicians and engineers to help improve navigation, ship-design, and the technical aspects of warfare. Princes and nobles also often provided patronage to their personal physicians who could use the position to engage in scientific writing. An example is the astronomer and physician Jean Fernel (1497–1558) who served as the king's personal physician at the court of Henry II. In the sixteenth century, the great naturalist Conrad Gesner (1516–1565), referred to as "the Swiss Pliny," made his living by becoming chief physician of Zurich, as well as professor at the local Carolinum University. The French physician and polymath Pierre Michon Bourdelot (1610–1685) served as the personal physician of Queen Christina of Sweden and later became both the personal physician and protegé of the rich and powerful French general the Prince de Condé. Francesco Redi served as the court physician of the

[39] Jan Jonston, the Polish physician, who enjoyed the patronage of a Polish prince, built a reputation sufficient to generate offers of professorships at a number of Dutch and German universities (which he declined). To build up that reputation, he published textbooks on medicine and natural history, as well as (tellingly enough) a guidebook for the tutors of the children of noble patrons (Margóczy, 2014b). Or consider the case of the distinguished Florentine mathematician Vincenzo Viviani (1622–1703), the aging Galileo's student and protegé. In 1666 his reputation was such that he was offered lucrative positions by both Louis XIV and John II Casimir of Poland, whereupon Grand Duke Ferdinand de Medici made him a counteroffer and appointed him court mathematician.

[40] Galileo, while working in Padua, freelanced for the Venetian arsenal and invented his famous geometric and military compass (used for gunnery) as well as other militarily useful devices. Similarly, Giovanni Domenico Cassini, one of the most eminent astronomers of the second half of the seventeenth century, while professor of astronomy at Bologna in the 1650s, was employed by Pope Alexander VII to investigate the hydraulics of the Po river and the means to avoid flooding, as well as to consult on military matters (he was appointed superintendent of fortifications in Perugia). Prince Maurice of Nassau retained the services of the engineer Simon Stevin, who tutored him in mathematics, served as his quartermaster general, and revamped the prince's finances using new methods of bookkeeping.

Medicis in Florence, as well as secretary and supervisor of their pharmacy and foundry.

Another kind of learning in demand by courts concerned geography, driven by patriotic and colonial motives by some princes. The young British Crown Prince Henry Frederick, prince of Wales, who died in 1612 at age nineteen, assembled an impressive collection of geographers around him, motivated by a "burgeoning patriotism" (Cormack, 1991, p. 81). But in addition to those direct services, patronage involved image and reputation. The concept of "the wise prince," combining learning with power, was laid out by Machiavelli, projecting the image of a Platonic philosopher-king, and thus providing legitimacy for many local Italian rulers in Florence, Milan, and Mantua, many of whom were little more than warlords (Eamon, 1991, p. 33). German princes likewise were involved in practical matters or scientific pursuits (Moran, 1991b, p. 169). Newton was made warden and later master of the English mint in London and conducted a merciless campaign against counterfeiters. The eighteenth-century German physicist and mathematician Franz Aepinus (1724–1802), who enjoyed the patronage of the Czarina Catherine the Great, was appointed head of her cryptographic services. John T. Desaguliers enjoyed the patronage of the Duke of Chandos, whom he advised on a variety of technical projects. At the same time he was engaged by Queen Caroline (King George II's spouse), who had deep scientific interests to instruct her on a variety of scientific subjects.[41]

Patronage provided more than material incentives. Biagioli (1990) has made this a central argument in his "new view" of patronage, in which he explicitly tried to minimize economic motives by scientists. Instead he, as well as Moran (1991a, p. 3), have argued that being associated with the mighty and rich elite provided scientists with "social and intellectual legitimacy." Patronage in this view was a means to an end. By carrying out their work in high-prestige locales, at the courts of people at the social pinnacle, experimentalists would put a "seal of good housekeeping" on their results and gain credibility. Patronage, as Biagioli has argued, helped natural philosophers acquire social status. Whether social status was the password to cognitive legitimization, as he argues remains to be seen. His assertion that the reputations earned by men like Galileo, Kepler, and Clavius were not the result of the quality of their scientific work but only of the social status and the patrons associated with them seems so over the top that it may have been made tongue-in-cheek (Biagioli, 1990, pp. 5, 28). If we take Biagioli's views too literally, we should observe that court philosophers would have

---

[41] The art of fawning and groveling before people in power that intellectuals at the time sometimes had to engage in is illustrated by Desaguliers's allegorical poem "The Newtonian System" written in 1728 for the ascension of King George II, in an attempt to ensure the continuation of the queen's support, in which he compared Newtonian astronomical certitude with Hanoverian stability (Fara, 2004).

worked for free or perhaps even paid their patrons for the right to be at their court and enjoy their protection.[42] Biagioli's interpretation of patronage contains an important truth, but there is no denying (nor any need to deny) that for many scientists patronage provided income and security and such patronage depended on the legitimization by peers who were best positioned to evaluate the contribution, as Westfall (1985) has argued.

Patronage could take different forms. Much of it was handed out by the princes and kings of Europe who collected intellectuals at their courts in part just for prestige reasons. The otherwise rather inept Habsburg Emperor Rudolf II (ruled 1572–1612) collected a large number of scientists and artists at his court in Prague (at that time the Imperial capital). The astronomers Tycho Brahe and Johannes Kepler were both members of the Habsburg court, as was Carolus Clusius, né Charles de l'Écluse (1526–1609). Clusius, one of the founders of modern botany, was by all accounts a paradigmatic member of the sixteenth-century Republic of Letters: cosmopolitan, widely traveled, extremely well connected, he worked for both Rudolf II and Rudolf's father Maximilian II (Evans, 1973, pp. 119–20).[43] Galileo was perhaps the most famous case: in 1610 he was appointed as court mathematician and philosopher by Grand Duke Cosimo II of Florence, and as such he was free to pursue his research (as long as it did not conflict too much with religious doctrine—but that is another story). As Westfall (1985) has shown, Galileo lobbied seriously for this position and in fact to some extent may have directed his research to increase his chances of obtaining the coveted court position. But other academic superstars found remunerative appointments based on their reputation as well. The Dutch mathematician Christiaan Huygens and the Italian astronomer Giovanni-Domenico Cassini were appointed to the French Royal academy in the

---

[42] Nor can one accept literally Biagioli's (1990, p. 5) claim that "patronage was a voluntary act only in the sense that by not engaging in it one would commit social suicide." For one thing, some of the leading scientists of the seventeenth century were sufficiently financially independent to not need patronage in the narrow sense of the word, yet no one seriously questioned the legitimacy of Spinoza or Newton. Reputations were built on intellectual achievement, and their relation with patronage was a two-way street. Moreover, Biagioli fails to recognize fully the voluntary nature of exchange in a competitive market with many actors on both the supply and the demand side, in which the action of exchange between two agents is consensual and welfare-improving even if participating in the market itself may be inevitable.

[43] The politics of patronage could be complex and as a source of income it could be fickle, as rulers could be capricious, or be replaced by others with different tastes. Rudolf II employed a Czech court physician named Tadeás Hajek (Hagecius, 1525–1600) who was well-connected and known throughout Europe and had the emperor's ear. It was through his influence that Brahe settled in Prague in 1599. Hajek's knowledge of astronomy, like many scientists at this time, was driven by a deep commitment to astrology much in demand at the Habsburg court (Evans, 1973, p. 152).

1660s at annual salaries of 6,000 and 9,000 livres, respectively. But much patronage was also handed out by rich nobles and merchants.[44]

Tutoring the children of the rich and noble was another common service rendered by intellectuals in search of a secure and peaceful existence: Thomas Hobbes was originally hired by the Cavendish family to teach their children, as was the mathematician William Oughtred, who was a member of the household of the earl of Arundel. Isaac Casaubon (1559–1614), a prodigiously learned French scholar who found refuge in England, was frequently summoned to one of the lodges of King James to entertain his majesty and his retainers with learned conversation. René Descartes was hired by the Queen of Sweden to tutor her children. The Biagioli theory that patronage served above all as a form of legitimization is clearly incomplete: a complex and multifaceted exchange of services between patron and scientist took place.

Patronage was both complex and adaptable. Courtly patronage provided intellectuals with an alternative to the often intellectually stifling environment of universities (Moran, 1991b, p. 169). At other times, they provided them with some measure of political protection against their intellectual (and personal) enemies. The aforementioned Tommaso Campanella could survive and accomplish much of his work because the Emperor Rudolf, Duke Maximilian of Bavaria, and other Catholic notables were exerting influence to protect him. Galileo relied on the powerful princes of Florence to protect him from his intellectual foes, although he may have overestimated their power in the end. Moreover, not all scientists were motivated and incentivized by patronage. Then, as now, scientific research and intellectual innovation were motivated by a combination of financial incentives, personal curiosity, a search for recognition and respect from one's peers, a moral commitment to revealing what was felt to be true, and a feeling of responsibility toward a collective entity such as one's country or humankind in general. Robert Boyle was a wealthy landowner and a dispenser rather than a recipient of patronage. Antonie van Leeuwenhoek was a well-to-do merchant in his native city of Delft and despite peppering the Royal Society with his observations using his improved microscope, there is no evidence that he sought anything in return except recognition. Spinoza, his famous contemporary, made his income from lens grinding

---

[44] There are many well-known examples of patrons who were not heads of state. One of the best known was the Prince de Condé, the famous French rebel and later successful general (1621–1686), whose intellectual tastes were quite eclectic: he engaged at his court the authors Molière and Racine, the rather radical theologian Isaac La Peyrère (1596–1676), who served as his secretary, as well as conservative mainstream Catholic intellectuals such as Bishop Bossuet. Cardinal Mazarin hired the bibliophile physician Gabriel Naudé (1600–1653) as his personal librarian and book-collector. Pierre Gassendi, a peasant's son, enjoyed the protection of the wealthy intellectual Peiresc (and for years lived in his house), and after the latter's death he acquired the patronage of Louis Emmanuel de Valois, governor of Provence.

and instrument making (and some tutoring and gifts from friends). He never accepted a patronage position despite his reputation. René Descartes lived comfortably, if not extravagantly, off assets that he inherited.[45] Marin Mersenne was a friar in the order of the Minims and was supported by his fellow monks. Pierre Bayle, the publisher of the *News from the Republic of Letters,* had the only patron he needed, namely, his Rotterdam publisher Reiner Leers and the existence of a large audience all over Europe (Eisenstein, 1979, p. 138).

The relationship between intellectuals and their political environment was complex, and more was at stake for patronage than display and amusement. The competition to attract the best minds of Europe to one's court reflected the belief that highly intelligent and well-read individuals could prove useful to the state, because their insights provided rulers with sage advice and helped guide policies. Their intelligence and expertise could come in handy in affairs of state. Indeed, many of the prominent scientists of the time were active as diplomats or advisors. Leibniz, an intellectual superstar, was hired in 1676 by the Duke of Brunswick-Lüneburg (after 1692 elector of Hanover), whom he served for the rest of his life in a variety of capacities.

The Republic of Letters, then, functioned as a competitive market for ideas. Like all well-working markets, it would settle on a single equilibrium best-practice idea if the knowledge was tight enough. However, because it was a market for ideas, it was subject to what economists call "network externalities." What one intellectual accepted as truth could affect the demand for the ideas of others. Many of the cultural evolution biases in chapter 5 were operative, and both direct bias (accepting the opinions of others because of their reputation) and frequency-dependent bias (joining a growing consensus) suggest that in many cases, the competitive process would settle on a dominant view even if it took many decades, as was the case with the Copernican Revolution, and even if eventually it would be judged as mistaken (such as the phlogiston theory of combustion, proposed by German natural philosophers in the seventeenth century). Much like many markets for goods with network externalities, the market for ideas

---

[45] According to Project Galileo, "Descartes asserted that he had received enough property from his family that he was free to choose where and how he would live. And he did. Note that in 1633 he withdrew *Le Monde* [a manuscript written between 1629 and 1633] from publication lest it compromise his freedom and leisure. The decision makes it clear that he felt no need to establish a name for himself." See http://galileo.rice.edu/Catalog/NewFiles/descarts.html (accessed Aug. 18, 2013). The additional point made by Richard Westfall (the compiler of project Galileo) regarding the essay that Descartes dedicated the *Principles* to Princess Elizabeth of Bohemia. "The whole relation with the Princess is surely revealing of the patronage system. She had no monetary rewards to give, just the prestige of a royal name" seems far-fetched; the princess was an exile from her native Bohemia and an accomplished intellectual. She spent the last twenty years of her life as abbess of a Lutheran convent in Germany. It is hard to see how much legitimization her royal name could convey.

normally settled on an equilibrium in which one doctrine became pre-dominant. This depended on how tight the knowledge was. Everything was contestable, but if a proposition was tight enough and could be verified at a reasonable level of certainty, the system tended toward it as an equili-brium cultural variant, making it "conventional wisdom." If it was untight, that is, if prevailing best-practice scientific methods were inadequate to decide between competing views, such a convergence would not occur. Even when it did, however, the market environment was rarely sufficiently stringent to rule out many niches occupied by non-conformists and crack-pots insisting on cultural variants that most people had abandoned (such as a belief that all answers about the history of life are in the book of Genesis). This, perhaps, is desirable, since a small fraction of such crackpot beliefs may end up generating ideas that turn out after all to be scientifically important—though that outcome is unlikely to emerge from the creationist museum in Petersburg, Kentucky.

The discourses that took place in the Republic of Letters were not just about content but also about the methods and means of acquiring knowledge that were more trustworthy and accurate. Better experiments, more careful calculations, and exact observations all became part of the scientific discourse. As noted earlier, in the Republic of Letters, between 1500 and 1700, a number of scientific debates took place that illustrate the effectiveness of the market for ideas to arbitrate and decide disputes. These debates were a form of *persuasion*, that is, various biases in cultural evo-lution. At least some of those disputes were decided by content bias: those with the best evidence and logic won out. In other words, when the accumulating evidence for a particular belief was sufficiently strong so that no attempt to falsify it had succeeded, it became increasingly accepted and thus could be considered tight knowledge. Such competitions could, of course, take decades and even centuries to be decided. Some have not been decided to the present day. Precisely because many issues were insufficiently tight to be thus decided, the market for ideas depended on other biases, especially direct bias. But direct bias was especially important because it saved information costs. Difficult mathematical proofs were accepted, because it was assumed that those who had vetted the theorems had checked them. Experimental results, as we have seen above, were often accepted and not reproduced because the buyers in the market for idea "trusted" those who had carried them out.[46]

---

[46] Shapin and Schaffer (1985, pp. 55–67) describe in detail the steps taken by Boyle to establish the trustworthiness of his experiments. Boyle's descriptions were also described in extreme detail in order to facilitate replication, to convince readers that the experiments could be trusted, and to offer the possibility of "virtual witnessing." Moreover, to further establish his trustworthiness, Boyle reported even failed experiments, wrote modestly, and ensured that his statements did not overreach.

The competition in the market for ideas and the importance of knowledge tightness and content bias is well illustrated by the rise and fall of a mystical religious movement known as Hermeticism, which counted as its followers such notable intellectuals as Giordano Bruno and John Dee. It was widely condemned as heretical and based on black magic, but for a while it competed seriously in the European market for ideas. The core of Hermetic beliefs was based on a set of ancient writings attributed to a mythical writer named Hermes, consisting of a mix of religious doctrines, astrology, and occult practices, such as talismans with great powers and the virtues of certain plants and stones (Yates, 1964, p. 2). Its followers believed that the writings attributed to Hermes were Egyptian in origin and predated the books of Moses, and their alleged antiquity gave them an aura of sacredness. The Hermetic books were part of a larger body of what was known as *prisca theologia*, books believed to be by ancient sages antedating both the Hebrew Bible and the earliest Greek sages and containing a body of knowledge that reflected the pure ur-religion from which all later wisdom originated. The rules of evidence and persuasion of the Republic of Letters and the principle of contestability did not spare this movement, however. In 1614 the Huguenot classical scholar Isaac Casaubon published a devastating analysis of the Hermetical writings. He established beyond serious doubt that they dated from the second or third centuries AD and were a Greek pastiche of ancient and biblical texts rather than a divinely inspired book by a much more ancient Egyptian writer (Grafton, 1983).[47] As Yates and others have pointed out, the strong belief in mystical and occult powers was widely shared in early modern Europe among learned people, from the Neapolitan philosopher and experimentalist Giambattista della Porta (1535–1615) to Isaac Newton himself.[48] Subsequent generations, embarrassed by what they regarded to be the superstitions of their predecessors, tried to minimize this element: intellectual history, too, is written by the winners.

The belief in magic and the occult was not necessarily retrograde: they constituted in Yates's words another illustration of the growing conviction that whereas "in the Middle Ages ... the true end of man was contemplation," the occult and magic of the Renaissance changed the purpose of intellectual activity. It now was "religious and not contrary to the will of God that man, the great miracle, should exert his powers" (Yates, 1964, p. 156). Many scholars have pointed out that these attitudes constituted a

---

[47] Yates (1964, p. 398) goes as far as seeing Casaubon's book as a watershed event, separating the Renaissance world from the modern one.

[48] Many Renaissance intellectuals were fascinated by the mystical numerology, known as *Kabbalah* or *Cabala* practiced by Jewish scholars since the publication of the *Zohar* book in thirteenth-century Spain. Among the writers fascinated by Cabalism were the fifteenth-century humanist scholar Giovanni Pico della Mirandola (1463–1494), the French classical scholar and astronomer Guillaume Postel (1510–1581), Athanasius Kircher, and Giordano Bruno.

novel bridge between the theoretical and the practical, but these bridges could take many forms. The gap between magic and science in early modern Europe was not nearly as wide as it became during the Enlightenment. Occult, mysticism, and magic coexisted and intersected with experimental methodology and empirical testing. It often employed advanced mathematics. Very slowly, what we call today modern science gained the upper hand and led to the Industrial Enlightenment, but the victory was never final and complete (Tambiah, 1990). All the same, by the second quarter of the eighteenth century, the occultist tradition had lost its intellectual respectability and contemporaries, much as they adulated Isaac Newton, avoided mentioning his occultist interests (Copenhaver, 1978, p. 34).

The market for ideas was the arena in which philosophical doctrines battled one another for acceptance. By the early eighteenth century the scientific world of the Continent had trifurcated into a Newtonian, a Cartesian, and a Leibnizian camp, which battled one another over important points. By the second half of the century the Newtonians had for all intents and purposes won this battle. It was a battle fought, at least north of the Alps, with only minimal intervention by the authorities, secular or religious. Instead, the weapons were persuasion, evidence, logic, political arm-twisting, and academic haggling on a playing ground that was at least reasonably level.[49]

Within the larger European context, the competition within the market for ideas was between conservative forces and the *nuova scienza*. Conservative forces did all they could to stop what they considered heretical views that contradicted the scriptures and other authorities. In the vanguard of the forces of reaction stood the Inquisition and the Jesuit order, the tormentors of the aging Galileo and the fierce opponents of heliocentrism, corpuscularianism, and infinitesimals. The fate of the Jesuits is especially telling. In many ways their best scientific minds considered themselves bona fide members of the Republic of Letters. They were torn between the formal rules of the order and their formidable intellectual abilities, which often created a contradiction between the scriptures and their scientific insights. Some Jesuits, for instance Christoph Grienberger, Clavius's successor as the professor of mathematics at the Collegio Romano, may have secretly

---

[49] An illustrative example is the late seventeenth-century dispute between the Newtonians and Cartesians on the shape of the earth. Johann Bernoulli had shown that Newtonian theory suggested an oblate (flattened at the poles) shape as opposed to the prolate (oblong) theory of the Cartesians. The great mathematician and Enlightenment genius Pierre Louis Maupertuis and his mathematician colleague Alexis-Claude Clairaut went to Lapland in 1736 to make the appropriate measurements (comparing the length of the meridian degree in Lapland with that in Paris), finding the evidence in favor of Newton's theory. Some minor anomalies remained, and new mathematical and geodesic tools were applied to the question until the matter of the degree of flattening was settled by the early nineteenth century. The point is, however, that these measurements settled the matter.

sympathized with Galileo's work, but the order's discipline to which the Jesuits were committed demanded deference to its theological principles (Castellano, 2004, pp. 10–11, 20). Rodrigo Arriaga, a Spanish Jesuit scientist, who taught in Prague for much of his life, published in 1632 a widely read textbook, *Cursus Philosophicus*, which had sympathetic passages about both the new astronomy and the new infinitesimal mathematics (Grant, 2003; Alexander, 2014, pp. 139–41). It was prohibited by the Jesuit's Board of Revisors led by the very conservative Jesuit General Muzio Vitelleschi. Within the Catholic world, many astronomers and mathematicians were sympathetic to Copernicus, Galileo, and other exponents of the heretical cosmology, such as Diego de Zuñiga's (1536–1598), who argued that texts in the Bible actually supported heliocentrism, but their works found themselves on the Index of prohibited books.

Not all reactionaries were Catholic: Descartes complained in 1642 about conservative Dutch Calvinist professors who rejected the new philosophy because it was opposed to and had undermined the traditional doctrines that universities had taught hitherto and because it was "in conflict with other disciplines and faculties and above all with orthodox theology" (Descartes, 2000, p. xiv).[50] Many of the great thinkers of the era, including Descartes himself, were concerned that their work might be misinterpreted as potentially atheistic and cause them to get into serious trouble. In the Paris of the 1620s, where there was little Jesuit influence and no Inquisition, too blatant an attack on approved thinkers could lead to the threat of capital punishment (MacLean 2006, p. 272). An opinion that clearly threatened to devalue existing dogma could bring with it serious risks. As a result, the most heterodox thinkers needed to keep a clear path to retract their views or had to find powerful protectors, or else they could find themselves on trial, in jail, or worse.

The market for ideas decided not only which ideas were to be accepted but also engaged in meta-arguments about the legitimate criteria and tools through which disputes among competing cultural variants were to be decided. As noted in chapter 5, the rise of the concept of experiment, so ardently advocated by the Baconians, was a major breakthrough. The commitment to experimentation as a tool to settle disputes and create the

---

[50] A case in point is his clash with the orthodox Calvinist theologian Voetius, who forced the University of Utrecht, where he was rector, to condemn Descartes's work and to enforce its nothing-but-Aristotle teaching policy. In Leyden, too, a demand was made in 1642 to stop teaching Descartes's works, on account of accusations of blasphemy and atheism. The pugnacious Descartes and his acolytes fought these limitations tooth and nail. Philosophers were instructed to stay clear of theology which in practice meant a serious limitation on what they could teach (Stewart, 1994, p. 41). In the long term, however, the competitive nature of the Republic of Letters left these intellectuals no choice: by the 1670s Cartesian science had become quite influential in Leyden, which was becoming the most prominent scientific center on the Continent (Jacob, 1988, p. 68).

kind of content bias that would make others change their mind emerged in full bloom in the seventeenth century. In England the work of Harvey and Gilbert, in Italy that of Galileo and Torricelli, and in France in a variety of circles and groups, all exchanged notes and results. To repeat, experiments were not an entirely new phenomenon, and experiments were conducted in antiquity and in the Middle Ages. But, as Wootton (2015, p. 346) has stressed, what was new was a scientific community that recognized the experimental method and the replication of experimental results as a powerful means of persuasion.

There were others important debates in this competitive marketplace. One of these was the dispute about the role of mathematics in the growth of propositional knowledge. Such Renaissance scholars as Erasmus and Juan Luis Vives counseled against the study of mathematics, fearing that it would withdraw the mind from the practical concerns of life. The many followers of Paracelsus, one of the most rebellious intellectuals of his age, condemned mathematical abstraction in the study of natural phenomena and favored a more inductive and observational method such as practiced in the chemistry and alchemy of the age (Debus, 1978, p. 21). Francis Bacon, as already noted, failed to see the opportunities that mathematics offered to natural sciences (Gaukroger, 2001, pp. 21–27). In contrast, Galileo, Descartes, and Huygens clearly realized that experiment and formal analysis complemented one another, and with Newton's work this faction resoundingly triumphed in the marketplace for ideas. But early in the seventeenth century there was also a debate about what one should use mathematics for: should it be used to study specific phenomena such as motion and force, as Galileo suggested, or should it be confined to a more ambitious study of the universe as a whole?[51] Here, too, the competitive process did its work: over time mystical and occultist approaches to natural philosophy, still very much in play by 1650, fell into disrepute, though their continued demise—to become a niche phenomenon, never quite disappearing—was an eighteenth century phenomenon. The market for ideas also had to determine what the agenda of research would be: should topics be picked because of their inherent metaphysical importance? Or were practical and economic considerations to be front and center?

Economics suggests that competitive and integrated markets breed global superstars, and some of those superstars can become cultural entrepreneurs. Such superstars can arise especially when the product of an individual is convex in output, and when production costs do not rise with the size of the market (Rosen, 1981). These conditions were satisfied in the Republic of Letters: convexity implies that the addition to knowledge by one

---

[51] A case in point is the English physician, occult philosopher, and mathematician Robert Fludd (1574–1637), who suggested that mathematics could be used to decipher the mystical harmonies of the universe (Debus, 1978, p. 12).

Galileo was larger than twice the contributions of two mediocre scientists, and the marginal costs of spreading new knowledge (that is, the costs incurred by adding one more person to the body of people already familiar with the new knowledge) were negligible thanks to the printing press and a large number of intelligencers, translators, and acolytes. In Europe, "superstar" intellectuals—from Erasmus, Paracelsus, and Luther in the early sixteenth century to Descartes, Newton, and Leibniz in the seventeenth—were famous throughout the Continent. And while they too only catered to an educated elite, they could access their audiences throughout the Continent and try to persuade scholars in different countries, thus not only selling books but also hopefully finding a powerful and rich sponsor who would underwrite their careers and provide a patronage appointment. Much like stellar sports figures and musicians today, a fairly small number of truly world-famous intellectuals attracted a disproportionate amount of the fame and patronage of the time. But the effect of the concentration of the payoffs among superstars had enormous externalities, because it demonstrated to young and ambitious intellectuals the rewards of winning this lottery. As with all superstars, those of science created a large cadre of would-be imitators, most of whom would never attain stardom. Society, however, would still benefit from their work, even if it amounted to little more than "normal science." In that sense, the superstars were the source of considerable model-based bias in cultural change: their fame and success made intellectual innovation respectable, even desirable.

The Republic of Letters, as MacLean (2008, p. 17) points out, could be seen from many different angles: a community of scholars, the content of the ideas they fostered, the means of disseminating them, the intellectual norms that set standards of persuasion (adequacy of proof, reproducibility of experiment), attitudes toward collaboration and disclosure, and so forth. Joining it meant that one had to accept a scientific ethic of sharing and communicating. For my purposes here, it can also be seen as a community that set incentives through social norms and informal rules, that is an institution. It was this institution that turned out to be one of the taproots of European technological change. In this regard the Republic of Letters should be regarded as the missing link that connects the growing literature that views institutions as the core difference between successful economies and less successful ones, and the literature that stresses the importance of technology and innovation in the origins of the Industrial Revolution and the generation of sustainable economic growth.

The institutionalists maintain, quite rightly, that one of the main ways that institutions fostered economic growth was by supporting markets. The Republic of Letters and its daughter, the eighteenth- and nineteenth-century Republic of Science, provided the institutional underpinning of a well-functioning market for ideas. It was in many ways a unique phenomenon: other civilizations made scientific advances and had functioning markets for ideas, but they always eventually ran into diminishing returns and eventually into a dead-end. There were built-in mechanisms that protected the status quo and resisted further innovation. In Europe that resistance was overcome, if not easily, rapidly, and universally. The result was a set of scientific and technological breakthroughs that was self-reinforcing and to date shows no signs of abating. Whether they merit the term "scientific revolution" or not is a moot point. It is the main explanation why ultimately Europe succeeded where no other society did, to break out of the Malthusian state of subsistence economies through the relentless power of accumulated useful knowledge.[52]

To repeat: the key to Europe's success was its fortunate condition that combined political fragmentation with cultural unity. If it had had one without the other, the end result would in all likelihood have been profoundly different. Political fragmentation in a poorly integrated intellectual world implied that no cultural entrepreneur would have been able to cover the fixed cost catering to a "market" (or audience) of a few thousand local people. Nor would there have been networks of people from whom scientists could learn and on whose shoulders they could stand. Even a well-integrated and large market for ideas in which there is little competition and limited entry will eventually not be able to generate enough innovation and change, because incumbents would find ways to suppress challenges to their cultural positions.

This is not to argue that the Republic of Letters came into being or persisted because it was fulfilled this task. Such functionalism would be ahistorical. Originally it was no more than a network set up by intellectuals who wanted to share and test out new ideas on like-minded colleagues, persuade them of the merits of their insights (thus "making a sale" in the market for ideas) to enhance their reputations, and who wanted to find out what others were up to (so as to make sure they were up to date on other people's work). Its impact on the long-run cultural development of the European intellectual elite and the economic transformation of the European world was an unintended consequence of these needs. But whatever brought it about, it turned out eventually to be an institution unique in human history and a key to the understanding where the long road that led to modern economic growth began. If one believes in the importance of institutions as drivers of economic growth, one cannot fail to recognize the importance of the Republic of Letters. Small as it may be, it illustrates how in evolutionary change that takes place in tiny minorities can have cascading consequences for the population at large. It is the paradigmatic

---

[52] As a comparison, we may look at India, which was very far from being the scientific desert that European visitors described it to be. Historians of India, however, have pointed to the "usual secretiveness" of Indian scholars in the eighteenth century, and to the fact that when the validity of knowledge was put to the test, "the sacred texts were always the standard measure" (Dharampal, 1971, p. 5; Kumar, 2003, p. 687).

illustration of the pivotal role of Hooke's "Cortesian army" or upper-tail human capital.

Between 1500 and 1700, Europe thus experienced an accelerated rate of cultural development. It discovered Protestantism, the structure of the solar system, the circulation of blood, the atmosphere, calculus, the laws driving the motion of heavenly and earthly bodies, biblical textual criticism, and many things in between. The greatest and most fateful outcome of a well-functioning market for ideas, however, was a set of beliefs we refer to as the Enlightenment. I have elsewhere (Mokyr, 2002, 2009a) made an argument about the central role of the Enlightenment in the economic history of Europe. The Enlightenment was the final stage in the cultural evolution that eventually led to the Industrial Revolution and modern economic growth in Europe. It stressed the two elements needed for the material progress of the nation and society. One consisted of the growth of useful knowledge, and the interaction between theory and practice; the other of improving the political institutions that governed the rules of the economic game and how resources were allocated and income distributed.

Can the concepts of cultural evolution put forward in chapters 3–5 help us understand the role of the Republic of Letters in the triumph of Enlightenment ideas in eighteenth-century Europe? At first blush the answer is obvious: it lubricated the market for ideas and greatly speeded up changing beliefs among the European literate elite. The epistolary and publication networks facilitated horizontal transmission of beliefs and ideas. After all, for **content bias** (that is, persuasion) to be effective in shaping people's minds, they need above all to be exposed to the ideas of others. Access was the one thing that the Republic of Letters provided with increasing abundance. But content bias itself can be seen as subject to evolutionary forces. Shapiro (2000) and Poovey (1998) and more recently Wootton (2015, pp. 251–309) have argued that early modern Europe witnessed a growing respect for the concept of fact and its counterpart, verification. Perhaps the central phenomenon in the cultural evolution of the era was the transformation of how content bias in natural philosophy worked, that is, what was admissible as evidence. In the scientific community of early modern Europe, what counted as persuasive evidence was evolving itself: it became accepted to treat facts the way the legal system had always done, namely to infer facts logically from indirect observations even when the fact itself could not be seen directly (Shapiro, 2000). In Wootton's felicitous phrase, this was the age in which scientists began to "handle evidence in the way that lawyers and theologians had been handling it for many years" (Wootton, 2015, p. 407). Moreover, knowledge was always contestable and subject to challenge. If new and more persuasive evidence was brought to bear on an issue, useful knowledge would be revised. It became increasingly accepted that science was not a search for the Truth but a never-ending road advancing toward more plausible and effective ways of understanding the natural world.

This type of reasoning changed the way the Republic of Letters worked and how it handled content bias. While none of the new forms of persuasion was wholly new, the discourse changed. Experimental data became increasingly credible as a way of persuading skeptics. Mathematization and precise computation slowly became a way of defending new propositions, and where precision was hard, empirical regularities could be discerned through the collection of facts and specimens and their organization and cataloging. And finally, new tools and instruments, as noted, created new facts that were increasingly indisputable.

As Margóczy (2014b) notes, in some areas of knowledge, authentication was crucial; in others, such as natural history, less so. But, he notes, authentication itself could be unreliable if the evidence could be faked. Hence, experts were needed to confirm the reliability of the facts and the evidence. Hence the role of direct bias. By designating certain people as trustworthy experts, the Republic of Letters designated authorities who judged other ideas on the basis of logic and evidence and declared them valid. Peer review—far from perfect—is still the best method we have to determine the validity of intellectual innovations. Above all, what matters, is how exactly direct bias worked in different institutional settings. Until ca.1500 the classics had been the ultimate authorities and in cases of doubt they were consulted. What made them authoritative is a consensus that rested on a conservative ideology enforced by the Church. But these rules could change, and when they did, intellectual innovation could occur. They changed when the old authorities were increasingly undermined by better data, better observations, and better instruments to gather and analyze them. At times, the entire concept of authority was doubted: Pascal noted that in matters subject to reason and the senses authority was useless and he bewailed the blindness of those who in such matters relied on authority alone (Pascal, [1651] 2007, p. 446). But of course in a world of increasing specialization and a growing body of knowledge, specialization and a "division of knowledge" (akin to a division of labor) were indispensable. This required trust in *some* authority. But who was to become an authority? Who appointed them? And who was to appoint the appointers?

Yet the scholars of the age clearly were committed to the idea of the power to persuade through **rhetorical bias**. Bacon himself, in a remarkable pasage in Book two of *The Advancement of Learning* noted that the art of eloquence, while in true value inferior to wisdom, "with people it is the more mighty" and that "profoundness of wisdom will help a man to a name or admiration, but that it is eloquence that prevaileth in an active life." The duty of Rhetoric, he felt, was to apply reason to imagination (Bacon, [1605] 1996, pp. 237–38). The Republic of Letters, argues Schoeck, was based on a common foundation of rhetoric which "made possible free movement of ideas, genres and books" (Schoeck, 1982, p. 303). Eloquence was the means by which members of the Republic of Letters communicated and persuaded one another. Yet rhetorical bias had its limits: erudite and brilliant conversation taking place in the *salons* and coffeehouses of the Republic of Letters in the age of Enlightenment started to look pedantic to contemporaries, and were easy to make fun of, especially when taken on by a master-satirist like Jonathan Swift.

The Republic of Letters anointed a new set of experts whose knowledge required more that just familiarity with an existing canon but also with the methods by which *novel* knowledge was to be validated. To become an expert, one had to have made an important original contribution; only those with proven creativity could judge that of others. One had to innovate to become an authority, and becoming an authority conveyed both patronage and power over others precisely because of the dependence of the system on reputation among peers. The imprimatur of expertise was no longer awarded solely by rulers, priests, and the establishment. The Republic of Letters itself increasingly asserted the right to decide who were the authorities who declared knowledge to be valid.

In that way **direct bias** was responsible for the continuous development of useful knowledge under the umbrella of the Republic of Letters. Broman (2012, p. 192) points to the Enlightenment as the era in which the ideology "that scientific knowledge had to make itself useful for social improvement" emerged, so that a well-organized society that depended on this knowledge placed a great deal of authority in the hands of these experts. The concept of direct bias bestows new importance on the influence of Bacon: while not much of an authority on science himself, his work helped set the metabeliefs underlying the mechanisms that appointed some scholars as experts and judges on the validity of ideas and helped establish the reputation mechanism that propelled the system forward. Direct bias was used not only in persuading people to accept what was right, but also to rid the intellectual community of false knowledge. David Wootton (2015, p. 304) has pointed to many books published in this period that were compilations of past errors that now could be dismissed as nonsense. Whether that demonstrates a kind of Gresham's Law in reverse in which good facts drive out bad facts, as Wootton argues, depends on how tight the knowledge was. False facts and hypotheses that could not be readily refuted with the tools of the time survived for a long time.

Paradoxically, precisely because the writings of the superstars themselves were always subject to verifiability and contestability, they gained credibility, since the audience at large could assume that ideas had been vetted and examined by experts. The Republic of Letters did not produce an unassailable gospel, like the Jewish Bible or the Chinese Four Books, works that were subject to exegesis but did not permit doubt and did not allow for a real concept of heresy. Some writers were regarded as authorities, but as the case of Newton attests, only insofar as their views had withstood every possible critique.

A model of cultural evolution also supports an inclusive view regarding the value of patronage. The Biagioli view of legitimization through social status, appropriately shorn of its more extreme expressions, is consistent with direct bias (in which the patron becomes the authority adjudicating which scientific work is meritorious). Moreover, it serves as a prime example of model-based bias (in which the prince sets the tone for his subjects of what is right and just and what is not). Precisely because so much science was sponsored and protected by royal and aristocratic patrons, legitimization of science meant that some arguments were deemed by many to be valid because a person of high social status had blessed them. Moreover, patronage of science by a high-ranking member of society meant that useful knowledge and experimental philosophy themselves became higher-prestige activities. Many books of science and learning of the time displayed groveling dedications to nobles, who were not even remotely capable of understanding their contents. It is in this light that we should see not only the activities of patrons like Emperor Rudolf II and Duke Federico Cesi, the founder of the Accademia dei Lincei, as well as the young crown Prince Henry Frederick.

Other forms of "bias" in cultural evolution, too, can be seen to have affected the market for ideas. The rather sudden realization in the late fifteenth and early sixteenth centuries that the planet looked quite different from what everyone had believed, as we have seen, led to a serious re-examination of truths previously thought to be unassailable. A century and a half later the catastrophic bloodshed during the Thirty Years War convinced more and more people of the merits of tolerance and pluralism. Both can be seen as examples of salient event bias. The age, of course, also had its share of coercion bias, of which the "cuius regio eius religio" rule serves as an example. But the Republic of Letters also serves as a powerful demonstration that in the competitive environment of a politically fragmented world, progress cannot be blocked by the coercion of a few reactionary powers. Finally, rhetorical bias influenced readers when content alone was insufficient. It helped to have the sharp pen of Voltaire on one's side.

To return to the important work of Henrich (2009), the Republic of Letters underscores the critical importance of interconnectedness and access. The increasingly efficient and dense networks created communications among scholars slaving away on problems in mathematics, anatomy, astronomy, and botany, and allowed them to compare notes, avoid duplication, recombine different ideas into new ones, and argue from analogy and contrast with the work of others. In many other ways the existence of the scholarly network in the Republic of Letters stimulated intellectual innovations in ways that created a monstrously large synergy, in which the output of the intellectual community was far larger than the sum of the individual components had they all worked on their own.

The logic of cultural evolution suggests that contingency and chance played an important role in bringing about this outcome precisely because there was a highly competitive marketplace for ideas and because much of the innovation led to knowledge that was rather untight. When it was hard to prove a particular supposition beyond reasonable doubt, it was possible for "bad knowledge" to drive out "good knowledge" or for the two to coexist for generations. In medicine, chemistry, and biology, for instance, incompatible and competing views survived for centuries. We do not have a very good model to predict which idea will prevail in such markets any more than we have a good tool to predict in advance which biological variants will become fixed in the population or which operating system will end up dominating personal computers. A lot may have depended on the beliefs and abilities of a few key cultural entrepreneurs and on their rhetorically powerful disciples, who persuaded large numbers of people of the master's message, sometimes in modified form. Success was never assured. Cohen (2012, p. 150) states perceptively that there is "no inherent reason whatever for why the Renaissance-European upswing should in the end have escaped the destiny of every previous, large-scale endeavor to attain knowledge of nature ... and come to a standstill at some point." In 1600, it was indeed hard to foresee what the Republic of Letters and the competitive market for ideas it supported would lead to.

All the same, the model proposed here is that when knowledge becomes tighter, content bias and direct bias mean that certain beliefs will prevail in the market for ideas. Once the tools become available to test alternatives, the members of the Republic of Science would choose Lavoisier over phlogiston, Newton's cosmology over Descartes's, and Pasteur over miasmatic theories. The remarkable thing is not that such developments took a long time—it is that they happened at all. By the second half of the eighteenth century, magical and mystical doctrines and practices were vanishing from the intellectual discourse. The first edition of the *Encyclopaedia Britannica,* which appeared in 1771, gave only 132 lines, less than a full page, to articles on such topics as astrology, alchemy, Cabala, demons, divination, the word "occult," and witchcraft. In contrast, astronomy occupied 67 pages, and chemistry 115 (Copenhaver, 1978, p. 32).[53] But what was true for biology and astronomy was not true for other cultural variants: one cannot prove by experiment or mathematics that social progress is likely to continue, or that an inclusive, open, and democratic society is more likely to prosper than an extractive, autocratic one, much less metaphysical beliefs about the purpose of the universe.

It is thus important to stress that the victory of the beliefs we associate with the Enlightenment in the market for ideas was anything but foreordained. Neither the form nor the content of the European Enlightenment were inevitable. The contingent outcomes of wars may have played a role: had Spain prevailed in its struggle with the rebellious Dutch and the

---

[53] Copenhaver (1978, p. 31) adds that by the time of Newton's death (1727), "the occultist tradition, with all its claims about the powers of magic, alchemy, divination, witchcraft, Cabala, and the other secret arts, no longer demanded a serious response from serious thinkers."

recalcitrant English, had Jesuits and other Catholic conservatives been able to monopolize education and intellectual discourse, there may have been no Enlightenment, or perhaps a dramatically different one. Had the intellectual status quo succeeded in rejecting the novel ideas that constituted the core of the Enlightenment, the Industrial Revolution would probably have fizzled out as another ephemeral efflorescence. But whatever the Enlightenment was, it happened. Powerful minds used a combination of logic, evidence, and rhetoric to change the beliefs and values of the intellectual elite. Almost all the biases of cultural evolution came into play in this victory. They did not operate uniformly over time or across space. There were many different versions of the Enlightenment, to the point where some historians in desperation have questioned the usefulness of the concept altogether, although the belief in the power of knowledge and reasoning to improve life and society remains one of the most important common denominators of all its versions. What this exactly meant and how to bring it about were a different matter.

With hindsight, however, it is possible to see how Enlightenment ideas prevailed in Europe. By the middle of the seventeenth century, useful knowledge was increasingly recognized as a potentially powerful force for economic change, becoming a source of social optimism and a force for progress even if it had not come close to its full potential. The triumphs of experimental science and observations aided by new instruments were an illustration of human agency in nature. They supported the basic Enlightenment idea of an agenda to bring about economic improvement through an aggressive manipulation of natural forces made possible by useful knowledge. These ideas, in some form, had been around since the Middle Ages, but what counted was their triumph over what progressive intellectuals regarded as obscurantism and superstition. Religious warfare had been shown to have been a rather futile and destructive endeavor, and a growing number of people were advocating the need for religious tolerance rather than pious conformity. By the late seventeenth century such political philosophers as Locke were starting to lay out the parameters of a set of political institutions that could make their world a better and more prosperous place.

Beyond institutions, what mattered in the long run was the willingness and ability to harness nature to human material needs. Whatever its exact sources, more than ever the insights of natural philosophy and history confirmed the beliefs of a mechanistic, understandable universe and a controllable environment that could and should be manipulated for the material benefit of humankind. The Republic of Letters of the seventeenth century, then, prepared the ground for the Industrial Enlightenment by offering to the market for ideas the metaconcept that people's relationship with the environment was based on intelligibility and instrumentality (Dear, 2006). Instrumentality basically meant that at some level the metaphysics of the essence of a phenomenon mattered less than its full and detailed description, its modus operandi, and how it could be harnessed. Understanding its deep causes (or, as an economist might call it, its "microfoundations") may have been a fruitless endeavor.[54] Intelligibility, above all, depended on a mechanistic and deterministic view of the world.

These two trends, institutional improvement and technological progress, were the product of the thought and labors of many people, some famous, most obscure. What accounted for the success was the institution within which these intellectuals and scholars worked and which set the incentives that drove them and the constraints that disciplined them. That institution was the sixteenth- and seventeenth-century Republic of Letters.

The Republic of Letters that began to emerge in Europe around the time of the great voyages and reached a crescendo in the age of Enlightenment is the most significant institutional development that explains the technology-led quantum leap in economic performance heralded by the Industrial Revolution. But other institutions mattered as well. Britain in the eighteenth century has been dubbed the "Associational Society" by its leading historian (Clark, 2000). Many of these associations, of course, had little to do with the dissemination of useful knowledge but were social gatherings, eating and (mostly) drinking clubs, sports and musical organizations, and so on. The significance of these associations is in the creation of a civil economy, in which economic agents behaved in an honorable manner and thus minimized the need for third party (that is, the state) enforcement of contracts. Yet a surprising number of them were devoted to the useful arts and this led to the rise of "public science" in Britain, in which useful knowledge was made available to those who could make best use of it (Stewart, 1992, 1998). Some of these tales have been well told, especially that of the most famous one, the Birmingham Lunar Society. But the Lunar Society was the culmination, not the start of the rise of public science in Britain. By 1700 there were already 2,000 coffeehouses in London, many of which were sites of literary activity, discussions about natural philosophy, and political debates (Cowan, 2005). Coffeehouses remained important centers for the dissemination of knowledge and beliefs throughout the eighteenth century. Perhaps the most famous of these coffeehouse societies was the London Chapter Coffee House, the favorite of the fellows of the Royal Society, whose membership resembled (and overlapped with) the Birmingham Lunar Society.[55] Masonic lodges, too, proved a locus for the exchange of scientific and technological information, even if that was not

---

[54] Thus, when William Harvey was asked by the German physician Caspar Hofmann what the "final cause" (in an Aristotelian sense, that is, the ultimate purpose) of the circulation of the blood was, he replied that as he was a very bad philosopher, he was first and foremost keen on establishing that the phenomenon actually existed and then perhaps later would worry about the final cause (Wright, 2012, p. 202).

[55] See Levere and Turner (2002). Its membership reads like a veritable list of the "Who's who" of the British Industrial Enlightenment of the 1780s.

their primary mission.[56] Public lectures on scientific and engineering sub-jects attracted a surprising number of attendants. Lecturers performed enter-taining public experiments, in which electricity and magnetism played roles disproportionate to their economic significance, and their direct impact on the techniques in use at the time is questionable.[57]

What matters, however, is not whether there was any direct and immediate link from these cultural developments to economic change and the Industrial Revolution. What mattered was that the cultural develop-ments in the values and beliefs of the European economic elite toward a more growth-friendly culture began to spread and affect more and more people, and especially practical people who could make a difference to economic conditions. The Industrial Enlightenment was a Western Euro-pean phenomenon, and it was especially successful in Britain, where the environment was especially susceptible to the idea of progress under the term of "improvement" (Slack, 2015), though eventually these notions took firm root almost everywhere else in the North Atlantic region. Improvement meant, among many things, the application of natural philosophy to any-thing from agriculture and medicine to navigation. It was not the highbrow science of Newton, perhaps, that made the difference in the eighteenth century, but the lowbrow concepts of approaching the study of nature through careful measurement, precise formulation, well-designed experi-ments, empirical testing, mathematization, and above all the belief that such activities were virtuous, respectable, and could lead to economic and social rewards.

The significance of the cultural and technological developments in Europe in enhancing interconnectivity has been discussed at great length, even if the terminology is not always the same. The emergence of a "public sphere," a term coined by philosopher Jürgen Habermas, has caught the eye of historians. It is often equated with the Republic of Letters, and many authors have stressed how it differed as a public space from the territorial state (Goodman, 1994, pp. 14–15, 49). Such scholars as Jacob (1997, 2000b) and Stewart (1992, 1998, 2004) have made much of the emergence of a culture of public science, in which science was discussed and studied, in the hope—remote, perhaps, in most cases—that one day it could be put to good

---

[56] On the significance of Masonic lodges, see Jacob (1991) and Im Hoff (1994, pp. 139–45).

[57] Many of these lecturers structured their lectures around topics that had no immediate or even remote applicability, presented theories that were bogus even by the standards of the time, and at times they showed a bias toward the flashy and dramatic experiment over the strictly useful (Schaffer, 1983). John Desaguliers, who made a name for himself as a lecturer ex-plaining the new physics to general audiences, admitted that "a great many persons get a consider-able knowledge of Natural Philosophy by way of amusement" (cited by Schaffer, 1994, p. 159). But as Stewart (2004, p. 8) remarks, "a sense of practical consequence was not immediately excluded by the spectacular."

use. Meanwhile, it was to be enjoyed and its practice conveyed a certain social prestige. With some luck and a lot of patience and persistence, public science could eventually be transformed into technological progress and economic progress.

Part IV

Prelude to the Enlightenment

Chapter 13

Puritanism and British Exceptionalism

The Industrial Revolution, as every schoolchild knows, started in Britain. The discussion so far has emphasized a set of European phenomena to explain the exceptionalism of Europe. Was Britain somehow unique even within Europe? I have summarized much of this literature elsewhere (Mokyr, 2009a), but given the importance of culture and beliefs, a natural question that could and should be raised is whether British culture was somehow different from the rest of Europe. The problem is that much of European intellectual culture was transnational. Newton, Descartes, Spinoza, Galileo, and Leibniz were read by intellectuals from Stockholm to Madrid and from Dublin to St. Petersburg. Where Britain may have differed is in the emergence of the Puritan movement. The historical importance of Puritanism to the growth of useful knowledge in England was placed on the agenda of historians by Robert K. Merton ([1938] 2001) in his classic work linking Puritanism to the rise of modern science. He stressed the importance of Puritanism to the particular form that British scientific culture developed in the seventeenth century. Merton's unit of analysis was very much a set of cultural beliefs and values, not a formal set of theological propositions. These were shared by many individuals who were not formally Puritans and in this sense his thesis has led to a somewhat pointless debate about the role of religion in the Scientific Revolution and to what extent he can be proven wrong by showing that many of the key scientists in this period were not Puritans.

The advance of Baconianism among the British elite in the seventeenth century was an integral part of a religious cultural movement. A series of scholars in the 1930s made this point with great emphasis. Richard Foster Jones, in a book first published in 1936, argued for a growing influence of Baconianism in Britain that eventually would lead to the Scientific Revolution. In a memorable phrase he wrote that "our modern scientific utilitarianism is the offspring of Bacon begot upon Puritanism" (Jones, [1936] 1961, p. 88). Bacon's work was highly congenial to Puritan ideology, even though Bacon was no Puritan.

The term "sentiment," which Merton uses quite frequently, is much like the cultural elements I defined in chapter 1. He stressed that the seventeenth century was a profoundly religious age in which the concern about salvation permeated daily life to a degree that is quite unimaginable today, and that when religious beliefs were not in alignment with economic progress, one of the two had to give in (Merton, [1938] 2001, p. 91). The growth of Puritan culture in British society represents an example of choice-based social learning: people became committed to various versions of Puritanism, because they found its religious arguments compelling, its leaders inspiring, or because it was consonant with a set of prior beliefs. By itself, there was nothing unusual in the commitment of Puritans to scientific and technological progress. It was part of a much larger European movement in which intellectuals, including not just English Puritans but also many Italian Catholics and German Lutherans, found science consistent with their religious beliefs and indeed an attractive way to practice them. Religion guided and at times encouraged scientific progress, but it could also seriously constrain its agenda in unexpected ways. For instance, as we have seen, Jesuits were in many ways good and eager scientists, yet in the end the religious dogmas to which they were subjected imposed institutional constraints that doomed them as a progressive institution. Orthodox Calvinism, similarly, could be seriously problematic.

What is important is that Puritans were deeply attracted to experimental philosophy, which they found to be congruent with their beliefs. Cohen (2012, p. 574) has pointed out that experimental research was as remote an activity from sacrilege and atheism that one could find. Experimental scientists such as Boyle insisted that their investigations of nature would make no sense without a creator who in his wisdom designed a universe in which bodies obeyed rules that scientists themselves could not possibly understand and he explicitly invoked the clockmaker analogy, in which an intricate mechanism could not emerge without an intelligent designer (Boyle, 1664, pp. 71–72). As Shapin (1994, pp. 156 ff) has stressed, Boyle's Puritanism meant above all that his identity as a scholar was strongly flavored by his Christianity and that he fulfilled a holy mission by becoming "a priest of nature" and giving thanks and praises to his maker for all of creation. But his religiosity also served to enhance his trustworthiness in an age in which atheism was still equated by most people— including intellectuals—with amorality.

The importance of Merton's thesis is not that it explains the Scientific Revolution, which it does not. Puritanism was English, the Scientific Revolution was European. The growth of science in Europe required a transnational institution, such as the Republic of Letters. But it required more: the coevolution of culture and local institutions, a major example of which was the coevolution of Puritanism and the English part of the Republic of Letters. The significance of Merton's interpretation is that it explicitly rejected a materialist approach to religion at this age. It is based on the assumption that people adopted certain ideological beliefs in large part because they found their content persuasive and compelling or for any of the other evolutionary biases; any facile materialist notion that links their cultural choices directly to their being members of a "bourgeoisie" or a commercial class is rightfully rejected.[1] Such leading intellectuals as Wilkins, Boyle, the botanists John Ray and Francis Willughby, the mathematician John Wallis, the physician and chemist Jonathan Goddard, and the political economist William Petty were all committed Puritans. It is not easy to associate Puritanism as such directly with any specific scientific advance, but Puritans greatly enhanced the social prestige of experimental science and thus helped prepare the ground for the Industrial Enlightenment. Their political preeminence was short-lived, but in restoration England most of them were received into the Royalist camp supported by the "protection of a lenient King" (Jones, [1936] 1961, p. 270). They abandoned their hopes of taking control of the universities and instead created their own organizations and environment in which they could practice the experimental Baconian science they believed in.

Puritans embraced science, in part because it simultaneously "manifested the Glory of God and enhanced the Good of Man" (Merton, 1973, p. 232). For them, as Webster ([1975] 2002, p. 505) has remarked, the ideal life was one that efficiently deployed one's ability for personal advantage and public service and glorified God by maximizing one's material resources. These two objectives were not separable but complemented each other in ways that took until the end of the seventeenth century to be fully worked out. Devout individuals recognized the profound ethical implications of scientific investigation: the systematic and meticulous study of God's creation was the closest a Calvinist could get to an inscrutable deity that could not be grasped by the cultivated intellect. The Puritan ideology built upon the Baconian belief that experimental science was a Christian religious activity; Puritanism and Science thus found a common ground in empiricism and experimentalism. Robert Boyle placed on the title page of his book *The Christian Virtuoso* (1690) the statement that the book would show "that by being addicted to Experimental Philosophy, a Man is being assisted rather than indisposed to being a Good Christian." The Puritans were the beneficiaries of what has been called the "Baconian compromise," which held that the key to God's works (that is, the understanding of the physical environment) is the key to God's word, so that the

---

[1] Indeed, it is strking that even though the political influence of the commercial-financial class was rising with the success of the Whigs, in its early stages the Royal Society had few representatives of this class, despite its strong interest in manufacturing techniques.

study of nature instructs interpreters of the scriptures. Science could be pursued free from the constraints of metaphysical systems and the literal interpretation of biblical statements about the natural world, as long as the book of nature could be interpreted as divine revelation (Moore, 1986, p. 323).

All this was paired to the utilitarian belief, inspired by Bacon, that the study of natural regularities and phenomena would lead to breakthroughs in useful knowledge that would eventually "refer their Attainment to the Glory of the Great Author of Nature and to the Comfort of Mankind," as Boyle wrote in his will (quoted in Merton, 1973, p. 235). Merton stressed that Puritanism was especially compatible with a labor-intensive approach to science (as experimentalism no doubt was), because it inherently condemned idleness as morally repulsive.[2] Others have objected that it was not just Puritans who adopted this viewpoint, and that not all Puritans saw eye to eye on this point. Yet Puritanism was a powerful cultural innovation in the sixteenth century and gathered strength in the decades following Bacon's death in 1626. Its success in the competitive marketplace for ideas in England deserves special attention precisely because it was part of a larger cultural movement in Western Europe that searched for ways to reconcile their religious beliefs, the pressure of organized religion, and their scientific interests. Puritanism itself was not necessarily the taproot of the technological flourishing of the eighteenth century, but it was indicative of something much deeper that characterized the Republic of Letters.

Moreover, Merton argued that seventeenth century Puritanism, whether it was loyal to the Church of England, Presbyterian, or vacillating between them, associated a great deal of virtue with "good works," which were increasingly associated with utilitarian objectives and useful knowledge. Merton pointed to another highly successful cultural entrepreneur, the Puritan theologian Richard Baxter (1615–1691), as the source of these beliefs. It may seem odd for an economic historian to point to Baxter as an important figure in the economic development of the West, but Baxter's influence on both sides of the Atlantic in the eighteenth century was considerable, and Max Weber regarded him as the author who "stands out above many other writers on Puritan ethics, both because of his eminently practical and realistic attitude, and, at the same time, because of the

---

[2] Bishop Sprat, himself no Puritan but clearly reflecting the views of some of the dominant Puritan members of the early Royal Society, confronted head on the charge raised against experimental science that it spent too much effort on studying nature and not enough on reflecting on salvation and the next world. He argued strongly that "true and unfain'd Mortification [asceticism sanctified by abstemiousness and contemplation] is not at all inconsistent with mens consultation of their happiness in this world or being emploi'd about earthly affairs. The honest pursuit of the conveniences, decence, and ornaments of a mortal condition ... is by no means contradictory to the most real and severe duties of a Christian" and that "the happiness and security of mankind in this life" were profound Christian values (Sprat, 1667, pp. 367–68).

universal recognition accorded to his works" (Weber, [1905] 1958, p. 155). His idea of the glorification of God through "good works" focused on labor that was "useful and profitable in a worldly sense ... at first blush, sheer utilitarianism" (Merton, [1938] 2001, p. 62).[3] Baxter was a cultural entrepreneur relying above all on content-based bias: he tried to persuade people by using reason and argument in the belief that everyone was amenable to reason. He was the author of an estimated 130 books and pamphlets; a modern site lists 67 titles. His "works enjoyed an unprecedented popularity, many going through repeated printings. Puritanism had always utilized the press, but there had never been a literary career like this, either in scale or in success: Baxter was the first author of a string of best-sellers in British literary history" (Keeble, 2004).

Religion in Britain, then, was not just a permissive factor; for many of the scientists in the second half of the seventeenth century, scientific writing and research was a mode of worship. That basic tenet of Robert Merton seems to have survived close scrutiny. It took the Enlightenment to shift the weight of emphasis from the glorification of God to the material well-being of humankind, but the seeds had been planted. As has been pointed out many times (for example, Shapin, 1988a), Merton did not argue strict causality in the sense that Puritanism was a sufficient or necessary condition for the Scientific Revolution and the Industrial Enlightenment. Much of the pathbreaking scientific work in seventeenth-century Europe was carried out on the Continent, a substantial amount of it by scientists active in Catholic countries. But Merton's argument that a growing accommodation between religious beliefs and scientific endeavor was of considerable significance in the rise of British science has survived the test of time. Equally important, because of its increasingly pragmatic and empirical orientation and interest in prescriptive knowledge, and its diffusion to a wide circle through mostly private and spontaneous mechanisms, eighteenth-century British science may have been a more suitable background to the Industrial Enlightenment. Members of such dissenting religions such as Unitarianists and Quakers have been widely observed to have played a role much larger than their relative numbers would indicate (Inkster, 1991, pp. 42–45; Jacob, 2000a).

Puritan science, if such a concept can be defined at all, was deeply empirical and shied away from the highly deductive, logically rigorous constructs, such as those favored by Descartes in France and Hobbes in Britain. It relied heavily on Baconian experimental methodology, on observation, and on a careful examination of facts rather than on a rational, carefully argued set of propositions that follow from one another. This can be

---

[3] Baxter at some point told Robert Boyle that he took great pleasure in experimental learning, and Boyle commented that Baxter was not one of those "narrow-souled Divines" who was suspicious of natural philosophy (Jones, [1936] 1961, p. 323).

seen especially by examining the work of the most important Puritan mathematician, John Wallis (1616–1703), the first mathematician to join the Royal Society and a Puritan clergyman who worked as hard on his sermons as he did on his mathematical proofs. Appointed the Savilian Professor of Mathematics at Oxford in 1649, most of his important work came afterward. His mathematics was in many ways flavored by an experimental, Baconian approach. As Alexander (2014, pp. 262–78) points out, Wallis's mathematics was pragmatic and experimental. It "replicated the experimental practices of the Royal Society ... relied on induction and never claimed to arrive at a final truth; the ultimate arbiter of truth was the consensus of men" (Alexander, 2014, pp. 277–78). Early in his career he had written that "speculative knowledge [that is, deductive arguments] is found even in the Devils in as large and ample measure as in the Saints." In contrast, "experimentall knowledge, is of another nature, whereby we know what we know. ...We not only Know that it is so but we Tast and See it to be so ... For Truths thus clearly and sensibly (as it were) reveiled to the Soul, it seems not to be in the power of the will to reject" (Wallis, 1643, pp. 60–61). Such an empirical position may seem a curious one to take for a mathematician, but in fact his *Arithmetica Infinitorum* (1656) with its firm belief in infinitesimals was important to young Newton in developing his own mathematics of fluxions (Westfall, 1980, pp. 113–17). It is clear from Newton's own writings, and those of many of his contemporaries, that Newton's mechanical system of the world reflected a rational and powerful Deity, and in that regard his work is consistent with the ideas of Puritanism.

The advantage of models of cultural evolution is that they are contingent and concern ex ante probabilities rather than deterministic causal models. In other words, they force us to recognize that things could have turned out differently than they did with fairly minor changes in initial conditions or accidents along the way. The Puritans and the early members of the Royal Society were one set of players in a large European arena. Their idea of doing science was very different from that of their many opponents, who were not nearly as committed to the inductive and empirical modes. In England, they battled one of the most powerful intellects of the Puritan age, Thomas Hobbes (who never was elected to the Society but had a highly influential position in Charles II's court) and on the Continent they contended with Cartesians and the Jesuits alike. Had political and military developments taken different turns, conservative forces might have prevailed and taken a more hostile attitude toward the new interpretation of the world. There was nothing inexorable in the ultimate triumph of the desirability of scientific progress any more than, say, the eventual evolution of *Homo sapiens* (or any other specific species) on the planet.

At the same time, contingency should not be overdone, and evolutionary theory, while making substantial allowances for contingency, does not imply sheer randomness. We can make sense of the past.[4] Although there were logical alternatives to the emergence of the key cultural belief that a combination of formal and experimental science with pragmatic ends was a path toward virtue and salvation, most European societies (much less non-European ones) did not follow them. It is a testimony to the power of the cultural entrepreneurs, such as Bacon and Baxter (and their acolytes), that they were able to persuade enough people to adopt that point of view. Once this cultural element was sufficiently established, and the belief in the virtuousness and even sanctity of useful knowledge was sufficiently entrenched, it became a dominant cultural element. Its success in Western Europe created the cultural biases that accounted for its diffusion elsewhere in the world. Moreover, there was much resistance to Puritan science by intellectual incumbents, many of them established church clergymen and conservative intellectuals, who opposed the new empirical bend of natural philosophy. In the end, all we can say is that intellectual seeds planted in a fertile soil have a good chance of sprouting and flourishing. Even then, sudden shocks can change the course of history.

Yet beyond the specific beliefs of one group or another looms another factor: pluralism. One debate, the one about religious tolerance, seems to have been decided at this time once and for all. Late seventeenth-century Britain offered every individual a menu of metaphysical items, from which a religious affiliation could be chosen that was most suitable to his or her inclinations (at some cost, since nonconformists and Catholics were excluded from government service and the universities). In that regard, Britain was fortunate. Although the Puritans were a minority and lost their political influence after 1660, they remained free to practice their religion and had an impact beyond their numbers, precisely because they were an elite culture. Oliver Cromwell, hardly a paragon of religious tolerance, allowed the Jews to settle in England after more than three centuries. Moreover, even when its institutions changed again after 1660, Britain remained committed to tolerance (Zagorin, 2003, pp. 188–239). Tolerance had important economic consequences. The influx of highly skilled French Huguenots illustrates the difference: not only did some leading Huguenot intellectuals, such as Denis Papin, Abraham De Moivre, and John T. Desaguliers, find a home in Britain, but also much of the clock- and watchmaking industry originated with immigrants (Landes, 1983, p. 219). All in all, perhaps 80,000 Huguenots fled to Britain and about 43,000 to Germany, out of perhaps a million living in France (Hornung, 2014) and it seems plausible that the most skilled and educated of them were the ones to leave rather than give up their institutions of worship, though others, such

---

[4] Joseph Needham, originally trained in biological science, warned that to attribute "the origin of modern science" entirely to accidental factors would be tantamount to admitting the bankruptcy "of history as a form of enlightenment" (1969a, p. 216).

as the eminent botanist Pierre Magnol (1638–1715), who loved his plants more than he loved his religion, converted to Catholicism and remained in France undisturbed. In the market for ideas, one of the most successful ones that won out in the seventeenth century in much of Western Europe was the idea of tolerance. Religious bigotry did not die easily, as the follies of the aging Louis XIV attest, but in its most extreme and virulent forms, it was doomed. What was needed was not just a set of incentives and motives for those who did science, but also an ideology that protected them from those whose entrenched monopoly on explaining the world was being threatened by science and its insistence on evidence and logic. As we have seen, it took a long time and rather special circumstances for this resistance to be weakened enough for scientists and engineers to do their work undisturbed.

Beyond their interest in experimental science and its potential applications to technology, Puritan culture emphasized other elements that in the end contributed to economic performance. Merton emphasized two already noted above. One was a cultural attitude toward work. What we call leisure, the Puritans thought of as idleness. Again, Max Weber saw this: "Waste of time is thus the first and in principle the deadliest of sins. The span of human life is infinitely short and precious to make sure of one's own election. Loss of time through sociability, idle talk, luxury, even more sleep than is necessary for health, six to at most eight hours, is worthy of absolute moral condemnation. ... It is infinitely valuable because every hour lost is lost to labour for the glory of God. Thus inactive contemplation is also valueless, or even directly reprehensible if it is at the expense of one's daily work" Weber, [1905] 1958, pp. 157–58). These views were distinctly minority views; but it is interesting to note that they coincided with the beginning of a period in which more people worked for money and worked harder, largely to acquire more market-supplied consumer goods (De Vries, 2008). Even for those for whom material consumption rather than Puritan principles was the driving force, it was reassuring to know that God approved.

A similar cultural phenomenon can be seen regarding the investment in human capital. Puritans regarded education as deeply virtuous, as would be expected of members of an intellectual religion. But not all human capital was created equal. Besides religious studies, Puritans condoned the study of "things" as opposed to "words"—physics, science, mathematics, and languages were all approved of, but not "frivolous" areas of study such as poetry, theater, music, and belles lettres. Puritans were not the only religious group to emphasize education. Education became the battlefield for competing religions. The dissenting academies of the eighteenth century are widely regarded as one of the main sources of the human capital that was deployed in Britain in the Industrial Revolution. But again, the powerful force of competition did its work, and the established church could not afford to fall behind. As Lawrence Stone noted, "the educational lead had been taken by Dissenters and Methodists, and the Anglicans were 'aroused and stimulated by their example.' It was fear of competition for the minds and loyalties of the poor which prompted some detailed enquiries set on foot by the Anglican hierarchy, and the replies make clear that this fear was uppermost in the minds of the rectors, vicars and curates" (Stone, 1969, pp. 81–82).

The great Bohemian educational reformer and intellectual reformer Jan Amos Comenius, a self-declared disciple of Bacon, who spent years in England, was one of the prophets of a more pragmatic, science-oriented education. Early in life he was persuaded by Bacon's writings that the millennium could be achieved by advances in natural philosophy and he applied his belief in progress to educational reform. He fully recognized the importance of early-age socialization in human capital formation and cultural change, even if his terminology differed from what we would use today. He emphasized the importance of science and mathematics education, although clearly spiritual concerns motivated his teaching students about the presence of the infinite in the phenomena of the natural world (Murphy, 1995, p. 126).[5] In Britain, his main follower in promoting education reform was Hezekiah (Ezekias) Woodward (1591/1592–1675). Woodward, a puritan minister, was a member of Hartlib's wide circle of friends, and through him became acquainted with the writings of Bacon and Comenius. He published a number of books that reflected Comenius's influence. Woodward felt that education was to reflect the Baconian notions of an active and practical life and warned especially against "the Irish disease" by which he meant "idlenesse, which spoyles all, and ... eates great holes in the web of our life" (Woodward, 1641, pp. 140–41).[6] His younger contemporary, John Webster (1611–1682), launched a strong and influential attack on university science and made a detailed proposal to reform schools in a more practical and utilitarian direction. He felt that logic and syllogisms should only be taught when its principles could be "demonstratively clear and proved" and specifically called for youths to study mathematics and engage in the practical, hands-on study of nature.[7] Charles Webster (1975,

---

[5] Comenius stressed above all the value of classification and simplification of all knowledge to ensure "ease and rapidity in learning," a very Baconian idea. He advised a conscious and systematic organizing and sequencing of the subject matter to facilitate understanding in the fullest possible degree. "Taking as his axiom the principle that 'nature prepares the material before she begins to give it form,' he draws analogies between the teacher and the builder laying a sound foundation for his building" (Murphy, 1995, p. 123).

[6] Comenius later acknowledged Woodward as one of his English patrons who had supported his "Herculean labors" of educational reform (Greengrass, 2004).

[7] He referred to mathematics as "a noble and excellent Science, with all the parts of it, both general, and special, vulgar, and mystical, might be brought into use and practice in the Schools, that men might not idly lose their time in groundlesse notions, and vain *Chymeras*, but in those reall exercises of learning that would both profit themselves, succeeding generations, and other Sciences." He also urged teaching by using an experimental method, and for youth "not to be idly trained in notions, speculations, and verbal disputes but may learn to inure their hands to

p. 202) notes that his educational objectives would have "received almost universal approbation among puritan reformers" and above all that science was to be taught and expanded according to Bacon's notions of observation and experimental work.

The Puritan experience and its emphasis on education was critical to the choice-based cultural evolution in Britain and North America. Modern research has suggested that the content and quality of socialization at an early age can be crucial to the formation of cultural beliefs and to later-in-life outcomes. The economic consequences in the long run are important: what is it that young children are taught? And who does the teaching? In the Bisin and Verdier world (see chapter 4), parents choose either to socialize children themselves or to assign them to a "random" teacher, but it stands to reason that in the age of English Puritanism, parents insisted that the values and beliefs taught to their children were consonant with theirs. Puritan values were indoctrinated into children and widely disseminated to adults through sermons and pamphlets. The values instilled in them held that useful knowledge, hard work, frugality, and honesty were virtues and were demanded by God. But the education also often included a set of specific skills that allowed individuals to produce goods and services more efficiently and encouraged them to look constantly for more productive ways of doing so by applying useful knowledge. By way of comparison, an upper class that believes in human capital but teaches its youngsters fencing, poetry, hunting, and classical languages will create a different (if not necessarily "smaller") stock of human capital than one that teaches accounting, chemistry, woodworking, and mechanics as well as a high valuation of patience capital, that is, the willingness to delay gratification and invest in one's future (Doepke and Zilibotti, 2008).

How much of the subsequent economic development in England may be attributed to the kind of phenomena that the Merton thesis is concerned with? Did it prompt a program of research in natural philosophy that led to important technological advances? The evidence, as many of Merton's critics noted, is at times ambiguous and in some ways biased. Natural philosophers often claimed practical benefits for their research in the self-serving hope of securing sponsorship even when there was no chance of any such benefits materializing. Moreover, it is not always clear what defined a Puritan and who exactly is included, and whether the Merton thesis deals adequately with the changing nature of Puritanism. Within Puritanism there were various streams and factions, some more

labour and put their fingers to the furnaces that the mysteries discovered by *Pyrotechny* and the wonders brought to light by *Chymystry* may be rendered familiar unto them ... [and] truly be taught by manual operation and ocular experiments ... that walk in the center of nature's secrets ... that can never come to pass unless they have laboratories ... and work in the fire, better than build castles in the air" (Webster, 1654, p. 107).

radical and ascetic than others. Nor can we readily quantify the impact of religious beliefs on what motivated scientists. Pure scientific activity was often driven by complex motives and the role of religion and practical bene-fits in this age are not easy to disentangle. In the case of Newton, as Cohen (1990, p. 72) notes, his declared motivation of practical usefulness is highly suspect. It is striking that there is not a single scientist in this age who attri-buted a major discovery or breakthrough to specific religious motives (Abraham, 1983, p. 371).

The emergence of Puritan ideology in seventeenth-century England was far from all there was to cultural change in Western Europe in the period leading to the Industrial Enlightenment. Merton may have under-stated the cosmopolitan and secular elements in the scientific program in England, and non-Puritans shared some Puritan beliefs more than he gave them credit for. Others have pointed out, however, that "Puritans" in the narrow definition of the word covers only a small portion of the scientists who seemed to be affected by the "Puritan spirit" and that it might be better to speak of a general "English providential view of the natural order" than of the peculiar religious views held by radical Puritans (Mulligan, 1980, p. 468).[8]

The critique raised by Cohen (1990, p. 66), Rees (2000, p. 71), and others who asked to what extent the Puritan heritage of the seventeenth century was of any direct use for the "practitioners of mechanical arts" at first glance seems to be a serious objection to the Merton thesis. Moreover, one might well ask why, if Puritan science flourished in the middle third of the seventeenth century, did it take another century for the British Industrial Revolution to take off, and especially why so little progress seems to have been made between 1700 and 1750, sometimes referred to as the "lost half-century." Some of this chronology is due to our somewhat overly rigid periodization.[9] Even if we accept with some misgiving the tale of the lost half-century, however, regarding this chronology as a mortal blow to the significance of Merton's approach seems to miss the point. Historians of science such as Shapin (1988a, p. 604) have found it astonishing that the thesis "elicited such vigorous and at times intemperate opposition." After all, Merton's thesis was cast in prudent and qualified terms, and was careful

---

[8] Indeed, Thomas Sprat's book (1667) on the Royal Society explicitly tries to justify scientific practices on the basis of Establishment Church (Anglican) principles rather than on more radical Puritan ones. Sprat himself summarized many of the beliefs that Merton and others identify as "Puritan," although he himself was a (non-Puritan) Anglican cleric.

[9] The Industrial Revolution is supposed to have started in 1760 or so, but in fact the first half of the eighteenth century saw major technological advances in the introduction of new mining techniques (including of course Newcomen pumps), the use of coke in smelting, the flying shuttle, smallpox inoculation, and the crucible technique in steelmaking—among others.

to distinguish between theology and institutionalized religion on one side and cultural beliefs on the other.

Charles Webster, Merton's most eminent follower, has stressed that considerable differences of world view existed in the Puritan camp. A continuum of approaches can be roughly divided into a more radical group that followed Bacon's view to its logical extreme and advocated scientific progress to attain a systematic control over nature, and more moderate ones that first and foremost saw the practice of experimental science as a virtuous activity toward personal enlightenment and salvation (Webster, [1975] 2002, pp. 498–502). But their contributions clearly established an important link in an intellectual chain of development that starts with Bacon, continues with the Hartlib circle and the invisible college, and culminates in the Royal Society. Margaret Jacob, whose sensible and informed judgments on the emergence of an industrial culture in Britain are the standard of this literature, has shown how "Puritan science" transformed itself into "Anglican science" during the restoration, reaching maturity in the science of Isaac Newton (Jacob, 1997, pp. 60–61). Regardless of whether it wholly overlapped with Puritans beliefs, the cultural change in Britain that traced the influence of Bacon and Baconians on the science of Boyle, Wilkins, and Ray prepared the ground for the British Industrial Enlightenment of the eighteenth century. The lineage from Francis Bacon to the Industrial Revolution via Puritan science is easily discernible even if it was not a straight line. It was not the only channel through which cultural change affected technological outcomes, but it was an important one.

It is fair to be skeptical of a claim that the Puritans were true harbingers of the Enlightenment (Mosse, 1960). They were still far more concerned with metaphysics than with practical knowledge of people and most Puritans lacked the Enlightenment concern for improving institutions in ways that would benefit economic growth. With the exception of some radical groups, they were far less concerned than their eighteenth-century followers with concepts relating to human freedom and social justice. In the dual objectives of the pursuit of useful knowledge as formulated by Bacon, the Glory of the Creator and the Estate of Man, the former was still dominant. But in their stress on empirics, admiration for mechanical knowledge, faith in experimental discoveries, and devotion to education, they did a lot to raise the prestige of science. Thus they constitute an essential link between the early followers of Francis Bacon and the Industrial Enlightenment of the eighteenth century. By the second half of the seventeenth century, considerable anecdotal evidence suggests that a concern with and interest in science and technology had become a high prestige activity.[10]

---

[10] Thomas Sprat, in his *History of the Royal Society* (1667, p. 403), noted that "[Natural] Philosophy is now admitted into our exchange, our Church, our Palaces, our Court [and] has begun to keep the best company ... and become the Employment of the Rich and the Great."

Had that been only a short-lived fad, its effects would have been of no consequence. But even if in the eighteenth century the interests of the Royal Society turned away from a focus on practical and useful knowledge, those of British society—even the aristocratic and rich elite—at large did not. In the eighteenth century some very wealthy enlightened individuals, such as the Earl of Stanhope (1753–1816), who took out two patents on steamships and invented a pyrometer, the pathbreaking chemist Henry Cavendish (1731-1810), one of the wealthiest men in Britain, or the Scottish banker Patrick Miller (1731–1815), engaged in research and experimentation, perhaps as hobbies, perhaps in the sincere hope of doing good. These were models that others could and did follow.

Such an account will sound Anglocentric. The Republic of Letters was a pan-European institution, and while British intellectuals played an important role it, they did not dominate it in any sense. Yet, as we have already seen, Britain gave as good as it got. While Puritanism was a very British phenomenon, the science that it created easily disseminated abroad, and the irrelevance of national boundaries marks the scientific contributions of scholars from Boyle and Wallis to Kepler and Leeuwenhoek. Johannes Kepler was a pious Lutheran, as was Tycho Brahe. Catholic scholars contributed much to the development of science and its practical applications in this age. This is not just true for lay Catholics such as Galileo, Cassini, and Descartes, but also of Jesuits, who played an important role in early modern science. Puritanism is unlikely to have influenced a figure such as the Jesuit Athanasius Kircher, a German-born polymath of prodigious scholarly productivity who wrote important books on topics as different as natural history, mathematics, geology, and the history of ancient Egypt (Findlen, 2004), or his equally prodigious predecessor and fellow German, the eminent Jesuit mathematician Christopher Clavius (1538–1612), who single-handedly imposed the study of mathematics in Jesuit education and helped Pope Gregory XIII reform the calendar to what is now named after him.[11] French Catholic clerics were able to combine a life of serious research and scientific activity with unwavering piety. Marin Mersenne was a member of the Minim order, an ascetic and ritualistic order, which did not stop him from becoming a pillar of the French

---

[11] The project of reforming the obviously defective Julian calendar was one of the great successes of sixteenth-century mathematics and observational astronomy, but some non-Catholic nations, such as Britain, were reluctant to adopt the Gregorian Calendar because of its patently papal origin (Britain switched to the Gregorian calendar in 1752, more than a century and a half after its introduction in 1582). Other examples of resistance to innovations merely because of their religious origins are hard to find. In nearly all cases, members of the Republic of Letters cared little about the religion of the originator of an intellectual innovation.

scientific establishment.[12] His colleague, Pierre Gassendi, was an ordained Catholic priest who found no contradiction between his beliefs and his embracement of an atomistic interpretation of the universe. Religion seems to correlate poorly with scientific interests: the Lutheran Danish polymath intellectual Ole Worm (1588–1654) shared his widespread and eclectic interests with the Jesuit Kircher and the German Calvinist Johann Heinrich Alsted (1588–1638), famous as an early encyclopedist (Grell, 2007, p. 215).

Cohen (2012, pp. 438–40, 565–68) has drawn a picture of a Continent in crisis in the mid-seventeenth century. He thinks that the conservative reaction might have snuffed out the new science and led "to a loss of momentum such as might have become the first step in a process of decay, petrifaction, and ultimate extinction" (Cohen, 2012, p. 439). He argues that the crisis was overcome, against all expectations, thanks to British science. To be sure, at some stage it seemed that the reaction could win out: in the 1670s a wave of French-speaking universities banned the teaching of Descartes's works and in Italy certain fields of investigation, especially mathematics and chemistry, declined fearing the heavy hand of the Curia. The harassment and persecution of the great (Catholic) chemist, Jan-Baptist van Helmont (1580–1644) in the 1630s is considered to have snuffed out serious chemical research in Italy (Ashworth, 1986, pp. 150–53). In the long run, however, these blows had no lasting serious effect. Research and scholars simply moved to locations where they were more welcome, and in the end the rulers who had persecuted intellectual innovators or made their repression possible had the choice between relenting on their conservative policies or risking falling permanently behind.

It would thus be misleading to point to the British experience as evidence for the cultural impact of religion as a key to economic success even if differences in nuances between British and Continental science can be seen. The Continent adopted, in different forms, many of the same cultural ideas. René Descartes, often pointed to as the paradigm of continental science, had adopted some of Bacon's views in a famous passage in his *Discourse on Method*: "instead of the speculative philosophy taught in the Schools, a practical philosophy can be found which ... we might put them in the same way to all the uses for which they are appropriate ... and to invent an infinity of devices which should make it possible to enjoy the fruit of the earth and especially to preserve human health" (Descartes, 1965 [1637], p. 50). Catholic France also produced its version of Samuel Hartlib, namely, the amazingly prolific letter-writer, mathematician, priest, and Descartes acolyte Marin Mersenne (1588–1648). Mersenne, despite his deep commitment to Catholicism, was a convinced Copernican, spread many of

---

[12] Mersenne tried to persuade himself that both Galileo and the Catholic Church were right, and he famously stated that there were 50,000 atheists in Paris in 1630, to which a wag responded that his circle of friends must have been quite wide (Caton, 1988, p. 78).

Galileo's beliefs and findings in France, and brought to France the news of Torricelli's barometer, which spurred Pascal's famous experiments pointing not only to the existence of the atmosphere but also to the possibility of a vacuum.

Puritanism may, however, have helped cement the division of labor between British and Continental science that emerged in the age of Enlightenment. Kuhn (1976, pp. 26–27) has argued that British science tended to be more experimental and directly "Baconian" (and less formal) than its Continental counterpoint.[13] It is common to stress the differences between the two cultures. French science, as the old truism has it, was more formal, deductive, and abstract than British science, which had a pragmatic and more experimental bent.[14] French academies had a somewhat different objective than that of British institutions: it is often argued that the *Académie Royale* (founded in 1666) linked the aspirations of the scientific community to the utilitarian concerns of the government, creating not a Baconian society open to all comers and all disciplines but a closed academy limited primarily to Parisian scholars and a few select foreign superstars.[15] It was, like almost everything else in France, more directed and more *étatist* than in Britain: members who dared criticize some aspect of the regime risked expulsion, as happened to the Abbé Saint Pierre in 1715. But the common elements are equally instructive, and the differences between France and Britain were one of emphasis and nuance, not of essence. Intellectuals in both nations shared a utilitarian optimism of people's ability to create wealth through knowledge and acknowledged the responsibility of leading scientists to set an agenda that contained practical and useful elements for the state and for society as a whole. This notion seems obvious, even almost banal, to us, but was far from a consensus in early modern Europe.

By the time of the Enlightenment the practical responsibilities of scientists to engage the needs of industry and agriculture were widely accepted. The bridges between the propositional knowledge created by the *savants* and the practical needs of industrialists, farmers, and navigators were

---

[13] Kuhn feels that after Newton, British mathematics has no figure that can compare to such Continental figures as Euler, the Bernoullis, and Laplace, while Continental experimentalists comparable to the best British ones such as Boyle, Black, Hales, and Priestley are absent before 1780 (Kuhn, 1976, p. 25). This seems, however, more of a matter of minor differences in comparative advantage than of essence, and in the end modern chemistry, the ultimate Baconian triumph, was mostly a Continental product. It was France that produced Lavoisier and his students such as Berthollet and Chaptal, though the contributions of Joseph Priestley and John Dalton illustrate the transnational character of the project.

[14] For a recent restatement of this view, see Jacob and Stewart (2004, p. 119).

[15] The French *Académie* was in large part patterned after the *Académie Française*, founded in 1635, which was in charge of setting rules for the French language under the auspices of Cardinal Richelieu. See Lux (1991).

occupied in large part by engineers, mathematicians, doctors, and chemists or scientists with a strong and deliberate practical bend. The great Leibniz himself was a prolific inventor and tinkerer, working, among others, on propellers, mining machines, pumps, and his famous calculating machine. Leonhard Euler, the most prominent mathematician of the age, was concerned with ship design, lenses, the buckling of beams, and (with his less famous son Johann) contributed a great deal to hydraulics.[16] Among the engineers, the aforementioned John T. Desaguliers is the best known, but there were many others, such as the watchmaker and mechanic Edward Barlow (1639–1719), the engineer Henry Beighton (1687–1743), the chemist William Cullen (1710–1790), and in eighteenth-century France such applied mathematical physicists as Jean-Charles de Borda (1733–1799) and Charles-Augustin de Coulomb (1736–1806). The development of an Industrial Enlightenment in France serves as a useful reminder of the transnational character of the cultural transformation: different national versions evolved over the long eighteenth century (say, 1660–1789), but they constantly interacted and influenced one another, freely mixing and exchanging cultural beliefs across national boundaries. To be sure, there were different national styles of engaging in scientific pursuits just as there were different political and cultural styles in different countries. The size, power, and degree of centralization of the state may have mattered too (Porter and Teich, 1992). It should be stressed again that one of the factors making the transnational character of the scientific community possible was that little of the new knowledge generated was seen as strategic or even of great economic significance, so that the authorities saw little harm in revealing what otherwise would have been treated as a state secret. Whatever the case, in the end both the Scientific Revolution and the Industrial Revolution were multinational collaborative efforts, in which the multiple national styles can be seen as a source of diversity and strength. As one authority would have it, if British empiricism transformed French rationalism, French scientific propaganda transformed Europe (Gay, 1966, p. 11). Yet one should not slight the work of Italians, Germans, Swedes, the Swiss, and the Dutch in

---

[16] A striking example, among many, of French Industrial Enlightenment was the mathematician René Réaumur (1683–1757) who was a member of the *Académie* from age twenty-four for fifty years. Among the many topics he investigated were insects, animal behavior, the chemical properties of steel, the possibility of making paper from wood pulp (instead of more costly rags), the manufacturing of porcelain, and meteorology. His work was inspired and motivated by potential applications. Thus his lifelong study of insects was motivated by a well-intentioned if sometime naive utilitarianism and the potential economic value of entomological research. He pointed to silk, wax, honey, lacquer, and cochineal, to name just a few useful products that justified his studies. He even seems to have believed that it might be possible to derive useful techniques from imitating insect activities. For instance, he was convinced that caterpillars and spiders have something to teach us about weaving. He also, of course, pointed out that the study of insects was profitable from another point of view as well—pest control (Gough, 2008).

this endeavor. In the end, it was *Europe* that was the locus of the Republic of Letters and experienced its consequences.

Thus the Republic of Letters, by construction, transcended national boundaries. For instance, Dutch intellectuals maintained close connections with their British colleagues despite three wars (Cook, 2007, p. 413), and the almost incessant wars between England and France following the publication of Newton's *Principia* in 1687 did not prevent Newton's message from spreading to France. Major breakthroughs in one country spread almost immediately to others, as did for example Harvey's work on blood circulation, which was cited less than ten years after the publication of *De Motu Cordis* by Descartes in his *Discourse on Method* (1637). In the end what emerged was a European synthesis, in which Bacon was as widely acknowledged by French *philosophes* as Descartes and Voltaire were by British writers. Gibbon noted in a famous passage in his chapter "General Observations on the Fall of the Roman Empire" that the philosopher, unlike the patriot, was permitted to consider Europe as a single "great republic" in which the balance of power may continue to fluctuate and the prosperity of some nations "may be alternately exalted or depressed," but which guaranteed a "general state of happiness, system of arts and laws and manners" which "advantageously distinguished" Europe from other civilizations (Gibbon, 1789, vol. 3, pp. 633–34). Some of this integrated community was wishful thinking on the part of intellectuals, and much of it fell apart after the French Revolution and the ensuing wars, but it was reconstituted in modified form after 1815.

A good example of how national cultures could blend seamlessly into one as early as the mid-seventeenth century is given by the famous Cavendish circle organized in Paris in the late 1640s by the playwright and natural philosopher Margaret Lucas Cavendish and her husband, the royalist William Cavendish (later duke of Newcastle), who had gone into exile after the royalist defeats of the English Civil War. The circle around them included Mersenne, Gassendi, Descartes, Hobbes, Petty, and Kenelm Digby (1603–1665), an English royalist Catholic diplomat and natural philosopher and a founding member of the Royal Society. In the early 1650s a similar role was played by John Evelyn who lived in Paris between 1649 and 1652 and had close ties with leading French intellectuals and was very active in bringing French ideas to Britain (Hunter, 1995d, p. 68). In the eighteenth-century Enlightenment this blending through travel was even more pervasive. Bacon, Newton, and Locke had such splendid reputations on the Continent that they often overshadowed the revolutionary ideas of Descartes and Fontenelle. Gay (1966, p. 13) quotes the German poet and literary critic Christoph Martin Wieland (1733–1813) to the effect that only the true cosmopolitan can do the great work to which humanity has been called: to cultivate, enlighten, and ennoble the human race. In this context, a discussion of any nation's cultural "exceptionalism" seems off the mark.

The roots of British leadership in the Industrial Revolution have to be sought elsewhere.[17]

To be sure, on the Continent, cultural evolution took slightly different routes from that of England and Scotland. In many places intellectual innovators there encountered more resistance than in Britain, but even without Britain's leadership Western Europe would eventually have found the path from the Republic of Letters to economic growth. The Industrial Enlightenment prepared the ground for nations to apply useful knowledge and align their institutions with economic modernization and growth (Mokyr, 2002, 2006a). There was no intentionality here: cultural beliefs were accepted in the market for ideas through the various biases proposed by the framework of cultural evolution (see chapter 5). But no one could have foreseen what was to come, and as the evolutionary framework suggests, this was anything but a deterministic process with foreordained outcomes. Indeed, in many cases the market for ideas came up with cultural variants that were anything but "modernizing" by anyone's definition. In Germany, for instance, an influential movement in the Lutheran church known as Pietism became influential in the late seventeenth and eighteenth centuries. Merton ([1938] 2001, p. 124) felt that Pietism "might almost be called the Continental counterpart of Puritanism" and attributed to it much of the scientific progress in Germany. Given the slowness of eighteenth-century technological progress in Germany and its heavy dependence on technology that originated elsewhere in the early stages of industrialization, this seems somewhat surprising. There is serious doubt, moreover, as to whether Pietism was on the whole a salutary force for the growth of useful knowledge and the emergence of the Industrial Enlightenment. Becker (1984) has pointed out that Pietism, while surely an influential religious movement in Germany, preached a simpler and more heartfelt version of Lutheranism, but not one that was particularly friendly to useful knowledge. While in Britain a more or less natural transition took place from seventeenth-century Puritan science to restoration Anglican science to eighteenth-century Enlightenment, the German Pietist movement was ambivalent and in many ways opposed to many aspects of the Enlightenment and specifically to research in and the teaching of useful knowledge. Even in education, which was an important item in the Pietist agenda, their stress on science and mathematics was limited and equivocal. Unlike Puritans, science for Pietists was an essential means toward religion, but wholly subordinate to theological doctrines, and it did not lead naturally into something we would

---

[17] For an attempt to understand British leadership, see Kelly, Mokyr, and Ó Gráda (2014).

recognize as the Industrial Enlightenment.[18] Pietist theologians were responsible for the dismissal of Christian Wolff, a German philosopher from his university position in Halle. Wolff, a disciple of Leibniz's, had a background in mathematics that had led him to a rational philosophy that was an application of mathematics and science.[19] The failure of Francke to suppress Wolff's views is a testimony to the effectiveness of the European states system in preserving intellectual pluralism. All the same, German Pietism, rather than serving as another illustration of the widespread power of religion to encourage and stimulate science postulated by Merton, actually may serve as a reminder that there were alternative paths in cultural evolution, and many led to technological and scientific dead-ends. The same can be said about the Jesuits, even if their case is of course different.

The relationship between religion and useful knowledge changed in the age of Enlightenment. The transformation of a deeply ethical and devout approach to science and technology, as it still was in the second half of the seventeenth century, into an increasingly secular (if not necessarily atheist) approach to useful knowledge of the later Enlightenment is in itself an interesting development. It is another example of the characteristic of evolutionary systems to produce unforeseen and unintended consequences. Neither Bacon nor any of his Puritan followers would have been totally comfortable with the admiration that the atheistic Diderot felt for them. Religious sentiments may have been a major factor in Puritan science, but at some point science could shed religion and advance on its own steam. It did not have to do this: many of the great British scientists in the age of the Industrial Revolution were still deeply religious, none more than Joseph Priestley, a shining example of the progressive English Enlightenment, the Quaker John Dalton, and Michael Faraday, an Elder in the Sandemanian

[18] In a telling remark, August Hermann Francke (1663–1727), the leader of Pietism, wrote that knowledge was worthy of pursuit only if it strengthened religious conviction or was subject to immediate practical application in good works (cited by Becker, 1984, p. 1070).

[19] Wolff's views annoyed his Pietist colleagues at Halle, who in 1723 persuaded the rather undereducated King Friedrich Wilhelm that Wolff's views represented a danger to the realm. The king commanded Wolff to leave his realm in forty-eight hours or be hanged; Wolff got out in time, and immediately found himself another position in Marburg. Even Wolff's Halle opponents professed to be shocked by the king's energetic action against the philosopher. In 1740 Frederic the Great (Friedrich Wilhelm's son) invited him back to Halle, illustrating both the frequent capriciousness of governments in their attitudes to heterodox ideas and their impotence—certainly by that time—in suppressing it.

Church (a fundamentalist protestant sect).[20] The connection between a
scientist and his or her religion, however, became increasingly incidental.[21]

    The roots of Britain's success as the economic leader of Europe in
the Industrial Revolution is a complex issue that has been dealt with elsewhere. But its cultural environment in the late seventeenth and early
eighteenth centuries was particularly conducive to technological creativity
(Jacob, 2014). Unitarians, a relatively small group of dissenters, were especially prominent. Again, this was not a religion for the masses, but mostly
an elite phenomenon. As Jacob has emphasized, this religion was especially
appropriate for this age: it believed in a rational and enlightened Deity, who
wanted people to advance economically and supported economic and social
progress (Jacob, 2000). But the more liberal wings of Anglicanism were in
the same camp. It was a religion that stressed stability and harmony, but
also the assurance that prosperity and material rewards for hard work and
ingenuity were perfectly virtuous and moral (Jacob, 1986, pp. 244–46;
McCloskey, 2006, passim). Religious leaders increasingly stressed the
virtuousness of economic activity and the study of mundane natural phenomena.[22] Far from being atheistic and anticlerical, Enlightenment religion in
Britain continued the tradition of having metaphysics make technological
progress and the concomitant economic growth look virtuous, following a
trail blazed by Bacon and the Puritans who admired him. It pictured a
progressive society as the realization of God's will, and in this sense, too,
it was a natural continuation of the Baconian program.

---

[20] Priestley (1733–1804), who is widely regarded to be one of the prophets of progress
of the eighteenth century, produced a large number of religious pamphlets. For him the historical
path of science was a gradual advance through experiment, observation, and reason. In religion,
however, the Truth had already been revealed, but had subsequently been corrupted by
philosophers and priests, and it needed to be cleansed to be restored (Schofield, 1997, p. 187).

[21] Lydia Barnett (2015, p. 153) has suggested that religious content began
disappearing from the scientific discourse (in this case, natural history) because of the persistence,
not the waning, of religious beliefs. For the early eighteenth century this was clearly the case for
many scholars—especially the ultra-orthodox Calvinist Louis Bourguet.

[22] Bishop Sprat, whose writing reflected the views of the members of the early Royal
Society, wondered whether "it be indispensably necessary for us to be always thinking of heavenly
things ... what Traffic, what Commerce, what Government, what secular Employment could be
allowed. ... How can it be imagin'd to be a sinful and carnal things to consider the object of our
Senses; when God, the most *spiritual Being*, did make them all" (Sprat, 1667, p. 369). For a
survey see McCloskey (2006, pp. 461–68).

Chapter 14

A Culture of Progress

Of all the ideas that were debated in the market for ideas in the Republic of Letters, perhaps none was more critical to later economic outcomes than the idea of progress: scientific, technological, and eventually social and economic as well. The growth of useful knowledge (both propositional and prescriptive) was considered to be central to this concept of progress. The dominant view that emerged as a product of the market for ideas was that the search for useful knowledge would be conducted as a collaborative project within a competitive system, but the ultimate beneficiary of these uncoordinated and individualistic efforts was "the whole human race" and the knowledge accumulated was itself more important than the individuals who generated it (Rossi, 1970, p. 63). As Bietenholz (1966, p. 20) has noted, the concept of *veritas filia temporis* (truth is the daughter of time) was first expressed by such sixteenth century humanists as Erasmus, but from Giordano Bruno and Francis Bacon to the Enlightenment, the statement summarized the belief that historical progress means that history consists of a progression from obscurity to lightness, not the reverse.

The concept of progress has been closely associated with the culture of the Enlightenment in the historical literature, but until recently economic historians have not tried to relate its growing popularity to the Industrial Revolution and subsequent economic growth. An important exception is Slack (2015), who traces the term "improvement" through seventeenth-century English culture and correctly observes that while economies and cultures move together, in this case improvement came first, because the "frame of mind" encouraged the kinds of economic behavior that led to its realization (Slack, 2015, p. 4). It should be conceded from the outset that a prevalent belief in progress by itself is, strictly speaking, neither a necessary nor a sufficient condition for economic development to occur. After all, markets evolved and expanded and new techniques diffused in medieval and Renaissance Europe without much of a deep sense of progress, and the same was true, a fortiori, in Song China. At the same time, the belief in progress, especially the version that saw the accumulation of useful knowledge as central to material improvement, was a hallmark of Enlightenment Europe, and it provided cultural lubrication to the innovation-creating machinery. But the belief that it could and should take place did not guarantee that it would.

Scholars have understandably differed about what is meant by the term and what kind of and whose progress is involved. Nisbet ([2008] 1994), for instance, distinguishes between "progress as freedom" (which includes material progress) and "progress as power," which we might think of as the emergence of the nation state and institutional change. More controversially, Lasch (1991) dismisses the idea of progress due to human ingenuity and the progress of arts and sciences as "vaporous tributes to the power of reason" produced by "second-rate thinkers." Instead he stresses the demand side of progress, a positive assessment of the proliferation of wants, rising expectations, newly acquired tastes and standards of personal comfort, which he attributes to Hume and Smith (Lasch, 1991, pp. 45, 52–54).[1] But the idea that stood at the very center of the progress movement of the seventeenth and eighteenth centuries was the Baconian program, which purported to increase and disseminate natural philosophy and other forms of knowledge to benefit "the useful arts."[2] In the end, anyone with the hope to understand the economics of the Industrial Revolution needs to confront its cultural roots.

The idea of progress is logically equivalent to an implied disrespect of previous generations. As Carl Becker noted in a classic work written in the early 1930s, "a Philosopher could not grasp the modern idea of progress ... until he was willing to abandon ancestor worship, until he analyzed away his inferiority complex toward the past, and realized that his own generation was superior to any yet known" (Becker, 1932, p. 131). As noted, the critical evaluation of the classical canon became more widespread in the sixteenth century, and with it came a sense that their own age knew more than past generations. Some sixteenth-century writers can be regarded as pioneers of these ideas, for instance the French humanist writer, Loys (Louis) Le Roy (1510–1577). After disputing the myth of the infallibility and completeness of ancient writings, Le Roy in his *Vicissitudes* (1575) goes on to discredit the general idea of decay or exhaustion in nature. He declared that there is nothing to prevent his age from producing men as brilliant and original as any of the ancients (Gundersheimer, 1966, p. 118).

---

[1] See Lasch (1991, pp. 45, 52–54). Among the minds that Lasch would have to classify as "second rate" are Descartes, Pascal, Priestley, and Condorcet.

[2] David Wootton points out that Shakespeare knew a lot of history, but unlike his contemporary Bacon, who was already grasping what useful knowledge might accomplish, had no sense of irreversible historical change (Wootton, 2015, pp. 5, 511).

Secular advances in material conditions largely depended on the advances made in useful knowledge. The idea of progress, as noted, is inextricably linked to the cultural issue of how one should rate the capabilities and wisdom of one's contemporary generation relative to the wisdom of one's ancestors. The same age that fostered a belief in progress shed its excessive respect for earlier thinkers, exuding a confidence that "we can do better." Bacon sensed that the deepest obstacle to the advance of science was the stubborn belief that knowledge has its ebbs and flows and that when it reaches a certain point "[it] can advance no further." The only hope against such a static view of the world was "a new science" that would raise knowledge continually and do things that have not been done or even thought of (Bacon, [1620], 1999, pp. 126–29, aphorisms 92, 97).[3] The writers of the half-century following Bacon's death credited Bacon as the prophet of such confidence: one of them wrote that "it is the great occasion of the title progress that hath been made in all other sciences, as well as that of Physick; and the incomparable Lord Bacon, among the several Causes of the non-advancement of all manner of Sciences, reckons this for one, *An extream Affection to Antiquity*" (Nedham, 1665, p. 6, emphasis in original). The superior knowledge of geography following the transoceanic voyages undermined the authority of the classical canon like nothing else. Many of the ironclad propositions made by ancient writers on geography were shown to be false—so what could be believed? "Whatsoever the ancients out of their glimring reason have conjectured, our times have sufficiently decided this controversy," Nathanael Carpenter (1625, p. 231) declared.

Such beliefs were strongly resisted by those who in some form or another were drawing rents from established knowledge, and it is not at all clear that the triumph of progressive intellectuals was preordained or inevitable. Certainly, the eventual triumph would have been hard to predict in 1679, when one of the charter members of the Royal Society, John Evelyn, complained that "T'is impossible to conceive, how so honest and worthy a design should have found so few promoters and so cold a welcome in a nation whose eyes are so wide open" (Evelyn, [1664] 1679, unpaginated preface). Decades later, Hume noticed a general tendency: "The humour of blaming the present, and admiring the past, is strongly rooted in human nature, and has an influence even on persons endued with the profoundest judgment and most extensive learning" (Hume, [1754] 1985, p. 464).

Nowhere is this struggle better illustrated than by the famous "battle of the books" that erupted in much of Europe in the late seventeenth

---

[3] Hill (1965, pp. 89–90) credits Bacon with a "breath-taking utopian vision" of progress that even his seventeenth-century followers did not quite enunciate, namely that he gave practical persons a theory that united a coherent optimism for humanity with a critique of Aristotle and scholastics, "turning the tables on the theological opponents of the new science."

century between the "ancients" and the "moderns."[4] Were modern scholars and authors nothing but midgets standing on the shoulders of giants, or were they giants themselves? The debate was widely regarded, then as now, as a tempest in a teapot (Levine, 1981, p. 73).[5] But it was not; it reflected a watershed in cultural evolution that had been two centuries or more in the making (Bury, [1920] 1955, ch. IV; Spadafora, 1990, ch. 2; Lecoq, 2001; Goldstone, 2012).[6] Modern scholars have regarded the debate in somewhat odd terms. In a remarkable but not uncharacteristic passage, the philosopher Stanley Rosen strongly disagrees with the dismissive attitudes with which some scholars have treated the *Querelle des Anciens et des Modernes,* and notes with bemusement the "extreme vigor with which twentieth-century spokesmen for the Enlightenment banished the ancients from a position of respect" (quoted in DeJean, 1997, p. 155).[7] Levine (1991, p. 414) notes that the story was "once famous, although it is now largely forgotten and misunderstood" and concludes that the battle ended in a draw though he gingerly concedes that the ancients had given some ground in the sciences and philosophy. Many modern scholars have strained to see parallels between the battle between ancients and moderns and events in our age (DeJean, 1997, pp. 124–50). Such a parallel seems far-fetched, to say the least, in an age when

---

[4] The literature on this issue is quite substantial. The classic statement remains R. F. Jones ([1936] 1961). For a recent assessment, see Levine (1981).

[5] There seems to be a certain coyness among modern authors to admit the obvious, which is that the "moderns" had an irrefutable case in terms of useful knowledge, just as much as their case was unprovable and silly as far as literature and poetry are concerned. Even Nisbet (1979), after describing Georges Sorel's ludicrous characterization of the idea of progress as a shabby piece of bourgeois trickery based on circular reasoning, feels the need to admit that "the reasoning (supporting progress) was certainly circular." It was not; insofar as progress in science and technology was based on a cumulative process and there was no knowledge "lost" in the course of history, the moderns had access to ancient knowledge but not the reverse.

[6] Auguste Comte noted that "the idea of continuous progress had no scientific consistency, or public regard, till after the memorable controversy at the beginning of the last [that is, eighteenth] century about the general comparison of the ancients and the moderns ... that solemn discussion constitutes a ripe event in the history of the human mind which thus, for the first time, declared that it had made an irreversible advance" (Comte, 1856, p. 441).

[7] DeJean (1997, p. 15) claims in the context of France that "the emphasis on the causal role of science is misleading—progress rather than science was the determining factor for the first Moderns." Regardless of what is meant by "determining factor," this separation between progress and science makes little sense. She may well be right in arguing that recent critics of the Enlightenment, by making science alone responsible for the modern success of the notion of progress, have placed on it a weight its original proponents never intended it to bear. But the fundamental insight of the cumulativeness of useful knowledge belies the notion that the moderns felt that by their time, progress was already over (DeJean, 1997, p. 17). That may well have been the case for the leader of the French literary moderns, Charles Perrault (1628–1703), who regarded the age of Louis XIV as the peak of human achievement, but it had little to do with the more general human and social progress that, as DeJean points out (1997, p. 22) became the hallmark of the Enlightenment.

Classics departments' faculty are reduced to single digits and in which the History of Science, Medicine, and even Economics are no longer taught outside a few history departments.

Many of the "ancients" viewed modern science as a possible attack on learning and made a point of dismissing the efforts of moderns as futile. Henry Stubbe (1632–1676), a pugnacious physician and political pamphleteer dismissed the entire scientific endeavor of his age as futile: "All that is said about the erecting of Mechanical or Sensible Philosophy of Nature is but empty talk. Human nature is not capable of such atchievements" and then accused modern authors ("virtuosi") of being ignorant of Aristotle and other classical writers (Stubbe, 1670, p. 15).[8] Conservative writers, such as Stubbe and the Geneva-born Anglican minister and scholar Méric Casaubon (1599–1671), paradoxically tried to associate experimental philosophy with both Puritanism and atheism. They worried about the enthusiastic Baconians throwing out the baby with the classical bath water and the materialistic implications of a mechanistic and utilitarian approach to knowledge. They resented the undeniable arrogance and self-righteousness that many of the Baconians evinced. They fought a hard fight. As late as 1704, the bookseller's introduction to Jonathan Swift's famous *Battle of the Books*, a satirical essay on the battle of the ancients and moderns, concluded that "we cannot learn to which side Victory fell" (Swift, [1704], 1753, p. 170).[9]

One major battle was fought in the medical world among physicians, in which the ancients remained loyal to their trusted Galenian traditions, while the moderns adhered to the iatrochemical ideas originally proposed by Paracelsus and expanded by van Helmont. The conservative Galenists, such as John Twysden (1607–1688), were outraged by the impudence that the Baconians showed toward their beloved classical authorities.

[8] Stubbe even argued that Harvey's discovery of the circulation of the blood, widely cited by the moderns as one of the outstanding achievements of the age, was neither all that original nor as pathbreaking as was alleged (Frank, 1979, pp. 130–31).

[9] One cannot help but surmise that the classic Monty Python skit "The Philosophers World Cup" in which Greek and German philosophers compete in an absurd soccer match, was inspired by a paragraph such as "The Moderns were in very warm debates upon the choice of their leaders, and nothing less than the fear impending from their enemies could have kept them from mutinies upon this occasion. The difference was greatest among the horse, where every private trooper pretended to the chief command, from Tasso and Milton to Dryden and Wither. The light horse were commanded by Cowley and Despreaux. There came the bowmen under their valiant leaders, Descartes, Gassendi, and Hobbes, whose strength was such that they could shoot their arrows beyond the atmosphere, never to fall down again, but turn, like that of Evander, into meteors, or, like the cannon ball, into stars. Paracelsus brought a squadron of stinkpot flingers from the snowy mountains of Rhaetia. ... The army of the Ancients was much fewer in number, Homer led the horse, and Pindar the light horse, Euclid was chief engineer, Plato and Aristotle commanded the bowmen, Herodotus and Livy the foot, Hippocrates, the dragoons, the allies, led by Vossius and Temple, brought up the rear" (Swift, [1704] 1753, pp. 186–87).

Twysden argued that classical medicine had stood the test of time and urged physicians to stick to the old and tried and not experiment with novel and unknown techniques. Even if the ancients did not always get it right, he argued, the medications they prescribed were known to be effective against a variety of maladies. Against them the chemical school heaped scorn on the classical authorities, and described Galenian medicine as a building having, in the words of the physician and alchemist George Starkey (1628–1665), "rotten foundations, ruinous arches and pillars, mouldering and tottering walls, and a leaky and almost fallen roof ... fit only to make a habitation for Birds of darkness" (Starkey, 1665, pp. 37–38). Even more stridently, the combative physician Nedham wrote that "there lies the Bane of our Profession, that because of a Book-knowledge of Hippocrates, Galen, and the rest that are counted Classick, is admitted in the Universities as a sufficient Test, to try a mans fitness to become a Doctor of Physick ... it cannot but Nauseate any ingenious man, to read the Superstitious Fooleries of Authors, and to see how they puzzle one another with petty quarrels about the Doctrinal part of this sort of Criticisms" (Nedham, 1665, pp. 253–54, 311–12). The vituperative tone of the debate among medical doctors perhaps reveals the lack of any actual substantial results in curing disease that either side could boast. It was a classic instance of untight knowledge: neither side had any persuasive evidence to support its beliefs, and thus substituted thunderous rhetoric for proof. Medicine in this age, whether Galenian or chemical, was unable to cope with the substantial challenges it faced. As far as effective therapy or experimental evidence was concerned, there was little to choose from between the ancient humoral theories and the more modern iatrochemical ones. The hope was that the new experimental science would help physicians cope with these challenges, but the options that the marketplace of ideas offered here were both equally unattractive.

As so often happens with intellectual disputes, the exact lines between the two camps are not always easy to draw. In some ways Isaac Newton, the arch-hero of the modern camp, ironically belonged more to the ancients than to the moderns. He believed (expressed in a set of propositions known as *scholia*) that much of what he had discovered had already been known in antiquity but had been subsequently lost (McGuire and Rattansi, 1966). Another paradigmatic modern, Robert Hooke, in his posthumous "Discourse on Earthquakes," wrote respectfully of the ancients with an explicit stab at his more enthusiastic "modern" colleagues that "howmuchsoever there may be some who slight and neglect and villify the Knowledge, Doctrines and Theories of the Ancients, which Humor I am apt to think proceeds from their ignorance ... yet certainly former times wanted not Men altogether as eminent for Knowledge, Invention, and Reasoning as any of this present Age affords" and singled out Ovid's *Metamorphosis* as an "account of the ages and duration of the earth" (Hooke, 1705b, pp. 379–80).

Much of the "battle of the books," of course, was about taste, and an argument whether one should prefer Shakespeare to Sophocles or Milton to Virgil seemed as otiose in 1700 as it does today. As might be expected, perhaps, the classic texts remained part of the basic education of anyone claiming to be an intellectual. While the ancients may have been defeated in the sciences and philosophy, they "held fast to literature and the arts" (Levine, 1991, p. 414), although even in that area the achievements in the visual arts, literature, and music of the age of baroque slowly drove home the message that indeed their own age could eclipse almost anything that the classics had to offer. The debate fizzled out in the early eighteenth century, because it became increasingly clear that scientific and material advance would go on apace, and that the idea of progress had emerged victorious even if its victory was more marked in "areas where reason and experiment reigned" (Levine, 1991, p. 414). Those areas, the legacy of Galileo and Bacon, were expanding continuously. From that point on, it was beyond any question that a reference to Aristotle or any other author in the canon, from the Bible down, would not be regarded as sufficient proof of an argument in a serious conversation in natural philosophy. Hence, dismissing the historian R. F. Jones as "whiggish," because he felt sympathy for those seventeenth-century intellectuals who thought that there were good grounds to prefer Galileo to Archimedes or Harvey to Galen, seems indefensible. Swift's amusing pamphlet marks the epilogue of a battle that had been fought for two centuries and had been won conclusively. Despite a few nostalgic romantic authors in the nineteenth century and the modern age, the moderns have won, and decisively so. Their triumph was already visible by the time they were being ridiculed in *Gulliver s Travels* and was complete by the end of the age of Enlightenment. It is to this victory that we owe the modern economy.

One of the debaters, the linguist and biographer William Wotton, indeed made the crucial distinction between areas that were cumulative (such as science and technology) and those that were not (such as rhetoric and poetry). Even in biblical studies, he argued, superior training in ancient languages would restore the true meaning of the scriptures, and hence reinforce Christian conviction (Levine, 1991, p. 410). The age of Enlightenment never abandoned the classics altogether, but it tried to combine the best of that civilization with the best of their own, hoping to preserve the baby of classical literature and philosophy while tossing out the bathwater of its obsolete cosmology and physics.[10] Ferrone (2015, p. 99) observes that the

---

[10] The "battle of the books" was in fact a rearguard action that shows how strong the position of the moderns had become. In the words of one scholar, "to sample a few of Temple's [William Temple, one of Wotton's main opponents] opinions about ancients and moderns gives one a sense of the genteel arrogance the Enlightenment had to put up with and overcome ... Temple served up a pastiche of pseudo-intellectual commonplaces. The ancients had said it all; advances in learning and art were unlikely when the originals were so perfect ... Where now is the great music of the past when Orpheus could move the stones and tame the beasts? Where today are the ancient arts of magic? How can the fortuitous circumstances that produced such excellences of the past ever come together again in these diminished times? Did Harvey and

Enlightenment writers used classical antiquity to contrast the past with the present "with the aim of constructing the future." A strong belief in progress, however, inevitably implied that the relative share of classical culture in education would decline over time, and that is precisely what has happened in our modern age.

The roots of the triumph of the moderns are easy to see in retrospect. The combination of geographical discoveries, technological advances, a better understanding of nature, and rapidly rising access to information persuaded more and more intellectuals in the period after 1500 that their own age was wiser and better informed than the era of antiquity. An intellectual superiority complex was essential if the age was to cast off the yoke of classical authority in technology and science. By the middle of the sixteenth century this sense was expressed most explicitly among French writers. Jean Bodin (1530–1596), famous for the first cogent formulation of a monetary theory of inflation, for instance, wrote in 1566 that while the ancients deserve a lot of credit as the inventors of all arts and sciences, they left a lot of problems unsolved, and "where we look more closely, there is no doubt that our discoveries surpass those of the ancients." Another French writer, the diplomat, cryptographer, and general-purpose intellectual Blaise de Vigenère (1523–1596), added in 1571 that "it is reasonable to make a place for antiquity, but from this it does all follow that we must read or praise only the works of the ancients" (both quoted in Rossi, 1970, pp. 75–74). The tone is still less cocky and more respectful toward the classics than it was to become a century later, but clearly the signs of a sense of progress are visible in these writings.

By the seventeenth century, the slavish veneration of classical learning was slowly fading, and statements that must have sounded downright insolent to admirers of classical civilization were expressed more and more often. The newly found confidence of western Europeans was in part based on the ever growing emphasis that European intellectuals placed on the social value of technological advances. The Italian poet and publicist Alessandro Tassoni (1565–1635) wrote in 1620 "what did the Greeks and Romans ever invent that can be compared to the printing press? If the Romans gloried in the transport of their armies to the island of England ... what glory is owed to him who taught the Portuguese to navigate to an unknown pole from one horizon to another," and the French physician and polymath Pierre Borel (ca. 1620–1671) added in 1655 "let therefore ancient Athens keep silent with her famous lyceum, let the fables go untold according to which men exist whose eyes penetrate the bowels of the earth ... today the most noteable and truest lynx eyes have appeared from whose sight nothing can escape" (quoted in Rossi, 1970, pp. 89, 90).

Copernicus have anything new to say? Who can tell whether it is the sun or the earth that moves?" (Traugott, 1994, pp. 504–5).

The notion that progress was an apt description of their own age spread also among the British writers of the seventeenth century, including the work of the (non-Puritan) clergyman Joseph Glanvill, who wrote a famous book titled *Plus Ultra, or, The Progress and Advancement of Knowledge since the Days of Aristotle*, in which he proudly listed area by area the advances that science had made since antiquity, much of which he ascribed to the work of the Royal Society and its members. A great admirer of Francis Bacon, he noted with some exuberance that "a ground of high expectation from Experimental Philosophy is given, by the happy genius of this present Age ... and that a ground of expecting considerable things from Experimental Philosophy is given by those things which have been found out by illiterate tradesmen or lighted by chance" (Glanvill, 1668, pp. 194–95).[11] Equally unambiguous was John Wilkins who felt that ancient knowledge on theology was still unassailable, but that as far as sciences that advance by either discoveries or experimentation, *we* are the ancients (Hooykaas, 1972, p. 113).

Not all authors of the late seventeenth and eighteenth centuries subscribed to a belief that progress was possible or even likely, and such doubting Thomases as Hobbes never quite bought into it. In the eighteenth century doubts were still expressed by some of the most eminent Enlightenment *philosophes* including Rousseau.[12] But on the whole, there was a growing consensus about the possibility of progress and its desirability. What was still very much up in the air were questions of detail: what kind of progress that was envisaged, what was the best way to bring it about, whom the progress was for, and whether progress in useful knowledge must be accompanied by progress in institutions to avoid the inequality and inevitable conflicts and disruptions that economic growth entailed.

It was the essence of the Enlightenment that by the middle of the eighteenth century few doubts about past and present progress could survive. John Clarke (1687–1734), an enlightened educational reformer, who advocated the teaching of mathematics and science, wrote disrespectfully in 1731 that "The Antients were indeed but very poor Philosophers ... with regard to the Knowledge of Nature, the thing is too notorious to admit of any

---

[11] Elsewhere, Glanvill (1665, p. 140) noted, somewhat insolently, that "that discouraging maxim, nil dictum quod non dictum prius, hath little room in my estimation. Except Copernicus be in the right, there hath been new under the sun ... the last ages have shewn us what antiquity never saw." Furthermore, he believed explicitly that "the Goods of Mankind may be much increased by the Naturalist's insights into trade"—essentially an early statement of one of the central assumptions of the Industrial Enlightenment. Glanvill would, however, not be counted as "enlightened" by our standards—he staunchly defended the existence of witches and spirits and wrote a book vehemently attacking those who doubted their existence.

[12] Rousseau was a complicated intellectual, and the merciless depiction of him as an embittered spokesman for a reactionary nostalgia longing for a primitive state of bliss that never was, is somewhat overdrawn (Nisbet, 1979).

Dispute at all. The discoveries of Sir Isaac Newton ... amount to a hundred times more than what all the antient Philosophers knew put together" (Clark, 1731, p. 47). Similarly, Richard Helsham, who held the Erasmus Smith professorship of natural and experimental philosophy at Trinity College Dublin from 1724 to 1738, started his highly successful textbook in natural philosophy (still taught in Dublin as late as 1849) by stating that "it is a matter of no small surprize to think how inconsiderable a progress the knowledge of nature had made in former ages ... compared with the vast improvements it has received ... of latter times. ... Philosophers of former ages buried themselves in framing hypotheses ... without any foundation in nature [and] so lame and defective as to not answer those very phaenomena for whose sakes they had been contrived" (Helsham, 1755, p. 1).

The idea of progress is thus inextricably linked to the cultural issue of how people regard the capabilities and wisdom of their own generation relative to the wisdom of previous ones. Many cultures, including some rabbinical Jewish and fundamentalist Muslim traditions, believed that truth had been fully revealed to individuals living in the remote past, and that the best current scholars can do is to interpret and exegesize earlier writings and search for deeper meaning in ancient texts. Chaney (2015) shows that the Sunni Revival in the Muslim world in the eleventh and twentieth centuries was accompanied by a sharp rise in the percentage of books that were commentaries on previous work rather than original work, and that they tended increasingly to concentrate on religious rather than scientific topics. True, within those constraints a fair amount of dispute and innovation was possible, but the constraints were binding all the same. Despite their vast advantage in literacy and human capital for many centuries, Jews played an almost negligible role in the history of science and technology before and during the early Industrial Revolution. Apart from an elaborate but absurd *kabbalist* numerology, in which hidden meanings were attached to the words in ancient texts according to the values associated with their letters in a desperate search for coded signs of the date for the coming of the Messiah, it is hard to find important achievements credited to Jewish mathematicians before the nineteenth century. There were a few exceptions to this rule, such as Jacob ben Immanuel (Bonet) Lates, physician to the late fifteenth-century popes and the inventor of an important instrument to measure astronomical altitudes and the mathematicians who helped the Portuguese navigators in computing latitude at sea.[13] But the great advances in science and mathematics between 1600 and 1750 do not include work associated with Jewish names. An exception is Joseph Solomon Delmedigo (1591–1655), a Jewish doctor who actually studied in Padua with Galileo, to whom he referred as

---

[13] See Seed (2001, pp. 73–82). The best-known of those astronomer-mathematicians was Abraham Zacuto (1452–1515), the inventor of a new and improved astrolabe to measure latitude at sea, and the compiler of detailed astronomical tables for ocean navigation.

"Rabbi Galileo," and who wrote in his *Sefer Elim* that only a complete fool (*"peti moochlat"*) would deny the Copernican cosmology (Delmedigo, 1629, p. 304).[14] Similarly, despite a number of notable Jewish physicians, it is hard to find any significant innovations associated with them. By the eighteenth century, to be sure, some learned Jews came to realize that the universe was not quite as their Talmudic sources had described it, but this acceptance came slowly and late.[15]

The same may be said about technology. Jews were readmitted into Britain after 1656, and it stands to reason that if more of them had had mechanical interests, more enterprising Jewish innovators would have found their way to Britain, where the atmosphere was conducive to inventors in the second half of the eighteenth century—as did many other Continental engineers. Only after they shook off their obsession with the writing of past generations during the Jewish *haskala* (education movement) did the share of Jews among leading scientists and inventors rise steeply.[16] But in the annals of the British Industrial Revolution, Jews are hard to find. Education, literacy, and learning did not amount to material progress unless they were accompanied by a willingness to abandon venerated traditions and slaughter sacred cows, no manner how many generations had believed in their truth.[17]

[14] Delmedigo railed against the failure of the Ashkenazi Jews to participate in the Scientific Revolution because of their obsessive focus on the study of the Talmud. He found their attitude toward secular learning deplorable. The rabbis, he complained, were so engrossed with halakhic casuistry and midrashic innovations that they completely ignore everything else. They consider such studies as logic, grammar, rhetoric, mathematics, science, and philosophy alien, even inimical to Judaism, and treat them with utter disdain. He searched among contemporary Jews and found very few with an interest either in science or mathematics (Barzilay, 1974, pp. 310–11).

[15] The leading Jewish intellectual of the sixteenth century, Judah Loew ben Bezalel, also known by the acronym the *Maharal* of Prague (1525–1609), was familiar with Copernicus but remained faithful to the rabbinical (Ptolemaic) view of the universe, which, in his words, was received from Moses at Sinai and thus sacrosanct. One could also mention Tobias Cohn (or Toviyyah ben Moshe ha-Kohen, 1652–1729), who wrote an encyclopedic work on medicine and natural philosophy published in 1707 and who criticized some of his fellow Jewish intellectuals for being too devoted to Kabbalah; at the same time, however, he viciously attacked heliocentrism as opposed to the scriptures (Neher, 1977).

[16] Among the more notable names (beside Einstein and Freud) are those of the physical chemist Fritz Haber, inventor of the Haber-Bosch process, arguably one of the most important inventions of all times; Lazar L. Zamenhof, the inventor of Esperanto; Paul Ehrlich, the originator of modern Immunology; the flight pioneer Otto Lilienthal; Theodore von Kármán, the father of supersonic flight; László Bíró, the inventor of the ballpoint pen; and Carl Djerassi, the pioneer of birth control pills.

[17] Neher (1977, p. 213) claims implausibly that within the Jewish community "freedom of thought was not an inaccessible value" and that it was an integral part of the Jewish conception of science. There is, indeed, little evidence that Delmedigo was systematically ill-treated by the Amsterdam Jewish community despite his trenchant critique of "the Jewish *esprit de corps* and its parochial orientations" and his view that "while the Jews share with other peoples

To return to Triandis's (1995) terminology, by comparison to their neighbors in the European setting, Jews in the sixteenth and seventeenth centuries were a tight society, in that there was widespread agreement on what was true and what was false, and there was a consensus on who was to make the judgment call in cases of doubt.

Elsewhere in Europe, however, the paralyzing uncritical respect for the classics was showing signs of evaporating in the sixteenth century despite the risks associated with heterodoxy in this century of intolerance.[18] A telling case is the career of Guillaume Postel (1510–1581), a French freethinking polymath and one of the most erudite and original thinkers of the sixteenth century. He advocated a universal Christian faith, in addition to his deep interest in Jewish mysticism, cartography, and studies of Islamic science. He was repeatedly arrested by the inquisition and the *parlement* of Paris, and escaped execution only by being declared insane rather than a heretic. The more powerful minds of the seventeenth century realized, much as Pascal (in his pre-Jansenist and more progressive days) noted, that it would be unjust to show the ancients more respect than they themselves had shown to those who had preceded them, a logical point entirely missed by Jewish theologians (Bury, [1920] 1955, p. 68). Progress, the moderns emphasized, was driven by improved tools of research, experimental methods, and instruments of observation that had come on line in the seventeenth century. Galen had no microscope, Ptolemy no telescope, Archimedes no calculus. More than anything, the moderns stressed, knowledge was cumulative. Cumulativeness was, of course, itself a variable that society to some extent controlled and constructed, and was a function of the mechanisms to preserve knowledge by ensuring its intergenerational transmission and the technological capability to store knowledge at low cost and high searchability. It is here that the printing press may have played an important role, as each book was published in hundreds of identical copies, so that copyist errors

many prejudices and superstitions, they partake little of their wisdom" (Barzilay, 1974, pp. 321–22). Delmedigo in many ways was a typical citizen of the Republic of Letters, one of the few Jews who could be counted as such. A peripatetic physician and intellectual, he represented an odd combination of conservative views and new ideas, and it seems possible that his criticism of Jewish culture was not regarded quite as provocative and notorious as that of Spinoza (Haberman, 2007, p. 543). Barzilay, indeed, points out that by 1630 or so, "whatever views Delmedigo may have harbored he kept to himself and never divulged in public. ... By that time, his travels and experiences must have convinced him at last that the Jewish world was not yet ready for his kind of views and learning" (Barzilay, 1974, p. 4).

[18] Europe's intellectuals did not, of course, abandon the classic legacy; Latin was still taught even if it was no longer the lingua franca of intellectuals after 1700, and classical civilization was still studied. Indeed, few did more to bring the riches of classical civilization to the attention of the French-reading public than Pierre Bayle, one of the emblematic figures of the Republic of Letters of his age. In his famous *Dictionary*, he concentrated heavily on classical writers, although he often used them as vehicles to propose his own ideas. See also Fumaroli, 2015, p. 66.

and omissions that had marred so many ancient texts vanished and that the inevitable loss of books over time through wear and tear would not affect the availability of the knowledge.

Indeed, in many past civilizations knowledge could be and had been lost resulting in technological regress. One of Bacon's inspirations, the law professor Guido Panciroli (1523–1599), wrote a book titled *Two Books of Things Lost and Things Found*, in which he listed the products and techniques that ancient civilization was believed to have possessed and subsequently lost. After all, as Keller (2012, p. 242) remarks, "the value of the inventor's knowledge for society was so great that the state could not afford its loss." For that reason Bacon, much of his life a civil servant and politician, proposed to move control of technological knowledge from the individual to the community. What Bacon failed to see was that such a community could be a private order institution, such as the Republic of Letters, that would be self-governing and yet could be relied on to preserve most of what was worth retaining. One component of the belief in progress is that the new mechanisms of the Republic of Letters would not only disseminate knowledge but at the same time also preserve it from oblivion and thus ensure cumulativeness.

While the idea of progress was based on the retention of past useful knowledge which guaranteed that there would be more and more of it, the conditions for its sustained and accelerating growth are fairly strong, and it took Enlightenment intellectuals many decades to figure them out. Moreover, eighteenth-century *philosophes* disagreed among themselves as to precisely what progress would consist of and how it would be brought about (Israel, 2010, esp. pp. 3–15), but if there was one item on which all but a few retrograde writers in the age of Enlightenment could agree on, it was that material progress would consist of practical advances relying on the growth of useful knowledge. In other words, science and technology combined were one of the two engines of material progress, and evidence was slowly mounting about the huge potential of these forces to change the daily material existence of humankind. At the same time, it was also realized that the other engine, political and legal reforms, what we would call today institutional change, would encourage commerce, capital accumulation, and innovation. This second engine of economic growth in many ways turned out to be less reliable and more likely to misfire and stall. For that reason, economists today speak of technological progress but institutional change: the directionality of the latter is much less self-evident.

The Enlightenment program was based on the implicit assumption that technological and institutional changes were mutually reinforcing, that is, there was a deep complementarity and synergy between technological and institutional change (Mokyr, 2006a). Advances in useful knowledge that were unaccompanied by institutional change could fizzle out or lead to a disastrous abuse of this knowledge. For example, when institutions are not aligned to support an economically productive research agenda, the growth in useful knowledge may continue apace, but be diverted into welfare-neutral or welfare-reducing directions, such as numerology, astrology, or more destructive weaponry. Moreover, intellectual innovation will eventually end up being increasingly resisted by an incumbent technology; if that resistance is not overcome, technological progress may be extinguished. If it is not, there is the further danger that the new technology, when it becomes dominant, will in its turn resist the next round of innovation. The net result is what I have called "Cardwell's Law"—the empirical regularity that no society remains at the cutting edge of technological creativity for very long (Mokyr, 1994).

However, the West was not stricto sensu "a society"—it was an agglomeration of disparate societies, which competed in some spheres and cooperated in others. Given this competition, and the diversity in institutions, it was far less likely for the forces that opposed progress to successfully coordinate and mount an effective campaign to slow it down and for the system as a whole to slip into stagnation, even if some of its components might. Nations that somehow were taken over by reactionary regimes realized eventually that resisting innovation was not a sustainable strategy in a competitive environment.

All the same, the powers of reaction and resistance in early modern Europe were far from negligible. Between 1500 and 1700, many of the heterodox scientists and innovators were threatened by some authority that sensed a challenge. Religion had not yet divorced itself from physics, astronomy, and even medicine and chemistry, and it represented powerful forces that supported the status quo. Some of the accounts of persecutions of innovators have been exaggerated, but enough of them remains to demonstrate that incumbents did not concede willingly to intellectual challenges and that things could have turned out differently had a few crucial battles in Europe gone the other way.[19] The reversal of fortunes experienced by Galileo Galilei was the result of a combination of his own blatant disrespect for his opponents as well as the reversal of fortunes of Catholic Europe in the early 1630s, which forced the papacy to take a more aggressive stand against heterodoxies. Whether this setback actually turned Italy into a scientific backwater as much as claimed by Alexander (2014, p. 179) remains in doubt, but obviously the struggle over the *libertas philosophendi* in southern Europe remained much

---

[19] The instances in which scientific heretics actually lost their lives were rare and often the result of severe recklessness, as was surely true in the celebrated cases of Miguel Servetus and Giordano Bruno, and both were in trouble for their religious apostasy rather than their science (though these were hard to separate in this age). Some lesser-known cases of radical philosophers losing their lives because of their beliefs include Lucilio Vanini, burned alive in Toulouse in 1619 for atheist beliefs, and Ferrente Pallavicino, executed in Avignon in 1642 for disrespect to the pope. Other cases are apocryphal. Thus Terence Kealey (1996, p. 3) uncritically repeats the legend of the great anatomist Andreas Vesalius being condemned to death by the Inquisition, eventually commuted to a lethal pilgrimage to the Holy Land.

more fluid than elsewhere. Wherever reactionary regimes were in power, innovative research could be threatened.[20] The eventual defeat of the conservative forces, culminating in the suppression of the Jesuits in 1773, was in large part caused by the palpable success of Enlightenment philosophy in the market for ideas and the growth of the concept of progress on the European Continent in the eighteenth century, including the nominally Catholic nation of France.

In late seventeenth- and eighteenth-century France, many of the leading thinkers were convinced that some kind of progress was taking place around them, although few of them believed that the growth of useful knowledge would necessarily lead to a more moral or enlightened society. Many doubts tempered the belief in progress. Voltaire, Diderot, and most of the *philosophes* believed that human nature was determined by its *histoire naturelle* and hence incurably morally deficient (Dupré, 2004, p. 204). Before the French Revolution, French realistic expectations of social and economic progress were based on little more than an envious glance at Britain and much wishful thinking. And yet, progress became a dominant theme among the *philosophes* of the ancient régime. France had no experience with Puritanism, but its increasingly secular intellectual culture was consonant with a faith in the progressiveness of civilization at large, including but not limited to science. The young Blaise Pascal, for instance, deeply influenced by Descartes, saw the world of knowledge as a single infinitely lived individual, "incessantly learning" (cited by Bury, [1920] 1955, p. 68). In an unpublished fragment written in 1647, Pascal added that the unit that did the learning was not a single individual but a collective entity, which he described as "all of mankind" but really must be understood as the Republic of Letters (Rossi,

---

[20] Jan Baptist van Helmont was a Flemish physican and chemist, the first to identify "gases" as such and one of the first to conduct careful quantitative experiments in biology. He was repeatedly threatened and penalized for his adherence to heterodox views of nature and medicine and for being a (skeptical) follower of Paracelsus. His book *De magnetica vulnerum* was impounded, and in 1624 the inquisition in the Spanish Netherlands began formal proceedings against him for "heresy and impudent arrogance." Helmont was condemned by the Louvain Theological Faculty in 1633–1634 for adhering to the "monstrous superstitions" of the school of Paracelsus (that is, the devil himself), for "perverting nature by ascribing to it all magic and diabolic art, and for having spread more than Cimmerian darkness all over the world by his chemical philosophy (*pyrotechnice philosophando*)." He spent four days in jail in March 1634, and was interrogated repeatedly. It seems that his good political connections protected him against worse consequences (he was closely associated with Marie de Medici, the queen mother of France, who was then in exile in the Spanish Netherlands). In the end, he was released but placed under house arrest. This was finally lifted in 1636, but church proceedings against him were not formally ended until 1642, two years before his death (Pagel, 1982, p. 14). In the preface of his 1644 work *Opuscula Media Inaudita*, van Helmont remarks "that the main body of his work was written in the full blast of persecutions" (quoted in Pagel, 1982, p. 154).

1970, p. 99).[21] As Israel (2010, p. 4) has recently put it, Enlightenment theories of progress were tempered by a sense of the dangers and challenges facing the attempts to improve society, and their "optimism rested on man's ability to create wealth by inventing technologies capable of raising production."

Among the most notable and influential French intellectuals who believed strongly in the progressiveness of human knowledge was Bernard LeBovier Fontenelle. In 1688, Fontenelle published a short essay titled *Digression sur les Anciens et les Modernes* in which he postulated that scientific progress, and the economic progress that will go with it, were not just possible but in fact inevitable.[22] He asserted that in his age a truth (*justesse*) ruled that had been hitherto unknown. He predicted that in the future this would go much further, and that one day the current generation would themselves be ancients and it would be fair and reasonable for posterity to outdo them. It was above all the modern age's superior methodology, logical rigor, and critical facilities that allowed the modern age to have the upper hand. By that he meant the "geometrical method that ruled the intellectual exchanges in the Republic of Letters" (Fumaroli, 2001, p. 193).

Fontenelle's argument implied a strong rejection of the conservative (pro-ancients) position in the debate on the extent to which the wisdom and science of their age could compare and compete with that of the classical writers. Regardless of whether he was "the first to formulate the idea of the progress of knowledge as a complete doctrine" as Bury ([1920] 1955, p. 110) has maintained, his little pamphlet was part of an intellectual movement that reached its zenith with Condorcet. Fontenelle was no towering intellect, but he was eloquent, well positioned, and influential.[23] Unlike Voltaire, he avoided being unnecessarily biting and provocative, which reinforced his position as one of the more effective epigones of the great cultural entrepreneurs responsible for the Enlightenment, the personification of direct and rhetorical bias.[24] He became secretary of the *Académie* in 1697 and held that

---

[21] In later years, Pascal underwent a religious experience amd was converted to Jansenism, a religious creed that was far more contemplative and morally oriented, and he renounced his earlier views and wrote of the "vanity of science"—a good illustration of how conservative religious beliefs, had they prevailed in the competitive market for ideas, might have thwarted the progress toward more advanced science and technology.

[22] See http://www.eliohs.unifi.it/testi/600/fontenelle/digression.htm, accessed July 23, 2010. The English translation, by Glanvill, is appended to Fontenelle (1719).

[23] DeJean (1979, p. 180) notes that "one cannot overestimate the crucial new role" that popularizers such as Fontenelle and his fellow modern Charles Perrault had in establishing the case for the moderns in France simply by outlining the scientific achievements of their age.

[24] Peter Gay (1966, p. 317) noted that "as Cicero had naturalized Greek philosophy among the Romans, Fontenelle spread Cartesian—and be it remembered, Baconian—ideas among civilized men and women in elegant and eloquent prose."

position for more than four decades. His contemporary, Abbé Saint Pierre (1658–1743), represents an even more optimistic view of society, pointing to the kind of phenomena that in Britain were associated with Bacon: printing, academies, and the organized division of knowledge, and in some ways was a French version of William Petty (Perkins, 1959, pp. 78–79). Saint Pierre's work represents a bridge between the Baconian sense of progress and a late Enlightenment view by being the first to elucidate the idea of utilitarianism, the greatest happiness for the most people, based on the notion that it was within the power of the state to improve the morals of humanity (Pollard, 1971, p. 42).[25]

An even more optimistic writer of the French Enlightenment was Anne-Robert-Jacques Turgot (1727–1781), who experienced few fruits of social progress in his own life. In an early work, *On the Successive Advances of the Human Mind*, the twenty-three-year old Turgot elegantly ([1750] 1808, vol. 2, pp. 52–92) expressed the source of progress: the art of invention was to be combined with Reason and Experience to create an inexorable path forward. For him progress was very much the continued advance of science, technology, and economic growth. When the successive masses of artisans end up meeting some man of genius, he felt, technology would inexorably advance to produce more riches. Even if different nations had different approaches to this progress, in the end they would come together in some massive feat of technological globalization (pp. 84–85). As Louis Dupré (2004, p. 207) summarizes Turgot's position, "history moves slowly toward greater perfection, though not in all respects. Knowledge and technique advance steadily; arts and morality do not." The idea of progress here is insightful but still rather naive; much like Saint Pierre, Turgot failed to see why the unbalanced advance between technological progress and institutions is actually a structural feature of history and the Achilles' heel of the belief in progress. He also seems to fall in the Candidesque error of thinking that almost any event in history, no matter how calamitous, led to progress in some fashion.[26]

[25] Saint Pierre was an outstanding polymath and typical citizen of the Republic of Letters, with a wide network of correspondence and a broad interest in political and scientific thought. His main concern was with progress in ethics and politics, and he argued that while even mediocre *savants* of his age knew far more than Socrates and Confucius, there had been little progress in the moral sciences. It was, he somewhat naively felt, a shame that the great geniuses of his age such as Descartes and Newton had not devoted themselves to the moral sciences, but he was convinced that this discrepancy would soon be resolved. He was a pioneer in insisting on quantification wherever possible, and he proposed a proto-Benthamite kind of utilitarian calculus, much like the quantitative analytical mechanics developed by contemporary mathematicians in France at that time (Perkins, 1959; Shank, 2004). He was also one of the first proponents of a perpetual peace, an Enlightenment idea later taken up by Rousseau and Kant.

[26] Nisbet (1979, p. 181) points out something interesting about the Sorbonne lecture of 1750 on which Turgot's book was based: six months earlier he had given a lecture based on Christian Providence, which was quite remote from the secularized Enlightenment notions in his

French optimism came to a crescendo, as is well known, in the works of Turgot's friend and biographer, Condorcet. His famous *Sketch of a Historical Picture of the Progress of the Human Mind* was translated almost immediately into English (Condorcet, 1795). A much longer work, it mirrored many of the same ideas as Turgot's essay. Much like Turgot, he acknowledged the wisdom of Bacon for revealing the "true method" of sciences, although he realized that his inductive methodology had little direct impact (Condorcet, 1795, pp. 230–31). But he explicitly linked progress in the accumulation of knowledge to social progress more widely defined, in the firm belief that ignorance and error had been the source of all misery in the past. Condorcet, much like Pascal a century before him, was a mathematician and knew little history; his ambitious overview of all of human history in ten progressive stages reads flat and artificial. His naive notions of human perfectability, although common to his age, are not the reason subsequent ages are grateful to Enlightenment thought. Yet his thinking brought to a crashing crescendo a century of thought that not only established a widespread belief in social and economic improvement through human agency, but also proposed an agenda as to how this progress was to be achieved. The details, however, were first worked out successfully across the channel in the more pragmatic and sober style of Enlightenment practiced in Britain.

British belief in progress in the century before the Industrial Revolution was more pragmatic, more down-to-earth than on the Continent, but it reached somewhat deeper into society, beyond the crème de la crème of the intelligentsia, into the ranks of educated entrepreneurs, literate mechanics, trained engineers, and high-skill artisans, who actually made the Industrial Revolution. Unlike much of the Continent, most of the educated elite in Britain were not working in opposition to the existing regime and retained their religious beliefs and affiliations. Progress was to be achieved not by social revolution but by relatively incremental cumulative practical advances in science, technology, and institutional reforms. The debate on whether England had an "Enlightenment" only makes sense if we believe that there was indeed just a single model that defines the movement in the eighteenth century, and that that model was French. There were differences between the English and the French models, but they were much closer to each other than the cultural elements predominant, say, in the Ottoman or Chinese empires.

Scotland and France were widely recognized centers of intellectual activity associated with the Enlightenment, but there was an English Enlightenment as well, practical, materialist, and adaptable. It did not seek perfection, just a continuous flow of relatively minor incremental steps toward an improved, if still imperfect, society. It is in this kind of environment that the continuous advance of technology could emerge and ironically cause the

later lecture. Within six months of being exposed to Paris's intellectual circles at the Sorbonne, he seems to have been dramatically affected by the secular culture of Paris intellectuals.

most disruption. The question of whether we can meaningful speak of a "European Enlightenment" or not remains in dispute. There were national nuances and differences, and beliefs everywhere evolved over the eighteenth century so that the Enlightenment of the 1780s that underpinned the American and French Revolutions was quite different from that of the 1690s. Yet as Withers (2007, p. 45) has stressed, the Republic of Letters in the eighteenth century remained a coherent and well-defined "space," defined by its customs, modes of communication, and rules of conduct. Moreover, the various European versions of the Enlightenment strongly influenced and imitated, blended with, and modified and complemented one another. It retained its open and transnational character, although the cosmopolitan nature of the Republic of Letters was always under threat and in the closing years of the century fell victim to nationalist proclivities.

Optimism and a belief in progress were not the only cultural beliefs that competed in the eighteenth-century market for ideas. Various forms of non-progressive thinking gained influence, and not just the desperate convulsions of a moribund, benighted religious reaction. Thus there was a growing nostalgia for a simpler, rural age (a sentiment known as primitivism) which can be found in the writings of Rousseau and Vico, among others. Yet such doubts were confined to niches. Spadafora (1990, p. 17) aptly defines the social climate in Britain as "confidence without complacency." Knowledge was the key to progress, and as long as it grew, the material condition of the human race would as well. As Erasmus Darwin, a key player in the English Enlightenment, stated in 1784, the "common heap of knowledge ... will never cease to accumulate so long as the human footstep is seen upon the earth" (cited by Musson and Robinson, 1969, p. 192). It was, however, one thing to have faith in the eventual occurrence of progress and quite another to provide the initiative to bring it about. Yet that is precisely what the many national and local "improving societies" founded in Britain intended to do.[27] How much they actually helped achieved what they hoped for is another matter.

What accounts for the eighteenth-century triumph of the idea of progress? On the demand side, the expansion of the economies in Western Europe after 1500 gave rise to an increasingly strong contingent of *homines novi*, for whom progress meant above all economic advantage for themselves.

---

[27] Among the major organizations set up with the explicit and conscious purpose to improve society, the Society of Arts (established in 1754) was meant to enhance "such Productions, Inventions or Improvements as shall tend to the employing of the Poor and the Increase of Trade." The Act of founding the British Museum of 1753 stated that it was meant to bring about "advancement and improvement" in useful knowledge (quoted in Spadafora, 1990, p. 79). The Royal Institution, established in 1799 by Count Rumford, similarly described its purpose as "the speedy and general diffusion of all new and useful improvements in whatever quarter of the world they may originate, and teaching the application of scientific discoveries to the improvements of arts and manufactures in this country and to the increase in domestic comfort and convenience" (quoted in Jones, 1871, p. 121).

The urban-mercantile classes naturally felt that progress meant— however indirectly—more commerce, more urbanization, and greater permeability of the upper classes by *arrivistes*. Yet there was more to it than economic change: the idea of progress proved consonant with Western Christianity in ways that seemed to have eluded Islam and Judaism. Judeo-Christian beliefs in mille-narianism provided a sense of a historical dynamic that had an endpoint that was different from current reality. Medieval Europe was suffused with mille-narian beliefs of history leading to a "better" world in which a Paradise would be reinstated at the end of history.[28] At the same time, Christianity turned out to be sufficiently flexible and agile to accommodate strong com-mitments to devoutness as well as powerful support for the moderns over the ancients, of experimental science over Aristotelian dogma, and of the Baconian application of useful empirical knowledge to production and the "arts" over arid scholasticism. Nisbet ([2008] 1994) has emphasized the devoutness of some of the major figures of the Enlightenment, such as Priestley and Herder. It was a fortiori true for the seventeenth century.

The Enlightenment, especially the British Enlightenment, retained an element of millenarianism, a belief in "a new heaven to replace the old," as Carl Becker (1932, p. 129) put it. A celestial heaven was to be rebuilt on earth, but the main idea of some kind of utopian dream remained. As Joseph Priestley wrote, "whatever was the beginning of this world, the end will be glorious and paradisiacal, beyond what our imaginations can now conceive" (Priestley, 1771, pp. 4–5). In part, this millenarian rhetoric was adopted to make the Baconian vision of sustained technological progress more persua-sive and appealing. After all, Britain in the age of Enlightenment was still a religious nation, and to be persuasive, the advocates or progress had to dep-loy religious metaphors. Many of them surely believed this language themselves.[29]

---

[28] One medieval writer who tried to produce a "dynamic" vision of the history of the world that led toward some kind of chiliasm was Joachim of Fiore (1135–1202), whose three-stage theory of history (each stage corresponding to one entity of the Holy Trinity) reappeared centuries later in the works of Auguste Comte and Karl Marx (Cohn, 1961, p. 101). Whether this eschatological prophecy was a true theory of progress (as Nisbet believes) or not, it demonstrates that in Christianity such dynamic theories were possible even if they were attacked by St. Thomas and denounced formally in 1263 by the Church as heretical.

[29] Priestley, a Unitarian clergyman in addition to being a scientist and philosopher, was in some ways an endearingly naive man. He added that "Extravagant as some may suppose these views to be, I could show them to be fairly suggested by the true theory of human nature ... the contemplation [of this subject] always makes me happy" (Priestley, 1771, p. 5).

Chapter 15

The Enlightenment and Economic Change

The market for ideas and the cultural entrepreneurs of the seventeenth century who emerged from it gave rise to the intellectual movement known as the Enlightenment: a complex, heterogeneous, and at times mutually incompatible set of cultural beliefs, but all the same a cultural sea change that uniquely marked Europe to become the locus of economic modernity. For the economist asking questions about the roots of European economic development, however, consistent themes in the elite culture all point in the same direction: a culture of practical improvement, a belief in social progress, and the recognition that useful knowledge was the key to their realization. These beliefs were complemented by other cultural elements we see as enlightened: the idea of political power as a social contract, formal limits on the executive branch, freedom of expression, intellectual contestability, religious tolerance, basic human legal rights, the realization that exchange was a positive-sum game, the virtuousness of economic activity and trade, the sanctity of property rights, and the folly of mercantilist notions that placed the state (and not the individual) as the ultimate object of society.

The increased prevalence of these beliefs, which fit uneasily but conveniently under the big umbrella of the Enlightenment, was the cultural underpinning of economic growth, the scaffold on which new and more prosperous economic buildings could be erected. Of all those beliefs, the notions about the power of useful knowledge to transform the economy constituted the driving force in bringing about the Great Enrichment. Economic growth could take place (and still does) in economies in which human rights are trampled on, with little freedom of expression or equality before the law, in which property rights are enforced only for the rich and powerful and in which government is tyrannical and corrupt. What counts for economic history was the beginning of a long and drawn-out rise in the belief in the transformative powers, social prestige, and virtuousness of useful knowledge.

Without the continuous emergence of new techniques based on a better understanding of natural processes, growth will inexorably grind to a halt.[1]

The central messages of the Enlightenment that mattered to subsequent economic change were products of the competition in the market for ideas and were a direct continuation of the Republic of Letters. The economic dimensions of the European Enlightenment, discussed in Mokyr (2002, 2009a), are sufficiently important to merit special monikers, such as the "Industrial," the "Medical" Enlightenment, and the "Commercial" Enlightenment.[2] The impact of the cultural change was decisive, especially in Britain, in which a scientist (Newton) and later an engineer (Watt) became symbols of a national spirit and a heroism that had nothing to do with the battlefield and everything to do with the creation of useful knowledge. In most other European societies, such prestige was still associated with other activities, primarily military or artistic, but over time the British example and influence led to the dissemination of these beliefs throughout most of the Continent. In the North American colonies and the United States, the odd mixture of Puritan values with elements of the French and Scottish Enlightenment were decisive in setting the culture of the young republic in the 1780s.

The strength of the ideology of progress in the eighteenth century was in its hope, not its realization. Indeed, the technological experience of the age of the early Industrial Revolution shows the Baconian program to be a disappointment (Mokyr, 2009a, p. 59). Yet even in those early decades of modern economic growth, the cultural changes in the sphere of useful knowledge interacted with the world of production through many channels and the two reinforced each other. In some sense, the statement that economic progress was affected by technological change is so obvious as to be almost trivial, but the insight has been clouded by the somewhat dated dispute on the role of science in the Industrial Revolution.[3] As economic historians have known for many years, it is difficult to argue that the Scientific Revolution of the seventeenth century we associate with Galileo, Descartes, Boyle, Newton, and others had a direct and major impact on the pivotal technological breakthroughs of the eighteenth-century Industrial Revolution,

[1] One reflective modern scientist, wondering about the long-term evolution of knowledge, has argued that pessimism has been an endemic part of every society, "with the single, tremendous exception (so far) of the Enlightenment" (Deutsch, 2011, p. 216).

[2] The concept of a Medical Enlightenment was first proposed by Roy Porter (1982) and refers specifically to the belief that growing useful knowledge could and would reduce the incidence of disease. The concept of an Agricultural Enlightenment was first proposed in Mokyr (2009a, pp. 171, 186); see also Jones (2016). The concept of a Commercial Enlightenment is proposed by Abbattista (2016).

[3] The *opus classicus* arguing for a key role for science in the Industrial Revolution remains Musson and Robinson (1969). For the best, more recent, statement arguing for the importance of science see Jacob (1997, 1998, 2014) and Jacob and Stewart (2004). For arguments to the contrary, see Hall (1974), Mathias (1979), and Landes (1969).

especially in the key sectors of textiles and iron. Technological progress in the Industrial Revolution, most students are taught, was the result of inspired tinkering by brilliant and dexterous craftsmen with no more than a smattering of best-practice science (which was not very good to start with).[4] Many modern historians see it the same way. As Charles Gillispie (1980, p. 336) has remarked, in the eighteenth century, whatever the interplay between science and production may have been, "it did not consist in the application of up-to-date theory to techniques for growing and making things."[5] More recently, Roberts and Shaffer (2007, pp. xxi– xxii) have stressed the importance of a "practical intelligence" or what they choose to call "cunning" (meaning dexterity and intuition) as a source of innovation and point out that it could easily combine with science. And yet, dexterity and practical intelligence by themselves would have run into diminishing returns; whether it was soap boiling, hydraulics, or fireworks making, in the end economic history confirms Bacon's statement that by themselves "neither the bare hand nor the unaided intellect has much power" adding that "human knowledge and human power come to the same thing because ignorance of cause frustrates effects" (Bacon, [1620] 2000, p. 33 aphorisms ii and iii). Had skilled artisans and dexterous workers by themselves been able to make more than local and marginal changes in technology, the Industrial Revolution might have taken place in India.

On the eve of the Industrial Revolution, it was not easy to see the fruits of science translated into practical uses. In 1704, one of Jonathan Swift's protagonist ancients makes the devastating remark that "if one may judge of the great genius or inventions of the *Moderns* by what they have produced, you will hardly have countenance to bear you out" (Swift, [1704] 1753, pp. 185–86). Half a century later, Dr. Johnson, writing an essay titled "What Have You Done?" in *The Idler* in December 1759, expressed the disappointment of the age: "When the Philosophers of the last age were first congregated into the Royal Society, great expectations were raised of the sudden progress of useful arts; the time was supposed to be near when

---

[4] Voltaire ([1733--34] 2007, p. 39) felt that the most useful inventions are not "those that do the most honor to the human mind" and that "we owe all the arts [technology] to mechanical instinct and not to orthodox philosophy."

[5] John R. Harris, one of the leading historians of the technology of the Industrial Revolution, has been even more skeptical of the importance of science relative to the "tacit" skills that he regarded as crucial to technological advances in the eighteenth century. He has even argued that France's backwardness in steelmaking was in part due to its reliance on scientists, who at first gave misleading and later rather useless advice to steel makers. See Harris (1998, pp. 219–21). For a powerful recent statement doubting the role of scientific progress in the technological advances of this period, see McCloskey (2010, ch. 38) who denies that "high-brow science" made much of a difference before the late nineteenth century, which still leaves a lot of room for low-brow science, from Watt's friend and advisor Joseph Black to Eugène Chevreul, the French chemist (whose scientific understanding of fatty acids made important improvements to the manufacture of soap and candles).

engines should turn by a perpetual motion, and health be secured by the universal medicine; when learning should be facilitated by a real character, and commerce extended by ships which could reach their ports in defiance of the tempest. But improvement is naturally slow. The society met and parted without any visible diminution of the miseries of life. The [gout] and [stone] were still painful, the ground that was not ploughed brought no harvest. ... The truth is, that little had been done compared with what fame had been suffered to promise; and the question ["what have you done?"] could only be answered by general apologies and by new hopes, which, when they were frustrated, gave a new occasion to the same vexatious enquiry" (Johnson, 1759). Steam power, perhaps the most spectacular technological offspring of the scientific breakthroughs of the seventeenth century, was as yet an exciting but economically marginal technique.

To be sure, a few important inventions, even before 1800, can be directly attributed to scientific discoveries or were dependent in some way on scientific insights. Yet the bulk of the most significant advances in physics, chemistry, biology, botany and other areas occurred too late to have an effect on the great changes of the last third of the eighteenth century we associate with the Industrial Revolution. Crucial as they were to the understanding of the universe and the evolution of nineteenth- century technology, they were largely peripheral to the main thrust of the eighteenth-century Industrial Revolution. Yet this was not for lack of trying. During the age of Enlightenment, and especially the decades after 1750, much of Europe witnessed a flourishing of interest in the application of useful knowledge to the arts and crafts as well as to agriculture. The important thing about the culture of useful knowledge in Europe, however, was not that it yielded immediate economic benefits, but that most practitioners believed that in the very long run it would. Bacon's vision was to be realized, but it became a matter of centuries, not decades.

Moreover, there were exceptions, and these were important, less in their direct economic impact (though it was there in a few cases) than in demonstrating the potential of the Baconian promise. As already noted earlier, Newcomen's atmospheric engine required some notions that had been developed by experimental philosophers, above all the realization of atmospheric pressure and that a vacuum was possible and could be exploited (Wootton, 2015, pp. 500–8). This is not to suggest by any means that the concepts of energy were well understood: the well-worn adage that science owed more to the steam engine than the steam engine owed science is certainly apt. Yet it still is undeniable that without the work of a long line of well-trained natural philosophers beginning with that of the Neapolitan Giambattista della Porta via the discovery of the atmosphere by Torricelli in 1643 and all the way to Denis Papin, who built the first workable model of an atmospheric engine in the 1690s, it is hard to see Newcomen's device succeeding (Kerker, 1961; Cohen 2012, pp. 476–78, 729; Wootton, 2015, pp. 490–95). Advances in the chemical industry, such as the soda-making process and chlorine bleaching came relatively later (1780s) and were based on a very partial understanding of the chemistry involved. Yet again: without any input from scientifically trained chemists such as Scheele and Berthollet, it may be doubted that chlorine bleaching would have evolved when it did (Musson and Robinson, 1969, pp. 251–337). Wootton (2015, p. 489) remarks that early modern science solved two of the most difficult problems it set for itself: the calculation of the trajectory of a projectile, and the determination of longitude at sea. I would add to that a third: the means of preventing smallpox, first through inoculation, and later by vaccination.

Much depended on the capabilities of eighteenth-century science and mathematics to come to grips with difficult problems of energy, materials, and biology. When it could be done, however, it was successful. Consider the work of a relatively obscure figure of the Industrial Enlightenment, Benjamin Robins (1707–1751). Robins was a self-taught mathematician, who renounced his Quaker background to apply best-practice mathematics and physics to engineering and then to ballistics. In the words of his biographer, "his *New Principles of Gunnery* [1742] transformed ballistics into a Newtonian science" (Steele, 2012). His work was quite influential, winning him the Copley Medal, and translated into many languages (into German by none other than Leonhard Euler who was working on similar problems). His ideas were widely implemented and led to military reforms in the Austrian and French artillery.[6] An example of a vexing practical problem that the advances in both propositional and prescriptive knowledge between 1500 and 1700 helped solve was the measurement of longitude at sea. The issue had been on the forefront of natural philosophy, and some of the greatest minds had worked tirelessly to solve it using new insights in astronomy and the new tools that had become available. Galileo, for one, hoped to use his discovery of the moons of Jupiter in determining longitude. The invention of the spiral-spring balance in watches by two of the best minds in the seventeenth-century, Huygens and Hooke, was another contribution to this effort. Without the insights of propositional knowledge, Harrison's marine chronometer (completed in 1759) would never have been made. None of this argument detracts from the contribution of the brilliant clockmaker. It points to the basic fact that skills and theory cooperated and complemented one another in making the Industrial Revolution possible.

Another successful application of increased scientific understanding to a directly useful purpose was the growth of gas lighting in the late eighteenth century (Tomory, 2012). The scientific basis for the controlled burning of gases was pneumatic chemistry, a branch of science that went back to van

---

[6] Steele (1994) sees Robins's work as an example that "contradicts the perception that rational mechanics had little effect on early modern mechanical technology" (p. 380) and that "The ballistics revolution ... contradicts the popular idea that the experimental and mathematical sciences remained essentially separate until the 19th century" (p. 381).

Helmont in the early seventeenth century. It was taken further by giants of the Industrial Enlightenment such as Joseph Black, Antoine Lavoisier, and especially Alessandro Volta. New scientific instruments and a growing need for lighting public areas and factories produced a major multinational effort in the use of gas lighting in the closing decades of the eighteenth century. As Tomory notes, the actual industrial process developed turned out to be an accidental by-product of distillation of hydrocarbons. But as so often was the case, the role of science was captured by Pasteur's famous dictum that Fortune favors prepared minds (and, one might add, prepared minds coupled to dexterous hands). In many ways, gas lighting is a perfect illustration of the economic impact of the Industrial Enlightenment, and not just in a literal sense. It was based on a combination of imperfect but experiment-based scientific understanding and artisanal brilliance; it was geared toward the solution of a recognized practical need; it was multinational in nature and very much an outcome of open science.

The same can be said about hydraulics, another area where theory and practice came together in the kind of fashion that the Baconians had dreamed about a century earlier. Here the pioneering figure was the French mathematician Antoine Parent (1666–1716), a somewhat underappreciated polymath, who published an influential paper on the efficiency of water wheels (1704) that soon became the standard text on hydraulics. Parent had applied the newly-invented differential calculus to find the maximum efficiency of water wheels, and it became a cornerstone of one of the first major engineering handbooks published, B. F. de Bélidor's *Architecture Hydraulique* (1737–1753). Parent's findings were adopted by eminent mathematicians, such as d'Alembert and Leonhard Euler (Reynolds, 1983, p. 207). Yet his work also serves as a good illustration of the highly erratic and nonlinear trajectory of the much-touted collaboration of theory and practice, as it contained a number of errors first pointed out by Daniel Bernoulli in the 1730s. It took many more decades to straighten out the theoretical basis of water power, and the pathbreaking work on hydraulics by the French mathematician Jean-Charles de Borda (1733–1799) remained unrecognized for many years.[7] Yet the eighteenth-century Republic of Letters never wavered in its belief that such a basis would eventually be attained, and that an understanding of hydraulics would serve to build more efficient machines. That belief was Bacon's legacy and it was a consensus that the age of Enlightenment inherited from the market for ideas of the centuries before 1700.

---

[7] David Wootton remarks that the case of water wheels is especially interesting because hydraulic technology had developed very slowly for a thousand years and yet the efficiency of water power took off in the age of Enlightenment. Wootton (2015, pp. 486–89) attributes this advance to the experimental methods as embodied in the work of John Smeaton, but the theoretical work of (mostly French) physicists complemented these experiments.

How essential was formal scientific knowledge to the emergence of modern growth? Could high-skilled artisans by themselves have brought about the Industrial Revolution? Hilaire-Pérez (2007) and Berg (2007) have argued that an artisanal "economy of imitation" could have led to a self-sustaining process of improvement. Artisans by themselves normally reproduced existing technology, and in that process at times an incremental micro-inventive sequence led to significant improvements, but in the end these advances were limited.[8] The institutional arrangements of the artisanal economy (mostly the craft guilds) helped diffuse techniques spatially, but Epstein's (2013, p. 67) view that regards them as inherently dynamic and progress oriented—and that the acceleration of technical innovation in the eighteenth century was more likely to have been caused by "technicians" than by an intellectually driven Industrial Enlightenment—is not persuasive. It was not one *or* the other: useful knowledge and artisanal dexterity were strongly complementary, and they created a synergy that changed the history of humankind, precisely as Bacon had hoped for. Had technological progress remained entirely unconnected to what happened at a higher intellectual level, had it consisted purely of disseminating and incrementally improving best-practice existing artisanal procedures, standardizing them, and hoping for learning-by-doing effects, the process would eventually have run into diminishing returns and fizzled out. A counterfactual world of technological progress entirely carried by skilled and imaginative artisans, without any input from Baconian-minded intellectuals and natural philosophers, might have seen some local technical advances in textiles and metals in the eighteenth century, but it would not have produced a sustainable and self-reinforcing Industrial Revolution. Many societies we associate with technological stasis were full of highly skilled artisans, not least of all Southern and Eastern Asia.

Without artisanal skill, however, the insights of natural philosophers would have had no economic impact. Artisans were an indispensable element in the progress of technology and a complement to radical inventions. They were the ones who carried out designs to specification, scaled up models, and materialized blueprints into new industrial equipment and materials. They installed and debugged complex mechanisms, made them work, fixed delicate machinery when it broke, and in general provided the tacit knowledge sometimes referred to obscurely as "skill" or "dexterity." But without the infusion of radical new ideas from natural philosophy, and eventually chemistry and mathematics, such capabilities would not have amounted to the "phase transition" that they became.

---

[8] Francis Bacon, who was an early believer in the value of artisanal knowledge, all the same complained that artisans confined themselves to the matters that pertained to the immediate tasks at hand, did not trouble themselves with more general issues, and would not raise their minds or stretch out their hands for anything else (Bacon, [1620] 1999, p. 130, aphorism 99).

Hilaire-Pérez (2007) emphasizes the innovative capacity of French artisans in their guilds, and the examples she cites are interesting. There can be no doubt that in a purely artisanal world, evolutionary sequences of microinventions did take place that led to considerable technological progress, both product and process innovation. Moreover, some of the more interesting "great inventors" of the age—starting with Newcomen and his assistant John Calley, the clockmaker John Harrison and the instrument maker James Watt—were skilled artisans themselves. Yet artisans, unless they were as unusually gifted and well educated as the brilliant inventor Jacques de Vaucanson (1709–1782) or the ingenious French armorer and inventor Edme Régnier (1751–1825), were good at making incremental improvements to existing processes, not in expanding the epistemic base of the techniques they used or applying state-of-the-art scientific knowledge to their craft. In other words, a purely artisanal knowledge society will not create a cluster of macroinventions that revolutionized production from the foundation.[9] Artisans were also not well positioned to rely on the two processes of analogy and recombination, in which technology improves by adopting or imitating tricks and gimmicks from other, unrelated, activities. If all that were needed for the Industrial Revolution had been enlightened and ingenious artisans, it could have occurred centuries earlier. Skilled artisans, after all, had been around for centuries, and could be found in India, the Middle East, and China. Focusing on artisans alone makes it difficult to understand why things moved so rapidly after 1750 and continued to do so after 1820. In textiles, the technical problems were on the whole less complex than in the chemical industry or in power engineering, but even there some help from mechanical science found its way to the shopfloor with important consequences for productivity and efficiency (Jacob, 2007).

When all is said and done, the technological revolutions that brought the world economic growth and prosperity were not the result of either artisanal ingenuity or scientific method and discovery, but from the confluence of the two. That confluence is the essence of the Industrial Enlightenment. It saw in the successful application of useful knowledge (including, but not confined to, Newtonian science) the empirical validation of the principles it tried to discover, but its science depended on the tools that technology supplied and the agenda that production difficulties and human needs provided. Enlightenment mathematicians, such as Euler and Borda, worked on ways to make water wheels more efficient. Natural historians, such as René Réaumur, looked for ways to understand insects and prevent their damage to farming, and the great naturalist the Comte de Buffon (1707–1788) studied

---

[9] Watt knew this all too well and sought contact with the best natural philosophers he could find in his milieu, especially the Scottish scientists Joseph Black and John Robison. Less well known is his reliance on the discovery of another Scottish scientist, William Cullen, that within a vacuum the boiling temperature of water is much reduced, which inspired his insight of the separate condenser.

the mechanical properties of wood used in naval construction. Benjamin Franklin and Franz Aepinus, among many others, struggled to try to understand electrical phenomena. It was understood by Enlightenment thinkers that the marriage between science and production could yield enormous benefits to humankind. But the courtship was to last for centuries.

What is it that natural philosophy brought to the table in the decades during and following the burst of macroinventions we identify with the classic Industrial Revolution? And why is the role of science so controversial? In part, it is our own way of thinking of "science" that is at fault, since we tend to think of science as more analytical than descriptive. The eighteenth century, however, spent an enormous amount of intellectual energy on describing what it could not understand. The three "Cs"—counting, classifying, cataloging—were typical of the Baconian program that the seventeenth century bequeathed to those who came after them. In that sense Carl Linnaeus and the versatile and productive Swiss physician and botanist Albrecht von Haller (1708–1777) were perhaps the more obvious carriers of the Baconian program than the Newtonians, as was Jean Jacques d'Ortous de Mairan (1678–1771) in France and Hans Sloane in England.[10] Organizing such knowledge in accessible ways, it was felt, would make it more intelligible and potentially more useful. The chemist Étienne François Geoffroy who claimed to have been inspired by Newton, wrote a famous paper that provided the first tabular arrangement of chemical substances according to their ability to dissolve another substance. It emphasized not the understanding of chemical facts but the ordering of the "brute phenomena themselves," as Dear (2006, p. 42) put it. It was devoid of any attempt to speculate on the reason why materials displayed different solubilities. Botany and zoology were treated in the same way: by cataloging and classifying, it was hoped, some patterns and regularities would emerge. In the absence of a clear concept of evolution, to say nothing of more advanced physiological concepts, many skeptics such as Buffon thought such a project foolhardy. Yet Linnaeus and his many disciples persisted in what became a central project of Enlightenment science. Linnaeus, as a physician, was above all interested in the materia medica. But he went beyond that: his belief that skillful naturalists could help transform farming was widely shared, and it inspired the establishment of agricultural societies and farm improvement organizations throughout Europe. By the second half of the eighteenth century, botany, horticulture, and agronomy were working hand-in-hand through publictions, meetings, and model gardens to introduce new crops, adjust crop

---

[10] Sloane's defense of a purely empirical science was that "the Knowledge of Natural History, being Observations of Matters of Fact, is more certain than most others and ... less subject to Mistakes than Reasoning, Hypotheses and Deductions are ... these are things we are sure of so far as our senses are not fallible and have been ever since creation" (Sloane, 1707, vol. I, unpaginated preface). Mairan was the founder of chronobiology and discovered among others the existence of circadian rhythms in plants.

rotations, and improve tools and farm management.[11] The empirical work of naturalists, such as Linnaeus, and eighteenth-century agricultural experts, such as Arthur Young and John Sinclair, were very widely read, if perhaps rarely with direct results on agricultural productivity. But there is no question that these scientists had recast their role in human society. As Koerner (1999, p. 11) observes about Linnaeus and his students, they "understood the dynamic of history to be the interplay of *natura* and *patria*, and how they (Enlightenment improvers to a man) cast *themselves* as agents of historical change" (emphasis in original). The Baconian origins of this attitude seem beyond question.

Beyond that, however, the role of natural philosophy in the intellectual evolution of the Enlightenment is more subtle than the rather simplistic search for the scientific origins of cotton-spinning equipment. The distinction between natural philosophers and "men of letters" was not nearly as sharp as the distinction between scientists and humanists is today. Montesquieu and Rousseau both had scientific training; Voltaire was a scientific amateur; and Adam Smith, Turgot, and Condorcet all had knowledge of astronomy and physics. As a result, scientific ideas and methods penetrated other intellectual discourses, and scientific terminology entered the debates on institutional reforms (Wuthnow, 1989, p. 174).

The Industrial Enlightenment, then, should be understood as a primarily empirical project, with only occasional flashes of analytical insight before the nineteenth century. Yet the collection and analysis of data was obviously of help in many practical applications. The search for empirical regularities in the data, to use a modern term, inspired Edward Jenner to see why some people seemed immune to smallpox. In animal breeding, in which British farmers scored significant advances, empirics was all they had to go by in the absence of any theory of evolution, let alone genetics. In metallurgy and engineering, the individuals doing the inventing on the ground (such as Henry Cort and Richard Trevithick) consulted empirical scientists, such as Joseph Black and Davies Giddy (Gilbert).

In short, the cultural beliefs that had been slowly ripening in the sixteenth and seventeenth centuries affected technology and eventually output, productivity, and economic performance, even if sometimes through roundabout mechanisms. One might legitimately ask whether the causality was not reversed. Culture might have been malleable and endogenous to the economy, as historical materialism would suggest. Even Merton, who was suspicious of historical materialism, felt that the Puritans' belief in progress was "a profession of faith which stemmed from their growing social and

---

[11] One source of confirmation of the belief in the possibility of economic progress may have been perceptions of agricultural progress. As John Gascoigne has noted, "as the land bore more, better, and increasingly diversified fruits as a consequence of patient experiment with new techniques and crops, so, too, the need to apply comparable methods to other areas of the economy and society came to seem more insistent" (Gascoigne, 1994 p. 185).

economic importance" (Merton, [1938] 2001, p. 81). The difficulty with choice-based cultural evolution is that at the end of the day, it is hard to know why some people are persuaded by certain novel beliefs and values and why others cling loyally to those of their parents or more generally to the ruling orthodoxy. Not all cultural choices were based solely on economic interest. At times, materialist arguments based on a *cui bono* logic can be shown to be demonstrably false, and enlightened thought at times defeated naked greed. Consider the debates in Britain around the abolition of the slave trade (1807) and slavery in the colonies (1833). Both of these were decisions in which a certain set of ideological persuasions defeated economic interests. It is telling that some leaders of the antislavery movement in Britain were enlightened industrialists, such as Josiah Wedgwood and his partner Thomas Bentley and the ironmonger Richard Reynolds.[12]

Yet the timing suggests, however tentatively, that the causality ran primarily from cultural change to the growth of useful knowledge, and not the reverse. At the time that Bacon was persuading (posthumously) men like Hartlib and Boyle about the control of nature, the idea that technological change could actually become a rising economic tide that lifted all boats still seemed far-fetched. Major technological breakthroughs, albeit important, had been rare and few in between, and there was little evidence that they made a significant difference in terms of economic growth. All the same, as noted, there had been successes in the late Middle Ages, including the introduction of the printing press, gunpowder, and the great voyages made possible by better charts, the compass, and improved ship design, and clearly these fostered a belief in human ability to control nature. But the role of systematic research in the creation of those advances had been small, and Bacon knew it (Gaukroger, 2001, p. 81).

Even Adam Smith, it is often remarked, did not realize that innovation was about to become an important (and eventually the central) source of economic growth. While he believed that Britain had been experiencing economic expansion in the centuries before, he did not foresee that useful knowledge would become the overwhelmingly powerful force it became. The hope of enlightened men and women in the early eighteenth century that useful knowledge would become the central factor in economic change was based not so much on experience and historical facts as much as on a metaphysical belief that the universe was knowable and manipulable, and the hope that the accumulation of natural knowledge would eventually pay off. Small advances bolstered this belief. In 1780 Benjamin Franklin wrote to his friend Joseph Priestley that "the rapid progress true Science now makes, occasions my regretting sometimes that I was born so soon. It is impossible

---

[12] James Watt, too, expressed his view that "the system of slavery (is) so disgraceful to humanity" which he hoped would be "abolished by prudent though progressive measures" and other members of the Lunar society mostly agreed (Dick, n.d., p. 10).

to imagine the Height to which may be carried, in a thousand years, the Power of Man over Matter. ... O, that Moral Science were in as fair a way of Improvement" (Franklin, [1780] 1840, p. 418). Priestley felt the same way, but it is hard to believe that the views of these two men who epitomized the Industrial Enlightenment in the English-speaking world were as yet common-place in this era.[13] Some salient events may have helped to create a bias in this direction. Two of the most spectacular inventions of the eighteenth cen-tury, the steam engine and the hot air balloon, may have had that effect des-pite their marginal economic importance in the eighteenth century because of their visually awe-inspiring and revolutionary nature. Those inventions set imaginations racing, reinforced the belief in the human ability to understand and manipulate nature in ways never imagined before, and reinforced the hope that similar advances could be made in other fields, such as agriculture and medicine—hopes that were largely disappointed in the medium run and led to a great deal of frustration.

Moreover, the victory of the belief in technological progress as a benevolent and progressive phenomenon over the forces of resistance and inertia was far from a done deal even during the Industrial Revolution. There was considerable doubt about the desirability of technological progress. In the age of mercantilism, which was receding slowly but was still very much in force by the early nineteenth century, it was believed above all that employ-ment and jobs were a central responsibility of ecnomic policy and thus often felt ambivalent about labor-saving technological progress because it was feared that such advances might lead to unemployment (Berg, 1980). Even David Ricardo, one of the great prophets of liberal political economy, ex-pressed a deep concern that technological progress could throw workers out of work and that the "discovery and use of machinery may be attended with a diminution of gross produce; and whenever this is the case, it will be injurious to the labouring class as some of their number will be thrown out of employment" (Ricardo, [1821] 1971, p. 382). Resistance to technological progress, for a variety of reasons, has survived until the present. It has multiple roots, some of them purely material, other ideological (Bauer, 1995; Mokyr, 2009a, ch. 6).

The Industrial Enlightenment was a movement explicitly committed to the diffusion and dissemination of knowledge and ideas, that is, to exposing people to larger menus of cultural variants from which they could make informed and hopefully rational cultural choices. Here the rhetoric, the way people persuade one another, was central. The Enlightenment benefited from earlier changes in how novel cultural elements were evaluated before

---

[13] Priestley wrote in 1771 that "All things (and particularly whatever depends on science) have of late years been in a quicker progress toward perfection than ever ... in spite of all the fetters we can lay upon the human mind... knowledge of all kinds ... will increase. The wisdom of one generation will ever be the folly of the next" (Priestley, 1771, pp. 253, 562).

they were accepted or rejected, that is to say, what forms content bias took. In this regard the progression from the seventeenth century Scientific Revolution seems natural. The rebellion against the authority of ancient scriptures and sages was continued by tightening the standards of evidence, making them more rigorous. What counted as persuasive evidence and proof itself underwent a process of cultural change: experimental methods were made more explicit and precise, and higher accuracy and more precise measurement became the rule.[14] The more reliable and accurate instruments were a key part of the persuasion process. For instance, the progress made in the understanding of heat transfer in the late eighteenth century owed much to improved thermometers (Heilbron, 2003b).

The Enlightenment invented the concept of *data*: an increasing number of scientific and technological works included a great deal of tabular material, examining, testing, and comparing (Headrick, 2000). In the second half of the eighteenth century, those in charge of augmenting the set of propositional knowledge and convincing others of the correctness of their innovations increasingly relied on quantification and formal mathematical methods (Frängsmyr, Heilbron, and Rider, 1990). The increasing reliance on mathematics and graphical representation in technical works supported this need for precise and effective communication. As Rider puts it, "mathematics was eminently rational in eighteenth-century eyes, its symbols and results were truly international ... in an age that prized the rational and the universal, mathematics ... offered inspiration and example to the reformers of language" (Rider, 1990, p. 115). Formal methods and quantification were an efficient language for communicating facts and relationships, and its rules are more or less universal (at least within the community that counted for the processing and application of useful knowledge). Computation and formal methods were necessary because they were an efficient way of persuasion and helped increase the tightness of knowledge: what was known became more certain, even if in many areas scientific disputes and bogus theories blossomed like never before. Theories lent themselves more readily to falsification and thus the knowledge generated by science became tighter.

Through meticulous procedures and sophisticated equipment, a rhetoric of precision emerged that facilitated scientific consensuses, if not always in straightforward manner.[15] Heilbron (1990, p. 9) submits that in the seven

---

[14] An early example of this is provided by van Helmont. A supporter of the iatrochemical school started by Paracelsus, he challenged his Galenist opponents to take out 200 or 500 patients from hospitals and elsewhere, divide them into two equal groups, and then randomly assign one group to his treatment and the other to theirs, and submit them to the different treatments "and we shall see how many funerals both of us shall have" (Debus, 2002, p. 377).

[15] The triumph of Lavoisier's chemistry over its British opponents in the later 1790s is a good example. Golinsky (1995) shows how his methods of quantification and precision helped persuade some skeptics (or in some cases failed to do so), but either way, precision and

teenth century most of "learned Europe" was still largely innumerate, but that in the second half of the eighteenth century propositional knowledge, from temperature and rainfall tables, to agricultural inputs and yields, the hardness and softness of materials, and economic and demographic information, was increasingly presented in tables. Readers were expected to be comfortable with that language or at least be willing to learn.[16] Tables not only made the presentation of information more efficient, they also organized and analyzed it by forcing the author to taxonomize the data. A booklet such as John Smeaton's famous *Treaty on Water and Wind Mills* used tables lavishly to report his experiments.

An important way in which the age of Enlightenment built on the Republic of Letters and improved the market for ideas was by organizing and formalizing the institutions of science. The seventeenth-century Republic of Letters was at first almost entirely virtual and had few formal organizations before 1660, the unofficial founding of the Royal Society. Renaissance academies such as the famous Accademia della Lincei were often virtual organizations.[17] Many informal, mostly short-lived, academies preceded the founding of formal academies after 1660. In addition to the Hartlib and Cavendish circles already mentioned, there were a number of groups of intellectuals organized by some leading figure such as the scholarly salon known as the *Cabinet des Frères Dupuy* organized by the learned bibliophile brothers Pierre Dupuy (1581–1652) and his brother Jacques (1591–1656). Among others, it was attended by Peiresc (who later maintained a detailed correspondence with the salon). It was a place in which letters and news from all of Europe converged and were discussed on a daily basis (Delatour, 2005a, p. 291). Its other regulars included the exiled Dutch jurist Hugo Grotius and leading French scientists of the age such as Pierre Gassendi and Marin Mersenne (Delatour, 2005b, p. 295). Another focus of the Republic of Letters in Paris was the group around Pierre Michon Bourdelot in the 1640s. The so-called *Académie Bourdelot* was a biweekly meeting in Paris attended by nobles, people of letters, philosophers, and people interested in science, and

---

measurement became an integral part of scientific discourse in the eighteenth century.

[16] Scattered but persuasive evidence suggests that formal and precise methods filtered down to some parts of the production sphere and were applied to mundane purposes. An example is the work of the Irish-born mathematician and land surveyor John Dougharty (1677–1755), who wrote a widely used book on quantitative methods in gauging areas and volumes, replete with ready-to-use tables. The work was first published in 1707 and went through six editions until 1750 (Dougharty, 1750). While the work was dedicated to the commissioners and officers of the excise tax and composed for the "edification of young officers," it was clearly aimed at a much wider audience.

[17] The Lincei academy did not meet often and did not have formal memberships or a brick-and-mortar center, except the palace of its patron, Duke Federico Cesi; it did give its members a sense of common purpose and the right to place a picture of a lynx on the title page of their books (Heilbron, 2003a, pp. 2–3).

it continued meeting until a year before Bourdelot's death in 1685. Among the attendees were the mathematician Gilles de Roberval (1602–1675), Gassendi, and Pascal. A bit earlier the circle around Marin Mersenne, known as the *Academia Parisiensis*, emerged, in which French and foreign intellectuals met to discuss science and mathematics (it was there that Blaise Pascal first met Descartes).

Outside France, one of the first academies of scholars was the *Accademia degli Incogniti* in Venice, founded in 1630 by intellectuals inspired by the teachings of Cesare Cremonini (1550–1631), a popular and heterodox University of Padua philosopher and close friend of Galileo's (Muir, 2007). The *Accademia del Cimento,* founded in 1657, was the private venture of Prince Leopold of Tuscany; it was mostly a group of Galileo's students and followers. It consisted of little more than a handful of notable experimental scientists such as Giovanni Alphonso Borelli and Vincenzo Viviani meeting in Florence under the auspices of the prince. Much like the earlier *Lincei*, it did not outlast its patron. In Germany, the first academy was founded in Schweinfurt in Franconia by a small group of medical doctors, and was named the *Academia Naturae Curiosorum,* later known as Leopoldina when it was officially sponsored by Emperor Leopold I in 1687. In the best traditions of the Republic of Letters, it claimed its objective to be the exploration of nature for the glory of God and the good of mankind. It had no permanent location, and worked mostly by correspondence but it published a scientific journal.[18] In that sense it was an intermediate form between the earlier spontaneous epistolary networks and the brick-and-mortar academies that emerged later. In England, Gresham College in London was established in 1598 under the will of Thomas Gresham, with the purpose of bringing together skilled artisans and scholars outside the universities, and its lectures were given in both Latin and English.[19] In the seventeenth century it became closely affiliated with the groups that later formed the Royal Society, which met at its premises before the great fire of London in 1666.

As Hunter (1989) notes, what brought about the formalization of these gatherings was a combination of the influence of Bacon's *New Atlantis* with its detailed depiction of a scientific academy, and a general movement toward more formalized and enduring forms of organization of all social activities in England culminating in the founding of the Royal Society in 1660. That change, however, hardly explains the almost simultaneous founding of the *Académie Royale des Sciences* in 1666 (and the *Académie de Peinture*

---

[18] The journal was the *Miscellanea Curiosa Medico-Physica*, first published in 1670 in Wroclaw (then the German city of Breslau), the world's first journal of natural science and medicine and still in print today.

[19] Hill (1965, pp. 37–52) describes Gresham College with great enthusiasm, but Harkness (2007, p. 120) has noted that the lectures were not very popular and the lecture halls were often half empty.

et de Sculpture in 1648). Institutionalization implied a modified and perhaps more efficient functioning of the Republic of Letters. Henry Oldenburg, the Society's secretary, became one of the most effective "intelligencers" ever, even more effective as a node in the communications network of the age than his predecessors Hartlib and Dury. As secretary of an official and formal organization, he acquired an authority reinforced by the publication of the *Philosophical Transactions* starting in 1665. Moreover, the Royal Society, by placing its stamp of approval on scientists, served de facto as an accrediting agency, which in turn increased its own status (Hunter, 1995b, pp. 130–31).

In the eighteenth century the movement toward formalized and sponsored organizations grew, not only in Britain but also through all of Europe. None of this was easy and smooth. The academies struggled with funding, sponsorship, and at times were resisted by universities, who viewed the academies as rivals (Heilbron, 2003a). The *Preußische Akademie der Wissenschaften* was founded in Berlin in 1700 at the suggestion of Leibniz, but it was not until 1744 that it was reorganized in an effective way and funded by Frederick the Great (who appointed a French scientist, Maupertuis, as its director). Informal organizations and *salons* remained major centers for the diffusion of knowledge. As Stewart (1992) has shown in great detail, public science involved a variety of informal groups meeting in coffeehouses, taverns, and people's homes as well as itinerant lectures presented to ad hoc audiences. The transformation from the informal Renaissance academies to the formal and official bodies sponsored by the state was far from complete by the end of the eighteenth century. And yet formal and official academies and centers of learning conveyed many advantages to the scientific community, not least of which was the social prestige and possible patronage associated with being a FRS or an *académicien*. To some extent, formal academies replaced the princely courts as the locus of patronage and the source of legitimacy for intellectuals (Biagioli, 1990, p. 36), and they coordinated and organized the reputation mechanism that remained central to the functioning of the Republic of Letters. However, there was a great deal of continuity here between the age of Enlightenment and the previous century, and informal meetings in salons and country inns remained part of public science.

When all is said and done, cultural evolution and the growth of useful knowledge, whether codified or tacit, was shared by only a minute percentage of the population in only a few nations. The cultural changes affected first a few thousand, then a few tens of thousands of people in pre-Industrial Revolution Europe; democratic instincts notwithstanding, we must concede that what the large majority of workers and peasants knew or believed mattered little as long as there were enough of them to do what they were told by those who knew more. Economic change was driven by upper-tail human capital. Adam Smith expressed this kind of elitism when he noted that "to think or to reason comes to be, like every other employment, a particular business, which is carried on by very few people who furnish the public with all the thought and reason possessed by the vast multitudes that labour." The benefits of the "speculations of the philosopher ... may evidently descend to the meanest of people" if they led to improvements in the mechanical arts (Smith, 1978, pp. 569–72).[20]

Just as the Republic of Letters was an elite phenomenon, the technological thrust of the Industrial Revolution was the result of the actions of a small and select group. Some economic historians, in their justified anxiety to get away from the absurd Victorian hagiography of a few key inventors having carried the entire Industrial Revolution, have tended to go too far in the other direction by implying that unless much or most of the population had access to education and technical knowledge and were richly endowed with human capital, the emergence and spread of new techniques would be limited. The truth is somewhere in between; it is undeniable that technological progress during the Industrial Revolution was an elite phenomenon, carried not by a dozen or two of big names who made it to the textbooks, but by the thousands—but not hundreds of thousands—of trained engineers, capable mechanics, and dexterous craftsmen on whose shoulders these inventors could stand, the upper tail of the human capital distribution (Meisenzahl and Mokyr, 2012; Squicciarini and Voigtländer, 2015). Technological advance in the period of the Industrial Revolution was a minority affair; most entrepreneurs and industrialists of the time were not like Matthew Boulton or Josiah Wedgwood and had little knowledge of or interest in science or even innovation, just as most landowners were not improvers. But the dynamics of competition in a market economy are such that in the long run, the few drag along the many.

---

[20] Soame Jenyns, a mid-eighteenth-century writer, advocated ignorance for the poor as "the only opiate capable of infusing the insensibility which can enable them to endure the miseries of poverty and the fatigues of the drudgeries of life." See Jenyns (1761, pp. 65–66). As Rosenberg points out, the Smithian view was that such a division of knowledge was increasingly pertinent to a sophisticated ("civilized") society in which specialized "philosophers" would account for technological progress. Compare Rosenberg (1965, pp. 134–36).

Part V

Cultural Change in the East and West

Chapter 16

China and Europe

Why did China not have an Industrial Revolution? The debate on the issue has been with us for many decades, and while it has stimulated a great deal of important research (Pomeranz, 2000; Rosenthal and Wong, 2011; Vries, 2013; Brandt, Ma and Rawski, 2014), little consensus has emerged on precisely what the key differences between China and western Europe were. Modern Chinese scholarship has successfully fought the notion that the West's Scientific and Industrial Revolutions implied that China somehow "failed" and has denounced it as imposing European standards on a society with very different values and norms. The famous "Needham question"—why Chinese science and technology, after first pulling ahead of Europe, were unable to keep pace—remains, however, irrepressible (Needham, 1969a, p. 16; Sivin, [1984] 2005). Needham (1969b, pp. 82–83) phrased the question in very stark terms: "why did the Chinese society in the eighth century A.D. favour science as compared with Western society, and that of the eighteenth century A.D. inhibit it?" Even though few modern scholars would quite phrase it so baldly, the question itself refuses to go away. A recent issue of *History of Technology* features some long essays dedicated to the very question.[1] One conclusion that seems acceptable to most participants in the debate is that there was nothing particularly exceptional about China; the flourishing of science and technology during the Tang and Song dynasties was followed by entrenchment and stagnation during the Ming and Qing dynasties, but such a retreat was not unusual. Goldstone's summary is that it is typical for science to advance when different cultural

---

[1] It is worth noting that in his essay on the Needham question in that volume, O'Brien (2009, p. 23) can do no better than to return to the old Weberian chestnut that Confucian principles did not account for the world as a rational and explicable work of God, as if this philosophy had prevented science and technology from flourishing under the Song and as if "Confucian" did not refer to a highly diverse and often inconsistent set of principles (Bodde, 1991, p. 344).

and philosophical traditions are allowed to mix, but then for it to stagnate and even be reversed when conflict and disorder occur (Goldstone, 2009, p. 141). What was exceptional was not what happened in China but what happened in Europe, where no such retrenchment occurred. Not only did the growth of useful knowledge not run into a barrier that stopped it in its tracks, but European methods for acquiring, vetting, disseminating, and applying it spread world-wide and eventually disrupted the equilibria that had settled in the Middle East, in China, and elsewhere.[2]

Before the Industrial Revolution in Europe, China and Europe had both experienced spells of technological progress. It is impossible to say where technology was more developed by 1700 and "who was ahead." In some areas Europe had advanced beyond China, in others it was still trying to catch up. The effort to catch up with the "other" was more intensive in Europe, but the presence of Jesuits at the Chinese court and the reforms they introduced in the Chinese calendar, as well as the introduction of western inventions such as eyeglasses and fire-fighting pumps into China from Europe (Elvin, 1996, pp. 83–84) demonstrate that imitation was not all one-sided. The full economic symptoms of the divergence between the two cultures, whatever its historical roots, become apparent only after 1700 when the dynamic of innovation in Europe underwent what could be called a "phase transition." While Chinese technology may not have been quite as stagnant as has been suggested by some, it experienced nothing of the sort. In this formulation, the Needham Question remains at the center of the agenda. Yet the insistence of the so-called California School that before the Industrial Revolution there were no signs whatsoever of any divergence between the two, and that differences in culture were immaterial to the divergence flies in the face of Needham's insistence on a slowdown in Chinese science and technology from the Ming dynasty on.[3]

A plethora of explanations have been suggested for the undeniable fact that at some point the two societies diverged and European technology caught up and then surpassed that of China, even if the date at which this happened is in dispute. Geographical explanations have been put forward by Pomeranz (2000) and Morris (2010), pointing to location, the presence of natural resources, and bellicose neighbors. More doubtfully, there is a stubborn argument that somehow technological creativity in China was slowed down by low wages, the mirror image of the argument that labor-

[2] Needham cites (with some disapproval) Einstein's 1953 letter in which he says that "In my opinion one need not be astonished that the Chinese sages did not make these steps [the invention of formal logical systems and the search for causal relationships through controlled experiments]. The astonishing thing is that these discoveries were made at all" (quoted in Needham, 1969a, p. 43).

[3] As De Vries (2015, p. 47) points out, if the dating of some of the aspects of the divergence between China and Europe are dated to 1600 instead of 1800 the resistance to relying on "culture as a variable in the story" could be overcome.

saving technology stimulated by high wages was the driving force behind the British Industrial Revolution (Allen, 2009). The argument has been demolished effectively by economists (McCloskey, 2010, pp. 186–96; Kelly, Mokyr, and Ó Gráda, 2014) as well as historical sociologists (Vries, 2013, pp. 184–89), but its superficial attractiveness seems irresistible to some scholars (Rosenthal and Wong, 2011, pp. 36, 120; Slack, 2015, p. 9). The evidence suggests that by most measures Chinese real wages were lower than most European ones. But to infer from low wages some kind of pervasive disincentive to innovate is simply mistaken economics. First and foremost, if wages were low because labor productivity was low, unit labor costs (which ought to be the relevant variable) might be quite high. But even if that were not the case, even cheap labor still costs *something*, and if it was cheap, it would be used more intensively, and thus any innovation that would make it more efficient across the board would be welcome.[4] Moreover, there is no evidence that technological progress before, during, or after the Industrial Revolution was on balance labor-saving. At times, it saved labor; at times, it saved capital and energy; at times it did neither and just made better or altogether new products (Styles, 2016).

One of the more sensible and little-noticed answers to the Needham Question was provided by Lin (1995).[5] Lin distinguished between past technological progress that was based purely on learning-by-doing and thus was the by-product of production (which could be called *experience-based* technological change), and advances that resulted from the deliberate application of science-based research and development (*knowledge-based* technological change). He points out that the former was characteristic of all technological change before the Industrial Revolution, and that because progress was an unintended by-product of the act of production, larger (and more integrated) populations had an advantage. Hence China, which was far larger than Western Europe, had a technological lead in the medieval period and before. Only when Europe began to apply systematic research in propositional knowledge to production did the balance tilt in its direction.

---

[4] Elvin (1996, pp. 88, 92) repeatedly rejects the notion that cheap labor in China was an impediment to technological progress, and is surprised by the failure of Chinese farmers to adopt certain labor-saving pumps that were described in Chinese books on agricultural technology.

[5] It is striking that Lin sees the Needham puzzle as "why the Industrial Revolution did not originate in China," whereas Needham himself and most subsequent scholars were first and foremost concerned with the rise of science. The implicit notion that a failure to develop "modern science" (whatever is meant by that) led to the absence of an Industrial Revolution in China and that the two are more or less interchangeable in this context is itself an interesting assumption. Needham himself clearly saw the two questions as separate (Needham, 1969a, p. 190). Much of the ensuing debate seems to have adopted the assumption that scientific and technological developments inevitably progressed cheek by jowl.

The sharp distinction between the two forms of technological progress made by Lin may be a bit overdrawn. Even in the eighteenth century,
as we have seen above, the relationship between science and technology in
Europe was subtle and complex, with industrial and agricultural processes
based on poorly understood natural phenomena. Experience-based technological change was not just dependent on raw numbers, but also on the quality
of the training and willingness of skilled artisans to innovate. The Industrial
Revolution of the eighteenth century was in considerable part still based on
artisanal knowledge, much of it tacit, and scientific inroads were still rather
rare. Only after 1815 did formal, codified knowledge begin to affect technology in a wider segment of production, but learning-by-doing and serendipitous discoveries that are the by-product of normal production remain
important until the present day. All the same, Lin's paper was a pioneering
effort and moved the literature in the right direction. What it left unex-
plained, of course, was why and how the difference in the way innovation
was generated in the two worlds emerged in the first place. If Europe's
success resulted from its ability to generate propositional knowledge that
eventually became capable of dramatically affecting output and productivity,
why did this not happen elsewhere?

China in the mid-eighteenth century was hardly a backward economy in any meaningful sense of the word. It was commercial, monetized,
educated, run by a trained and professional bureaucracy, and was able to
generate and accommodate a substantial population increase after 1680 or so
without obvious Malthusian effects. In terms of the kind of institutions that
underlay Smithian growth, the puzzle of strong institutions coupled to a
stagnant economy is manifest. China's institutions, while different, seemed
by most measures not to be inferior to Europe's. It had a central administration based on a meritocratic imperial civil service, well-enforced property
rights in land, and a functional system of law and order enforced mostly by
local authorities.

Yet some European thinkers, who may not have known much about
China beyond the accounts of travelers and missionaries, sensed a difference
even on the eve of the Industrial Revolution. David Hume, for one, in his
essay on *The Rise of Arts and Sciences* made an argument contrasting Europe's
diversity and pluralism with China's alleged homogeneity and unified state.
He felt that political fragmentation was the main reason behind European
flourishing of useful knowledge. He was well aware of China's past achievements in science and technology and its sophisticated culture ("politeness"
in eighteenth-century parlance), but in his day he felt that Chinese science
was making slow progress compared to Europe. The reason seemed clear to
him. In China, he argued, the authority of one teacher was propagated easily
from one corner of the empire to another and "none had the courage to resist
the torrent of popular opinion, and posterity was not bold enough to dispute
what had been universally received by their ancestors" (Hume, [1742] 1985,
p.122). The idea has resonated among many: Qian (1985, pp. 25, 114) sees

unified China as politically and intellectually "intolerant," whereas Europe's pluralism eventually resulted in a political structure and ideology that were more propitious for "the rise of modern science." Fragmentation, he argued, provided Europe with a set of political authorities that were "mutually restraining" and thus gave nonconformist thinkers in Europe substantial degrees of freedom.[6] What Hume grasped was an important difference: in China intellectual activity was controlled by and transmitted through the central administration far more than in Europe, and as a result the Chinese market for ideas operated in a different fashion.

How far "behind" was China? In a pathbreaking paper, Shiue and Keller (2007) have pointed out that in terms of allocative efficiency, as late as 1750, China did not lag significantly behind Europe. They show that at least by the criteria of market integration (as measured by the comovements of prices), China was roughly speaking on par with Europe (though behind Britain). They thus add reasons to doubt that improved allocative efficiency (Smithian Growth) by itself led to accelerated technological progress. Instead, their findings show how subsequent industrialization (which included improvements in transportation networks) and institutional changes (which included the reduction or elimination of internal barriers to trade and a movement toward freer international trade) led to higher market integration in Europe in the first half of the nineteenth century. In other words, the data suggest that trade did not cause technological progress, but technological progress and institutional change did lead to more effective markets.

Moreover, Qing China had "sprouts of capitalism" especially in mining where advanced methods of financing and management were introduced. Larger workshops in textiles and paper employing wage labor were slowly beginning to threaten domestic cottage manufacturing in eighteenth-century China, much as was happening in Europe (Rowe, 2009, pp. 125–26). Many scholars have shown that while the Chinese relied on different institutional forms of contract enforcement and dispute resolution, these were strong enough to create a well-functioning market economy.[7] Furthermore, the Chinese state administration served far more as a third-party enforcement mechanism of property right`s than had been previously

---

[6] The idea that European states and religions were in a purely competitive market while Asia was ruled by large homogeneous empires is of course overdrawn (Goldstone, 2009, pp. 99–102). Persia, the Ottoman Empire, and the Mughals in northern India and their nemesis to the south, the Maratha Empire, competed as hard and as bloodily with their neighbors as Louis XIV and Frederick II did in Europe, with the great battle of Panipat (north of Delhi) of 1761 being one of the most extensive and bloody clashes of the time. Religious competition, too, was comparable to Europe's, with Islam divided among Sunni, Shiite, and other factions, yet competing with Hinduism in southern Asia.

[7] Madeleine Zelin has concluded that "China's property rights regime played a key role in rural and urban capital accumulation. From the late Ming these institutions provided an environment that fostered entrepreneurship" (Zelin, 1994, p. 32). A convenient summary of this literature is provided by Brandt, Ma, and Rawski (2014, pp. 56–58, 63–64).

believed. Local officials resolved property disputes over water, land tenure, and contracts even in the absence of a formal civil code (Rowe, 2009, p. 58). While there were craft guilds (*hang*) in China, there is no evidence that they played a serious role at excluding others from their trade, as they often did in Europe, thus leading to local cartels generating rents for the incumbents before the late nineteenth century (Pomeranz, 2013, pp. 106–8). Using the traditional definitions of what "good" institutions do, namely underpinning and supporting well-functioning markets, it is hard to see much daylight between China and the most advanced parts of Europe. Perhaps the most striking difference is the absence of anything resembling copyright or any other formal intellectual property right in China (Alford, 1995). Yet this absence was a consequence and a symptom of deeper cultural differences and by itself is probably of second-order significance for the growing gap in the development of useful knowledge between Europe and China.

China was also a relatively well-educated and literate nation. Estimates of literacy rates in Qing China in the nineteenth century range from 30 to 45 percent of the male population and 2 to 10 percent of the female population, which meant at least one literate person per family (Rawski, 1979, p. 23, 140; Woodside and Elman, 1994, p. 531).[8] This was not a new phenomenon. As early as the eleventh century under the Northern Song, China experienced a new emphasis on education, with both government and private schools proliferating. This development was so far-reaching that "even in the poorest and most remote rural places there gradually appeared lower-level country schoolteachers in the smaller villages ... the norms of the higher levels of culture, transmitted through the various kinds of local education, broadly penetrated the level of the ordinary people" (Mote, 1999, pp. 159–60). As Liu (1973, p. 484) noted, the progress of printing technology made books accessible to those who were not necessarily wealthy. He adds that for the first time in history, a centralized government established schools beyond the capital in various regions. Furthermore, individual initiatives and community or kinship group initiatives set up and maintained private schools of various sizes.

Under the Qing, too, education expanded. Both by top-down "organized socialization" and by the private acquisition of knowledge through various forms of learning (still guided by the state), education increased in variety and reach between 1644 and 1911 (Woodside and Elman, 1994, p. 526). The concept of organized socialization from above is critical here. In Europe, education was a decentralized and competitive business, with no single entity having much market power. Religious educational institutions

---

[8] It is possible that these numbers are overly optimistic, in view of the relatively small market for new imprints of books in Qing China (Van Zanden, 2013, p. 337). It should also be kept in mind that reading Chinese could range between a full literacy, as enjoyed by the educated elite, and knowledge of just a few hundred characters, which would mean reading at a rudimentary level only.

competed with one another, as well as with secular schools. Any top-down socialization was thus severely limited not by the policies of officials but by their inability to impose their will on educational institutions. In China, the state, though constrained in its capacity to implement its decisions on the people, was still the central entity setting the rules of education. By the late Ming period, the private academies, which previously had been a force for reform, were losing their autonomy, and the Mandarin bureaucracy laid down the rules: the academies were "to serve the needs of the administration" and became part of the establishment, utterly opposed to anything that would disturb the order of society (Meskill, 1982, quotation on p. 151). Even when foreigners arrived in China in the form of Jesuits, they could operate only at the pleasure of the emperor and his court. One could see this influence as a classic case of coercion bias. The Chinese emperors, no more than their European peers, could not coerce their subjects to think and believe in the ways the rulers wanted. But they could set the boundaries of the permissible intellectual conversation and the parameters of what was taught in the schools.

Moreover, China was a land of books. Already during the Song era, it had a thriving book trade, but after 1500 there occurred what the leading expert has called an "explosive expansion" of printing. By 1800 "scholarship, book production, and libraries were central to Chinese culture" (Elman, 2006, p. 81). Chinese printers used both xylography (woodprints) and moveable type (which had been known in China since the eleventh century), although the nature of Chinese written language made the use of moveable font rather awkward and expensive (Angeles, 2014). Various kinds of books were printed, including novels, almanacs, encyclopedias, as well as the Chinese classics. By the eighteenth century a specially designated street in south Beijing had specialized in the book trade and became the book emporium of China. Lively book markets, however could be found throughout the Yang-zhi delta. These facts clearly refute any kind of facile explanation of the Great Divergence based on a human capital advantage that the West may have had over China.[9] Chow (2004, pp. 248–52) points to the many apparent advantages enjoyed by Chinese publishers. They could choose between two alternative printing techniques (woodblock and moveable type) suitable for different print runs, and before the Qing revolution there was little formal censorship in China, even if politically sensitive publications could be risky. Chow also argues that unlike the strict guild system and licensing requirements in Europe, in China there was essentially free entry into the industry.

And yet recent attempts to compare the number of books published in China and Europe, despite many pitfalls in interpreting the numbers, have

---

[9] In this regard the non-Western world is quite diverse: in the Islamic world, for mostly religious reasons, printing and publishing in Arabic and Turkish were delayed by centuries. For a recent survey of differences in access to books among different cultures in early modern Europe, see Van Zanden (2013).

shown that the number of volumes published in China was a small fraction of what was published in Europe (McDermott, 2006, pp. 70–71).[10] Van Zanden, who has done the most careful quantitative work on book publishing in China and the West, has concluded that "movable type printing did not really take off in China before 1800" (Van Zanden, 2013, p. 336). For the Chinese ideographic script, with its many thousands of characters, moveable type was simply not cost effective and printing remained largely confined to block printing.[11] To be sure, this ratio is affected by the multiple editions and translations of the same book in Europe, so that the actual difference in the size of the intellectual menu was probably less than the large gap in the number of titles suggests.

In China printing took off more slowly as Van Zanden's dramatic diagram of the number of imprints in Europe and China shows abundantly (Van Zanden, 2013, p. 327). Although the real cost of Chinese books (in terms of the wage of an unskilled laborer) was probably only half that in Europe (Angeles, 2014), there is reason to think that access to the books published was in many ways easier and less costly in Europe. Chow (2004) points to institutional constraints (such as censorship) in Europe as an impediment on the diffusion of books in Europe, but this loses sight of the fact that these constraints were not coordinated across political units and were hard to enforce, so that as a limitation on what the entire continent could publish, the constraints were ineffective. In China, the limitations on heterodox writings may have appeared less severe by comparison, but because it was initiated by the imperial court there was less coordination failure in suppressing them, as Hume pointed out. The crackdown of the Qing emperors on real or suspected political dissent and the mistrust of "foreigners" had real consequences on the market for ideas (Koyama and Xue, 2015). In short, while in Europe the negative incentives for intellectual innovation were becoming weaker after the middle of the seventeenth century and had largely vanished a century later, they became stronger in China at almost the same time.

All in all, there can be little doubt that the Chinese intellectual elite during the Ming and Qing dynasties was literate, educated, creative, and sophisticated. And yet, one may ask, if everything was so good, why was

[10] Buringh and Van Zanden (2009, pp. 436–37) have estimated that for the period 1522–1644 (the later Ming dynasty), the annual number of books published was between twenty-seven and forty-seven annually. This estimate, however, is based on books extant in libraries today, and because Chinese print runs were smaller and a lot more cultural destruction occurred there than in Europe, the Chinese figure is a serious underestimate. Yet, as they note, given that the European number of books published was forty times larger, it is hard to believe that differential survival alone can fully explain the gap (all the more so in view of China's larger population). The gap for the Qing period is equally impressive.

[11] As Angeles (2014) points out, the actual number of type pieces in a European printshop was not that much smaller (because each type was used repeatedly on any given page). The difference in cost was due to the fact that the Chinese characters were all different and could therefore not be mass produced.

everything so bad? Different cultures can be educated and sophisticated in different ways. Can we infer that there was no human capital difference between the two cultures, and that the Great Divergence should be explained by purely locational and geographical variables? Differences in human capital can occur both in quantity and content. Some kinds and modes of education are more conducive to skepticism, innovation, and thinking outside the box.[12] The concepts of choice-based cultural evolution suggest that socialization is a pivotal process in which beliefs and values are transmitted, and it is quite possible that some of the critical differences lie in this area. Modern students of education such as Li (2012) stress the importance in Chinese learning of such concepts as *zunshi* (respect for teachers), which she feels has been seen as a sign of docility and lack of critical thinking. A related virtue is *qianxu* (humility), which views pride as an obstacle to improvement (Li, 2012, pp. 51–52). In the Western traditions, what could be viewed as pride was correlated with trying to build a reputation among peers. Such differences in cultural approaches to socialization could create deep differences in cultural outcomes in every other dimension, as cultural differences to learning can be regarded as analogous to differences in the way somatic cells are structured— they become the root cause of many other differences later in life.

Moreover, it has been argued that Qing China actually overproduced human capital. A classical education in China prepared one for a career in the civil service, but in 1800 there were 1.4 million degree holders competing for no more than 20,000 posts. Even the very best scholars, those who made it to the Hanlin Academy (an intellectual honor society) could face unemployment. Rowe feels that the state's reduced demand for officials and its venal fashion of distributing the offices was at fault (Rowe, 2009, p. 152), but the deeper problem was that Chinese education was almost entirely aimed at preparing civil servants. Unlike Europe, there were no schools or academies that taught useful knowledge and prepared young men for a life of commerce or industry. Although it was slow in the making, by the eighteenth century much of Europe was making that transition, and other cultures, China included, increasingly lagged behind.[13]

Can we identify a set of cultural differences between Europe and China that would help explain why Europe experienced a successful Enlightenment and forged ahead in its economic modernization during and after the

---

[12] As McCloskey points out, education can be counterproductive when it is overly focused on venerable but antiquated knowledge and produces a "rote-learning bureaucracy hostile to innovation." Without the appropriate values, which she feels are embodied in a "bourgeois rhetoric," education becomes a desirable human ornament, not the route to riches (McCloskey, 2010, pp. 162–63).

[13] Malkom Khan (1833–1908), an Iranian diplomat and social reformer, noted in the late 1850s with some envy that "Europe has advanced by virtue of possessing two kinds of factories: one for producing goods, the other for producing men where they take ignorant children and turn out engineers and accomplished thinkers" (quoted in Algar, 1973, p. 28).

Industrial Revolution, creating a two-century gap between Europe and Asia?[14] Greif and Tabellini (2014) have argued that in China the social unit that organized cooperation was the extended family or clan, while in Europe it was a voluntary group of unrelated (by blood) people, which they term "corporations." They associate these two groups with a stronger "general morality" in Europe and a "limited morality" in which cooperative norms and customs hold mostly for a smaller group of relatives. As I argued in chapter 2, one could make a case that a general morality is more conducive for a private, decentralized effort of producing intellectual innovation. Indeed, the concept of generalized morality can be used to understand how the European Republic of Letters worked. Its members had to deal largely with strangers in a network of weak ties, yet the rules of a general morality— not faking results, not copying without attributing, responding to letters, and so on—applied and were observed.

The gap between China and the West should not be overstated here: China had a market for ideas in which people who did not know one another well corresponded and swapped ideas and information. All the same, the historical record of China indeed shows that much of the growth of useful knowledge during the Tang and Song dynasties was generated and diffused by civil servants (Mokyr, 1990, pp. 209–38). That does not make such knowledge less valuable, but it does make its continued development more vulnerable to political changes, and the rise of conservative governments in China indeed may imply a sharper slowdown than in a culture in which science and technology were largely controlled by the private sector. The Greif-Tabellini framework suggests indeed a divergence between Europe and China that is driven by deep cultural and institutional differences, but they have to do with the basic organization of society, not the metaphysical differences between Confucianism and Judeo-Christian religions. In their model, much as in the story told here, "endogenous social institutions and cultural traits mutually reinforced each other" (Greif and Tabellini, 2014, p. 21). It is significant, perhaps, that the prominent role of clans in the organization of Chinese economic life came to its full bloom in the Song era, after which the technological momentum began to slow down.

What mattered is above all the choice-based cultural evolution of intellectual elites, choices that were shaped by the different institutional structures, and in turn helped create these institutions. The point that should be addressed is not anything like "why China failed" (it did not) or "why China was not capable of generating more technological progress" (it was and it did). Rather, the question is how during the centuries known as the

---

[14] Among the modern economic historians who have squarely blamed Chinese culture for China's falling behind Europe the most prominent is David Landes (1998, ch. 21; 2000). Many modern economic historians interested in global history have taken a skeptical view of his position as "virtually unsupported assertions" (O'Brien, 2009, p. 7) and "essentialist explanations" (Goody, 2010, p. 97).

early modern period (1500–1700), Europe and China differed sufficiently to create a gap in technological and economic capabilities that lasted for much of the modern era.[15] There was nothing wrong with China per se, but in Europe and in Europe alone something quite unusual took place: the set of intellectual changes that led to the Enlightenment. The unique power of the European Enlightenment was that it eventually affected not only Europe but also every corner of the planet. To stress this asymmetry cannot be dismissed as Eurocentric or "essentialist," no matter how much such revisionist scholars as Blaut (1993) or Goody (2010) may insist.[16]

One can discern two extreme positions in this literature. One is that the roots of European exceptionalism and economic superiority go all the way back to classical antiquity and that see non-European societies as "primitive" and "backward."[17] This interpretation is denigrated by revisionist California School historians who propose the opposing extreme, namely that there was no real difference between East and West, and that the Great Divergence was just a kind of alternating equilibrium in which one side gained a temporary advantage over the other. Between the two there is room for a third interpretation. That interpretation holds that at some point in early modern Europe, the cultural environment began to change sufficiently to create a climate in which a variety of cultural entrepreneurs and their followers could affect the attitudes and beliefs, and the institutions consistent with them, of a significant part of Europe's elite in a way that was uniquely favorable to innovation and technological progress. It thus prepared the ground for a fateful change in the way useful knowledge was regarded in society. Eventually it led to the breakdown of the Malthusian ceilings and other constraints that had kept living standards from rising very much before 1800. It also led to two centuries of European global dominance.

The cultural transformation of Europe ended up changing global history in ways that would never have occurred had it not been for the impact of the exposure of non-Europeans to Western culture. Of course, Western influence was resisted, modified, blended with local elements, and transformed to create different outcomes. The great exchanges between West and East were a two-way street. In an earlier time, the West adopted many of the tech-

---

[15] Mote (1999, p. 970) notes that the breakdowns in Chinese society in the nineteenth century were the result of foreign industrial technology, which lowered China's capacity to compete.

[16] Peter Perdue (2007, p. 145) has remarked that while Needham was correct that Western historians might be criticized for their Eurocentric ("Orientalist") biases, Chinese writers in the late nineteenth century themselves held even more fervent Orientalist views of their own past as stagnant and worthy of rejection.

[17] The depiction of this school is little more than a straw man. Goody (2010, p. 95) from whom the adjectives are quoted significantly provides no references here, and it is hard to think of any recent scholars who held such extreme views and saw, for instance, Song China or Tokugawa Japan as "primitive" relative to the medieval West.

nological insights of the East, from gunpowder and porcelain to umbrellas and smallpox variolation. In more modern days, it still has no qualms about adopting Chinese technology, from acupuncture to Asian cuisine. But it had, by and large, no interest in copying the philosophical and institutional underpinnings of Chinese useful knowledge. The West's brand of aggressive Baconianism, in which nature is investigated and researched to expose exploitable natural regularities and alter the physical world so as to improve material welfare, has remained to date triumphant.

In Europe, as we have seen, the Enlightenment can be regarded as the culmination of the triumph of the moderns over the ancients, the deep belief that their own generation was creating a culture and a body of knowledge superior to what anyone had possessed before and that was a gateway to a better world. Was anything comparable taking place in the East? Despite the absence of a strong theocratic organization such as the Christian church or Islamic government, the heavy hand of the respect for "ancients" was felt throughout much of Chinese history. In the era known as the "age of warring states" between 475 and 221 BC, China produced many of its most successful cultural entrepreneurs, whose heritage became central pillars of its culture: Confucius himself, and some of his most influential followers such as Mengzhi (Mencius) and Xunzi. The establishment of this philosophical canon in China set the cultural parameters for Chinese society for many centuries, but within Confucianism there was a great deal of heterogeneity and room for flexibility, and surely it allowed for different degrees of openness to innovation and foreign influences. Confucianism itself emerged as the winner in the market for ideas during the Qin (221–207 BC) and the subsequent Western Han dynasties (202 BC–9 AD) and the later or Eastern Han dynasty (25– 220 AD). During the era of the warring states, a competitive market for ideas existed in which adherents of different schools tried to "persuade one ruler after another that their particular Way was best suited as a guideline for political action" (Cohen, 2012, pp. 36–37). With unification, a convergence to a particular set of ideas was imposed, and arguably a coherent single interpretation "of the constitution of the world" emerged in Han China, which lasted until modernization.[18] The Confucian view held that social and political stability and continuity were fundamental values and objects of

---

[18] Alford (1995, pp. 18–29) links the absence of intellectual property rights in China to a "sense of power of past," in which the rules of propriety (*li*) had been inherited from the ancients and the imperial structures were legitimized by the past. As a consequence, he argues, the need to interact with the past and control access to it restricted the extent to which anyone except in an official capacity was allowed to limit access to it (Alford, 1995, p. 25). He cites as evidence Confucius himself on his *Analects*: "I transmit rather than create. I believe in and love the Ancients." Alford's argument implies that the establishment of copyright in Europe by itself signals a triumph of the moderns, because new knowledge and ideas were now regarded as valuable property, and the absence of copyright in China signified the opposite.

social policy, and thought of proper government as directed toward virtue and justice as opposed to disruptive progress.[19]

Needham (1969a, p. 119) argued that there was a certain spontaneous homeostasis about Chinese society, and good historical materialist that he was, attributed it first and foremost to the nature of agriculture and the need for large-scale hydraulic control. But the triumph of the conservative ideology was to some extent contingent, as was any outcome in a competitive market for ideas. Arguments about interpretation took place repeatedly, but the fundamental outlines of Chinese intellectual life remained unchallenged (Cohen, 2012, p. 37). Its main competitor was Mohism, and some scholars have felt that had Mohism not lost the battle and vanished almost completely from the Chinese market for ideas, Chinese history might have looked very different.[20]

Daoism remained highly influential in Chinese history, and to some extent was a rival of Confucianism. Daoism rose and declined in the long course of Chinese history, but finally fell out of favor in the Qing dynasty. Needham felt that Daoism was more empirical and respectful of technology and craftsmanship, and thus had a strong positive effect on technological progress in China. No Confucian scholar would ever stoop down to the details of manual labor, he felt, whereas for the Daoist this was part of the "Way" (Ronan and Needham, 1978, pp. 85–113). Needham and Bodde have both pointed to the somewhat paradoxical support of Daoism for manual labor and craftsmanship coupled to its putative distrust of technological innovation. Needham explained the paradox by noting that they objected to the social abuses that technological innovation made possible (Ronan and Needham, 1978, pp. 106–7). The sharp contrast he drew between Daoism and Confucianism as far as their attitudes to science and technology has been disputed by more recent scholarship (Mote, 1999, pp. 325–26). In any event, while at times Confucianism and Daoism were antagonistic, the syncretic nature of the neo-Confucianism that emerged during the Song dynasty made the rivalry between them less prominent. As a popular religion, Daoism was quite pervasive in Chinese society, but it did not have distinct boundaries,

[19] Kublai Khan, the Yuan emperor, reputedly asked the poet and mathematician Li Ye in 1257 how the empire (which he was in the process of consolidating) should be ruled. Li responded that it should have sound institutions and just laws and procedures, and that corruption should be eliminated, so as to establish trust between the ruler and his subject. Indeed, Li explained, the recent earthquakes experienced in the Mongol region were caused by the presence of too many "whores, sycophants, and wicked people at court" (Chan and Ho, 1993, p. 321).

[20] Bodde (1991, p. 169) has argued that in that case China might eventually have developed a mechanistic philosophy and science, "perhaps in the end not too unlike that which eventually arose in Western Europe."

and the sharp religious distinctions in European religions and the fierce competition among them were absent in China.[21]

In China, after its reunification by the Mongol Yuan dynasty and the subsequent rise of the Ming in 1368, competition in the market for ideas gradually weakened, and intellectual innovation was largely constrained by the limits of accepted philosophical tenets, perpetuated by the neo-Confucian orthodoxy formulated in its ultimate form by Zhu Xi (1130–1200) in the twelfth century. Zhu was, by any definition, a true cultural entrepreneur.[22] A superlative teacher who had hundreds of students and disciples, he was also an able social organizer and had an uncanny gift to persuade and get others to implement his programs. In his lifetime, Zhu did not enjoy much success, but in the first half of the thirteenth century his views were adopted by more and more literati, and it penetrated the Imperial examinations. The Yuan and the subsequent Ming dynasties adopted his work as the ruling orthodoxy of the Chinese Empire. By the early fifteenth century this process was complete.[23]

If and when this orthodoxy was challenged, it was usually on the basis of alleged inconsistency with the classic teachings, not because it flew in the face of new observations. European advances in science did filter into China through the activity of the Jesuits, but apart from recalibrating their calendars and predicting eclipses, their impact was highly selective and not dramatic.[24] Had the Chinese authorities allowed other gates of entry for European knowledge besides the Jesuits, it is likely that the new science of Galileo and Newton might have made more of an inroad. In Ming and Qing China there was a market for ideas, but the barriers to entry were high, and the competition between intellectual incumbents and intellectual innovators was biased in favor of the former. This may sound odd in a land where there was no Holy Inquisition (though the Qing emperors at times persecuted intellectuals whom they suspected of subversion), no concepts of blasphemy or

[21] Needham (1969b, pp. 75–76) speaks of an "extraordinary syncretism" in China's religious history, in which scholars dressed up in Buddhist robes, donning Confucian hats with a Taoist staff, maintaining that the three religions "were essentially parts of one and the same truth."

[22] Bol (2008, p. 88) refers to him as "an intellectual entrepreneur" who wrote, compiled, and published a body of work that "gave Neo-Confucianism a firm textual foundation"—in other words, he coordinated and standardized a number of competing interpretations of neo-Confucianism, produced by his predecessors, especially the brothers Cheng Hao and Cheng Yi. After him, Bol notes, it is "almost right" to refer to neo-Confucianism as "Zhu Xi-ism."

[23] Bol (2008, p. 97) points to 1415, when the Yongle emperor issued the "great Compendia" of neo-Confucian learning, as the time at which the establishment of the state orthodoxy was complete and it "narrowed and closed literati minds."

[24] Deng (2009, p. 62) goes so far as to argue that the European influence on China's "knowledge stock" was hardly noticeable and that China "did not need European knowledge on a large scale."

sacrilege in the European sense. But perhaps the sharp rise of these institutions in the early modern West was a sign that in Europe the intellectual incumbents felt (justly) that they were under threat. In China the Jesuits were allowed to operate, but they were controlled and constrained at the emperor's discretion. Qian (1985, pp. 57–58), suggests, with some exaggeration, that Chinese scientists in Ming and Qing times were wholly focused on "textual and archaeological research," and that instead of advancing science, the Chinese were obsessed with their history. He adds that "one can imagine that a man who advocated an experimental, critical methodology would look an eccentric to the public as well as to his peers."

Such a skeptical attitude toward intellectual innovators surely existed in Europe as well, but the Republic of Letters provided an institution in which innovation, even radical innovation, was not only not frowned upon but even encouraged. Such attitudes were perhaps held only by a minority of the entire set of intellectuals, many of whom remained quite conservative and backward-looking. But there were enough of them to overcome the built-in inertia of intellectual systems, and arguably that was not the case in China. As Derk Bodde (1991, p. 190) has maintained, the greater intensity of the persecutions of heretics in Europe indicated a highly diverse and competitive intellectual environment "peculiarly favorable to scientific development." It remains an open question whether the conservative bent of Chinese learning dominated because the resistance to radical innovations in China was stronger, and that therefore the number and energy of innovators and game-changing intellectual entrepreneurs were lower than in Europe.

The Chinese experience illustrates the fact that a competitive and open market for ideas was not the only road to progress in useful knowledge, it was just the most sustainable and effective one. When a dominant single ruler sponsored and encouraged top-flight scientists, useful knowledge could advance significantly. The Yuan Emperor Kublai Khan, much like European rulers three centuries later, provided patronage to a number of important engineers and scientists, of whom the brilliant and prodigiously creative polymath Guo Shoujing (1231–1316) is the best known. Guo was an outstanding hydraulic engineer and mathematician, and the emperor made heavy use of his skills on projects including the repair of the Grand Canal that supplied Beijing with grain and the redesign of the Chinese calendar, a matter of supreme importance to the rulers. His astronomical instruments and clocks continued the grand traditions of the Song dynasty and his armillary spheres were still in existence in the early seventeenth century when they were described by Matteo Ricci.[25] Yet Guo's work can equally be seen as a sign of

---

[25] Among the other engineers and scientists sponsored by the Yuan, Liu Bingshong (1216–1274) should be mentioned as the engineer who planned and designed the city of Dadu (now Beijing) as the capital of the new dynasty. The mathematician Li Ye (also known as Li Zhi or Li Chih, 1192–1279) also enjoyed the patronage of Kublai Khan, though he soon retired from it, citing ill health. Much as was the case in Europe, imperial patronage in China involved access

the fragility of the institutional setup of monopolistic patronage; when the regime changed in 1368, few talented Chinese engineers and scientists had the opportunities that Guo had. Needham comments on his work on spherical trigonometry that after Guo's time, no progress of any importance was made until the arrival of the Jesuits from Europe and that Guo's astronomy "suffered in the general standstill of science during the Ming" (Ronan and Needham, 1981, pp. 45, 82).[26]

Although the term "standstill" may overstate the case, there is a consensus that the cultural climate rigidified in Ming and Qing China, and became increasingly unaccommodating to intellectual innovation. Whereas in Europe the victory of the moderns relegated the classical canon to a position in which the classics were admired and taught but ancient science was treated with skepticism, in China the two schools fought to a stalemate. The institutions simply differed. The Chinese State was far less despotic and oppressive than some have depicted it (for example, Balazs, 1964, pp. 3–27, who views imperial China as an proto-totalitarian bureaucracy). Ming and Qing China was a decentralized market economy with a centralized imperial bureaucracy, the ultimate culmination of the *junxian* (top-down) administrative system, which encouraged a commercial economy with relatively free markets, even if toward the end it suffered from an increasingly ineffective political authority (Sng, 2014). It did not, however, have to compete with neighboring states for the best citizens and generals. Stability and domestic peace were increasingly regarded as an overriding value, and this included intellectual stability. The neo-Confucian annotated "four books" (*Sishu Jizhu*), compiled by Zhu Xi in the twelfth century, remained as rigid a canon as the West ever had.[27] It became a kind of dynastic ideology, a formal alliance between the politics of status quo and a conservative philosophy forged under the Ming and carried to its extremes by the Qing.[28] More important, the kind of heterodox and iconoclastic writers such as Ramus, Copernicus, and Bacon, who overthrew conventional wisdom in Europe in the sixteenth and early seventeenth centuries, did not succeed in China to a degree comparable with Europe. Unlike Europe, there was no competitive political pluralism that heretics and intellectual innovators could exploit to create an open and competitive market for ideas.

---

to the advice and wisdom to scholars renowned for their sagacity and erudition.

[26] Ho (1993, p. 299) agrees that Guo may be regarded as the last of the great traditional astronomers and mathematicians in Chinese history.

[27] As Bol (2008, pp. 105–6) points out, the four Zhu Xi books (which included the *Analects* and Mencius's dialogues) partially supplanted the "five classics," which previously had occupied central stage.

[28] The terms "dynastic ideology" and "dynastic orthodoxy" to describe the culture of intellectuals in Imperial China are due to Elman (2000, pp. 67, 70) and capture very well the synergy between court, the bureaucracy, and the examination system that perpetuated it.

Of course, dissent and critique of Chinese orthodoxy did occur in some corners. Thus for instance Yan Yuan (1635–1704), head of an academy in Hopei, rejected much of the neo-Confucian doctrines of Zhu Xi and saw them as sterile ivory-tower exercises. Instead, he harked back to earlier classical texts in which Confucian learning had been, in his view, more practical. The curriculum he put in place included more mathematics, archery, wrestling, and geography. Yan was just as disrespectful of Zhu Xi as some of his contemporaries in Europe were of their classical authorities (Ching, 2000, pp. 197–198). His critique, and that of his main follower Li Gong (1659–1733), was that Zhu had misread the classics, and much of their work was based on textual critiques. Their dissent did not really catch on in the Chinese market for ideas, and the anti-Zhu movement in China never became very influential among Chinese intellectuals, much less in the state bureaucracy. The civil service remained loyal to the neo-Confucian orthodoxy, and there was never any danger of an intellectual undermining of the political status quo in the same way that the European Enlightenment undermined autocratic rule in Western Europe.

China was a meritocracy in its own way. The system of the anonymous imperial examinations (*keju*) tested candidates mostly on their knowledge of the classical canon. In its early stages, the meritocracy was set up to curtail the power of entrenched aristocrats in the politics of the central government and seems to have worked well. Many of the leading intellectuals of the Song dynasty rose to occupy leading positions through the examination system. These include Zhu Xi himself, his predecessors the Cheng brothers—Cheng Hao (1032–1085) and Cheng Yi (1033–1107)—and the Su brothers (two other leading *literati* in the eleventh century), as well as the influential sixteenth-century critic of Zhu's thought, Wang Yangming. Elman (2000, p. 14) summarizes the rise of the examination system in Tang and Song years as the transformation of the *Shih* (the class of gentry-literati) "from men of good birth to men of culture." Ability rather than hereditary ascription became the criterion for advancement in government.

As often happens, however, institutions that were established originally for one purpose end up having very different and probably unanticipated consequences. The imperial service examination system eventually turned into a powerful tool to defend incumbent literati against the threat of intellectual innovators who threatened their political influence and the value of their human capital. Ironically, Zhu Xi and other founding fathers of neo-Confucianism criticized rote learning as useless for intellectual development, yet the core of the imperial examination system was the mindless memorization of Zhu Xi's commentaries on which every ambitious Chinese lad had to waste his childhood (Elman, 2000, pp. 261–69, 373). The Mandarin civil service examinations, Needham insisted with some hyperbole, caused the system to "perpetuate itself through ten thousand generations" (Needham,

1969a, p. 202).[29] These examinations, another scholar has argued, remained the instrument through which the ancient texts became "an instrument of repressive conformity" (Huang, 1981, p. 210).[30] In a society in which public office remained "the most important source of prestige and wealth" (Brandt, Ma, and Rawski, 2014, p. 77), the best and brightest young men allocated their time and efforts to preparing for these examinations. More precisely, many historians believe that it was "a test of refined literacy," and its curriculum became increasingly disjoint from the administrative skills that those who passed had to acquire (Rowe, 2009, p. 46) although questions about law and policy remained on the examinations during the Ming dynasty (Elman, 2013, pp. 250–79). In the absence of any serious threat to the monopoly of power, Nathan Sivin has observed, a social system that valued civil service above every other career, philosophers ... understood the danger of proposing alternatives to the current dispensation of power" (Lloyd and Sivin, 2002, p. 245).

In a famous passage, the head of the Jesuit mission in Beijing, Matteo Ricci, wrote ca. 1600 that in China "Only such as have earned a doctor's degree or that of licentiate are admitted to take part in the government of the kingdom ... no one will labor to attain proficiency in mathematics or in medicine who has any hope of becoming prominent in the field of philosophy [that is the classics]. The result is that scarcely anyone devotes himself to these studies ... the study of mathematics and medicine are held in low esteem, because they are not fostered by honors as is the study of philosophy" (Ricci, 1953, p. 32).[31] It is now known, however, that questions on natural studies such as mathematics, astronomy, and medicine remained on the Ming civil service examination as "policy" and "natural studies"

---

[29] It is telling that in 1713 the Kangxi emperor proscribed questions dealing with natural studies in the civil examinations in an effort to keep divination and portents out of public discussion. While the Qing administration encouraged the study of historical geography, mapmaking was kept secret by the imperial authorities, a good example of how the government could limit the access to useful knowledge (Elman, 2000, p. 485). Under the Qing, natural studies and court translation projects on mathematical harmonics and astronomy were off-limits to examiners and examination candidates (Elman, 2005, p. 168). For a further discussion, see De Saeger (2008).

[30] Other scholars have similarly seen the examination as a primary explanation of the Needham Question and expressed themselves just as emphatically as Needham. "The eight-legged essay of the Ming-Qing examination system hobbled men's minds just as clearly as footbinding hobbled Chinese women" (John King Fairbank, in his preface to Qian, 1985, p. vi). Baark (2007, p. 346) concludes that the Chinese market for ideas was subservient to the political system and thus discouraged innovation and that scientific knowledge remained "susceptible to the scrutiny of 'political correctness.'"

[31] It might be added that the meritocracy, as it always does, favored the sons of the wealthy and powerful and that the rhetoric of impartiality and egalitarianism in the Confucian ideals could not reverse the obvious disadvantage that the sons of peasants, artisans, and clerks labored under compared to the sons of the gentry (Woodside and Elman, 1994, p. 546).

essays and only disappeared in Qing times (Elman, 2000, pp. 461–85; 2013, pp. 261–72). The answers, however, were more often than not backward looking: questions about calender reform were answered using dynastic histories rather than technical manuals. Technical learning, Elman explains, was not the ultimate object of the question—the candidates were expected to place such questions within the classical canon (Elman, 2013, p. 269). Moreover, natural studies were kept strictly within the neo-Confucian orthodoxy, and any intellectual innovation that threatened the political status quo was considered heterodox and led to a candidate failing his examination.

Such an approach was a prescription for stagnation. In the end, China, with all its learning and literacy, had to rely on the Jesuits to set their calendars and astronomy right. By the early eighteenth century, natural studies had disappeared from the formal curriculum. To be sure, as Bol (2008, p. 109) remarks, even if everyone taking the examinations would have to be familiar with the Four Books, that does not mean that this was all that one knew, much less that it would dictate beliefs and behavior. Moreover, the nature of the examinations changed repeatedly during the Ming and Qing dynasties, and the growing narrowness of the curriculum was not inevitable. As it happened, however, it increasingly became an agenda-setting device of incumbents to protect their turf.

The teaching of the sons of elite families in China seems rigid even by the standards of the time. Small boys were required to read and recite certain sections of the Four Books and Five Classics—the summary of the Chinese canon—in a certain sequence, a hundred times each. Rote learning supported the orthodoxy and the "rote reception of that orthodoxy" (Woodside and Elman, 1994, pp. 532–33). If the purpose was continuity and stability, however, it functioned well. The Mandarinate consisted of individuals who had voluntarily submitted to intensive indoctrination by an orthodox ideology (Rowe, 2009, p. 48). The unassailability of these texts remained the most effective bulwark against troublesome innovators. In China, Sivin has remarked, until the nineteenth century we cannot find scientists willing to abandon values and beliefs that had evolved for thousands of years in the view of "proven facts."[32] This is not to say that such conservative forms of learning were not prevalent in Europe, nor that the Chinese system was totally frozen and incapable of any reform; but because

---

[32] Oddly enough, Sivin ([1984] 2005, p. 13) has little patience with an argument that purports to explain "why China failed to beat Europe in the Scientific Revolution," namely, the predominance in China of a scholar-bureaucrat class immersed in books, faced toward the past and oriented toward human institutions rather than nature. In Europe, too, he notes, the universities were full of schoolmen and dons much like the Chinese. "They did not prevent the great changes that swept over Europe." But this argument is weak: there were conservative scholars in Europe, but they were increasingly challenged by innovators, and eventually lost out in the market for ideas. Universities may have been (with some notable exceptions) conservative and static places, but much of the intellectual fermentation took place in scientific societies, academies, and of course through private channels as part of the Republic of Letters.

of its higher levels of diversity and competition, the European market for ideas allowed innovative and nonconformist minds to thrive and eventually to generate pluralism and intellectual innovation on a scale that the Chinese system suppressed.

It is unwarranted to see the Chinese examination system as a totally rigid and fixed institution, an antimodern monolith that had crystallized in its place until its demise in the early twentieth century. Elman (2000, pp. xx, xxiv) rightly warns against such interpretations and notes that the examination system was the product of a give and take between the imperial administration and local elites that was adjusted and adapted over time to reflect new realities and needs. While the system was meant to reproduce the social, political, and cultural status quo, it was never unmitigated and absolute in its effects (Elman, 2000, p. xxix). It always involved a competitive market for ideas and attempts to challenge existing authorities in some measure. The neo-Confucians competed with their critics as well as with one another. At times, they took courageous stands against the abuse of imperial power, and attempts were made to create networks of opposition, especially at the local level (Bol, 2008, p. 151).

That said, there were clear time-tested limits to such challenges, and these limits became more stringent with the ascent of the Qing dynasty after 1644. The competitive market for ideas was hamstrung by the fundamental understanding of all philosophers that "open divergences of view were limited to area that did not threaten the political status quo" (Lloyd and Sivin, 2002, p. 245). Hence, an argument, popular in some modern historiography, that a comparison between the outcomes of the different cultural systems generating and disseminating intellectual innovations in China and in Europe is otiose because it is "teleological" and a "Eurocentric development narrative" should be dismissed as patently ahistorical—as if the Great Divergence never happened or is not worthy of an explanation, or as if cultural explanations of this sort should be ruled out a priori.

To what extent was Chinese conservatism an endogenous outcome, determined by external events? There surely was no fixed "Chinese model" that set the parameters of Chinese cultural development. Elman (2000, p. 64) asserts that the memorization of orthodox texts and rote learning modes of Chinese education were a political act in which the Han Chinese asserted the higher ground of moral truth over the warrior tribes who ruled them in the Yuan and Qing dynasties. Be that as it may, human capital was available in large quantities in China, but it was seriously misallocated—if the purpose was to augment useful knowledge and eventually generate a technology-driven process of economic development.[33] There was nothing in Chinese

---

[33] The misallocation was exacerbated by the growing rigidity of the examination system in Ming and Qing times. The highest degree, known as *Jinshi* became required for the top offices in the Civil Service. At the same time there was a substantial excess of holders of the lowest degree, *Shengyuan*, who had no chance for office. Elman (2000, p. 140) notes that the

culture that made this outcome inevitable. Between ca. 1000 and ca. 1200, indeed, China went through a period of economic and intellectual flourishing, of optimism and even a notion in progress and reason that we tend to associate with the European Enlightenment. In the Song period, a belief in improvement was much in the air in China. There was a belief in the benefits of education, the improvability of political institutions, and a faith in reason's capability to make society better (Gernet, 1982, p. 345). Some philosophers, such as Wang Anshi (1021–1086), argued that economic progress was quite possible, although his view was that it should be initiated by the state and was contingent on a reform of the bureaucracy. Others were more conservative, especially Wang's nemesis, Sima Guang (1019–1086), who opposed commercialization and any policy favoring economic progress, taking a rigid "zero-sum" approach. Wang's policies, dubbed by Morris (2010, p. 376) as "the New Deal and Reaganomics rolled into one," were progressive and clearly aimed at reforming and streamlining the Chinese economy. The struggle between the two parties in the eleventh century serves as an example that a competitive market for ideas could exist in China. Yet as Rowe (2001, p. 286) notes, in this struggle most neo-Confucians felt that Sima won "hands down."[34] While a progressive minority never quite disappeared from the Chinese intellectual stage, it always had to operate in the shadow of conservative giants.

To be sure, China was a mercantile and in some ways even a "bourgeois" society, but even more than in Europe, its merchants were conservative. As Mote (1999, pp. 764–65) stresses, the Chinese merchants did not foster an intellectual culture that encouraged radical heterodoxy. They eagerly adopted the lifestyles of the scholar-elite, and "unlike the eighteenth century European Enlightenment thinkers, they did not make war on the establishment" (Mote, 1999, p. 765). It was the ultimate *trahison de la bourgeoisie*. What Chinese elite culture created was, in the memorable phrase of Woodside and Elman (1994, p. 551) "a bittersweet wedding of Confucian/Neo-Confucian moral discourse to an imperially prescribed view of state power drawn from classical Legalism." In that culture, it was hard for the market for ideas to generate the kind of tradition-shattering innovations that the European cultural environment generated after 1500.

The cultural foundations of China's polity were rooted in a secular ideology that was inherently neither hostile nor conducive to the growth of useful knowledge. It could be either progressive or reactionary, depending on the circumstances. Morris (2010, pp. 423–26) argues that "Zhu Xi gave his

---

relative number of *shengyuan* degree holders increased from 1 licentiate per 2,200 persons in 1500 to 1 per 300 in 1700. For more on this human capital surplus, see Huang (1998, p. 108).

[34] Wang Anshi tried to reform the civil service examinations to make them more practical. He was strongly opposed by the brothers Su Shi and Su Zhe, Sima Guang's close allies. While during the Song dynasty the Wang school was dominant, the Mongol rule reestablishment of the examination system meant that in the end, the conservatives prevailed in this struggle.

age the ideas it needed" (p. 423) and that his philosophy did not cause
Chinese elite culture to become more conservative, but rather that growing
conservatism caused his ideas to become dominant (after his death, to be
sure, and under Mongolian rule). Whatever the exact causal mechanism, the
neo-Confucian project or the *Song Lixue* (School of Principle), of which Zhu's
work was the core, has been defined as a "reassertion of Chinese values"
(Mote, 1999, p. 147) in a marketplace for ideas in which the Confucian ways
were threatened by other cultural ideas. It was inherently conservative,
because it was based on a learned tradition, on exegesis and philology. It was
backward-looking and restorationist. Zhu Xi's writings mark the *summa
theologica* of neo-Confucianism and became the main material on which
prospective members of the Chinese civil service were tested.[35] The triumph
of his conservative views is often regarded as a major element in China's
inward turn by the end of the Song dynasty. In the market for ideas, competing ideologies confronted one another, and the neo-Confucianists came
out on top, especially during the Yuan (Mongol) dynasty (1279--1368), which
first abolished the examinations and then re-instated them. The neo-
Confucian orthodoxy became the main basis for the restored civil service
examinations in 1313 by decree of the Renzong emperor.[36] By the 1370s, the
exclusive emphasis on neo-Confucian texts were extended to "a degree of
orthodoxy that even Zhu Xi had not advocated" (Elman, 2000, p. 37).
Perhaps the outcome was not predetermined. Perhaps the more enlightened
ideology of Wang could have won out under different circumstances.[37]

As it turned out, late Ming and especially Qing scholarship became
increasingly conservative and backward looking. Elman (2006, pp. 36–37)
points out that eighteenth-century Chinese scholarship was reminiscent of
early Renaissance scholarship that translated ancient Greek texts into Latin
to forge a new scholastic synthesis. Yet Europeans, he notes, "went beyond
their ancient masters to make significant breakthroughs" while the Chinese
"focused on the distant past to overcome recent failures."[38] Unlike the

[35] Many China scholars have explicitly compared Zhu Xi's influence on Chinese
thought to the "sterilizing effects" in the West of the philosophy of Aristotle and Thomas Aquinas
in the late Middle Ages. The comparison with Aquinas, another great synthesizer, is of course
attractive (for example Needham, 1969b, p. 66; Gernet, 1982, p. 346). Much like Aquinas, Zhu
Xi offered what Bol (2008, p. 102) calls a coherent "unified field theory" capable of defining
wisdom and explaining both human society and heaven and earth.

[36] Even then, as Elman (2000, p. 33) points out, the victory of the Zhu Xi orthodoxy
was incomplete, and other fields remained in the curriculum. Literary ability in the ancient rhyme-
prose style was kept on the examinations until 1366.

[37] The contingent nature of the triumph of the neo-Confucian school is stressed by
Liu (1973).

[38] It seems attractive to argue, as does Goldstone (2012), that precisely because
European science first lost and then rediscovered most of its classical heritage, medieval scholars,
of whom Aquinas was the most important, had to create an ingenious but rigid and ultimately

rediscovery and resurrection of classical learning in early modern Europe, the Chinese orthodoxy never came under the withering criticism of observation and experimentation, augmented by better instruments and more advanced mathematics.

Cultural change went hand in hand with other factors. Thirteen- and fourteenth-century China was subject to a variety of exogenous shocks, such as Mongol invasions and plague. Observing the collapse of civil society around them, scholars turned more conservative because "antiquity became less a source of renewal than a source of refuge" (Morris, 2010, p. 426). However, by the time of the rise of the Ming dynasty (1368) the worst was over, and yet the Chinese did not pursue an aggressive policy of overseas expansion despite the Zheng He expeditions, nor did they seriously return to a reformist agenda in the tradition of Wang. China was able to keep Europeans and their ideas out when it wished, and Chinese intellectuals seemed on the whole more interested in reproducing the existing cultural order than in challenging it, and critics of the status quo rarely had much influence.

In China, politics was inherently conservative because most emperors and their bureaucracies found radical ideas destabilizing. Zhu Xi's neo-Confucian ideology was an instrument that maintained order and stability and it allowed the Ming and Qing dynasties to survive at a fairly low cost to society. But there was more than just a functionalist explanation for its tenacity. Choice-based cultural evolution can shed light on this tendency for conservatism. Salient event bias, driven by such horrible events as the fourteenth-century plague and the destruction inflicted on China by Genghis Khan and later by the post-1644 anti-Qing rebellions may well have led to the growing demand for stability and a positive conformist bias. The aversion to radical destabilizing ideas was probably no less pronounced among European rulers. But because they did not exert much power to direct the market for ideas, they were in the long run powerless to stop their proliferation.

The prevalence of Chinese conservatism is not a big riddle. Great respect for the inherited wisdom of the past was the default option for most societies, and the odd man out was not China but Europe, and its ever-increasing tendency to show a willingness to overthrow old ideas if they were found to be unacceptable. What mattered here was that in Europe they were found unacceptable not only because the economic and social realities were changing, but because they were tested by evidence and logic and more often than not found to be incorrect, inconsistent, or unproven. The better

fragile syncretic construct that reconciled existing religious dogma with classical knowledge. China, India and Islam, he maintains, never lost their classical dogma and responded to challenges by an intellectual retrenchment. In the seventeenth century, because of internal disorders in all Asian empires (as in Counter-Reformation Europe), Goldstone argues, "a conservative enforcement of orthodox and religious authorities took over as a means to keep order."

Europeans got at observing, experimenting, and computing, the more impertinent they became about the wisdom of ancient venerable authorities. As we have seen, this deep skepticism in Europe was the flip side of the belief in progress. Was there such a belief in Chinese culture? Needham argued that in Song China this was very much the case. The "idea of cumulative dis-interested cooperative enterprise in amassing scientific information was much more customary in medieval China than anywhere in the pre- Renaissance West," he wrote, adding that "no mathematician or astronomer in any Chinese century would have dreamed of denying a continual progress and improvement in the sciences they professed" (Needham, 1969a, p. 277). Other scholars have disagreed: Bodde pointed out that Daoist thought felt overall that if there was a trend in history at all, it led from paradise to corruption. Accordingly the decline began only after early sage-kings had completed their "civilizing work" on society and that while both "cyclical" and "linear" dynamics can be found in Chinese reflections on history, the cyclical element clearly dominated (Bodde, 1991, pp. 122–33). In general, most Chinese thinkers, insofar that they recognized a trend, felt that the past was better than the present or that at worst history was a cyclical but station-ary process. For the neo-Confucians, who gained definitive control of the intellectual world of China under the Ming, antiquity was the ideal period, followed by a decline, with no guarantee that the world would ever be better (Bol, 2008, p. 101). Strikingly, Needham's evidence for belief in progress is entirely taken from pre-Ming China, and the idea withered in China just as it was slowly but certainly emerging triumphant in parts of Europe.

After the Song, then, China did not have a very competitive market for ideas, and incumbents were able to erect high barriers to entry to potential entrants who wanted to contest the status quo and become cultural entre-preneurs. In China, science remained in many ways an activity controlled and regulated by the state administration. It would be incorrect to say that nothing like a Chinese Republic of Letters existed: there was a community of scholars who corresponded with one another, read one another's publi-cations, and formed a scholarly network dedicated to a shared collection of Confucian learning (McDermott, 2006, p. 118). Although some serious disputes arose among Chinese intellectuals, truly radical innovations that re-presented a complete rejection of previous paradigms and the classical canon did not occur. There was no Chinese Paracelsus, Descartes, or Spinoza. Ideas were much less contestable, and the Chinese intellectual community lacked autonomy and a competitive marketplace in which intellectual consumers exercised their cultural choices. Moreover, whereas in Europe useful knowl-edge of all kinds was made increasingly accessible as people came to realize that its dissemination would maximize its social benefits, in China, what Catherine Jami (2012, p. 389) has called "the Imperial Monopoly" on scholarship determined much of what went on in the market for ideas. Nor was there a competitive states system, which would have forced the authorities to adopt and encourage innovations, however reluctantly, so that they could continue to hold their own in international affairs.[39]

One reason for the low competitiveness of the Chinese market for ideas was that the mobility across political boundaries was rarely an option in China. Consider the example of the seventeenth-century Chinese scholar Zhu Shunshui (Chu Shun-shui, 1600–1682), one of the few Chinese intellectuals who can be compared with a European intellectual in his itinerancy. His knowledge was quite broad and extended to fields of practical knowledge such as architecture and crafts. Fleeing from China (he had remained a supporter of the Ming dynasty, overthrown in 1644), he arrived first in Annam (Vietnam) and then in Japan, where he had quite a following and eventually became advisor and mentor to the daimyo Mitsukuni. Zhu, as Julia Ching notes, was hardly a purely abstract philosopher, but "the investigation of things referred less to the metaphysical understanding of principle of material forces, and more to coping with concrete situations." At the same time, the extension of knowledge applied not only to knowledge of the Confucian classics, but also to "all that is useful in life" (Ching, 1979, p. 217). This, again, sounds promising, but Zhu's work remained unknown in China until his rediscovery in the late nineteenth century. Having left his homeland, he became a nonentity; this is in sharp contrast with Europe where intellectual reputations disregarded national boundaries.

Other explanations for the conservative bias in Chinese culture have been put forward. Some of those explanations strike one today as a bit bizarre. One of the most eminent Sinologists of our time, Derk Bodde (1991), has made a startling argument in which he points to the Chinese language as an impediment to a more innovative culture. He pointed out the inherent weaknesses of the Chinese language as a mode of transmitting precise information and its built-in conservative mechanisms. The Chinese language, he felt, placed a number of obstacles in the way of the growth of useful knowledge in China. One was the large gap between literary Chinese and spoken Chinese. This made written documents far less accessible for people without considerable training and thus made it difficult for artisans and technicians to draw on the useful knowledge accumulated by scholars and scientists. One might wonder whether the gap between written Latin and the spoken vernaculars in Europe was not at least as large. Second, he argues that the absence

---

[39] A striking case is the one of Hong Lianji (Hung Liang-Chi, 1746–1809), a powerful intellectual who launched a strong critique of the Qing dynasty and was sentenced to death, a sentence commuted to exile (and soon pardoned). Hong is known as the "Chinese Malthus" for producing an essay—in the same year as the first edition of Malthus's famous *Essay on Population*—making very similar points. The difference was in its reception. While Malthus became something of a celebrity in his time, respected and honored, his work widely discussed and read all over Europe, Chinese scholars disregarded Hong's work despite the rapid population growth in the century before his work and the clear signs of population pressure in nineteenth-century China (Silberman, 1960, pp. 257–60).

of inflection and punctuation created considerable ambiguity over what texts exactly meant. While Bodde's critics are right to point out that much of this ambiguity could be resolved if one knew the context, the point is that efficient communication must be able to provide as much information as possible with little context. Furthermore, the lack of alphabetization handicapped, in his view, the organization and classification of knowledge. Finally, Bodde pointed out that written Chinese was itself a formidably conservative force: it created a cultural uniformity over time and space that was the reverse of the dynamic diversity we observe in Europe. In his view, the Chinese characters "achieved a prestige and mystique ... unrivaled in any other civilization ... Ideologically the effect of [Chinese literary language] was strongly conservative ... and discouraged cultural variation especially within the small but dominant literate minority" (Bodde, 1991, p. 90). The way a nineteenth-century official would describe Western barbarians was very similar in metaphor and illustration to the way this would be done by a Han statesman two millennia earlier (Bodde, 1991, p. 31). Whether language was itself an autonomous factor affecting culture, or whether it was a reflection of deeper conservative forces remains unresolved.[40]

The other perplexing issue in Chinese culture was Chinese attitudes toward Western knowledge and their ambiguity about learning from Westerners. To what extent was the development of Chinese useful knowledge impeded by their suspicion of foreign ideas? The hostility of Chinese elites to "barbaric" cultural elements can surely be overstated. Even David S. Landes (1998, pp. 341–42), who stresses that the rejection of foreign technology was all the more serious because China itself had slipped into a "technological and scientific torpor," concedes that "intellectual xenophobia did not apply to all Chinese." As Elman (2005) has demonstrated in detail, for much of the seventeenth century Jesuit mathematicians and astronomers taught the Chinese literati a great deal. But in the end it all depended on the goodwill of the emperor and his court, and they remained suspicious of the Jesuits' religious objectives and eventually turned against them.

---

[40] It is telling that Bodde, after explaining at length that the absence of punctuation in Chinese was a recondite instrument to ensure that communication remained within a group of insiders rather than reached a large number of people, then admits that punctuation in Chinese became universal in the twentieth century as a result of Western influence.

Initially, the Jesuits contributed a great deal to China.[41] The Jesuits came to China to spread Catholicism, not to disseminate best-practice Western science and technology. After 1670, moreover, their knowledge was no longer at the cutting edge (Elman, 2005, pp. 105, 148). The Jesuits in Europe became gradually weaker, and much of the growth of useful knowledge in Europe passed them by, as they tried to stick to outdated Aristotelian notions to avoid conflict with the doctrinaire orthodoxy of the Holy See. George Macartney commented in his journals in 1793 that the Jesuits in China did not grasp Newtonian science and knew little math. Western knowledge was deemed to be part and parcel of Europe's religious and political objectives, and by the early eighteenth century a partial reaction set in: the Kangxi emperor banned all questions on natural studies from the civil service examination and his successor, the Yongzheng emperor, began a closed door policy that lasted until after the Opium Wars in the 1840s (Elman, 2005, p. 168).

The dependence on the Jesuits illustrates a basic issue with Chinese importation of Western culture: it had to be controlled, filtered, and sorted by the authorities, and so the narrow channel of Jesuit missionaries suited them well, but it also limited what they could learn. One could wonder what prevented the Chinese from hiring foreign engineers and mathematicians and sending ambassadors and spies to Amsterdam, Paris, and London to study best-practice European useful knowledge in the same way that the Russians and later the Japanese did. It is hard not to see a supreme irony in the role of the Jesuits in China: while in Europe after 1600 they constituted a conservative force fighting rearguard actions to maintain a moribund body of obsolete knowledge, in China they would still have been considered a force for progress. It is worth noting that the Jesuits did not expose China to the heliocentric view of the world till 1760. Sivin ([1973] 1995, p. 13) summarized the irony by noting that "although the Jesuits' Chinese writings at first reflected conservative but open-minded current thinking, they gradually became hopelessly obsolete, out of touch with practice as well as theory. But the constraints under which they wrote, and the lack of competition from lay

[41] Mote (1999, p. 959) goes so far as to assert that the quality of the Jesuits at the Chinese court was as good as anything that European learning could offer anywhere. This may have been partially true for the years that the ingenious Flemish Jesuit Ferdinand Verbiest was at the early Qing court (1659–1688), although even Verbiest was constrained by his Jesuit commitments to a Tychonic world view, and by the 1650s both the instrumentation and the theory the Jesuits deployed in China were obsolete. While he managed to convince the Kangxi emperor in 1670 to prefer his calendar to that of the Chinese astronomer Yang Guangxian, his attempts to place Western (mostly Aristotelian) philosophy and science on the agenda for the revision of the imperial examinations curriculum were declined by the same emperor in 1683 (Elman, 2005, pp. 103, 146; Kurz, 2011, pp. 79–88).

authors, ... meant that no one acknowledged or corrected crucial mis-statements before the mid-nineteenth century."[42]

Any argument based on some inherent superiority of Western or Christian culture flies into the face of much of history.[43] The best counter-example is of course the prodigious flourishing of China's material culture during the Song dynasty in the eleventh and twelfth centuries, during which China came, in some views, within a hair's width of embarking on an Industrial Revolution. Certainly, if we see the British Industrial Revolution as an era of increased use of fossil fuels, iron, textiles, improved transportation, rising agricultural productivity, and enhanced internal commerce, China in the Song era qualified. It will remain a long and hard debate to determine why Song China, instead of taking off and becoming the workshop of the world, slid back into a technologically more stagnant economy. China's inability to withstand the attacks of nomads and semi-nomads, such as the Jurchen and Mongols, played a major role. But this raises the question of why such a powerful and ingenious society was unable to develop the kind of defense that would keep invaders at bay.[44] Morris's (2010, p. 392) description of the decline of China in late Song years as the result of the "four horsemen of the apocalypse that stalked China in the thirteenth century"—migration, the collapse of the state, famine, and disease—is evocative, but in the end does not explain why the nation did not bounce back after peace was restored under the Ming after 1368.

The alternative interpretation is that the positive-feedback self-reinforcing explosive technological trajectory experienced by Britain and Europe after 1750 was inherently a radically novel phenomenon, a sui generis, unlike the earlier technological efflorescences that Song China, Renaissance Europe, and other societies had experienced (Goldstone, 2002). Cohen (2012, p. 28), in his survey of the rise of modern science, repeatedly touches upon the issue of a slowing-down of scientific flourishing, and for all episodes of such advances that subsequently fizzled out, his explanation is "what else would you expect?" In that interpretation, an Industrial Revolution was never in the cards for Song China. A free and open market for ideas, such as emerged in Europe in the sixteenth century, leading eventually to the Enlightenment and a cultural transformation that created a new set of attitudes toward useful knowledge did not develop in China—or anywhere else.

---

[42] Needham, 1956, p. 294, notes that "one of the ironies of histories is that the Jesuits were proud of introducing to China the correct [Aristotelian] doctrine of the four elements–just half a century before Europe gave it up forever."

[43] For a recent example of such theories, see Stark (2003, 2005).

[44] To some extent, of course, it did. With the disastrous fall of Kaifeng, its capital and industrial center in 1127 to the Jurchen, the Song capital moved southeast to Hangzhou establishing the Southern Song, which was besieged and captured in 1276 by Mongols but remained a large and thriving city under the Yuan dynasty (1279–1368).

Such an explanation is far from arguing that it *could* never have taken place given enough time, though it is unlikely that its shape would have been very similar to what actually emerged. The question is a bit like whether some form of intelligent life on the planet would ever have emerged if *homo sapiens* had never emerged and become the dominant species. Presumably the answer is that given enough time, this is quite likely, but whatever different culture would have emerged was unlikely to have written the *Eroica* symphony or *Finnegans Wake*. In the political configuration in Europe, a fragmented political system combined with an intellectual unity ensconced in the transnational Republic of Letters created unique opportunities for dramatic cultural changes. Such changes were led and coordinated by cultural entrepreneurs from Luther and Paracelsus to Marx and Darwin. The most important product of these changes was the European Enlightenment.

The importance of the Enlightenment for Europe's subsequent economic development goes beyond its impact on the exploitation of useful knowledge for material progress, the essence of the Industrial Enlightenment. It also codified and formalized the kind of institutions any society needed to maintain its technological momentum: the rule of law, checks and balances on the executive, and severe sanctions on more blatant and harmful forms of rent-seeking through corruption and highly inefficient forms of redistribution, although the Enlightenment was never able to eradicate rent-seeking altogether. As Brandt, Ma, and Rawski (2014) make clear, such institutions were lacking in post-1750 China and prevented it from taking advantage of the opportunities created by technological progress in the West, the way Japan did. Qing China, as already noted, was above all a society in which the major players sought "stability and prosperity" (Brandt, Ma, and Rawski, 2014, p. 105). The historical irony is that prosperity as it was experienced after 1750 required creative destruction, the very opposite of social and economic stability.

In the pre-1750 economies, periods of relative rapid growth and rising prosperity occurred quite frequently. The problem with these earlier efflorescences was always negative feedback: prosperity and development bred the very forces that would undo it. The best known of those forces is Malthusian: population growth led to resource pressure and thus to a variety of positive checks such as environmental disasters, famines, and diseases that would wipe out any progress. The other form of negative feedback was institutional: the prosperity of a region or a society attracted predators and parasites, both external (greedy and well-armed neighbors, many of them tough horsemen or sailors) and internal (corrupt officials, rapacious rulers and priests, and various other rent-seekers). In the end such parasites tended to slaughter many golden-egg-laying geese, not just by destroying infrastructural capital but by permanently changing the incentives of society to engage in hard work and investment, a classic example of salient event bias (see chapter 5). In that sense, to be sure, culture is endogenous to such events, but this feedback tends to amplify the economic consequence of a Genghis

Khan or a Tamerlane. It is hard to know which of those two feedbacks, the demographic or the institutional, was more important in the decline of Song China. None of this means that prosperity could not be sustained for many decades or even centuries. Many economies were able to put off negative feedback through a variety of mechanisms. They could mitigate the nemesis of diminishing returns by intensifying agriculture, increasing the real and effective supply of land by eliminating fallows and double-cropping; they could slow down the growth of population by a variety of preventive means, from postponing first marriage to infanticide; they could try to buy off potential invaders or hire mercenaries to fight them.

None of those solutions worked in the long run, because a third fundamental ceiling to economic growth remained in place: an overly narrow epistemic base of technology, that is to say, a lack of understanding of why production techniques in use actually worked. It was only in the nineteenth and twentieth centuries that the ceiling was broken through in the Western world, in large part caused by the changing cultural beliefs about useful knowledge and how it was deployed in the economy which created a positive feedback mechanism (Mokyr, 2002). These changing beliefs about science and technology were complemented by changing views about the role of the state, law and order, violence, and human rights that the Enlightenment triggered (Pinker, 2011, pp. 133–34, 184–86).

As late as the middle of the seventeenth century, the differences between the epistemic bases on which technology rested in the West and China were probably not large.[45] The divergence between Europe and China occurred because the culture that generated and diffused useful knowledge in Europe and the institutions that supported it in the age of Enlightenment caused the epistemic bases of technology to become eventually ever wider. Needham (1954, p. 18), at the very outset of his monumental magnum opus, states that the purpose of his work was to understand why Chinese science, both ancient and medieval, showed the clearest development of experimental and observational inductive science, "though they were always interpreted by theories and hypotheses of primitive type." Yet before the seventeenth century, Europe was not all that different. Derk Bodde makes this point strongly when he claims that by 1668, "the traditional technologies of Europe and China alike were both based more on practice than on theory and had both reached approximately the highest point possible for such technologies before the advent of modern science" (Bodde, 1991, p. 235). Whatever is meant by "theory" here, the gap in propositional knowledge was becoming wider. By 1700, Europeans had already vastly expanded the horizons of their useful knowledge in geography, hydraulics, optics, the manipulation of dom-

---

[45] Like Needham, Bodde seems too closely wedded to a linear connection between "scientific knowledge" and technical progress. His view that "in 1687 Newton's *Principia* was published ... less than a century after, steam was beginning to turn the wheels of Britain" implies a linear causal connection between the two that cannot be defended (Bodde, 1991, p. 235).

esticated animals, graphical representation, astronomy, scientific instruments, crop rotations, and so on. Propositional knowledge and prescriptive knowledge mutually reinforced each other. This coevolution created a self-reinforcing virtuous cycle that created the rapidly growing gap between West and East in technology in a relatively short time in the late eighteenth and early nineteenth centuries.[46]

We will never know whether without the rise of the West, the Orient would have been able to replicate something similar, given enough time. It seems unlikely, but there is no way of knowing if they would have stumbled upon steam power or the germ theory of disease. It is true that the consensus of modern scholarship has remained of the opinion that by 1800 the bulk of output in Chinese industry employed a technology very little different from that under the Song (Richardson, 1999, pp. 54–55). At the level of the economy as a whole, this is an overstatement: Chinese agriculture adopted new crops such as peanuts and sweet potatoes, some of which were introduced by the intercontinental ecological arbitrage practiced by European explorers in the sixteenth century. Stagnation is therefore too strong a word, but comparing Chinese technological achievements not only with those of the West but also with its own successes during the Song clearly indicates a decelerating progress. Elvin (1996, p. 93), after studying the missed opportunities of hydraulic technology adoption in China, concludes that there were strong and perceived needs, and few constraints in adopting such techniques. And yet there was minimal advance. China's technological somnolence was rudely interrupted by the exposure to Western technology in the nineteenth century.

The failure of radically heterodox views to catch on in China underlines the fundamental difference between China and Europe: there were repressive and reactionary regimes galore in Europe, but the interstate competitiveness constrained their ability to enforce a specific orthodoxy. Such a suppression would have negative effects on their military power and political prestige, and it might deprive them of some of their most useful citizens. If all rulers had been rational, therefore, we would never have seen any suppression in Europe. In fact, such events did occur ("off the equilibrium path" as economists would call it), the most notorious being the revocation of the edict of Nantes in 1685 in France. But in Europe's institutional environment, all such decisions did was to shift around where intellectual innovation would occur, but it could not suppress it altogether. France's Huguenots, as we have seen, simply took their creativity elsewhere. In short, what was missing in China's institutions was a high level of competitiveness, both in the market for ideas and at the level of political power.

[46] Bodde (1991, p. 362) provides a list of Chinese inventions, such as the astronomical clock, mathematical navigation, and the seismograph, which became "magnificent dead ends" (to use David Landes's term) and were not further developed. Bodde ascribes this to a Chinese lack of interest in "theory."

Other cultural answers in the literature to the question of why Chinese science after 1600 moved at a slower pace than Europe's have been proposed. Needham was the first to argue cogently that because China did not have a strong theistic tradition with a Supreme Lawgiver, it never established the idea of a universal law of nature. Instead, he felt, they believed in an organic world of primary forces that interacted organically much like an endocrine system in which causality is hard to pin down. He noted that modern science cannot do without a set of mechanical forces in the ways that Galileo and Newton formulated them (Needham, 1969a, p. 311). While he conceded that the idea of a Supreme Being was not absent in China, it was "depersonalized" and "lacking in ideas of creativity." As a result, the Chinese lacked the concept of a rational celestial legislator whose laws could be deciphered by people using scientific methods (Needham, 1969a, p. 328).

How serious was this obstacle? The idea that there are regularities in nature that are predictable and exploitable is too obvious to be completely cast aside by any culture, and no production is possible without it.[47] Whether these laws are truly universal or are just usable empirical regularities may matter less to technology than to phenomenology. Belief in an omnipotent being that controls all laws can backfire, as it can lead to occasionalism and other metaphysical beliefs that get in the way of progress. Translation becomes a key here, as the Chinese employ words like *thien fa* (laws of heaven), yet, as Needham insisted, these are laws without a lawgiver. In that sense, of course, the Chinese may have been closer to a twentieth-century way of thinking about nature than to the thinking of Kepler and Newton.[48] For the ancient Chinese, the world looked more like a "vast organism, with all parts cooperating in a mutual service which is perfect freedom" (Ronan and Needham, 1978, p. 167).

To sum up, then, what could explain the Needham puzzle? One tantalizing clue is a famous remark by Nathan Sivin that China had sciences but no Science (Sivin [1984], 2005, p. 4). In this view, China paradoxically lacked a unifying single coordinating mechanism such as a competitive market in which new ideas were tested. In Europe, despite the political fragmentation,

---

[47] Needham (1969a, p. 322) cites Wang Pi, a Chinese writer from 240 AD: "We do not see Heaven command the four seasons and yet they do not swerve from their course, so we also do not see the sage ordering the people about, and yet they obey and spontaneously serve him." The thought, he adds, is extremely Chinese. Yet the regularity of the seasons can be interpreted as a "law" even if it is unclear who legislated it. Other texts confirm the recognition of such regularities (*Ch'ang*) such as the one cited in Bodde (1991, pp. 332–43). Bodde, however, stresses that such texts do not invalidate Needham's belief in the absence of a Chinese equivalent of natural laws, because such views remained a minority view and could not have survived the rise of neo-Confucian thinking from the eleventh century on.

[48] The idea that the ancient world failed to come up with laws of nature because of the absence of an single divine lawgiver is similarly dismissed by Wootton (2015, p. 378), pointing to the profound influence of such thinkers as Lucretius on seventeenth-century science.

the market for ideas worked well enough to allow new entrants to challenge incumbents. At times, such new entrants coordinated a wholesale overthrow of a paradigm. Europe's market for ideas allowed such cultural entrepreneurs to flourish, even if they were perhaps few and far between. Such a focal point in a market for ideas, as long as it does not degenerate into an incontestible authority figure, is a sign of a well-functioning competitive market (comparable in some ways to a single price). The competitive process compared the logic and evidence, and the various biases of cultural evolution ended up settling on certain paradigmatic beliefs, coordinated on key players. Isaac Newton played exactly that role, as did Paracelsus, Vesalius, Descartes, Galileo, Lavoisier, Linnaeus, Darwin, Einstein and numerous others. What made such successful entrepreneurs possible was that in Europe the market for ideas was not just contestable, but that ideas were actually continually contested. Intellectual sacred cows were increasingly being led to the slaughterhouse of evidence.

What early European intellectuals did to Aristotle, Ptolemy, and Galen, their Ming-Qing colleagues could not do to Confucius, Mencius, and Xunzi until the waning days of the empire in the closing decades of the nineteenth century. In China, the tradition of respect for classical leaning was even stronger that in Europe. Nathan Sivin has pointed out that it was widely accepted that the Chinese ancient classics "contained all possible wisdom"and that "scientific pursuits on China thus did not aim at stepwise approximation to an objective reality but a recovery of what archaic sages already knew" (Lloyd and Sivin, 2002, p. 193).

Moreover, the rise of open science in Europe almost guaranteed that existing knowledge would not disappear or be forgotten the same way that many pieces of useful knowledge that existed in classical civilization were no longer extant in medieval Europe. In China, despite a vibrant intellectual life, some techniques—most famously in shipbuilding and clockmaking—seem to have fallen into disuse and disappeared, possibly as those few who possessed the knowledge died before the knowledge was passed on and no documents or models were preserved. Perhaps the best example was the famed Su Sung clock, probably the most advanced and sophisticated water-driven clock ever built, yet by the time the Jesuits arrived in China the memory of it had disappeared. It was, in Landes's felicitous if slightly inaccurate phrase, "a magnificent dead end." It is worth reciting his explanation for the astonishing disappearance of what appears to have been a technological triumph: "there was no marketplace of ideas, no diffusion or exchange of knowledge, no continuing and growing pool of skills or information—hence a very uneven transmission of knowledge from one generation to the next" (Landes, 1983, p. 33).[49] Open science was the best guarantee for the continuous cumulative nature of the useful knowledge: every discovery and every invention was expected to be placed in the public realm. The Patent Offices of Europe, despite their declared purpose as an organization that constrained the adoption of new technology, reinforced this trend, since detailed descriptions of inventions had to be submitted with the applications.

[49] Landes's interpretation of Chinese technological history could be seen as one-sided and a bit simplistic; he fails to mention the continued improvement of Chinese clocks under the Yuan (Mongol) dynasty in the thirteenth and fourteenth centuries, especially through the work of Guo Shoujing. Yet even experts critical of Landes's approach concede that after the fall of the Yuan, while clockmaking was not altogether eradicated, there remained little evidence of its former glory: "when the Jesuits arrived carrying their 'bells that rang by themselves,' there was little evidence remaining to disprove their impression that the Chinese had no knowledge of clockwork" (Pagani, 2001, pp. 12–15)

Chapter 17

China and the Enlightenment

If the argument that the European Enlightenment was a critical factor in Europe's subsequent development is accepted, even in part, the question why other civilizations did not undergo a similar transformation must arise. One answer is that it would be Eurocentric to suggest that just because Europe experienced this cultural transformation and just because it was a stage in the path to economic growth, no other paths were available. Another argument, which I find more appealing, is that China indeed experienced a movement comparable to the European Enlightenment, but it was sufficiently different that it led to a rather different set of outcomes. The advance of science and technology that enrich a nation depends critically on the cultural beliefs of those in the upper tail of the human capital distribution, that is, the intellectual and technical elite. Could it be that one of the keys to the Needham puzzle is to be found there?

A simple argument that China never had an Enlightenment and therefore did not have an Industrial Revolution is incomplete and misleading. Some of the developments that we most closely associate with Europe's Enlightenment remarkably resemble events in China, but the differences between the European and the Chinese Enlightenments are as revealing as the similarities. Late Ming China experienced the rise of an intellectual movement known as *shixue* or "concrete studies." Given the ambiguities in the meaning of the term, we should not read any modern concepts into it. Yet it is often taken to mean "practical matters" such as water control, military science, and administration, as well as knowledge that is in some sense verifiable. It expressed an antipathy for cramming for imperial exams and the detached and pedantic textual scholarship dominating intellectual life in China at the time (Rowe, 2009, p. 59). Either way, a great deal of intellectual innovation was associated with it. Some of that knowledge was borrowed from the West (mostly through the Jesuits and the books they brought along), some of it was indigenous (Jami, Engelfriet, and Blue, 2001, pp. 12–14).

Another crucial element largely missing in China was the institutional bridges that eighteenth-century Europe built between those who possessed propositional knowledge and those who controlled prescriptive knowledge. In engineering, mechanics, chemistry, mining, and agriculture, the *savants* and the *fabricants* in China were as far or further apart as they ever were in Europe.[1] The information flows between those who knew things and those who made things were far narrower and weaker in China than in Europe, and the realization that this connection held the key to progress in the future was missing in the East.[2] Needham noted that the real work in engineering was "always done by illiterate or semi-literate artisans and master craftsmen who could never rise across that sharp gap which separated them from the 'white collar literati'" (Needham, 1969a, p. 27).[3] The Baconian emphasis on creating communications not just within the scholarly community and between scholars and people in power, but eventually also between the realm of the scholar and those of the manufacturer, the farmer, and the navigator, redefined the agenda of research in Europe. Needham (1969a, p. 142) notes that Chinese scholars, masters of the ideographic characters but quite far removed from their own artisans, continued for a long time to "harp on the primitive theories of the five elements and the two principles of *yang* and *yin*." Only rarely, he notes, did exceptional individuals in China break through these barriers. In Europe, as we have seen, such individuals were more common. Moreover, European culture strove to place best-practice scientific knowledge and the investigative techniques used by natural philosophers at the disposal of technological innovators, thus aiding and supporting technological progress. We cannot say that no attempts were made in this direction in the last two centuries of the Chinese Empire, but in the end they could not overcome the obstacles that the entrenched incumbency placed in its way.

---

[1] Needham points out that the Greek distinction between theory and practice, the former suitable to a gentleman and the latter not, has a precise equivalent in the Chinese distinction between *hsüeh* and *shu* (Needham, 1969a, p. 142).

[2] In the early eighteenth century Hu Hsu, a famous scholar in his time, complained that the vast bulk of peasants, artisans, and merchants were not part of the educational system and left almost entirely ignorant (Woodside and Elman, 1994, p. 529). The matter is well summarized by Nathan Sivin (1995, ch. VII): "Science was done on the whole by members of the minority of educated people in China, and passed down in books. Technology was a matter of craft and manufacturing skills privately transmitted by artisans to their children and apprentices. Most such artisans could not read the scientists' books. They had to depend on their own practical and esthetic knowledge."

[3] Bodde (1991, pp. 224, 367) has similarly argued that there was an "enormous distance between 'white collar' and 'blue collar' workers" in China, and that Chinese science was pursued primarily by learned scholars schooled in the classics. Hence technological progress was carried primarily by poorly educated artisans and skilled craftsmen and not by intellectuals. That served China well as long as innovation was carried out primarily by skilled artisans through experience and serendipity, and did not require injections of propositional knowledge—as was the case in Europe before 1700 as well. The gap between the two began to widen precisely after that, when insights from science were needed to keep the momentum of technological change going instead of petering out, as they did in China (Lin, 1995).

The Chinese counterpart to an Enlightenment movement in the seventeenth and eighteenth centuries was known as the school of *kaozheng* or "evidentiary research." In this school, abstract ideas and moral values gave way as subjects for discussion to concrete facts, documented institutions and historical events (Elman, 2001, p. 4). Chinese scholarship of this period was "not inherently antipathetic to scientific study or resistant to new ideas" (De Bary, 1975b, p. 205). It was based on rigorous research, demanded proof and evidence for statements, and shunned leaps of faith and speculation. It all sounded quite promising, but in the end it led to a different outcome than in Europe. Chinese scholars were primarily interested in philology, linguistics, and historical studies, "confident that these would lead to greater certainty about what the true words and intentions of China's ancient sages had been and, hence, to a better understanding of how to live in the present" (Spence, 1990, p. 103).[4] Equally significantly, unlike the European Enlightenment, the Chinese movement remained by and for the Mandarinate, the ruling neo-Confucian elite, which by most accounts had little interest in material progress.

An early attempt at intellectual innovation that was more or less contemporaneous with Europe's growing criticism of the ancients can be traced to the writings and career of Li Zhi (1527–1602), a philosopher of heterodox inclinations, who actually seems to have felt that one did not have to be a Confucian scholar to be a philosopher, a truly iconoclastic position for the time (Jiang, 2001, p. 13). Views that are similar to those we associate with the European radical Enlightenment were expressed by Li, including that self-interest was part of human nature and was not to be condemned, and that the pleasures of the flesh might be both virtuous and therapeutic. In his correspondence with Geng Dingxian (1524–1594) he makes a point supporting the moderns against the ancients. He quotes Confucius's *Analects* to say that it is better to be "impetuous and uncompromising" than "sanctimoniously orthodox" and accuses Deng of "following old paths and treading in earlier footsteps" (Brook, 2010, p. 180). Huang (1981, p. 204) points out that Li's views were a threat to the neo-Confucian orthodoxy built on the writings of Zhu Xi, and that if it were accepted that individuals could achieve the Great Unity in their own minds, much of the Confucian formal canon could be dispensed with. Such views would constitute a serious threat to the empire, "the integration of which relied to a large degree on the general acceptance of orthodox teachings by the educated elite." At least in that sense Li might have been regarded by the establishment to be as serious a threat as Martin Luther was in Europe a generation or two earlier. Yet in China, the

---

[4] Specifically, *kaozheng* learning was focused on exegesis of the ancient canon: determining authenticity and meaning, and analyzing the etymology and paleography of ancient Chinese characters. This turn toward the ancients affected the civil service examinations throughout the empire. See Elman (2013, p. 275).

battle faced by potential cultural entrepreneurs was far much more uphill.[5]
Even the enfeebled late Ming empire could coordinate the suppression of
subversive ideas better than the European states could.

Moreover, Li was no Galileo or Bacon. His concern was almost
entirely an attempt to reconcile the undeniable private needs and desires of
human beings with the obvious constraints of public morality (Huang, 1981,
p. 198). In any event, his heterodox views were extremely costly to him:
following the publication of his heretical book *A Book to Burn*, he was arrested
by the emperor's guard, jailed, and committed suicide in prison (Huang,
1981, pp. 189–221). It is not entirely clear to what extent Li's heretical
writings contributed to his fate, as opposed to his lifestyle and his pugnacious
character. Moreover, there were other late Ming writers whose works were
quite heterodox: Jiang provides a list of innovative writers of that period led
by Wang Yangming (1472–1529). Wang was a successful and influential
critic of Zhu Xi's thought, proposing a more idealist and egalitarian philosophy, arguing that morality was innate and not learned, and complained that
Zhu Xi and his school had replaced moral action with the study of morality.
Wang's followers concluded that studying the classics was less useful to
moral knowledge than meditation—a view that was quite anathema to the
neo-Confucian unity (Brook, 2010, pp. 163, 183). There seems to be little
evidence that such criticism hurt his career as a general and administrator.
Wang's views established a competing form of neo-Confucianism, with Zhu
Xi-ism associated with the status quo and the established authority (Bol,
2008, p. 99). For a while the more liberal approaches of Wang and those
influenced by him might have seemed to open the door to a more pluralistic
approach to knowledge in China, all within the traditions of neo-Confucianism.[6] Wang's career shows that the market for ideas in China clearly was to
some extent competitive and not invariantly hostile to critique of the
orthodoxy. Yet intellectual life remained dominated by the civil service examination system, in which innovation, pluralism, and contestability were
largely stigmatized—indeed the growing monopoly of neo-Confucianism
provided the administration with a tool to fight off challenges to the status
quo posed by Wang and his followers (Elman, 2013, p. 81).

Other attempts at serious intellectual reform were made in China in
the period under discussion. It could well be argued that the seeds of a
Chinese Enlightenment were sown by Fang-Yizhi (1611–1671), the author
of a book meaningfully titled *Small Encyclopedia of the Principles of Things*,

---

[5] Brook (2010, p. 182) assesses that Li may be seen by modern scholars as a martyr
for intellectual autonomy, but to his contemporaries he was "a crazy old man."

[6] Needham compares Wang's views to those of such giants of Western philosophy as
Berkeley and Kant, but adds that "unfortunately all this, sublime though it was, could hardly be
sympathetic to the development of natural science. ... Wang could never understand the basic
principle of scientific method" (Ronan and Needham, 1978, p. 252).

which discussed potentially useful forms of propositional knowledge such as meteorology and geography. He was familiar with Western writing and was in close touch with Johann Adam Schall von Bell, a Jesuit missionary scientist residing in China. Early on, Fang was quite influential in the *kaozheng* school of the eighteenth century and his life and works serve as a good reminder of the different history China could have had if circumstances had been different. Peterson (1975, pp. 400–1) has gone so far as to suggest that Fang was representative of the possibility in the seventeenth century that the realm of "things" to be investigated would center on physical objects, technology, and natural phenomena.[7] He argued that Fang's work paralleled the secularization of science in Europe. The real question, then becomes, what was different about China that prevented Fang from becoming a cultural entrepreneur comparable to Bacon or Galileo, so that his new ideas remained only a "possibility"?[8] The *shixue* movement representing a strong interest in natural phenomena and technical writing, in the view of modern scholars, "all but disappeared during the subsequent [Qing] dynasty" to make room for more textual, backward looking intellectual activity (Jami, Engelfriet, and Blue, 2001, p. 14), although the exact difference between the *shixue* and *kaozheng* schools is still in dispute. There is a consensus today that with the rise of the Qing, Chinese science, in Elman's words "turned inward towards native traditions of classical learning" and "during the Newtonian century in Europe Chinese scholars simultaneously focused on restoring native medicine, mathematics, and astronomy to admired fields of classical learning worthy of literati attention. ... These developments were not challenged until the middle of the nineteenth century, when modern Western medicine and technology became insuperable and irresistible" (Elman, 2005, pp. 220–21).

All the same, the literature about the "Chinese Enlightenment" may have overstated its bias toward literary and philological topics. The arrival of the Jesuits to China in the late sixteenth century stimulated a revival of interest in astronomy and mathematics, and Chinese scholars carefully examined useful knowledge that seeped in from the West (Jami, 1994). *Kaozheng* scholars such as Mei Wending (1633–1721) compared Western mathematics and astronomy to Chinese knowledge, and pointed to the advances that the West had made. Yet Mei's rhetoric in his book *Lixue yiwen* (*Doubts Concerning the Study of Astronomy*, 1693) illustrates the fundamental constraints that the accumulation and application of useful knowledge in China was subject to.

---

[7] Sivin (1975, note n) is far more skeptical of Fang's abilities and has compared him with European scholasticism, feeling that his work was "antiquated."

[8] Fang himself ended up spending his last twenty years as a Buddhist monk, perhaps because he did not want to serve the new Qing rulers. He seems to have lost his interest in Western learning in later years, and there is no evidence that his ideas were pursued further (Engelfriet, 1998, p. 358). Peterson (1979, p. 12) stresses that Fang was considerably less influential than his contemporaries Gu Yanwu (1613–1682) and Huang Zongxi (1610–1695).

In Mei's work, the moderns are in no way superior to the ancients, and there is no progress in history; indeed "the accumulation of human knowledge is merely a token of the ancients' superior merit" (Jami, 2012, p. 220). While the *kaozheng* scholars recognized that the study of mathematics and astronomy was essential to their documentary studies, their ideas were not translated into action and they were focused on understanding ancient texts rather "than in applying their knowledge to practical concerns" (Jami, 1994, p. 227).

Perhaps most remarkable was the late Ming dynasty official Xu Guangqi (1562–1633). Xu's career and views in some ways mirror those of his contemporary Francis Bacon and shared Bacon's belief in what is known in China as *shiyong*, the practical application of knowledge in pursuit of social order (Bray and Métailié, 2001, p. 323). His commitment to learning was motivated by the conviction that it could be used to save the country, not only by military means, but also by applying science and technology to make the country prosperous and powerful (Qi, 2001, p. 361). In that regard, his beliefs are distinctly reminiscent of Bacon's, despite the obvious differences. Xu was a high-level official in the imperial administration (at the time of his death he was both deputy prime minister and minister of "rites," roughly speaking, culture and education). He was responsible for reforming the Chinese calendar based on more accurate astronomical data he learned from the Jesuits, who had access to the work of Brahe and Kepler. Remarkably, he converted to Christianity in 1603 (subsequently becoming known as "Dr. Paul") and was a close collaborator of the Jesuit missionary Father Matteo Ricci, with whom he translated Euclid's *Elements of Geometry*. Perhaps his most astonishing contribution was his monumental *Nongzheng quanshu*, an agricultural treatise published posthumously in 1639 that summarized much existing knowledge of Chinese agriculture, but also illustrated his firm belief in the importance of experimentation to augment agricultural knowledge. The book was vast, containing 700,000 Chinese characters (Bray, 1984, p. 66). It was, by the standards of that time on any continent, full of progressive ideas. Xu reported a great deal of agricultural experimentation, at least some of which he carried out himself. He also advocated the new crops that were being introduced into China from the New World, and condemned conservative farmers reluctant to adopt new crops, such as sweet potatoes because of their mistaken belief that crops will only grow well where they originated (Bray and Métailié, 2001, p. 341). He had a practical intellect and endorsed concrete studies (*shixue*); Xu's work perhaps serves as an indication of where Chinese intellectual innovators could have gone had they lived in a different polity (Zurndorfer, 2009, p. 82).

None of the late Ming writers directly challenged and refuted the basic canon of Chinese metaphysics. All the same, De Bary (1975a, p. 5) and Jiang (2001) note that the various modernizing and innovative views of the world thrived in a limited way in the late Ming period.[9] Jami (2012) and others have suggested that the rise of the Qing dynasty was decisive for the fate of the development of science in China and that what little there was of a stirring of intellectual progress before 1644 could not survive what De Bary has called the "Manchu suppression." In the late eighteenth century, the Qianlong emperor's administration cracked down on intellectuals in what has become known as the "literary inquisition." The suppression was aimed more at scholars suspected of anti-Qing sympathies than at intellectual innovators per se, but it is believed to have inflicted long-lasting damage on the Chinese intellectual class and the formation of human capital (Koyama and Xue, 2015).[10]

Moreover, to make Western learning more acceptable, Chinese scholars had to convince the officials, especially those of the Qing dynasty, that most of it had Chinese origins, thus conferring on it a status comparable to Chinese traditional knowledge and thus legitimizing it. Mei Wending convinced the Kangxi emperor that European learning was derivative from the Chinese and that the only source of reliable knowledge was the ancient learning of China (Elman, 2005, pp. 231, 236). The new astronomical knowledge, such as the precise shape of the earth, while in its current version originating in Europe, was said to have been present in China all along and thus was not foreign at all (Jami, 2012, p. 222). The need of Chinese scholars to show that Western knowledge had already existed in ancient China indicated the difficulty they had in ridding themselves of the burden of the ancients. No such need to assert their own originality seems to have been present in Europe. Europeans borrowed useful knowledge freely and shamelessly from foreign civilizations, acknowledged their debts to earlier generations, but then went on to expand this knowledge and improve the techniques. The contrast with China is stark: one scholar has concluded (with some exaggeration) that "by 1800, there was no sign that China had been persuaded to adopt European knowledge on a large scale ... and that European knowledge was able to fundamentally affect ordinary Chinese life" (Deng, 2009, p. 62).

While the Chinese scientists did at times adopt European tools that they clearly did not possess, they did little to improve them beyond what the Europeans had done. An example is the adoption of the telescope, clearly a European invention, to the study of astronomy (Huff, 2011, pp. 110–14). While the telescope was introduced into China by the Jesuit missionaries,

---

[9] All the same, the death of Li Zhi and a similar fate that befell another heterodox writer of his age, Tzu-po Ta-kuan (1544–1604), led a contemporary to note that "if anyone behaved like a heretic, he will of course be killed. Li Zhi and Ta-kuan are good object lessons" (Kengo, 1975, p. 60).

[10] Mote (1999, p. 928) notes that pervasive fear of persecution led many intellectuals to destroy books in their possessions rather than face the chance of discovery and punishment.

their star catalogs were not expanded at a rate comparable to that achieved by telescope-equipped European astronomers, such as John Flamsteed. Huff attributes this difference to a "curiosity deficit" in China, but one cannot understand this difference without a deeper examination of the institutional and political environment in which the accumulation of useful knowledge operated.

The tradition of *kaozheng* scholarship contained many elements that we associate with the European scientific revolution and the subsequent Enlightenment (Elman, 2001). Kaozheng scholars developed an efficient network of information exchange and correspondence. The Jiangnan (Yangzi delta) area, in which many of the kaozheng scholars resided, counted many libraries, and the lending of books was a universal custom. In Beijing an entire street was a major book emporium, and much like in Europe, the publishing industry printed novels as well as classical texts. In the late Ming period Jiangnan books fell in price and attained wide popularity and circulation (Elman, 2005, p. 29). Much like their European counterparts, Chinese scholars agreed that mathematics was one of the keys to concrete studies, as Jiao Xun (1763–1820) put it. Much like in Europe, too, information was organized in tabular form, and often illustrated by diagrams and maps. Gu Donggao's (1679–1759) book used them for information on the pre-Qin and Han periods (722–481 BC) and Yan Roju (1636–1704) counted and analyzed citations from classical poetry. The scientists of the early Qing period were convinced that their mathematical tools (trigonometry and geometry) had the power to explain nature as well as to predict it. Yet, as Nathan Sivin (1975, p. 161) notes, "in China the new tools were used to rediscover and recast the lost mathematical astronomy of the past and thus to perpetuate traditional values rather than to replace them."

Unlike Europe, Chinese intellectuals found it difficult to shake loose from the iron grip of the past. Mathematics, medicine, and most other forms of useful knowledge were studied and reflected on, but remained mostly a branch of classical studies. Attempts to apply this knowledge to practical uses were taking place, and when new ideas or products appeared, the Chinese were not averse to them. But unlike their European counterparts, Chinese scholars never came to believe that useful knowledge and its capacity to generate material progress through its applications was one of the raisons d'être of natural philosophy. The wholesale shredding of the wisdom of earlier writers, at times quite impudently so, that was characteristic of many European writers, did not catch on in China. Even Xu Guangqi's massive treatise on agriculture consisted of more than 90 percent citations of earlier writers (Bray and Métailié, 2001, p. 337).

The work of Gu Yanwu (1613–1682), one of the founding intellectuals of the *kaozheng* school, is revealing. Sometimes pictured as a kind of Chinese version of Arthur Young (see for example Morris, 2010, p. 473), Gu's work was emblematic of the new Chinese scholarship in the late Ming era: it was far more rigorous and rational, and was based on extensive traveling in China, where he acquired first-hand information. And yet Gu's writing provided mostly information based on philology, archaeology, and the careful analysis of early works, and his interests were mostly in historical and textual studies and politics.[11]

An early enlightenment-type author in China was Song Yingxing (1587–1666), the author of *Tiangong Kaiwu* (*The Creations of Nature and Man*), a lavishly illustrated encyclopedic volume on technology completed in 1637 (Song [1637], 1966). Song, who repeatedly failed his civil service examinations, was an astonishingly learned man who was termed "the Chinese Diderot" and the "Chinese Agricola" by Joseph Needham (1959, p. 154; 1986, p. 102). Song's work is especially interesting, because his thinking in some ways was very much in line with his European contemporaries. Precisely because the road to success and social prestige led through scholarship of ancient texts in which ambitious youngsters were trained, most Chinese intellectuals had little interest in new technology and in the expansion of practical useful arts and sciences. Chinese intellectuals were more interested in matters of public administration and governance, and were glad to leave technological issues to craftsmen. Song, perhaps because he never was able to join the ranks of the elite, broke the barrier between natural philosophy and technical knowledge (Cullen, 1990, p. 315). In his preface he states baldly that "an ambitious scholar will undoubtedly toss this book onto his desk and give it no further thought; it is a work that is in no way concerned with the art of advancement in officialdom" (Song, [1637] 1966, p. xiv). Song regarded issues of ritual and morality irrelevant to discussions on human-heaven interconnectedness. As Schäfer points out, this seems to be consistent with the values that came out of the Baconian program, and, in her words, "fits our modern conception of a scientist: someone who suspects indoctrination, challenges contemporary thought, and systematically searches for a rational order in the world that surrounds him" (Schäfer, 2011, p. 54). Cullen notes that his views made him a soulmate of some of the more progressive Europan thinkers such as Bacon, whose influence on the Industrial Enlightenment, as we have seen, was immense. But the difference between the two is as striking as the similarity: Song was not to become the "Chinese Bacon." His work had little impact on the intellectual life of his contemporaries (Cullen, 1990, p. 316).[12] It is also important to realize that even a progressive

---

[11] His magnum opus, *Ri-zhi-lu* or *Jih-chih lu* (*Daily Accumulation of Knowledge*) is a treasure trove of information, but is definitely stronger on Confucian classics, history, ceremony and administration than on matters of great practical knowledge. See Peterson (1979, pp. 9–12) for details.

[12] Schäfer (2011, pp. 258–82) notes that the book was published twice, with about fifty copies made, though it was not totally ignored either and seems to have circulated among a small circle, where it was of some "quizzical and inadvertent" interest—a far cry indeed from the vast impact that the writings of Francis Bacon made on his contemporaries. No reprints of his magnum opus were made in the Qing period (after 1644), and the resurrection of the work was thanks to the discovery of a copy in Japan that had been brought there in the 1880s.

scholar such as Song thought very differently from his Baconian contemporaries. Schäfer (2011, p. 117) notes that he would have "laughed at any suggestion that the talented scholar should engage in the practice of craftsmanship or vice versa that a craftsman should try scholarly work. In fact, he insisted that ... the idea that a person from one group could appropriate the knowledge of the other would not work." China, much like Europe, had multi-talented individuals who spanned both theoretical and practical knowledge, but unlike Europe the vast majority of intellectuals regarded themselves entirely as scholars and their discourse was solely with other learned persons.

Another example of how the Chinese Enlightenment differed from Europe's is a later scholar, the philosopher Dai Zhen (or Tai Chen, 1724–1777). Dai Zhen was one of the dominant figures in the *kaozheng* movement, and his insistence on evidence and his mathematical capabilities would appear to make him comparable to European contemporaries. One historian described him as someone who was "a truly scientific spirit ... whose principles hardly differed from those which in the West made possible the progress of the exact sciences" (Gernet, 1982, p. 513). Yet while Dai was sharply critical of the neo-Confucian school sometimes known as the Cheng-Zhu school (after the names of its founders), Gernet immediately adds that the erudition of this research went hand in hand with the renunciation of any attempt at reflection and synthesis and that its research into historical details became an end in itself (Gernet, 1982, p. 516). Thus, Dai reinterpreted the writings of Confucius and tried to reconcile the teachings of two of Confucius's most illustrious followers, Mencius and his opponent Xunzi. He criticized the writings of Song era authorities such as Zhu Xi, but largely on the grounds that the latter had misinterpreted earlier sages, not on the basis of observation or experiment. While insisting on evidence, Dai did not mean by it anything that Galileo or Boyle would have been interested in—for him the focus of research was philology and phonology, exegesizing the writings of earlier generations.[13] Nothing was to come between the scholar and his careful study of the classics, and what "the student of the Way needs to do is to approach the classical text with an open mind, without preconceptions." He thus objected to the neo-confucian orthodoxy, but purely out of fundamentalism, and he viewed education as "utterly and eternally dependent on the classics" (Brokaw, 1994, pp. 269, 277).

A generation before Dai, and no less impressive, was Chen Hongmou (1696–1771), a professional administrator who wrote widely on what may best be called political economy and public administration. As Rowe (2001, p. 114) shows, Chen was an unusually progressive scholar, who in some ways resembled the physiocrats and Adam Smith and decried the

---

[13] As Elman (2005, p. 259) points out, Dai Zhen engaged in a systematic research agenda "that built on paleography and phonology to reconstruct the meaning of classical words." His followers extended his approach and attempted to use etymology to reconstruct the true intentions of the sages, defending them from the neo-Confucian philosophy of the state.

ivory-tower antiquarianism of the *kaozheng* scholars, who he thought were too "mired in the past." He strongly believed in markets and the power of commerce to bring out efficiency in production and came close to Smith's concept of an invisible hand. Rowe (2001 p. 214) points out that the one element that Enlightenment Europe had, which was entirely missing in Chen, is the strong belief in the economic virtue of emulation, which was a central element of the European Enlightenment ideology. But equally striking is the absence in his work of a concept of useful knowledge as a source of economic progress.[14] Chen was deeply interested in creating prosperity, and his proposals included active economic policies to encourage mining, commerce, and manufacturing. He instinctively understood incentives and tried to bring more rural workers into a system of domestic manufacturing, in which state intervention at the provincial level would be the main moving part. But significantly, technological progress and a more active role for useful knowledge were not central to his thinking. Agriculture, where technology was perhaps most important in his thought, would be improved by introducing crops already cultivated elsewhere into Shaanxi province. But the emphasis was not on innovation per se as much as it was on the dissemination of existing knowledge. The "Confucian moral tone" assumed the short-sightedness of an ignorant population of local peasants, "which the better-educated and more widely experienced official was beholden to overcome" (Rowe, 2001, p. 232).[15]

The *kaozheng* medical literature had its own debate on ancients vs. moderns, but ironically it differs from Europe's in two critical dimensions: first, the ancients were the classical writers of the Han dynasty (206 BC to 220 AD), and the moderns were the writers of the Song era (still three or four centuries in the past), and second, that the *kaozheng* scholars favored the *earlier* writers (Elman, 2005, pp. 232–36). There were no Chinese equivalents of Paracelsus, Vesalius, and Harvey, who threw all caution to the wind and trusted only what they (believed they) saw. Little wonder, then that the verdict of historians has been that "this scientific spirit was applied almost exclusively to the investigation of the past"(Gernet, 1982, p. 513).

It might be thought that the backward looking character of China's intellectual life during the Ming and Qing dynasties is surprising. After all, China was a society without an institutionalized religion. It did not have a

---

[14] To be sure, such a concept is also largely (if not entirely) absent from Smith, whose vision of economic growth was primarily based on trade and the division of labor.

[15] It is striking that Chen was a "loyal devotee" of the conservative Song era historian and statesman Sima Guang, whose biography he wrote and whose works he edited. While he was, in Rowe's terms, more "developmental" than Sima, there is little in his writings that suggests a Baconian belief in the progressive powers of useful knowledge (Rowe, 2001, p. 287). It is indeed striking that his discussion on "accumulation" includes almost nothing on an expansion of new productive assets and techniques, and it is instead wholly focused on the topic of price stabilization through granaries.

caste of priests, rabbis, or mullahs whose power and livelihood depended on their interpretation of the sacred writings of the past making them highly intolerant of apostasy. But religiosity is neither a necessary nor a sufficient condition for intellectual conservatism. One explanation of its backward-looking orientation surely is the large investment of human capital of ambitious and bright Chinese youngsters in the learning of the past, in the hope of passing the civil service examinations. The bulk of candidates failed these exams in local competitions, and hence large reservoirs of classically trained men were desperately looking for ways to extract some rents from their human capital. These people also constituted a vast audience for the books published at the time. Furthermore, the first three Qing emperors, who ruled for more than a century, sought to appropriate the classical legacy to "establish their dynastic prestige and political legitimacy" (Elman, 2005, p. 238). But more generally, the skepticism toward the knowledge of earlier generations that awoke in Europe after 1500, as more and more beliefs of ancient authorities were questioned, tested, and found wanting by European scientists and physicians, was rarely allowed to arise in China.[16]

A telling example is the publication of Chinese encyclopedias. As I have argued elsewhere (Mokyr, 2005), European encyclopedias are emblematic of a main theme of the Industrial Enlightenment in that they were explicitly meant to reduce access costs and make useful knowledge available to those who could make use of it. By organizing large bodies of knowledge in single publications, they showed their eagerness to distribute the knowledge to the curious and to those who might want to use it. Yet such compendia also contained conservative elements, because they present a snapshot of present accumulated knowledge, unless they were constantly updated and replaced. European encyclopedias, it was universally realized, went out of date almost as soon as they were published, and hence they were quickly replaced.

Europeans were not the only ones to realize the importance of reference books. But there was a critical difference: while European reference books were made accessible to a wide public, in China they were typically limited to a very narrow audience of mandarins in power. Wang Zhen's *Nong Shu* (*Treatise on Agriculture*), completed in 1313, foreshadowed the best works of the European Enlightenment: its more than 300 illustrations of tools and machinery were rendered with such accuracy that they could be made from the illustrations, as was the author's intention (Elvin, 1973, p. 116). However, in 1530 there was just one copy left in all of China, and it had to be reprinted. Another early example was the vast *Yongle Dadian,* compiled by the Ming Emperor Yongle between 1403 and 1408, which contained a massive amount

---

[16] Even an author like Jack Goody, who goes out of his way to condemn "essentialist" interpretations of Chinese history, writes that "characteristic of the cultural history of China has been a constant looking back to the Confucian classics, to 'Antiquity,' providing a continuous point of reference for both conservatives and reformers" (Goody, 2009, p. 238).

of information on science, technology, religion, history, and literature among other things. Because of the size of the work, it could not be blockprinted, and only three copies were made, the third one in 1557 after a palace fire threatened the survival of the work. Access to the work was limited to the emperor himself, unless special dispensation was granted (McDermott, 2006, pp. 126–27). Another example is the equally voluminous *Bencao Gangmu* (*Compendium of Materia Medica*), written by the herbalist Li Shizhen in the late sixteenth century, which contained a complete list of all medical plants, herbs, and substances (1,892 of them, in fifty-three volumes) believed to have medicinal properties. This was not just a regurgitation of old materials, as it includes references to syphilis, and sweet potatoes, both of which had New World (and thus recent) origins. Even larger was the *Gezhi congshu*, a "repository of classical, historical, institutional, medical, and technical works from antiquity to the present [i.e., late Ming times]" (Elman, 2005, p. 34), a collection of books (completed ca. 1603) that included all knowledge important to educated people prior to the arrival of the Jesuits. These books embodied the great respect in which the Chinese held the learning of previous generations, and they crystallized as much as disseminated the body of useful knowledge.

Unlike Diderot's encyclopedia, these compilations were not widely disseminated. One widely traveled early Qing scholar, Lio Xanting (1648–1695), complained that in ten years of searching he had not been able to find a single copy of Xu Guangqi's *Nongzheng quanshu* (Bray and Métailié, 2001, p. 355).[17] No new edition appeared for two centuries. As we have seen, Song Yingxing's magnificent *The Creations of Nature and Men*, survived only because an accidental copy had found its way to Japan. Of the enormous collection put together by Hu Wenhuan, the compiler of *Gezhi Congshu*, only 181 of 346 remained extant in the late eighteenth century (Elman, 2010, p. 381).

The efforts to organize knowledge in a systematic way were continued after the overthrow of the Ming in 1644. The vast efforts of the Chinese Qing emperors to publish encyclopedias and compilations of knowledge under the Kangxi and Qianlong emperors—above all the massive *Gujin tushu jicheng* compiled by Chen Menglei and published in 1726 (one of the largest books ever produced, with 10,000 chapters, 850,000 pages and 5,000 figures)—indicate an awareness of the importance of access to information. It was printed at the Wuyingdian, the Imperial Printing Office in Beijing. Altogether about 60 copies were made of it, a number that pales in comparison to the European encyclopedias, which were sold in large numbers.[18]

---

[17] Bray also notes (1984, p. 70) that Xu's detailed program of reforming agricultural administration was never put into practice.

[18] Darnton (1979) has estimated that in total, d'Alembert and Diderot's *Encyclopédie* sold about 25,000 copies. Given the many competitors in many languages that came out in the eighteenth century, and not counting the many compendia, dictionaries, lexicons, and similar

It is also revealing that Chen was arrested and deported (twice), and his name was removed from the project by the emperor whose wrath he had incurred. The entire project was carried out under imperial auspices and was a project of, by, and for the imperial bureaucracy.[19] Chen Yuanlong's (1652—1736) parallel project, an equally vast compilation named *Mirror of Origins,* contained almost no European learning, because the Kangxi emperor believed that all learning originated in China and his son, the Yongzheng emperor, disliked the Jesuits. The last of those massive works, commissioned by the Qianlong emperor in 1773 and completed in 1782 was the *Siku quanshu* (*Library of the Four Treasuries*), another huge work with 360 million words, filling 36,000 large folio volumes. Altogether seven copies of this work were made, four of which were kept at the imperial palace, although after 1787 access for scholars and literati opened up (McDermott, 2006, p. 168). In Europe, by and large, encyclopedias and reference books were the product of private enterprise, sometimes published very much against the will of authorities powerless to stop them. It stands to reason that some of the reference books produced in China served candidates for the state examinations and perhaps "to help the mandarins in their work" (Burke, 2000, p. 175).

Even ordinary books, moreover, did not circulate much. China had public libraries, and in the Song years they were reasonably accessible and promising young scholars were allowed to spend a few years studying in them. Over time, however, theft, fires, and wear and tear reduced the size of the collections. By Ming times, these libraries were reduced to a small fraction of the books they were supposed to own. Public libraries were hardly centers of learning, and the big concentrations of books that were in private collections were carefully guarded and thus were inaccessible (McDermott, 2006, pp. 127–47). Things improved under the Qing, when officials sponsored more than 150 editorial projects, with the Qianlong emperor's famous *Four Treasuries* project its crowning achievement, and book-sharing among bibliophiles developed in the mid-eighteenth century (McDermott, 2006, pp. 167–68). Even then, however, access remained a major problem for scholars, especially those living far from the urban centers in the lower Yangzi valley.

The one historical case that purports to illustrate the great divergence of Enlightenment Europe and retrograde China is the famous failed mission of Lord George Macartney to China in 1793, in which the friendly gestures and samples of British ingenuity were allegedly spurned by the aging Qianlong Emperor. The traditional view of this event is that it is an

---

books published in the eighteenth century, the total number of encyclopedic reference books published in Europe was a large multiple of the sales of the *Encyclopédie.*

[19]   One scholar has suggested that, much different from the works of European encylopedists, the *Gujin tushu jicheng* arose from the idea that the emperor's task was to join the whole knowledge of the world to a unified Cosmos (Bauer, 1966, p. 687).

illustration of the large cultural gap that had opened between East and West. In a classic paper, Cranmer-Byng and Levere (1981) argued that the British, "confident in their Industrial Revolution" were committed to an "ideology of progress through science," and Macartney noted in his diary his obvious belief in the superiority of the culture the fruits of which he was carrying to the Chinese. This stood in complete opposition to "the policy of the present [Chinese] government to discourage all novelties." The Chinese were seemingly unable to appreciate the intellectual and theoretical content of natural philosophy, with its potentially enormously useful application (Cranmer-Byng and Levere, 1981, pp. 516, 518). The mission was doomed from the start, because the two countries possessed different cultures with totally different sets of values. This view may overstate the real gap. Cranmer-Byng and Levere (1981) concede that the aging Qianlong emperor had far less interest in science and technology than his grandfather Kangxi, and thus the failure of the Macartney mission might to some extent be explained by accidental factors and was more contingent than was previously thought. More recent scholarship is cautious: "neither Lord Macartney nor the Qianlong emperor could foresee that the Industrial Revolution in England would produce British military superiority ... we should not read the events of the first and second Opium Wars back into the eighteenth century" (Elman, 2005, p. 254). It is also true that Macartney did not actually display some of the most advanced industrial machinery available in Britain at the time. The steam engine model, the Smeaton pulleys, and "assorted chemical, electrical and philosophical apparatus" never reached the Chinese court. In short, it stands to reason that the Macartney delegation brought with it an unrepresentative sample of British mechanical triumphs, and that what they brought had little appeal to the Chinese court.

Yet that the Macartney mission failed, even if it was in part the fault of bad organization and bad luck, is an indication of a deep difference between the celestial empire and the European nations. Chinese officials may still have sensed that the Europeans had something they did not have, as Mote (1999, p. 961) stresses. But they did not react because they felt they did not have to. They were committed to the Chinese model of slow change of what Mote has eloquently described as "self-renovating change that was constant and gradual, not sudden and disruptive, and was always justified by reference to past models" (Mote, 1999, p. 966).[20] An eighteenth-century Confucian scholar named Cheng Tingzuo had nothing but contempt for European science: "Far-off Europe!... Its people are known for their many-sided cleverness, excelling particularly in mathematics. Apart from this

---

[20] Father Ricci, one of the keenest observers of Chinese society in the late Ming period, noted that when the Chinese realized the superior quality of a foreign product, they might prefer it; but "their pride ... arises from an ignorance of the existence of higher things and from the fact that they find themselves far superior to the barbarous nations by which they are surrounded" (Ricci, 1953, p. 23).

everything else is excessive ingenuity" (cited by Elvin, 1996, p. 97). In that regard, Chinese society was not all that different from Jewish society in early modern Europe: slow development and marginal increments in knowledge within rigid boundaries were tolerated within the constraints of the past. It was a model that worked well and was sustainable and stable, except for one thing: in eighteenth-century Europe a new culture had emerged that questioned and then rejected the wisdom of its canonical forefathers and rebuilt much of the body of useful knowledge from scratch. Such a culture turned out to be more aggressive and was subject to sudden and disruptive changes such as the Industrial Revolution. It inevitably spilled over and affected other cultures that by themselves had a much more quiescent dynamic. There was nothing wrong with China except for what happened in Europe.

To see how China and Europe may have been different, it is useful to return to the concept of cultural entrepreneur. In some eras, especially during the era of the warring kingdoms, China's most creative and original philosophers attained considerable influence and were instrumental in changing the outlook of society and through that, the institutions and performance of the economy. As noted in chapter 16, the most prominent cultural entrepreneur that China produced was Zhu Xi, the synthesizer of neo-Confucianism. The orthodoxy established by Zhu came to its full bloom under the Ming. One fifteenth-century Chinese writer noted that "since the time of Zhu Xi, the Way has been clearly known. There is no more need for writing; what is left for us is to practice" (quoted in Hucker, 1975, p. 373).[21] Such views are exaggerated: the seventeenth century witnessed a flourishing of a diverse and sometimes contentious literature, which one scholar has described as a "vibrant and innovative culture" (Schäfer, 2011, p. 14). Some differences of opinion were possible within the neo-Confucian orthodoxy, which may have been a "fluctuating concept" and not a rigid, fixed body of thought.[22] Within the fluid boundaries of the Zhu Xi orthodoxy, late Ming China experienced a flourishing of studies on a host of natural phenomena including magnetism, hydraulics, and medicine. Yet at the end of the day we do not find a major break with the past and a willingness to shed much of accepted wisdom. Scholarship was not meant for the eventual "relief of Man's estate," as Bacon famously phrased it, but in understanding "the works of heaven" and the "inception of things." That is, when meticulously describing crafts and technology, late Ming scholars hoped that they could learn the principles that would bring about order in the world. In the final analysis, human affairs were not their focus (Schäfer, 2011, pp. 17–18). The

---

[21] Needham (1969b, p. 66) notes that Zhu has been termed both the Thomas Aquinas and the Herbert Spencer of China.

[22] Thus, for instance, the Ming philosopher Chen Chianzhang (1428–1500) disagreed with Zhu on many points, but "was not a complete break from the dominant trend of his time" (Ng, 2003, p. 36). He was accused of heresy and of being influenced by Daoist and Buddhist thought, but the ruling orthodoxy was sufficiently entrenched that it was not overly concerned.

country, literate and learned as it was, teemed with powerful intellectuals and astonishing polymaths who brilliantly straddled abstract philosophy and mundane areas, comparable with Europe's most admired superstars. All the same, it is hard to discern many spectacularly successful cultural entrepreneurs in imperial China after Zhu. Only after the overthrow of the empire, in the twentieth century, has China seen a number of influential cultural entrepreneurs, although men like Mao and Deng also attained enormous political power, and some of their influence may well have depended on coercion bias. Such intellectual continuity was anything but a weakness, much less a failure. It was the normal state of affairs in human history, only to be broken by exceptional circumstances.

The Chinese approach to knowledge was different in some important nuances from European. It did not "posit the existence of a uniform and predictable order in the physical universe" (Dikötter, 2003, p. 695) and did not rely on the new mathematical tools that allowed the Europeans increasingly to apply their useful knowledge to engineering problems.[23] The nature and characteristics of useful knowledge as it developed in China were not "less" or "worse" than what emerged in the West, just *different*. The ability of Chinese science to serve as an epistemic base for Chinese technology clearly did not work as well if our criterion for working well is the ability to generate economic growth.[24]

Pre-modern Chinese technology, no matter how sophisticated and advanced compared to the European variety, remained grounded on a narrow epistemic base.[25] Except for medicine, where practice and theoretical knowledge inevitably intertwined, and a few Leonardo-like universal geniuses who could do and did everything—such as the astonishing Song dynasty polymaths Shen Kuo (1031–1095) and Su Song (1020–1101)

---

[23] In a famous essay, Needham (1969a, pp. 299–330) argued that the Chinese never had a concept of a universal scientific law because its religion did not include the concept of a supreme lawgiver. The best they could do, he thinks, is the Taoist concept of empirical regularities that were wholly "inscrutable" and context-dependent and he concludes (p. 311) that "by that path science could not develop." He noted that the European Scientific Revolution was accompanied by the rise of the concept of immutable laws of nature (see also Ronan and Needham, 1978, pp. 290–91). It is hard to see that the centrality of a supreme and omnipotent law giver was much of an advantage to Judeo-Christian theistic religions in developing their useful knowledge. After all, it did little for Islam after Al Ghazali's *kalam* occasionalism became increasingly influential, nor for Jewish science before the nineteenth century.

[24] Nathan Sivin ([2005] 1984, p. 542) has rightly criticized "a saga of Europe's success and everyone else's failure." Yet he himself notes a few pages earlier (p. 537) that "the privileged position of the West comes ... from a head start in the technological exploitation of nature." It is unreasonable to explain such a head start without admitting that something that Westerners learned about nature was different from what was learned in China.

[25] Needham (1970, p. 39) cites with approval the verdict of a ninth-century Arab author that "the curious thing is that the Greeks are interested in theory but do not bother about practice, whereas the Chinese are very interested in practice and do not bother much about the theory."

—Chinese science during that time remained largely separate from technology and production (as it was in Europe at the time).[26] On the whole, Chinese science had little interest in finding out *why* and *how* techniques worked. One might wonder, moreover, whether Chinese craftsmen and engineers might have found much of the science of their world very helpful. It is perhaps telling that although a considerable number of Chinese inventions and techniques found their way to the West in one form or another, there are comparatively fewer instances of Chinese propositional knowledge (not to mention science proper) being adopted in Europe.

As noted, the growing consensus that characterized Enlightenment Europe was a mechanistic view of the universe. There were fixed and clear rules by which nature operated, and humankind's challenge was to discover these knowable rules and take advantage of them. Yet the view that these differences somehow handicapped the Chinese and caused a "failure" can be criticized as an example of the hindsight bias that just because Europe created what became known as "modern science," this was the *only* way that technological progress and economic growth could have occurred. Evolutionary theory suggests that the actual outcomes we observe are but a small fraction of the outcomes that are feasible, and we simply have no way of imagining how Chinese useful knowledge would have evolved in the long run had it not been exposed to Western culture and whether it would not have produced a material culture comparable to the one produced by the European Industrial Enlightenment.

It is clear, in any event, that the Chinese Enlightenment, if that is the right term, did not produce what the European Enlightenment did. Its research agenda included little or no useful knowledge and instead, in one succinct formulation, they were "living out the values of their culture" (De Bary, 1975b, p. 205). Mathematics and astronomy were applied for instance to reconstruct the size and shape of historical ceremonial bronze bells or reconstruct ancient carriages. Even though the *kaozheng* movement was born in part as a rebellious movement protesting the Manchu conquest of 1644, it could not remove itself from the establishment, and its agenda remained largely confined to what the court sponsored. If China's imperial government was not interested in steering research in a direction that could benefit from useful knowledge or the economy, there seems to have been no other agency that had the interest or the capacity to do so. The agenda of Chinese scholarship remained predominantly retrospective: to prove ancient sages right and to perform exegesis on their writings was a worthwhile intellectual activity, but it did not bring about the technological developments that changed the course of world history. It seems wrong to dub the Chinese experience a "failure." What is exceptional, indeed unique, is what happened in eighteenth-century Europe.

[26] For a similar recent view, see Davids (2013, pp. 230–31).

Epilogue

Useful Knowledge and Economic Growth

Nations and their economies grow in large part because they increase their collective knowledge about nature and their environment, and because they are able to direct this knowledge toward productive ends. But such knowledge does not emerge as a matter of course. While most societies that ever existed were able to generate some technological progress, it typically consisted of one-off limited advances that had limited consequences, soon settled down, and the growth it generated fizzled out. In only one case did such an accumulation of knowledge become sustained and self-propelling to the point of becoming explosive and changing the material basis of human existence more thoroughly and more rapidly than anything before in the history of humans on this planet. That one instance occurred in Western Europe during and after the Industrial Revolution.

Many factors contributed to this unique event, and the transformation of elite cultural beliefs in the centuries before the Industrial Revolution was only one of them. The big difference between Europe and the rest of the world was the Enlightenment and its implications for scientific and technological progress. But the rise of the Enlightenment in the late seventeenth century was the culmination of a centuries' long process of intellectual change among the European literate elite. The changes in the market for ideas were the crucial events that set Europe apart from the rest of the world. Europe was not in every respect a better-organized or a more dynamic society than other Eurasian societies. Goldstone (2012, p. 238) suggests that the "intellectual shift that began around 1500, ... limited for centuries to a small circle of scholars and theologians, ... by 1660 had started producing significant changes in the way elites acquired and validated knowledge." Changes in cultural beliefs for a while could move almost independently from changes in other economic variables, such as commercialization, urbanization, and economic growth. Eventually, however, they would feedback into the economy in a direction and with a magnitude that even the most ebullient of the seventeenth-century moderns and most committed believer in progress could not have imagined. In that sense, at least, we can see a major correction to the view that insists that the Great Divergence was a late and temporary phenomenon due mostly to fairly minor and accidental differences in geography. Culture, after all, mattered.

In this book, I have outlined a model of cultural change that explains why the Enlightenment took place in Europe. The question that will inevitably be raised is whether the Enlightenment in Europe was a necessary or a sufficient condition for the great breakthroughs that led to explosive economic growth and the modern economy. Could another and different civilization have eventually broken the Malthusian and knowledge barriers that kept human society at living standards close to subsistence since the beginning of humanity?

We may never know, because the Islamic world, Africa, China, India, and the original societies of America were all exposed to European culture, and their trajectories were irreversibly perturbed. But most societies that ever existed were subject to what I have called elsewhere Cardwell's Law (Mokyr, 1994, 2002), which is a generalization of the phenomenon that technology in any economy crystallizes at some point, and progress slows down and then fizzles out. The stagnation occurs because the status quo can suppress further challenges to entrenched knowledge and blocks nonmarginal advances using a range of means, from the threat to persecute heretics and the burning of their books, to subtle but effective mechanisms, such as meritocracies in which the key to personal success was the uncritical expertise in the existing body of knowledge inherited from the past.

Breaking out of Cardwell's Law requires, above all, a community that combines pluralism and competition with a coordination mechanism that allows knowledge to be distributed and shared, and hence challenged, corrected, and supplemented. Ancient Greece and the Hellenistic culture it created in the eastern Mediterranean, at least for a while, may have enjoyed these attributes and perhaps if it had not been consolidated into Roman rule, it might have evolved into something different. Perhaps medieval Islam, had it avoided the cruel hands of benighted religious beliefs and of the Mongols who destroyed so much of the infrastructure and so many of the institutions that explain its initial flourishing, could have morphed into a world enjoying self-propelled progress.

The correct way to think about the rise of modern science and technology in Europe is to see it not just as the natural continuation of ancient, medieval, and Renaissance culture but also, paradoxically, as its repudiation (Goldstone, 2012). There was nothing inexorable about this turn of events; indeed, it was a closely fought outcome. Fairly minor rewrites of history could have secured Europe for an obscurantist Catholic regime in which the Republic of Letters would have turned into a benighted theocracy dominated by Jesuits, as imagined for instance in the counterfactual novel of Kingsley Amis (1976). In such a world, out-of-the-box thinkers from Newton and Spinoza to Toland and La Mettrie might have been silenced or sufficiently discouraged, and the Enlightenment might never have taken off.

Would it have been possible for a totally different set of institutions to have created a modern economy? Instead of a decentralized community of competitive scientists and inventors, imagine a New Atlantis run by a central administration in which technological progress is brought about by civil servants supported and sustained by a benign and progress-minded bureaucracy. Could such an organization have brought about the modern world without anything resembling the European Enlightenment? The economist's logic would probably judge such a scenario as unlikely. It is one thing for such a political situation to be brought about in a single period; the likelihood that it could be sustained and avoid being corrupted and disrupted by greedy and ignorant outside invaders or inside rent-seekers in the long run seems dim.

To see the true importance of the European Enlightenment in the economic developments that followed it, recall that it involved two highly innovative and complementary ideas: the concept that knowledge and the understanding of nature can and should be used to advance the material conditions of humanity, and the belief that power and government are there not to serve the rich and powerful but society at large. The combination of these two and their triumph in the market for ideas created a massive synergy that led to the economic sea changes we observe, from industrialization and the growth in physical and human capital to the discovery and mastery of natural forces and resources that were still beyond imagining in 1750. It is a tale that will be told, and retold many times, and surely the arguments I have advanced here will be challenged and questioned by many others. That, in the end, is what illustrates the glory of a well functioning market for ideas.

References

Aarsleff, Hans. 1992. "John Wilkins." In Joseph L. Subbiondo, ed., *John Wilkins and 17th-Century British Linguistics*. Philadelphia: John Benjamins, pp. 3–41.

Abbattista, Guido. 2016. "China, the West, and the 'Commercial Enlightenment.'" Presented to a Conference on "Global Perspectives in a European 'long Enlightenment,' 1750 to 1850." Unpublished.

Abraham, Gary A. 1983. "Misunderstanding the Merton Thesis: A Boundary Dispute between History and Sociology." *Isis* Vol. 74, No. 3, pp. 368–87.

Acemoglu, Daron, Simon Johnson, and James Robinson. 2005a. "Institutions as a Fundamental Cause of Economic Growth." In Philippe Aghion and Steven Durlauf, eds., *Handbook of Economic Growth* Amsterdam: Elsevier, pp. 385–465.

———. 2005b. "The Rise of Europe: Atlantic Trade, Institutional Change, and Economic Growth." *The American Economic Review* Vol. 95, pp. 546–79.

Acemoglu, Daron, and Matthew O. Jackson. 2015. "History, Expectations and Leadership in the Evolution of Social Norms." *Review of Economic Studies* Vol. 82, No. 2, pp. 423–56.

Acemoglu, Daron, and James Robinson. 2006. "De Facto Political Power and Institutional Persistence." *American Economic Review* Vol. 96, pp. 325–30.

———. 2012. *Why Nations Fail: The Origins of Power, Prosperity, and Poverty*. New York: Crown.

Agrippa, Heinrich Cornelius. [1527] 1676. *The Vanity of Arts and Sciences*. London: Printed for Samuel Speed.

Aldrich, Howard E., Geoffrey M. Hodgson, David L. Hull, Thorbjørn Knudsen, Joel Mokyr, and Viktor J. Vanberg. 2008. "In Defence of Generalized Darwinism." *Journal of Evolutionary Economics* Vol. 18, pp. 577–96.

d'Alembert, Jean LeRond. [1751] 1995. *Preliminary Discourse to the Encyclopedia of Diderot*, translated and edited by Richard S. Schwab. Chicago: University of Chicago Press.

———. 1821. *Oevres Complètes de d Alembert*. Vol. 3, pt. I (Historical Eulogies). Paris: A Belin.

Alesina, Alberto, and Paola Giuliano. 2016. "Culture and Institutions." *Journal of Economic Literature,* forthcoming.

Alexander, Amir. 2002. *Geometrical Landscapes: The Voyages of Discovery and the Transformation of Mathematical Practice*. Stanford, CA: Stanford University Press.

———. 2014. *Infinitesimal: How a Dangerous Mathematical Theory Shaped the Modern World*. New York: Farrar, Straus and Giroux.

Alford, William P. 1995. *To Steal a Book is an Elegant Offense: Intellectual Property Law in Chinese Civilization*. Stanford, CA: Stanford University Press.

Algar, Hamid. 1973. *Mirza Malkum Khan: A Study in the History of Iranian Modernism*. Berkeley: University of California Press.

Algarotti, Francesco. 1739. *Sir Isaac Newton s Philosophy Explain'd for the Use of the Ladies. In Six Dialogues on Light and Colours*. London: Printed for E. Cave.

Allen, Robert C. 1983. "Collective Invention." *Journal of Economic Behavior and Organization* Vol. 4, No. 1, pp. 1–24.

————. 2009 . *The British Industrial Revolution in Global Perspective.* Cambridge: Cambridge University Press.

Amico, Leonard N. 1996. *Bernard Palissy.* New York: Flammarion.

Amis, Kingsley. 1976. *The Alteration.* London: Jonathan Cape.

Angeles, Luis. 2016. "The Economics of Printing in Early Modern China and Europe." *Economic History Review,* forthcoming.

Anstey, Peter R. 2002. "Locke, Bacon and Natural History." *Early Science and Medicine* Vol. 7, No. 1, pp. 65–92.

Arbuthnot, John. 1701. *An Essay on the Usefulness of Mathematical Learning.* Oxford: Printed at the Theater in Oxford for Anth. Peisley Bookseller.

Ariew, Roger. 2003. "Descartes and the Jesuits: Doubt, Novelty, and the Eucharist." In Mordechai Feingold, ed., *Jesuit Science and the Republic of Letters.* Cambridge, MA: MIT Press, pp. 157–94.

Ashworth, William B. Jr. 1986. "Catholicism and Early Science." In David C. Lindberg and Ronald L. Numbers, eds., *God and Nature: Historical Essays on the Encounter between Christianity and Science.* Berkeley: University of California Press, pp. 136–66.

Aubrey, John. 1898. *Brief Lives, Chiefly of Contemporaries, Set Down by John Aubrey between 1669 and 1696.* Edited from the author's mss by Andrew Clark. Oxford: Clarendon Press.

Baark, Erik. 2007. "Knowledge and Innovation in China:Historical Legacies and Emerging Institutions." *Asica Pacific Business Review* Vol. 13, No. 3, pp. 337–56.

Bacon, Francis. [1592] 1838. "In Praise of Knowledge." In *The Works of Lord Bacon.* London: William Ball. Vol. 1, pp. 216–17.

————. [1603] 1838. "Valerius Terminus: of the Interpretation of Nature." In *The Works of Lord Bacon,* London: William Ball.Vol. 1, pp. 218–31.

————. [1605] 1875. *The Advancement of Learning, Books 2–6.* Reprinted in *Works of Francis Bacon,* edited by James Spedding et al. London: Longmans and Co. Vol. IV, pp. 283–498.

————. [1605] 1996. *The Advancement of Learning, Books 1 and 2.* Reprinted in *Francis Bacon: the Major Works.* Oxford World Classics. Oxford: Oxford University Press.

————. [1620] 1861–79. *Preparative towards a Natural and Experimental History.* In Reprinted in *Works of Francis Bacon,* edited by James Spedding et al. Boston: Houghton Mifflin and Co., Vol. VIII pp. 351–71 (http://onlinebooks.library.upenn.edu/webbin/metabook?id=worksfbacon, accessed Sept. 10, 2014).

————. [1620] 1999. *The Great Instauration.* Reprinted in *Selected Philosophical Works,* edited by Rose-Mary Sargent. Indianapolis, IN: Hackett Publishing.

————. [1620] 2000. *The New Organon.* Edited by Lisa Jardine and Michael Silverthorne. Cambridge: Cambridge University Press.

————. [1623] 1996. *The Advancement of Learning,* Book One. Reprinted in Brian Vickers, ed., *Francis Bacon, Major Works.* Oxford World Classics, Oxford University Press, pp. 120–68.

————. [1627] 1996. *New Atlantis.* Reprinted, *Francis Bacon, Major Works* edited by Brian Vickers. Oxford World Classics. Oxford: Oxford University Press.

Baechler, Jean. 2004. "The Political Pattern of Historical Creativity." In Peter Bernholz and Roland Vaubel, eds., *Political Competition, Innovation and Growth in the History of Asian Civilizations.* Cheltenham, UK: Edward Elgar, pp. 18–38.

Bala, Arun. 2006. *The Dialogue of Civilizations in the Birth of Modern Science.* New York: Palgrave Macmillan.

Balazs, Etienne. 1964. *Chinese Civilization and Bureaucracy,* translated by H. M. Wright. New Haven, CT: Yale University Press.

Barnett, Lydia. 2015. "Strategies of Toleration: Talking across Confessions in the Alpine Republic of Letters." *Eighteenth-Century Studies* Vol. 48, pp. 141–57.

Barzilay, Isaac. 1974. *Yoseph Shlomo Delmedigo (Yashar of Candia): His Life and Works.* Leiden: E. J. Brill.

Basalla, George. 1988. *The Evolution of Technology.* Cambridge: Cambridge University Press.

Baten, Joerg, and Jan Luiten van Zanden. 2008. "Book Production and the Onset of Modern Economic Growth." *Journal of Economic Growth* Vol. 13, No. 3, pp. 217–235.

Bateson, Gregory, 1979. *Mind and Nature: A Necessary Unity.* New York: Dutton.

Bauer, Martin, ed. 1995. *Resistance to New Technology.* Cambridge: Cambridge University Press.

Bauer, Wolfgang. 1966. "The Encyclopedia in China." *Cahiers d Histoire Mondiale* Vol. 9, pp. 665–91.

Bayle, Pierre. [1696–97] 1734. *The Dictionary Historical and Critical of Mr Peter Bayle.* Second edition, collated ... by Mr Des Maizeaux. London: printed for J. J. and P. Knapton.

———. [1696–97] 1740. *Dictionaire Historique et Critique.* Fifth edition, revised, corrected and expanded, *avec la vie de l'auteur,* by Mr. Des Maizeaux. Amsterdam: P. Brunel.

Becker, Carl L. 1932. *The Heavenly City of the Eighteenth-Century Philosophers.* New Haven, CT and London: Yale University Press.

Becker, George. 1984. "Pietism and Science: A Critique of Robert K. Merton's Hypothesis." *American Journal of Sociology* Vol. 89, pp. 1065–90.

Becker, Sascha O., and Ludger Wöeßmann. 2009. "Was Weber Wrong? A Human Capital Theory of Protestant Economic History." *Quarterly Journal of Economics,* Vol. 124, No. 2, pp. 531–96.

Belfanti, Carlo Marco. 2004. "Guilds, Patents, and the Circulation of Technical Knowledge." *Technology and Culture* Vol. 45, No. 3, pp. 569–89.

Bell, A.E. 1947. *Christian Huygens and the Development of Science in the Seventeenth Century.* London: Edward Arnold.

Benabou, Roland. 2008. "Ideology (Joseph Schumpeter Lecture)." *Journal of the European Economic Association* Vol. 6, Nos. 2-3, pp. 321–52.

Benabou, Roland, Davide Ticchi, and Andrea Vindign,. 2014. "Forbidden Fruits: The Political Economy of Science, Religion and Growth." Unpublished working paper, Princeton University.

Benhabib, Jess and Spiegel, Mark M. 2005. "Human Capital and Technology Diffusion." In Philippe Aghion and Steven N. Durlauf, eds., *Handbook of Economic Growth.* Amsterdam: North Holland, Vol. 1A, pp. 935–66.

Benrath, Karl. 1877. *Bernardino Ochino of Siena.* New York: Robert Carter and Brothers.

Benz, Ernst. 1966. *Evolution and Christian Hope: Man s Concept of the Future from the Early Fathers to Teilhard de Chardin.* Garden City, NJ: Doubleday.

Berg, Maxine. 1980. *The Machinery Question and the Making of Political Economy, 1815–1848.* Cambridge: Cambridge University Press.

———. 2007. "The Genesis of Useful Knowledge." *History of Science* Vol. 45, pt. 2, No. 148, pp. 123–34.

Bernholz, Peter, Manfred Streit, and Roland Vaubel, eds. 1998. *Political Competition, Innovation, and Growth.* Berlin: Springer.

Bertucci, Paola. 2013. "Enlightened Secrets: Silk, Intelligent Travel, and Industrial Espionage in Eighteenth- Century France." *Technology and Culture* Vol. 54, No. 4, pp. 820–52.

Biagioli, Mario. 1990. "Galileo's System of Patronage." *History of Science* Vol. 28, No.1, pp. 1–62.

Bietenholz, Peter. 1966. *History and Biography in the Work of Erasmus of Rotterdam.* Geneva: Librairie Droz.

Birse, Ronald M. 1983. *Engineering at Edinburgh University: A Short History, 1673–1983.* Edinburgh: School of Engineering, University of Edinburgh.

Bisin, Alberto, and Thierry Verdier. 1998. "On the Cultural Transmission of Preferences for Social Status." *Journal of Public Economics* Vol. 70, pp. 75–97.

———. 2001. "The Economics of Cultural Transmission and the Dynamics of Preferences." *Journal of Economic Theory* Vol. 97, pp. 298–319.

———. 2011. "The Economics of Cultural Transmission and Socialization." In Jess Benhabib, Alberto Bisin and Matthew O. Jackson, eds.: *Handbook of Social Economics*, Vol. 1A. Amsterdam: North-Holland, pp. 339–416.

Blackmore, Susan. 1999. *The Meme Machine.* Oxford: Oxford University Press.

Blaut, James M. 1993. *The Colonizer s Model of the World.* New York: Guilford Press.

Blom, Philip. 2010. *A Wicked Company: The Forgotten Radicalism of the European Enlightenment.* New York: Basic Books.

Bodde, Derk. 1991. *Chinese Thought, Society, and Science.* Honolulu: University of Hawaii Press.

Bol, Peter K. 2008. *Neo-Confucianism in History.* Cambridge, MA: Harvard University Press.

Botticini, Maristella, and Zvi Eckstein. 2012. *The Chosen Few: How Education Shaped Jewish History 70–1492.* Princeton, NJ: Princeton University Press.

Bowles, Samuel. 2004. *Microeconomics: Behavior, Institutions, and Evolution.* Princeton, NJ: Princeton University Press.

Bowles, Samuel, and Gintis, Herbert. 2011. *A Cooperative Species: Human Reciprocity and Its Evolution.* Princeton, NJ: Princeton University Press.

Boyd, Robert, and Peter J. Richerson. 1985. *Culture and the Evolutionary Process.* Chicago: University of Chicago Press.

———. 2005. *The Origins and Evolution of Cultures.* Oxford and New York: Oxford University Press.

Boyd, Robert, Peter J. Richerson, and Joseph Henrich. 2013. "The Cultural Evolution of Technology." In Peter J. Richerson and Morten H. Christiansen, eds., *Cultural Evolution: Society, Technology, Language, and Religion.* Cambridge, MA: MIT Press, pp. 119–42.

Boyle, Robert. 1664. *Some Considerations Touching the Usefulnesse of Experimental Natural Philosophy. Propos d in a Familiar Discourse to a Friend, by way of Invitation to the Study of it.* second ed. Oxford: Hen. Hall for Ri. Davis.

———. 1669. "A Proemial Essay, Wherein, With Some Considerations Touching Experimental Essays in General, Is Interwoven Such an Introduction to All Those Written by the Author, as is Necessary to be Perus'd for the Better Understanding of them." In *Certain Physiological Essays and Other Tracts Written at Distant Times, and on Several Occasions.* Second ed. London: Blew Anchor in the Lower Walk of the New-Exchange: Henry Herringman.

————. 1671. *Some Considerations Touching the Usefulnesse of Experimental Natural Philosophy*. Oxford: Henry Hall for Ric. Davis.

————. 1682. *A Continuation of New Experiments, Physico Mechanical. The Second Part*. London: Printed by Miles Flesher.

————. 1690. *The Christian Virtuoso*. London: Printed for Edw. Jones.

————. 1744. *The Works of the Honourable Robert Boyle*, (5 vols). London: Printed for A. Millar.

Brandt, Loren, Debin Ma, and Thomas G. Rawski. 2014. "From Divergence to Convergence: Re-evaluating the History Behind China's Economic Boom." *Journal of Economic Literature* Vol. 52, No. 1, pp. 45–123.

Bray, Francesca. 1984. *Agriculture*. In Joseph Needham, ed., *Science and Civilization in China*. Cambridge: Cambridge University Press, Vol. 6, part 2.

Bray, Francesca, and Georges Métailié. 2001. "Who Was the Author of the Nongzhen Quanshu?" In Catherine Jami, Peter Engelfriet, and Gregory Blue, eds., *Statecraft and Intellectual Renewal in Late Ming China: the Cross-Cultural Synthesis of Xu Guangqi (1562–1633)*. Leiden: Brill, pp. 322–59.

Breger, Herbert. 1998. "The Paracelsians—Nature and Character." In Ole Peter Grell, ed., *Paracelsus: the Man and his Reputation, his Ideas and their Transformation*. Leiden: Brill, pp. 101–15.

Brock, William H. 1992. *The Norton History of Chemistry*. New York: W. W. Norton.

Brockliss, L.W.B. 2002. *Calvet s Web: Enlightenment and the Republic of Letters in Eighteenth-century France*. Oxford: Oxford University Press.

Brokaw, Cynthia J. 1994. "Tai Chen and Learning in the Confucian Tradition." In Alexander Woodside and Benjamin A. Elman, eds., *Education and Society in Late Imperial China, 1600–1900*. Berkeley: University of California Press, pp. 257–90.

Broman, Thomas. 2012. "The Semblance of Transparency: Expertise as a Social Good and an Ideology in Enlightened Societies." *Osiris* Vol. 27, No. 1, pp. 188–208.

————. 2013. "Criticism and the Circulation of News: The Scholarly Press in the Late Seventeenth Century." *History of Science* Vol. 51, pp. 125–50.

Brook, Timothy. 2010. *The Troubled Empire: China in the Yuan and Ming Dynasties*. Cambridge, MA: Harvard University Press.

Broomé, Per, Benny Carlson, Holmberg Ingvar, and Charles Schewe. 2011. "Do Defining Moments Leave their Mark for Life? The Case of Sweden." Malmö, Sweden: Malmö Institute for Studies of Migration, Diversity, and Welfare.

Browne, Sir Thomas. [1646] 1964. *Pseudodoxia Epidemica or Enquiries into Very Many Received Tenents and Commonly Presumed Truths*. In Geoffrey Keynes, ed., *The Works of Sir Thomas Browne*, Chicago: University of Chicago Press, Vol. II.

————. [1680] 1964. "Harveian Anniversary Oration." In Geoffrey Keynes, ed., *The Works of Sir Thomas Browne*, Chicago: University of Chicago Press, Vol. III, pp. 195–205.

————. 1964. *The Works of Sir Thomas Browne*, edited by Geoffrey Keynes. Chicago: University of Chicago Press.

Buringh, Eltjo, and Jan Luiten Van Zanden. 2009. "Charting the 'Rise of the West': Manuscripts and Printed Books in Europe, a Long-Term Perspective from the Sixth through Eighteenth Centuries." *Journal of Economic History* Vol. 69, No. 2, pp 409–445.

Burke, Peter. 2000. *A Social History of Knowledge*. Cambridge: Polity Press.

Bury, J. B. [1920] 1955. *The Idea of Progress: An Inquiry into Its Growth and Origin.* New York: Dover.

Bynum, W. F. 1993. "Nosology." In W.F. Bynum and Roy Porter, eds., *Companion Encyclopedia of the History of Medicine.* London and New York: Routledge, pp. 335–56.

Campanella, Tommaso. [1602] 1981. *The City in the Sun: A Poetical Dialogue.* Translated by Daniel J. Donno. Berkeley: University of California Press.

Cantoni, Davide, and Noam Yuchtman. 2014. "Medieval Universities, Legal Institutions, and the Commercial Revolution." *Quarterly Journal of Economics* Vol. 129, pp. 823–87.

Cardwell, Donald S. L. 1972. *Turning Points in Western Technology.* New York: Neale Watson, Science History Publications.

Carlos, Edward Stafford. 1880. *The Sidereal Messenger of Galileo and a part of the Preface to Kepler's Dioptrics.* London: Dawson's of Pall Mall.

Carpenter, Nathanael. 1625. *Geographie Delineated.* Oxford: Printed by John Lichfield and William Turner.

Castellano, Daniel J. 2004. "The Reception of Copernicanism in Spain and Italy before 1800." Masters thesis, Department of History, Boston University.

Caton, Hiram. 1988. *The Politics of Progress: The Origins and Development of the Commercial Republic, 1600–1835.* Gainesville: University of Florida Press.

Cavalli-Sforza, Luigi L., and M. W. Feldman, 1981. *Cultural Transmission and Evolution: a Quantitative Approach.* Princeton, NJ: Princeton University Press.

Cavalli Sforza, Luigi L., M. W. Feldman, K. H. Chen, and S. M. Dornbusch. 1982. "Theory and Observation in Cultural Transmission." *Science* Vol. 218, pp. 19–27.

Chambers, Douglas D. C. 2004. "Evelyn, John (1620–1706)." In *Oxford Dictionary of National Biography.* Oxford: Oxford University Press.

Chan, Hok-lam, and Peng Yoke Ho. 1993. "Li Chih, 1192–1279." In Igor de Rachewiltz et al., eds., *In the Service of the Khan: Eminent Personalities of the Early Mongol-Yüan Period (1200–1300).* Wiesbaden: Harrassowitz Verlag, pp. 316–35.

Chaney, Eric. 2008. "Tolerance, Religious Competition and the Rise and Fall of Muslim Science." Mimeo, Harvard University.

———. 2015. "Religion and the Rise and Fall of Islamic Science." Unpublished ms., Harvard University.

Childrey, Joshua. 1660. *Britannia Baconia or the Natural Rarities of England, Scotland, and Wales.* London: Printed for the author.

Ching, Julia. 1975. "Chu Shun-Shui, 1600–82. A Chinese Confucian Scholar in Tokugawa Japan." *Monumenta Nipponica* Vol. 30, No. 2, pp. 177–91.

———. 1979. "The Practical Learning of Chu Shun-shui, 1600–1682." In W. Theodore de Bary and Irene Bloom, eds., *Principle and Practicality: Essays in Neo-Confucianism and Practical Learning* New York: Columbia University Press, pp. 189–229.

———. 2000. *Religious Thought of Chu Hsi.* New York: Oxford University Press.

Chitnis, Anand. 1976. *The Scottish Enlightenment.* London: Croom Helm.

Chow, Kai-Wing. 2004. *Publishing, Culture, and Power in Early Modern China.* Stanford: Stanford University Press.

Christopoulou, Rebekka, Ahmed Jaber, and Dean R. Lillard. 2013. "The Intergenerational and Social Transmission of Cultural Traits: Theory and Evidence from Smoking Behavior." NBER Working Paper 19304.

Cipolla, Carlo M. 1972. "The Diffusion of Innovations in Early Modern Europe." *Comparative Studies in Society and History,* Vol. 14, No. 1, pp. 46–52.

———. 1980. *Before the Industrial Revolution: European Society and Economy, 1000–1700.* Second ed. New York: W. W. Norton.

Clark, Gregory. 2007. *A Farewell to Alms.* Princeton, NJ: Princeton University Press.

Clark, Peter. 2000. *British Clubs and Societies, 1580–1800: The Origins of an Associational World.* Oxford: Clarendon Press.

Clarke, John. 1731. *An Essay upon Study.* London: Printed for Arthur Bettesworth.

Clifton, Gloria. 2004. "Dollond Family (per. 1750–1871)." In *Oxford Dictionary of National Biography,* Oxford: Oxford University Press.

Coase, Ronald. 1974. "The Market for Goods and the Market for Ideas." *American Economic Review* Vol. 64, pp. 384–91.

Cobb, Matthew. 2006. *Generation: Seventeenth-Century Scientists Who Unravelled the Secrets of Sex, Life, and Growth.* New York and London: Bloomsbury.

Cohen, Bernard I. 1990. "Introduction: The Impact of the Merton Thesis." In Bernard I. Cohen, ed., *Puritanism and the Rise of Modern Science.* New Brunswick, NJ: Rutgers University Press, pp. 1–111.

Cohen, H. Floris. 1994. *The Scientific Revolution: A Historiographical Inquiry.* Chicago: University of Chicago Press.

———. 2012. *How Modern Science Came into the World.* Amsterdam: Amsterdam University Press.

Cohen, Jack, and Ian Stewart. 1994. *The Collapse of Chaos.* New York: Penguin.

Cohn, Norman. 1961. *The Pursuit of the Millennium.* New York: Harper Torchbooks.

Colie, Rosalie. 1955. "Cornelis Drebbel and Salomon De Caus: Two Jacobean Models for Salomon's House." *Huntingdon Library Quarterly* Vol. 18, pp. 245–60.

Collins, Randall. 1998. *The Sociology of Philosophies: A Global Theory of Intellectual Change.* Cambridge, MA: Harvard University Press.

Comte, Auguste. 1856. *Social Physics from the Positive Philosophy.* New York: Calvin Blanchard.

Condorcet, Jean-Antoine-Nicolas de Caritat, Marquis de. 1795. *Outlines of an Historical View of the Progress of the Human Mind: Translated from the French.* London: Printed for J. Johnson.

Constant, Edward W. 1980. *The Origins of the Turbojet Revolution.* Baltimore: Johns Hopkins University Press.

Cook, Harold J. 2007. *Matters of Exchange: Commerce, Medicine and Science in the Dutch Golden Age.* New Haven, CT and London: Yale University Press.

Copenhaver, Brian P. 1978. *Symphorien Champier and the Reception of the Occultist Tradition in Renaissance France.* The Hague and New York: Mouton.

Cormack, Lesley B. 1991. "Twisting the Lion's Tail: Practice and Theory at the Court of Henry Prince of Wales." In Bruce T. Moran, ed., *Patronage and Institutions: Science, Technology and Medicine at the European Court, 1500–1750.* Rochester, NY : Boydell Press, pp. 67–83.

Cosmides, Leda, and John Tooby. 1994. "Better than Rational: Evolutionary Psychology and the Invisible Hand." *American Economic Review* Vol. 84, pp. 327–32.

Cowan, Brian. 2005. *The Social Life of Coffee: The Emergence of the British Coffeehouse.* New Haven, CT and London: Yale University Press.

Cranmer-Byng, J.L., and Trevor Levere. 1981. "A Case Study in Cultural Collision: Scientific Apparatus in the Macartney Embassy to China, 1793." *Annals of Science*, Vol. 38, No. 5, pp. 503–25.

Cullen, Christopher. 1990. "The Science/Technology Interface in Seventeenth-century China: Song Yingxing on Qi and the Wu Xing." *Bulletin of the School of Oriental and African Studies* (University of London) Vol. 53, No. 2, pp. 295–318.

Damon, S. Foster. 1988. *A Blake Dictionary: The Ideas and Symbols of William Blake*. London: Brown.

Daniel, Stephen H. 2004. "Toland, John (1670–1722)." In *Oxford Dictionary of National Biography*. Oxford: Oxford University Press.

Darnton, Robert. 1979. *The Business of Enlightenment*. Cambridge, MA: Harvard University Press.

———. 2003. "The Unity of Europe: Culture and Politeness." In *George Washington s False Teeth*. New York: W. W. Norton, pp. 76–88.

Darwin, Charles. 1859/1871. *The Origin of Species by Means of Natural Selection* and *The Descent of Man and Selection in Relation to Sex*. New York: Modern Library edition.

Dasgupta, Partha, and Paul A. David. 1994. "Toward a New Economics of Science." *Research Policy*, Vol. 23, No. 5, pp. 487–521.

Daston, Lorraine. 1990. "Nationalism and Scientific Neutrality under Napoleon." In Tore Frängsmyr, ed., *Solomon s House Revisited*. Canton, MA: Science History Publications, pp. 95–119.

———. 1991. "The Ideal and Reality of the Republic of Letters in the Enlightenment." *Science in Context* Vol. 4, No. 2, pp. 367–86.

David, Paul A. 2004. "Patronage, Reputation, and Common Agency Contracting in the Scientific Revolution." Unpublished manuscript, Stanford University.

———. 2008. "The Historical Origins of 'Open Science': An Essay on Patronage, Reputation and Common Agency Contracting in the Scientific Revolution." *Capitalism and Society* Vol. 3, No. 2, pp. 1–103.

Davids, Karel. 2013. *Religion, Technology and the Great and Little Divergences*. Leiden and Boston: Brill.

Davy, Humphry. 1840. "Sketch of the Character of Lord Bacon." In *The Collected Works of Sir Humphry Davy*, edited by John Davy. London: Smith, Elder & Co., Vol. 7, pp. 121–22.

Dear, Peter. 1995. *Discipline and Experience: the Mathematical Way in the Scientific Revolution*. Chicago: University of Chicago Press.

———. 2006. *The Intelligibility of Nature: How Science Makes Sense of the World*. Chicago: University of Chicago Press.

Deaton, Angus. 2011. "Aging, Religion, and Health." In David A. Wise, ed., *Explorations in the Economics of Aging*. Chicago: University of Chicago Press, pp. 237–62.

De Bary, W. Theodore. 1975a. "Introduction." In W. Theodore De Bary, ed., *The Unfolding of Neo-Confucianism*. New York: Columbia University Press, pp.1–36.

De Bary, W. Theodore. 1975b. "Neo-Confucian Cultivation and the Seventeenth-century 'Enlightenment.'" In W. Theodore De Bary, ed., *The Unfolding of Neo-Confucianism*. New York: Columbia University Press, pp. 141–206.

Debus, Allen G. 1978. *Man and Nature in the Renaissance*. Cambridge: Cambridge University Press.

————. 2002. *The Chemical Philosophy: Paracelsian Science and Medicine in the Sixteenth and Seventeenth Centuries.* Second ed. New York: Science History Publications.

DeJean, Joan. 1997. *Ancients Against Moderns: Culture Wars and the Making of a Fin de Siècle.* Chicago: University of Chicago Press.

Delambre, J. B. [1816] 1867. "Notice sur la vie et les ouvrages de M. le comte J. L. Lagrange." In *Oeuvres de Lagrange,* Paris: Gauthiers-Villars, Vol. 1, pp. ix–li.

Delatour, Jérôme. 2005a. "Le Cabinet des Frères Dupuy." *Sciences et Techniques en Perspective* Vol. 9, No. 1, pp. 287–328.

————. 2005b. "Le Cabinet des Frères Dupuy." *Revue d Histoire des Facultés de Droit et de la Science Juridique* Vol. 25–26, pp. 157–200.

Delmedigo, Joseph Salomon. 1629. *Sefer Elim.* https://archive.org /stream/ seferelim00delmuoft#page/135/mode/2up, accessed Nov. 23, 2014.

Deming, David. 2005. "Born to Trouble: Bernard Palissy and the Hydrologic Cycle." *Ground Water* Vol. 43, No. 6, pp. 969–72.

Deng, Kent. 2009. "Movers and Shakers of Knowledge in China during the Ming-Qing Period." *History of Technology* Vol. 29, pp. 57–79.

Denonaine, Jean-Jacques. 1982. "Thomas Browne and the Respublica Litteraria." *English Language Notes* Vol. 19, No. 4, pp. 370–81.

Desaguliers, John Theophilus. 1745. *A Course of Experimental Philosophy,* second ed. London: Printed for W. Innys and others.

Descartes, René. 2000. *Philosophical Essays and Correspondence.* Edited by Roger Ariew. Indianapolis, IN: Hackett.

————. [1641] 2005. *Discourse on Method and Meditations on First Philosophy.* Translated by Elizabeth Haldane. Stilwell, KS: Digireads.

Deutsch, David. 2011. *The Beginning of Infinity: Explanations that Transform the World.* New York: Penguin.

Devlin, Keith. 2000. *The Language of Mathematics: Making the Invisible Visible.* New York: Henry Holt.

De Vries, Jan. 2008. *The Industrious Revolution: Consumer Behavior and the Household Economy, 1650 to the Present.* Cambridge: Cambridge University Press.

————. 2015. "Escaping the Great Divergence." *Tijdschrift voor Sociale en Economische Geschiedenis* Vol. 12, No. 2, pp. 39–49.

De Pleijt Alexandra M., and Jan Luiten van Zanden. 2013. "The Story of Two Transitions: Unified Growth Theory and the European Growth Experience, 1300-1870." Unpublished ms., Utrecht University.

De Saeger, David. 2008. "The Imperial Examinations and Epistemological Obstacles." *Philosophica* Vol. 82, No. 2, pp. 55–85.

Dharampal. 1971. *Indian Science and Technology in the Eighteenth Century.* Goa: Other India Press.

Dibon, Paul. 1978. "Communication in the *Respublica literaria* of the 17th Century." *Res Publica Litterarum: Studies in the Classical Tradition.* Vol. I, pp. 43–55.

Dick, Malcolm. n.d. "The Lunar Society and the Anti-slavery Debate." http:// www.search. revolutionaryplayers.org.uk, accessed Nov. 23, 2013.

Diderot, Denis. [1751] 2003. "Arts" in the *Encyclopédie ou Dictionnaire raisonné des sciences, des arts et des métiers.* Vol. 1 Reprinted in *The Encyclopedia of Diderot & d Alembert, Collaborative Translation Project,* translated by Nelly S. Hoyt and Thomas Cassirer. Ann Arbor: Michigan Publishing, University of Michigan Library. <http://hdl.handle.net/2027/spo.did2222.0000.139>, accessed June 24, 2014, n.p.

Dieckmann, Herbert. 1943. "The Influence of Francis Bacon on Diderot's *Interprétation de la Nature.*" *Romanic Review* Vol. 34, pp. 303–30.

Dijksterhuis, Fokko Jan. 2007. "Constructive Thinking: A Case for Dioptrics." In Lissa Roberts, Simon Schaffer, and Peter Dear, eds., *The Mindful Hand: Inquiry and Invention from the Late Renaissance to Early Industrialization.* Amsterdam: Royal Netherlands Academy of Arts and Sciences.

Dikötter, Frank. 2003. "China." In Roy Porter, ed., *The Cambridge History of Science,* Vol. 4: *Eighteenth-century Science.* Cambridge: Cambridge University Press, pp. 688–98.

Dittmar, Jeremiah. 2011. "Information Technology and Economic Change: The Impact of the Printing Press." *Quarterly Journal of Economics* Vol. 126, No. 3, pp. 1033–72.

Dobbs, Betty Jo Teeter. 2000. "Newton as Final Cause and Prime Mover." In Margaret J. Osler, ed., *Rethinking the Scientific Revolution.* Cambridge: Cambridge University Press, pp. 25–39.

Dobbs, Betty Jo Teeter, and Margaret C. Jacob. 1995. *Newton and the Culture of Newtonianism.* New York: Humanity Books.

Doepke, Matthias and Zilibotti Fabrizio. 2008. "Occupational Choice and the Spirit of Capitalism," *Quarterly Journal of Economics* Vol. 123, No. 2, pp. 747–93.

Dooley, Brendan. 2003. "The *Storia Letteraria d Italia* and the Rehabilitation of the Jesuit Science." In Mordechai Feingold, ed., *Jesuit Science and the Republic of Letters.* Cambridge, MA: MIT Press, pp. 433–73.

Dougharty, John. 1750. *The General Gauger: or, the Principles and Practice of Gauging Beer, Wine, and Malt,* sixth ed. London: Printed for John and Paul Knapton.

Dupré, Louis. 2004. *The Enlightenment and the Intellectual Foundations of Modern Culture.* New Haven, CT: Yale University Press.

Durham, William H. 1992. "Applications of Evolutionary Culture Theory." *Annual Reviews of Anthropology* Vol. 21, pp. 331–55.

Eamon, William. 1985. "Science and Popular Culture in Sixteenth Century Italy: The 'Professors of Secrets' and Their Books." *The Sixteenth Century Journal* Vol. 16, No. 4, pp. 471–85.

———. 1991. "Court, Academy and Printing House: Patronage and Scientific Careers in Late Renaissance Italy." In Bruce T. Moran, ed., *Patronage and Institutions: Science, Technology and Medicine at the European Court, 1500–1750.* Rochester, NY: Boydell Press, pp. 25–50.

———. 1994. *Science and the Secrets of Nature.* Princeton, NJ: Princeton University Press.

Easterlin, Richard. 1981. "Why Isn't the Whole World Developed?" *Journal of Economic History* Vol. 41, No. 1, pp. 1–19.

Easterly, William. 2001. *The Elusive Quest for Growth.* Cambridge, MA: MIT Press. *Edinburgh Review,* 1851. "Review of the Official Catalogue of the Great Exhibition of the Works of Industry of All Nations." *Edinburgh Review* No. 192, pp. 285–306.

Eisenstein, Elizabeth. 1979. *The Printing Press as an Agent of Change.* Cambridge: Cambridge University Press.

Eldredge, Niles. 1995. *Reinventing Darwin: The Great Evolutionary Debate.* London: Weidenfeld and Nicholson.

Elman, Benjamin A. 1994. "Changes in Confucian Civil Service Examinations from the Ming to the Ch'ing Dynasty." In Alexander Woodside and Benjamin

A. Elman, eds., *Education and Society in Late Imperial China, 1600–1900*. Berkeley: University of California Press, pp. 111–48.

———. 2000. *A Cultural History of Civil Examinations in Late Imperial China*. Berkeley: University of California Press.

———. 2001. *From Philosophy to Philology: Intellectual and Social Aspects of Change in Late Imperial China*, second ed. Los Angeles: UCLA Asia-Pacific Institute.

———. 2005. *On Their Own Terms: Science in China, 1550–1900*. Cambridge, MA: Harvard University Press.

———. 2006. *A Cultural History of Modern Science in China*. Cambridge, MA: Harvard University Press.

———. 2010. "The Investigation of Things, Natural Studies, and Evidential Studies in Late Imperial China." In Hans Ulrich Vogel and Günter Dux, eds., *Concepts of Nature: A Chinese-European Cross-Cultural Perspective*. Leiden and Boston: Brill, pp. 368–99.

———. 2013. *Civil Examinations and Meritocracy in Late Imperial China*. Cambridge, MA: Harvard University Press.

Elvin, Mark. 1973. *The Pattern of the Chinese Past*. Stanford, CA: Stanford University Press.

———. 1996. *Another History: Essays on China from a European Perspective*. Broadway, NSW, Australia: Wild Peony Press.

———. 2004. *Retreat of the Elephants: an Environmental History of China*. New Haven, CT: Yale University Press.

Engelfriet, Peter M. 1998. *Euclid in China: The Genesis of the First Chinese Translation of Euclid's Elements*. Leiden: Brill.

Epstein, Stephan R. 2013. "Transferring Technical Knowledge and Innovating in Europe, c. 1200–c. 1800." In Maarten Prak and Jan Luiten van Zanden, eds., *Technology, Skills and the Pre-modern Economy*. Leiden: Brill, pp. 25–67.

Evans, R.J.W. 1973. *Rudolf II and His World*. Oxford: Oxford University Press. Rep. ed., 1997.

Evelyn, John. 1661. "Translator's Preface." In Gabriel Naudé, *Instructions Concerning Erecting of a Library*. London: G. Bedle and T. Collins.

———. [1664] 1679. *Sylva or a Discourse of Forest Trees*. London: Printed for John Martyn, printer for the Royal Society.

Fara, Patricia. 2002. *Newton: The Making of a Genius*. New York: Columbia University Press.

———. 2004. "Desaguliers, John Theophilus (1683–1744)." In *Oxford Dictionary of National Biography*. Oxford: Oxford University Press.

Farrington, Benjamin. [1951] 1979. *Francis Bacon: Philosopher of Industrial Science*. New York: Farrar, Straus and Giroux.

Feingold, Mordechai. 2003. "Jesuits: Savants." In Mordechai Feingold, ed., *Jesuit Science and the Republic of Letters*. Cambridge, MA: MIT Press, pp. 1–45.

———. 2004. *The Newtonian Moment: Isaac Newton and the Making of Modern Culture*. New York: Oxford University Press.

———. 2010. "The War on Newton." *Isis* Vol. 1010, No. 1, pp. 175–86.

Fernández, Raquel. 2008. "Culture and Economics." In Steven N. Durlauf and Lawrence E. Blume, eds., *The New Palgrave Dictionary of Economics*, second edition http://www.dictionaryofeconomics.com/article?id=pde2008_E000282, accessed July 12, 2015.

————. 2011. "Does Culture Matter?" In Jess Benhabib, Matthew O. Jackson, and Alberto Bisin, eds., *Handbook of Social Economics*. Amsterdam: North-Holland, Vol. 1A, pp. 481–510.

Ferrone, Vincenzo. 2015. *The Enlightenment: History of an Idea*. Princeton, NJ: Princeton University Press.

Findlen, Paula. 2004, ed. *Athanasius Kircher: The Last Man Who Knew Everything*. New York: Routledge.

Fontenelle, Bernard Le Bovier de. 1719. *Conversations with a Lady, on the Plurality of Worlds, to Which is Also Added, a Discourse Concerning the Antients and Moderns. Written by the Same Author*. London: Printed for J. Darby.

————. [1727] 1728. "Éloge de M. Neuton." In *The Life of Sir Isaac Newton*, London: printed for James Woodman, pp. 1–23.

Fowler, James and Darren Schreiber. 2008. "Biology, Politics, and the Emerging Science of Human Nature." *Science*, Vol. 322 (Nov. 7), pp. 912–14.

Frängsmyr, Tore, J.L. Heilbron, and Robin E. Rider. 1990. *The Quantifying Spirit in the 18th Century*. Berkeley: University of California Press.

Frank, Robert G. Jr. 1979. "The Image of Harvey in Commonwealth and Restauration England." In Jerome Bylebyl, ed., *William Harvey and His Age*. Baltimore: Johns Hopkins University Press, pp. 103–44.

Franklin, Benjamin, [1780] 1840. "True Science and its Progress—Inconveniences Attend all Situations in Life." In *The Works of Benjamin Franklin*, edited by Jared Sparks. Boston: Hilliard, Gray and Company, Vol. 8, p. 418.

Freud, Sigmund. [1930] 1961. *Civilization and Its Discontent*. New York: W. W. Norton.

Fumaroli, Marc. 2001. "Les Abeilles et les Araignées." In Anne-Marie, Lecoq, ed., *La Querelle des Anciens et des Modernes*. Paris: Gallimard, pp. 7–220.

————. 2015. *La République des Lettres*. Paris: Gallimard.

Futuyma, Douglas J. 1986. *Evolutionary Biology*. Sunderland, MA: Sinauer Publishers.

Galor, Oded. 2011. *Unified Growth Theory*. Princeton, NJ: Princeton University Press.

Galor, Oded and Omer Moav. 2002. "Natural Selection and the Origins of Economic Growth." *Quarterly Journal of Economics* Vol. 117, No. 4, pp. 1133–91.

————. 2006. "Das Human Kapital: A Theory of the Demise of the Class Structure." *Review of Economic Studies* Vol. 73, No. 1, pp. 85–117.

Gans, Joshua S. and Scott Stern. 2003. "The Product Market and the 'Market for Ideas': Commercialization Strategies for Technology Entrepreneurs" *Research Policy* Vol. 32, pp. 333–50.

Gascoigne, John. 1994. *Joseph Banks and the English Enlightenment*. Cambridge: Cambridge University Press.

————. 2003. "Ideas of Nature: Natural Philosophy." In Roy Porter, ed., *The Cambridge History of Science*, Vol. 4: *Eighteenth-Century Science*. Cambridge: Cambridge University Press, pp. 285–304.

Gaukroger, Stephen. 2001. *Francis Bacon and the Transformation of Early-Modern Philosophy*. Cambridge: Cambridge University Press.

————. 2006. *The Emergence of a Scientific Culture*. Oxford: Oxford University Press.

Gauss, Christian, ed., 1920. *Selections of the Works of Jean-Jacques Rousseau*, second ed. Princeton, NJ: Princeton University Press.

Gay, Peter. 1966. *The Enlightenment*. Vol 1: *An Interpretation: the Rise of Modern Paganism*, New York: Alfred A. Knopf.

————. 1969. *The Enlightenment*. Vol. 2: *The Science of Freedom*. New York: W. W. Norton.

Gernet, Jacques. 1982. *A History of Chinese Civilization*. Cambridge: Cambridge University Press.

Gibbon, Edward. 1789. *The History of the Decline and Fall of the Roman Empire*, new ed., 3 vols. London: Printed for A. Strahan and T. Cadell.

Giglioni, Guido. 2010. "The First of the Moderns or the Last of the Ancients? Bernardino Telesio on Nature and Sentience." *Bruniana & Campanelliana* Vol. 16, No. 1, pp. 69–87.

Gilbert, William. [1600] 1893. *De Magnete*, translated by P. Fleury Mottelay. London: Bernard Quaritch.

Gillispie, Charles Coulston. 1960. *The Edge of Objectivity: An Essay on the History of Scientific Ideas*. Princeton, NJ: Princeton University Press.

———. 1980. *Science and Polity in France at the End of the Old Regime*. Princeton, NJ: Princeton University Press.

Giuliano, Paola. 2016. Review of Peter J. Richerson and Morten H. Christiansen, 2013. *Journal of Economic Perspectives* Vol. 54, No. 2, pp. 522–33.

Glaeser, Edward L. 2005. "The Political Economy of Hatred." *Quarterly Journal of Economics* Vol. 120, No. 1, pp. 45–86.

Glaeser, Edward L, R. La Porta, F. Lopez-de-Silanes, and Andrei Shleifer. 2004. "Do Institutions Cause Growth?" *Journal of Economic Growth* Vol. 9, pp. 271–303.

Glanvill, Joseph. 1661. *The Vanity of Dogmatizing*. London: Printed by E. C. for Henry Eversden.

———. 1665. *Scepsis Scientifica, or, Confest Ignorance, the Way to Science*. London: Printed by E. Cotes for Henry Eversden.

———. 1668. *Plus Ultra, or, The Progress and Advancement of Knowledge since the Days of Aristotle*. London: Printed for James Collins.

Glass, Bentley. 2008. "Maupertuis, Pierre Louis Moreau De." In Charles C. Gillispie, ed., *Complete Dictionary of Scientific Biography*. Detroit: Charles Scribner's Sons, Vol. 9, pp. 186–89.

Goldgar, Anne. 1995. *Impolite Learning: Conduct and Community in the Republic of Letters, 1680–1750*. New Haven, CT: Yale University Press.

Goldschmidt, Richard B. 1940. *The Material Basis of Evolution*, reprinted, 1982. New Haven, CT: Yale University Press.

Goldstone, Jack A. 2002. "Efflorescences and Economic Growth in World History: Rethinking the 'Rise of the West' and the Industrial Revolution." *Journal of World History* Vol. 13, No. 2, pp. 323–89.

———. 2009. *Why Europe? The Rise of the West in World History, 1500–1850*. Boston: McGraw-Hill.

———. 2012. "Divergence in Cultural Trajectories: The Power of the Traditional within the Early Modern." In David Porter, ed. *Comparative Early Modernities*. New York: Palgrave-Macmillan, pp. 165–92.

Golinsky, Jan. 1995. "'The Nicety of Experiment': Precision of Measurement and Precision of Reasoning in late Eighteenth-Century Chemistry." In M. Norton Wise, ed., *The Values of Precision*. Princeton, NJ: Princeton University Press, pp. 72–91.

Goodman, Dena. 1991. "Governing the Republic of Letters: The Politics of Culture in the French Enlightenment." *History of European Ideas* Vol. 13, No. 3, pp. 183–99.

———. 1994. *The Republic of Letters: A Cultural History of the French Enlightenment*. Ithaca, NY: Cornell University Press.

Goody, Jack. 2009. *Renaissances: The One or the Many?* Cambridge: Cambridge University Press.

———. 2010. *The Eurasian Miracle.* Cambridge: Polity Press.

Gorodnichenko, Yuriy and Gerard Roland. 2011. "Culture, Institutions, and the Wealth of Nations." NBER Working Papers 16368, unpublished ms.

Gough J. B. 2008. "Réaumur, René-Antoine Ferchault de." In Charles C. Gillispie, ed., *Complete Dictionary of Scientific Biography.* Gale Virtual Reference Library. Detroit: Charles Scribner's Sons. Vol. 11, pp. 327–35.

Grafe, Regina. 2012. *Distant Tyranny: Markets, Power, and Backwardness in Spain, 1650–1800.* Princeton, NJ: Princeton University Press.

Grafton, Anthony. 1983. "Protestant versus Prophet: Isaac Casaubon on Hermes Trismegistus." *Journal of the Warburg and Courtauld Institutes* Vol. 46, pp. 78–93.

———. 2009a. "A Sketch Map of a Lost Continent: the Republic of Letters." *The Republic of Letters: a Journal for the Study of Knowledge, Politics, and the Arts,* Vol. 1, No. 1, pp. 1–18. Reprinted in *Worlds Made by Words: Scholarship and Community in the Modern West.* Cambridge, MA: Harvard University Press, pp. 9–34.

———. 2009b. "Where was Salomon's House? Ecclesiastical History and the Origins of Bacon's New Atlantis." Reprinted in *Worlds Made by Words: Scholarship and Community in the Modern West.* Cambridge, MA: Harvard University Press, pp. 98–113.

———. 2015. "A Hero of the European Mind." *New York Review of Books."* Nov. 19.

Granovetter, Mark S. 1973. "The Strength of Weak Ties." *American Journal of Sociology* Vol. 78, no. 6, pp. 1360–80.

———. 1983. "The Strength of Weak Ties: A Network Theory Revisited." *Sociological Theory* Vol. 1, pp. 201–33.

———. 2005. "The Impact of Social Structure on Economic Outcomes." *Journal of Economic Perspectives* Vol. 19, No.1, pp. 33–50.

Grant, Edward. 2003. "The Partial Transformation of Medieval Cosmology by Jesuits in the Sixteenth and Seventeenth Centuries." In Mordechai Feingold, ed., *Jesuit Science and the Republic of Letters.* Cambridge, MA: MIT Press, pp. 127–55.

Greene, Kevin. 2000. "Technological Innovation and Economic Progress in the Ancient World: M. I. Finley Re-considered." *Economic History Review* Vol. 53, No. 1, pp. 29–59.

Greengrass, Mark. 2004. "Woodward, Hezekiah (1591/2–1675)." *Oxford Dictionary of National Biography.* Oxford: Oxford University Press.

Greengrass, Mark, Michael Leslie, and Timothy Raylor, eds. 1994. *Samuel Hartlib and Universal Reformation.* Cambridge: Cambridge University Press.

Greif, Avner. 1994. "Cultural Beliefs and the Organization of Society: a Historical and Theoretical Reflection on Collectivist and Individualist Societies." *Journal of Political Economy* Vol. 102, No. 5, pp. 912–50.

———. 2005. *Institutions and the Path to the Modern Economy: Lessons from Medieval Trade.* Cambridge: Cambridge University Press.

———. 2009. "Morality and Institutions." Unpublished ms., Stanford University.

———. 2012. "A Theory of Moral Authority: Moral Choices under Moral Networks Externalities." unpublished ms., Stanford University.

Greif, Avner, and Guido Tabellini. 2014. "The Clan and the City: Sustaining Cooperation in China and Europe." Unpublished ms.

Greif, Avner, and Steven Tadelis. 2010. "A Theory of Moral Persistence: Crypto-Morality and Political Legitimacy." *Journal of Comparative Economics* Vol. 38, pp. 229–44.

Grell, Ole Peter. 2007. "In Search of True Knowledge: Ole Worm (1588–1654) and the True Philosophy." In Pamela H. Smith and Benjamin Schmidt, eds., *Making Knowledge in Early Modern Europe*. Chicago: University of Chicago Press, pp. 214–32.

Guerrini, Anita. 2004a. "Keill, James (1673–1719)." In *Oxford Dictionary of National Biography*. Oxford: Oxford University Press.

———. 2004b. "Cheyne, George (1671/2–1743)." In *Oxford Dictionary of National Biography*. Oxford: Oxford University Press.

Guiso, Luigi, Paola Sapienza, and Luigi Zingales. 2006. "Does Culture Affect Economic Outcomes?" *The Journal of Economic Perspectives* Vol. 20, No. 2, pp. 23–48.

———. "Social Capital as Good Culture." Proceedings of the Twenty-Second Annual Congress of the European Economic Association. *Journal of the European Economic Association,* Vol. 6, No. 2/3, pp. 295–320.

Gundersheimer, Werner L. 1966. *The Life and Works of Louis Le Roy*. Geneva: Librairie Droz.

Haberman, Jacob. 2007. "Delmedigo, Joseph Solomon." In *Encyclopaedia Judaica,* Michael Berenbaum and Fred Skolnik, eds., second ed. Detroit: Macmillan Reference Vol. 5, pp. 543–44.

Habermas, Jürgen. 1989. *The Structural Transformation of the Public Sphere*. Cambridge, MA: MIT Press.

Hahn, Roger. 1986. "Laplace and the Mechanistic Universe." In David C. Lindberg and Ronald L. Numbers, eds., *God and Nature: Historical Essays on the Encounter between Christianity and Science*. Berkeley: University of California Press, pp. 256–76.

———. 1990. "The Age of Academies." In Tore Frängsmyr, ed., *Solomon s House Revisited*. Canton, MA: Science History Publications, pp. 3–12.

Hakewill, George. 1627. *An Apologie of the Power and Providence of God in the Government of the World*. Oxford: Printed by John Lichfield and William Turner.

Hall, A. Rupert. 1974. "What Did the Industrial Revolution in Britain Owe to Science?" In Neil McKendrick, ed., *Historical Perspectives: Studies in English Thought and Society*. London: Europa Publications, pp. 129–51.

Halley, Edmund. [1687] 1934. "Ode to Newton," translated by Leon J. Richerson. http://www.vrijmetselaarsgilde.eu/Maconnieke%20Encyclopedie/NMAP~1/Newtonis/EHOde.html.N.p. accessed Aug. 28, 2013.

Hankins, Thomas L. 2008. "Lalande, Joseph-Jérôme Lefrançais de." In Charles C. Gillespie, ed. *Complete Dictionary of Scientific Biography*. Detroit: Charles Scribner's Sons, Vol. 7, pp. 579–82.

Harford, Tim. 2016. "How Politicians Poisoned Statistics." *Financial Times* April 16/17 2016, pp. 16–17.

Harkness, Deborah. 2007. *The Jewel House: Elizabethan London and the Scientific Revolution*. New Haven, CT and London: Yale University Press.

Harris, Judith Rich. 2009. *The Nurture Assumption: Why Children Turn Out the Way They Do,* second edition. New York: Free Press.

Hauk, Esther, and Maria Saez-Marti. 2002. "On the Cultural Transmission of Corruption." *Journal of Economic Theory* Vol. 107, pp. 311–35.

Headley, John M. 1997. *Tommaso Campanella and the Transformation of the World.* Princeton, NJ: Princeton University Press.

Headrick, Daniel R. 2000. *When Information Came of Age: Technologies of Knowledge in the Age of Reason and Revolution, 1700–1850.* New York: Oxford University Press.

Hegel, Georg Wilhelm Friedrich [1805–1806] 1892-6. *Lectures on the History of Philosophy* translated by Elizabeth S. Haldane, 3 vols. London: Kegan Paul, Trench, Trübner and Co.

Heilbron, J. L. 1990. "Introductory Essay." In Tore Frängsmyr, J. L. Heilbron, and Robin E. Rider, eds., *The Quantifying Spirit in the 18th Century.* Berkeley: University of California Press, pp. 1–23.

———. 2003a. "Academies and Learned Societies." In J. L. Heilbron, ed., *The Oxford Companion to the History of Modern Science.* Oxford and New York: Oxford University Press, pp. 1–5.

———. 2003b. "Experimental Philosophy." In J. L. Heilbron, ed., *The Oxford Companion to the History of Modern Science.* Oxford and New York: Oxford University Press, pp. 286–88.

Helsham, Richard. 1755. *A Course of Lectures in Natural Philosophy.* London: Printed for J. Nourse at the Lamb.

Henrich, Joseph. 2001 "Cultural Transmission & the Diffusion of Innovation." *American Anthropologist* Vol. 103, pp. 992–1013.

———. 2004. "Demography and Cultural Evolution: How Adaptative Cultural Processes Can Produce Maladaptive Losses—the Tasmanian Case." *American Antiquity* Vol. 69, No. 2, pp. 197–214.

———. 2009. "The Evolution of Innovation-Enhancing Institutions." In Stephen Shennan and Michael O'Brien, eds., *Innovation in Cultural Systems: Contributions from Evolutionary Anthropology.* Altenberg Workshops in Theoretical Biology. Cambridge, MA: MIT Press.

Henrich, Joseph, and Natalie Henrich. 2006. "Culture, Evolution, and the Puzzle of Human Cooperation." *Cognitive Systems Research* Vol. 7, pp. 220–45.

Henrich, Joseph, Robert Boyd, and Peter J. Richerson, 2008. "Five Misunderstandings about Cultural Evolution." *Human Nature* Vol. 19, No. 2, pp. 119–37.

Henrich, Joseph et al. 2001. "In Search of Homo Economicus: Behavioral Experiments in 15 Small-Scale Societies." *American Economic Review* Vol. 91, No. 2, pp. 73–78.

Henry, John. 2002. *Knowledge Is Power: How Magic, the Government and an Apocalyptic Vision Inspired Bacon to Create Modern Science.* Cambridge: Icon Books.

———. 2008. *The Scientific Revolution and the Origins of Modern Science*, third ed. Basingstoke, UK: Palgrave Macmillan.

Hetherington, Norriss S. 1983. "Isaac Newton's Influence on Adam Smith's Natural Laws in Economics." *Journal of the History of Ideas* Vol. 44, No. 3, pp. 497–505.

Hilaire-Pérez, Liliane. 2007. "Technology as Public Culture." *History of Science* Vol. 45, pt. 2, No. 148, pp. 135–53.

Hill, Christopher. 1965. *Intellectual Origins of the English Revolution.* Oxford: Clarendon Press.

———. 1967. *Reformation to Industrial Revolution.* Harmondsworth, UK: Penguin.

Ho, Peng Yoke. 1993. "Kuo Shou-Ching." In Igor de Rachewiltz et al., eds., *In the Service of the Khan: Eminent Personalities of the Early Mongol-Yüan Period (1200–1300)*. Wiesbaden: Harrassowitz Verlag, pp. 282–99.

Hodgson, Geoffrey M. and Thorbjørn Knudsen. 2010. *Darwin s Conjecture: the Search for General Principles of Social and Economic Evolution*. Chicago: University of Chicago Press.

Hoffman, Philip T. 2015. *Why Did Europe Conquer the World?* Princeton, NJ: Princeton University Press.

Home, R. W. 2003. "Mechanics and Experimental Physics." In Roy Porter, ed., *The Cambridge History of Science*, Vol. 4: *Eighteenth-Century Science*. Cambridge: Cambridge University Press, pp. 354–74.

Hont, Istvan. 2005. *Jealousy of Trade: International Competition and the Nation-State in Historical Perspective*. Cambridge, MA: Harvard University Press.

Hooke, Robert. 1667. *Micrographia: Or Some Physiological Descriptions of Minute Bodies Made by Magnifying Glasses*. London: Printed for John Martyn.

———. 1705a. "The Present state of Natural Philosophy, and How Its Defects May Be Remedied." In *The Posthumous Works of Robert Hooke, M.D. S.R.S.* London: printed by Sam. Smith and Benj. Walford, pp. 3–185.

———. 1705b. "A Discourse on Earthquakes." In *The Posthumous Works of Robert Hooke, M.D. S.R.S.* London: printed by Sam. Smith and Benj. Walford, pp. 250–429.

Hooykaas, R. [1956], 1990. "Science and Reformation." *Journal of World History* Vol. 3, pp. 109–39. Repr. in I. Bernard Cohen, ed. 1990. *Puritanism and the Rise of Modern Science*. New Brunswick: Rutgers University Press, pp. 189–208.

———. 1972. *Religion and the Rise of Modern Science*. Edinburgh: Scottish Academic Press.

Hornung, Erik. 2014. "Immigration and the Diffusion of Technology: The Huguenot Diaspora in Prussia." *American Economic Review* Vol. 104, No.1, pp. 84–122.

Houghton, Walter E., Jr. 1942. "The English Virtuoso in the Seventeenth Century, pts. I and II," *Journal of the History of Ideas* Vol. 3, No. 1, pp. 51–73, 190–217.

Huang, Martin W. 1998. "Stylization and Invention: the Burden of Self-Expression in *The Scholars*." In Roger T. Ames, Thomas P. Kasulis, and Wimal Dissanayake, eds., *Self as Image in Asian Theory and Practice*. Albany: State University of New York Press, pp. 89–112.

Huang, Ray. 1981. *1587: A Year of No Significance*. New Haven, CT: Yale University Press.

Hucker, Charles O. 1975. *China s Imperial Past*. Stanford, CA: Stanford University Press.

Huff, Toby. 2011. *Intellectual Curiosity and the Scientific Revolution*. Cambridge: Cambridge University Press.

Hughes, Jonathan R. T. 1986. *The Vital Few: the Entrepreneur and American Progress*. Expanded Edition. Oxford: Oxford University Press.

Huizinga, Johan. [1924] 1984. *Erasmus and the Age of Reformation. With a selection from the letters of Erasmus*. Translated from the Dutch by F. Hopman. Princeton, NJ: Princeton University Press (Princeton Legacy Library).

Hume, David. [1742] 1985. "Of the Rise and Progress of the Arts and Sciences." In David Hume, *Essays: Moral, Political and Literary*, edited by Eugene F. Miller. Indianapolis: Liberty Fund, pp. 111–37.

———. [1754] 1985. ""Of the Populousness of Ancient Nations." In *Essays: Moral, Political and Literary*, edited by Eugene F. Miller. Indianapolis: Liberty Fund, pp. 377–464.

Hunter, Michael. 1981. *Science and Society in Restoration England*. Cambridge: Cambridge University Press.

———. 1989. *Establishing the New Science: the Experience of the Early Royal Society*. Woodbridge, UK: Boydell Press.

———. ed. 1994. *Robert Boyle Reconsidered*. Cambridge: Cambridge University Press.

———. 1995a. "The Debate over Science." *In Science and the Shape of Orthodoxy: Intellectual Change in Late Seventeenth-Century Britain*. Woodbridge, UK: Boydell Press, pp. 101–19.

———. 1995b. "First Steps in Institutionalization: The Royal Society of London." In *Science and the Shape of Orthodoxy: Intellectual Change in Late Seventeenth-Century Britain*. Woodbridge, UK: Boydell Press, pp. 120–34.

———. 1995c. "The Early Royal Society and the Shape of Knowledge." In *Science and the Shape of Orthodoxy: Intellectual Change in Late Seventeenth-Century Britain*. Woodbridge, UK: Boydell Press, pp. 169–79.

———. 1995d. "John Evelyn in the 1650s: a Virtuoso in Search of a Role." In *Science and the Shape of Orthodoxy: Intellectual Change in Late Seventeenth-Century Britain*. Woodbridge, UK: Boydell Press, pp. 67–98.

———. 2009. *Boyle: Between God and Science*. New Haven, CT: Yale University Press.

Iliffe Robert. 1995. "'Is He Like Other Men?' The Meaning of the *Principia Mathematica* and the Author as Idol." In Gerald MacLean, ed., *Culture and Society in the Stuart Restoration*. Cambridge: Cambridge University Press, pp. 159–76.

———. 2003. "Philosophy of Science." In Roy Porter, ed., *The Cambridge History of Science*, Vol.4: *Eighteenth-century Science*. Cambridge: Cambridge University Press, pp. 267–84.

Im Hoff, Ulrich. 1994. *The Enlightenment*. Oxford: Blackwell.

Inkster, Ian. 1991. *Science and Technology in History: An Approach to Industrial Development*. New Brunswick, NJ: Rutgers University Press.

Israel, Jonathan. 2010. *A Revolution of the Mind*. Princeton, NJ: Princeton University Press.

Itard, Jean. 2008. "Clairaut, Alexis-Claude." In Charles C. Gillespie, ed., *Complete Dictionary of Scientific Biography*. Detroit: Charles Scribner's Sons, Vol. 3 pp. 281–86.

Jablonka, Eva, and Marion J. Lamb. 2005. *Evolution in Four Dimensions: Genetic, Epigenetic, Behavioral, and Symbolic Variation in the History of Life*. Cambridge, MA: MIT Press.

Jacob, Margaret C. 1986. "Christianity and the New Worldview." In David C. Lindberg and Ronald L. Numbers, eds., *God and Nature: Historical Essays on the Encounter between Christianity and Science*. Berkeley: University of California Press, pp. 238–55.

———. 1988. *The Cultural Meaning of the Scientific Revolution*. New York: Alfred A. Knopf.

———. 1991. *Living the Enlightenment: Freemasonry and Politics in Eighteenth-Century Europe*. New York: Oxford University Press.

———. 1997. *Scientific Culture and the Making of the Industrial West*. second ed., New York: Oxford University Press.

———. 1998. "The Cultural Foundations of Early Industrialization." In Maxine Berg and Kristin Bruland, eds., *Technological Revolutions in Europe*, Cheltenham, UK: Edward Elgar, pp. 67–85.

———. 2000a. "Commerce, Industry, and the Laws of Newtonian Science: Weber Revisited and Revised." *Canadian Journal of History* Vol. 35, No. 2 pp. 275–92.

———. 2000b. "The Truth of Newton's Science and the Truth of Science's History." In Margaret J. Osler, ed., *Rethinking the Scientific Revolution*. Cambridge: Cambridge University Press.

———. 2006. *Strangers Nowhere in the World: The Rise of Cosmopolitanism in Early Modern Europe*. Philadelphia: University of Pennsylvania Press.

———. 2007. "Mechanical Science of the Factory Floor." *History of Science*, Vol. 45, part 2, No. 148, pp. 197–221.

———. 2014. *The First Knowledge Economy*. Cambridge: Cambridge University Press.

Jacob, Margaret C., and Larry Stewart. 2004. *Practical Matter: Newton s Science in the Service of Industry and Empire, 1687–1851*. Cambridge, MA: Harvard University Press.

Jami, Catherine. 1994. "Learning Mathematical Sciences during the Early and Mid-Ch'ing." In Alexander Woodside and Benjamin A. Elman, eds., *Education and Society in Late Imperial China, 1600–1900*. Berkeley: University of California Press, pp. 223–54.

———. 2012. *The Emperor s New Mathematics: Western Learning and Imperial Authority during the Kangxi Reign (1662–1722)*. Oxford: Oxford University Press.

Jami, Catherine, Peter Engelfriet, and Gregory Blue. 2001. "Introduction." In Catherine Jami, Peter Engelfriet, and Gregory Blue, eds., *Statecraft and Intellectual Renewal in Late Ming China: The Cross-Cultural Synthesis of Xu Guangqi (1562–1633)*. Leiden: Brill, pp. 1–15.

Janiak, Andrew. 2006. "Newton's Philosophy." In Edward N. Zalta, ed., *The Stanford Encyclopedia of Philosophy*, http://plato.stanford.edu/archives/win2009/entries/Newton-philosophy/, accessed Nov. 29, 2013.

Jefferson, Thomas. 1789. "Letter to John Trumbull, dated Feb. 15, 1789." http://www.loc.gov/ exhibits/jefferson/18.html, accessed Sep. 3, 2013.

Jenyns, Soame. 1761. *A Free Inquiry into the Nature and Origin of Evil*, fourth edition. London: R. and J. Dodsley.

Jiang, Jin. 2001. "Heresy and Persecution in Late Ming Society: Reinterpreting the Case of Li Zhi." *Late Imperial China* Vol. 22, No. 2, pp. 1–34.

Jin, Dengjian. 2016. *The Great Knowledge Transcendence: The Rise of Western Science and Technology Reframed*. New York: Palgrave Macmillan.

Johnson, Dominic D.P. 2009. "The Error of God: Error Management Theory, Religion, and the Evolution of Cooperation." In Simon A. Levin, ed., *Games, Groups, and the Global Good. Springer Series in Game Theory*. New York: Springer, pp. 169–80.

Johnson, Dominic D.P., and Oliver Krüger. 2004. "The Good of Wrath: Supernatural Punishment and the Evolution of Cooperation." *Political Theology* Vol. 5, No. 2, pp. 159–76.

Johnson, Samuel. 1759. "What Have You Done? (With Your Life)." *The Idler* no. 88, 22 December 1759. http://www.ourcivilisation.com /smartboard /shop/johnsons/idler/chap88.htm, accessed May 11, 2015.

Jones, Bence. 1871. *The Royal Institution: Its Founder and Its First Professors*. London: Longmans Green and Co.

Jones, Eric L. 1981. *The European Miracle*. Cambridge: Cambridge University Press.

———. 2006. *Cultures Merging: a Historical and Economic Critique of Culture*. Princeton, NJ: Princeton University Press.

Jones, Richard Foster. [1936] 1961. *Ancients and Moderns: a Study in the Rise of the Scientific Movement in 17th Century England*, second ed., St. Louis, MO: Washington University Press.

Jones, Peter M. 2016. *Agricultural Enlightenment: Knowledge, Technology, and Nature*. Oxford: Oxford University Press.

Jonston (Johnstone), John. 1657. *A History of the Constancy of Nature*. London: Printed for John Streater.

Kant, Immanuel. [1784] 2010. *Principles of Politics and Perpetual Peace*. Translated by W. Hastie. n.p.: Digireads.com.

Karayalçin, Cem. 2008. "Divided we Stand, United we Fall: the Hume-North-Jones Mechanism for the Rise of Europe." *International Economic Review* Vol. 49 No. 3, pp. 973–99.

Kealey, Terence. 1996. *The Economic Laws of Scientific Research*. New York: St. Martin's Press.

Keeble, N. H. 2004. "Baxter, Richard (1615–1691)."In *Oxford Dictionary of National Biography*. Oxford: Oxford University Press.

Keill, James. 1708. *An Account of Animal Secretion, the Quantity of Blood in the Humane Body, and Muscular Motion*. London: Printed for George Strahan.

Keller, Vera. 2012. "Accounting for Invention: Guido Pancirolli's Lost and Found Things and Desiderata." *Journal of the History of Ideas* Vol. 73, No. 2, pp. 223–45.

Kelly, Morgan, and Cormac Ó Gráda. 2013. "The Waning of the Little Ice Age: Climate Change in Early Modern Europe." *Journal of Interdisciplinary History,* Vol. 44, No. 2 (Autumn), pp. 301–25.

Kelly Morgan, Joel Mokyr, and Cormac Ó Gráda. 2014. "Precocious Albion: a New Interpretation of the British Industrial Revolution." *Annual Review of Economics* Vol. 6, pp. 363–91.

Kengo, Araki. 1975. "Confucianism and Buddhism in the late Ming." In W. Theodore De Bary, ed., *The Unfolding of Neo-Confucianism*. New York: Columbia University Press, pp. 39–66.

Kerker, Milton. 1961. "Science and the Steam Engine." *Technology and Culture* Vol. 2, No. 4, pp. 381–90.

Kesten, Hermann. 1945. *Copernicus and his World*. New York: Roy Publishers.

Keynes, John Maynard. 1946. "Newton the Man." http://www-groups. dcs.st-and.ac.uk /~history/Extras/ Keynes_Newton. html, n.p., accessed September 17, 2010.

Khan, B. Zorina. 2006. "The Evolution of Useful Knowledge: Great Inventors, Science and Technology in British Economic Development, 1750–1930." Unpublished paper, Bowdoin College.

Klemm, Friedrich. 1964. *A History of Western Technology*. Cambridge, MA: MIT Press.

Ko, Chiu Yu, Mark Koyama, and Tuan-Hwee Sng. 2015. "Unified China and Divided Europe." Unpublished ms., National University of Singapore.

Koerner, Lisbeth. 1999. *Linnaeus: Nature and Nation*. Cambridge, MA: Harvard University Press.

Koyama, Mark, and Xue, Melanie Meng. 2015. "The Literary Inquisition: the Persecution of Intellectuals and Human Capital Formation in China." Unpublished ms.

Koyré, Alexandre. 1965. *Newtonian Studies.* Chicago: University of Chicago Press.

Kroeber, Alfred L., and Clyde Kluckhohn. 1952. *Culture: A Critical Review of Concepts and Definitions.* Cambridge, MA: Harvard University Peabody Museum of American Archeology and Ethnology Papers No. 47.

Kronick, David. 1962. *A History of Scientific and Technical Periodicals.* New York: Scarecrow Press.

Krugman, Paul. 1991. *Geography and Trade.* Cambridge, MA: MIT Press.

Kuhn, Thomas S. 1976. "Mathematical vs. Experimental Traditions in the Development of the Physical Sciences." *Journal of Interdisciplinary History* Vol. 7, No. 1, pp. 1–31.

Kumar, Deepal. 2003. "India." In Roy Porter, ed., *The Cambridge History of Science: Vol. 4: Eighteenth-Century Science.* Cambridge: Cambridge University Press, pp. 669–87.

Kuran, Timur. 1987. "Preference Falsification, Policy Discontinuity, and Collective Conservatism." *Economic Journal* Vol. 97, No. 387, pp. 642–65.

———. 1997. *Private Truths, Public Lies: The Social Consequences of Preference Falsification.* Cambridge, MA: Harvard University Press.

Kurz, Joachim. 2011. *The Discovery of Chinese Logic.* Leiden: Brill.

Labrousse, Elisabeth. 1983. *Bayle,* translated by Dennis Potts. Oxford: Oxford University Press.

Landa, Janet Tai. 1981. "A Theory of the Ethnically Homogeneous Middleman Group: An Institutional Alternative to Contract Law." *Journal of Legal Studies* Vol. 10, pp. 349–62.

———. 1995. *Trust, Ethnicity, and Identity: Beyond the New Institutional Economics of Ethnic Trading Networks, Contract Law, and Gift-exchange.* Ann Arbor: University of Michigan Press.

Landes, David S.1983. *Revolution in Time: Clocks and the Making of the Modern World.* Cambridge, MA: Harvard University Press.

———. 1998. *The Wealth and Poverty of Nations.* New York: W. W. Norton

———. 2000. "Culture Makes almost all the Difference." In Lawrence E. Harrison and Samuel P. Huntington, eds., *Culture Matters: How Values Shape Human Progress.* New York: Basic Books, pp. 1–13.

Lasch, Christopher. 1991. *The True and Only Heaven: Progress and Its Critics.* New York: W. W. Norton.

Lecoq, Anne-Marie, ed. 2001. *La Querelle des Anciens et des Modernes.* Paris: Éditions Gallimard.

Leighton, Wayne A., and Edward J. López, 2013. *Madmen, Intellectuals, and Academic Scribblers: The Economic Engine of Political Change.* Stanford: Stanford University Press.

Levere, T. H., and G. L'E. Turner, 2002. *Discussing Chemistry and Steam: The Minutes of a Coffee House Philosophical Society 1780–1787.* Oxford: Oxford University Press.

Levin, Daniel Z., and Rob Cross. 2004. "The Strength of Weak Ties You Can Trust: The Mediating Role of Trust in Effective Knowledge Transfer." *Management Science* Vol. 50, No. 1, pp. 1477–90.

Levine, Joseph M. 1981. "Ancients and Moderns Reconsidered." *Eighteenth-Century Studies* Vol. 15, No. 1, pp. 72–89.

———. 1991. *The Battle of the Books: History and Literature in the Augustan Age.* Ithaca, NY: Cornell University Press.

Levine, Robert. 1997. *A Geography of Time.* New York: Basic Books.

Li, Jin. 2012. *Cultural Foundations of Learning: East and West*. Cambridge: Cambridge University Press.

Lin, Justin Yifu. 1995. "The Needham Puzzle: Why the Industrial Revolution Did Not Originate in China." *Economic Development and Cultural Change* Vol. 43, No. 2, pp. 269–92.

Lindberg, David C. and Ronald L. Numbers. 1986. "Introduction." In David C. Lindberg and Ronald L. Numbers, eds., *God and Nature: Historical Essays on the Encounter between Christianity and Science*. Berkeley: University of California Press, pp. 1–18.

Liu James T. C. 1973. "How Did a Neo-Confucian School Become the State Orthodoxy?" *Philosophy East and West* Vol. 23, No. 4, pp. 483–505.

Livingstone, David N. 1994. "The Historical Roots of Our Ecological Crisis—a Reassessment." *Fides et Historia* Vol. 26, No. 1, pp. 38–55.

Lloyd, Geoffrey, and Nathan Sivin. 2002. *The Way and the Word: Science and Medicine in Early China and Greece*. New Haven and London: Yale University Press.

Locke, John. [1693] 1812. "Some Thoughts Concerning Education." In *The Works of John Locke*, London: John Otridge and Son. Vol. 9, pp. 1–205.

Long, Pamela O. 2011. *Artisan/Practitioners and the Rise of the New Sciences, 1400–1600*. Corvallis: Oregon State University Press.

Lowengard, Sarah. 2006. *The Creation of Color in Eighteenth-Century Europe*. New York: Gutenberg-ebooks. http://www.gutenberg-e.org/lowengard/ index.html, accessed October 4, 2010.

Lux, David S. 1991. "The Reorganization of Science, 1450–1700." In Bruce T. Moran, ed., *Patronage and Institutions: Science, Technology and Medicine at the European Court, 1500–1750*. Rochester, NY: Boydell Press, pp. 185–94.

Lynch, William T. 2001. *Solomon s Child: Method in the Early Royal Society of London*. Stanford: Stanford University Press.

Lyons, Anthony, and Kashima Yoshihisa. 2001. "The Reproduction of Culture: Communication Processes Tend to Maintain Cultural Stereotypes." *Social Cognition* Vol. 19, No. 3, pp. 372–94.

Lyons, Henry George. 1944. *The Royal Society, 1660-1940, A History of Its Administration under Its Charters*. Cambridge: Cambridge University Press.

Macaulay, Thomas Babington. [1837]. 1983. "Lord Bacon," *Edinburgh Review*, repr. ed., Kessinger Publishing.

Maclaurin, Colin. 1750. *An Account of Sir Isaac Newton s Philosophical Discoveries, in four books*. second ed. London: printed for A. Millar.

MacFarlane, Alan. 1978. *The Origins of English Individualism*. Cambridge: Cambridge University Press.

MacLean, Ian. 2006. "The 'Sceptical Crisis' Reconsidered: Galen, Rational Medicine and the *Libertas Philosophandi*." *Early Science and Medicine* Vol. 11, No. 3, pp. 247–74.

———. 2008. "The Medical Republic of Letters." *Intellectual History Review* Vol. 18, No. 1 (Special Issue: Humanism and Medicine in the Early Modern Era), pp. 15–30.

MacLean, Gerald, ed. 1995. *Culture and Society in the Stuart Restoration*. Cambridge: Cambridge University Press.

MacLeod, Christine. 2007. *Heroes of Invention: Technology, Liberalism and British Identity*. Cambridge: Cambridge University Press.

Malcolm, Noel. 2004. "Private and Public Knowledge: Kircher, Esotericism, and the Republic of Letters." In Paula Findlen, ed., *Athanasius Kircher: The Last Man Who Knew Everything.* New York: Routledge, pp. 286–98.

Malherbe, Michel. 1985. "Bacon, l'Encyclopédie, et la Révolution," *Études Philosophiques* No. 3, pp. 387–404.

Mandelbrote, Scott. 2004. "Ray, John (1627–1705)." In *Oxford Dictionary of National Biography.* Oxford: Oxford University Press.

de Mandeville, Bernard [1724] 1755. *The Fable of the Bees.* ninth ed. Edinburgh: W. Gray and W. Peter.

Manuel, Frank E. 1963. *Isaac Newton: Historian.* Cambridge, MA: Belknap Press of Harvard University Press.

Margóczy, Daniel. 2014a. *Commercial Visions: Science, Trade and Visual Culture in the Dutch Golden Age.* Chicago: University of Chicago Press.

———. 2014b. "Certain Fakes and Uncertain Facts: Jan Jonston and the Question of Truth in Religion and Natural History." In Marco Beretta and Maria Conforti, eds., *Fakes, Hoaxes, Counterfeits and Deception in Early Modern Science.* Sagamore Beach, MA: Science History Publications, pp. 190–225.

Mason, Stephen F. 1992. "Bishop John Wilkins, FRS (1614–72): Analogies of Thought-Style in the Protestant Reformation and Early Modern Science." *Notes and Records of the Royal Society of London* Vol. 46, No. 1, pp. 1–21.

Mathias, Peter. 1979. *The Transformation of England.* New York: Columbia University Press.

Mayr, Ernest. 1982. *The Growth of Biological Thought.* Cambridge, MA: Harvard University Press.

———. 1989. "Speciational Evolution or Punctuated Equilibria." In Albert Somit and Steven A. Peterson, eds., *The Dynamics of Evolution.* Ithaca, NY: Cornell University Press, pp. 21–53.

———. 1991. *One Long Argument: Charles Darwin and the Genesis of Modern Evolutionary Thought.* Cambridge, MA: Harvard University Press.

Mayr, Otto. 1986. *Authority, Liberty & Automatic Machinery in Early Modern Europe.* Baltimore: Johns Hopkins University Press.

Mazzotti, Massimo. 2004. "Newton for Ladies: Gentility, Gender, and Radical Culture." *British Journal for the History of Science* Vol. 37, No. 2 (June), pp. 119–46.

McClellan, James E., III. 1979. "The Scientific Press in Transition: Rozier's Journal and the Scientific Societies in the 1770s." *Annals of Science* Vol. 36, No. 5, pp. 425–49.

McCloskey, Deirdre N. 1985. *The Rhetoric of Economics.* Madison: University of Wisconsin Press.

———. 2006. *The Bourgeois Virtues: Ethics for an Age of Commerce.* Chicago: University of Chicago Press.

———. 2010. *Bourgeois Dignity: Why Economics Can t Explain the Modern World.* Chicago: University of Chicago Press.

———. 2016a. *Bourgeois Equality: How Ideas, Not Capital or Institutions, Enriched the World.* Chicago: University of Chicago Press.

———. 2016b. "Max U vs Humanomics: a Critique of Neo-Institutionalism." *Journal of Institutional Economics,* forthcoming.

McDermott, Joseph P. 2006. *A Social History of the Chinese Book.* Hong Kong: Hong Kong University Press.

McElreath, Richard, and Joseph Henrich. 2007. "Modeling Cultural Evolution." In Robin Dunbar and Louise Barrett, eds., *Oxford Handbook of Evolutionary Psychology*. Oxford: Oxford University Press, pp. 571–86.

McGuire, J.E., and P.M. Rattansi. 1966. "Newton and the 'Pipes of Pan.'" *Notes and Records of the Royal Society of London* Vol. 21, No. 2, pp. 108–43.

McMains, H. F. 2000. *The Death of Oliver Cromwell*. Lexington: University Press of Kentucky.

Meisenzahl, Ralf R., and Joel Mokyr. 2012. "The Rate and Direction of Invention in the British Industrial Revolution: Incentives and Institutions." In Scott Stern and Joshua Lerner, eds., *The Rate and Direction of Innovation*. Chicago: University of Chicago Press, pp. 443–79.

Melton, James Van Horn. 2001. *The Rise of the Public in Enlightenment Europe*. Cambridge: Cambridge University Press.

Menand, Louis. 2010. *The Marketplace of Ideas: Reform and Resistance in the American University*. New York: W. W. Norton.

Merchant, Carolyn. 1980. *The Death of Nature*. New York: Harper & Row.

Merton, Robert K. [1938] 2001. *Science, Technology, and Society in Seventeenth-Century England*. New York: Howard Fertig Press.

———. 1973. *The Sociology of Science*. Chicago: University of Chicago Press.

Meskill, John. 1982. *Academies in Ming China: A Historical Essay*. Tucson: University of Arizona Press.

Mesoudi, Alex. 2011. *Cultural Evolution*. Chicago: University of Chicago Press.

Mesoudi, Alex, Andrew Whiten, and Kevin Laland. 2006. "Towards a Unified Science of Cultural Evolution." *Behavioral and Brain Science* Vol. 29, pp. 329–83.

Mesoudi, Alex et al. 2013. "The Cultural Evolution of Technology and Science." In Peter J. Richerson and Morten H. Christiansen, eds., *Cultural Evolution: Society, Technology, Language, and Religion*. Cambridge, MA: MIT Press, pp. 193–216.

Mill, John Stuart. [1845] 1967. "The Claims of Labor." In John M. Robson, ed., *The Collected Works of John Stuart Mill*, Vol. 4, *Essays on Economics and Society*, part I. Toronto: University of Toronto Press, London: Routledge and Kegan Paul, pp. 370–80.

———. [1848] 1929. *Principles of Political Economy,* edited by W. J. Ashley. London: Longmans, Green and Co.

Millar, John. 1790. *An Historical View of the English Government, from the Settlement of the Saxons in Britain to the Accession of the House of Stewart*. Dublin: printed for J. Jones.

Miller, Peter N. 2000. *Peiresc s Europe: Learning and Virtue in the Seventeenth Century*. New Haven, CT: Yale University Press.

———. 2015. *Peiresc s Mediterranean World*. Cambridge, MA: Harvard University Press.

Mitch, David. 1999. "The Role of Education and Skill in the British Industrial Revolution." In Joel Mokyr, ed., *The British Industrial Revolution: An Economic Perspective*, second ed. Boulder, CO: Westview Press, pp. 241–79.

Mitchell, Wesley Clair. 1974. "Bentham's Felicific Calculus." In Bhikhu Parekh, ed., *Jeremy Bentham: Ten Critical Essays*. London: Frank Cass, pp. 168–86.

Mokyr, Joel. 1990. *The Lever of Riches: Technological Creativity and Economic Progress*. New York: Oxford University Press.

———. 1991. "Was There a British Industrial Evolution?" In Joel Mokyr, ed., *The Vital One: Essays Presented to Jonathan R. T. Hughes*. Greenwich, CT: JAI Press, pp. 253–86.

———. 1994. "Cardwell's Law and the Political Economy of Technological Progress." *Research Policy* 23, No. 5 pp. 561–74.

———. 2000. "Innovation and Selection in Evolutionary Models of Technology: Some Definitional Issues." In John Ziman, ed., *Technological Innovation as an Evolutionary Process*. Cambridge: Cambridge University Press, pp. 52–65.

———. 2002. *The Gifts of Athena*. Princeton, NJ: Princeton University Press.

———. 2005. "The Intellectual Origins of Modern Economic Growth." [Presidential address.] *Journal of Economic History* Vol. 65, No. 2, pp. 285–351.

———. 2006a. "The Great Synergy: The European Enlightenment as a Factor in Modern Economic Growth." In Wilfred Dolfsma and Luc Soete, eds., *Understanding the Dynamics of a Knowledge Economy*. Cheltenham, UK: Edward Elgar, pp. 7–41.

———. 2006b. "Useful Knowledge as an Evolving System: The View from Economic history." In Lawrence E. Blume and Steven N. Durlauf, eds., *The Economy as an Evolving Complex System* Vol. III: *Current Perspectives and Future Directions*. New York: Oxford University Press, pp. 307–37.

———. 2006c. "Mobility, Creativity, and Technological Development: David Hume, Immanuel Kant and the Economic Development of Europe." In G. Abel, ed., *Kolloquiumsband of the XX. Deutschen Kongresses für Philosophie*. Hamburg: Felix Meiner, pp. 1131–61.

———. 2007. "The Market for Ideas and the Origins of Economic Growth in Eighteenth Century Europe." [Heineken Lecture.] *Tijdschrift voor Sociale en Economische Geschiedenis*, Vol. 4, No. 1, pp. 3–38.

———. 2009a. *The Enlightened Economy*, New York and London: Yale University Press.

———. 2009b. "Intellectual Property Rights, the Industrial Revolution, and the Beginnings of Modern Economic Growth," *American Economic Review* Vol. 99, No. 2 (Papers and Proceedings), pp. 349–55.

———. 2014. "Culture, Institutions, and Modern Growth." In Itai Sened and Sebastian Galiani, eds., *Economic Institutions, Rights, Growth, and Sustainability: The Legacy of Douglass North*. Cambridge: Cambridge University Press, pp. 151–91.

Monod, Jacques. 1971. *Chance and Necessity: An Essay on the Natural Philosophy of Modern Biology*. New York: Alfred A. Knopf.

Montes, Leonidas. 2008. "Newton's Real Influence on Adam Smith and Its Context." *Cambridge Journal of Economics* Vol. 32, pp. 555–76.

Moore, James R. 1986. "Geologists and Interpreters of Genesis in the Nineteenth Century." In David C. Lindberg and Ronald L. Numbers, eds., *God and Nature: Historical Essays on the Encounter between Christianity and Science*. Berkeley: University of California Press, pp. 322–50.

Moran, Bruce T. 1991a. "Introduction." In Bruce T. Moran, ed., *Patronage and Institutions: Science, Technology and Medicine at the European Court, 1500–1750*. Rochester, NY: Boydell Press, pp. 1–4.

———. 1991b. "Patronage and Institutions: Courts, Universities, and Academies in Germany; an Overview 1550–1750." In Bruce T. Moran, ed., *Patronage and Institutions: Science, Technology and Medicine at the European Court, 1500–1750*. Rochester, NY: Boydell Press, pp. 169–83.

Morris, Ian. 2010. *Why the West Rules—For Now*. New York: Farrar, Strauss and Giroux.

Mosse, George L. 1960. "Puritan Radicalism and the Enlightenment." *Church History* Vol. 29, No. 4, pp. 424–39.

Mote, F. W. 1999. *Imperial China: 900– 1800*. Cambridge, MA: Harvard University Press.

Muir, Edward. 2007. *The Culture Wars of the Late Renaissance*. Cambridge, MA: Harvard University Press.

Mulligan, Lotte. 1980. "Puritans and English Science: A Critique of Webster." *Isis* Vol. 71, No. 3, pp. 456–69.

Murphy, Daniel. 1995. *Comenius: A Critical Reassessment of His Life and Work*. Portland, OR: Irish Academic Press.

Musson, A. E. and Eric Robinson. 1969. *Science and Technology in the Industrial Revolution*. Manchester: Manchester University Press.

Nakayama, Shigeru. 1969. *A History of Japanese Astronomy: Chinese Background and Western Impact*. Cambridge, MA: Harvard University Press.

Nedham, Marchamont. 1665. *Medela Medicinæ: A Plea for the Free Profession, and a Renovation of the Art of Physick*. London: For Richard Lownds at the White-Lion in S. Pauls Church-yard, neer the little north-door.

Needham, Joseph. 1954. "Plan of the Work." In Joseph Needham, ed., *Science and Civilization in China*. Cambridge: Cambridge University Press, Vol. 1, pp. 18–41.

———. 1956. "The Fundamental Ideas of Chinese Science." In Joseph Needham, ed., *Science and Civilization in China*. Cambridge: Cambridge University Press, Vol. 2, pp. 216–345.

———. 1959. *Mathematics and the Sciences of the Heavens and the Earth*. In Joseph Needham, ed., *Science and Civilization in China*. Cambridge: Cambridge University Press, Vol. 3.

———. 1969a. *The Grand Titration*. Toronto: University of Toronto Press.

———. 1969b. *Within the Four Seas: The Dialogue of East and West*. London: Allen and Unwin

———. 1970. *Clerks and Craftsmen in China and the West*. Cambridge: Cambridge University Press, 1970.

———. 1986. *Chemicals and Chemical Technology*. In Joseph Needham, ed., *Science and Civilization in China*. Cambridge: Cambridge University Press Vol. 5 pt. 7.

———. 2004. *The Social Background,* Part 2, *General Conclusions and Reflections*. In Joseph Needham, ed., *Science and Civilization in China*. edited by Girdwood Robinson. Cambridge: Cambridge University Press, Vol. 7.

Neher, André. 1977. "Copernicus in the Hebraic Literature from the Sixteenth to the Eighteenth Century." *Journal of the History of Ideas* Vol. 38, No. 2, pp. 211–26.

Nelson, Richard R., and Edmund S. Phelps. 1966. "Investment in Humans, Technological Diffusion, and Economic Growth." *American Economic Review* Vol. 56, pp. 69–75.

Nelson, Richard R., and Sidney Winter. 1982. *An Evolutionary Theory of Economic Change*. Cambridge, MA: The Belknap Press.

Neusner, Jacob. 1980. "Scriptural, Essenic, and Mishnaic Approaches to Civil Law and Government: Some Comparative Remarks." *Harvard Theological Review* Vol. 73, No. 3/4, pp. 419–34.

Newton Isaac. 1721. *Opticks or A Treatise of the Reflections, Refractions, Inflections and Colours of Light*, third edition. London: Printed for William and John Innys.

———. 1729. *The Mathematical Principles of Natural Philosophy*, translated by Andrew Motte. London: Printed for Andrew Motte.

Ng, William Yau-nang. 2003. "Chen Xianzhang." In Antonio S. Cua, ed. *Encyclopedia of Chinese Philosophy*. New York: Routledge, n.p.

Nickerson, Raymond S. 1998. "Confirmation Bias: A Ubiquitous Phenomenon in Many Guises." *Review of General Psychology* Vol. 2, No. 2, pp. 175–220.

Nielsen, Rasmus, et al. 2010. "Sequencing of 50 Human Exomes Reveals Adaptation to High Altitude," *Science* Vol. 329, pp. 75–78.

Nisbet, Robert. 1979. "The Idea of Progress: A Bibliographical Essay." *Literature of Liberty: A Review of Contemporary Liberal Thought*, vol. II, no. 1, January/March. http://oll.libertyfund.org/ ?option=com _content&task = view&id=165&Itemid=259, accessed June 8, 2013.

———. [1994] 2008. *History of the Idea of Progress*, second ed. New Brunswick, NJ: Transactions Publishers.

North, Douglass C. 1981. *Structure and Change in Economic History*. New York: W. W. Norton.

———. 2005. *Understanding the Process of Economic Change*. Princeton, NJ: Princeton University Press.

Nowacki, Horst. 2008. "Leonhard Euler and the Theory of Ships." *Journal of Ship Research* Vol. 52, No. 4, pp. 274–90.

Nowak, Martin A. 2006. "Five Rules for the Evolution of Cooperation." *Science* Vol. 314, pp. 1560–63.

O'Brien, Patrick. 2009. "The Needham Question Updated: a Historiographical Survey and Elaboration." *History of Technology* Vol. 29, pp. 7–28.

Ochs, Kathleen. 1985. "The Royal Society of London's History of Trades Programme: An Early Episode in Applied Science." *Notes and Records of the Royal Society of London* Vol. 39, No. 2 (April), pp. 129–58.

Ogilvie, Sheilagh. 2014. "The Economics of Guilds." *Journal of Economic Perspectives* Vol. 28, No. 4, pp. 169–92.

Oldenburg, Henry. 1665. "The Introduction." *Philosophical Transactions of the Royal Society* Vol. 1.http://www.gutenberg.org/files/28758/28758-h/28758 -h.htm.

O'Malley, C. D. 2008. "Vesalius, Andreas." In Charles C. Gillispie, ed., *Complete Dictionary of Scientific Biography*. Gale Virtual Reference Library. Detroit: Charles Scribner's Sons, Vol. 14, pp. 3–12.

O'Malley, M. 1990. *Keeping Watch: A History of American Time*. New York: Viking Books.

Ostrom, Elinor. 1990. *Governing the Commons: The Evolution of Institutions for Collective Action*. Cambridge: Cambridge University Press.

Ostrom, Elinor, and Charlotte Hess. 2007. "A Framework for Analyzing the Knowledge Commons." In Charlotte Hess and Elinor Ostrom, eds., *Understanding Knowledge as a Commons*. Cambridge, MA: MIT Press, pp. 41–81.

Pagani, Catherine. 2001. *Eastern Magnificence & European Ingenuity: Clocks of Late Imperial China*. Ann Arbor: University of Michigan Press.

Pagel, Walter. 1982. *Joan Baptista Van Helmont: Reformer of Science and Medicine*. Cambridge: Cambridge University Press.

Palissy, Bernard. [1580] 1957. *Discours Admirables* (*Admirable Discourses*) translated by Aurèle La Rocque. Urbana: University of Illinois Press.

Pancaldi, Giuliano. 2003. "Priority." In J. L. Heilbron, ed., *The Oxford Companion to the History of Modern Science*. Oxford and New York: Oxford University Press, pp. 676–77.

Parker, Samuel. 1666. *A Free and Impartial Censure of the Platonick Philosophie*. Oxford: Printed by W. Hall, for Richard Davis.

Parthasarathi, Prasannan. 2011. *Why Europe Grew Rich and Asia Did Not: Global Economic Divergence, 1600–1850*. Cambridge: Cambridge University Press.

Pascal, Blaise. [1651] 2007. "Preface to the Treatise on Vacuum." In *Thoughts, Letters and Minor Works*. New York: Cosimo Books, pp. 444–58.

Paterson, Timothy H. 1987. "On the Role of Christianity in the Political Philosophy of Francis Bacon," *Polity* Vol. 19, No. 3 pp. 419–442.

Perdue Peter C. 2007. "Chinese Science: a Flexible Response to the West?" *East Asian Science, Technology and Society: An International Journal* Vol. 1, No. 1, pp. 143–145.

Pérez-Ramos, Antonio. 1988. *Francis Bacon s Idea of Science and the Maker s Knowledge Tradition*. Oxford: Oxford University Press.

———. 1996. "Bacon's Legacy." In Markku Peltonen, ed., *The Cambridge Companion to Bacon*. Cambridge: Cambridge University Press, pp. 311–34.

Perkins, Merle L. 1959. *The Moral and Political Philosophy of the Abbé de Saint-Pierre*. Geneva: Librairie Droz.

Perkinson, Henry J. 1995. *How Things Got Better: Speech, Writing, Printing, and Cultural Change*. Westport, CT: Bergin and Garvey.

Peterson, Willard. 1975. "Fang-I-Chih: Western Learning and the 'Investigation of Things.'" In W. Theodore De Bary, ed., *The Unfolding of Neo-Confucianism*. New York: Columbia University Press, pp. 369–411.

———. 1979. *Bitter Gourd: Fang I-Chih and the Impetus for Intellectual Change*. New Haven, CT: Yale University Press.

Petty, William. 1647. *The Advice of W. P. to Mr. Samuel Hartlib. for the Advancement of Some Particular Parts of Learning*. London: n.p.

Pinker, Steven. 2011. *The Better Angels of Our Nature*. New York: Penguin.

Pocock, J.G.A. 1999. *Barbarism and Religion,* Vol. 1: *The Enlightenments of Edward Gibbon, 1737–1764*. Cambridge: Cambridge University Press.

Polanyi, Michael. 1962. "The Republic of Science: Its Political and Economic Theory." *Minerva* Vol. 1, pp. 54–73.

Pollard, Sidney. 1971. *The Idea of Progress: History and Society*. Harmondsworth, UK: Penguin.

Pomeranz, Kenneth. 2000. *The Great Divergence: China, Europe, and the Making of the Modern World Economy*. Princeton, NJ: Princeton University Press.

———. 2013. "Skills, 'Guilds,' and Development: Asking Epstein's Questions to East Asian Institutions." In Maarten Prak and Jan Luiten van Zanden, eds., *Technology, Skills and the Pre-Modern Economy*. Leiden: Brill, pp. 93–127.

Poni, Carlo. 1993. "The Craftsman and the Good Engineer: Technical Practice and Theoretical Mechanics in J.T. Desaguliers." *History and Technology* Vol. 10, pp. 215–32.

Poovey, Mary. 1998. *A History of the Modern Fact*. Chicago: University of Chicago Press.

Porter, Michael E. 2000. "Attitudes, Values, Beliefs, and the Microeconomics of Prosperity." In Lawrence E. Harrison and Samuel P. Huntington, eds.,

Culture Matters: How Values Shape Human Progress. New York, Basic Books, pp. 14–28.

Porter, Roy. 1982. "Was There a Medical Enlightenment?" *British Journal for Eighteenth-Century Studies* Vol. 5, pp. 49–63.

Porter, Roy, and Mikuláš Teich, eds. 1992. *The Scientific Revolution in National Context.* Cambridge: Cambridge University Press.

Poynter, F. N. 1973. "Sydenham's Influence Abroad." *Medical History* Vol. 17, No. 3, pp. 223–34.

Prak, Maarten, and Jan Luiten Van Zanden. 2013. "Introduction." In Maarten Prak and Jan Luiten van Zanden, eds., *Technology, Skills and the Pre-Modern Economy.* Leiden: Brill, pp. 1–22.

Priestley, Joseph. 1771. *An Essay on the First Principles of Government.* London: Printed for J. Dodsley.

Pritchett, Lant. 2001. "Where Has All the Education Gone?" *World Bank Economic Review*, Vol. 15, No. 3, pp. 367–91.

Qi, Han. 2001. "Astronomy, Chinese and Western: The Influence of Xu Guangqi's views in the Early and Mid-Qing." In Catherine Jami, Peter Engelfriet, and Gregory Blue, eds., *Statecraft and Intellectual Renewal in Late Ming China: the Cross-Cultural Synthesis of Xu Guangqi (1562–1633).* Leiden: Brill, pp. 360–79.

Qian, Wen-yuan. 1985. *The Great Inertia: Scientific Stagnation in Traditional China.* London: Croom Helm.

Rawski, Evelyn S. 1979. *Education and Popular Literacy in Ch'ing China.* Ann Arbor: University of Michigan Press.

Reed Christopher A. 2004. *Gutenberg in Shanghai: Chinese Print Capitalism, 1876–1937.* Honolulu: University of Hawaii Press.

Rees, Graham. 2000. "Baconianism." In Wilbur Applebaum, ed., *Encyclopedia of the Scientific Revolution.* New York and London: Routledge, pp. 69–71.

Rescher, Nicholas. 1978. *Scientific Progress.* Oxford: Basil Blackwell.

Reston, James. 1994. *Galileo: A Life.* New York: Harper Collins.

Reynolds, Terry S. 1983. *Stronger Than a Hundred Men: A History of the Vertical Water Wheel.* Baltimore: Johns Hopkins University Press.

Ricardo, David. [1821] 1971. *Principles of Political Economy*, third ed., edited by R.M. Hartwell. Harmondsworth, UK: Pelican Classics.

Ricci, Matteo. 1953. *China in the Sixteenth Century: The Journals of Matthew Ricci, 1583–1610.* Translated by Louis J. Gallagher. New York: Random House.

Richardson, Philip. 1999. *Economic Change in China, c. 1800–1950.* Cambridge: Cambridge University Press.

Richerson, Peter J. and Robert Boyd. 2005. *Not by Genes Alone: How Culture Transformed Human Evolution.* Chicago: University of Chicago Press.

Richerson, Peter J. and Morten H. Christiansen, eds. 2013. *Cultural Evolution: Society, Technology, Language, and Religion.* Cambridge, MA: MIT Press.

Rider, Robin E. 1990. "Measure of Ideas, Rule of Language: Mathematics and Language in the 18th Century." In Tore Frängsmyr, J. L. Heilbron, and Robin E. Rider, eds., *The Quantifying Spirit in the 18th Century,* Berkeley: University of California Press, pp. 113–140.

Ridley, Matt. 2010. "When Ideas Have Sex." http://designmind.frogdesign.com/articles/and-now-the-good-news/when-ideas-have-sex.html, accessed Dec. 27, 2014.

Ringmar, Erik. 2007. *Why Europe Was First: Social Change and Economic Growth in Europe and East Asia, 1500–2050.* London: Anthem Press.

Roberts, Lissa and Simon Schaffer. 2007. "Preface." In Lissa Roberts, Simon Schaffer, and Peter Dear, eds., *The Mindful Hand: Inquiry and Invention from the Late Renaissance to Early Industrialization*. Amsterdam: Royal Netherlands Academy of Arts and Sciences, pp. xiii–xxvii.

Robertson, John. 2000. "Unenlightened England: A Review." *Prospect*, Dec. 21.

Rodrik, Dani. 2014. "When Ideas Trump Interests." *Journal of Economic Perspectives* Vol. 28, No. 1, pp. 189–208.

Roe, Shirley. 2003. "The Life Sciences." In Roy Porter, ed., *The Cambridge History of Science,* Vol. 4: *Eighteenth-Century Science.* Cambridge: Cambridge University Press, pp. 397–416.

Roetz, Heiner. 2010. "On Nature and Culture in Zhou China." In Hans Ulrich Vogel and Günter Dux, eds., *Concepts of Nature: A Chinese-European Cross-Cultural Perspective.* Leiden: Brill, pp. 198–219.

Roland, Gérard. 2004. "Understanding Institutional Change: Fast-Moving and Slow-Moving Institutions." *Studies in Comparative International Development* Vol. 38, No. 4, pp. 109–31.

Ronan, Colin A., and Joseph Needham. 1978. *The Shorter Science and Civilisation in China.* Cambridge: Cambridge University Press, Vol. 1.

———. 1981. *The Shorter Science and Civilisation in China.* Cambridge: Cambridge University Press, Vol. 2.

Rosen, Sherwin. 1981. "The Economics of Superstars." *American Economic Review* Vol. 71, No.5, pp. 845–58.

Rosenberg, Nathan. "Adam Smith on the Division of Labour: Two Views or One?" *Economica*, Vol. 32, No. 126, pp. 127–39.

Rosenberg, Nathan, and Birdzell, L.E. 1986. *How the West Grew Rich*. New York: Basic Books.

Rosenthal, Jean-Laurent, and R. Bin Wong. 2011. *Before and Beyond Divergence: The Politics of Economic Change in China and Europe.* Cambridge, MA: Harvard University Press.

Rossi, Paolo. 1970. *Philosophy, Technology and the Arts in the Early Modern Era*. New York: Harper Torchbooks.

———. 1978. *Francis Bacon: From Magic to Science.* Chicago: University of Chicago Press.

Rowe, William T. 2001. *Saving the World: Chen Hongmou and Elite Consciousness in Eighteenth-century China.* Stanford, CA: Stanford University Press.

———. 2009. *China s Last Empire: The Great Qing.* Cambridge, MA: Belknap Press.

Sandberg, Lars G. 1979. "The Case of the Impoverished Sophisticate: Human Capital and Swedish Economic Growth before World War I." *Journal of Economic History* Vol. 39, No. 1, pp. 225–41.

Saviotti, Pier Paolo. 1996. *Technological Evolution, Variety, and the Economy.* Cheltenham, UK: Edward Elgar.

Schäfer, Dagmar. 2011. *The Crafting of the 10,000 Things.* Chicago: University of Chicago Press.

Schaffer, Simon. 1983. "Natural Philosophy and Public Spectacle in the Eighteenth century." *History of Science* Vol. 21, No. 1, pp. 1–43.

Schaffer, Simon. 1994. "Machine Philosophy: Demonstration Devices in Georgian Mechanics." *Osiris* Vol. 9, pp. 157–82.

Schich, Maximilian, Chaoming Song, Yong-Yeol Ahn, Alexander Mirsky, Mauro Martino et al., 2014. "A Network Framework of Cultural History." *Science* No. 345 (Aug. 1), pp. 558–62.

Schliesser, Eric. 2007. "Hume's Newtonianism and Anti-Newtonianism." *Stanford Encyclopedia of Philosophy*. http://plato.stanford.edu/entries/hume-Newton/ accessed September 7, 2010.

Schoeck, R.J. 1982. "Sir Thomas Browne and the Republic of Letters: Introduction." *English Language Notes* Vol. 19, No. 4, pp. 299–312.

Schofield, Robert E. 1997. *The Enlightenment of Joseph Priestley: A Study of His Life and Work from 1733 to 1773.* University Park, PA: Penn State University Press.

Schumpeter, Joseph A. 1954. *History of Economic Analysis.* Oxford: Oxford University Press.

Schwartz, Shalom H., and Sipke Huismans. 1995. "Value, Priorities, and Religiosity in Four Western Religions." *Social Psychology Quarterly* Vol. 58, No. 2, pp. 88–107.

Scott, H. M., ed. 1990. *Enlightened Absolutism: Reform and Reformers in Later Eighteenth Century Europe.* Houndmills, UK: Palgrave Macmillan.

Seed, Patricia. 2001. "Jewish Scientists and the Origin of Modern Navigation." In Paolo Bernardini and Norman Fiering, eds., *Jews and the Expansion of Europe to the West, 1450–1800,* New York: Bergahn Books, pp. 73–85.

Seki, Motohide and Yasuo Ihara. 2012. "The Rate of Cultural Change in One-to-Many Social Transmission When Cultural Variants are Not Selectively Neutral." *Letters on Evolutionary Behavioral Science* Vol. 3, No. 2, pp. 12–16.

Sened, Itai and Sebastian Galiani, eds., *Economic Institutions, Rights, Growth, and Sustainability: The Legacy of Douglass North.* Cambridge: Cambridge University Press.

Settle, Jaime E., Christopher T. Dawes, Nicholas A. Christakis, and James H. Fowler. 2010. "Friendships Moderate an Association between a Dopamine Gene Variant and Political Ideology." *Journal of Politics* Vol. 72, No. 4, pp. 1189–98.

's Gravesande, Willem Jacob. 1720. *Mathematical Elements of Natural Philosophy Confirmed by Experiments, Or an Introduction to Sir Isaac Newton's Philosophy.* London: J. Sene and W. Taylor.

Shank, J. B. 2004. "The Abbé Saint-Pierre and the 'Quantifying Spirit' in French Enlightenment Thought." In Mary Jane Parrine, ed., *A Vast and Useful Art: The Gustave Gimon Collection on French Political Economy.* Stanford, CA: Stanford University Libraries, pp. 29–47.

———. 2008. *The Newton Wars and the Beginnings of the French Enlightenment.* Chicago: University of Chicago Press.

Shapin, Steven. 1988a. "Understanding the Merton Thesis." *Isis* Vol. 79, No. 4, pp. 594–605.

———. 1988b. "Robert Boyle and Mathematics: Reality, Representation, and Experimental Practice," *Science in Context* Vol. 2, No. 1, pp. 23–58.

———. 1991. "'A Scholar and a Gentleman': The Problematic Identity of the Scientific Practioner in early modern England." *History of Science* Vol. 29, No. 3, pp. 279–327.

———. 1994. *A Social History of Truth.* Chicago: University of Chicago Press.

———. 1996. *The Scientific Revolution.* Chicago: University of Chicago Press.

———. 2003. "The Image of the Man of Science." In Roy Porter, ed., *The Cambridge History of Science* Vol. 4: *Eighteenth-Century Science.* Cambridge: Cambridge University Press, pp. 159–83.

Shapin, Steven, and Simon Schaffer. 1985. *Leviathan and the Air Pump: Hobbes, Boyle, and the Experimental Life.* Princeton, NJ: Princeton University Press.

Shapiro, Barbara J. 2000. *A Culture of Fact.* Ithaca, NY: Cornell University Press.

Shariff, Azim F., Ara Norenzayan, and Joseph Henrich. 2009. "The Birth of High Gods: How the Cultural Evolution of Supernatural Policing Agents Influenced the Emergence of Complex, Cooperative Human Societies, Paving the Way for Civilization." In M. Schaller, Ara Norenzayan, Steven J. Heine, Toshio Yamagishi, and Tatsuya Kameda, eds. *Evolution, Culture and the Human Mind.* New York: Psychology Press.

Shaw, George Bernard. 1903. "Maxims for Revolutionists." http://www.gutenberg.org/ cache/ epub/26107/ pg26107.html, accessed Sept. 1, 2012.

Shennan, Stephen. 2013. "Long-Term Trajectories of Technological Change." In Peter J. Richerson and Morten H. Christiansen, eds., *Cultural Evolution: Society, Technology, Language, and Religion.* Cambridge, MA: MIT Press, pp. 143–155.

Shiue, Carol H., and Wolfgang Keller. 2007. "Markets in China and Europe on the Eve of the Industrial Revolution." *American Economic Review* Vol. 97, No. 4, pp. 1189–216.

Silberman, Leon. 1960. "Hung Liang-Chi: a Chinese Malthus." *Population Studies* Vol. 13, No. 3, pp. 257–65.

Simonson, Tatum, Yingzhong Yang, Chad D. Huff, Haixia Yun, Ga Qin, David J. Witherspoon, et al. 2010. "Genetic Evidence for High-Altitude Adaptation in Tibet." *Science* Vol. 329, July 2, pp. 72–75.

Sivin, Nathan. [1973], 1995. "Copernicus in China or Good Intentions Gone Astray." *Studia Copernicana* Vol. 6, pp. 63–122, reprinted in Sivin, 1995, ch. IV.

———. 1975. "Wang Hsi-shan." In Charles Coulson Gillispie, ed., *Dictionary of Scientific Biography.* New York: Charles Scribner's Sons, Vol. 14, pp. 159–68.

———. 1995. *Science in Ancient China.* Aldershot, UK: Variorum.

———. [1984] 2005. "Why the Scientific Revolution Did Not Take Place in China —or Didn't It?" in Everett Mendelsohn, ed., *Transformation and Tradition in the Sciences.* Cambridge: Cambridge University Press, pp. 531–54. Revised version, 2005, http://ccat.sas.upenn.edu/~nsivin/scirev.pdf, accessed Nov. 30, 2013.

Skempton, Alec. 2002. *A Biographical Dictionary of Civil Engineers in Great Britain and Ireland,* Vol. 1: *1500–1830.* London: Thomas Telford Publishing.

Slack, Paul. 2015. *The Invention of Improvement: Information and Material Progress in Seventeenth- Century England.* Oxford: Oxford University Press.

Slezkine, Yuri. 2004. *The Jewish Century.* Princeton, NJ: Princeton University Press.

Sloane, Hans. 1707. *A Voyage to the Islands Madera, Barbados, Nieves, S. Christophers and Jamaica,* 2 vols. London: Printed by B.M. for the author.

Smith, Adam. [1759], 1976. *The Theory of Moral Sentiments,* edited by D. D. Raphael and A. L. Macfie. Oxford: Oxford University Press.

———. [1762–1763] 1978. *Lectures on Jurisprudence,* edited by R. L. Meek. Oxford: Oxford University Press.

———. 1799. "The History of Astronomy." In *Essays on Philosophical Subjects.* Edinburgh: Printed for the Editor of the Collection of English Classics, pp. 1–124.

Smith, Pamela H. 1994. *The Business of Alchemy: Science and Culture in the Holy Roman Empire.* Princeton, NJ: Princeton University Press.

Smith, Pamela H., and Schmidt, Benjamin. 2007. "Knowledge and Its Making in Early Europe." In Pamela H. Smith and Benjamin Schmidt, eds., *Making Knowledge in Early Modern Europe.* Chicago: University of Chicago Press, pp. 1–16.

Sng, Tuan Hwee. 2014. "Size and Dynastic Decline: The Principal-Agent Problem in Late Imperial China 1700-1850." *Explorations in Economic History,* Vol. 54, pp. 107–27.

Snobelen, Stephen D. 1999. "Isaac Newton, Heretic: the Strategies of a Nicodemite." *British Journal for the History of Science* Vol. 32, pp. 381–419.

———. 2012. "The Myth of the Clockwork Universe: Newton, Newtonianism, and the Enlightenment." In Chris L. Firestone and Nathan Jacobs, eds. *The Persistence of the Sacred in Modern Thought.* Notre Dame, IN: University of Notre Dame Press, pp. 149–84.

Song, Yingxing [Sung, Ying-Hsing]. [1637] 1966. *T ien-Kung K ai-Wu [Tiangong Kaiwu]: Chinese Technology in the Seventeenth Century.* University Park, PA: Pennsylvania State University Press.

Sorbière, Samuel. [1664] 1709. *A Voyage to England, Containing Many Things Relating to the State of Learning, Religion, and Other Curiosities of That Kingdom.* London: J. Woodward.

Sorrenson, Richard. 2001. "Dollond and Son's Pursuit of Achromaticity." *History of Science* Vol. 39, pp. 31–55.

Spadafora, David. 1990. *The Idea of Progress in Eighteenth-Century Britain.* New Haven, CT: Yale University Press.

Spence, Jonathan. 1990. *The Search for Modern China.* New York: W. W. Norton.

Sperber, Dan. 1996. *Explaining Culture: A Naturalistic Approach.* Oxford: Blackwell's.

Spolaore, Enrico, and Romain Wacziarg. 2013. "How Deep Are the Roots of Economic Development?" *Journal of Economic Literature* Vol. 51, pp. 1–45.

Sprat, Thomas. 1667. *History of the Royal Society of London.* London: Printed for J. Martyn.

Squicciarini, Mara P., and Nico Voigtländer. 2015. "Human Capital and Industrialization: Evidence from the Age of Enlightenment." *Quarterly Journal of Economics,* Vol. 130, No. 4, pp. 1825–83.

Stark, Rodney. 2003. *For the Glory of God: How Monotheism Led to Reformations, Science, Witch-hunts and the End of Slavery.* Princeton, NJ: Princeton University Press.

———. 2005. *The Victory of Reason: How Christianity Led to Freedom, Capitalism, and Western Success.* New York: Random House.

Starkey, George. 1665. *An Epistolar Discourse to the Learned and Deserving Author of Galeno-pale.* London: R. Wood, for Edward Thomas.

Stearns, Raymond Phineas. 1943. "The Scientific Spirit in England in Early Modern Times (c. 1600)." *Isis* Vol. 34, No. 4, pp. 293–300.

Stebbins, G. Ledyard. 1969. *The Basis of Progressive Evolution.* Chapel Hill, NC: North Carolina University Press.

Steele, Brett D. 1994, "Muskets and Pendulums: Benjamin Robins, Leonhard Euler, and the Ballistics Revolution." *Technology and Culture* Vol. 35, pp. 348–82.

———. 2004. "Robins, Benjamin (1707–1751)." *Oxford Dictionary of National Biography.* Oxford: Oxford University Press.

Stevin, Simon. [1585], 1608. *Disme: the Art of Tenths,* translated by Robert Norton. London: printed by S. S[tafford] for Hugh Astley.

Stewart, Dugald. [1793] 1829. *Account of the Life and Writings of Adam Smith ... from the Transactions of the Royal Society of Edinburgh.* In *The Works of Dugald Stewart.* Cambridge: Hilliard and Brown, Vol. 7, pp. 3–75.

Stewart, Larry. 1992. *The Rise of Public Science.* Cambridge: Cambridge University Press.

———. 1998. "A Meaning for Machines: Modernity, Utility, and the Eighteenth-Century British Public." *Journal of Modern History*, Vol. 70, No. 2 (June), pp. 259–94.

———. 2004. "The Laboratory and the Manufacture of the Enlightenment." Unpublished, University of Saskatchewan.

Stewart, M. A. 1994. "*Libertas Philosophandi*: From Natural to Speculative Philosophy." *Australian Journal of Politics and History* Vol. 40, No. 1, pp. 29–46.

Stigler, George J. 1965. "The Intellectual and the Marketplace." *Kansas Journal of Sociology*, Vol. 1, No. 2 (Spring) pp. 69–77.

Stigler, Stephen J. 1999. *Statistics on the Table: The History of Statistical Concepts and Methods.* Cambridge, MA: Harvard University Press.

Stone, Lawrence. 1969. "Literacy and Education in England 1640–1900." *Past & Present* No. 42, pp. 69–139.

Storr, Virgil Henry. 2011. "North's Underdeveloped Ideological Entrepreneur." In Emily Chamlee-Wright, ed., *Annual Proceedings of the Wealth and Well-being of Nations* Vol. 1, pp. 99–115.

Strasser, Gerhard F. 1994. "Closed and Open Languages: Samuel Hartlib's Involvement with Cryptology and Universal Languages." In Mark Greengrass, Michael Leslie, and Timothy Raylor, eds., *Samuel Hartlib and Universal Reformation.* Cambridge: Cambridge University Press, pp. 151–61.

Stubbe, Henry. 1670. *Campanella Revived or an Enquiry into the History of the Royal Society,* London: n.p.

Styles, John. 2016. "Fashion, Textiles and the Origins of Industrial Revolution." Unpublished ms., University of Hertfordshire.

Sutton, Robert B. 1953. "The Phrase *Libertas Philosophandi.*" *Journal of the History of Ideas* Vol. 14, No. 2, pp. 310–16.

Swedberg, Richard. 2006. "Social Entrepreneurship: the View of the Young Schumpeter." In Chris Steyaert and Daniel Hjorth, eds., *Entrepreneurship as Social Change.* Cheltenham, UK: Edward Elgar, pp. 20–34.

Swift, Jonathan. [1704] 1753. *A Tale of a Tub. Written for the Universal Improvement of Mankind. To which is added, An Account of a Battle between the Antient and Modern Books in St. James's Library,* thirteenth edition. Glasgow: printed by R. Urie.

Szostak, Rick. 2009. *The Causes of Economic Growth: Interdisciplinary Perspectives.* Berlin: Springer.

Tabellini, Guido. 2008. "Institutions and Culture." [Presidential Address]. *Journal of the European Economic Association* Vol. 6, Nos. 2–3, pp. 255–94.

———. 2010. "Culture and Institutions: Economic Development in the Regions of Europe." *Journal of the European Economic Association* Vol. 8, No. 4, pp. 677–716.

Tambiah, Stanley Jeyaraja. 1990. *Magic, Science, Religion, and the Scope of Rationality.* Cambridge: Cambridge University Press.

Teich, Mikuláš, and Roy Porter, eds. 1996. *The Industrial Revolution in National Context.* Cambridge: Cambridge University Press.

Tomory, Leslie. 2012. *Progressive Enlightenment: The Origins of the Gaslight Industry, 1780–1820.* Cambridge, MA: MIT Press.

Trail, R. R. 1965. "Sydenham's Impact on English Medicine." *Medical History,* Vol. 9, No. 4, pp. 356–64.

Trattner, Walter I. "God and Expansion in Elizabethan England: John Dee, 1527–1583." *Journal of the History of Ideas* Vol. 25, No. 1, pp. 17–34.

Traugott, John. 1994. "Review of Joseph Levine, *The Battle of the Books: History and Literature in the Augustan Age.*" *Modern Philology* Vol. 91, No. 4, pp. 501–8.

Triandis, Harry C. 1995. *Individualism and Collectivism.* Boulder, CO: Westview Press.

Turgot, Anne-Robert-Jacques. 1808. *Oeuvres de Mr. Turgot.* 9 vols. Paris: Imprimerie de Delance.

Tuschman, Avi. 2014. "Political Evolution: Why Do Young Voters Lean Left? It's in the Genes." *Bloomberg Business Week,* April 17. http://www.bloomberg.com/bw/articles/2014-04-17/liberal-or-conservative-brain-development-may-be-key-factor.

Ultee, Maarten. 1987. "The Republic of Letters: Learned Correspondence, 1680–1720." *Seventeenth Century* Vol. 2, pp. 95–111.

Unger, Richard W. 2013. "The Technology and Teaching of Shipbuilding." In Maarten Prak and Jan Luiten van Zanden, eds., *Technology, Skills and the Pre-modern Economy.* Leiden: Brill, pp. 161–204.

United States Department of Education. 2008. "1.5 Million Homeschooled Students in the United States in 2007." National Center for Education Statistics, *Issue Brief,* December.

Van Berkel, Klaas. 2013. *Isaac Beeckman on Matter and Motion: Mechanical Philosophy in the Making.* Baltimore: Johns Hopkins University Press.

Van Zanden, Jan Luiten. 2013. "Explaining the Global Distribution of Book Production before 1800." In Maarten Prak and Jan Luiten van Zanden, eds., *Technology, Skills and the Pre-modern Economy.* Leiden: Brill, pp. 321–40.

Vermeij, Geerat J. 2004. *Nature: An Economic History.* Princeton, NJ: Princeton University Press.

Vickers, Brian. 1992. "Francis Bacon and Progress of Knowledge." *Journal of the History of Ideas* Vol. 53, No. 3, pp. 495–518.

Vincenti, Walter G. 1990. *What Engineers Know and How They Know It.* Baltimore: Johns Hopkins University Press.

Voigtländer, Nico, and Joachim Voth. 2015. "Nazi Indoctrination and Anti-Semitic Beliefs in Germany." *Proceedings of the National Academy of Sciences* Vol. 112, No. 26, pp. 7931–36.

Voltaire. [1733–34] 2007. *Philosophical Letters or Letters Concerning the English Nation,* edited by John Leigh, translated by Prudence L. Steiner. Indianapolis, IN and Cambridge: Hackett Publishing.

———. 1738. *The Elements of Sir Isaac Newton's Philosophy,* translated from the French, revised and corrected by John Hanna. London: Printed for Stephen Austen.

———. [1751] 1785. *Siècle de Louis XIV.* In *Oeuvres Complètes de Voltaire.* Basel: Jean Jacques Tourneisen, Vol. 21.

Vries, Peer H.H. 2001. "The Role of Culture and Institutions in Economic History: Can Economics be of Any Help?" *NEHA Jaarboek* Vol. 64, pp. 28–60.

———. 2013. *The Escape from Poverty.* Vienna: Vienna University Press.

Wallace, Anthony F. C. 1982. *The Social Context of Innovation.* Princeton, NJ: Princeton University Press.

Wallis, John. 1643. *Truth Tried or, Animadversions on a Treatise Published by the Right Honorable Robert Lord Brook, Entituled, The Nature of Truth*. London: Printed by Richard Bishop for Samuel Gellibrand.

———. 1656. "Arithmetica Infinitorum." In John Wallis, *Operum Mathematicorum*. Oxford: Leon Lichfield, pp. 109–200.

Waquet, Françoise. 1989. "Qu'est-ce que la République des Lettres? Essai de Sémantique Historique." *Bibliothèque de l'École des Chartes*, Vol. 147, pp. 473–502.

Wason, P. C. 1960. "On the Failure to Eliminate Hypotheses in a Conceptual Task." *Quarterly Journal of Experimental Pscyhology* Vol. 12, pp. 129–40.

Watson, Foster. 1913. *Vives, On Education: A Translation of the* De Tradendis Disciplinis *of Juan Luis Vives*. Cambridge: Cambridge University Press.

Weber, Max. [1905] 1958. *The Protestant Ethic and the Spirit of Capitalism*. New York: Charles Scribner's Sons.

Webster, Charles. 1970. *Samuel Hartlib and the Advancement of Learning*. Cambridge: Cambridge University Press.

———. [1975] 2002. *The Great Instauration: Science, Medicine and Reform, 1626–1660*, second ed. Bern: Peter Lang.

Webster, John. 1654. *Academiarum Examen, or the Examination of Academies*. London: Giles Calvert.

Wesson, Robert. 1991. *Beyond Natural Selection*. Cambridge, MA: MIT Press.

Westfall, Richard S. 1980. *Never at Rest: A Biography of Isaac Newton*. Cambridge: Cambridge University Press.

———. 1985. "Science and Patronage: Galileo and the Telescope." *Isis* Vol. 76, No. 1 (March), pp. 11–30.

———. 1986. "The Rise of Science and the Decline of Orthodox Christianity." In David C. Lindberg and Ronald L. Numbers, eds., *God and Nature: Historical Essays on the Encounter between Christianity and Science*. Berkeley: University of California Press, pp. 218–37.

———. 2000. "The Scientific Revolution Reasserted." In Margaret J. Osler, ed., *Rethinking the Scientific Revolution*. Cambridge: Cambridge University Press, pp. 41–55.

Westman, Robert. 1986. "The Copernicans and the Churches." In David C. Lindberg and Ronald L. Numbers, eds., *God and Nature: Historical Essays on the Encounter between Christianity and Science*. Berkeley: University of California Press, pp. 76–113.

White, Andrew Dickson. 1896. *The Warfare of Science with Theology*. New York: D. Appleton and Company.

White, Lynn. 1978. *Medieval Religion and Technology*. Berkeley: University of California Press.

White, Michael. 1997. *Isaac Newton, The Last Sorcerer*. New York: Helix Books.

Wigelsworth, Jeffrey R. 2003. "Competing to Popularize Newtonian Philosophy: John Theophilus Desaguliers and the Preservation of Reputation." *Isis* Vol. 94, No. 3, pp. 435–55.

Wilkins, John. 1648. *Mathematicall Magick, or, The Wonders That May Be Performed by Mechanicall Geometry*. London: Printed by M. F. for Gellibrand.

———. [1648], 1684. *A Discourse Concerning a New Planet*, fourth ed. London: Printed by T.M. & J.A. for John Gillibrand.

———. 1668. *An Essay towards a Real Character and a Philosophical Language*. London: John Martin.

———. [1641] 1984. *Mercury, Or, The Secret and Swift Messenger*, edited by Brigitte Asbach-Schnitker. Amsterdam and Philadelphia: J. Benjamins.

Williams, David. 2004. *Condorcet and Modernity*. Cambridge: Cambridge University Press.

Wilson, Andrew. 2002. "Machines, Power and the Ancient Economy." *Journal of Roman Studies* Vol. 92, pp. 1–32.

Wiseman, Richard. [1676] 1719. *Eight Chirurgical Treatises*, fifth ed. London: Printed for B. Tooke and others.

Withers, Charles W. J. 2007. *Placing the Enlightenment*. Chicago: University of Chicago Press.

Wojcik, Jan. 1997. *Robert Boyle and the Limits of Reason*. Cambridge: Cambridge University Press.

Woodside, Alexander and Benjamin A. Elman. 1994. "Afterword: The Expansion of Education in Ch'ing China." In Alexander Woodside and Benjamin A. Elman, eds., *Education and Society in Late Imperial China, 1600–1900*. Berkeley: University of California Press, pp. 525–60.

Woodward, Ezekias. 1641. *A Gate to Sciences Opened by a Naturall Key*. London: Printed for John Bartlet.

Wootton, David. 2015. *The Invention of Science: A New History of the Scientific Revolution*. London: Allen Lane.

Wotton, William. 1694. *Reflections Upon Ancient and Modern Learning*. London: Printed by J. Leake.

Wright, Thomas. 2012. *Circulation: William Harvey s Revolutionary Idea*. London: Vintage Books.

Wuthnow, Robert. 1989. *Communities of Discourse*. Cambridge, MA: Harvard University Press.

Yates, Frances. 1964. *Giordano Bruno and the Hermetic Tradition*. Chicago: University of Chicago Press.

———. 1967. "Vicissitudes." *New York Review of Books*, Aug. 24.

Zagorin, Perez. 1998. *Francis Bacon*. Princeton, NJ: Princeton University Press.

———. 2003. *How the Idea of Religious Toleration Came to the West*. Princeton, NJ: Princeton University Press.

Zak, Paul J., and Stephen Knack. 2001. "Trust and Growth." *Economic Journal* Vol. 111, No. 470, pp. 295–321.

Zelin, Madeleine. 2004. "A Critique of Rights of Property in Prewar China." In Madeleine Zelin, Jonathan K. Ocko, and Robert Gardella, eds., *Contract and Property in Early Modern China*. Stanford, CA: Stanford University Press, pp. 17–36.

Zilsel, Edgar. 1942. "The Sociological Roots of Science." *American Journal of Sociology* Vol. 47, no. 4, pp. 544–60.

Ziman, John. 2000. "Selectionism and Complexity." In John Ziman, ed., *Technological Innovation as an Evolutionary Process*. Cambridge: Cambridge University Press, pp. 41–51.

Zittel, Claus, Gisela Engel, Romano Nanni, and Nicole C. Karafyllis, eds. 2008. *Philosophies of Technologies: Francis Bacon and His Contemporaries*. Leiden and Boston: Brill.

Zurndorfer, Harriet T. 2009. "China and Science on the Eve of the 'Great Divergence' 1600–1800." *History of Technology* Vol. 29, pp. 81–101.

Index

Aarsleff, Hans, 94
Abbattista, Guido, 268
Abraham, Gary, 237
Academia Leopoldina, 281
Academia Parisiensis, 281
Académie Bourdelot, 281
Académie de Peinture et de Sculpture, 282
Académie des Inscriptions et Belles-Lettres, 90
Académie des Sciences, 90, 109, 262
Académie Française, 241
Académie Royale, 181, 196, 206, 241, 282
academies, 173, 182
Accademia degli Incogniti, 281
Accademia dei Lincei, 219, 280
Accademia del Cimento, 95, 281
Accademia della Traccia, 95
access costs, 183
access to knowledge, 219
Acemoglu, Daron, 5, 10-12, 60, 61, 174
achromatic lens , 108
Acquaviva, Claudio, 130
The Advancement of Learning, 95, 104, 146, 152, 217
Aepinus, Franz, 205, 275
agenda for progress, 20
agriculture, 91, 278
    in Chen Hongmou's work, 331
Agrippa, Cornelius, 75
Aikenhead, Thomas, 177
air pump, 162
Al Ghazali, 66, 67, 337
alchemy, 220
Alcinous, 197
alcohol, 146
Aldrich, Howard, 24, 28
Aldrich, Howard E., 9
Alesina, Alberto, 7, 10, 13, 32
Alexander, Amir, 130, 131, 146, 147, 156, 212, 232, 260
Alexander VII, Pope, 204
Alford, William P., 292, 298
Algar, Hamid, 295
Algarotti, Francesco, 110
algebra, 146
Alhazen, 148
Allen Robert C., 185, 289
Alps, 169
Al-Razi (Rhazes), 145
Alsted, Johann Heinrich, 240
Amico, Leonard, 138
Amis, Kingsley, 341
Amsterdam, 176, 189, 257
Anabaptists, 175

ancient learning, attitudes toward, 150
ancients, 101
    in China, 327
ancients and moderns
    battle of, 250
    in *kaozheng* medical literature, 331
Angeles, Luis, 293, 294
Anglican Church, 235
Anglicanism, 113, 246
Anstey, Peter R., 91
apostasy, 165
Aquinas, Thomas, 145, 336
    compared to Zhu Xi, 308
Arabic numerals, 146
Arbuthnot, John, 105
Archimedes, 32, 258
architects, 204
Arianism, and Newton, 115
Ariew, Roger, 130, 166
Aristotelian doctrine, 150
Aristotelian dogma, 77
Aristotelian methodology, 72
Aristotelian orthodoxy, 171
Aristotelians, 75, 156
Aristotle, 73, 74, 151, 152, 162, 172, 308, 319
armillary spheres, 301
Arriaga, Rodrigo, 212
artisanal knowledge, 137, 139, 160, 290
artisanal technology, 143
artisans, 81, 119, 136, 269, 274
    and the Industrial Revolution, 273
Asbach-Schnitker, Brigitte, 94
Ashworth, William B., 240
Asian civilizations, contact with, 147
Associational Society, 222
astrology, 220
astronomical instruments, 301
astronomy, 220
atheism, 127
atmospheric engine, 203
attitudes, 17, 20
    toward progress, 20
Aubrey, John, 93
auctoritates, 172
authorities, 49
    ancient, 194
authority, 56
    concept of, 217
Averroes, 148
Avignon, 260

Bacon, Francis, 67–69, 70–98, 99, 101,

396 Index

Opium Wars, 335
Opticks , 108
Optics, 101
Orta, Garcia de, 145
Ostrom, Elinor, 122, 185, 187
Ottoman Empire, 188, 291
Oughtred, William, 207
Oxford University, 151

Padua, 110, 174, 204
Padua, University of, 173, 188, 256, 281
Pagel, Walter, 261
Palissy, Bernard, 138
Pallavicino, Ferrente, 260
Pancaldi, Giuliano, 201
Panciroli, Guido, 259
Panipat, battle of, 291
Papin, Denis, 203, 233, 270
Paracelsus, 73, 105, 151, 156, 157, 162,
    213, 214, 251, 261, 310, 331
Parent, Antoine, 272
Paris, 151, 175, 176, 188, 212, 281
    salons in, 200
Parker, Samuel, 80
Parthasarati, Prasannan, 164
Pascal, Blaise, 162, 241, 248, 261, 262, 264,
    201, 217, 281
Pasteur, Louis, 158
patent offices, 320
patent system, 202
patents, 16
patience capital, 140
patronage, 16, 87, 106, 109, 111, 172, 176,
    177, 179, 181-183, 188, 203-208
    and scientific prestige, 219
Paul IV, Pope, 170, 171
Paul V, Pope, 176
peanuts, 317
peer review, 217
Peiresc, Nicolas C.F. de, 95, 130, 137, 161,
    162, 194, 198, 200, 201, 207, 280
Pemberton, Henry, 110
pendulum clocks, 83, 162
penny post, 195
Perdue, Peter, 297
Pérez-Ramos, Antonio, 70, 77, 79, 95, 98
Perkins, Merle L., 263
Perkinson, Henry J., 159, 161, 179
perpetual peace, ideal of, 263
Perrault, Charles, 250, 262
Persia, 291
persuasion, 20, 23, 33, 35, 44, 45, 190, 211
    and biases in cultural evolution, 209
    and the market for ideas, 190
    in the Industrial Enlightenment, 279
Perugia, 204

Pestré, Abbé Jean, 79, 96
Peter the Great, Czar, 199
Peterson, Willard, 325, 329
Petty, William, 86, 87, 88, 229, 243, 263
phase transition, in European innovation,
    288
Phelps, Edwin, 123
phenotype, 28
Philosophical Transactions, 87, 282
phlogiston theory, 177, 208, 220
Phoenicia, 132
physical sciences, Newton's impact on,
    103
physicians, 125, 158, 162, 251, 252
    and patronage, 204
    Jewish, 257
physiocrats, 330
Pietism, 244, 245
Pinker, Steven, 316
Pitcairne, Archibald, 102
plague, 309
Planck, Max, 65
plasmids, 144
Plat, Sir Hugh, 74, 97, 185
Pleijt, Alexandra M. de, 124
Pleiotropy, 28
Pliny, 151, 152
pluralism, 13, 53, 80, 129, 131, 156, 166,
    170, 174, 219, 233
    European, 290
pneumatic chemistry, 271
Po river, 204
Poland, 95, 126, 171, 175, 188
Polanyi, Michael, 62
Pole, Reginald, 170
polite society, 155
Pollard, Sidney, 263
Pomeranz, Kenneth, 287, 288, 292
Poovey, Mary, 84, 216
Pope, Alexander, 111
Popper, Karl, 75
population thinking, 31
porcelain, in China, 148
Porter, Michael, 14
Porter, Roy, 242, 268
positive checks, 315
positive-sum game, 267
postal networks and services, 36, 195, 196
Postel, Guillaume, 258
potatoes, 145
Potsdam, 178
Poynter, F.N., 91
practical intelligence, and innovation, 269
Prague, 212
Prak, Maarten, 148, 173
precision, rhetoric of, 279